LEARNING DISABILITIES
in Perspective

LEARNING DISABILITIES
in Perspective

Howard S. Adelman and Linda Taylor
University of California, Los Angeles

Scott, Foresman and Company
Glenview, Illinois

Dallas, Texas   Oakland, New Jersey   Palo Alto, California
Tucker, Georgia   London

To the children who teach us
how much more there is to learn:
Kim and Craig, Jim, Wagner,
Bruce, Jack, Kathy, Donovan, Bill,
Donna, Patrick, Wendy, Mike,
Alesia, Tim, Janice, . . .

Library of Congress Cataloging in Publication Data

Adelman, Howard S.
   Learning disabilities in perspective.

   Bibliography: p. 343
   Includes index.
   1. Learning disabilities.   I. Taylor, Linda.
II. Title.
LC4704.A33   1982   371.9   82-10690
ISBN 0-673-15398-3

1   2   3   4   5   6—RRC—86   85   84   83   82

The authors and the publisher would like to thank the following sources for the use of their material: **(pp. 26, 45)** From "Remedial Classroom Instruction Revisited" by Howard S. Adelman, *The Journal of Special Education*, 1971, vol. 5, no. 4. Copyright © 1971 by Buttonwood Farms Inc. Reprinted by permission. **(pp. 82–83)** From "Initial Psychoeducational Assessment and Related Consultation" by Howard S. Adelman and Linda Taylor, *Learning Disabilities Quarterly*, Fall, 1979, vol. 2, no. 4. Copyright © 1979 by Learning Disabilities Quarterly. Reprinted by permission. **(p. 180)** From "Enhancing Motivation for Over-coming Learning and Behavior Problems" by Howard S. Adelman and Linda Taylor, previously unpublished article in press. Reprinted by permission of Professional Press, Inc., 11 E. Adams St., Chicago, Illinois 60603. **(p. 267)** From *The Change Agent's Guide to Innovation in Education* by Ronald G. Havelock. Copyright © 1973 by Educational Technology Publications, Inc., Englewood Cliffs, New Jersey 07632. Reprinted by permission. **(p. 277)** "About School" by R. Mukerji from *Colloquy*, January 1970, vol. 3, no. 1. Copyright © 1970 by the United Church Press. Reprinted by permission. **(p. 304)** From "The Countenance of Educational Evaluation" by Robert Stake, *Teachers College Record*, April 1967, vol. 68, no. 7. Copyright © 1967 by Teachers College, Columbia University. Reprinted by permission. **(p. 305)** From *Educational Evaluation* by W. James Popham, pp. 31–32. Copyright © 1975 by Prentice-Hall, Inc. Reprinted by permission of Prentice-Hall, Inc., Englewood Cliffs, N.J. **(pp. 331–32)** "The Expert Trap" by Howard S. Adelman from the *Journal of Learning Disabilities*, October 1978, vol. 11, no. 8. Copyright © 1978 by Professional Press, Inc., 11 E. Adams St., Chicago, Illinois 60603. Reprinted by permission.

Preface

Since 1921 the Fernald School (formerly the Psychology Clinic School) at UCLA has been a major clinical research and training center that has focused on learning problems. The facility has been best known for techniques developed by its founder, Grace Fernald. In keeping with the innovative spirit of her pioneering work, the staff continues to explore new directions in dealing with learning problems.

When Fernald published her work on multisensory remedial techniques in 1943, a number of other theoretical and intervention approaches were evolving which led to eventual establishment of the label and field of *learning disabilities* (LD). In the 1960s, along with others in the field, the Fernald staff found itself caught up in the rapidly expanding LD movement. In a research and training center, however, the staff's responsibility is not to reify a movement, but to explore issues and problems. Recent conceptual and empirical activities at Fernald have evolved a broad perspective of learning disabilities that differs from the perspective of most textbooks. It is from this perspective that our book explores prevailing views of the field and suggests alternative models and practices.

When we first began to work with individuals manifesting learning problems, we were interested primarily in the subgroup that might appropriately be labeled *specific learning disabled* (SLD). We wanted to understand this phenomenon and contribute to its correction and prevention. Unfortunately, these straightforward motives were confounded by the difficulty of validly distinguishing specific learning disabilities from the diversity of learning problems referred for help. This reality soon led us to realize that those labeled *learning disabled* represent a wide range of learning problems.

Thus, our focus broadened to investigation of the diverse types of learning problems and to an understanding of learning disabilities within this context.

Most professionals working with diverse learning problems are expected to diagnose, assess, prescribe, and treat. They also are asked to provide data to prove that their actions are beneficial. In pursuing such activities, whether explicitly stated or not, they rely on specific views of what causes and what can correct learning problems. Their actions also are based on views of what constitutes ethical practice. These and related topics are the major focus of this book:

Part 1 explores causes of learning problems;

Part 2 focuses on diagnosis, screening, and placement practices with special emphasis on related assessment procedures;

Part 3 discusses the planning and implementation of corrective interventions;

Part 4 presents an experimental intervention approach designed to systematically personalize and provide remediation for learning problems in classroom settings; and

Part 5 provides a general discussion of sociopolitical, social-philosophical, and moral perspectives of helping, and highlights concepts and concerns related to evaluating intervention efficacy.

Three recurrent themes are presented in this book: (1) prevailing views and practices in the LD field, (2) basic concepts and concerns, which must be understood if the limitations of prevailing approaches are to be comprehended, and (3) alternative perspectives and procedures that can help improve current thinking. Thus, this book discusses learning disabilities and much more.

Our intent is to counter the trend toward using the term *learning disabilities* as a synonym for all learning problems. Continuing this trend could have disastrous results for both the research and the practice related to those who have—and those who do not have—specific disorders. Adopting a broad perspective, however, could help advance understanding of specific learning disabilities as well as other types of learning problems. In particular, a broader perspective should help clarify critical differences in causality and interventions.

Throughout this book we stress the importance of basic concepts that can be used to generate a wide variety of innovative practices. Putting learning disabilities into perspective, we have included many viewpoints not often discussed in the LD literature. There is particular emphasis, first, on the value of understanding human behavior in terms of motivation as well as developmental functioning and, second, on the value of exploring problems and practices in terms of interactions, sequences, and hierarchies. For example, as a basis for classifying the range of learning problems, we discuss causes as stemming not only from factors within the person (such as neurological and emotional problems), but from environmental variables (such as school procedures and curricula) and from the interaction of person and environmental variables. This view of etiology suggests that who or what is to be assessed and is to change is not a priori the person currently manifesting the problem. Therefore the environment also may need to be assessed and changed and may even be the sole focus of intervention. This emphasis on the environment may sound similar to behaviorist approaches. However, the view presented here goes beyond behaviorism by clarifying socioeconomic-political causes and by suggesting interventions to alter environments to make them more accommodating or less hostile or both.

This book is intended for readers approaching the study of learning disabilities for the first time *and* for those seeking to broaden their perspectives. Only with the aid of such a broadened perspective can one understand why there are diverse answers to such apparently simple questions as What is the cause of my child's learning problems? and What is the best way to correct the problem? For each professional ready to give answers to these questions, there is another ready to contradict the answers, and still another who will suggest that there is now no satisfactory answer available. This is not comforting, but it is the state of the field. We have had to learn to live with the discomfort and frustration these circumstances produce, while doing the best we can to help those who are experiencing problems. As Stevenson points out, "Having partial answers does not mean that we are helpless, nor does it keep us from attempting to put what we do know into practical application; it does mean we must be aware of the limitations of our knowledge, of where fact leaves off and beliefs begin" (1972, p. 1).

This is a field with considerably more questions than answers. To arrive at validated answers, the reader must first develop a general awareness of major issues and problems that currently exist. We want this volume to contribute to that end. We hope the reader will come to appreciate the need for acquiring critical awareness and for avoiding premature resolution of these complex concerns.

Every book is the product of more persons than ever can be individually acknowledged. Our biggest debt is to all those whose work we have had the opportunity to read or observe. We also are greatly indebted to those who typed, commented on drafts, edited, and so on. Since there would be nothing to relate without the cooperation of the children and adults who have perplexed us and inspired us to explore and to learn, this book is meant as partial payment; our ongoing debt is to them.

OVERVIEW

Contents

PART 2
_____
CLASSIFICATION AND SELECTION FOR LEARNING DISABILITIES   55

LEARNING DISABILITIES
in Perspective

PART 1
PERSPECTIVES ON THE CAUSES OF LEARNING DISABILITIES

A small circus, traveling from town to town, arrived in a village where the wonders of such performers and animals had never before been seen. As word spread, people from the surrounding area turned out. Among them was a group of blind children.

To make certain these children had a memorable time, the circus folk brought out their elephant, who was a gentle beast, so that the blind youngsters could touch and explore the creature. The children were fearful, for they had never been taught about elephants and, even after much reassurance, only three had the courage to venture forth.

Together they were led to the elephant, and each gingerly felt the part of the elephant that could be readily grasped. When the three brave ones returned, the others pleaded for them to describe the elephant.

The girl who had felt the elephant's leg said, "The elephant is like a tree, round, tall, and solid."

"That's not so!" blurted the boy who had felt the trunk. "The elephant is like a person's arm, soft, caressing, and strong."

The child who had explored the ear was indignant. "No! No! The elephant is like a rug, flat and rough."

Dissatisfied by the different descriptions, their friends demanded to know who was right. Relentlessly, the three explorers argued for the correctness of his or her individual perception.

Finally, someone suggested that the three go back and once again examine the elephant. Fortunately, this time each encountered a different part. It was only then they came to understand the parts that make up an elephant, and the nature of understanding.

Adapted from an old fable

Over the last fifteen years, the number of individuals diagnosed as learning disabled (LD) has increased dramatically. As more and more programs have been initiated, differing definitions have been formulated. Conflicting theories have implicated a variety of causes, and many controversial remedies have been proposed. One result of the rapid growth of competing views is widespread debate and confusion over what is or is not a learning disability.

It is acknowledged widely that every person experiencing learning problems is not learning disabled. Unfortunately, few agree on how to differentiate among types of learning problems.

In principle, one way to make appropriate distinctions between types of problems is to group individuals according to the causes of their difficulties. Our intent in Part I is to present alternative views of causality as a basis for clarifying how learning disabilities differ from other learning problems. We begin with a discussion of prevailing definitions of LD.

Chapter 1

Learning Disabilities: Definitions and Causes

"What's the use of their having names," the Gnat said, *"if they won't answer to them?"*

"No use to them," said Alice; *"but it's useful to the people who name them, I suppose. If not, why do things have names at all?"*

Lewis Carroll, *Through the Looking Glass*

What is a learning disability? What causes learning disabilities? These questions have proven to be as complex to answer as they are simple to ask. We can begin to understand why by surveying contemporary efforts both to define *learning disabilities* and to identify their causes.

DEFINING LEARNING DISABILITIES

The definition adopted in federal legislation in the United States identifies children with specific learning disabilities as those who have

> *a disorder in one or more of the basic psychological processes involved in understanding or in using language, spoken or written, which may manifest itself in an imperfect ability to listen, think, speak, read, write, spell or to do mathematical calculations. The term includes such conditions as perceptual handicaps, brain injury, minimal brain dysfunction, dyslexia, and developmental aphasia. The term does not include children who have learning problems which are primarily the result of visual, hearing or motor handicaps, of mental retardation, or emotional disturbance, or of environmental, cultural, or economic disadvantage.* (Federal Register, 1977, p. 65083)

This definition has been the subject of continual debate since its inception.[1] In particular, many professionals are distressed by use of the phrase "basic psychological processes" in the definition, since there is little agreement about what constitutes a basic psychological process.

The definition also is criticized for implying a minor disorder in neurological functioning despite current inability to verify such minor disorders. This inability is due to tremendous methodological problems involved in assessing brain-behavior relationships.

Another major criticism is directed at the definition's exclusionary clauses. As it is widely interpreted and applied, it excludes persons who are not of at least average intelligence as well as those whose learning problems are attributed to emotional disturbance, environmental or economic disadvantage, motor handicaps, and so forth. While there is a reasonable conceptual and political basis for these exclusions, they can be and have been misleading. For example, they have been interpreted as indicating that the causes and correction of learning disabilities differ for the excluded groups.

Despite such criticisms, it is this definition that has been most frequently cited in relation to practical and research activities over the past decade. During this time, the concept of LD has gained considerable prominence. Widespread acceptance and application attest to the usefulness of the concept. Unfortunately, pervasive usage has led to overgeneralization. Thus, the irony is that, while the definition is exclusionary, the term tends to be applied in an overinclusionary manner. This tendency, of course, is detrimental to increasing knowledge of etiology and appropriate corrective strategies.

Because of various conceptual and methodological problems, the population labeled *learning disabled* is widely acknowledged to be heterogeneous in terms of the factor(s) that initially caused the learning problem and, therefore, also in terms of appropriate interventions. Stated differently, several types of learning problems are being subsumed under a single label, masking major group differences that have important implications for practice and research.

Critics have recognized this problem, and more restricted definitions have been offered. For example, in one of the position papers prepared for the National Project on the Classification of Exceptional Children (Hobbs, 1975a, 1975b), a group of noted professionals proposes the following definition:

> Specific learning disability, *as defined here, refers to those children of any age who demonstrate a substantial deficiency in a particular aspect of academic achievement because of perceptual or perceptual-motor handicaps, regardless of etiology or other contributing factors. The term* perceptual *as used here relates to those mental (neurological) processes through which the child acquires . . . basic alphabets of sounds and forms. (Wepman, Cruickshank, Deutsch, Morency, & Strother, 1975, in Hobbs, 1975a, p. 306)*

Elimination of exclusionary clauses and etiological considerations and restriction to perceptual functioning would undoubtedly reduce the types of persons likely to be labeled *learning disabled*. At the same time, this alternative definition simply highlights the fact that learning problems are associated with a variety of correlates which may or may not be importantly related to cause or correction. While restricting the term to persons manifesting one or more correlates

---

[1]Education for All Handicapped Children Act of 1975, Public Law 94–142. The definition incorporated into this act is only slightly modified from its original formulation by the National Advisory Committee on Handicapped Children (1968).

probably would be helpful for research purposes, exclusive focus on perceptual correlates may be too limiting.

Other attempts to improve the prevailing definition have emphasized operational diagnostic criteria. For example, a proposal made by the Bureau of Education for the Handicapped in 1976 stated:

A specific learning disability may be found if a child has a severe discrepancy between achievement and intellectual ability in one or more of several areas: oral expression, written expression, listening comprehension or reading comprehension, basic reading skills, mathematics calculation, mathematics reasoning, or spelling. A "severe discrepancy" is defined to exist when achievement in one or more of the areas falls at or below 50% of the child's expected achievement level, when age and previous educational experiences are taken into consideration. (Federal Register, 1976, p. 52405)

A severe discrepancy level was further defined mathematically as CA(IQ/300 + 0.17) – 2.5, where CA is chronological age, IQ is intelligence quotient, and the numbers are constants.[2]

As Norman and Zigmond (1980) note, resistance to this definition was formidable:

Critics objected to a mathematical formula as theoretically unsound; others claimed that the students identified under the proposed definition would not be the same as those students being served in existing programs; still others were concerned that strict federal guidelines infringed on states' rights to establish criteria based on local norms or clinical judgments. Following lengthy hearings and considerable debate, the proposed definition was rejected.

The definition of Learning Disabilities published in the final regulations (Federal Register, 1977, p. 65083) retained the concept of a severe discrepancy between achievement and intellectual ability, but was as broad, loosely structured, and open to interpretation as the definition established more than a decade ago. (p. 10)

IDENTIFYING CHARACTERISTICS AND CAUSES

Much of the confusion in defining learning disabilities is due to the lack of certainty about cause. A significant factor related to maintaining this uncertainty is that many professionals are extremely pessimistic about the usefulness of identifying causes. Some dismiss the topic because of absence of proof for existing etiological theories. Others are discouraged by how procedures based on causal theories have been misused. Many, perhaps the majority, believe that knowing cause is of little help in treating problems.

While understandable, ultimately these attitudes do a disservice to efforts to advance knowledge and improve practices related to the prevention and treatment of learning disabilities and other learning problems.[3] Rather than ignore the topic of etiology, one should seek better conceived theories and more comprehensive etiological research.

Essentially, the study of causality encompasses three stages of research activity. The first stage is that of description. What are the characteristics of phenomena in which we are interested? In the instance of learning disabilities, what are the characteristics of

[2]Cone and Wilson (1981) provide a critical analysis of this and three other basic methods of quantifying severe discrepancy.

[3]A prominent example of the value of etiological knowledge is seen in connection with mental retardation caused by phenylketonuria (PKU). Knowledge of the genetic bases for this problem suggests genetic counseling as a preventive step, and knowledge of the chemical mechanisms involved in the disorder allow direct intervention to minimize mental retardation (See Abroms, 1981).

FOR EXAMPLE

THE CREATION OF "LEARNING DISABILITIES"

The term learning disability *became popular when the Association for Children with Learning Disabilities (ACLD) was organized under the name in 1963. During the period just prior to that, parents throughout the United States became concerned because their children who were not learning in school were rejected from special education since they were not mentally retarded, deaf or blind, or otherwise handicapped. Local parent groups were organized. Parent-sponsored schools were initiated. They were called by different names such as schools for the neurologically handicapped, brain-injured, alphasoid, dyslexic, and perceptually handicapped. Parent organizations met in Chicago in 1963 to discuss their mutual problems, one of which was the need for a national organization and an appropriate name.*

Discussing the problem and the difficulties of labels for these children, Kirk (1963) explained that sometimes classification labels block our thinking. It is better, he told the conference, to state that a child has not learned to read than to say the child is dyslexic. He

continued that it may be more scientific to say "a child has not learned to talk" than to say the child is aphasic or brain injured. He advised that a name should be functional and that if the parents were interested in research on the relation of the brain to behavior, they could use a neurologic term. He suggested further that if they were interested in service to their children, it might be preferable to use a term related to teaching or learning and that a term such as learning disability *might be preferable to some currently used terms such as* cerebral dysfunction *and* brain injured.

The term learning disabilities struck a receptive chord with the parent groups since it implied teaching and learning and since they were interested primarily in service for their children. They selected the name Association for Children with Learning Disabilities, and from that point on, learning disabilities became a new category of exceptional children and crept into federal, state, and local legislation.

Kirk and Gallagher (1979, p. 287)

persons who have such problems? What variables and factors are important? The second stage involves looking for relationships. Are there patterns? Are there characteristics and clusters of characteristics that are systematically associated with each other? What variables and factors are systematically associated with these characteristics? The third and most complex stage of etiological research focuses on establishing cause-effect relationships. Is a characteristic or cluster of characteristics a direct symptom of an underlying disorder? Is a variable causing the problem, caused by the problem, or simply a common but not causally related correlate? All that goes on prior to this third stage is but preamble. Until it has been accomplished successfully, there is no proof of causality. In the field of learning

disabilities, the study of causality is still in its earliest stages, involving efforts to describe and categorize clusters of characteristics.

Characteristics

It is a commonplace notion that persons having problems learning also will manifest a variety of other problem characteristics, e.g., activity level too high or too low, poor attention span, aggression, poor self-image, visual and auditory problems, poor coordination, and so forth. However, as Deshler (1978) points out, despite the variety of characteristics that have been cited, there has been a sparsity of well-designed and large-scale studies. As a result, many unfounded assumptions are perpetuated about the characteristics of the learning disabled.

VIEWPOINT

RE-CREATION OF "LEARNING DISABILITIES" BY REPRESENTATIVES OF THE NATIONAL JOINT COMMITTEE FOR LEARNING DISABILITIES

The National Joint Committee for Learning Disabilities (NJCLD) consists of six major organizations concerned with learning problems: the American Speech-Language-Hearing Association (ASHA), the Association for Children and Adults with Learning Disabilities (ACLD), the Council for Learning Disabilities (CLD), the Division for Children with Communication Disorders (DCCD), the International Reading Association (IRA), and The Orton Dyslexia Society. In 1981, official representatives of the six organizations agreed to propose a new definition of learning disabilities.

> *Learning disabilities is a generic term that refers to a heterogeneous group of disorders manifested by significant difficulties in the acquisition and use of listening, speaking, reading, writing, reasoning or mathematical abilities. These disorders are intrinsic to the individual and presumed to be due to central nervous system dysfunction. Even though a learning disability may occur concomitantly with other handicapping conditions (e.g., sensory impairment, mental retardation, social and emotional disturbance) or environmental influences (e.g., cultural differences, insufficient/inappropriate instruction, psychogenic factors), it is not the direct result of those conditions or influences. (Hammill, Leigh, McNutt, & Larsen, 1981, p. 336)*

As Hammill, Leigh, McNutt, and Larsen (1981) indicate, the NJCLD believed that a new definition was needed because of inherent weaknesses in the definition enacted into law in the United States. (*Federal Register*, 1977). Among the weaknesses cited are that (1) the term *children*, makes the definition unnecessarily restrictive, (2) the phrase "basic psychological processes" is too closely associated with "mentalistic process" and "perceptual-motor ability" training programs, (3) the list of inclusive "conditions" (e.g., perceptual handicaps, minimal brain dysfunction) is ill-defined, controversial, and confusing, and (4) the "exclusion" clause is ambiguous and has led to widespread misconceptions (i.e., that learning disabilities cannot occur in conjunction with other handicapping conditions or environmental, cultural, or economic disadvantage).

In developing the proposed definition, the NJCLD wanted one which was

> *basically a theoretical statement specifying the delimiting characteristics of conditions called learning disabilities. These attributes had to be broad enough to include all known examples of learning disabilities, yet narrow enough to permit the distinction of learning disabilities from other conditions. The purpose of the definition was to establish learning disabilities theoretically—not to set up specific operational criteria for identifying individual cases. Important as operational criteria may be to school placement, research subject selection, and funding practices, the theoretical statement must come first, because it serves as a*

Furthermore, some widely mentioned characteristics, such as high levels of activity, have been clustered prematurely into separate syndromes, such as the hyperkinetic behavior syndrome. In general, evidence is sparse about a given characteristic's relative frequency, severity, and area of occurrence (1) at different ages (stages of development), (2) within different subgroups of persons with learning problems, and (3) between those with and those without learning problems.

guide for generating actual objective identification procedures. To be practical, the abstract contents of the definition must be
implemented in administrative rules and regulations. (Hammill et al., 1981, pp. 338–39)

To minimize misinterpretation of the proposed
definition, Hammill et al., (1981, pp. 339–40) offer
the following phrase-by-phrase rationale.

"Learning disabilities is a generic term" The
Committee felt that learning disabilities was a
global ("generic") term under which a variety
of specific disorders could be reasonably
grouped.
"that refers to a heterogeneous group of disorders" The disorders grouped under the
learning disability label are thought to be specific and different in kind, i.e., they are
"heterogeneous" in nature. This phrase implies
that the specific causes of the disorders are also
many and dissimilar.
"manifested by significant difficulties" The
effects of the disorders on an individual are
detrimental to a consequential degree; that is,
their presence handicaps and seriously limits
the performance of some key ability. Because
the NJCLD was concerned that "learning disabled" is often used as a synonym for "mildly
handicapped," the Committee wanted to emphasize that the presence of learning disabilities in an individual can be as debilitating

as the presence of cerebral palsy, mental defect, blindness, or any other handicapping
condition.
"in the acquisition and use of listening, speaking, reading, writing, reasoning or mathematical abilities." To be considered learning disabled, an individual's disorder has to result in
serious impairment of one or more of the listed
abilities.
"These disorders are intrinsic to the individual" This phrase means that the source of
the disorder is to be found within the person
who is affected. The disability is not imposed
on the individual as a consequence of economic deprivation, poor child-rearing practices, faulty school instruction, societal pressures, cultural differences, etc. Where present,
such factors may complicate treatment, but
they are not considered to be the cause of the
learning disability.
"and presumed to be due to central nervous
system dysfunction." The cause of the learning disability is a known or presumed dysfunction in the central nervous system. Such
dysfunctions may be by-products of traumatic
damage to tissues, inherited factors, biochem-
ical insufficiencies or imbalances, or other
similar conditions that affect the central nervous system. The phrase is intended to spell
out clearly the intent behind the statement
that learning disabilities are intrinsic to the
individual.

A government-sponsored task force in the
1960s (Clements, 1966) generated what has
become the most widely reported specification of characteristics. This group categorized the various descriptions cited in the
literature and came up with ten general

symptoms: (1) hyperactivity, (2) perceptual-motor impairments, (3) emotional lability, (4) general coordination deficits, (5) disorders of attention, (6) impulsivity, (7) disorders of memory and thinking, (8) specific learning disabilities, (9) disorders of

speech and hearing, and (10) equivocal neurological signs and encephalographic irregularities.[4]

One recent example of research on characteristics is provided by Kaluger and Kaluger (reported in Kaluger and Kolson, 1978). The potential value of investigating characteristics is reflected in this study—so are the problems. These investigators identified fifty-two characteristics among a sample of three hundred children who had been identified as learning disabled. The characteristics are classified under five general headings:

1. *Difficulties in academic learning*—achievement in reading is one or more years below mental age level; poor oral reading fluency; poor reading comprehension; poor ability in phonetic analysis of new words; reversal of letters, words, sounds of syllables in reading; reversal of letters and numbers in writing; spelled words that show little relationship to the sound they contain; achievement in arithmetic below mental age level; little or no application of skills learned in reading and arithmetic.

2. *Perceptual-motor difficulties*—poor auditory perception (awareness, discrimination, memory, sequence, etc.); poor visual perception (discrimination, memory, sequence, etc.); confusion about left and right and directional orientation; no consistent use of preferred hand or preferred foot (cerebral dominance); preferred hand and foot not on same side of body (laterality); gross motor awkwardness or clumsiness; uncoordinated use of hands or feet or both (e.g., inability to skip); poor vi-

sual-motor coordination (fine motor); illegible or distorted handwriting; mild tremor upon exertion of hands, fingers, or feet; uses only one hand (or side of body) with no assistance from the other; cannot pull main visual or auditory stimulus from background stimuli (figure-ground); cannot discriminate among different phonetic sounds; impaired form perception, space conception, and/or poor recall of form or space; ocular imbalance or poor adjustment.

3. *Language and speech disorders*—speech defect beyond immature articulation; indistinct or distorted speech (omits or adds sounds); distortion in repeating sounds; poor ability in blending sounds; long, rambling conversation or storytelling; poor word or sentence structure; halting, stumbling, or very slow oral delivery; miscalls word, but gives appropriate substitute (e.g., "Dad" for "man").

4. *Difficulties with thought processes*—takes a long time to organize thoughts before responding; capable of concrete thinking, but poor at abstractions; unable to pay attention or respond in an orderly fashion (poor ego control); unable to shift attention or to change behavior, ideas, or words (perseveration); pays too little attention to details or to the internal construction of words; pays too much attention to details; cannot see the total pattern of form, thought, or idea; poor organization of work time and work space; cannot follow or remember directions; cannot understand or remember gestures or words; cannot transfer learning from isolated skills to application.

---

[4]Other studies and reports discussing LD characteristics include: Crinella, 1973; DeLoach, Earl, Brown, Poplin, and Warner, 1981; Dykman, Ackerman, Clements, and Peters, 1971; Kass 1966; Owen, Adams, Forrest, Stolz, and Fisher, 1971; Routh and Roberts, 1972; Vande Voort, Senf, and Benton, 1972; Werry, 1972; Wolff and Hurwitz, 1973; and Yule and Rutter, 1976.

5. *Behavior and affective characteristics*—excessive body or verbal activity (hyperactive or hyperkinetic); rather lethargic and nonactive (hypoactive); easily distracted visually; easily distracted by sound (auditorally); short attention or concentration span; works better when someone is standing by, but not when the person moves away; takes much more time than others to do work; one day seems capable and remembers, but the next day does not (variability of performance); unplanned, impulsive, or "forced" motor responses which appear meaningless or inappropriate (impulsivity or disinhibition); overreaction or overflow of an emotional response (emotional lability).

As the above study illustrates, the problems associated with studying characteristics are numerous. On a conceptual level, investigators must decide which characteristics to describe and correlate. (Does one focus on those which are mentioned by parents, teachers, psychologists, and M.D.s? Does one look only at areas of functioning which have been identified by currently popular theories? In general, how does one decide what to look for and how to describe what is found?) On a methodological level, three critical problems are highlighted by the above study. First and foremost, the validity of procedures used in making differential diagnoses among persons with learning problems is extremely dubious. Therefore, it is impossible to know how many of those included in Kaluger and Kaluger's sample actually were learning disabled. There simply are no widely agreed-upon criteria for deciding who should be designated as having a learning problem or for designating the severity of the problem. Second, there is no way to know whether the characteristics cited are more prevalent at one age without sampling and analyzing by age. Third, it is generally acknowledged that children without learning problems also manifest some of these characteristics to a degree. In the absence of normative comparison data, it is impossible to know which characteristics and what degree of severity actually are descriptive of any particular subgroup of persons with learning problems. Indeed, some characteristics might not even be viewed as problems, especially at certain ages, if the persons were not also manifesting problems learning (Adelman, Taylor, Fuller, & Nelson, 1979).

While present statements of characteristics have little practical value, descriptive and relational research on characteristics can provide direction for subsequent etiological investigations. For example, Kaluger and Kaluger hypothesize that the particular characteristics manifested by some youngsters in their study are systematically related to the youngsters' learning disability. Based on this hypothesis, subsequent investigation could be directed at determining whether any particular cluster of characteristics is caused by a specific learning disability and central nervous system (CNS) disorder. If it could be proven that this was the case, identification of such characteristics, at as early an age as is feasible, might allow for intervention to minimize subsequent learning problems.

In summary, then, the characteristics listed above can only be viewed as frequently mentioned *correlates*. And they are probably correlates of learning problems in general, rather than of any specific subgroup of learning problems such as the learning disabled. Whether there is a cluster of correlates unique to any subgroup of persons with learning problems, or to all persons with such problems, has not been established. What criteria should be used in determining whether a behavior is a severe enough problem to be designated as a significant correlate of the learning problem has not been determined. Whether a correlate is a symptom of underlying disabilities and disorders or whether it is only a secondary problem stemming from a performance problem related to a particular learning activity also is unknown. All these unknowns are ample reasons for pursuing major programs of etiological research.

Causal Models

Studies of causality are guided by causal models. The specific models most often relied upon in discussing the etiology of learning and behavior problems can be designated as (1) the disordered or "ill" person model (or medical model), (2) the slow maturation model, and (3) the pathological or inadequate environment model. The first two models localize the cause of problems within the person and are in marked contrast to the environmental model.

The person-focused models view the causes of an individual's problems as biological or psychological in nature. However, the two models differ in the variables they emphasize. In the case of the disordered or "ill" person model, the key causal factor is postulated to be a disorder (traumatically or genetically instigated) that results in a handicapping disability which eventually produces the manifested problems.

The slow maturation model implies no disorder. Rather, due to the same types of instigating factors, a child's rate of maturation in one or more areas of development is slow (but not disrupted or limited) compared with those of other children the same age. One result of developmental lag is that the child cannot keep up with a normally accelerating school curriculum and thus soon manifests a learning problem.

In general, both models imply some interdependence between person and environmental determinants, but the major focus is on an individual's disorders, disabilities, and deficiencies. At the same time, the person variables stressed in each model represent a very limited set of biophysical and developmental factors.

In contrast to person-focused models is the view that learning and behavior problems stem primarily from inappropriate (e.g., pathological or inadequate) environmental experiences. Among the most extreme proponents of this position have been those whose primary emphasis is on the individual's previous learning opportunities and related reinforcement contingencies (rewards and punishments). Proponents of environmental determinism have drawn heavily on the work of Skinner (e.g., 1953, 1969). Many stress that in treating existing learning and behavior problems nothing can be done about preceding etiological factors. Therefore, their primary concern is not causality but how to deal with the manifested problems as they arise (e.g., Haring & Bateman, 1977).

Of the three causal models, the disordered person model has been the most dominant view of learning problems. As a result, the tendency has been to localize such problems within the individual and, in the case of LD, to assume that the problem stems from a specific disorder in the central nervous system. Indeed, according to Tarnopol and Tarnopol (1976), the most frequently cited causes, worldwide, have been CNS disorders.

CNS Disorders

Neurological damage and dysfunctioning related to learning problems are regarded as CNS disorders. They are seen as resulting from either (1) trauma to the system which produces damage or dysfunction or (2) genetic inheritance which produces dysfunction. Such disorders can have disabling effects that may hinder development in specific areas, thereby resulting in learning problems. These are manifested as performance problems in specific areas which, subse-

Figure 1-1

Sequence of events related to CNS disorders as implied by the dominant literature on learning disabilities.

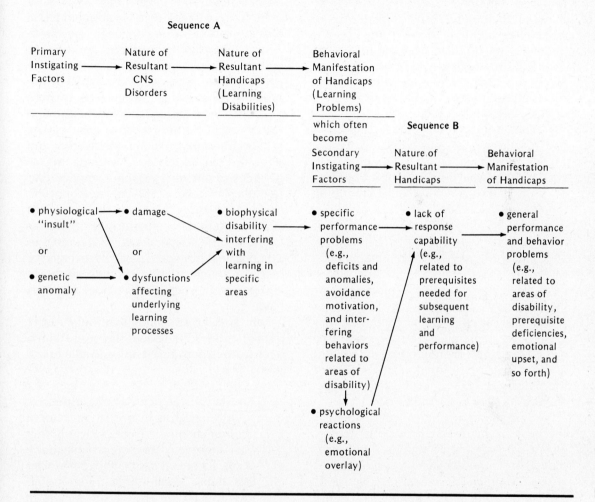

quently, may impair performance in other indirectly related areas.

As diagrammed in Figure 1-1, the sequence of events related to CNS disorders can be described as beginning with a primary instigating factor that produces a *disorder* (Sequence A). The disorder, in turn, produces a handicapping *disability* that interferes with learning and is manifested as a *problem* in performance related to learning. It should also be noted that once a problem

occurs it can become an instigating factor in a sequence leading to additional learning problems (Sequence B).

In keeping with this schema, the term *learning disorders* refers to CNS damage or dysfunction that causes learning disabilities that result in learning problems. The most frequently cited definitions of *specific learning disabilities* are consistent with the schema in that they refer to a cluster of developmental areas, such as perceptual, cognitive, and/or language areas, where normal growth and learning are blocked or interfered with because of CNS disorders.

Since CNS disorders vary in how extensive and pervasively disabling they are, it is important to differentiate between major and minor disorders. Major or gross CNS disorders certainly will interfere with learning. As examples, major disorders can severely disable development related to (1) the motor area, as in cerebral palsy; (2) cognitive functioning, as in mental retardation; (3) sensory and perceptual functioning, as in auditory and visual disabilities; (4) language, as in aphasia; and (5) social-emotional functioning, as perhaps is the case in autism. A major CNS disorder usually does result in disabilities that are related to learning, and often in pervasive disabilities. In such cases, however, the disorder so clearly manifests itself—for example, as gross motor disability, pervasive intellectual disability, or severe hearing and sight impairment—that persons are primarily labeled as cerebral-palsied, mentally-retarded, deaf, blind, and so forth. Because of the dramatic nature of the primary disability, related learning disabilities are seen as secondary concerns.

For a person to be primarily designated as specific learning disabled, dramatic signs of gross CNS disorders are supposed to be absent. That is, the damage or dysfunction is viewed as minimal; therefore, the labels minimal cerebral dysfunctioned (MCD) and minimal brain damaged or dysfunctioned (MBD) also have been used in designating

persons believed to have disorders (de la Cruz, Fox, & Roberts, 1973).[5] Similarly, terms like dyslexia and developmental aphasia seem to have been originally adopted to indicate reading and language problems which stem from minimal CNS disorders. In current usage, however, the terms often are applied without regard to the cause of the problem. Dyslexia, in particular, is used to describe almost any type of reading problem (Money, 1962; Tansley & Panckhurst, 1981).

In addition to minimal CNS disorder and primary disability related to learning, the label specific learning disabled implies that resultant learning problems must not be pervasive. That is, a person designated as SLD is supposed to be performing comparatively well in some areas and poorly in others. The prototype is a person, average or better in intellectual functioning, performing poorly in such basic school skills as reading.

Four specific examples may help clarify the types of CNS-related theories which have been hypothesized as causing learning disabilities.

1. Anoxia (oxygen deprivation), especially at birth, is seen as an instigating factor of minimal brain damage. Obviously, if anoxia is severe, gross brain damage will occur. Rabinovitch (1959) hypothesizes that anoxia leading to learning disabilities affects the association centers in parietal and parietal-occipital areas of the brain. Damage to these areas is be-

---

[5]Types of minimal CNS disorders resulting from trauma or genetic inheritance include damage or dysfunctions in such specific areas of the brain as (a) the second frontal gyrus (Wernicke, 1874), (b) the angular gyrus (Geshwind, 1968; Hinshelwood, 1917), (c) the connection between the cortical speech mechanism and the brain stem centrencephalic system (Penfield & Roberts, 1959), (d) the area immediately surrounding the thalmus (Lennenberg, 1967), (e) the parietal and parietal-occipital areas and the parietal-occipital temporal lobe junction (Drew, 1956; Geshwind, 1968; Rabinovitch, 1959); and (f) the midbrain, especially the reticular formation (Dykman, Walls, Suzuki, Ackerman, & Peters, 1970). Also suggested have been disorders related to such nonspecific factors as (a) nonlocalized minimal brain damage (Strauss & Lehtinen, 1947), (b) lack of cerebral dominance (Delacato, 1963; Orton, 1928), (c) underdevelopment of directional functions (Hermann, 1959), (d) slow tempo of neuromuscular maturation (Eustis, 1947; Harris, 1957), and (e) endocrine disturbance and chemical imbalance (Green & Perlman, 1971). As more is learned about brain-behavior relationships, other hypotheses are being formulated. For instance, theories about the differential functions of left and right hemispheres of the brain lead to speculations of disorders in hemispheric functioning which produce learning disabilities (Geshwind, 1979; Kinsbourne, 1975; Ornstein, 1977; Vellutino, 1979; Witelson, 1976, 1977).

lieved to result in a specific disability related to learning to associate symbols with meaning, but it is not seen to produce difficulties in symbol recognition. This type of difficulty in reading has been frequently described and has been offered as evidence that a brain disorder is present. It has also been suggested that, on the average, males have larger heads at birth than females, and that this increases the probability of difficult births and a higher frequency of anoxia. The fact that there are more boys than girls identified as specific learning disabled sometimes is suggested as evidence to support the cause-effect mechanism described above. However, as we will see in the next section, correlational findings such as these are not sufficient evidence of cause-effect relationships.

2. Endocrine disturbance and chemical imbalances related to acetylcholine and chloresterase have been postulated as causing dysfunctions in neural impulse transmission (Smith & Carrigan, 1959). Such dysfunctioning is seen as resulting in perceptual inefficiency. For instance, it has been hypothesized that, if synaptic transmission is too rapid, neural impulses are transmitted too quickly for adequate traces to be established in the brain. This has been offered as an explanation for the behavior of persons who manifest rapid shifts in attention and resultant learning problems.

3. It is widely hypothesized that persons whose rate of neurological development is comparatively slow will lag behind their peers with regard to maturation and development, especially in the early, formative years. This often is referred to as the maturational or developmental lag hypothesis. According to this view, children whose neurological development is much slower than others their age are not ready to cope

effectively with the same tasks as the majority of their peers. Most classrooms cannot accommodate children who are lagging considerably behind other students. For instance, the first-grade reading curriculum begins with the assumption that all students have developed to a certain level of auditory and visual perceptual abilities. If students have not yet developed these capabilities, chances are they will not be able to handle aspects of the reading curriculum. In such classrooms, as the curriculum moves on, these children fall further behind. Consequently, when their neurological development finally advances to a point where they can cope successfully with the earlier curriculum, they are confronted with more advanced demands for which they do not have the prerequisites. A similar line of reasoning has been suggested related to the impact of relatively brief delays in maturation that result from minor CNS damage and dysfunctions that have been compensated for or corrected (Bender, 1968; Bryant, 1972; Reitan & Boll, 1973; Schilder, 1935; Slingerland, 1971).

4. As a final example, a number of nutritional factors recently have been hypothesized as directly affecting CNS development and functioning, and have been implicated specifically as possible causal factors of learning disabilities. Protein, vitamin, and mineral deficiencies all have been suggested as resulting in CNS disorders, either as a result of the absence of nutrients needed to facilitate development or because substances ingested—such as food dyes—upset the body's chemical balance (Cravioto & DeLicardie, 1975; Feingold, 1976; Lipton & Wheless, 1981; Runion, 1980; Spring, Vermeersch, Blunden, & Sterling, 1981; Swanson & Kinsbourne, 1980; Wunderlich, 1973).

These examples all directly implicate CNS disorders instigated by trauma or inheritance as the causal mechanism underlying manifested learning problems. Some views, however, have only indirectly implied disorders and have focused mostly on resultant disabilities as the cause of a current performance deficit or learning problems. Examples are found in the work of those who stress perceptual (visual and auditory) disabilities (e.g., Frostig & Horne, 1964; Kephart, 1971; Wepman, 1964), psycholinguistic disabilities (Kirk & Kirk, 1971), and difficulties related to sustaining selective attention (Berlyne, 1970; Ross, 1976; Senf, 1972). While such theories touch upon the CNS bases of the disabilities and resultant learning problems, the emphasis has been on describing a disability and its causal relationship to performance.

Critical reviews of theory and research that directly or indirectly implicate CNS disorders as causal factors related to learning problems are found in the work of Tansley and Panckhurst (1981) and Vellutino (1979).

The predominant view of the cause of LD, then, localizes the problem in the CNS and postulates a variety of traumatic and genetic factors that might instigate CNS disorders. It should be stressed, however, that prevailing causal hypotheses related to LD are all based on theory. Factual evidence supporting the cause as being localized in a CNS disorder is difficult to generate, especially with regard to minor disorders. Moreover, emphasizing such terms as *learning disorders*, such labels as *specific learning disabilities*, and such sequences of events as those presented in Figure 1–1 leaves the impression that all learning problems are caused by CNS dis-

VIEWPOINT

DYSLEXIA AND CAUSALITY

There are apt to be fundamental differences in both description and prediction between the so-called brain-injured child and the child with the kinds of central nervous sytem (CNS) peculiarities of management and attention that have been referred to [as dyslexia]. Some of the most subtle clinical problems in speech and hearing are those which do not show classical neurological symptoms, and which are therefore not subjects for classical presumptions about brain injury. These children usually have CNS peculiarities; somewhere in the various reverberatory circuits of the brain, possibly involving several systems, there are inadequacies in the feedback circuitry. It seems entirely reasonable that this is what is involved in much of dyslexia—not just a twisting of orthographic details because of some lack of cerebral dominance, and not necessarily anything to do with a focal lack of tissue; but an inadequacy

in the reinforcing mechanisms which make processing, pattern-formation, and retention possible and productive.
Hardy (1962, p. 175)

Dyslexia is used . . . to mean any or all degrees of reading impairment from nonreading to delays in the normal acquisition of reading of sufficient degree that the subject is considered a reading problem. . . . The relationships we seek to clarify between concept formation, oral language acquisition and reading or its impairment, are viewed in the context of the development of the neurological substrata which serve the increasing needs of the maturing child. . . .

A sizable number of dyslexic children are so, not because of any specific brain damage, personality problem or immaturity, but rather because they have been improperly taught.
Wepman (1962, pp. 180–86)

orders and that all persons manifesting such problems are thus learning disabled. Not so. In fact, learning problems are of *several* types and stem from a *variety* of sources. The type of learning problem which is a behavioral manifestation of a biophysical disability is only one type and is perhaps the smallest proportion of the large number of learning problems seen daily in school programs (Dalby, 1979; Thompson, 1981). In Chapters 2 and 3, we place this type of learning problem within the context of the full range of such problems and summarize a number of other biological, psychological, and environmental factors that are seen as possible causes of learning disabilities as well as other types of learning problems.

FALLACIES IN DETERMINING CAUSE

Given the difficulty of measuring brain functions and their relationship to human behavior, it is not surprising that measuring minimal brain disorders has proven a rather difficult task to achieve. Because of the measurement problems involved in assessing minor brain disorders, there has been an unfortunate tendency to extrapolate and overgeneralize from cases of major brain damage. The fact is, leading theories regarding minor CNS disorders have not been adequately researched (Chall & Mirsky, 1978; Knights & Bakker, 1976; Luria & Majovski, 1977; Rourke, 1975).

Until needed research is carried out, practitioners should not act as if correlated characteristics are causally connected to a person's learning problems. With particular regard to professional practices, what must be understood and acted upon is the knowledge that, while all causes and symptoms are correlates, all correlates are not causes and symptoms. That is, just because a behavior such as mixed dominance or laterality is found to exist concurrently with a learning problem does not necessarily mean it is a

symptom of the problem, is caused by the problem, or is a cause of the problem. Even when a behavior is generally accepted as negative and a problem unto itself—as is, for example, gross motor awkwardness or clumsiness—it is not necessarily causally connected to any academic learning problems. These very elementary points are at the core of many mistakes currently made in discussing causes of learning problems and in assessment and corrective intervention practices. To prevent perpetuation of such errors, it is critical that the differences between causal and noncausal correlates be clearly understood.

Reichmann (1961) cites the example of the housewife who complained that whenever her telephone rang, the sound level on the television set went down. Investigation disclosed that the pitch of the telephone bell affected the remote control device on the set. Thus, these correlated events were indeed in an unexpected cause-effect relationship with each other. In contrast, Chase cites the example of a tribe of South Pacific natives who believe lice keep a person healthy:

> They observe that practically all healthy natives have lice, while sick people often do not, ergo lice must be the cause of good health. The real explanation, however, is quite different. When a person falls sick in that tropical climate [the person] usually runs a fever. Lice do not like it that hot and they leave. (1956, p. 74)

Thus, these correlated events were not in a cause-effect relationship, although it clearly was intuitively appealing for the natives to think they were. The traditional moral of these examples should be clear: just because two events or characteristics occur simultaneously, even though this happens consistently, is not sufficient evidence that they are causally related.

To really understand correlated characteristics, it is important to be clear about what a correlate is. If one variable is systematically *associated* with another variable, then the variables are designated as correlates. While there are a number of statistical operations used to investigate correlations between variables, basically they all are designed to describe the *degree* of relationship (i.e., association) between the variables (Nunnally, 1978). A correlation coefficient (e.g., r = .71) is a descriptive statement of the *degree* of relationship. The coefficient may or may not be statistically significant. In either case, it is not evidence that the relationship is one of cause and effect. Nor does a correlation coefficient by itself offer any guidance as to whether a cause-effect relationship may exist between variables.

As Chase (1956) points out, there are three kinds of situations where correlates may lead to errors in post hoc cause-effect interpretations. The first is when one event regularly follows another. For example, "Chantecleer, the cock in Rostand's famous play, observed that after he crowed the sun came up. Therefore, he reasoned, his crowing caused the sun to rise" (Chase, 1956, p. 71).[6] The second kind of error occurs when one event *may* affect another, but only in a minor way, as part of a much more complex set of causal events. For example, when a person frequently overeats and has stomach pains afterwards, and because carrots are always part of the meal, the person comes to believe that carrots are the cause of the pains. The third error involves two events which occur together over a period of time, but on a post hoc basis it is not possible to tell if one causes the other or whether both are caused by a third factor.

Misuses of correlational findings abound. In the quest for answers to complex phenomena such as learning problems, there is

VIEWPOINT

PREMATURE BELIEF THAT CAUSE IS KNOWN

In the last analysis, we see only what we are ready to see, what we have been taught to see. We eliminate and ignore everything that is not a part of our prejudices.
Charcot, 1857

Why there should be a widespread belief that evidence exists proving causality is itself a matter worth investigating. At this point, we can only speculate about some of the reasons. For one, it can be seen that the question "What causes learning disabilities?" presumes that an answer is currently available, and this presumption may well contribute to the tendency of the asker to prematurely assume that etiological hypotheses have been proven. Also, for over forty years, the most prevalent hypotheses in this area have been related to CNS disorders (Cruickshank, Bentzen, Ratzeburg, & Tannhauser, 1961; Fernald, 1943; Strauss & Lehtinen, 1947; Strauss & Werner, 1942; Werner & Strauss, 1940). Since learning is seen as a function of CNS activity, it is not difficult to see why there would be widespread acceptance of the idea that problems in learning stem from CNS disorders.

The lack of widely accepted alternative theories also seems to have contributed to the

a tendency to interpret any set of correlated variables as having a cause-effect relationship as long as the direction of that relationship appears "logical." Unfortunately, the logic used too often is that generated from simplistic theories or intuition; more generally, such logic may simply reflect the tenor of current sociopolitical-economic thinking and pressure.

---

[6]There is a Latin phrase, *post hoc, ergo propter hoc*, which is used to identify the fallacy whereby one event is assumed to cause another for no more logical reason than that the first event preceded the second. The literal translation is "After this, therefore because of this."

adoption of the CNS theory. With increasing discussion of the one theory, there appears to be an increasing tendency to believe it has been proven.

There are tremendous sociopolitical-economic pressures on researchers and practitioners to determine what causes psychoeducational problems. Society expects professionals to have answers in order that clients, parents, and policymakers can make decisions on the basis of facts, not unproven or conflicting theories.

Such pressures parallel a psychological need for answers to complex questions of cause and effect. Because of these factors, both the asker and the responder may not be sufficiently critical in discussions of causality, discussions that could lead to premature belief that sufficient evidence about the cause of learning disabilities exists.

While other factors could be cited, what is of concern is the tendency to inappropriately accept theory as fact. This unfortunate tendency has had and continues to have negative consequences. One example of the negative impact, which already has occurred, is the profound way that premature and widespread acceptance of CNS views of causality has shaped and limited intervention strategies. This fact is reflected in the preponderance of special programs and techniques advocated over the past forty years which have been designed to correct or minimize the impact of neurological disorders. These include visual perceptual assessment and training, major reductions of environmental stimuli, techniques to assess and improve cerebral dominance, visual-auditory-kinesthetic-tactile techniques, stimulant drug treatment, special diets, and so forth. Lack of evidence for the effectiveness of such procedures is discussed in Part 3 of this book. The point for emphasis here is that many procedures have been implemented on a large scale based on the illusion (and at the same time perpetuating the belief) that the theory which generated them has been proven. We may, however, be overlooking important causal factors.

I remember how a professor of genetics many years ago showed me published drawings of cell nuclei before and after the discovery and description of chromosomes. Chromosomes kept showing up in the later drawings, not in the earlier. In other words, microscopes do not reveal concepts until the concepts have been invented.

Boring (1953, p. 176)

All individuals have some problems with reference to learning and performing in some areas. All individuals have problems at times interacting with teachers, friends, and parents. The decision as to when these problems should be designated as severe and in need of treatment is neither logically nor empirically a simple matter. Even after they are so designated it still usually is not logically or empirically evident what caused the problems or how they are causally connected to other manifested problems that the person has in common with most people. It is clear, however, that once any problem has become designated as in need of treatment, other problems the person is experiencing come under special scrutiny, and it often is compelling to think they are all connected in some cause-effect relationship. The more intuitively logical it becomes to think that a set of problems are causally related, the less compelling it often is to understand that they may not be.

CONCLUDING COMMENTS

Evidence regarding a possible causal connection between a variable and a learning problem may be statistically impressive, clinically dramatic, and often compelling in terms of one's personal experiences and beliefs. However, unless there is an invariant causal relationship, the fact that two events are present in the situation is insufficient evidence of cause and effect.

The example of brain damage and CNS dysfunctioning is a case in point. Since persons with gross brain damage have been found to manifest problems learning, it may seem logical to assume that when similar learning problems are observed, they, too, are caused by brain damage or at least CNS dysfunctioning. This logic may be bolstered by the view that learning involves the CNS and thus learning problems must reflect CNS dysfunctioning. In the first instance, there is a problem in formal logic. Direct evidence that A (e.g., brain damage) causes B (e.g., learning problems) is not proof that B is always caused by A. Specifically, the suggested causal relationship between learning problems and CNS dysfunctioning is not susceptible to conclusive empirical testing. Thus, evidence cannot be generated to prove or disprove the hypothesis. Inability to generate proof does not mean the hypothesis is untrue. Equally, lack of disproving evidence does not mean the hypothesis is true. Despite logical arguments against prematurely accepting the causal hypothesis, however, the intuitive appeal of the relationship between learning problems and CNS dysfunctioning seems to be so great that many find it hard to believe it is not an adequate causal explanation.

To complicate the matter further, even when research evidence regarding a cause-effect relationship among variables is found, the causal relationship probably will not be invariant. Thus, while previous findings can be used to *suggest* that variables *may* be causally related in a new situation, each new case requires independent proof.

A great deal of current diagnostic activity related to learning problems does no more than identify correlates and cannot validly assess causal relationships. Moreover, these correlates too often are the bases for arriving at major decisions about what needs to be treated. (A major discussion of this point is offered in Chapter 7. Here it should suffice to emphasize that, obviously, if diagnoses are in error, corrective interventions based on them may be inappropriate.)

As the above discussion indicates, in most cases no one is currently in a position to provide with a very high degree of certitude a specific answer regarding *the cause* of a particular person's learning problems. This is the challenge that lies ahead for etiological research. However, lack of adequate research in this area does not mean that causality should or has to be ignored in practice. Practitioners can contribute to the continuing exploration of cause through interventions with persons who have learning problems. To do so, they need to (1) be cautious about inferring that correlates are causes, (2) extrapolate from current theories and research related to understanding the causes of human behavior in general and use a number of paradigms in thinking about what may be causing observed problems, and (3) gather data about what appears to work in correcting a problem since intervention elements that lead to progress may be important clues as to what caused the problems. Moreover, they will find that by going beyond the perspective that the predominant view of the cause of learning disabilities has perpetuated, the range of useful implications for practice can be greatly expanded. In Chapter 2 we present a broad perspective of causality as a basis of placing learning disabilities into context vis-à-vis other types of learning problems.

Chapter 2
Determinants of Learning and Learning Problems

*Models of causality are merely analogies—
potentially useful myths—but the power
they have to shape thoughts and actions is
awesome.*
Adelman

I wouldn't have seen it if I hadn't believed it.
Foster, Ysseldyke, and Reese (1975, p. 469)

Theories specifying the determinants of
human learning and behavior are more
complex and comprehensive than most
causal models used to explain problems. General theories encompass not only broad sets
of person and environmental variables, but
also complex interactions.[1] In this chapter,
we briefly sketch the range of determinants
implied by general paradigms, with particular emphasis on contemporary interactional
models and their implications for understanding learning and learning problems.

GENERAL PARADIGMS FOR EXPLAINING HUMAN BEHAVIOR

As with the causal models used to explain
problems, some general theories of the determinants of human behavior can be classified as either person- or environment-
focused. For example, there are general
theories that primarily emphasize behavior

---

[1]The terms *interaction* and *transaction* are used throughout the book and are defined as follows: Interaction denotes
any time that factors are acting on each other. This may occur between factors in one category (e.g., person variables
acting on each other) or across categories (e.g., environmental variables affecting person variables). Transaction
denotes that subclass of complex interactions where factors are continuously and reciprocally interacting (e.g., one
variable influencing another which in turn affects the first factor and so forth).

as determined by variables within the person. However, unlike their problem-oriented counterparts, these general theories go beyond biophysical and developmental variables and stress the impact of thoughts, feelings, and motivations (Manosevitz, Lindzey, & Thiessen, 1969). The important role played by psychological factors has been the specific concern of humanistic, existential, and some cognitive and affective arousal theorists (Atkinson, 1964; Buhler & Allen, 1972; May, 1961; Young, 1961). Recently, some theorists have stressed that an individual's overt actions also should be considered as potential determinants of subsequent behavior (e.g., Bandura, 1978).

With regard to environmental models, radical behaviorists exemplify the extreme proponents of environmental determinism. Skinner (1971) usually is identified as the leading representative of this position which suggests, first, that situational influences control behavior and, second, that the person interacts with the environment only in the sense of reacting to it. Currently, however, the emerging cognitive behaviorist view recognizes that person variables play a key role in mediating an individual's responses to stimuli (e.g., Mahoney, 1974).

In addition to behaviorists, ecologically oriented theorists (Altman, 1975; Barker, 1968; Moos & Insel, 1974) have emphasized the impact of other kinds of environmental variables. These psychologists have focused on such factors as living, learning, and working space; number of persons interacting; number and types of available activities; nature of dynamics in social situations; and so forth. Situational variables also are the focus of social psychology and personality theorists who look at cross-situational consistencies in behavior (Bem & Allen, 1974;

FOR EXAMPLE

COGNITIVE BEHAVIORISM

With occasional renegade exceptions (e.g., Wolpe, 1958; Bandura & Walters, 1959; Mowrer, 1960), early behavior modifiers were content to restrict their analyses and operations to discrete and blatantly observable phenomena. The terms "mental" and "unobservable" acquired classically conditioned negative connotations through association with the terms "soft," "unscientific," and "unparsimonious." The avoidance of inferred variables assumed near-religious proportions, hence the "Cognitive Inquisition." While explicitly modeling their paradigm after that of classical physics, behavioral researchers energetically criticized all forms of psychological inference. One wonders if they were aware that none of their respected colleagues in physics had ever actually observed an electron. The pervasiveness of this ban on mediational inferences sometimes approached that of religious dogma. After a recent colloquium on cognitive behav-

ior modification, my host took me aside and said, "I've been waiting seven years for someone to say what you just said—that it's okay to examine covert events as factors in human behavior. We have been waiting for someone to lift the ban." Careless and wholesale reliance on unjustified inference can, of course, cripple an empirical enterprise, particularly one as young and unstable as behavior modification in the early 1960's. The fact remained, however, that critics could legitimately contend that 'significant private phenomena' were functionally absent from the early behavioral framework. While their absence was often cited as an asset by enthusiastic behaviorists, their exclusion constituted a serious limitation in both the comprehensiveness and clinical relevance of the then-current behavior theory.
Mahoney (1974, p. 3)

VIEWPOINT

AN ORGANISMIC PERSPECTIVE OF THE ROLE OF PERSON VARIABLES IN DETERMINING BEHAVIOR

Thoughts and feelings are not determiners of behavior, according to Skinnerians. They are either concomitant with behavior or consequences of it. . . .

Using a mechanistic approach, one could view thoughts or feelings as behavior and could then analyze them in the same way that [one] would analyze eating or throwing a ball. In doing this, one gives up the fundamental policy of dealing only with observable behaviors, and in fact this is being done more frequently by advocates of the mechanistic approach. . . .

The organismic approaches differ from mechanistic ones in that they consider humans to be active organisms. Whereas the mechan-istic approaches assume that humans are passive and under the control of the environment, organismic approaches assert that they act on their environment. In their continual interaction with the environment, humans will be acting to bring about changes in the environment, and they will also be adapting to the environment. (See, for example, the work of Piaget, 1951, 1952). The organismic approaches differ from those of behaviorism by placing primary importance on cognitive and/or affective processes as determiners of behavior. Humans act on their environment in a lawful and ordered way, as determined by their thoughts and feelings.

Deci (1975, pp. 9–13)

Mischel, 1973). Increasingly, environmentally oriented psychologists have been concerned with the tendency to focus on the immediate or primary environment in which a person acts. A more complex picture emerges when it is recognized that environmental factors, which may in themselves be causal variables (or which may interact with person factors), can be conceived as encompassing (1) a primary environment, such as the classroom or home; (2) a secondary environment, such as the school or neighborhood; and (3) a tertiary environment, such as national culture, policies, and economic conditions (Adelman & Taylor, in press).

Even though they encompass a broader range of factors than the causal models used to explain problems, general theories that are primarily oriented to person or environment have been found by most psychologists to be unsatisfying explanations of the causes of human behavior. For instance, after many years of debate among personal-ity and social psychology theorists, most of them have given up paradigms that suggest behavior is determined by person or environmental factors alone. The trend has been to adopt the position that behavior results from an interaction of person and situational factors (Bandura, 1978; Bowers, 1973; Endler & Magnusson, 1975).

With regard to interactional models, Lewin's (1951) view that behavior is a function of person-environment interaction, expressed as B = f(P,E), has been very influential. As Bandura (1978) points out, interactional models may describe a unidirectional or bidirectional interaction between the person (P) and the environment (E). That is, one may influence the other (unidirectional) or they both may influence and change each other in a transactional manner (bidirectional). In early theories, P was defined as encompassing cognitive and other internal factors affecting perception and action. When P is so defined, the resulting interactional paradigm is conceptually weakened because it fails to recognize that overt actions are a potential causal determinant. For example, each action of a student, such as not being able to complete a task, is perceived by the student and becomes a determiner of subsequent behavior. To correct the conceptual deficiency, Bandura's social learning theory describes behavior as determined by reciprocal interactions of environmental influences, internal factors, and overt actions. In the next section, we apply this type of paradigm in order to outline an interactional view of learning and learning problems.[2] The framework presented provides a basis for placing LD in perspective with regard to other learning problems.

AN INTERACTIONAL VIEW OF LEARNING AND LEARNING PROBLEMS

The potential value of an interactional model of causality for broadening our understanding of human problems is as old as the nature-versus-nurture debate. However, as any cursory review of current literature related to learning and behavior problems demonstrates, interactional paradigms remain a minority position.

Discussion of how the specific nature of person-environment interactions results in learning or learning problems requires a lengthy and complex presentation. To condense the discussion, our initial focus is restricted to processes involved in cognitive development because of their obvious importance in understanding success and failure in school.[3] After discussing appropriate and negative learning patterns, we describe

sequences and categories of causal events that are consistent with an interactional paradigm.

Appropriate Learning

As a first step toward understanding the causes of learning problems, it is well to begin with some understanding of the process of learning per se. Cognitive learning involves modification and growth of psychological structures. These structures are referred to variously as *centrally organized processing structures, cognitive maps,* or *schemata.* These structures are presumed to be mediated by neurophysiological processes.

Individuals' cognitive structures affect both their experience of and response to stimuli. The stimulation may come from external environmental variables. However, the stimulation also may come from variables that can be called the *internal environment,* including physiological, emotional, and cognitive stimuli. In learning situations, the learner experiences both external and internal stimuli. That is, there is a complex pattern of stimulation that acts on and is acted upon by the learner's cognitive structures. Contact with stimuli designed to produce learning is supposed to result in specific modifications and growth in the learner's cognitive structures (see Figure 2-1). For example, a student comes to class with certain information, skills, and a specific way of understanding the world in which he or she functions. These cognitive structures are used to deal with the material, tasks, and activities encountered in the

---

[2]The interactional paradigm we use in analyzing the determinants of learning and learning problems encompasses both an individual's overt actions and internal activity as person (P) variables that may interact with environmental (E) variables. Behavior (B) is seen as an integrated whole which is a function of P reciprocally transacting with E, i.e., $B = f(P \leftrightarrow E)$. The strength of this model is that it suggests that the way an individual behaves may be caused by either situational influences or person variables (including overt actions and internal factors) or an interacting combination of both. With regard to the paradigm $B = f(P \leftrightarrow E)$, learning is a specific type of behavior. Thus, in rather simplistic terms, learning and learning problems can be conceptualized as a function of person-environment interactions.

[3]The formulation outlined has been evolved from J. McV. Hunt's (1961) extensive review and expansion of Piaget's general concepts, from Bandura's (1977a) social learning theory, and from research on children's learning (e.g., Stevenson, 1972).

VIEWPOINT

A SOCIAL LEARNING PERSPECTIVE OF PERSON-ENVIRONMENT INTERACTIONS

Social learning theory (Bandura, 1974, 1977b) analyzes behavior in terms of reciprocal determinism. The term determinism is used here to signify the production of effects by events, rather than in the doctrinal sense that actions are completely determined by a prior sequence of causes independent of the individual. Because of the complexity of interacting factors, events produce effects probabilistically rather than inevitably. In their transactions with the environment, people are not simply reactors to external stimulation. Most external influences affect behavior through intermediary cognitive processes. Cognitive factors partly determine which external events will be observed, how they will be perceived, whether they have any lasting effects, what valence and efficacy they have, and how the information they convey will be organized for future use. The extraordinary capacity of humans to use symbols enables them to engage in reflective thought, to create, and to plan foresightful courses of action in thought rather than having to perform possible options and suffer the consequences of thoughtless action. By altering their immediate environment, by creating cognitive self-inducements, and by arranging conditional incentives for themselves, people can exercise some influence over their own behavior. An act therefore includes among its determinants self-produced influences. . . .

It is true that behavior is influenced by the environment, but the environment is partly of a person's own making. By their actions, people play a role in creating the social milieu and other circumstances that arise in their daily transactions. Thus, from the social learning perspective, psychological functioning involves a continuous reciprocal interaction between behavioral, cognitive, and environmental influences. . . .

It is within the framework of reciprocal determinism that the concept of freedom assumes meaning (Bandura, 1977b). Because people's conceptions, their behavior, and their environments are reciprocal determinants of each other, individuals are neither powerless objects controlled by environmental forces nor entirely free agents who can do whatever they choose. People can be considered partially free insofar as they shape future conditions by influencing their courses of action. By creating structural mechanisms for reciprocal influence, such as organizational systems of checks and balances, legal systems, and due process and elective procedures, people can bring their influence to bear on each other. Institutional reciprocal mechanisms thus provide not only safeguards against unilateral social control but the means for changing institutions and the conditions of life. Within the process of reciprocal determinism lies the opportunity for people to shape their destinies as well as the limits of self-direction.

Bandura (1978, pp. 345–47)

---

school environment. At the same time, the student is experiencing personal feelings of happiness or anxiety and physiological sensations related to whether the student is rested or tired, hungry or well fed, and so forth. In such instances, cognitive learning and development result from the complex reciprocal interactions of all these factors.

As primary concepts for explaining how cognitive structures operate and change,

Piaget (e.g., 1952) has postulated two complementary processes, *assimilation* and *accommodation*. Assimilation is the process by which an individual incorporates stimuli without having to modify cognitive structures (schemata). This occurs when something new is perceived as familiar or when one responds to new situations in the same way one has responded to other situations. During assimilation, cognitive structures al-

Figure 2-1

An interactional view of the process of cognitive learning and development.

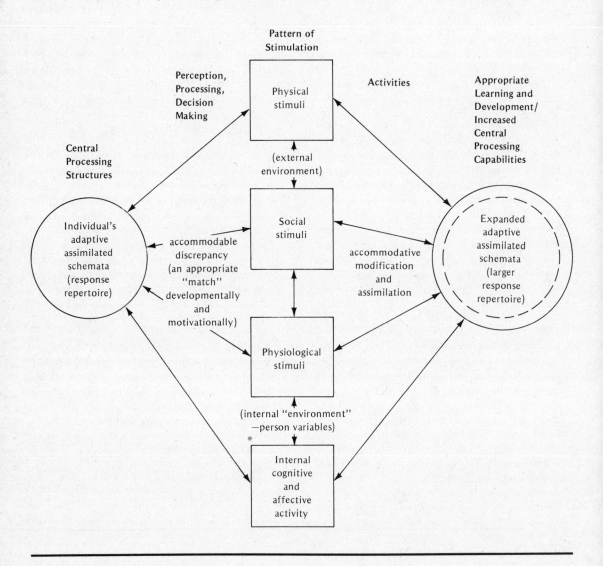

ter the perception of stimuli to fit current ways of understanding experiences.

Accommodation is the process by which one modifies current ways of understanding in order to meet demands that cannot simply be assimilated. This occurs when something is perceived as unfamiliar or when familiar stimuli are experienced in a new way. Adults

encountering new math for the first time are expected to make accommodative modifications. The numbers are familiar, but the problems must be responded to differently. In such situations, adults find they must change their way of thinking about mathematics. As new math is explained and practiced, they do learn to cope with the problems. The resultant modifications in their schemata reflect new cognitive structures or changes in old structures or both.

Piaget's view is that when the assimilative and accommodative processes oppose each other, tension is produced. It is resolution of this tension that leads to accommodative modification and growth in cognitive structures. In this way, one's central processing capabilities and one's capacity of accommodation are increased. That is to say: (1) learning has occurred; and (2) the individual is ready to learn something else to build on this, for example, the next step in a sequence or something more complex.

Of course, what is learned may be long lasting or only temporary. For structural changes to be solidified, there must be continued use of new learning. Accommodative modifications must become integrated to be useful in coping with future events. Integration results from repeated use of newly learned knowledge and skills as occurs in practice and play situations.

The following simplified examples, compared with Figure 2–1, should help illustrate and summarize the above points. A classroom environment may contain a variety of novel and vivid materials and tasks (physical stimuli) that arouse curiosity and excitement (internal cognitive and affective activity) that the person experiences (assimilates) as similar to feelings previously encountered in successful learning situations. This awareness leads to subsequent thoughts and feelings (internal cognitive and affective activity) which motivate the student to attend to new concepts being taught (physical and social stimuli) and results in learning (accommodation that expands the schemata). If the student has the opportunity to apply newly learned concepts as part of other activity at school or at home, the concepts become an integrated (assimilated) part of her or his way of understanding future experiences. In contrast, an overcrowded classroom (physical and social stimuli) arouses discomfort or anxiety (physiological stimuli and affective activity) which the student experiences (assimilates) as similar to emotions felt in previous failure situations. This leads to thoughts and feelings (internal cognitive and affective activity) interfering with attention to reading instruction (physical and social stimuli) and learning is disrupted (accommodation does not occur).

As formulated by Hunt (1961), "accommodative modification and growth [is] a function of the match between environmental circumstances and existing schemata" (p. 267).[4] The concept of the "match" provides a heuristic way of understanding how accommodation does or does not occur. This principle implies that a pattern of stimulation produces learning (accommodative modification and growth in schemata) when—and only when—there is an appropriate discrepancy between the pattern of stimulation the individual experiences and the person's assimilated cognitive structures. More specifically, appropriate learning is dependent upon (1) the discrepancy being within the limits of an individual's capacity for accommodation, and (2) the appropriate operation of accommodative and assimilative processes. Thus an appropriate "match" for successful learning is one in which there is a discrepancy that can be accommodated between one's existing structures and the pattern of stimulation experienced (see Figure 2–1).

By definition, a discrepancy that can be accommodated is one that is within the individual's cognitive capabilities and is sufficiently motivating to activate and direct be-

---

[4]In adapting this principle, we view *environmental circumstances* as encompassing the combined impact of external (e.g. physical, interpersonal, organizational, cultural) and internal (e.g. physiological and emotional) stimuli. Thus, as a broader term, we have adopted the phrase *pattern of stimulation*.

havior. The appropriate match for peak learning is a discrepancy that demands the fullest use of one's accommodative capacity. A discrepancy producing an appropriate match for learning may result "spontaneously" from the types of cognitive and affective stimuli described as curiosity, striving for competence, and feelings of self-determination (Berlyne, 1971; Deci, 1980; White, 1959). Schools, however, do not rely on spontaneous occurrences. A major concern of teachers is how to produce an appropriate match. This usually involves finding ways to enable students to pursue what social learning theorist Bandura (1977a) has conceived of as four forms of activity: (1) direct experimentation, (2) vicarious experiences (e.g., attending to live or symbolic models), (3) attending to and accepting others' verbalized experiences and judgments (experiencing verbal persuasion), and (4) logical verification (e.g., reasoning). Each of these can be seen as a response to a pattern of stimulation. Other responses include physiological activity, especially that related to emotional arousal. In turn, any response can become part of a new pattern of stimulation that can inform and motivate the individual and lead to learning.

What we have described above applies not only to "normal" learners; it is a model of learning that is relevant to all learners. Whatever the range of individual differences or disabilities, the same processes apply. The critical factor is whether the pattern of stimulation experienced by a specific individual facilitates learning.

Negative Patterns of Learning
As diagrammed in Figure 2-1 (see also Figure 2-2[a]), *appropriate* learning is a function of a discrepant pattern of stimulation that can be accommodated. In contrast, when inap-

propriate stimulation is experienced, negative patterns of learning occur.

The absence of an appropriate discrepancy between the pattern of stimulation encountered and the person's adaptive assimilated schemata results in *arrested learning* or a delayed rate of learning. In this case, there is little or no accommodative modification and growth (see Figure 2-2[b]). This is the situation, for example, when there is inadequate stimulation. In such situations the already assimilated schemata can be strengthened, or there will be a lag in the learning process, or both. If stimulus deprivation is not prolonged, the lag in learning is temporary. If the period of inadequate stimulation is lengthy, the resulting lag will be more severe. With infants, the result may be totally arrested development. With older individuals, there is the stultifying impact of boredom. In general, inadequate stimulation is associated with the relative absence of experiences which the individual perceives as interesting and valued.

If there is a discrepancy beyond accommodative capacity, distress and avoidance responses are evoked. This is the situation when there is overstimulation or extreme discontinuity related to such factors as task difficulty or motivation. If the individual cannot avoid the stimulation and must meet the demands, the result may be (1) *inappropriate learning* (inappropriate accommodation, assimilation, or both); or (2) *disrupted learning* (accommodative and assimilative failure). Thus, if there is a lengthy period of confrontation with stimulation that must be accommodated, the individual will either acquire faulty assimilated schemata (such as heightened ego defense mechanisms and strategies of lying or cheating) for adapting to such circumstances, or will psychologically decompensate (see Figure 2-2 [c]).[5]

---

[5]Selye (1956) has formulated the general adaptation syndrome to describe decompensation. While Selye's formulation is concerned mainly with physiological breakdown, psychological decompensation seems to follow a similar pattern. The model describes the individual's reaction to excessive stress as following three stages: (a) an alarm reaction stage (e.g., the individual is continuously tense and anxious), (b) a stage of resistance (e.g., excessive use of ego defense mechanisms), and (c) a stage of exhaustion (e.g., psychotic break).

Figure 2-2

Patterns of Learning and Development.

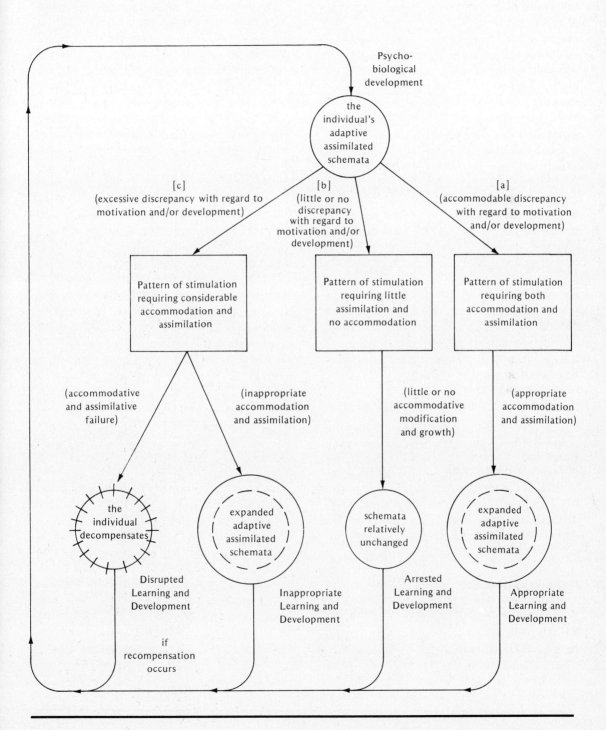

Figure 2-3

Sequence of events related to learning and behavior problems.

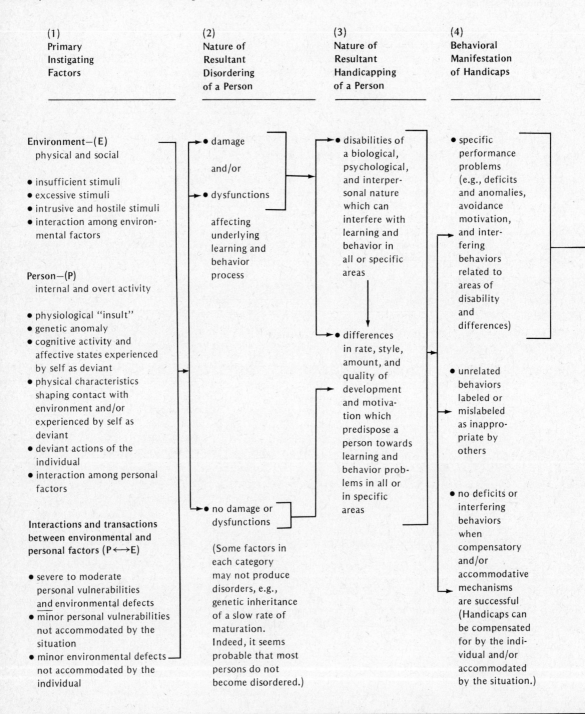

(1) Primary Instigating Factors	(2) Nature of Resultant Disordering of a Person	(3) Nature of Resultant Handicapping of a Person	(4) Behavioral Manifestation of Handicaps
Environment—(E) physical and social • insufficient stimuli • excessive stimuli • intrusive and hostile stimuli • interaction among environmental factors **Person—(P)** internal and overt activity • physiological "insult" • genetic anomaly • cognitive activity and affective states experienced by self as deviant • physical characteristics shaping contact with environment and/or experienced by self as deviant • deviant actions of the individual • interaction among personal factors **Interactions and transactions between environmental and personal factors (P←→E)** • severe to moderate personal vulnerabilities and environmental defects • minor personal vulnerabilities not accommodated by the situation • minor environmental defects not accommodated by the individual	• damage and/or • dysfunctions affecting underlying learning and behavior process • no damage or dysfunctions (Some factors in each category may not produce disorders, e.g., genetic inheritance of a slow rate of maturation. Indeed, it seems probable that most persons do not become disordered.)	• disabilities of a biological, psychological, and interpersonal nature which can interfere with learning and behavior in all or specific areas • differences in rate, style, amount, and quality of development and motivation which predispose a person towards learning and behavior problems in all or in specific areas	• specific performance problems (e.g., deficits and anomalies, avoidance motivation, and interfering behaviors related to areas of disability and differences) • unrelated behaviors labeled or mislabeled as inappropriate by others • no deficits or interfering behaviors when compensatory and/or accommodative mechanisms are successful (Handicaps can be compensated for by the individual and/or accommodated by the situation.)

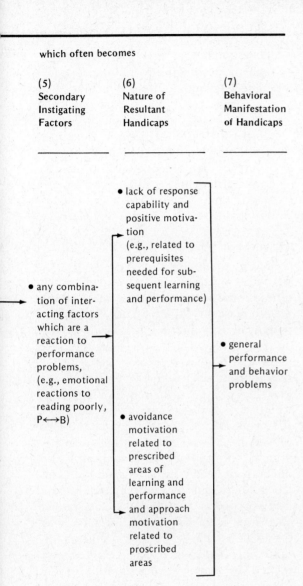

which often becomes

(5) Secondary Instigating Factors	(6) Nature of Resultant Handicaps	(7) Behavioral Manifestation of Handicaps

- any combination of interacting factors which are a reaction to performance problems, (e.g., emotional reactions to reading poorly, P↔B)

- lack of response capability and positive motivation (e.g., related to prerequisites needed for subsequent learning and performance)

- avoidance motivation related to prescribed areas of learning and performance and approach motivation related to proscribed areas

- general performance and behavior problems

Sequence of Causal Events Related to Learning Problems

In contrast to the sequence of events implied by prevailing causal models of learning disabilities (see Figure 1-1), Figure 2-3 graphically portrays the causal sequence implied by the reciprocal interaction model of learning problems. As can be seen, this view continues to recognize that a problem may be caused primarily by person (P) variables. Thus, learning disabilities instigated by a physiological trauma that disorders the CNS are encompassed. Problems stemming primarily from environmental (E) variables such as poor instruction also are recognized. Furthermore, it is stressed that the causal sequence of events may be instigated by complex interactions of environment and person factors (P ↔ E). Over time, as the sequence progresses, the interactions become even more complex.

A few comments are necessary to highlight some key implications of what is portrayed in Figure 2-3.

1. The primary instigating factors (E, P, or P ↔ E) may disorder a person and result in disabilities that interfere with growth and thereby accentuate developmental and motivational differences. However, in many, if not most, instances instigating factors do not produce damage or dysfunction, but directly result in developmental and motivational differences that are extreme enough to handicap a person.

2. Whenever environmental instigating factors have an immediate effect on the biological or psychological functioning of the individual, it is usually the resulting person variables that are of immediate practical concern. Thus, they are most emphasized in discussing the causal sequence of events. Nevertheless, it should be clear that environmental instigating factors are conceptually, if not empirically, quite distinct from person

instigating factors and both categories need to be distinguished from resultant person disorders and handicaps (see Figure 2–3, columns 1 and 2).

3. Disabilities, developmental differences, and motivational differences do not always result in specific performance problems. In general, the nature and scope of learning and behavior problems that result from disabilities and differences depend on the degree to which an individual can overcome (or correct or compensate for) such disabilities and differences, or the degree to which the situation accommodates the individual (see Figure 2–3, columns 3 and 4).[6] For example, a learning problem may indeed stem from such a simple sequence of events as a head injury instigating minimal brain damage and producing a disability that interferes with learning and performance. At the same time, it is clear that not all head injuries produce brain damage and that not all damage to the brain is severe enough to interfere with learning.

4. Learning problems may also stem from a complex set of events. For instance, the instigating factor may be a genetically determined rate of development that is slower than the standard set by accepted age norms. When the individual experiencing this condition is placed in an environment where there is a continuing demand to keep up with age norms, learning problems result. The problems that do result will be in performance related to areas of disabilities, developmental differences, and motivational differences. Given a more accommodating environment or a better

match, the problems might never be manifested.

5. Emotional reactions and related behavior problems are common negative effects stemming from difficulties with learning. From our perspective, such reactions become secondary instigating factors. That is, the behavioral manifestations of handicaps eventually begin to interact with other behavioral, environmental, and person variables to produce additional handicaps and resultant problems (see Figure 2–3, columns 5 and 6).

Before concluding our discussion of the sequence of causal events, the likelihood of attributional and pathological biases should be emphasized. It is hard to discriminate empirically among the sources of problems, and once a handicap has been identified, it is likely that unrelated problem behavior will be misattributed to it; that is, an attributional bias may exist. Furthermore, a pathological bias may be established resulting in the overevaluation of the severity of disapproved behaviors; behavior that would be seen as bothersome, but would fall within limits of normalcy if manifested by a nonlabeled individual, is identified as pathological when manifested by a labeled individual. Once secondary instigating factors are present, the range of real problems undoubtedly expands to areas not directly related to handicapping disabilities and differences. As real problems increase, the tendency toward falsely identifying other behaviors as problems seems likely to increase as does the tendency to misapprehend causality.

---

[6]Even when there are severe disabilities, there have been dramatic examples of individuals minimizing the impact of handicaps (e.g., Helen Keller).

With reference to differences, it should be noted that they will be in developmental areas *and* in motivational areas. This point is emphasized because motivational differences have not been sufficiently discussed as a potentially critical handicapping condition, especially with regard to learning problems.

Categories of Hypothesized Causes of Learning Problems

In the absence of empirical evidence, models of causality are used to generate hypothesized etiological variables. Given an interactional model, the list of possible specific causes is staggering. Therefore, there is need for categorization. Table 2-1 presents a conceptual (as contrasted with empirical) categorization as an aid in organizing the wide range of potential causes. It also highlights specific examples related to each category.

As Table 2-1 shows, major types of instigating factors exist on different levels and within different areas of focus. In addition to the interaction between major categories of variables (P and E), there are interactions within each category (between type, level, and area) and between elements of each type, level, and area. Moreover, interactions include concurrent and sequential transactions between and within categories.

There are very few instigating factors that can be postulated a priori as inevitably causing learning or behavior problems. Moreover, as is evident from Figure 2-3 and Table 2-1, it is much easier to speculate about etiology than it is to determine the cause of any individual's specific learning or behavior problem.

It will be some time before research on learning and behavior problems provides satisfactory evidence regarding various hypothesized causal relationships and establishes practical procedures for validly assessing relationships in specific clinical cases. Because a reciprocal interaction model encompasses person, environmental, and interactional causes, we see it as the most useful paradigm for generating hypotheses to guide such research. For example, it is only from the perspective of such a complex set of interacting variables that differences in problem incidence that are related to such variables as sex, race, and socioeconomic status truly can be appre-

VIEWPOINT

SEX, RACE, AND CULTURAL DIFFERENCES

We are not shackled by our biology unless we fail to understand it. . . . It develops with use and becomes inflexible with disuse and misuse. At present it seems that our schools fail to develop all of girls' abilities and misuse some of the abilities of boys.
McGuinnes (1979, p. 88)

We need to exert our efforts to make the school a place where differences, between and among people, are not merely tacitly accepted but are celebrated as a national blessing.
Smith (1974, p. vii)

ciated. With regard to sex, for instance, there is the reported high incidence of learning problems which appear early among boys and the underachievement patterns of girls which appear in later schooling. The focus on person factors has led to suggestions of biological differences related to neurological development and hemispheric specialization (e.g., see Dalby, 1979, for a discussion of differences related to hemispheric myelination). In contrast, interactional views have led to speculation that cultural expectations for boys and girls at different ages vary and interact in ways that shape childrens' attitudes and behaviors toward learning and performance (e.g., sextyping, modeling, vocational choices). Thus, many boys come to school with behavior patterns, such as high activity levels and attitudes about certain kinds of activities, that frequently make them less than motivated for academics. Girls, as they get older, have found that sex-role stereotypes often conflict with achievement behavior (Horner, 1974). Hypotheses also have been generated about even more complex causal interactions between biological differences and sex-role expectations (Williams, 1974).

TABLE 2-1

Hypothesized Causes of Learning and Behavior Problems:
Primary Instigating Variables Based on an Interactional Model (B = f[E ⟷ P])

	Environment (E)	Person (P)	Interactions and Transactions Between E and P*
Levels of Focus	1. Primary (e.g., home; classroom) 2. Secondary (e.g., neighborhood; regional area) 3. Tertiary (e.g., national; international)	1. Molecular (e.g., synaptic transmission; genetic structure) 2. Molar activity of varying units (e.g., small bits of activity, such as eye movements and directionality; complex units, such as amount of bodily activity, manners, morality, mores)	Molecular or molar activity of the individual in the primary or secondary environment or with reference to tertiary environmental factors. (combinations of E and P examples cited under Levels of Focus, such as the amount of physical activity in a classroom, the impact on one's behavior of the value placed on education in one's society)
Areas of Focus	1. Physical (e.g., geographical; architectural) 2. Social (e.g., interpersonal; organization; socio-cultural; political; economic)	1. Internal—biological and psychological (e.g., CNS; thoughts, choice and decision making; feelings) 2. Overt actions—motor and verbal (e.g., physical movement, such as gait, posture, facial expressions, activity level; spoken language, such as verbal fluency, articulation, content)	Internal or external activity of the individual with reference to the physical or social environment (combinations of E and P examples cited under Areas of Focus, such as the effect of architectural design on feelings, political policies shaping personal decision making)

Similar complex interactions have been hypothesized in efforts to explain the reported disproportionate incidence of students from minority and lower socioeconomic groups who have been labeled as problems and are not performing well in academic work (Mercer & Brown, 1973). For example, besides cultural differences and biological factors, the causes of their problems have been explained as the result of a mutual incompatibility between their attitudes toward school as it currently exists and the traditional attitudes of school personnel toward such groups (e.g., Gordon & Shipman, 1979).

CONCLUDING COMMENTS

Psychological theories and data indicate that it is inevitable for people to think in causal terms about their own and others' behavior (Heider, 1944, 1958; Jones & Nisbett, 1971; Ross, 1977). In doing so, each individual is employing one or more models of what determines human behavior. The model of causality to which one subscribes profoundly shapes one's perceptions, thoughts, beliefs, decisions, and actions. Different models generate different concepts, frameworks, and methods that guide research, practice, and everyday living.

	Environment (E)	Person (P)	Interactions and Transactions Between E and P*
Types of Instigating Factors	1. Insufficient stimuli (e.g., prolonged periods in impoverished environs; deprivation of learning opportunities at home or school such as lack of play and practice situations and poor instruction; inadequate diet) 2. Excessive stimuli (e.g., overly demanding home or school experiences, such as overwhelming pressure to achieve and contradictory expectations) 3. Intrusive and hostile stimuli (e.g., medical practices, especially at birth, leading to physiological impairment; conflict in home or faulty child rearing practices, such as long standing abuse and rejection; migratory family; language used in school is a second language; social prejudices related to race, sex, age, physical characteristics and behavior)	1. Physiological "insult" (e.g., cerebral trauma, such as accident or stroke; endocrine dysfunctions and chemical imbalances; illness affecting brain or sensory functioning) 2. Genetic anomaly (e.g., genes which limit, slow down, or lead to any atypical development) 3. Cognitive activity and affective states experienced by self as deviant (e.g., lack of knowledge or skills, such as basic cognitive strategies; lack of ability to cope effectively with emotions, such as low self-esteem) 4. Physical characteristics shaping contact with environment and/or experienced by self as deviant (e.g., visual, auditory, or motoric deficits; excessive or reduced sensitivity to stimuli; easily fatigued; factors which produce stereotypical responses such as race, sex, age, unusual appearance) 5. Deviant actions of the individual (e.g., performance problems, such as excessive errors in reading and speaking; high or low levels of activity)	1. Severe to moderate personal vulnerabilities and environmental defects and differences (e.g., person with extremely slow development in a highly demanding, understaffed classroom, all of which equally and simultaneously instigate the problem) 2. Minor personal vulnerabilities not accommodated by the situation (e.g., person with minimal CNS disorders resulting in auditory perceptual disability enrolled in a reading program based on phonics; very active student assigned to classroom which does not tolerate this level of activity) 3. Minor environmental defects and differences not accommodated by the individual (e.g., student is in the minority racially or culturally and is not participating in many school social activities and class discussions because he or she thinks others may be unreceptive)
Interactions of Variables Within Categories	1. Concurrent environmental transactions (e.g., overly punitive parent, demanding teachers, and racially isolated school) 2. Sequential environmental transactions (e.g., special school placement, subsequent negative expectations of others and long range impact of political policy decisions which affect resources available)	1. Concurrent personal transactions (e.g., awareness of poor skills and of lack of ability to cope with anxiety; problems reading and speaking) 2. Sequential personal transactions (e.g., stroke and subsequent awareness of loss of some basic cognitive coping skills; performance problems in making visual perceptual discriminations and in doing school assignments)	*May involve only one (P) and one (E) variable or may involve multiple combinations.

VIEWPOINT

MODELS DEFINE AND SHAPE

By embracing and acting on a society's or an organization's definitions of problems and of deviants, interveners work to maintain the status quo.
Bermant and Warwick (1978, p. 392)

Society defines what is exceptional or deviant, and appropriate treatments are designed quite as much to protect society as they are to help the child.
Hobbs (1975a, p. 20)

The guiding nature of models can be both helpful and misleading. With regard to everyday living, an individual's informal model of causality, valid or not, can inhibit or facilitate change, learning, or growth (Frank, 1961). Thus, it must be accounted for in any effort to correct learning and behavior problems. Practitioners and researchers who rely on formal models of causality, valid or not, also find their work facilitated or inhibited by their adopted perspective. The products of their work must be evaluated to determine whether the model is appropriate or misleading.

Since models of causality are merely analogies or potentially useful myths, one's decision to continue to rely on a particular model cannot be based strictly on available scientific data. Instead, with reference to learning and behavior problems, the best decision would be based on which model will be most helpful and least harmful to individuals and most likely to advance scientific understanding and upgrade social policy.

From the perspective of prevailing psychological theories, models of human behavior that incorporate only person or environmental variables currently are judged as of limited heuristic value and as often misleading with regard to research and practical methodology. Philosophically and politically, narrow causal models of problems are criticized as favoring society's needs over those of the individual (Hobbs, 1975a; Kittrie, 1971; Szasz, 1969). Psychological, philosophical, and political analyses converge in suggesting that old myths have outlived their value and that broader interactional models of causality should take their place. To aid in the transition, in Chapter 3 we present, in interactional terms, additional perspectives relevant to understanding the causes of learning and behavior problems.

Chapter 3
Learning Disabilities as One Type of Learning Problem

I suppose teachers have always been intuitively aware of the fact that when they change their method of teaching, certain children who have appeared to be slow learners or even non-learners become outstanding achievers. . . .
Torrance (1965, p. 253)

While learning is not restricted to any time or place, it is most often seen as a "problem" in the classroom. In recent years an increasing number of school children have been identified as having learning and behavior problems. Some have been labeled *learning disabled*; others, *emotionally disturbed, educationally handicapped, educable mentally retarded, learning handicapped, dyslexic, hyperactive,* and so forth. Despite all that has been written about students variously labeled, little is known about how they differ from each other, and there is growing recognition that some individuals assigned different labels may be very similar to each other. The important implications of similarities (homogeneity) among persons differently labeled and differences (heterogeneity) among persons labeled the same are just beginning to be discussed. In particular, little attention has been paid to the likelihood that each of the labeled groups currently includes more than persons who have within themselves disorders that interfere with learning.

From an interactional perspective, the following general proposition has been formulated to aid understanding the heterogeneity in learning problem populations. *A given student's success or failure in school is a function of the interaction between the individual's motivational and developmental status* (such as interests, expectations, strengths, and limitations) *and specific classroom situational factors encountered* (such as individual differences among teachers and differing approaches to instruction). That is, learning and behavior problems are seen as resulting not only from predispositions of the learner but from characteristics of the specific teacher, instructional program, and setting. This interactional view of factors that determine school success and failure, and some of its implications, are the focus of this chapter. Specifically, we explore how the learning environment in schools may be a causal determinant of many learning and behavior problems, and we emphasize that these types of problems need to be distinguished from specific or severe learning disabilities.

THE LEARNER AND THE CLASSROOM

All students differ from each other in terms of motivational and developmental status and, therefore, in terms of the willingness and capability to learn and perform. As we saw in Chapter 2, key learner predispositions encompass assimilated cognitive structures and cognitive, affective, and physiological activity that the student experiences at the time learning occurs.

Among the important characteristics of classroom situations are objectives, personnel, procedures, and materials. These situational factors combine to produce classrooms that vary in the degree to which the program (1) accommodates the wide range of developmental, motivational, and performance differences among students and (2) provides an appropriate match for each student's learning. In particular, programs vary

in their ability to detect existing and potential problems and to correct, compensate for, or tolerate extreme differences among learners. For the purposes of this discussion, these program variations are understood to be the degree to which the program is personalized.

The degree to which school environments *do not* personalize their programs has great etiological significance with regard to learning problems. To clarify this point, we highlight below both the process of facilitating learning and the even more complex task of facilitating learning in the classroom. Then, we formulate and discuss the implications of formal propositions about the relationship between the learner, the degree of personalized instruction, and school success and failure.

Facilitating Learning

One goal of teaching is obviously to avoid the negative learning patterns discussed in Chapter 2.[1] Stated positively, teaching is the process of arranging environmental opportunities in a way that appropriately facilitates learning. According to Hunt,

> The principle that environmental circumstances force accommodative modifications in schemata only when there is an appropriate match between the circumstances that a child encounters and the schemata . . . already assimilated [is] only another statement of the educator's adage that teaching must start where the learner is. (1961, pp. 267–68)

In interactional terms, then, the intent of teaching is to establish a pattern of stimulation that appropriately challenges the student's assimilated way of adapting to circumstances and thus results in accommodative growth and learning, i.e., developing new ways to cope with situations. The ideal in facilitating learning would be to pro-

---

[1]The term *teaching* is used in the generic sense. A *teacher* is anyone who intervenes to help another learn, e.g., a teacher, tutor, therapist, or parent.

vide an *optimal* match. However, there is no satisfactory way to specify the optimal match for any student. To say that the process is complex is a gross understatement. Appreciating the complexity of establishing an optimal match is actually the first step in understanding how easily a poor match can occur and can cause learning problems. Although each component is discussed in detail in Parts 3 and 4, we will highlight a few key components.

Motivation. If a student is to perform and learn, a student must be motivated. Thus, every teacher must be concerned about motivational readiness—not in the old sense of waiting for the student to become interested, but in the contemporary sense of providing environments that elicit curiosity and facilitate exploration. In general, students must value and expect to succeed in the situation (Atkinson, 1964; Berlyne, 1971; Bruner, 1966; Deci, 1975). This view of motivation emphasizes that the student may value an activity because of awareness of potential satisfaction in the form of extrinsic (material or social reinforcers) or intrinsic motivation (curiosity, desire to feel competent and self-determining). If the student is not aware of potential satisfaction related to an activity, such as reading, then it is unlikely that behavior will be directed toward that area, and learning problems can be expected. Another complexity, however, is suggested by recent research findings on the relationship between extrinsic rewards and intrinsic motivation. Overreliance on extrinsic rewards, while clearly shaping behavior, also may undermine a student's intrinsic valuing of an activity. This, in turn, may produce subsequent problems with learning and performance (Adelman, 1978a; Condry, 1977; Deci, 1975, 1980; Lepper & Greene, 1978; Levine & Fasnacht, 1974).

VIEWPOINT

MOTIVATION

Adults see activities from a success-failure view of things. A child lives more with an interesting-uninteresting view of things. Remember?
Nyberg (1971, p. 166)

Development. Problems in both motivation and development arise when the individual must deal for prolonged periods either with environmental discrepancies that are so great they cannot be accommodated or with situations that result in so little discrepancy they are too easily assimilated (see Figure 2–2). Providing an accommodative match for development involves dealing with differences in such variables as rate, style, amount, and quality of performance in various developmental areas, for example, sensory, perceptual, motor, language, cognitive, social, and emotional areas. One example of efforts to accommodate developmental levels comes from work on cognitive differences. Hunt and Sullivan (1974) have presented an elaborate theoretical model of conceptual-level matching. In a recent research review, Miller (1981) summarizes findings which show that negative learning patterns result from mismatches between teaching procedures and predispositions of the student. Other evidence for this idea comes from work on aptitude-treatment interactions (e.g., Cronbach & Snow, 1977; Hunt, 1975; Tobias, 1976). As with recent research on motivation, interaction-oriented efforts to establish an appropriate match for developmental differences have been more successful in suggesting the potential problems that can arise from not accomplishing this objective than in providing guidelines for effective teaching.

Range of options and mutual contracts.   In our work exploring the teaching process as a cause of learning problems (Adelman & Taylor, 1977), we have identified two key procedural errors: failure to provide a range of options from which a student can choose and failure to establish a mutually satisfactory agreement or contract between student and teacher. More specifically, we stress that learning and behavior problems are associated with failure to accomplish such process objectives as (1) establishment and maintenance of an appropriate instructional relationship (e.g., trust, communication, meaningful choices, mutual decision making, support and direction); (2) clarification and agreement about purposes of instruction; and (3) clarification and agreement about learning opportunities, teaching procedures, why these experiences can be expected to be effective, and so forth.

The process of facilitating learning is complex, and there is little agreement on how it should be accomplished.[2] Given the complexity of the process, it is impressive that so many people learn so well. At the same time, it seems evident that they do so despite how little is understood about learning and teaching.

Facilitating Learning in the Classroom
There can be little doubt that efforts to facilitate learning may be deficient. A student who experiences poor teaching will experience many mismatches. The more frequent, extensive, and long-lasting such experiences are, the more the negative learning patterns, as illustrated in Figure 2-2, are likely to result.

In classrooms, the complexity of establishing an appropriate match and avoiding significant mismatches (between the pattern of stimulation and a student's assimilated schemata) is increased. To approximate a satisfactory match for all students would require a great deal of specific and active interaction between teacher and students; of course, the number of children in most classrooms precludes much one-to-one interaction. Even with one-to-one instruction, nobody claims that current teaching practices are optimal or that all teachers are equally competent. We conclude that, given the prevailing classroom practices and the number of students in most classes, it is unlikely that many students experience an appropriate match. Therefore, while some students develop problems as a result of their deficits, it seems likely that others develop problems because of the deficiencies and limitations of classroom programs.

In summary, then, the process of facilitating learning is a problem. Facilitating learning in existing classrooms is even more so. This is an accepted fact that discourages many teachers and has led to widespread demands for improvement in school instruction. While classroom programs have been acknowledged to be deficient, however, the significance of this deficiency in terms of understanding the causes of learning problems is too often overlooked in practice and research.

FORMAL PROPOSITIONS ABOUT SCHOOL SUCCESS AND FAILURE

The nature of the interaction between the individual and the classroom program may be viewed as the major determinant of school success or failure. The hypothesized relationship can be stated formally as follows:

---

[2]For example, Joyce & Weil (1972) discuss the process of teaching in terms of sixteen models, grouped into four categories, to show the range of procedures currently in use.

1a. The more optimal the match between a student's assimilated adaptive schemata and the pattern of stimulation in the classroom program in which he or she is required to perform, the greater the likelihood of school success.

1b. Conversely, the less optimal the match between the student's schemata and stimulation experienced in the program, the greater the likelihood of poor school performance. (It should be emphasized that these hypotheses do not indicate *why* the match is a poor one. The following secondary hypotheses do address this matter.)

2a. The greater a disorder and handicap that the individual brings to the situation, the more difficult it is likely to be to establish an appropriate match to facilitate learning and appropriate behavior.

2b. The greater the teacher's ability and school's resources in personalizing instruction and thus facilitating appropriate matches, the fewer will be the number of students who exhibit learning or behavior problems or both.

2c. Conversely, the poorer the teacher's and school's ability in personalizing instruction, the greater will be the number of students with learning or behavior problems.

Types of Learning Problems

One implication of hypothesis 2 above is the obvious point that poor classroom programs can cause even nonhandicapped students to have learning and behavior problems. It is not known how many youngsters without disorders are diagnosed as learning disabled (LD) or emotionally disturbed (ED), or are assigned some other label during their schooling. However, with the growing interest in diagnostic classification of children's problems, it seems probable that the number of youngsters with classroom-caused problems assigned to one

VIEWPOINT

LEARNING IN THE CLASSROOM

It is not difficult to learn to read. It is very difficult to learn to read in school. It is very difficult to learn to read in school because schools are institutions and institutions suffer from numbers. Learning to speak is far more difficult than learning to read. First, the learner must break down reality into the objects, actions, and more abstract things that speakers around [the learner] refer to. Second, [the learner] must discriminate among sounds until [the learner] can recognize those vocal sounds that mean something. Third, [the learner] must pair off the objects and other things with the vocal sounds referring to them, despite ambiguities in both the sounds and the meanings. Fourth, [the learner] must infer for himself [or herself] the basic grammatical regularities by which sentences are constructed from these words. Unless defective, every child of whatever background does all this in the first years of life with no deliberate instruction and no special lures. If [one] tried to do this under present school conditions, we would no doubt be having crash programs in learning to speak as we have in reading.

Moffet (1970, p. 7)

or more of these categories has increased almost exponentially in the last decade. As a result of current diagnostic practices, a label such as *LD* or *ED* (or for that matter *educable mentally retarded, educationally handicapped, hyperactive,* or *dyslexic*) encompasses a continuum with regard to the primary instigating factors that initially caused their problems. At one end of the continuum are those students who *do* have fairly severe disorders which predispose them to school difficulties. At the other end are those students who *do not* have such internal disorders and whose problems stem primarily from the deficiencies of the learning environment. Toward the middle of the continuum are youngsters who do have very minor disorders, but who are able to com-

Figure 3-1

Two views of the populations diagnosed as learning disabled and emotionally disturbed.

Prevailing View:
Learning disabled and emotionally disturbed students are categorized as separate populations

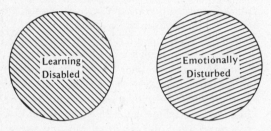

Hypothesized View:
The diagnosed learning disabled and emotionally disturbed populations are seen as overlapping and as consisting of a continuum encompassing three major subgroups of youngsters with learning or behavior problems, or both.

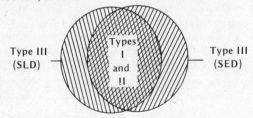

Type I
No disorder—problem results primarily from the deficiencies of the learning environment.

Type II
Minor disorder—problem results from deficiencies in both the individual and the learning environment.

Type III
Severe disorder—problem results from the individual's disorders and handicaps, i.e., a specific or severe learning disability (SLD) or severe emotional disturbance (SED).

pensate for such disorders in performing and learning school tasks under appropriate circumstances, for example, when the instructional process is appropriately motivating.[3] For the purposes of this discussion, the non-disordered individuals are referred to as having Type I problems; the individuals with minor disorders, Type II problems; and the individuals with serious disorders, Type III problems. Students with Type I problems and other students on their end of the continuum may have been assigned a variety of diagnostic labels, but most of these labels inappropriately suggest that the students' problems were caused by a disorder. It is only students with Type III problems who are seen as appropriate recipients of diagnostic labels implying person disorders, such as specific learning disabilities and specific or severe emotional disturbance.

In order to keep these points from getting lost in too much complexity, it may be helpful just to use two groups of labeled students, the learning disabled and the emotionally disturbed, as an example. These labels imply that each group consists of a different and relatively homogeneous population. In fact, however, some pupils diagnosed *LD* and some diagnosed *ED* may be quite similar in terms of what caused their problems. That is, they may be students without disorders who have experienced relatively poor classroom programs. They may even be quite similar in terms of the learning and behavior problems they manifest and have been labeled differently only for such reasons as assessor predilections and program availability.[4]

[3]The issue of compensatory mechanisms has not been well studied, but there are many examples of highly motivated individuals who have overcome severe handicaps in their efforts to understand and to communicate with others.
[4]As we discuss in Part 2, current assessment procedures do not have the capability of validly detecting the cause of a problem that may have been developing gradually over several years; often the procedures cannot even provide a valid assessment of the student's current performance capabilities. Despite these diagnostic problems, the assessment can be designed to fit in with the practical decision that must be made about whether the student is to receive special help. And, chances are, if the assessor believes the individual is deserving and knows help is only available if the student is assigned a particular label, the "correct" diagnosis will be made.

Proportions of Type I, II, and III Problems

The question of actual percentages for the three types of problems hypothesized above is an intriguing one.[5] As an estimate, the Type III group (students with serious disorders) probably is the smallest proportion of the total population currently labeled LD and ED. This remains conjecture, however, until research data on the matter are available.

Figure 3-1 summarizes the prevailing hypothesized views of the LD and ED populations. The hypothetical view shows the two populations overlap. Most students labeled LD and ED are seen as representing Type I and II learning and behavior problems. The small remaining percentage is seen as those actually having a severe enough disorder to warrant its being assigned the discrete classifications of *specific* or *severe learning disability* or *severe emotional disturbance*, i.e., a Type III problem. Another way to picture hypothetically the types and proportions of learning problems based on an interactional model is portrayed in Figure 3-2.

To expand the point further, Figure 3-3 portrays the entire population of school-age children in terms of the degree of personalization needed in learning to read. The instructional needs of students learning to read in the classroom differ. In particular, the support and direction (structure) and instructional methods needed to teach each student satisfactorily varies dramatically.

VIEWPOINT

FAILURE OF SCHOOLS

Most children in school fail.

For a great many, this failure is avowed and absolute. Close to forty percent of those who begin high school, drop out before they finish. For college, the figure is one in three.

Many others fail in fact if not in name. They complete their schooling only because we have agreed to push them up through the grades and out of the schools, whether they know anything or not. There are many more such children than we think. If we "raise our standards" much higher, as some would have us do, we will find out very soon just how many there are. Our classrooms will bulge with kids who can't pass the test to get into the next class.

But there is a more important sense in which almost all children fail: Except for a handful, who may or may not be good students, they fail to develop more than a tiny part of the tremendous capacity for learning, understanding, and creating with which they were born and of which they made full use during the first two or three years of their lives.

Holt (1964, p. xiii)

Thus, the student population as a whole can be seen to differ in terms of instructional needs along a continuum ranging from those who are learning satisfactorily to those who manifest the three types of learning problems described above (see Figure 3-3).

---

[5]Because of the imprecise way the label *learning disability* is used, incidence figures fluctuate markedly. Various expert estimates and empirical reports provide figures ranging from 1 to 30 percent of the school population. With regard to the United States, Canada, and Great Britain, Tansley and Panckhurst (1981) suggest that 2 to 5 percent are learning disabilities. Japan and China have reported the lowest incidence, approximately 1 percent (Makita, 1968; Tarnopol & Tarnopol, 1976).

Legislation in the United States has tended to reflect the estimate of the National Advisory Committee on Handicapped Children (1968) that places the figure at 1 to 3 percent of the school-age population. Federal agencies use the 3-percent figure in estimating those who need special education services. We lean toward the 1-percent estimate. Recent federal statistics indicate that 1.89 percent of the school-age population have been designated as learning disabled. Based on the 3-percent estimate, another 1.11 percent are being sought.

Current estimates, while not based on adequate data, go so far as to suggest that almost 50 percent of the current school population is not performing satisfactorily in reading. This percentage obviously is not true for most schools, but it may be a reasonable guess and even an underestimate with regard to schools in economically disadvantaged areas.

Figure 3-2

Hypothesized types and proportions
of learning problems.

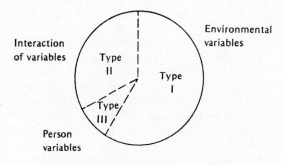

This typology is meant to represent different initial
causes (primary instigating factors) of learning problems
in the population of persons presently labeled *learning
disabled.*

CONCLUDING COMMENTS

In summary, we want to stress two major
points from the preceding discussion.

First, students labeled *LD* and *ED* are seen
as consisting of a heterogeneous group in
terms of both the cause of their problems
and intervention implications. The continuum ranges from those pupils whose problem stems initially from the learning environment to those who actually have severe
disorders that interfere with school performance. For convenience, the continuum
may be described as encompassing three
major subgroups of youngsters with problems. With regard to LD, this analysis implies
that many students so labeled are misdiagnosed. From our perspective, we believe the
label needs to be used more discriminately
and should be reserved for that subgroup of
learning problems that actually have severe
disorders and handicaps, i.e., Type III learn-

ing problems. Moreover, to avoid confusion
with all those currently being misdiagnosed
as LD, the complete label of *specific* or *severe* learning disability (SLD), seems more
appropriate for this type of problem.

Second, a significant relationship exists
between teachers' ability to personalize instruction and the type and relative proportion of problem students who are likely to be
found in classrooms. Specifically, it is suggested that the more personalized the classroom, the fewer the number of Type I and
II learning problems precipitated and the
greater the number of all types of problems
helped. This interactional view of the causal
relationship between the nature of instruction and the range of learning problems
likely to be found in a classroom emphasizes
the importance of environmental changes in
preventing and remedying such problems.
Moreover, the interactional perspective underscores the idea that the nature and scope
of environmental changes needed differ
with each of the three types of problems.
For example, changes designed to personalize a program for nondisordered students
(Type I problems) may focus on improvements in regular teaching practices rather
than specialized remedial and therapeutic
treatments, whereas many of the latter approaches will be tried in working with a severely disordered pupil (Type III problems).
These points are amplified in Parts 3 and 4.

Of course, schools are not the only environment that can be thought of as causally
related to learning and behavior problems
(see Table 2-1). Schools have been used as
the primary example because they are one of
the most pervasive influences in children's
learning and they are the place learning is
most often seen as a problem. However, in
using this example and by focusing on
classrooms in particular, there is a danger
that some of what we have said will be

viewed as criticism of teachers. Nothing could be farther from our intent. As the discussion in this chapter emphasizes, classroom teaching is one of the hardest tasks imaginable. It is a task which the best knowledge available cannot prepare a person to do in a highly successful fashion. Moreover, the resources needed to do the job optimally simply are not available in most classrooms. Teachers are sent forth to do a task that, due to current circumstances, has a fair degree of failure built into it; then teachers are lambasted for the inevitable degree of failure that occurs. No wonder there is so much talk of teacher "burn-out."

Certainly, many teachers, like many persons in any field, could do a better job. Given that this statement is a truism, it may seem to some legislators that all that is needed is to demand accountability. But what is being demanded may be something that no one knows quite how to do. Thus, it may be impossible to meet the substance of the demands. It is still an unanswered empirical question as to how wide a range of individual differences in motivation and development can be accommodated in public school classrooms by a highly competent, regular teacher using the most optimal procedures that can be made available. (Despite the fact that this is the concept underlying the move to "mainstream" exceptional children, regular school programs have not demonstrated that a very wide range of individual differences can be accommodated.) While the question is an empirical one, whether it is to be answered is a political matter. No answer can be forthcoming unless our society is ready to invest in sponsoring relevant research and recruiting the most gifted teaching personnel. Current policies and priorities suggest we are not yet ready.

Figure 3-3

A hypothetical representation of the student population.

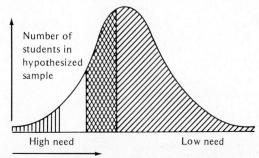

Number of students in hypothesized sample

High need   Low need

Degree of personalized instruction the pupil needs

 Students who are learning satisfactorily, though not optimally, with current broadband practices

 Students who are not learning satisfactorily primarily because current broadband practices are too limited or used in ways which do not accommodate an appropriate range of motivational and developmental differences (Type I and some Type II learning problems)

 Students who are not learning satisfactorily because they have relatively minor disabilities or motivational/developmental differences and therefore need a higher degree of specific and active one-to-one interaction with a teacher than is possible when broadband teaching practices are used exclusively (some Type II learning problems)

 Students who are not learning satisfactorily because they have more severe disabilities or motivational/developmental differences and therefore must have the highest degree of specific and active one-to-one interaction with a teacher (Type III learning problems)

Chapter 4

Etiology and Learning Problems: Current Status and Future Directions

A RESPONSIBLE ANSWER TO THE
   QUESTION OF CAUSALITY

FACTORS MAINTAINING THE
   STATUS QUO
Reactions Against Identifying Causes
Psychosocial Biases
Methodological Problems

FUTURE APPROACHES TO
   ETIOLOGICAL RESEARCH

CONCLUDING COMMENTS

*We cannot perceive unless we antici-
pate, but we must not see only what we
anticipate.*
Neisser (1976, p. 43)

*Until the cause is known, contemporary un-
derstanding and wisdom are not only limited, but may be misguided and misleading.*
Adelman

By this point, it should be evident why there
are no simple answers to the question, What
causes learning disabilities? Many people are
asking for, and would be comforted by, a
straightforward answer. Those parents and
teachers who worry they have done something to cause a child's problems may
even be somewhat relieved by a suggestion
that the problems are due to factors such as
minor brain damage or dysfunction for
which they were not responsible.

When a large number of people want an
immediate and acceptable answer, considerable pressure is put on "experts" to provide it. In response to such pressure, the
disordered-person model of causality has
been generalized to account for an increasing number of school learning problems. In
turn, the general public, professionals, and
policymakers have been uncritically receptive to this perspective.

In this chapter, we discuss what can now
be said in answering questions about causality and what inhibits improving answers to
these questions. We then conclude our discussion of etiology by exploring how the
state of the art might be improved.

A RESPONSIBLE ANSWER TO THE QUESTION OF CAUSALITY

Our discussion of etiology has emphasized that the causes of the most commonly encountered learning and behavior problems are known only in theory; if a person has problems, currently available assessment procedures cannot validly detect what originally caused them. As a result, populations labeled *learning disabled, emotionally disturbed, educationally handicapped, dyslexic, hyperactive,* and so forth, are quite heterogeneous with regard to etiology and appropriate corrective strategies. Indiscriminate use of ambiguous labels, of course, is detrimental to efforts directed at developing a comprehensive and meaningful body of knowledge about learning problems. Moreover, it seems clear that as long as this tendency continues, it is not one's ability to assess as much as it is one's theory of causal and contributing factors that will shape assessment practices, diagnostic classifications, and intervention approaches.

Given the state of the art, a responsible answer to the question What causes learning disabilities? appears to be that, for most persons presently labeled *LD*, the primary instigating cause of the problem can only be

VIEWPOINT

ANSWERS COME EASY

The parents of a child who has been labeled and is physically, psychologically, or academically deficient are usually avid consumers of ideas that promise help. These parents are struggling to understand what may be incomprehensible. But answers come easy, and all too often they are given by individuals with well-lubricated ethics in a forceful, professional, quasi-scientific and logical manner.
Pihl (1975, p. 23)

inferred. The only certainty associated with LD is that those so labeled are not satisfactorily learning something someone is trying to teach them.

Stated differently, the LD label as presently applied should be acknowledged as an uncertain indicator of why a person is not learning satisfactorily and what should be done about it. The person so labeled probably does not differ very greatly from many others who manifest similar behavior in learning situations, but who are assigned different labels or are simply described as problems and underachievers.

Obviously, inability to assess cause validly does not prevent the formulation of hypotheses about causality. There is a vast array of hypotheses, including many that implicate the environment at home and at school and some that stress that sociopolitical-economic factors may be causally related. Many of these hypotheses are unlikely to be very satisfying to those who are looking for person-oriented answers. Moreover, unresearched hypotheses can never instill the confidence that comes from being told the evidence has been found. However, offering causal theory as theory certainly represents a more appropriate response than one that in any way prematurely implies that "research has proven —— ." The uncritical acceptance and use of limited etiological research data as proof only colludes with prevailing myths and mystifications to bolster the positions of those who argue against striving to identify causes.

FACTORS MAINTAINING THE STATUS QUO

The search for a better understanding of the causes of learning problems is hampered by a variety of factors. Prominent among these are (1) reactions against identifying the causes of an individual's learning problems, (2) psychosocial biases that help maintain

VIEWPOINT

ETIOLOGY

Based on analysis of the current state of the LD field, it seems reasonable to conclude the following.

> While it is common practice to theorize about neurological disorders causing most learning problems, there currently are no reliable and valid procedures for determining a causal relationship in most cases in which it has supposedly been identified;

> Because of widespread, premature adoption of the label *learning disabilities* by legislatures, administrators, and practitioners, there probably have been many false positive identifications. That is, it is likely many persons currently so labeled do not have a disorder/disability that initially caused their learning problems.

> There is a pervasive tendency to view causes of learning problems from a relatively narrow perspective that emphasizes factors within the person. A more appropriate perspective is seen as adopting a broad model of causation that emphasizes not only person factors, but environmental variables and causes that stem from complex interactions across categories of variables.

> Persons whose learning problems currently are seen as caused by neurological dysfunctions (e.g., currently labeled *learning disabled, dyslexic, hyperkinetic*, etc.) probably constitute at least three different groups of learning problems when classified with reference to the general class of variables initially causing the problem. We have categorized these three groups as follows: Type I learning problems (caused by environmental variables); Type II learning problems (caused by an interaction of person and environmental variables); and Type III learning problems (caused by person variables that produce either major processing dysfunctions, and thus are seen as producing problems appropriately labeled *specific* or *severe learning disabilities,* or major social or emotional dysfunctions, and thus are seen as producing problems more appropriately labeled *severe emotional disturbance*).

> With regard to all types of learning problems, the causal role of motivational factors has been ignored. An environment may be too limited in the range of motivationally relevant learning opportunities; there may be a mismatch between a particular individual's interests and a particular learning environment; or an individual's learning problems may reflect a strong avoidance motivation to most learning environments, such as most classrooms.

prevailing practices and beliefs, and (3) methodological problems associated with identifying cause-effect relationships. We discuss these factors in hopes of an increased awareness of their existence that will lead to efforts to diminish their negative impact.

Reactions Against Identifying Causes

Because of inadequate data about causal factors and detrimental effects of labeling practices, many writers and practitioners have argued against pursuing the identification of causes. Some have taken the pragmatic stance that teaching a student who has a learning problem requires no more than knowing what the youngster needs to learn. A great deal of the negative reaction, however, comes from those who are concerned about negative side effects of diagnostic labeling.

As the report of the project on classification of exceptional children (Hobbs, 1975a) concludes:

There is growing public concern over the uses and abuses of categories and labels as applied to children.... Categories and labels are powerful instruments for social regulation and control, and they are often employed for obscure, covert, or hurtful purposes: to degrade people, to deny them access to opportunity, to exclude "undesirables" whose presence in some way offends, disturbs familiar custom, or demands extraordinary effort. (pp. 8-11)

On the other hand, the report also emphasizes that

classification of exceptional children is essential to get services for them, to plan and organize helping programs, and to determine the outcomes of intervention efforts.... Categories and labels may open up opportunities for exceptional children, facilitate the passage of legislation in their interest, supply a rallying point for volunteer organizations, and provide a rational structure for the administration of government programs. (pp. 5-13)

Thus, the report acknowledges that there are both problems *and* benefits related to labeling.

While research has yet to clarify for whom and under what circumstances, there is little doubt that labeling can result in negative side effects for the individual labeled. Possible negative effects raise major ethical dilemmas which cannot be ignored by any responsible professional. If negative effects cannot be avoided, subsequent benefits must be judged to outweigh potential harm to the individual.

Critics who argue responsibly against labeling suggest that negative effects outweigh the benefits. Their arguments, however, tend to ignore ethical concerns related to neglecting etiological research. Professionals have an ethical responsibility to advance knowledge, particularly knowledge that can improve the state of professional practice. From this perspective, labeling done as part of etiological studies can be considered as potentially benefiting future generations. Specifically, successful

etiological research can result in improved prescriptions for alleviation of problems, including preventive action. For example, while identifying and labeling causes may lead to what Merton (1948) describes as a self-fulfilling prophecy, such activity also is the basis for the opposite phenomenon, the suicidal prophecy. Suicidal prophecies are the foundation of preventive practices. That is, potential problems are identified for a population, subgroup, or individual and then efforts are directed at preventing the prophecy from occurring. In such instances, labeling may be viewed not only as positive but as absolutely necessary if learning problems are to be prevented.

The above discussion highlights the intricacies of the ethical case for and against labeling causality. Ethical judgments related to all intervention practices require complex analyses (see Chapter 16; see also Beauchamp & Childress, 1979; Bermant, Kelman, & Warwick, 1978). Indiscriminant labeling always is irresponsible and is to be avoided. Equally as irresponsible would be the elimination of labeling (especially as related to etiological research) in situations where important benefits can result, if not immediately, at least for society in the future. Thus, labeling per se is not the issue; as we will discuss more fully in Chapter 5, the issue is *when* and *how* labeling should be used.

The danger in the negative reactions against current labels designed to identify causes is that such reactions tend to bolster the positions of those who argue that it is not worth studying causes. This extreme position obviously is anti-scientific and detrimental to both applied and basic research efforts.

Psychosocial Biases

As has long been noted by psychologists (e.g., Dewey, 1929; Festinger, 1957), people do not like to feel uncertain. Lack of an answer or complex answers to pressing problems usually is discomforting and leads to activity designed to eliminate the discomfort. When the cause of a problem is uncertain, post hoc reasoning is an extremely common way for people to fill an explanatory vacuum. Sometimes even a rather flimsy answer seems better than nothing. As we discussed in Chapter 1, the current conclusion that CNS disorders are the cause of LD reflects a considerable amount of post hoc reasoning. The premature and widespread acceptance of this conclusion well may reflect the tendency to adopt unproven answers as long as they appear logical.

Other psychological theories suggest a variety of reasons for maintaining belief in a limited set of person variables as causes of learning problems. Attribution theory, for instance, suggests that the actors and observers in a situation have access to quite different information, and this leads them to conflicting conclusions about causality. Specifically, Jones and Nisbett have hypothesized that "there is a pervasive tendency for actors to attribute their actions to situational requirements, whereas observers tend to attribute the same actions to stable personal dispositions" (1971, p. 80). Thus persons with problems tend to "blame" the environment, while those observing the problem see the cause as based in the person with the problem. As Jones (1979) recounts, several theoretical explanations have been offered for this tendency: (1) the salience of the actor's behavior may "engulf" the observer's perception (Heider, 1958); (2) only limited information about preceding events is available to observers; and (3) an observer may have numerous reasons (motivational biases) for wanting to believe an actor's dispositions are the causal factor. The professionals who assess learning and behavior problems, of course, are "observers" in this sense, as are parents. Thus, for many of us, the psychological tendency is to see person variables as causes and to ignore indications that the environment might be a contributing cause.

Related to attributional tendencies are theories about where responsibility for one's actions generally resides. That is, people differ in terms of whether they tend to see control of major life events as residing within themselves or as due to external factors (internal versus external locus of control). In addition to locus of control, concepts such as field dependence and field independence have been discussed as highly related to competence and self-direction. A great deal of what has been written about a person's tendencies to externalize causality implies, or at least is interpreted as, suggesting that individuals who accept personal responsibility for their problems are somehow better human beings than those who do not. This makes it difficult to keep a fair balance in looking at the relative contribution of environmental and person variables.

Another reason for ignoring environment and overemphasizing person variables is that professionals who intervene to help persons are not usually in a position to make major changes in the environment (especially secondary and tertiary environments). Therefore, they tend to focus on "helping" persons (1) understand the problems they are experiencing (usually from the observer's perspective that problems are within the person) and (2) change in ways that will make them fit in with the environment or learn to live with their problems.

Going beyond psychological and pragmatic factors, many writers have emphasized the relativity of deviance and, thus, of causal attributions based on analyses of sociopolitical-economic shifts. Hobbs, for example, succinctly concludes:

Normality and exceptionality (or deviance) are not absolutes; both are culturally defined by particular societies at particular times for particular purposes (Benedict, 1934). Becker (1963, p. 9) describes the process in the following way: "Social groups create deviance by making the rules whose infraction constitutes deviance, and by applying these rules to particu-

lar people and labeling them as outsiders. . . . The deviant is one to whom that label has successfully been applied; deviant behavior is behavior that people so label."

When the country is in a conservative mood, when established values and institutions go unquestioned, then the difficulties of an individual are likely to be attributed to . . . personal weaknesses and deficiencies. The child or adult who experiences difficulty will be seen as somehow inadequate, as unable to take advantage of existing opportunities until those inadequacies are remedied. The institutional forms that evolve will emphasize helping individuals to adapt themselves to existing social conditions (Levine and Levine, 1970, p. 279). Solutions to exceptionality or deviance will be basically philanthropic and oriented toward doing something about the deficits of the individual.

When, however, increasing numbers of persons become discontented and begin to challenge the legitimacy of specific social norms and to advocate social change, then the individual will be viewed as basically good. Problems in living will be attributed largely to the inadequate circumstances of an individual's life rather than to . . . personal failings. Helping forms then will emphasize the need to modify existing social institutions to increase their relevance to current, general conditions of life. New social institutions to provide for personal growth and development will emerge (Levine and Levine, 1970). Solutions to deviance will be basically political and oriented toward doing something about society, toward improving individual opportunities rather than toward removing individual deficits. (1975a, pp. 21–22)

FOR EXAMPLE

PERSONAL BIAS IN EXPLAINING THE CAUSES OF LEARNING PROBLEMS

There is no question that many people feel they know what caused their successes and failures. That is, they have a clear sense of causal connections and they confidently explain what causes past events. Unfortunately, the clarity of hindsight is not always matched by its validity (Fischoff, 1976; Ross, 1977; Tversky & Kahneman, 1974).

As an example, if you are a good reader, you may believe it is because of the way you were taught, say, with a phonics method. While your belief may be correct, all that is known for certain is you are a good reader and you remember that at some point you received phonics instruction. Chances are that some of the others in the same phonics program do not read well. Is that because of phonics instruction? From your perspective, this would appear doubtful. After all, you believe your success is due to phonics. However, it could be that instruction was not the critical factor in either case. For instance, the key to your effective learning may have been that you did a great deal of reading at home.

That is, amount of practice may have been the difference between reading success and failure. Or, perhaps what was a good instructional match for you was not so good for everyone. For instance, some students may not have been developmentally ready to make the type of auditory perceptual discriminations needed to learn phonics at the time it was presented. Because the instructional system poorly matched the learner's stage of development, they were deprived of skills that would have allowed for self-improvement in reading. The developmental lag in auditory perception might not be identified as a possible causal factor if the person were not assessed soon after onset of reading problems. This is because all but extremely slow or disabled developers acquire adequate perceptual abilities by about age 10 (Wepman et al., 1975) and thus are no longer perceptually lagging. Thus, ironically, the original cause may have disappeared, but the learning problem which was created remains.

Methodological Problems

Another fundamental factor that tends to maintain the status quo related to understanding etiology is the methodological difficulties that arise in investigating cause-effect relationships. Two key difficulties are (1) the sparsity of satisfactory measurement procedures and (2) "design" complications involved in distinguishing cause and effect.

As we will discuss in Part 2, causal factors that produce extremely severe biological dysfunctioning, such as gross brain trauma or major endocrinal and chemical disturbances, usually can be assessed. However, minor biological and most psychological and environmental factors that probably are responsible for most learning problems are notoriously difficult to measure. Many measurement devices are too insensitive; for example, the EEG is unable to detect minor cerebral dysfunctioning. Some procedures readily identify differences between individuals, but what is identified does not differentiate between problem and nonproblem populations (e.g., as when mixed dominance is identified). Other measures produce reliable findings indicative of dysfunctioning, but what the specific nature of the problem is remains highly debatable (e.g., as when a measure claims to identify problems in visual perception or psycholinguistic abilities). Most measures are affected by the lowered motivation (often avoidance motivation) of individuals who have problems. There is no effective way to measure what people are capable of doing unless they are motivated to perform. Thus, poor performance may not be indicative of disorders or lagging development, but may simply reflect the person's degree of motivation.

The timing of etiological assessments and the existence of several possible causal factors can make the situation even more complex. Establishing a cause-effect connection between contemporaneous events is difficult enough; with any significant time interval between the primary instigating factor

and etiological assessment, the complexity of gathering valid data can become insurmountable. The presence of several possible instigating factors makes discrimination of the actual cause even harder.

It is unlikely that proof of causal relationships can be found using only post hoc rational analysis or psychometric measurements. The design and measurement problems that permeate current efforts to assess causality indicate the need for developing new methodological strategies.

FUTURE APPROACHES TO ETIOLOGICAL RESEARCH

The feasibility of pursuing new directions in studying the causes of learning problems depends not only on overcoming factors maintaining the status quo; it also involves adopting alternative conceptual models and methods. In Chapters 2 and 3, we explored an interactional model and how it could be used systematically to generate and categorize causal hypotheses. In this section, we suggest two methodological approaches as especially promising for investigating major causes of learning problems: (1) a cautious, unobtrusive approach in studies related to prediction or to identification as soon after onset of problems as is feasible and (2) research on intervention related to prevention and to sequential and hierarchical approaches to correction after onset of problems.

While predictive research has not yet been highly successful (Adelman, 1978b; Satz & Fletcher, 1979), prediction represents a useful approach to studying causality. This approach involves assessing hypothesized causal variables, under appropriately controlled conditions, prior to the anticipated onset of problems and then monitoring learning to identify problems as they appear. If one, having ruled out major alternative causes, can repeatedly and accurately predict, then the case for cause-effect conclusions is bolstered greatly. Similarly, studies to identify problems shortly after onset can reduce the time lapse between cause and effect sufficiently to increase confidence about causal connections.

Predictive and early-identification research helps rule out many compelling correlates and strengthens the case for further investigation of more probable hypothesized causes. The next steps include determining, under controlled conditions, whether modifying or removing certain variables prevents the problem.

Of course, even without findings of predictive research, preventive programs can be inaugurated. If preventive programs are successful, clarification of the specific effective variables should aid in understanding causes of problems. Similarly, corrective interventions designed to alleviate problems soon after onset can offer major insights into etiology. One example of such a strategy is a sequential and hierarchical approach to intervention based on an interactional model of causality. Since this approach is discussed and diagrammed in Parts 2 and 4, only a brief outline is offered here. As used in our laboratory (Adelman & Taylor, 1978a), this approach first attempts to correct any general environmental deficiencies that may be interfering with an individual's learning. If this step is sufficient to correct the problem, then person variables can be ruled out as sole causes of current problems. If general environmental changes are not sufficiently effective, a hierarchical sequence of interventions is initiated. The first step in this sequence involves modifying instruction (e.g., increasing task alternatives, or using additional techniques) specifically to accommodate the learner's current motivational and developmental status. In doing so, there is no presumption that the student lacks prerequisites or has disabilities. If successful, this step points to potential interactions of person and environmental variables, that is, a mismatch between the previous approach

to teaching and the characteristics of the student. If this step is insufficient or unsuccessful, the next step emphasizes helping the student acquire any prerequisites that may not have been learned (such as sustaining attention, following directions, or communicating appropriately with others). Success after learning prerequisites points to readiness factors that may have been the current source of problems, but, of course, does not indicate primary instigating factors. Such success, however, does tend to rule out major biological disorders. If this step is unsuccessful, focus shifts to possible disorders, such as central processing dysfunctioning. At this point, instructional and special remedial and therapeutic strategies are used in attempts to establish ways to correct or compensate for such disorders. By screening out all but those individuals with the most intractable problems, the process helps identify the most likely sample for inclusion in subsequent studies of primary instigating factors hypothesized as producing disorders. That is, the probability that the sample actually contains a large percentage of disordered persons (i.e., those with specific or severe learning disabilities) should be markedly increased.

CONCLUDING COMMENTS

There are promising conceptual models and methodological strategies that can increase understanding of causes and their implications for practice. However, major programs of etiological study are not so much dependent on awareness of research strategies as they are a matter of political policy and priority. What now appears evident is that priority is being given to immediate service needs—and to programs of research that claim they can quickly meet these needs—rather than to long-term research. A sound program of etiological research might take twenty years to complete with no guarantee of success. This is not a long time by scientific standards, but much too long by the standards of funding agencies and legislative bodies responsible for underwriting needed research. The result of current policies emphasizing relatively short-term studies is that the knowledge base for understanding, preventing, and treating learning and behavior problems is grossly deficient. It is easy to accept the idea that more services and resources are needed to help persons experiencing problems; equal acceptance is needed for the idea that long-term research studies are indispensable if new and fundamental knowledge is to be made available to meet that need.

At the same time, it is important to stress that one does not need to abandon consideration of causality because of the lack of valid, systematic research data. It is preferable to have such an empirical basis for applied practices. However, even without direct evidence of causal relationships, current practices can be improved by moving beyond limited person or environmental models of causality. As we have illustrated, an interactional perspective provides a basis for broadening contemporary thinking about the range of potentially useful intervention approaches. For example, it should be now evident that attributing the cause of problems to environmental factors, or to an interaction between an individual's vulnerabilities and an actively hostile environment, implies different intervention than does attributing causality only to person factors. Specifically, any attribution that recognizes that environmental factors may be contributing to problems underscores the need for interventions designed to produce changes in the environment. Moreover, this perspective underscores the need not only for environmental changes designed to alter the individual, but for alternatives in the environment to accommodate specific individuals and to accommodate a wider range of individual differences.

PART 2

CLASSIFICATION AND SELECTION FOR LEARNING DISABILITIES

Some people are saying these days that we should not classify children or children's problems, but these good people are wrong. Classification is essential. . . . We cannot solve problems without classifying, and we can't communicate without classifying.
Hobbs (1979, p. 8)

The appropriate educational placement for individual children remains, of course, a matter for local determination. The new policy, however, does seem to rule out blanket judgments by school officials that all children with a particular kind of handicapping condition . . . shall be educated in self-contained classrooms, or that all handicapped youngsters should be placed in special schools. Instead, separate judgments must be made for each child, and these judgments must be based on an analysis of that child's individual needs.
Martin (1976, p. 14)

Much activity in the learning disabilities field is devoted to identifying individuals with problems and deciding whether they require special services. Assessment procedures are essential ingredients of this activity.

It is common for professionals to administer an extensive psychoeducational "test battery" which includes tests of visual and auditory perception, cognition, intelligence, achievement, psycholinguistic ability, and motor coordination. Poor performance on one or more tests is likely to lead either to a specific diagnostic label based on what the test claims to measure, such as *visual perceptual dysfunction*, or to a more encompassing label, such as *learning disabled*. In turn, the diagnostic label or pattern of assessment findings may be used to prescribe placement and treatment. Due to popular interest and legislated programs, procedures for diagnosis, screening, and placement have become highly marketable commodities. To meet the demand, an increasing number of persons, agencies, and companies are involved in supplying such services.

With demand increasing, both consumers and suppliers tend to ignore some of the limitations and negative effects of available procedures. In fact, some practices are accepted as valid simply because they are so widely used. The assumption is that the practice must be valid, or why would so many textbooks discuss it, professionals use it, companies sell it, legislative bodies endorse it, and the general public accept it? Such logic has led to the suggestion that some practices have a "market," "cash," and "vicarious" validity, which far exceeds their rational and statistical validity (Salvia & Ysseldyke, 1981; Ysseldyke & Algozzine, 1979).

Widespread acceptance of formal classification and selection practices is not sufficient evidence that the practices are beneficial, or even that they are at least more beneficial than harmful. Constructive critics point out many negative by-products of large-scale classification and selection programs. As discussed by Ebel (1964) and Messick (1965), five major concerns raised regarding current practices used in schools are: (1) invasion of privacy; (2) incorrect and/or indelible labeling of children as disordered or deficient, with negative consequences for self-esteem, motivation, and social status; (3) reduction in the range of individual characteristics and talent due to the tendency of test authors to focus only on what is readily measurable; (4) growing control over education and the futures of individuals by those responsible for testing programs; (5) mechanistic evaluation and decision making which, over time, may reduce essential freedoms.

These are important concerns for which many professionals in psychology and education continue to seek solutions. Unfortunately, criticism of specific practices often leads to irresponsible and indiscriminate attacks. For example, the well-founded concern that labeling persons as problems can lead to negative effects has led many critics to the ill-founded conclusion that all labeling should be abolished.

Given the widespread activity and controversy surrounding diagnosis, screening, and placement procedures used for learning disabilities, a general discussion of these matters is in order. Thus, our intent in Part 2 is not only to review current practices, but to discuss the general nature of assessment used in psychoeducational decision making and to suggest some alternative perspectives designed to improve understanding of learning disabilities.

Chapter 5
Assessment and Psychoeducational Decisions

Measurement procedures do not make decisions; people *make decisions.*
Thorndike & Hagen (1977, p. 3)

No list of "recommended tests" can eliminate the necessity for careful choice by the user.
Cronbach (1970, p. 116)

In answering the questions Who is learning disabled? and What should be done to help such persons?, assessment plays a critical role. Thus, every professional working in the learning disabilities field uses informal and often formal assessment processes to diagnose, screen, and make placement decisions. However, attitudes toward prevailing assessment practices vary considerably; they are defended and cursed with equal vigor. Parents and professionals alike often are confused by the conflicting claims. To the novice exploring the field, it must be even more confusing. One reason for the confusion is that the claims for many diagnostic and placement procedures are not tempered with presentations of concepts and concerns that clarify *why* assessment is essential and *why* the adequacy of specific practices continues to be debated.

The key to moving beyond the limitations of prevailing practices lies in comprehending distinctions that have been ignored or blurred during the rapid growth of the learning disabilities field. In this chapter (and in Appendix A), we briefly discuss basic concepts related to assessment for diagnosis, screening, and placement. Since there is presently no theory or model that broadly encompasses these concepts, our presentation (1) defines assessment and categorizes its purposes, (2) outlines the scope of assessment activities, (3) reviews technical considerations, (4) discusses biasing factors, (5) explores relevant ethical concerns, and (6) highlights reciprocal relationships between psychoeducational assessment and sociopolitical-economic decision making.[1]

DEFINITION AND PURPOSES OF ASSESSMENT

Assessment is something most people know about because they are involved in assessment processes many times each day. While such assessments are not as formalized or systematic as those performed by professionals, the essential features of the process are the same: information is perceived, judgments formulated, and decisions made.

Related to psychoeducational problems, assessment is a relatively new term. The terms *diagnosis*, *diagnostic testing*, and *screening* are more commonly used. Since words shape thoughts and practices, the term *assessment* represents a major shift in perspective.

Diagnosis and screening, following medical usage, imply that procedures (commonly tests) are given to the person designated as having a problem; then information about the person usually is gathered from others. The objectives are to analyze the person's problem, clarify causality if feasible, and prescribe treatment. These are commendable objectives. Unfortunately, as applied in education and psychology, this orientation leads to a narrow view of learning and behavior problems. Diagnosis and screening do not have to be restricted to persons; environments and person-environment interactions can be identified as well. Broadening the focus to these variables has proven helpful, but the primary emphasis has remained on diagnosis and screening and the presumption that problems stem from, and belong to, persons alone.

Diagnostic objectives are based on a pathological orientation—only problems are sought, and resultant prescriptions stress treatment and remediation. While a pathological focus using test data based on individuals can be justified in medical settings, more comprehensive practices are required in the fields of education and mental health. The need is for multifaceted processes to appraise strengths and limitations of individuals, environments, and their interactions. Diagnosis and screening, as terms and concepts, are too limited; thus assessment has emerged as an alternative.[2]

Formally defined, assessment is the process by which attributes of phenomena are *described* and *judged*. Descriptions take the form of data gathered by formal or informal measurements, such as test responses and observations of behaviors or settings. Judgments take the form of interpretive conclusions about the meaning of data, such as whether a phenomenon is good or bad, above or below norm, pathological or not. In practice, the overall aim of assessment is to describe and make judgments about decisions to be made. The judgments may represent a conclusion about the past (such as what caused an existing problem), a statement about the present (such as identifying a range of appropriate options), or a prediction about the future (such as which persons or settings will benefit from an intervention).

---

[1]Readers familiar with assessment concepts may be tempted to skip ahead, but we encourage at least skimming the core concepts discussed in this chapter for continuity with material subsequently presented.

[2]Origin of the term *assessment* as applied to psychoeducational practices is attributed to World War II activity of the Office of Strategic Services (OSS Staff, 1948). The task of psychologists assigned to the OSS was selection of personnel for special assignments calling for leadership abilities and other strengths. Assessment with its connotations of evaluating worth was seen in this context as a more appropriate rubric than diagnosis.

Figure 5-1

Assessment processes and purposes.

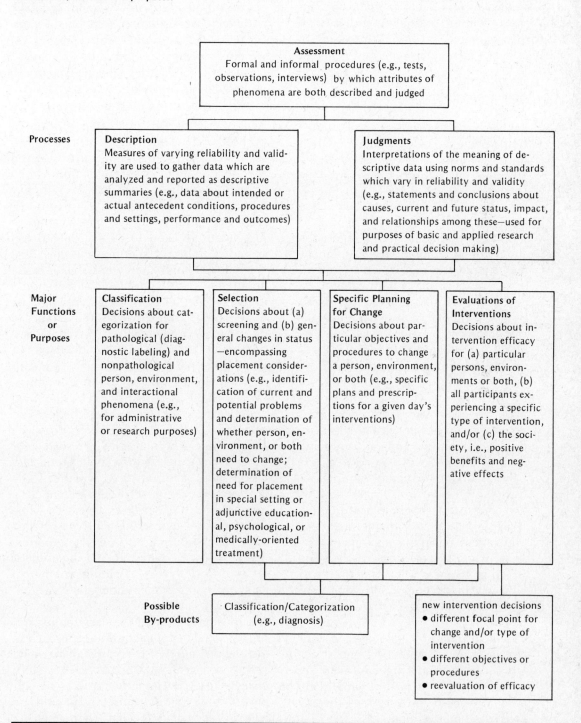

Assessment
Formal and informal procedures (e.g., tests, observations, interviews) by which attributes of phenomena are both described and judged

Processes

Description
Measures of varying reliability and validity are used to gather data which are analyzed and reported as descriptive summaries (e.g., data about intended or actual antecedent conditions, procedures and settings, performance and outcomes)

Judgments
Interpretations of the meaning of descriptive data using norms and standards which vary in reliability and validity (e.g., statements and conclusions about causes, current and future status, impact, and relationships among these—used for purposes of basic and applied research and practical decision making)

Major
Functions
or
Purposes

Classification
Decisions about categorization for pathological (diagnostic labeling) and nonpathological person, environment, and interactional phenomena (e.g., for administrative or research purposes)

Selection
Decisions about (a) screening and (b) general changes in status —encompassing placement considerations (e.g., identification of current and potential problems and determination of whether person, environment, or both need to change; determination of need for placement in special setting or adjunctive educational, psychological, or medically-oriented treatment)

Specific Planning for Change
Decisions about particular objectives and procedures to change a person, environment, or both (e.g., specific plans and prescriptions for a given day's interventions)

Evaluations of Interventions
Decisions about intervention efficacy for (a) particular persons, environments or both, (b) all participants experiencing a specific type of intervention, and/or (c) the society, i.e., positive benefits and negative effects

Possible
By-products

Classification/Categorization
(e.g., diagnosis)

new intervention decisions
• different focal point for change and/or type of intervention
• different objectives or procedures
• reevaluation of efficacy

As seen in Figure 5-1, we have grouped the major *purposes* of psychoeducational assessment into four categories. These represent the nature of the decisions upon which assessment activity is intended to have a bearing.

1. *Classification*—Decisions are made not only about diagnostic labeling but also about how to categorize nonpathological person, environmental, and interactional phenomena. Classification labels are developed with reference to descriptive characteristics or causal or predictive criteria.

2. *Selection*—Selection encompasses (a) screening and (b) general changes in status. Screening includes decisions about the focal point for assessment (i.e., should the person, environment, or person-environment interaction be assessed?), identification of current and potential problems, and whether current interventions are satisfactory. Decisions about general changes in status usually are discussed as placement decisions, but they go beyond the concept of placement to encompass decisions about general environmental and interactional changes. Specifically, these are decisions about the general nature and form of intervention needed (e.g., expansion and enrichment of environments, placement in a special setting, and educational, psychological, or medically oriented treatments), general preferences regarding implementation (e.g., who, where, and when), and which preferences will be fulfilled (e.g., who will be accepted, and what general environmental changes will be pursued).

3. *Specific planning for change*—Decisions are made about immediate and short-term objectives and procedures to accomplish long-term goals. Examples are specific plans or prescriptions for any given day's intervention.

4. *Evaluation of intervention*—Decisions are made about intervention effectiveness based on positive and negative effects. Decisions may be made with reference to (a) particular persons or environments or both, (b) all participants experiencing a specific type of intervention, or (c) society as a whole.

An example may clarify the above definition of assessment and categorization of purpose. Achievement tests often are used to assess reading performance in a given school. The number of right and wrong answers provides a *description* of performance on a given set of items at a given time. Based on these descriptive data, a variety of *judgments* are likely to be made. They will be based on available norms and prevailing standards. Different judgments will be made about individuals with identical scores who differ in age. Different judgments may be made about groups living in economically disadvantaged areas and in wealthy communities. Decisions will be made about whether to label diagnostically programs and individuals judged to be performing poorly. That is, a district could be identified as deficient, an individual labeled as learning disabled, and so forth. Such decisions usually reflect administrative, research, or other societal needs for classification. Decisions will be made as to whether some schools and individuals should be helped to improve and, if so, specific plans will be formulated. At a later date, achievement test data again will be used to evaluate performance. Thus, the same data may be used for (1) *classification* (e.g., deciding whether to categorize programs or individuals or both, and which labels to assign), (2) *selection* (e.g., deciding whether the class, school, and district should adopt a different approach to instruction and whether individuals need special services), (3) *specific planning for change* (e.g., deciding what specific approach to reading instruction should be adopted and what specific reading skills a

FOR EXAMPLE

PREVAILING ASSESSMENT PRACTICES

Alf, age 9, is given a note to take home. In it his teacher explains he's not performing as well in class assignments as other students. The teacher believes his daydreaming and inattentiveness indicate a learning disability. His parents come in for a conference. As a result, Alf visits the school psychologist who gives him an intelligence test, achievement test, projective/personality tests, and a perceptual motor test. The teacher receives a report from the psychologist which says Alf is of normal intelligence, achieves significantly below normal for his grade level in reading and math and significantly below age level with regard to visual perception. He also is seen as having some minor problems with self-esteem. The teacher and parents meet again. Alf will now work with the special resource teacher two days a week and the family will try to help with educational games and special family activities to help Alf feel good about himself.

Why was Alf tested?

Teacher's purpose—Classification, selection, and specific planning: to confirm there was a

problem, to determine the cause of the problem, to select resources for working on the problem, and, if possible, to find specific remedies.

Parents' purpose—Classification and selection: to understand the nature of the problem and what, if any, additional resources are needed.

Alf's purpose—?

Psychologist's purpose—Classification and selection: to determine which, if any, diagnostic category Alf fits, in order to decide on need and eligibility for additional resources.

Critics of prevailing testing practices suggest that the various assessment purposes mentioned above can be met appropriately (perhaps more appropriately) through use of alternative procedures.

given individual should be taught), and (4) *evaluation* (e.g., deciding whether a school's reading program and an individual's progress is adequate).

Choices about what data to gather and what to exclude usually are based on the types of judgments and decisions assessors must make. For instance, as the above example stresses, an assessor may be involved in making applied decisions of a political, administrative, instructional, or therapeutic nature.

While the same data may be used appropriately for several purposes, it also should be noted that there are many instances where such usage is inappropriate. For example, in a study of Child Service Demonstration programs for students with learning disabilities, Thurlow and Ysseldyke (1979) found data from tests, which were designed

for purposes of classification and selection, being used inappropriately for specific intervention planning and evaluation.

SCOPE OF ASSESSMENT ACTIVITY

Most books on assessment provide descriptions and summaries of (1) types of procedures such as interviews, observations, and objective and projective tests, and (2) specific uses such as diagnosis, prescription of treatment, or general evaluations of intelligence, achievement, and performance. Most literature reflects predominant practices; conceptual frameworks are not given high priority. People are the major focal point of assessment, and assessment of environments, and person-environment interactions tend to be ignored.

VIEWPOINT

SCOPE OF ASSESSMENT ACTIVITY

There is abundant evidence that many of the behavioral differences we find in test performance are largely the result of differences in the environments in which individuals have lived rather than of inherent differences in individuals themselves. . . . However, despite this accumulation of evidence, we have persisted in our view of testing in essentially individualistic terms. . . .

This is indeed an unfortunate state of affairs. All theories of learning and behavior make provision for the influence of the environment on the development of human characteristics, but . . . we have not had a corresponding emphasis in our measurement procedures. I would also submit that we have rarely attempted to systematically relate individual test data to environmental data in ways that are designed to increase our understanding of the interactive process between the individual and the environment.

Wolf (1966, pp. 508–9)

A few researchers, however, have been concerned with developing procedures for assessing environments (e.g., Barker, 1968; Bloom, 1964; Moos, 1979; Wolf, 1966) and person-environment interactions (e.g., Adelman, 1971; Cronbach, 1957, 1975; Cronbach & Snow, 1977; Hunt & Sullivan, 1974; Wolf, 1974). The result among some writers has been a broadening perspective regarding the nature and scope of assessment activity. Based on their expanded perspective, they have taken on the intriguing challenge of trying to develop broad assessment frameworks for categorizing variables, instruments, and processes. Systems-oriented thinkers have suggested that the stages in assessment activity be conceived in terms of an input-throughput-output-feedback paradigm.

In an effort to synthesize current assess-

ment activity, Sundberg (1977) suggests, as a tool for further exploration, a three-dimensional model which includes the following:

1. *five types of functions*—personnel selection and classification; training and education; counseling/therapy/system change; program evaluation/planning/data feedback; instrumentation for research/theory building;
2. *five system levels*—individual; small group; organization; community; region, state, or nation;
3. *five types of assessment methods*—projective techniques; objective techniques; observations of behavior; biopsychological techniques; interviews.

Sundberg portrays the three interacting dimensions as an "assessment cube" which illustrates that each method might be used at different system levels for different functions. Thus, the model draws attention to at least 125 combinations of assessment activity.

Building on the expanded perspectives of recent theory and research, we have synthesized the nature and scope of assessment into five dimensions: (1) functions or purposes served, (2) general processes and stages involved, (3) focus of activity, (4) types of procedures and instruments, and (5) variations in practices related to assessment situations, procedures, and instruments (see Table 5–1).

Most points outlined in Table 5–1 are discussed in some form in basic assessment texts and in many works dealing with clinical populations (e.g., Brown, 1976; Cronbach, 1970; Hersen & Bellack, 1981; Korchin, 1976; Salvia & Ysseldyke, 1981; Sundberg, 1977; Thorndike & Hagen, 1977). However, the perspective in most texts is narrower than that suggested by the definition and the purposes of assessment presented above. Thus, to underscore the broader perspective and highlight points not usually found in general sources, the following aspects of Table 5–1 are emphasized.

Rather than being the primary focus of classification, diagnosis is but one facet, and classification is but one of four major purposes toward which assessment activity is directed (see Table 5–1, I).

At its very foundation, most psychoeducational assessment activity is designed to contribute to a decision-making process. Thus, assessment processes and stages (II, A–D) logically should be shaped by the subsequent decisions to be made.

Particular note should be taken of the difference between the processes of description and judgment (II, B–C). The descriptive act involves only data gathering, analyses, and reporting and is distinguished from the interpretative facets involved in making judgments about the meaning of descriptive findings.

The five dimensions refer not only to the assessment of persons and problematic conditions but to environments, person-environment interactions, and non-problematic conditions (see Table 5–1, III, A–D).

Variations in practice not only influence the form of assessment activity but also affect the quality of data made available for decision making (V, A–H). Unreliable data clearly are not the most desirable basis for making important decisions.

While there are a great number of instruments on the market and procedures reported in the literature, there are relatively few types (IV, A–E), and for some decisions none of the available procedures may be appropriate.[3] For

VIEWPOINT

ASSESSING ENVIRONMENTS

[Just as it is possible to assess persons] environments can be similarly portrayed with a great deal of accuracy and detail. Some people are supportive; likewise, some environments are supportive. Some [people] feel the need to control others; similarly, some environments are extremely controlling. Order and structure are important to many people; correspondingly, many environments emphasize regularity, system, and order.
Insel and Moos (1974, p. 179)

example, no assessment procedure currently exists that can validly indicate that the primary instigating cause of an individual's reading problem stems from a minimal neurological dysfunction.

No one denies the value of, or need for, *valid* formal assessment procedures. Assessment is inevitable, and formal procedures of high validity can improve both effectiveness and efficiency of decision making. However, psychoeducational assessment currently is a seriously flawed enterprise. This fact cannot be ignored or wished away just because a great need for assessment exists. On the contrary, ethics demand consumers be aware of the concerns, and researchers and practitioners understand the issues and problems if they are to advance knowledge and improve practice. Informed use of prevailing LD assessment practices requires knowing basic technical concepts, which clarify the usefulness of assessment procedures, and being aware of factors that bias data gathering and interpretation. A brief discussion of these topics follows.

---

[3]The accelerated rate of test development has resulted in an interesting irony: many professionals are increasingly dissatisfied with, and critical of, widely used test instruments, and simultaneously there is an increasing demand by consumers for these very procedures. In response to demand and in spite of criticisms, inadequately developed procedures appear faster than they can be cataloged. Referring to the 1,270 tests reviewed in *The Seventh Mental Measurements Yearbook,* Buros (1972) states: "At least half of the tests currently on the market should never have been published. Exaggerated, false, or unsubstantiated claims are the rule rather than the exception" (pp. xxvii–viii).

TABLE 5–1

Nature and Scope of Assessment Activity

I. Functions and purposes served by assessment activity
  A. Classification
    1. Diagnostic labeling
    2. Nonpathological person, environment, and interactional categorizations
  B. Selection
    1. Screening decisions
    2. Decisions about general changes in status (including placements)
  C. Specific planning for change
    1. Objectives designed for each intervention (person, environment, interactions)
    2. Procedures designed for each intervention
  D. Evaluation of interventions
    1. Efficacy for a particular participant and interaction
    2. Programmatic efficacy related to all participants and interventions
    3. Impact on society
II. General processes and stages involved in assessment
  A. Preparatory decisions about what is to be assessed (implicit or explicit rationale for assessment activity)
  B. Description ("measurements" of specified variables and serendipitous data gathering, followed by analysis and descriptive summaries)
  C. Judgments (interpretations)
  D. Communication and decision making with reference to assessment purposes
III. Focus of assessment activity
  A. Focal point
    1. Person(s) (individual or groups of individuals)
    2. Environment(s)
    3. Person-environment interactions
  B. Nature of phenomena
    1. Problematic-nonproblematic conditions
    2. Observable-inferred
    3. Proximal-distal
    4. Historic-current-future expectations
  C. Levels
    1. Molecular-molar analyses of persons
    2. Primary, secondary, tertiary contextual analysis
    3. Interaction of person-environment levels
  D. Areas or domains
    1. Biological and psychological processes
    2. Motor and verbal functioning
    3. Physical environment
    4. Social environment
    5. Interaction of person-environment domains
IV. Types of procedures and instruments (standardized, semi-standardized, or unstandardized)
  A. Interviews and written personal reports (responses to oral or written questions, inventories of items, etc.)
  B. Observations
  C. Verbal and performance measures (e.g., objective instruments such as achievement tests; projective instruments such as ink blots and thematic pictures; instruments developed by teachers, psychologists, and M.D.s which have not been formally and

TECHNICAL CONSIDERATIONS AND UTILITY

A critical understanding of the adequacy of any assessment and decision-making practice requires knowledge of what is meant by the concepts of reliability, validity, norms and standards, and utility as applied to assessment. At this point we can only underscore the importance of these considerations.[4]

  1. *Reliability*—Good assessment procedures are expected to be able to gener-

---

[4]Appendix A offers a more complete discussion of reliability, validity, and norms and standards.

technically standardized)

D. Biological tests (e.g., electrorecording devices, chemical analyses)

E. Available records and data (e.g., analyses of current or cumulated records related to person, environment, interactions; analyses of natural performances and products)

V. Variations in practices related to assessment situations, procedures, and instruments

A. Normative-personalized assessment

B. Degree of control of and participation in assessment processes by person(s) or those responsible for environment(s) being assessed

C. Stimulus and response conditions
   1. Natural-simulated
   2. Formal-informal
   3. Number and complexity of variables assessed (involves breadth of focus and fidelity; perceptual selectivity)
   4. Ambiguity and subjectivity
   5. Number of objects (person, environment, interactions)
   6. Obtrusiveness
   7. Reactive impact (planned or unplanned)
   8. Status of referrers, assessors, and those assessed (e.g., socio-economic, race, age, gender, education and training)
   9. Degree of standardization with regard to administration, data collection, recording, and analysis (e.g., degree of interpretation/reliability involved in presenting instructions, scoring and coding data, etc.)

D. Source of data
   1. Directly from focal point or object assessed (e.g., person assessed)
   2. Indirectly from other sources (e.g., relatives, friends, objective observers)

E. Record used for analyses
   1. Degree to which a record is available (is produced or already exists) related to variables of interest
   2. Form (e.g., multiple choice answers, essays, verbal statements, graphs from electro recordings, ratings of person(s), environment(s), or interactions, cumulative personal and organizational records)
   3. Descriptive facts, correlates, or cause-effect signs
   4. Amount (e.g., length)
   5. Decipherability and perceptual distortion
   6. Units of analysis which can be employed

F. Level of interpretation involved in and degree of standardization with regard to norms for interpreting and communicating data and making judgments and decisions (e.g., content, criteria-related and construct validity; appropriateness of data used as standards for comparison; model and disciplinary biases in interpreting data)

G. Degree to which a procedure provides needed data over and above available information for making judgments and decisions (i.e., incremental validity or utility)

H. Single stage vs. multi-stage decision making (e.g., one-time assessment vs. sequential screenings)

ate consistent and reproducible data. The degree to which they do is called *reliability* and is expressed as a correlation coefficient ranging from .00 (not at all reliable) to 1.0 (perfectly reliable). No assessment procedure is perfectly reliable. Various authorities have suggested that reliability should be at least .90 when major instructional and treatment decisions are to be made about an individual. For individual screening, reliability should be at least .80 if there is to be follow-up assessment. Few of the prevailing assessment procedures in the LD field have reliability coefficients this high.

2. *Validity*—Reliability coefficients are not an indication that a procedure measures

what it purports to, nor do they indicate what decisions should be made. These matters are dependent on the validity of a procedure with regard to the purposes for which it is used. The processes involved in establishing validity are as much rational and subjective as they are empirical and objective. There are different types of validity:

a. *Content validity* is concerned with whether what is assessed constitutes a representative sample, for example, a sample of an area of human functioning such as knowledge and skills;

b. *Criterion-related validity* (encompassing predictive, concurrent, and diagnostic validity) is concerned with the extent to which currently assessed phenomena are related to future, concurrent, or past phenomena;

c. *Construct validity* is concerned with the extent a procedure measures some theoretical, not directly observable, concepts such as intelligence, anxiety, perception, or motivation.

That there are different types of validity reflects the fact that assessment procedures are used for different purposes. The same procedure may be used as an assessment of content learned, as a construct measure, or as a predictor. Prospective users need to be certain that satisfactory validation data exist for each intended purpose. For instance, an IQ test may have sufficient predictive (criterion-related) validity to use it as a predictor of subsequent performance in a particular type of school or classroom. It may not, however, have sufficient construct validity with regard to certain population subgroups to generate an accurate index of intelligence for individuals in that subgroup. This of course is what representatives of minority and clinical-problem populations have argued about IQ tests. When they complain that the tests are not valid (e.g., are culturally biased), they are referring to the *construct validity* not the *predictive validity* of the instrument. Indeed, the tests are often good predictors of the fact that large segments of such subgroups will have school problems. However, it is important not to lose sight of the reality that such predictions (1) will be in error in a significant number of cases, (2) may be made as accurately using base-rate information, and (3) do not clarify the reasons for the problems. With regard to this last point, the cause might be low intelligence. However, it also could be that the values and standards dominating public schools require behavior and perfor-

---

FOR EXAMPLE

VALIDITY

The psychologist gave Alf the Developmental Test of Visual Perception (commonly referred to as the Frostig Test). She gave this test because she believed that the test validly measures this psychological process and that poor visual perception, if found at Alf's age, is a cause of poor reading performance. In such cases, she had been taught that special visual perceptual training is a prerequisite to improving reading problems.

Many recent studies have questioned the validity of the Frostig Test. Specifically, it is not seen as having (1) *construct* validity, that is, as validly measuring visual perception, or (2) *predictive* validity, that is, as correlating significantly with reading success and failure. Moreover, the assumption that special visual perception training exercises are necessary to improve reading has not been supported by research. (See reviews by Arter and Jenkins, 1979; Coles, 1978; Salvia and Ysseldyke, 1981.)

mance which are incompatible with the particular subgroup's orientation to life.

As the above example highlights, validity is specific to assessment purposes and situations. Each assessment procedure must be judged with regard to the type of validity called for by the purpose and situation. Expert judgment plays a major role in all facets of validation processes. Given the biasing factors affecting expert judgment, a great many psychoeducational assessment procedures can be expected not to have been satisfactorily validated.

3. *Norms and standards*—Standards are theoretical or value referents used to make judgments about whether the current status of a phenomenon is as it *should* be, for example, whether it is good or bad, a problem or not. Norms are empirically based referents, such as a set of previously gathered data on a phenomenon which can be used for comparison with current findings.

To minimize variability related to interpretations and judgments, norms and standards must be standardized. The availability of explicit norms provides an empirical basis for interpreting data. Articulated standards help clarify theoretical, value, and motivational bases for judgments and resultant decisions. Analyses of the degree to which standardized norms and standards are reliable and valid provides a basis for evaluating their appropriateness and adequacy.

Norms used in interpreting psychoeducational assessment findings often are extremely inadequate. Even when norms are published in a manual accompanying an instrument, they may be extremely deficient. The criticisms by test publishers Seashore and Ricks (1950) seem as relevant today as they were when they were first made:

Inspection of test manuals will show (or would show if information about the norms

FOR EXAMPLE

NORMS AND STANDARDS

Of considerable interest and controversy is the topic of hyperactivity and its measurement (e.g., Plomin & Foch, 1981). Let us assume a child's gross motor activity has been assessed on a measure which produces scores from 1 to 10, with a score of 1 representing the lowest level and 10 the highest level of activity. The youngster scores 8. Is he or she hyperactive? Obviously, the score is toward the high end of the scale: however, this only indicates that the activity level is relatively *high*, not *hyper*. The score alone doesn't clarify whether the activity level was higher than most children typically manifest on the measure. Norms are needed to clarify this matter.

Let us assume the measure has been satisfactorily standardized and a good set of norms are available. According to the norms the median or average score of similar children (in terms of sex, age, socioeconomic status, and so forth) is 6. The child's score of 8 can now be interpreted. The activity level indeed is higher than average. However, we still do not know whether the activity level should be judged as hyperactive. (The prefix hyper tends to convey the idea pathology is present, such as in the term hypertense.)

To make such a judgment requires application of standards derived from theory or values. In this case, the assessor would apply a theory of hyperactivity. The theory might or might not be supported by studies usable as evidence that (1) the instrument reliably and validly measures hyperactivity and (2) a high proportion of children or a particular subgroup of children who score 8 have the type of problem characteristics which warrant a judgment of hyperactivity. In the absence of adequate theory and data or because of contradictory theories and data, values usually prevail. Users of the data may think the child's higher-than-average activity is inappropriate because this is a widely accepted attitude and belief. When this occurs, negative judgments usually will be made about the score, including assignment of labels which define it as pathological. Consequently, even in the absence of adequate normative data for interpreting activity level as above average, theory and value standards may be used to judge a specific person's activity level as a problem.

were given completely) that many such massed norms are merely collections of all the scores that opportunity has permitted the author or publisher to gather easily. Lumping together all the samples secured more by chance than by plan makes for impressively large numbers; but while seeming to simplify interpretation, the norms may dim or actually distort the counseling, employment, or diagnostic significance of a score. (As quoted in Cronbach, 1970)

In applying norms which have been provided, or in drawing on one's own experientially based norms, the assessor must be reasonably confident that the types of problems discussed above have not so severely limited reliability and validity as to render the norms potentially harmful. Norms must be appropriate both for the purpose of the assessment and for the phenomenon assessed.

Standards, too, vary in reliability and validity. Their reliability primarily is a function of how systematically they are applied. Their systematic application primarily is a function of the degree to which standards are explicit, widely understood, and accepted.

Since standards may come from theoretical or value-based sources, their validation is related to their source. Theoretical standards are constructs and need to be validated as such and then applied reliably. Value-based standards derive validity from widespread acknowledgment, namely consensual validation. A common example is use of IQ scores as a standard for judging the adequacy of current academic performance. In this case, the IQ score represents the theoretical construct of intelligence and is interpreted as an indication of potential. The current level of school functioning then is judged with reference to this standard.

VIEWPOINT
STANDARDS AND PERSPECTIVES

Ambient Adultomorphism—Adultomorphism is a strong tendency for interpreting a child's behavior in adult terms. It is to this malady that we owe most of the incredible variety of ways a child can "fail" at something. [Children know that they make] mistakes and blunders but they become other things to do, they change things around and point to new things, and they are just as intriguing (maybe more so) as straightaway accomplishments.
Nyberg (1971, pp. 165–66)

The technical inadequacies that characterize a large proportion of psychoeducational assessment activity are responsible for producing a great deal of questionable data. Decisions based directly on such data are highly fallible. What prevents the situation from being as bleak as it could be is that assessors and other decision makers apparently do not rely heavily on much of the data they gather when it comes time for decisions. (Adelman, 1978; Wade & Baker, 1977). If they did, the variability and inconsistencies in findings would confound decision making in many instances. The paucity of recent discussion of these problems in the assessment literature is distressing. In general, while there has been an interesting history of research and debate about what factors actually determine decision making and whether assessment data are useful in the process, there is still a need for further investigation (Dawes, 1979; Einhorn & Hogarth, 1978; Goldberg, 1970; Gough, 1962; Holt, 1958, 1967, 1970; Meehl, 1954, 1957, 1965; Meehl & Rosen, 1955; Sarbin, 1943, 1970; Sawyer, 1966).

4. *Utility*—Even when a procedure is technically adequate, the decision to use it should be based on evidence that it will add needed data not available through less costly, simpler, or already required procedures. The degree to which a procedure adds something important to the assessment usually is characterized as incremental validity or incremental utility (e.g. Sundberg, 1977).

In each assessment situation, a certain amount of information already is available. For instance, routine procedures in schools already provide data for certain types of decisions. Sometimes interviews provide all the information needed. When available information is not adequate, the need for more information provides almost overwhelming pressure for assessors to use another assessment tool. However, need and pressure are no guarantee that valid procedures, which can provide desired data, exist. When decisions involve predictions, incremental validity can be computed (e.g., through multiple regression analyses) to determine how much an individual piece of data adds to predictive efficiency.

Incremental validity studies have raised many questions about the utility of gathering and interpreting a large amount of assessment data as is commonly done in clinical test-battery approaches (Coles, 1978; Cronbach & Gleser, 1965; Dawes, 1979; Smith & Knoff, 1981). Some researchers have argued it is difficult to find even one reliable and valid assessment procedure which adds enough information beyond that provided by base rates (Meehl & Rosen, 1955). In general, then, to justify the addition of an assessment procedure, it must be evident that the procedure adds precision or certainty to interpretations and judgments about assessment findings and ultimately to the decisions made.

BIASING FACTORS

Potential for bias in assessment is great. Indeed, some degree of bias is inevitable. While certain forms of bias are idiosyncratic and correctable through individual effort, a broader concern is with pervasive influences affecting most psychoeducational assessment. Thus, in this instance, we are not concerned with the prejudiced and stereotypic thinking of an individual, but with factors that affect large numbers of assessors causing them to react in systematically biased ways.

Bias affects both the descriptive and judgmental phases of assessment. Selectivity and distortion, and therefore bias, in formal assessment stem from (1) weaknesses in the knowledge base used to guide assessment and from (2) psychological and societal factors which systematically influence information availability and processing.

Weak Knowledge Base

To comprehend why some degree of selectivity and distortion is inevitable, one need only recognize that assessors primarily look for what they have come to understand are the important aspects of phenomena. They cannot really afford to do otherwise. There is no time to describe everything, and random sampling of complex phenomena tends to produce random findings and little understanding. Thus, whether explicitly stated or not, each assessor is guided by some underlying rationale.

Prominent aspects of an assessor's rationale will be a theory or model of the phenomenon to be assessed, a model of how it can be assessed, and an understanding of specific methods for translating concepts into empirical findings. If there is widespread consensus acknowledging the soundness of underlying models and methods, assessment findings probably will not be seen as biased. That is, where there is, or at least appears to be, a strong base of knowledge related to a phenomenon and how to measure it (e.g., X-rays of broken bones), variations in procedures, findings, and interpretations will be minimized. Concomitantly, whatever selectivity and distortion are present will not be readily apparent.

In contrast, when the knowledge base is weak (i.e., theory and research are viewed as inconclusive), there will be diverse and competing models and methods. Assessors will differ, often markedly, in the perspectives they adopt as rationale for practices. They will be greatly influenced by the available (albeit weak) knowledge base in their respective disciplines. However, since no specific model, orientation, or trend will be dominant, even professionals from the same discipline and field can be expected to be guided by different ideas. Thus, assessors can be expected to look for different data, perhaps to use different methods, and often to arrive at different conclusions about the same phenomena. Moreover, it should not be too surprising that the tendency is to find and interpret data consistent with one's "theories."

Given a weak knowledge base, related research can only be in its early stages and unable to resolve debates over which ideas and practices are correct. In spite of data suggesting a given idea or practice is not effective and is perhaps even harmful, enough testimony often has appeared claiming its validity to allow advocates to justify its continuation.

Prior to the emergence of a body of research, the compelling "logic" underlying a practice, its intuitive appeal, or the proselytizing capabilities of its adherents appear to be the significant factors in its acceptance and maintenance. With time, many pioneering practices that lack validity become institutionalized through professional train-

FOR EXAMPLE

KNOWLEDGE BASE

With reference to the case of Alf, the weak knowledge base affected everyone involved in making the decisions.

While the teacher knew Alf was not performing as well as others in her class, she didn't know why or what to do about it. She recalled some of the "symptoms" she had learned about in education courses and recognized these in Alf. This led her to feel justified in referring him for help.

The psychologist duly noted Alf's symptoms. She administered the "standard battery" prescribed by the school district. Her diagnosis and recommendations were based on the current view that persons who test significantly below grade level on an achievement test and who score at least average on an IQ test can be diagnosed as learning disabled and might have a minimal brain dysfunction. Since Alf is a poor reader and did not do well on a test of visual perception, she thinks he might be dyslexic.

Alf's parents felt confused about the problems. They recalled various TV programs and magazine articles they had seen dealing with learning disabilities, dyslexia, and brain damage. They were both reassured and further mystified by the information provided by the school's "experts." They agreed to the recommendations because they know of no alternatives.

As for Alf, neither the parents nor the school personnel were certain about what to tell him or how to talk with him about the nature of the problem.

ing programs, unsupported expert opinion, publishing companies, and so forth. Such practices prevail until a strong body of research not only documents their inappropriateness but is used effectively to undermine their institutional support systems.

As long as psychology and education are dominated by relatively weak theories and methods with regard to operationalizing and measuring causes and correcting psychoeducational problems, the conflict among competing and resilient assessment rationales will continue. Concomitantly, selectivity and distortion are inevitable.

Coexistence of contradictory perspectives does not mean each enjoys equal status. A model may be in vogue, but vogues change. For example, for some time a pathological perspective (i.e., medical model, or disordered-person model) dominated psychoeducational assessment practices. Only in recent years has this view been challenged sufficiently to allow nonpathologically oriented assessment procedures to evolve. These procedures should gain stature as the prevailing trend is successfully countered by those subscribing to an alternative bias, such as the view that capitalizing on social competence is important in working with problem populations.

Psychological Bias
In addition to bias that stems from the knowledge base, there is selectivity and distortion from psychological factors systematically influencing information availability and processing. A few examples will illustrate this point.

As a general principle, the more complex and comprehensive the phenomena assessed, the more difficult it is to obtain an adequate sample of data. While some reasons for this are strictly procedural and practical, such as lack of instruments, time, and so forth, sometimes the difficulty is due to an assessor's cognitive, perceptual, and motivational functioning. An example of one such psychological factor of potentially great importance in understanding the bias in assessment comes from attribution theory.

Those who assume the role of gathering data, especially professional assessors, can be described as *observers* of phenomena. Persons observed can be designated *actors*. In discussing perceptions of the causes of behavior, attribution theorists have suggested a pronounced tendency for observers and actors to perceive differentially the causes of the actor's behavior. Specifically, Jones and Nisbett (1971) hypothesize that "there is a pervasive tendency for actors to attribute their actions to situational requirements, whereas observers tend to attribute the same actions to stable personal dispositions" (p. 80). With regard to assessment, there seems to be a corresponding tendency to believe that an observers' (assessors') perceptions are objective and accurate while the perceptions of persons assessed (actors) are subjective and biased.

When systematic observer-actor differences have been demonstrated, they often have been interpreted as arising from actor and observer differences with regard to information availability and processing and motivational predilections such as self-serving interpretations (Bradley, 1978; Miller & Ross, 1975; Monson & Snyder, 1977). While interpretations vary, research has found observer-actor differences frequently enough to warrant speculation that this might be an important assessment biasing influence. For example, a great many assessors may be predisposed to look for, and localize, causes of psychoeducational problems within those who manifest the problems, such as students. In contrast, students (actors) may tend to attribute cause to teachers, peers, task difficulty, and so forth. If this is to be expected as a result of psychological influences, how can one know whose perception is correct? Perhaps both are biased and incorrect. Selectivity and distortion resulting from actor-observer differences in perception related to assessment practices clearly need investigation (Compas, Adelman, Freundl, Nelson, & Taylor, 1982; Compas & Adelman, 1981).

Professional role demands also are potential factors causing selectivity and distortion. Psychologists and educators are under constant pressure to demonstrate greater competence than is possible given

FOR EXAMPLE

PSYCHOLOGICAL BIAS

In the case of Alf, the teacher, psychologist, and his parents started out with the assumption that something was wrong with him. What they looked for and found were problems within Alf. Then, it seemed only logical to help him deal with his problems.

the current knowledge base. This pressure often leads professionals to overstate expertise. In turn, as various psychological theories suggest, their public declarations often lead them to defend and subsequently believe in the unsubstantiated theories and practices they have defended. Other individuals oversell their expertise, not for ego defensive reasons, but for ego enhancing purposes, including such self-serving objectives as attaining status and financial rewards.

As these examples suggest, the cognitive-perceptual-motivational predispositions of assessors can be seen to combine in complex ways to shape their actions and conclusions.

Societal Bias

Prevailing societal values play a major role in defining what is exceptional, deviant, or a problem and how each should be dealt with. These values are translated into governmental policies that determine which psychoeducational problems will be attended to and which practices will be encouraged. As many writers have suggested (Adelman, Zimmerman, & Sperber, 1969; Coles, 1978; Foucalt, 1965; Haney, 1981; Hobbs 1975a; Kittrie, 1971; Szasz, 1969, 1970; Tobach, 1974), interventions are designed quite as much and perhaps more to serve and protect society's interests as they are to help an individual. In particular, it has been argued that the best developed assessment practices, especially the test instruments widely used today, are primarily a reflection of what society feels it needs to protect and advance its interests.

Mercer (1973) has stressed that the behavior of children whose background differs from the dominant culture will be assessed as deficient to the extent their subcultural values and norms, and thus their behaviors, are incompatible with those of the dominant culture. What evidence there is tends to support this view (Baratz & Baratz, 1970; Berschied & Walster, 1974; Burke, 1975; Coates, 1972; Franks, 1971; Mercer, 1972; Olmedo, 1981; President's Committee on Mental Retardation, 1970; Reschly, 1981; Rubin, Krus, & Balow, 1973; Rubovits & Maehr, 1973; Schmidt & Hunter, 1974). Black and Mexican-American children have been greatly overrepresented in special classrooms. Lower socioeconomic status groups have been more frequently diagnosed as mentally retarded than middle- or upper-class children. Similarly, it has been estimated that only 2 percent of suburban children are assessed as having severe reading

FOR EXAMPLE

SOCIETAL BIAS

In the case of Alf, a teaching assistant in the classroom had noticed that two other children seemed equally inattentive and behind in their work. The others, both girls, stared quietly at their books and drew little attention to themselves. Alf, on the other hand, got a bit noisy when bored and tapped his pencil, flipped pages, and talked to other children at his table. Since she was concerned with sex role discrimination, the assistant wondered whether noisy boys were more likely than quiet girls to be referred for testing and special programs. More generally, she wondered whether such a societal bias might be a significant factor in learning disabilities being seen as a boys' problem.

disabilities, while up to 60 percent of slum-area children are so diagnosed (Balow, 1971).

Chase (1977) presents the position that society, for self-serving purposes, has perpetuated biological explanations for problems that require social solutions. For example, Kamin (1974) proposes that IQ tests have been used in ways which support "the belief that those on the bottom are genetically inferior victims of their own immutable defects." He further suggests that

> the consequence has been that the IQ test has served as an instrument of oppression against the poor—dressed in trappings of science, rather than politics. . . . The poor, the foreign born, and racial minorities are shown to be stupid [and] born that way. The underprivileged are today demonstrated to be ineducable, a message soothing to the public purses as to the public conscience. (p. 2)

Similarly, Coles (1978) argues that the "biologizing" of social problems has resulted in the positing of

> organic causalities for poverty, aggression, and violence, as well as for educational underachievement (Anderson, 1972; Delgado, 1971; Jensen, 1969; Mark and Ervin, 1970; Wilson, 1975). . . . By positing biological bases for learning problems, the responsibility for failure is taken from the schools, communities, and other institutions and is put squarely on the back, or rather within the head, of the child. Thus, the classification (assessment leading to the diagnosis of learning disabilities) plays its political role, moving the focus away from the general educational process, away from the need to change institutions, away from the need to rectify social conditions affecting the child, and away from the need to appropriate more resources for social use toward the remedy of a purely medical problem . . . a classic instance of what Ryan (1971) has called "blaming the victim." (p. 333)

What is being so boldly stated by these various writers is that society has a large stake in how the causes and corrections of psychoeducational problems are understood. Bias

stemming from society's values seems so ubiquitous a phenomenon that someone (source unknown) has formulated the "Law of Selective Attention to Data" which postulates that the greater the ideological relevance of research or assessment findings, the greater the likelihood that the professionals involved in the activity will pay selective attention to the data gathered.

Prevailing biases are reflected in mandatory programs and in research and development activity supported by government. Because societal bias so pervasively shapes perceptions, it is likely that most people are unaware of the selectivity and distortion built into practices they support. This lack of awareness, of course, makes it difficult to counter the bias.

The fact that selectivity and distortion permeate current assessment practices again underscores that, in many instances, it is the model rather than valid findings that guides and shapes assessment decisions. Moreover, emphasis on methodological matters in the assessment literature has tended to focus on reliability, validity, and norms, especially in relation to test instruments. Generally ignored have been concerns about (1) what is actually being assessed, (2) overreliance on test procedures, (3) the value of data gathered for decision making, and (4) what factors actually play the most significant role in arriving at any particular type of decision. Current emphases in the literature seem to have created the impression that existing psychoeducational assessment procedures are more technically adequate than they actually are. This impression tends to contribute to the unquestioning use of these procedures as a primary basis for making major psychoeducational decisions. What has been stressed in this section are methodological matters that suggest that current procedures may be biased, technically inadequate, and generally not as useful as prevailing practices suggest. Obviously, work is needed to improve utility, to counteract bias, and to overcome technological hurdles (Duffey, Salvia, Tucker, and Ysseldyke, 1981).

The better an assessor's understanding of these concerns, the better equipped the assessor is to select from the multitude of available procedures or begin the arduous task of developing assessment procedures. In identifying what is available and as an aid in evaluating the technical adequacy of many instruments, one can turn to a variety of sources. For example, a major resource is the *Mental Measurements Yearbook* (e.g., Buros, 1978). This is a series of critical reviews and bibliographies of published psychometric tests. A companion work, *Tests in Print II* (Buros, 1974) provides a comprehensive bibliography, by category, of tests used in psychology, education, and industry. Tests specifically used with children manifesting learning and behavior problems are discussed in various texts (e.g., Palmer, 1970; Salvia & Ysseldyke, 1981). Since so many procedures are unpublished, efforts have been made to compile surveys (e.g., Comrey, Backer, & Glaser, 1973; Chun, Cobb, & French, 1975; Johnson & Bommorito, 1971). Because the focus on environmental assessment is comparatively so recent, compilations of procedures for this purpose have not yet been completed. For reference to and discussion of such procedures, one must turn to works by researchers (e.g., Moos, 1979) or by reviewers of new trends in assessment (e.g., McReynolds, 1975).

ETHICAL CONCERNS

One's right to education and treatment increasingly is recognized. From both an ethical and legal perspective, society is asked to accept responsibility for making certain that no one is deprived of such interventions because of race, gender, age, or financial status. This stance is a welcome affirmation of civil and human rights. At the same time, it is critical that emphasis on the value of pro-

VIEWPOINT

TESTS

At present, no matter how poor a test may be, if it is nicely packaged and if it promises to do all sorts of things which no test can do, the test will find many gullible buyers. When we initiated critical test reviewing in the 1938 Yearbook, we had no idea how difficult it would be to discourage the use of poorly constructed tests of unknown validity. Even the better informed test users who finally become convinced that a widely used test has no validity after all are likely to rush to use a new instrument which promises far more than any good test can possibly deliver. Counselors, personnel directors, psychologists, and school administrators seem to have an unshakable will to believe the exaggerated claims of test authors and publishers. If these users were better informed regarding the merits and limitations of their testing instruments, they would probably be less happy and less successful in their work. The test user who has faith—however unjustified—can speak with confidence in interpreting test results and making recommendations. The well-informed test user cannot do this; [the user] knows that the best of our tests are still highly fallible instruments which are extremely difficult to interpret with assurance in individual cases. Consequently, [the user] must interpret test results cautiously with so many reservations that others wonder whether [the user] really knows what he [or she] is talking about.
Buros (1974, p. xxxvii)

viding care does not result in losing sight of major ethical concerns.

Impetus for ethical concern about negative aspects of psychoeducational assessment procedures has come from reported misuses and abuses of personality and intelligence tests. In the 1960s and 1970s, attacks were common in the media and in legislative hearings. Criticism has come from political conservatives, liberals, and civil libertarians (see discussions by Cronbach, 1970; Freedman, 1965a, 1965b; Haney, 1981; Kamin, 1974; Westin, 1967). At the center of the controversy is the traditional tension between society's rights, responsibilities, and needs and individuals' rights and freedoms. Critics suggest individuals' rights and liberties are not sufficiently considered and safeguarded. Greater concern for human dignity is demanded. This demand has led to increased legal protection of rights and due process for students, patients, and clients. Ethically, the focus is on improvement of consent procedures and clarity of the ethics of mandatory (coercive) intervention such as involuntary assessment, treatment, and institutional placement.

Another line of ethical criticism stresses the errors, costs, and "negative side effects" of assessment. Some critics stress psychological, social, economic, and possible physical harm to individuals; others point out that subgroups are discriminated against; and a few have raised the spectre that the quality of life in society may be significantly lowered by institutionalizing assessment practices.

In contrast to the above are those professionals who underscore positive values of psychoeducational assessment activity. While acknowledging potential for misuse and abuse, advocates point out benefits for individuals, groups, and society as a whole. From their perspective, it is a core ethical responsibility of professionals to use assessment practices in ways which maximize benefits and minimize negative effects to individuals and society. Furthermore, they insist that professionals must also participate in activities designed to advance knowledge, skills, and standards of practice.[5]

In Chapter 16, we discuss each of these matters in the broader context of all psychoeducational intervention. Here we simply highlight concerns regarding privacy rights and negative consequences of assessment.

Privacy

Ethical concerns surrounding privacy rights have expanded in recent years. Not long ago the only major concern was for confidentiality; in many assessment situations such as schools, clinics, and personnel placement offices, it was presumed that persons implicitly gave consent for assessment by applying for a service or position. Thus, ethical concerns, such as who was to have access to the information, arose only after data were gathered.

Increasingly, practices presuming consent have been challenged. The issue of informed consent has come to the fore because of concern about privacy and negative consequences of assessment. With regard to privacy rights, there is a dual concern: (1) invasion of privacy and (2) misuse of information (Anastasi, 1966; Willingham, 1967). These concerns arise when the information is considered highly sensitive and could lead to negative diagnoses and evaluations. The situation is especially volatile when assessment is carried out primarily to serve society or institutional objectives.

VIEWPOINT

JILL: "What do you want to be when you grow up?"
JACK: "A psychologist."
JILL: "Oh, you want to help people who have problems."
JACK: "No, I'm just nosey!"

---

[5]Thorndike and Hagen (1977) categorize positive contributions in terms of individual and social good. Individual good includes determining the most effective content and method for education and career planning. The social good includes efficient use of social resources and educational procedures, protection from incompetence and ineptitude, discovering talent in all segments of the population, and adding to knowledge.

Power to assess—to obtain and use information about persons and environments—is power to shape lives. Legally and ethically, there is a need to keep such power in check. At issue is the "kind and degree of control a person ought to be able to exercise in respect to knowledge of or the disclosure of information about himself or herself" (Wasserstrom, 1976, p. 4)[6] From this issue springs a variety of questions. What kind of information is it reasonable to ask about an individual? What safeguards exist when highly personal and sensitive information is sought? Under what circumstances, and by whom, should needed information be gathered? What types of records should be kept and who should have access to them? What restrictions should be placed on how information can be used? Is anonymity provided when appropriate? Should children be asked to provide information without their parents' consent? Should parents consent for children who don't want to be assessed? When parents have given consent to assess their child, is separate consent needed in order to ask the child questions about the parents? In general, when and who can give consent for another?

The complexity of the ethical concerns is well illustrated when individuals come for help. A request for help often is seen as consent to ask about anything the assessor sees as relevant. Given adequate theory and empirical evidence about what information is relevant, it would be a relatively clear-cut matter to explain what is needed and why as a basis for obtaining consent. Unfortunately, the state of knowledge regarding many psychoeducational problems is not sophisticated enough to specify what information is absolutely needed and what is irrelevant. Thus there are considerable variations in assessment activity carried out by different assessors even when referral problems are similar. In the absence of an adequate scientific base, many assessors develop their own criteria for what should be assessed. Some feel free to ask anything that intuitively seems significant at the moment. While meaning well, they often pry into embarrassing and painful areas of a person's life to gather data which ironically may be irrelevant. Some data gathered amounts to little more than gossip, such as details of a divorce or sexual behavior, and may have no significant relationship to the problem being assessed. The abuse may be further compounded if the data inappropriately influence prescribed treatment.

For a variety of political and legal reasons, many school systems have moved away from presumption of consent. The result has been that (1) less assessment data are gathered and circulated in schools, (2) consent is sought more frequently when a need for assessment exists, and (3) due process is being established for student and parent access to student-related records and for complaints and corrections of data which may be inappropriate or in error. In the United States, an example of such activity is provided by the federal government's enactment of the Family Educational Rights and Privacy Act of 1974 and resultant actions incorporating the law into state and local educational codes.

Typically, the burden of protecting rights still falls to those assessed. It is left to students or parents to object if they dislike either what is asked or the procedures. To make matters worse, if they do object, they risk being refused services or may have their refusal interpreted as defensiveness, hostility, or lack of cooperation.

---

[6]In other words, when should society be able to mandate assessment and, in the process, infringe on individual privacy rights? Stated in this way, the question can be seen to be one aspect of the broader concern over when society should be allowed to coerce individuals and, in the process, deny a variety of rights and freedoms. This broader concern involves the "ethics of coercion," a topic we will discuss in Part 5.

FOR EXAMPLE

ETHICAL CONCERNS

Privacy—In the case of Alf, he and his parents were not informed or aware that some of the tests were projective/personality instruments designed to look for social and emotional problems. This raises such questions as, Was it ethical not to tell them? and, Given the nature of the referral problem, why was this information needed?

Negative consequences—Alf felt pretty anxious the day of the testing. When a few kids in class teased him about it, he made it sound like a special opportunity he was being given and laughed their comments off. Later, when he had been diagnosed as Learning Disabled and was going each day to the resource room, it wasn't possible to make it sound like a special opportunity or to laugh it off. The other kids had their own labels for students who needed special help. ("He's a retardo.") School officials judged this as an acceptable price for Alf to pay for the benefits they believe he is receiving from being assigned to the resource room.

The situation is further complicated where procedures have become routinized and institutionalized. Under such circumstances, those involved often see neither a "rights" issue nor a need for consent. For example, M.D.s, psychologists, educators, and a variety of other personnel in schools, clinics, etc., routinely administer batteries of tests and questionnaires with little or no explanation about why information is needed or about the procedures' validity or lack thereof. When procedures have become a natural part of an institution's operations, those administering them may be genuinely unaware of invading privacy or coercing. Those who are assessed generally assume the experience must be essential, and any discomfort is a necessary "negative side effect."

Negative Consequences

Every major intervention has some negative consequences. Assessment activity is no exception. It is customary to speak of "negative side effects," but this wording often ignores errors and economic costs and is more appropriately applied to minor and perhaps low-probability phenomena. Negative consequences encompass the range of potentially significant harm which may occur.

Negative consequences related to assessment, such as extreme anxiety, may occur during the process, or may be an immediate or long-term outcome. For example, persons who are assessed and labeled may be stigmatized, isolated, and excluded from important experiences, and this may negatively affect motivation and hinder full and healthy development. Specifically, the hypothesis of the self-fulfilling prophecy (Merton, 1948) suggests that attaching labels connoting disturbance and deficiency may negatively affect the attitudes and behavior of others, and increase the likelihood that problems will develop. Evidence suggests that certain subgroups are more likely than others to experience such negative effects. This occurs, for example, because of intentional and unintentional cultural and sex-role bias in intelligence testing and in career and vocational counseling. Civil rights hearings have highlighted the role of formal assessment in excluding minority groups and females from educational and economic opportunities. Judicial and legislative action have attempted to redress inequities and prohibit discrimination. Unfortunately, little data exist on the frequency of negative consequences, including inevitable errors, or about financial costs to individuals and to taxpayers (Guskin, Bartel, & MacMillan, 1975).

The cost to the society may be more than financial. As Illich (1977) aptly describes, overreliance on professionals leads to alarming incapacity among individuals and natural support systems to cope with problems. The rapid rise in number of children

VIEWPOINT

RIGHTS AND CONSENT

In discussing the competence and freedom of children to make choices regarding participation in research, Ferguson (1978) discusses assumptions which might lead to appropriate guidelines for assessment practices:

> Three principles are taken as basic assumptions in exploring this topic. First, the child is considered to be a person. This implies that she/he is not a chattel of her/his parents, of the state, or of any other institution of the society, but has rights as an individual to respect, to privacy, to legal protection, and to consideration as a valuable member of society. Also implied is a reasonable balance between opposing views of the child as vulnerable and dependent or as a rational and moral being.
>
> The second principle is that of self-determination. This requires "that each individual be given the opportunity to make an informed and uncoerced choice regarding participation in research activities" (National Commission for the Protection of Human Subjects, Note 1). search is intended to safeguard those whose guardians to children's participation in recapacity for self-determination is not yet fully developed or is temporarily or permanently impaired. Parental consent should be a necessary but not a sufficient condition for children's participation. Investigators should conduct research so as not only to respect but to enhance the child's developing capacity for informed choice.
>
> Third, the generation of knowledge and the discovery of scientific truth, whether or not the findings have immediate relevance to human welfare, is considered in itself a good. This implies that participation in research which

> meets acceptable criteria for scientific merit, provided the subject's basic human rights and welfare are not infringed upon, is desirable.

Given these premises, Ferguson raises the following issues:

> I. What constitutes informed consent for a child? Should deception ever be used with children?
> II. Proposed DHEW guidelines specify that no child of "sufficient understanding should participate in a non-beneficial research activity without his or her consent (or assent)." (Staff report, 1975, p. 6). The issue here is how to assess "sufficient understanding." The criteria to be proposed derive from our current knowledge of the general course of cognitive development. No specific "age of consent" would seem generally appropriate.
> III. Special problems of invasion of privacy arise in "naturalistic" observational research frequent in studies of young children.
> IV. What incentives may legitimately be offered to children in seeking their cooperation in research?
> V. Finally, since observance of principles is in practice impossible to legislate, it is of the utmost importance that those who conduct research with children be adequately qualified. The Division on Developmental Psychology of the American Psychological Association and the Society for Research in Child Development have developed very similar sets of ethical standards for the guidance of their members. (Ferguson, 1978, pp. 114–15)

diagnosed as learning disabled, and the highly specialized (though often inappropriate) treatments prescribed may be a most poignant example of such effects.

From a practical perspective, concern over negative consequences generally centers on how to minimize negative consequences and be certain that benefits outweigh harm. Unfortunately, frequently at issue are whether a given negative consequence should be tolerated at all and whether positives are actually outweighing negatives. Not at issue are the following ethical responsibilities: (1) assessors are obligated at least to be aware of potential negative consequences, such as immediate and long-term harm to individuals, groups, and society; (2) where consent is sought, assessors are required ethically and usually by legal guidelines to inform prospective consenters of potential positive and negative consequences; (3) as they attempt to maximize what they believe are benefits, assessors are obligated to minimize potential negative effects; (4) while they cannot follow a student around to prevent self-fulfilling prophecies, they can take steps to correct and guard records and equip students and parents to protect and advocate for themselves; and (5) finally, assessors are expected to acknowledge whenever findings are inconclusive and not rationalize or dismiss uncertainties and incongruities in findings.

While the preceding discussion of ethical concerns related to privacy and negative consequences could be interpreted as applying primarily to assessment of individuals, these concerns apply to assessment of environments as well. For instance, increasing demands for accountability and national assessment of school programs clearly focus on environmental variables. Data published in newspapers regarding achievement test levels from specific schools do more than inform the public. The public censure following low performance may have serious and unwarranted repercussions on institutions as well as on staff and students.

WHO DECIDES? THE POLITICS OF ASSESSMENT

Not only is decision making the final outcome of assessment, but decisions are made at each stage of the overall assessment process. For example, at the preparatory stage there are decisions about the need for as-

FOR EXAMPLE

WHO DECIDES?
THE POLITICS OF ASSESSMENT

With reference to the case of Alf, the teacher referred the case for testing and the psychologist agreed. Alf and his parents might have preferred to have the teacher's competence assessed. The situation raises such questions as:

When do parents have the information, competence, or legitimate power to decide? Should they have?

When do students, such as Alf, have the information, competence, or legitimate power to decide? Should they have?

sessment, selection decisions about the focal point for assessment, and planning decisions about what procedures and instruments to use. In many instances, these matters are resolved so routinely that those involved hardly are aware that decisions were made. In other cases, heated debates arise. An argument is raging, for instance, about the appropriateness of preschool screening programs to detect learning problems. (Can it be done appropriately?) Pivotal to all such debates are considerations about criteria and procedures for decision making. Where there is disagreement, a particularly critical concern is: who decides what the criteria and procedures should be?

When the objectives of the individual and the group or society are compatible, the question of who decides about criteria and procedures may be of little concern. However, when interests conflict, who decides becomes a profoundly important matter. Usually, control of decision making is maintained by those with greatest authority in a situation. This is a questionable practice whenever those in authority do not have a legitimate basis for assuming power or have interests that conflict with those of other participants. The former circumstance

VIEWPOINT

ASSESSMENT AND SOCIAL CONTROL

In the San Francisco schools in 1973, black children were greatly overrepresented in special classes. Although they comprised only 27.8 percent of the total student population, they comprised 47.4 percent of all students in educationally handicapped classes and 53.3 percent of those in the educable mentally handicapped classes [Rivers and others, 1975]. In a Riverside, California, study of persons identified as mentally retarded, there were 300 percent more Mexican-Americans and 50 percent more blacks but only 60 percent as many whites as would be expected from their respective proportions in the community (Mercer, 1972a). Socioeconomic status of the child also introduces a systematic bias. A child with an IQ score within the mild range of mental retardation who is from a low-socio-economic-status group is more likely to be diagnosed mentally retarded than a middle- or upper-class child with a similar score. . . .

Classification, then is not a simple, scientific, and value-free procedure with predictably

benign consequences. Rather, it arises from and tends to perpetuate the values of the cultural majority, often to the detriment of individual children or classes of children. The majority has traditionally made the rules, determined what is good, normal, or acceptable and what is deviant, exceptional, or unacceptable. Classification serves to identify children who do not fit the norms, who are not progressing normally, and who pose a threat to the equilibrium of the system, so that they may be changed or isolated. Seen in this light, classification becomes a mechanism for social control. It institutionalizes the values of the cultural majority, governs the allocation of resources and access to opportunity, protects the majority from undue anxiety, and maintains the status quo of the community and its institutions. Clearly, many of the negative consequences and abuses that prompted this study can be understood and remedied only within this broader cultural context.

Hobbs (1975a, pp. 29–30, 40–41)

---

includes instances when professionals assess and prescribe outside their area of competence, or in areas where the state of knowledge precludes sufficient expertise, and when professionals inappropriately presume consent of participants. The latter circumstance includes instances where professionals' values or financial interests are at variance with those seeking their services and when society pursues its rights and responsibilities at the expense of the rights and liberties of individuals.

It is when interests conflict that the "political" facets of assessment activity are underscored. Power conflicts and imbalances are apparent when those with authority are in a position to have their psychological, social, political, or economic interests prevail in decision making while those without such authority dislike the decisions and indicate their dissatisfaction.

Authority stems from a variety of psychological and sociopolitical-economic factors which may be institutionalized and legitimized. Therefore, it should be clear that political facets of assessment are not limited to power imbalances stemming from legislated authority.[7] What is being described

---

[7]The *overt* political facets of assessment activity are seen in the many instances when assessments are required by organizational (government, school, industry) policies and when assessment data are used for planning, evaluating, and policy-making purposes. *Covert* political facets are potentially present in all other assessment situations.

is any power imbalance inappropriately detrimental to the interests of one or more participants.

Concerns have been raised about the decision-making role of those assessed, especially children or persons seen as less than competent, such as those identified as having learning or emotional problems. Currently, the role students, clients, and their advocates should play in decision making is being widely debated in legal and professional circles. Efforts to ensure protection for those denied a decision-making role have been reflected in recent court cases and various advocacy programs. Clearer guidelines should soon emerge clarifying both the legitimate bases for denying individuals decision-making power and the protections safeguarding their interests when others have decision-making power. Since overt and covert power imbalances appear inevitable, stringent protection of individual rights is essential. There must be understanding of and commitment to ethical principles by professionals and the society as a whole if abuses are to be constrained.

CONCLUDING COMMENTS

Understanding conceptual, ethical, and methodological concerns is essential to wise decision making related to learning and behavior problems. This understanding provides a basis for selecting among assessment procedures and for assembling and interpreting information upon which decisions are made.

In exploring ideas pertinent to an assessment framework, we have grappled with problems of defining psychoeducational assessment, its purposes, nature, and scope. As outlined in Figure 5–1 and Table 5–1, psychoeducational assessment

involves a process by which attributes of phenomena are both described and judged as a basis for decision making;

FOR EXAMPLE
FOLLOW THROUGH ON DECISIONS

With regard to follow-through on decisions, we like to keep in mind the fable of the arthritic Bulgarian peasant who sells her only cow to go to a distant university clinic for help. A famous medical professor finds her case so interesting that he uses her in a demonstration for his students. After extensively examining her and describing and diagnosing her problem and symptoms, he prescribes a course of treatment. Naturally, the whole experience fills the woman with awe. At the conclusion, the doctor gives her a written prescription for medicine and details other treatment steps. The old woman is overcome with admiration for his expertise and says the Bulgarian equivalent of, "Gee, you're wonderful doctor!"

Many years later, the professor happens to be passing through the woman's village. She sees him and rushes out to kiss his hand and thank him for his marvelous help. He remembers the case and is gratified when she tells him how much good the treatment has done. Indeed, he is so pleased with the news that he fails to note that she is as crippled as before.

The fact is that she never had the prescription filled because she didn't have ready access to an apothecary nor did she have the money. In addition, she would never have been willing to part with the valuable piece of paper given to her by the great doctor. As to the other treatment steps, her village had no provision for hydrotherapy or stores which carried products needed for the prescribed special diet.

Regardless of her failure to improve her condition, the old woman continued to relate with pleasure to all who would listen about the great doctor and the wonderful treatment he prescribed. (Adapted from Berne, 1964.)

encompasses four major functions or processes—classification, selection, specific planning for change, and evaluation of interventions;

appropriately focuses on persons, environments, and interactions and on nonpathological as well as pathological conditions;

significantly varies in practice, which affects not only its form but the quality of data made available for decision making;

is limited in terms of the types of procedures available even though the marketplace is being flooded with some types of instruments.

Table 5–2 presents a summary of key concerns which are relevant in evaluating and selecting assessment procedures. No assessment activity is free of such concerns. That

TABLE 5–2

Key Conceptual, Ethical, and Methodological Concerns Related to Selecting Assessment Procedures

I. Conceptual concerns
Procedures will be shaped by decisions made with regard to the following issues:
A. What decisions are to be made?
B. Whose interests are to be served by the assessment activity (e.g., the society, individual students and clients, the assessor) and what criteria are to be used in judging phenomena?
C. What models of cause and correction are to be used as bases for planning assessment activity (e.g., person, environment, or interactional determinants of behavior)?
D. What information is needed to facilitate decision making?

II. Ethical concerns
Procedures must attempt systematically to detect and minimize:
A. Errors (e.g., false negatives and positives).
B. Misprescriptions related to subsequent intervention procedures (including over-identifying individuals and subgroups as the object of change).
C. Violations of rights (e.g., failure to provide help, failure to get consent appropriately, invasion of privacy, denial of access to assessment reports and of the right to correct the record).
D. Negative repercussions of assessment processes or products (e.g., increasing feelings of anxiety, incompetency, and lack of self-determination, increasing

overreliance and dependency on professionals, initiating self-fulfilling prophecies and stigmatizing effects).
E. Inappropriate financial costs and exclusion from services of those who can't afford services.
F. Failure of professionals to take responsibility for improving standards of practice and advancing knowledge (including collusion with an inadequate status quo).

III. Methodological (technical, practical) concerns
The following problems continue to place major limitations on assessment activity and assessments should be planned in ways to minimize their occurrence and to take them into account so that final decisions are made wisely.
A. The more complex the assessment objectives, the lower the *reliability* of the total set of measurement procedures tends to be.
B. *Construct validity* often has not been demonstrated satisfactorily by scientific standards for current practice, e.g., the "validation" procedures, when undertaken, often are tautological.
C. *Predictive and postdictive validity* appear to diminish, in some instances at an exponential rate, the more distant in time the assessment data being gathered are from the criterion being predicted to or from the

is, what is outlined are major issues and problems about which assessors need to be aware and with which they must be ready to deal.

Furthermore, as important as assessment is, it is necessary to recognize that psychoeducational decision making involves more than choosing a particular assessment procedure (Harber, 1981; Messick,

---

original factor causing the phenomena under investigation.

D. *Content validity* often is judged quite differently by experts and what one expert judges as highly valid may not be a satisfactory procedure for sampling what another assessor wants information about.

E. *Biasing factors* are to some degree inevitable (e.g., due to the weak knowledge base for psychoeducational procedures, because of psychological and societal factors which affect the perception and motivation of assessors and those assessed).

F. There is a sparsity of systematically gathered and agreed-upon *norms and standards* for interpreting findings and making judgments ("good-bad", "normal-abnormal", "success-failure") thereby resulting in idiosyncratic variations in judgments and resultant decision making.

G. The *utility* of a procedure may be judged as much, or more, on the basis of its marketability and the current absence of a feasible alternative as it is on its efficacy (e.g., its validity with regard to the decisions being made, its ability to add information beyond base-rate levels).

H. The *costs* of assessment practices are escalating; time demands often are extensive; referral practices tend to overrely on "old boy" networks; in general, standards for practice are not high.

Adapted from Adelman and Taylor (1979)

1981). Decisions before, during, and after assessment are shaped as much or more by the courses of future action which decision makers, such as assessors, clients, and policy makers, see as viable and beneficial. Of particular importance is that those who are asked to carry out decisions, especially when they have not had a meaningful role to play in decision making, have their own subjective view about what is viable and beneficial for others and for themselves. They may agree verbally, and even in principle, that a particular decision is correct, but this is not the same as agreeing to implement it. Decisions to lose weight, quit smoking, and New Year's resolutions all typify this point. In specific connection with psychoeducational concerns, placement decisions assigning students to remedial programs are not tantamount to students agreeing to work on overcoming problems. Concomitantly, teachers have long bemoaned the fact that assessors' reports recommending special instruction often fail to prescribe specific instructional objectives or they contain prescriptions which are meaningless to them.

In conclusion, even when based on relatively objective assessment procedures, decision making as it is usually practiced is an extremely subjective process. Decisions usually require more than data. Indeed, in extreme cases, data gathered may be ignored completely in order to make a decision which decision makers see as viable and beneficial. More often than not, complex value questions are involved in psychoeducational decision making. Assessment activity explicitly or implicitly reflects philosophical considerations about whether outcomes are to favor the majority's interests or those of the individual. From this perspective, it is evident that assessment and related decision making are influenced by and, in turn, influence major sociocultural and political-economic actions. As Thorndike and Hagen (1977) aptly state, "The wisdom of the decider is crucial" (p. 20).

Chapter 6

Diagnosis of Learning Disabilities

What's in a name?
When it comes to diagnosis, the label as-
signed may profoundly shape futures. Diag-
nostic labels attach names to problems. The
names often imply what caused a problem
and what to do about it. People tend to have
strong images associated with specific labels
and act upon those images. Sometimes the
images are useful generalizations; some-
times they are harmful stereotypes.
Adelman

A great deal of time and money is spent assessing the "learning disabled." Often an
extensive battery of tests is involved. Data
produced by tests may be augmented by the
assessor's observations, by medical, school,
and other existing reports, and by written
and oral interviews. Findings frequently are
used not only for screening and diagnostic
classification, but for placement and specific
intervention planning.

The various assessment procedures and
instruments used by a practitioner to diagnose, screen, and place persons as learning
disabled are so numerous that any attempt
to list them all here certainly would be inadequate. Table 6-1 lists some of the most
prominent examples, categorized by type.
No effort has been made to distinguish
between standardized, semistandardized, or
unstandardized procedures. If any general
statement characterizes the list, it is that
none of the measures has been satisfactorily
validated with regard to learning disabilities.
Thus, while such procedures are typically
used and widely discussed, their prominence should not be taken as an index of
their validity.

Assessment procedures used for diagnosis, screening, and placement of learning disabilities are subject to a variety of common methodological problems (see Chapter 5 and Appendix A). In addition, there are unique concerns related to each area which deserve emphasis. Those related to diagnosis are the focus of this chapter. Those related to screening and placement are discussed in Chapter 7.

DIAGNOSIS

Individuals who have not learned to read very well in spite of apparent ability and opportunity have, for about the last forty years, been assigned a variety of labels in addition to *learning disabled*. These include:

brain injured
dyslexic
educationally handicapped
hyperactive
hyperkinetic behavior syndrome
language disordered
learning disordered
minimal brain damaged
minimal cerebral dysfunctioned
perceptually impaired (dysfunctioned)
problem learner
problem reader
psycholinguistic disability
psychoneurological disorder
reading disability
slow learner
Strauss syndrome
underachiever

Less common appellations which have been used are:

auditory learner
choreiform child
developmental aphasia
developmentally imbalanced
driven child
dyssynchronous child
educationally maladjusted
interjacent child

VIEWPOINT

DIAGNOSTIC LABELS

Diagnosis is changing because we are changing our concepts of illness and disease [however] it is very difficult to rid our thinking and our language of the old entity concept of illness. We often speak in figurative terms of "fighting the disease," "facing it," of having a cancer, of suffering from arthritis, or of being afflicted with high blood pressure. This argot reflects the tendency to go on thinking of all diseases as a thing, a horrid, hateful, alien thing which invades the organism. . . .

What we are objecting to is the inference so easily drawn that the diagnostic labels in common use to describe psychiatric conditions are as definite and constant as those of Tay-Sachs disease. . . . Diagnostic name-calling may be damning. . . . The very word "cancer" is said to kill some patients who would not have succumbed (so quickly) to the malignancy from which they suffer. . . . We disparage labelling of all kinds in psychiatry insofar as these labels apply to supposed diseases or conditions of specific etiological determination. We deplore the tendency of psychiatry to retain its old perjorative name-calling functions. Patients who consult us because of their suffering and their distress and their disability have every right to resent being plastered with a damning index tab. Our function is to help people, not to further afflict them.

Menninger (1963, p. 41)

invisibly crippled child
kinesthetic learner
organic brain syndrome
performance disabled (handicapped)
visual learner

Many of the above "diagnoses" still are used. However, the institutionalization of the learning disabilities movement has made *learning disabled* the more likely diagnosis.

The immediate, practical purpose of diagnosis is to identify a problem so that it can be

TABLE 6-1

Types of Assessment Procedures and Instruments Used for the Diagnostic Classification, Screening, and Placement of Individuals[a]

I. Observations or rating of current behavior (by parents, students, or professionals)
A. In natural settings such as classrooms, home, or free play situations
   1. For prevention and identification
      a. Child Behavior Rating Scale (Cassel, 1962)
      b. Individual Learning Disabilities Classroom Screening Instrument (Giles, Meier, & Cazier, 1973)
      c. Student Rating Scale (Adelman & Feshbach, 1971; Feshbach, Adelman, & Fuller, 1977)
      d. The Pupil Rating Scale Revised (Myklebust, 1981)
      e. Devereux Child Behavior Rating Scale (Spivack & Spotts, 1966) and Devereux Adolescent Behavior Rating Scale (Spivack, Spotts, & Haimes, 1967)
   2. For diagnosis, treatment planning, or evaluation
      a. Burks' Behavior Rating Scale (Burks, 1969)
      b. Peterson-Quay Problem Behavior Checklist (Quay & Peterson, 1967)
      c. Target Behavior analysis procedures (O'Leary, 1972)
      d. Conners Rating Scale (Conners, 1969)
B. In special assessment situations
   1. For prevention and identification
      a. Early Detection Inventory (McGahan & McGahan, 1967)
      b. Gesell Developmental Tests (Ilg & Ames, 1964)
   2. For diagnosis, treatment planning, evaluation
      a. Checklist for Student's Behavior (Smith, Neisworth, & Greer, 1978)
      b. It is important to note that while standardized measures are almost nonexistent, observations of behaviors during psychological and medical examinations tend to be the most heavily relied on data in confirming presenting problems (Adelman, 1978c; Wade & Baker, 1977)

II. Interviews and written personal reports by parent, students, or professionals (responses to oral and/or written questions, or inventories of items, related to medical, psychological, educational, and socioeconomic background and status with emphasis on traumatic incidents and developmental problems)
Note: While some of the data elicited may be factual, there is undoubtedly an important bias toward subjective reinterpretation (Yarrow, Campbell, & Burton, 1970).
A. Histories
   1. Medical information related to pregnancies and birth, illnesses, and injuries (Seidel & Ziai, 1975)
   2. Developmental information related to social, emotional, motor, language, and cognitive areas, e.g., Gesell's Illustrative Behavior Interview (Gesell & Amatruda, 1947)
   3. School history focusing on important events or patterns regarding school experiences (Wallace & Larsen, 1978)
   4. Family information including socioeconomic data, relevant medical, developmental or school history of family members (Mercer & Lewis, 1977)
B. Current status (present concerns and perceived causes of problems)
   1. Medical status—current health status, recent illnesses, injury, or physical complaints (Schain, 1972)
   2. Developmental status—current social, emotional, motor, language, and cognitive status, e.g., Vineland Social Maturity Scale (Doll, 1953)
   3. School status—current school problems and perspectives by all participants as to the causes and possible corrections
   4. Family status—current family events, living arrangements, impending changes

III. Verbal and performance measures
A. For prevention and identification
   1. de Hirsch Predictive Index (de Hirsch,

Jansky, & Langford, 1966)
2. The Satz Battery (Satz, Friel, & Rudegeair, 1976)
3. Denver Developmental Screening Test (Frankenburg, Dodds, Fandall, Kazuk, & Cohrs, 1975)

B. For diagnosis, treatment planning, evaluation
1. Cognitive area and aptitudes
   a. Wechsler Intelligence Scales; WPPSI, WISC-R, WAIS (Wechsler, 1955, 1967, 1974)[b]
   b. Stanford Binet Intelligence Test (Terman & Merrill, 1973)
   c. Boehm Test of Basic Concepts (Boehm, 1970)
   d. Slosson Intelligence Test (Slosson, 1971)
   e. McCarthy Scales of Children's Abilities (McCarthy, 1972)
   f. Peabody Picture Vocabulary Test–Revised (Dunn & Dunn, 1981)
   g. Ravens Progressive Matrices (Ravens, 1956)
   h. System of Multicultural Pluralistic Assessment (Mercer & Lewis, 1979)
   i. Achievement tests such as the California Achievement Test (Tiegs & Clark, 1963)
   j. Psychoeducational tests such as the Woodcock-Johnson Psychoeducational Battery (Woodcock & Johnson, 1977)
2. Language area
   a. Illinois Test of Psycholinguistic Abilities (Kirk, McCarthy, & Kirk, 1968)[b]
   b. Wepman Auditory Discrimination Test (Wepman, 1973)[b]
   c. Slingerland Screening Test (Slingerland, 1974)
   d. Test of Written Language (Hammill & Larsen, 1978)
   e. Achievement tests such as Metropolitan Achievement Tests: Language Instructional Battery (Balow, Hogan, Farr, & Prescott, 1978)

f. Reading readiness tests such as Metropolitan Readiness Tests (Nurss & McGauvran, 1976)
3. Perceptual Motor area
   a. Bender Visual-Motor Gestalt Test (Bender, 1938; Koppitz, 1963, 1975)[b]
   b. Developmental Test of Visual Perception (Frostig, Lefever, & Whitlesey, 1964)[b]
   c. Lincoln-Oseretsky Motor Development Scale (Sloan, 1955)[b]
   d. Graham-Kendall Memory for Designs (Graham & Kendall, 1960)[b]
   e. Purdue Perceptual Motor Survey (Roach & Kephart, 1966)[b]
   f. Developmental Test of Visual Motor Integration (Beery & Buktenica, 1967)
4. Social and emotional areas
   a. Vineland Social Maturity Scale (Doll, 1953)
   b. California Test of Personality (Thorpe, Clark, & Tiegs, 1953)
   c. Kuder Personal Preference Record (Kuder, 1954)
   d. Goodenough-Harris Drawing Test (Harris, 1963)
   e. Children's Apperception Test (Bellak & Bellak, 1965)
   f. Early School Personality Questionnaire (Coan & Cattell, 1970)
   g. Piers-Harris Children's Self-Concept Scale (Piers & Harris, 1969)
5. School Performance
   a. California Achievement Test (Tiegs & Clark, 1978)
   b. Stanford Achievement Test (Madden, Gardner, Rudman, Karlsen, & Merwin, 1973)
   c. Metropolitan Achievement Tests (Prescott, Balow, Hogan, & Farr, 1978; Farr, Prescott, Balow, & Hogan, 1978; Hogan, Farr, Prescott, & Balow, 1978; Balow, Hogan, Farr & Prescott, 1978)
   d. Iowa Tests of Basic Skills (Hieronymus, Lindquist, & Hoover, 1978); Tests of Achievement and Profi-

TABLE 6-1 *continued*

ciency (Scannell, 1978)
  e. Gates-MacGinite Reading Tests
     (MacGinite, 1978)
  f. Wide Range Achievement Test (Jas-
     tak & Jastak, 1965; 1978)
  g. Peabody Individual Achievement
     Test (Dunn & Markwardt, 1970)
  h. Psychoeducational tests such as
     Woodcock-Johnson Psycho-educa-
     tional Battery (Woodcock & Johnson,
     1977)
  i. Skill diagnostic inventories such as
     Criterion Reading (Hackett, 1971),
     Brigance Diagnostic Inventories
     (1977, 1978, 1980), and Diagnostic
     Mathematics Inventory (Gessell,
     1977)
IV. Physiological Tests
  A. Physical examination—a nonspecialized
     exam including measurement of height,
     weight, head circumference, blood pres-
     sure, and exams of various physiological

systems including visual acuity using
Snellen wall or E charts
  B. Sensory Acuity—specialized tests
     1. Vision tests to assess refractive errors,
        nystagmus, faulty eye movement
        a. Keystone Telebinocular (e.g., Walton
           & Schubert, 1969)
        b. Massachusetts Vision Test (e.g.,
           Foote & Crane, 1954)
        c. Bausch and Lomb Orthorater (e.g.,
           Salvia & Ysseldyke, 1981)
     2. Hearing
        a. Sweep audiometry (e.g., Schain,
           1972)
        b. Pure tone audiometry (e.g., Northern
           & Downs, 1974)
  C. Neurological exam
     1. Evaluation of mental status, speech,
        muscle tone, fine and gross motor con-
        trol—"hard" neurological signs such as
        bilaterally exaggerated tendon reflexes,
        and various "soft" neurological signs

corrected. Unfortunately, efforts to carry out this simple intent produce many difficulties and are surrounded by controversy (e.g., see reviews by Guskin et al., 1975; Phillips & Draguns, 1971).

Diagnostic activity is criticized for ignoring individual differences and for being stigmatizing and dehumanizing. Critics claim psychoeducational diagnosis is irrelevant to effective treatment. Present diagnostic practices are decried as reifying and maintaining the status quo.

In response, it is argued that there is no satisfactory evidence for lasting negative consequences of diagnosing and that, without diagnosis, special help would not be available. Present diagnostic practices are

defended as doing a necessary job with reasonable effectiveness.

Both sides in the debate have made valid points. Diagnoses are needed and current diagnostic practices leave a great deal to be desired. In exploring these matters, we begin by looking at essential features of diagnostic labeling.

Nature of Diagnostic Classification
It is helpful to place diagnostic classification within a broad context. For precision in usage, the term *diagnosis* is restricted to the act of *classifying pathology*. Diagnosis represents only one major type of classification or labeling purpose.

From a treatment perspective, a diagnosis

such as confused dominance, asymmetrical reflexes, overflow or crossover movements. (e.g., Schain, 1972)[b]
2. Electroencephalogram—amplification, recording, and analysis of electrical activity of the brain (e.g., Ellingson, 1966)[b]

Note: As distinct from neurological exams, neuropsychological exams involve a battery of tests measuring intelligence, sensory and motor functioning and achievement, with the aim of relating performance to brain dysfunction (Reitan & Davison, 1974).

D. Special procedures to test hormonal, chemical, or structural defects (e.g., Schain, 1972)
   1. X-ray studies of the skull for intracranial calcification or tumor
   2. Metabolic tests, e.g., brain metabolism, ferric chloride test for PKU
   3. Chromosomal studies
V. Available records and data
   A. Past

1. Medical reports from pediatricians, neurologists, other medical specialists
2. Psychological—test data, results, and reports from school psychologists or other professionals
3. Educational
   a. Review of past school products (e.g., written papers, tests, projects)
   b. Reports from teachers and tutors
   c. Cumulative school records (grades, teacher comments, test scores, attendance, school health records)
B. Current (within the past three months)
   1. Medical—report from the most recent physical and/or neurological exam
   2. Psychological—test data, results, and reports from school psychologists or other professionals who have been consulted recently
   3. Educational
      a. Review of current school products (e.g., written papers, tests, projects)
      b. Reports from current teachers and tutors

a. Examples and specific references cited when relevant and available.

b. This item is one of the ten most frequently recommended tests and evaluations for a learning disabilities battery as noted by authoritative publications from 1968 to 1979 (Coles, 1978).

may or may not be needed. However, from a scientific perspective, diagnostic labeling is tantamount to the general task of classification or taxonomic sorting which is a basic characteristic of scientific activity. Classification is part of the process of organizing, bringing order to, and understanding what otherwise might be confusing, overwhelming, and incomprehensible. Classification is of major importance to advancing knowledge.

In discussing the purposes of diagnosis, Gough (1971) has suggested three levels. Level 1 is identification of a cluster of symp-

toms (a syndrome) for which symptomatic relief is about all that can be offered. Level 2 involves identifying pathology so that the possibility of arresting the reaction and curative efforts can be tried. Level 3 involves identifying etiology so that the possibility of prevention can be explored. These levels reflect the central conceptual concern related to diagnostic classification, namely, what is the diagnosis identifying? signs, symptoms, or a syndrome? pathological processes underlying the symptoms? severity of the problem? appropriate treatment objectives? procedures? prognosis? etiology? When

VIEWPOINT

CLASSIFICATION

Measurement is essential to science, but before we can measure, we must know what it is we want to measure. Qualitative or taxonomic discovery must precede quantitative measurement (Eysenck, 1952, p. 34).

In general, the conceptual process of classification essentially

involves the establishment of categories to which phenomena can be ordered. The number of class systems that potentially may be constructed is limited only by [one's] ability to abstract from [one's] experience. The principles employed to construct such classes may be inductive, deductive, or a combination of both, and may vary on a continuum from the closely descriptive to the highly abstract (Zigler & Phillips, 1961, p. 608).

Principles used to construct categories for labeling usually are related closely to the purposes for which the classification schema has been developed, such as basic and applied research objectives and practical administrative and treatment needs.

there is a lack of clarity as to what the diagnostic label identifies, its usefulness is greatly diminished, and many undesirable outcomes may result.

Broadly, classification of psychoeducational problems reflects the need to categorize past, present, or future status to ameliorate, prevent, or study such problems. For example, it often is important to categorize problems with reference to primary instigating cause (see Table 2-1) in order to prevent such problems in the future. Our synthesis of various perspectives suggests that the essential steps in developing classification categories and procedures involve determination of:

the range of phenomena (qualities, attributes) to be labeled;

a set of categories, based on (1) inductive and deductive theoretical principles, (2) empirically demonstrated usefulness, or (3) rationally defended need;

a working definition and empirical operations by which phenomena can be observed;

reliable and valid procedures for quantifying perceived phenomena;

reliable and valid criteria (norms, standards) by which quantified phenomena can be evaluated for classification; and

appropriateness of assigning a label.

In summary, classification, including diagnostic labeling, may be used for scientific and practical purposes and to meet the objectives of society, special-interest groups, and individuals. The various purposes and objectives may lead to competing schemes for categorization. For example, those adhering to different theoretical models often advocate different objectives and labels. Such differences contribute to situations where a particular diagnostic label is branded as useless and even as harmful by some, while others proclaim its value with equal vigor.

Learning Disabilities as a Classification Label

Labels such as *learning disabilities* are developed with a number of behavioral correlates and implications for research and practice in mind. In effect, these correlates and implications are hypotheses about symptoms, underlying processes, causes, and so forth. Ultimately the value of a label is judged by its contribution to research and practice. When a particular label's benefits (usefulness, economy, convenience, etc.) do not outweigh the costs (financial, negative

VIEWPOINT

The surprised principal, waving the achievement test scores, confronts Ms. Smith, the second-grade teacher.

"How did you get these low IQ students to do so well?"

"Low IQ?" she repeated with equal surprise. "What do you mean, low IQ?"

"Well, didn't you see their IQ scores on the list I sent you last fall?"

"Oh no!" Ms. Smith exclaimed, "I thought those were their locker numbers!"

---

effects, etc.), it is time to develop a better one—not to do away with classification.

The current situation with regard to the LD label is that it needs improvement. Since the category has been found useful at least by legislators, parent groups, administrators, and some practitioners, it obviously has met a practical and political need. Many practitioners and researchers, however, find it a poor category for their purposes and see the label as harmful. For example, as discussed in Part 1, a major criticism of the LD label (as well as most psychiatric and special education labels), is that the category encompasses a *heterogeneous* group including individuals who differ with regard to symptoms, causes, current performance capabilities, and prognosis (Bryan, 1974; Wepman et al., 1975). Another major criticism stresses the difficulties in using the label reliably and validly that result in frequent diagnostic *errors*.

Heterogeneity criticism. At its simplest level, the heterogeneity criticism points out that the group currently classified as LD encompasses important subclasses. At a more complex level, the criticism suggests the LD classification does not really capture the essence of a class of phenomena.

In discussing a similar point related to psychiatric diagnosis, Zigler and Phillips (1961) use the example of the biological classification of a genus that encompasses a number of species. Borrowing this example, we see that if LD is like a genus, it should not be criticized for encompassing a heterogeneous group of persons. It could be criticized, however, for not labeling the significant subgroups (species) encompassed by the label. On the other hand, LD may not possess the characteristics of a genus, but may be more akin to a species. In such a case, the group of which it is a subgroup should be clarified. If the current label is not analogous to either a genus or species, it should be replaced by a better classification schema. Clearly, research must determine whether the LD label is appropriate and whether specific labels for subgrouping are needed.

In any case, as Zigler and Phillips (1961) indicate, it is important to understand that homogeneity is not a quality inherent in a phenomenon, but a construction of the observer and classifier. Therefore, "it would perhaps be more fruitful to dispense entirely with the homogeneity-heterogeneity distinction, . . . allowing us to direct our attention to the underlying problem of the relative merits of different classificatory principles" (p. 611).

Sources of error. Assuming that the LD label is based on sound classification principles, the major concerns involve whether it can be, and is, applied reliably and validly for specific individuals with problems. Current evidence indicates it cannot and is not. Reliability is a necessary prerequisite for a diagnostic system (Zigler & Phillips, 1961). If professionals cannot consistently differentiate one phenomenon's characteristics from another, even the most potentially valuable set of classification labels cannot be put to use. More importantly, a label has to be valid. For instance, it must appropri-

VIEWPOINT

MOVEMENT TO DE-EMPHASIZE CATEGORIES RELATED TO SPECIAL EDUCATION

There is a movement among some special educators to shift away from the traditional categories which have evolved for designating exceptional individuals as handicapped (e.g., mentally retarded; visually, hearing, speech, or orthopedically impaired; emotionally disturbed; or learning disabled). This trend is referred to either as the cross-categorical or non-categorical movement (Dunn, 1968; Gallagher, 1971). Those who advocate this trend for special education stress that differential diagnoses using current categories and diagnostic procedures do not validly distinguish individuals with regard to treatment needs.

Two major factors which have bolstered this trend are (1) ethical and legal concerns about the role such categorization has played in segregat-

ing individuals with physical, cognitive, social, and emotional differences—including a disproportionate number from minority groups—in special classrooms and (2) an increasing doubt that significant benefits result from placement in self-contained special education classrooms.

The large-scale move toward mainstreaming reflects these concerns and has been bolstered by, and has given impetus to, the argument that traditional special education categories should be altered. Whereas traditional special education categories reflected the interest in placement of individuals into special classes, proposals for alternative classification systems tend to emphasize use of labels in planning instruction and treatment and identifying the severity of learning problems (Adelman, 1971; Hallahan & Kauffman, 1976; Lerner & James, 1974).

---

ately identify causes, treatment needs, or prognosis.

Use of LD as a label presupposes that assessment procedures can differentiate, reliably and validly, learning problems caused by minor CNS dysfunctioning. Unfortunately, procedures used to arrive at a diagnosis of LD are not able to assess cause directly. Rather, they rely heavily on measurement of a relatively limited range of controversial "symptomatic" behaviors and skills. The symptoms are controversial because research has yet to demonstrate how a particular symptom relates to either the causes or remediation of learning problems. Whenever diagnosis of cause must rely on ambiguous symptoms rather than direct diagnostic signs, errors are common.

It also is widely recognized that errors in applying the LD label result from traditional technical deficiencies associated with assessment procedures. These include rater or

tester or assessor bias, fluctuations in children's performance due to motivation and the degree of assimilation of new behaviors and skills, the limited range of behavior which can be sampled because of restrictions imposed by time and instrument availability, and so forth.

Another source of error, less frequently discussed, is the sparsity of norms and standards that can be used as guidelines in making judgments about children's behaviors and skills (Messick, 1975). Most commonly, this involves lack of specific criteria as to what constitutes "normal" and "abnormal" behavior and "success" or "failure." As Strupp and Hadley (1977) point out, what is identified as a problem depends on the values incorporated in the evaluation criteria as brought to bear by three "interested parties": society, the individual, and the professional intervener. Lack of specificity and differences in criteria mean that varying standards may be applied for labeling problems. Consequently, children with the same behaviors and skills could be seen as problems at one age but not at another, in one school or classroom but not in another, and so forth (Algozzine, 1977; Conners, 1970; Gersten, Langner, Eisenberg, Simcha-Fagan, & McCarthy, 1976; Lapouse and Monk, 1964; Werry & Quay, 1971). Similarly, different cut-off points often are used to maximize or minimize errors in labeling—depending on such factors as current administrative policies and research activity (Adelman & Feshbach, 1975).

Due to the sparsity of established cause-effect relationships and because of deficiencies associated with current assessment practices, assignment of the LD label is based more on theory and various professional orientations ("biases") than on valid assessment data. The perspective most frequently employed in developing and applying classification labels for learning and behavior problems reflects a tendency to view such problems as resulting from chronic, pathological disorders within the person. While this view will be a valid basis for diagnosis in some cases, in a significant number of others it leads to errors.

In sum, given the various sources of errors associated with diagnosing LD, a considerable number of misdiagnoses seems inevitable. Consequently, valid differential diagnostic classification of the subgroup whose learning problems stem from minimal neurological dysfunctioning remains a desirable, but elusive, objective.[1]

Fortunately many problems can be identified for treatment without being assigned sophisticated differential diagnostic labels. For example, as we will discuss in Chapter 7, screening and placement practices often require no more than gross discriminations among problems.

DIFFERENTIAL DIAGNOSTIC ASSESSMENT AND LEARNING DISABILITIES

The major difficulties related to assessment for classifying psychoeducational phenomena such as learning problems are twofold. One difficulty is the fact that currently used classification labels do not identify discrete problem populations; this alone would be sufficient to confound the assessor's classification efforts. The second difficulty is that most available assessment procedures are limited by severe methodological problems. To date, the main scientific impact of research designed to address these difficulties has been to underscore the weakness of the current knowledge base and prevailing practices.

Prevailing assessment procedures used for classification have been criticized as lacking validity for making differential diagnoses (e.g., Arter & Jenkins, 1979; Coles, 1978; Kaufman, 1981; Salvia & Ysseldyke, 1981). The process of *differential assessment*, including differential diagnosis, involves gathering data that validly exclude the phenomena from other categories and finding definite indications that the phenomena belong to a specific category. At the very least, contradictory data must be accounted for.

Despite their unsuitability, a variety of tests, ratings, and global observations are used for differentially diagnosing learning disabilities (Sattler, 1982). From the standpoint of practice, the result is numerous labeling errors and, consequently, wrongly prescribed treatment. Moreover, ready acceptance of unvalidated diagnostic classifications may contribute to premature,

---

[1]Our hypotheses and research regarding a continuum of learning problems in terms of person, environmental, and interactional causes represent one effort to identify this subgroup and explore other relevant subgroups (see Chapter 3). Other recent efforts to study subgroups in this area are reported by Gaddes (1980), Luick (1979), McIntyre, Murray, Blackwell, and Harris (1979), and Torgeson and Houck (1979).

widespread acceptance of other unvalidated interventions.

Research on populations diagnosed as LD also is profoundly affected by the deficiencies of current diagnostic assessment practices. Even when two studies purport to be sampling persons with learning disabilities, they may have selected individuals who differ significantly on such critical dimensions as type of learning problem, degree of severity, type of causation. At the same time, studies purporting to sample two different problems (e.g., minimal brain dysfunctions versus emotional disturbance) may be taking some subjects from the same population or even from a third problem population. Limitations of current diagnostic procedures make it very difficult to identify homogeneous groups of subjects with regard to critical variables, thereby almost guaranteeing that persons in any given sample will differ with respect to source of problem and syndrome manifested.[2] This of course limits analyses and generalizations of findings.

Specific Diagnostic Indicators

Differential assessment of learning disabilities requires seeking information that would exclude persons who should not be labeled *learning disabled,* such as those who should be diagnosed as mentally deficient, a behavior problem, and so forth. Other unique signs are sought that would indicate that the person indeed belongs in the LD category. Thus, classifying someone as learning disabled involves more than administering a battery of tests and interpreting patterns of data. There must be research that has clarified specific diagnostic indicators—for example, behavior and the degree of severity—*exclusively* associated with specific learning disabilities at various ages.

Which data are specifically sought and when usually depends on when, where, and by whom a problem is first noted. Problems recognized prior to enrollment in school generally are identified by parents or pediatricians and not uncommonly are assigned a diagnostic label by an M.D. or a psychologist. Problems noted after enrollment in school may be assessed by an educational specialist, a school counselor, a school or private psychologist, a social worker or psychiatrist, a general or special medical practitioner, or some combination working independently or as a team. Both the age of a person referred and the assessor's general field, and specific orientation within that field, will profoundly shape the procedures used and the diagnostic label assigned. Current political policies also have a major shaping influence. When legislation cites a specific label, diagnosticians use that label. If the law in a state or country were to provide services only for learning problems caused by minimal brain damage, that state or country would have an unusually high incidence of persons diagnosed as brain damaged.

From a psychoeducational perspective, assessment procedures for use in differential diagnosis should be validated with reference to a specific definition of learning disabilities. If the label is meant to denote ongoing neurological causality, then assessment procedures with demonstrated construct and criterion-related validity are needed.[3]

---

[2]It is worth noting that once individuals are involved in special treatment programs they may be relabeled by association, that is, they may be assigned a label consistent with that used to describe the population the program is designed and purports to serve. For example, it is not uncommon for researchers to refer to the sample in their study as learning disabled solely on the basis of the students' enrollment in a program that claims to serve an LD population. We have seen this done repeatedly. This practice alone should raise serious questions as to how much LD research actually has been carried out on validly classified LD samples.

[3]See Appendix A for a discussion of different types of validity relevant to understanding assessment activity of this nature.

Construct validation is necessary since minimal neurological dysfunctioning is only observable or measurable indirectly and subjectively. Criterion-related validation is necessary since the findings are meant to separate those whose learning problems are due to neurological dysfunctioning from those whose learning problems stem from other causes.

If the label is meant to designate, and to differentiate among, instruction or treatment objectives, the type of assessment validation needed varies with the nature of the intervention. For instance, intervention for persons manifesting learning problems may focus on (1) current tasks, such as learning to multiply; (2) prerequisite abilities needed to perform current tasks, such as following directions and ordering and sequencing events, or (3) psychological processes hypothesized as underlying human learning such as motivation, attention, perception, and psycholinguistic abilities. Content validity is necessary with regard to assessment of current academic deficiencies and instructional planning. Criterion-related and content validation are needed for assessing prerequisites. Construct, criterion-related, and content validation are required of any assessment procedure that purports to assess underlying process deficits.

In general, the types of assessment procedures used in differentially diagnosing learning disabilities are well exemplified by the list in Table 6–1. How valid are such procedures for making the necessary differential diagnostic classification? A growing body of literature addresses this question (Adelman, 1978c; Arter & Jenkins, 1979; Coles, 1978; Dudley-Marling, Kaufman, & Tarver, 1981; Salvia and Ysseldyke, 1981; Ysseldyke, Algozzine, Regan, & Potter, 1979). A central problem identified by several writers is that diagnosis of learning disabilities, as defined in Part 1, requires valid measurement of specific indicators of minor neurological dysfunction. Thus arises the question, can prevailing assessment procedures validly detect minor neurological dysfunctions?

Minor Neurological "Signs"

While the presence or absence of *major* brain dysfunctions usually can be validly diagnosed, it is increasingly conceded that diagnoses of *minor* neurological dysfunctions are arrived at only by inference from behavior and performance data. As yet, these minor dysfunctions cannot be detected reliably and validly using direct biological measures. For example, with respect to diagnosing minimal neurological dysfunctions in children, an important guideline is establishing that a previously acquired ability has been lost rather than that it has yet to develop. According to Schain (1972):

> Most of the traditional neurological examination of complex motor functions is based on demonstration of loss of abilities or of well-defined deviations from norm. These criteria are often not met in the diagnosis of borderline neurological abnormalities in children with learning disorders. There are little normative data meeting ordinary standards of reliability regarding the acquisition of abilities such as the performance of rapid alternating hand movements, performance of tandem walking, the behavior of outstretched hands, the occurrence of overflow movements and other "soft" neurological signs. When normative data are available, as in the establishment of laterality functions, there is often evidence of wide variations in the time-table of acquisition. (p. 10)

Since the key to diagnosing learning disabilities is identification of neurological signs, it is common for assessors to note finding "soft signs." This notion was first advanced by Bender in 1947. Strauss and Lehtinen (1947) also referred to such phenomena designating them "minor signs" and "slight neurological signs." The term *soft signs* is both misleading and indicative of the diagnostic problem in this area. In medicine, the term *signs* refers to objective evidence of disease, such as detection of a virus, and is contrasted with *symptoms,* such as nausea and dizziness, which are seen as subjective evidence. The adoption of the adjectives *hard* and *soft* to qualify the term *signs* stems from the fact that for minor neurological dysfunctions, "hard" signs simply are not present; therefore the term *soft signs* is used. A variety of other behaviors that are *inferred* to be correlates of minor neurological dysfunctioning are characterized as *soft* signs (sometimes referred to as equivocal or borderline signs).[4] Unfortunately, whatever they are called, they are no more than symptoms until they are validated as being associated solely, or at least primarily, with neurological dysfunctioning. However, based on available data, it seems unlikely that such validation will be forthcoming.

Symptoms referred to as soft signs apparently are found with considerable frequency among persons whose problems are unlikely to be the result of neurological dysfunctioning and even among persons with no significant problems at all (Gomez, 1967; Winkler, Dixon, & Parker, 1970). In reviewing the validation research on ten frequently recommended procedures for use in a battery to diagnose learning disabilities (see Table 6-1), Coles (1978) found that available evidence does not support the view that the procedures can differentially diagnose neurologically based learning problems from learning problems caused by other factors. This finding applies to psychoeducational procedures such as perceptual and intellectual measures and neurological evaluations, including EEGs. A similar point can be made with reference to neuropsychological test batteries, which have been gaining

FOR EXAMPLE
A NEW "OFFICIAL" DIAGNOSIS FOR HYPERACTIVITY

Because of the difficulties in validly diagnosing MBD (minimal brain damage or dysfunction) and because of dissatisfaction with the term *hyperactivity*'s primary emphasis on activity level, the American Psychiatric Association has developed a new label as part of its overall diagnostic schemata. The new designation—*attentional deficit disorder* (ADD) with and without hyperactivity—is defined, and diagnostic criteria are delineated, in the Diagnostic and Statistical Manual (DSM III) which is widely used by many professionals and agencies. This diagnostic label will probably be used with increasing frequency along with, or in place of, *learning disabilities.*

ADD with hyperactivity is described as a problem found in children and adolescents. Candidates for this diagnosis are those who display developmentally inappropriate inattention, impulsivity, and hyperactivity.

In the classroom, attentional difficulties and impulsivity are evidenced by the child's not staying with tasks and having difficulty organizing and completing work. The children often give the impression that they are not listening or that they have not heard what they have been told. Their work is sloppy and is performed in an impulsive fashion. On individually administered tests, careless, impulsive errors are often present. Performance may be characterized by oversights, such as omissions or insertions, or misinterpretations of easy items even when the child is well motivated, not just in situations that hold little intrinsic

---

[4]As listed by Schain (1972), "soft neurological signs" looked for in children are: (a) clumsiness in tasks requiring fine motor coordination, e.g. tying shoes and buttoning; (b) choreiform movements; (c) mild dysphasias and associated movements; (d) borderline hyperreflexia and reflex asymmetrics; (e) finger agnosia; (f) dysdiadochokinesis; (g) ocular apraxia and endpoint nystagmus; (h) tremor; (i) graphesthesias; (j) whirling; (k) extinction to double simultaneous tactile stimulation; (l) pupillary inequalities; (m) mixed laterality and disturbances of right-left discrimination; (n) unilateral winking defect; (o) awkward gait; and (p) avoiding response in outstretched hands.

interest. Group situations are particularly diffi-cult for the child, and attentional difficulties are exaggerated when the child is in the class-room where sustained attention is expected.

At home, attentional problems are shown by a failure to follow through on parental requests and instructions and by the inability to stick to activities, including play for periods of time appropriate for the child's age.

*Hyperactivity in young children is mani-fested by gross motor activity, such as exces-sive running or climbing. The child is often de-scribed as being on the go, "running like a motor," and having difficulty sitting still. Older children and adolescents may be extremely restless and fidgety. Often, it is the quality of the motor behavior that distinguishes this disorder from ordinary overactivity in that hy-peractivity tends to be haphazard, poorly or-ganized and not goal directed (*American Psy-chiatric Association, *1980, p. 41).*

Specific diagnostic criteria are:

I. *Inattention.* At least three of the following:
   A. Often fails to finish things he or she starts
   B. Often doesn't seem to listen
   C. Easily distracted
   D. Has difficulty concentrating on school-work or other tasks requiring sustained attention
   E. Has difficulty sticking to a play activity
II. *Impulsivity.* At least three of the following:
   A. Often acts before thinking

   B. Shifts excessively from one activity to another
   C. Has difficulty organizing work (this not being due to cognitive impairment)
   D. Needs a lot of supervision
   E. Frequently calls out in class
   F. Has difficulty awaiting turn in games or group situations
III. *Hyperactivity.* At least two of the following:
   A. Runs about or climbs on things exces-sively
   B. Has difficulty sitting still or fidgets ex-cessively
   C. Has difficulty staying seated
   D. Moves about excessively during sleep
   E. Is always "on the go" or acts as if "driven by a motor"
IV. Onset before the age of seven
 V. Duration of at least six months
VI. Not due to schizophrenia, affective dis-order, or severe or profound mental retar-dation (American Psychiatric Association, 1980, pp. 43–44)

The number of symptoms indicated above are for children from 8 to 10 years old. This is seen as the peak period for referral. Older children are seen as having less symptoms and younger chil-dren more. ADD without hyperactivity is iden-tified using the same symptoms, excluding the set related to hyperactivity and with fewer other symptoms required for diagnosis of the syndrome.

For a critical discussion of the ADD definition, see Ross and Pelham (1981).

---

in prominence and are being applied in diagnostic efforts related to learning prob-lems. A perspective on current limitations of these approaches is provided by Luria and Majovski (1977) in their comparison of the Halstead-Reitan Neuropsychological Test Battery (Reitan & Davison, 1974) and Soviet clinical approaches. These writers under-

score the potential of the methods for study-ing brain-behavior relationships *after* a neurological dysfunction has been iden-tified. At the same time, they implicitly ac-knowledge the severe limitations of such procedures for diagnosing whether learn-ing problems are caused by neurological dysfunctioning.

FOR EXAMPLE

DIAGNOSTIC LABELS

Curious about how the youngsters referred to our special school program came to be labeled, we conducted a small study (Adelman, 1978c, 1979). First, we asked 38 parents about the diagnostic labels which had been assigned to their children.

Parents indicated that 32 youngsters had been diagnosed with one or more of 10 different labels. That is, 32 students were assigned a total of 68 labels: 10 were diagnosed learning disabled/disordered, 7 dyslexic, 4 minimal brain dysfunctioned, 17 educationally handicapped, 17 hyperactive, 2 emotionally disturbed, 2 perceptual problems, 1 educable mentally retarded, 2 slow learner, and 6 disruptive. Nine had received only one label, 13 had two labels, 7 had three labels, and 3 had been assigned four labels.

As a second step, we asked parents to sign a release allowing us to contact professionals who had made the diagnoses. Twenty-six parents agreed, but professionals contacted provided sufficient information on only 15 students. (Getting even this modest proportion of responses required considerable follow-up efforts.) With reference to the specific bases upon which professionals assigned diagnostic labels, the sample clearly is inadequate and the variables investigated are fairly restricted. Still, the findings are suggestive. Perhaps most striking is the finding that only one diagnosis resulted from a consistent pattern of test results, while over half the diagnoses were based primarily on observations, and a third were arrived at despite contradictory evidence. Of the nine diagnoses resulting from observational data, six were based on unsystematic reports (e.g., from parents or teachers or both) which were later validated by the assessor's observations during one examination session. In a not untypical example (a boy age 7 at the time of the diagnosis), a pediatrician diagnosed the boy

as having a hyperactive behavior syndrome and minimal brain dysfunction based on "short attention span and distractible" behavior manifested during the examination and on reports from the mother and teacher stating that behavior and performance was a problem. "Cursory" neurological findings were normal. Once diagnosed, the youngster was placed on amphetamine medication. He was subsequently diagnosed as educationally handicapped and placed in a special class.

As an example of the four diagnoses made despite contradictory evidence (all were labeled LD), there is the case of a 9-year-old boy referred because of "learning problems in school." The LD diagnosis was based primarily on poor reading performance reported by the school (e.g., letter reversals, poor phonetic analysis skills, poor memory), below normal scores on standardized tests of reading, and a "highly significant difference between his verbal and performance IQ scores on the WISC-R," that is, his verbal score was in the low average range and the performance score was in the superior range. This diagnosis was made despite performance at or above the norm on the Bender Visual-Motor Gestalt Test, the Southern California Sensory Integration Tests, the Wepman Auditory Discrimination Test, and the Illinois Test of Psycholinguistic Abilities.

It is interesting to note that in the seven cases where physicians were involved in evaluating the bases for the problems, no abnormal neurological findings were reported even though complete or partial neurological testing was done with five of the youngsters. Generally, in validating that a problem existed, the physicians' findings stressed case-history material, parent and teacher reports of problems, and behaviors such as activity level, lack of cooperation, nervousness, etc., manifested during the physical examination.

The diagnostic reports themselves are worth commenting on. Extensive summaries of developmental histories, family status, peer relations, and specific test scores and responses were included without any clarification of how such matters might be causally related to the referral problems or diagnosis, or how they might rule out some factor as a cause. In several instances a total test score, which was clearly at or above norm for the youngster's age group without this fact being stated, was reported while, at the same time, a missed item from the same test was presented in support of the conclusion that the area tested was a problem area for the student.

It was particularly ironic to find extensive discussion of performance deficiencies on reading achievement tests in reports that were sent back to the teacher who had referred the child for assessment in the first place because of extensive deficiencies in reading noted in the classroom. Also, it was ironic to come across indications that the child was uninterested and manifested avoidance motivation when taking the diagnostic tests, for example, "——did not want to perform the tasks requested," and yet find that test scores were still reported and interpreted as valid indices of developmental capabilities (as contrasted to current motivational status). The selective omission of statements regarding strengths even when test performance was superior was a graphic demonstration of the prevalence and impact of pathological biases which appear to permeate assessment activity, thereby eliminating a major potential strength of such activity which is to disconfirm unwarranted attributions of causality. The major purpose of the various diagnostic assessments was that they allowed for the validation—by an "expert"—of the presence of the problem and the need for special attention to correct it.

If the cause of learning disabilities is seen as stemming from *minor* neurological dysfunctioning, then logically assessment would be of "hard" neurological signs. This, however, has not been the focus of diagnostic efforts; symptoms or "soft signs" have been. In research efforts to date, behaviors seen as symptoms of neurologically based learning disabilities are found as frequently among persons without learning problems. The problem in diagnosing learning disabilities caused by minor neurological dysfunctioning remains one of finding a set of symptoms that is predominantly associated with learning problems.

CONCLUDING COMMENTS

Valid classification is a critical step in advancing knowledge about learning and behavior problems. As the evidence accumulates indicating that widely used diagnostic procedures produce too many errors and too much confusion, it is necessary to consider new approaches. For example, it is unlikely that learning disabilities can be diagnosed validly until environmental and interactional causes of learning problems are identified and ameliorated. In turn, widespread understanding and acceptance of the implications of this point appear unlikely until there is a major shift in professional thinking and in practices and concomitant reallocation of political priorities and resources.

Chapter 7

Screening and Placement for Learning Disabilities

A sense of inferiority and not belonging affects the motivation of a child to learn. Segregation, even though perhaps well intentioned, under the apparent sanction of law and state authority, has a tendency to retard the educational, emotional and mental development of the children.
From Wolf v. Legislature of the State of Utah, 1969

Valid or not, a diagnosis of learning disabilities plays an important role in justifying application of specialized interventions, such as drug treatment, special class placement, and special funding. In this connection, the function of those who label often involves what sociologists refer to as gatekeeping. Assignment of diagnostic labels such as *LD* opens the gate to interventions not widely used or available to persons with "ordinary" learning and behavior problems.

The task of gatekeeping requires screening procedures not only to find but to label a problem and to prescribe treatment. Difficulties arise, however, when the same screening procedures are used to pursue these three functions simultaneously. While such an approach reflects commendable objectives (including enhanced utility, economy, and formulation of specific treatment and placement decisions), it also tends to obscure significant considerations associated with screening and placement. As the following discussion stresses, an understanding of each of these as separate functions is essential to good practice and research in the field of learning disabilities.

SCREENING

At the turn of the century, Alfred Binet and his co-workers undertook the task of developing procedures to identify school children unable to profit from regular instruction. Since that time, the need for such procedures generally has been viewed as extremely important and desirable. This perspective permeates psychology and education and in recent years has resulted in increasing emphasis on prediction and "early" identification screening. It is a perspective rapidly being institutionalized as the result of legislative and judicial actions.[1] Among the variety of problems that are the focus of screening are learning disorders and disabilities, hyperactivity, emotional disturbance, behavior problems, developmental lag problems, perceptual and language problems, central processing problems, cerebral dysfunctions, and reading and other basic skill problems. Children who have such problems are described as at risk, high risk, or as high challenges, underachievers, and school failures.

Given the historical, legislative, and judicial background, it is not surprising that screening has proliferated. Clearly, valid identification of problems is a highly desirable objective, for example, for purposes of prevention and correction. At the same time,

however, there have been negative reactions to the establishment of large-scale programs for screening learning and behavior problems.[2] Prominent among these reactions are concerns over errors (e.g., Gallagher & Bradley, 1972; Meehl & Rosen, 1955; Muehl & Di Nello, 1976; Satz, Friel & Rudegeair, 1976), negative side effects (e.g., Adelman & Feshbach, 1971; Adelman, 1978d; Goffman, 1961; Hobbs, 1975a; Illich, 1976; Laing & Esterson, 1970; Leifer, 1969; Schrag & Divoky, 1975; and Szasz, 1961, 1970) and failure to provide needed services following screening (e.g., Schaer & Crump, 1976).

Two Sequential Decisions

Screening for learning problems involves two sequential questions: (1) Is there a problem now or is there likely to be one in the near future? and (2) Are current interventions adequate or should they be altered? Tables 7-1 and 7-2 outline the focus of assessment (e.g., primary assessment questions, relevant data, types of procedures, and sources of data) and the bases for making these screening decisions. A few brief comments are offered below to clarify key concerns related to each sequential decision.

Significance of the problem. With reference to the first screening decision, the primary question to be answered is whether

---

[1]In the United States, for example, legislative pressures have been building for screening activity since 1967. In that year, the Social Security Act was amended requiring states to provide screening, diagnostic services, and appropriate treatment for all children who were eligible for Medicare. This legislation originally was permissive and subsequently made mandatory. Congressional action has continued to give impetus to such programs for special groups of children—most recently through the Education for All Handicapped Children Act (P.L. 94-142). Some states appear to have exceeded the federal mandate and already have begun massive screening programs. Within the next few years, it is anticipated that many more states will develop plans for screening.

[2]Screening also is referred to as prediction, early identification, early detection, and early warning. Because of the confusion caused by so many overlapping terms, it is helpful to make several distinctions. First, the process of predicting high risk (or at risk) individuals can be distinguished from the process of identifying individuals with current problems. As the word prediction implies, labeling as high risk is a future judgment—an act of prophesying a problem which is not yet present. In contrast, identification involves a current problem.

The term early identification, while intuitively appealing and widely used, only adds to conceptual confusion. The term refers to identification at an early age or early after onset, but it is often used as a synonym for prediction. In either case, the focus is on detecting a sign or a symptom of a problem in its incipient stages (before it becomes a full-blown syndrome). For example, a deficit in insulin metabolism is seen as an early stage of diabetes which if treated appropriately can prevent the later, more pathognomic stages of the disorder. By way of contrast, it should be noted comparable indicators of subsequent emotional, behavioral, and learning problems have not been validated.

something is *significantly* wrong (see Table 7–1). Prevailing practices are designed to identify persons with problems or who are "at risk." This may be accomplished through individual or group assessment. Group procedures usually are gross or first-level screens which are expected to overidentify problems. The errors are to be detected by follow-up assessments. The major concern in detecting such errors is that criteria for what constitutes a *significant* psychoeducational problem often depend on clinical judgment.

Another common concern associated with this stage of identifying problems is that screening procedures often are misused. For example, data from first-level screening tests and rating scales administered in infancy, at

TABLE 7–1

First Screening Consideration

Selection Decision:
   Is there a problem now or is there likely to be one in the near future?

Assessment Focus[a]

Primary Assessment Questions	Relevant Data	Type of Assessment Procedures	Source of Data
Is something *significantly* wrong?	Indices of dissatisfaction or concern over current status	Interviews and written personal reports (statements in response to specific questions, etc.)	Consumers, providers of interventions (e.g., M.D.s, administrators, evaluators, teachers, psychologists), knowledgeable others
	Recent samples of processes and outcomes related to performance (behavior, learning)	Requests for available records	As above
		Observation ratings[b]	As above
		If needed:[c] Standardized tests	Tests and assessors
	Data for comparison purposes regarding processes and outcomes of an appropriate normative, referent group	Intragroup comparisons using above procedures (if a large sample is screened)	As above
		Locating and requesting summary reports and available records on an appropriate referent group (including test norms)	As above plus Published norms (e.g., in test manuals and other published sources)

preschool level, in kindergarten, or in the primary grades have been used to generate tentative classifications. At times these labels have been interpreted as definitive diagnoses and even have been used to generate prescriptions. Most screening procedures have lower reliability and validity than procedures designed for diagnostic classification and for generating specific prescriptions. In particular, the validity of first-level screens is so low that they are expected to identify persons who do not even have significant problems. At best, most screening procedures provide a preliminary indication that something may be significantly wrong and that the possibility of initiating a change in the status quo should be considered. When diagnostic classifications and specific

Bases for Decisions[d]

Several successive screening assessments may be used. Those individuals whose data are judged as poor (e.g., at the lower end of a distribution of scores) are likely to be identified as problems or predicted as potential problems. The specific criterion (e.g., cut-off score) may be based on findings from research studies or clinical judgment regarding what is a significant (severe and pervasive) problem.

a. While this presentation implies that decisions will be based on assessment findings, it should be reemphasized that selection decisions can and probably often are made without considering the broad range of available data and may not be consistent with the implications of such data.

b. This presentation assumes that adequate medical assessment of visual and auditory acuity has been accomplished and that any necessary corrective actions have been dealt with appropriately. To be representative, data might include samples of performance over time and over situations such as the home, neighborhood, school, test and therapy settings, and so forth.

c. If records and observations do not provide adequate data on severity of learning problems, achievement tests may be administered. Similarly, personality tests and projective techniques may be given in an effort to clarify the severity of emotional problems.

d. If there is disagreement among decision makers (e.g., professionals, clients) about findings, criteria, or courses of action to be pursued, the final decision will depend on who is able to control the situation or else no active decision will be made. Furthermore, decisions may be based primarily and appropriately on other than assessment considerations. For example, current knowledge does not provide the basis for choosing between many specific forms of instruction and treatment for learning, behavioral, and emotional problems. Therefore, decisions about the use of various instructional strategies and psychological and medically oriented treatments usually depend on one, or more than one professional's current beliefs, not specific assessment findings. Also, if a diagnostic label is needed in order to admit or qualify someone for an intervention, usually the needed label will be generated. Current evidence suggests the basis for such diagnostic classification among children often is more a matter of situational need and professional belief than the valid application of assessment procedures.

(*Note:* Each of the above points is also relevant to Tables 7–2 to 7–5.)

prescriptions are sought, assessment procedures with greater validity are required.

Adequacy of current intervention. Given a commitment to correction, once a problem is detected additional assessment is required to determine whether current interventions are satisfactory or should be altered (see Table 7-2). The bases for deciding that change is indicated are dissatisfaction with current intervention and agreement that change is desirable. If there is disagreement, data can

TABLE 7-2

Second Screening Consideration

Selection Decision:

Are current interventions adequate or should they be altered?

Assessment Focus

Primary Assessment Questions	Relevant Data	Type of Assessment Procedures	Source of Data
(A) Are current forms of intervention perceived as *satisfactorily* ameliorating the problem or is a change desired?	Indices of (a) dissatisfaction or concern over rate of progress, intervention objectives, or processes and (b) desire to change the intervention	Interviews and written personal reports	Consumers, providers of interventions, knowledgeable others
(B) When there are significant differences in perception as to whether the current intervention is satisfactory, the assessment concerns become:			
What have been the actual progress and processes?	Samples of processes and outcomes, in situ, at various times since intervention was initiated, (e.g., work samples)	Requests for available records	*As above*
	Data for comparison purposes regarding severity and pervasiveness of learning and behavior problems prior to and during same period	Requests for records prior to current intervention, including data on formal IQ and achievement tests	Providers of interventions and other professionals who have made relevant assessments

be gathered to clarify reasons for the lack of agreement as a possible step in resolving the conflict.

A case example may help clarify the complexity and concerns which may arise in screening.

A first-grader in a regular classroom program is identified at the beginning of the school year as a high risk for reading problems. Identification resulted from a two-step process. First, a gross, first-level screening was done using a reading readiness test administered to all first-graders. Second, all students scoring sig-

Primary Assessment Questions	Relevant Data	Type of Assessment Procedures	Source of Data
Why are there differences in perception?	Delineation of perceptions of current progress and of what was desired (e.g., expectations and standards for progress and processes)	Interviews and written personal reports	Consumers, providers of interventions, knowledgeable others

Bases for Decisions

(A) Perceptions of satisfaction
1. If all parties are satisfied, there is no need to decide on a change in the way the problem is dealt with.
2. If all parties are dissatisfied, there is an obvious need for change.
3. If there are significant differences in perception, there is need for additional assessment to facilitate decision making about whether there is a need for change.

(B) Differences in perception
1. Differences may be due to lack of information or to errors or to differences in expectations and standards. Additional assesssment data is intended to facilitate decision making by providing missing data, replacing misinformation with accurate data, or clarifying the range of perspectives and thereby helping bring about agreement as to satisfaction or dissatisfaction.
2. If disagreement continues among those involved in decision making (e.g., professionals, clients), the final decision will depend on who is able to control the situation or else no active decision will be made.

nificantly below norm were given a battery of tests. The findings are reported to the parents and student, and they are interviewed to assess their concern and desire to explore various courses of action. The parents indicate they are quite happy with the current program. Moreover, the parents are not at all convinced that the tests are valid based on their observations of the student's reading activity at home. The teacher is consulted and is uncertain as to whether the student's rate of progress is satisfactory since the student has only been in class a month. The school psychologist and the principal both state that the current classroom reading program will be inadequate for any student detected by the screening program. At a conference, each party is given the opportunity to clarify his or her position by detailing the beliefs, "theories," and data upon which it is based. At the end of the conference, the participants' views remain unchanged, and no decision is made. After the family leaves, the principal and school psychologist agree that, in a few weeks, the school will want to explore and recommend a change in placement. The parents are later informed that an additional first-grade classroom has been established, and their child, along with others, has been reassigned to the new room.

This case is typical in that the problem is localized in the student and the student ends up in a different program to remedy the problem. Given that screening errors are common and that some students' problems are more the fault of the program, major concerns include how to increase the validity of the assessment and how to effectively challenge wrong decisions.

Referral: The Hidden Screening Procedure

Prior to any formal assessment, there often is an informal screening procedure in opera-tion. That procedure is referral. There are, of course, self-referrals, but a great many problems are referred by school, medical, and psychological personnel, as well as by the courts. Since such referral sources are aware of many more problems than they refer, how they make referral decisions is a critical matter.

The current ethos in our culture stresses that a person manifesting a problem ought to seek professional help. If an individual does not do so, persons in responsible positions in society, such as parents, teachers, legislators, and judges, usually see it as their duty to refer the person to a professional helper.

Observers tend to see causes of problems in terms of stable dispositions of actors; referral processes may reflect their bias. That is, observers may tend to ignore external causal factors and therefore overidentify and overrefer persons for assessment (Algozzine & Ysseldyke, 1981).

Moreover, the literature that emphasizes the societal context of who is designated as exceptional and deviant suggests that selection for referral is shaped significantly by the status of both the referrer and the person who might be referred. Specifically, it is widely argued that socioeconomic status, race, education and training, age, and sex of both the referrer and those referred can be major biasing factors. In general, individuals from nondominant groups are more likely to be identified and referred than those from the dominant group for manifesting behavior incompatible with prevailing cultural values and norms.[3]

---

[3]The evidence for referral bias is drawn from findings related to differential placement decisions. For example, black and Mexican-American children, lower socioeconomic status groups, and boys have been greatly overrepresented in special education programs, for example, labeled and segregated as retarded, emotionally disturbed, hyperactive. Women are overrepresented as clients in psychotherapy. Minority members and the lower class have been more likely to be hospitalized for psychiatric treatment than to be accepted for outpatient interventions. (For more on this topic, see discussion and references in Chapter 6; also see Chesler, 1972; Dohrenwend & Dohrenwend, 1974; Hobbs, 1975a; Lee & Temerlin, 1970; Mercer, 1973; Mitchell & Namenek, 1970; Scheff, 1974.)

A Prominent Example of Screening Practices

Because so much present-day emphasis is on predictive and early-age screening, this area provides a logical example to illustrate the current state of screening in general. There has been considerable research directed toward screening psychoeducational problems in children. Literally hundreds of studies have been reported over the past decade (e.g., see references cited in Adelman & Feshbach, 1971; Badian, 1976; Bower, 1960; de Hirsch et al., 1966; Gallagher & Bradley, 1972; Hobbs, 1975a; Jansky & de Hirsch, 1973; Keogh & Becker, 1973; Meier, 1975; Mercer, 1979; Rogolsky, 1968–69; Schaer & Crump, 1976).

The widespread and pervasive view among the general public seems to be that it is already, or shortly will be, feasible to make highly accurate identifications through massive screening of preschoolers and kindergarteners. Unfortunately, the need, pressure, and enthusiasm for new procedures are leading to inappropriate extrapolations of research findings and premature application of procedures and techniques. As Gallagher and Bradley (1972) state, "it is important to note that the enthusiasm which generated these tests has not carried over to the technical development of the instruments" (p. 104). Few of the procedures meet even the minimal standards set forth by the American Psychological Association and the American Educational Research Association (see American Psychological Association, 1974). As Hobbs (1975a) states in the summary report of the project on classification of exceptional children:

Every professionally competent report we have on early screening ... strongly qualifies most assertions concerning the reliability, validity, or applicability of screening procedures ... , especially for use in the early years of childhood. There are frequent references to the high level of clinical skill required to administer or interpret a test and to the need for sophisticated procedures or instrumentation. ... Tests are often described as "promising". Perhaps the most frequent recommendation of responsible reviewers is that more research is needed. ... Screening tests of sensory function (hearing, vision) are adequate for older children but difficult to use with younger children. Screening for retarded intellectual development in middle and late childhood is possible with a fair measure of confidence, although cultural backgrounds may render results problematic. Assessment of intellectual competence during infancy is highly unreliable. Early screening for affective or emotional development is extraordinarily difficult and perhaps impossible (except for extreme cases) with current knowledge. (pp. 92–93).[4]

The major concern of most researchers has been to find procedures which correctly identify a high percentage of children while at the same time not falsely identifying too many. Unfortunately the best research to date has failed to produce a set of procedures that meet these criteria (de Hirsch et al., 1966; Feshbach et al., 1977; Satz et al., 1976). In general, no currently available procedures intended for large-scale use can claim to identify a large number of problems without making many false positive errors.[5] The only way such procedures can reduce the number of false positives is to alter the cut-off scores used in making identifica-

---

[4]Concern over child screening has been expressed by a number of other writers (Faust, 1970; Freund, Bradley, and Caldwell, 1979; Hersh and Rojcewicz, 1974; Keogh and Becker, 1973; Meier, 1975; Satz and Fletcher, 1979), but perhaps none with greater fervor than Schrag and Divoky (1975) who go so far as to claim that "the prime function of all screening devices is mystification, a ritual conferring legitimacy on institutional decisions" (p. 129). This is a view which has been raised regarding comparable professional activity by such other socio-political critics as Laing (1967), Szasz (1961, 1970), Goffman (1961), and Illich (1976).

[5]False positive errors refer to those identified as problems or potential problems, but are not; false negative errors are those which have not been identified, but should have been.

tions, but by doing this, the number of correct identifications also is reduced. Cut-off scores can be adjusted so that the best of the current procedures could avoid almost all false positive identifications, while correctly screening a significant proportion of the most severe problems (Feshbach et al., 1977).

There is no question that severe learning and behavior problems can be identified through use of screening devices. However, detection of *severe* psychoeducational problems is neither difficult nor the best indicator that a screening procedure is valid. Research findings and clinical observation both indicate that even at very young ages, children with severe problems usually have been identified by parents, general medical practitioners, and nursery and kindergarten teachers without the use of complex and costly screening devices. Hobbs (1975a) has made a similar point:

> Most serious developmental problems get picked up in routine clinical practice . . . or are identified by parents or other untrained observers; mild and moderate problems (by far the greatest number), however, are difficult to detect and assess even by well-trained professional people administering complete examinations with the best equipment. (p. 94)

If this is the case, it seems reasonable to suggest that the standard for judging the efficacy of any screening procedure should be its ability to identify a significant number of problems beyond those commonly recognized. Using this standard, prevailing procedures would be judged even less efficacious than they are.

Critiques of screening procedures should not be construed as arguments against the desirability of preventing and correcting problems, especially in early childhood. In general, prevention and intervention in the earliest stages of a problem have the potential to be more effective and economical than later remediation. For some types of problems, undue delay can compound problems and even result in irreversible developmental damage. Often raised are concerns about the potential dangers of available screens and, more generally, about the need for screening as a component in prevention strategies. Many critics of current trends in screening would agree with Hobbs (1975a) that "ideally, special screening programs to identify health problems and developmental difficulties of children should not be necessary. All children regardless of economic status should be able to participate in a comprehensive health-maintenance program" (pp. 90–91). Thus, if ongoing psychoeducational maintenance programs could be developed, many would see this as preferable to mass screening of learning and behavior problems.

Given the status of prevailing screening procedures, future research should go beyond efforts to validate current assessment instruments. Studies also are needed to clarify the nature and appropriateness of current policies and practices. Research can aid in developing appropriate policies and safeguards. Among the questions in need of investigation are: To what degree are guidelines and procedures inconsistent and biased? To what extent do they produce inequities and injustices? Is there a way to *assess* or determine empirically whether environments, interactions, or persons should be the initial focal point of screening or must the decision remain solely a matter of political policy and professional beliefs?

PLACEMENT

While screening precedes placement decisions, the major practical objective of screening is to identify problems so that they can be ameliorated. Thus, the ultimate value of screening depends on the nature of subsequent intervention decisions and placements.

In this section, we explore three sequential placement decisions. Before doing so, however, we will clarify the types of placement options that might be considered and the guiding placement principle of least intervention needed.

Placement Options and the Principle of Least Intervention Needed

Listings of specific interventions advocated for persons manifesting learning/behavior/emotional problems can fill pages. Treatments, therapies, methods, and techniques have been developed by physicians, psychologists, educators, kinesiologists, social workers, and almost anyone else predisposed to do so. The range of options can generally be considered in terms of the nature and form of the interventions (see Figure 7–1).

As illustrated in Figure 7–1, essentially there are two sets of options. These involve decisions about (1) the nature of the *setting* and *primary intervention activities* and (2) whether *adjunctive interventions* are needed and, if so, what their general nature should be. Figure 7–1 highlights that decisions about these options often are best made sequentially.

A key principle intended to guide decision making about placement options is the notion that the least intervention needed (i.e., least restrictive, least disruptive) to do the job should be chosen (e.g., Kanfer & Goldstein, 1980). Special educators and clinical psychologists are particularly concerned with this principle but too often it is discussed narrowly in terms of "least *restrictive environment*" (e.g., Kaufman & Mona,

1978).[6] Whatever the context and breadth of its presentation, this principle is more complex than it may at first appear.

Most professionals would agree that placement decisions should be guided by a principle of least intervention needed. For example, a person who can receive equivalent help at a community clinic should not be in a psychiatric hospital. Similarly a child whose reading problem can be corrected by a regular classroom teacher should not be placed in a remedial class. Someone whose decision-making needs can be met by a short interview and consultation should not undergo extensive assessment. Recent trends in both mental health and education reflect a desire to adhere to this principle, for example, by establishing community mental health centers and "mainstreaming" exceptional children.

Unfortunately, however, interventions—by definition—disrupt the "natural" course of events. By implication, disruptions may be restrictive of other choices and options. Placements in special remedial classes or special schools clearly are disruptive and usually restrictive. While not generally mentioned in this context, many teaching activities—special remedial techniques, sex education, human relations training, assertion and effectiveness training, and so forth—also are potentially disruptive.

Since all interventions can be an appropriate avenue for change and, to this end, are intended to be disruptive, it is clear that disruption per se is not the issue. What is

[6]In the United States, current legislation mandates placement of handicapped children in the least restrictive environment in order to prevent them from being denied access to education in the regular environment unless there is a compelling educational justification for doing so. Thus, by law and federal regulations, handicapped children (including children in public and private institutions) must be educated with children who are not handicapped to the maximum extent appropriate. Special class and separate school placements or other removal of handicapped children from the regular educational environment is to occur only when the educational needs of the child, as determined by special processes established to identify such needs, cannot be met within the regular educational environment. Public agencies also must ensure that a continuum of alternative placements is available to meet such needs and that, unless a child's educational needs require some other arrangement, handicapped children will be educated in the school which they would attend if not handicapped. The assumption is that placement in regular public school classes and campuses, with necessary auxilliary services, is preferable to placement in any other setting. Justification for placement in a more restrictive setting must include demonstration that education cannot be achieved satisfactorily in the regular educational environment *and* can and will be achieved in the special setting.

Figure 7-1

Usual range of options related to general nature and form of interventions involving individuals.

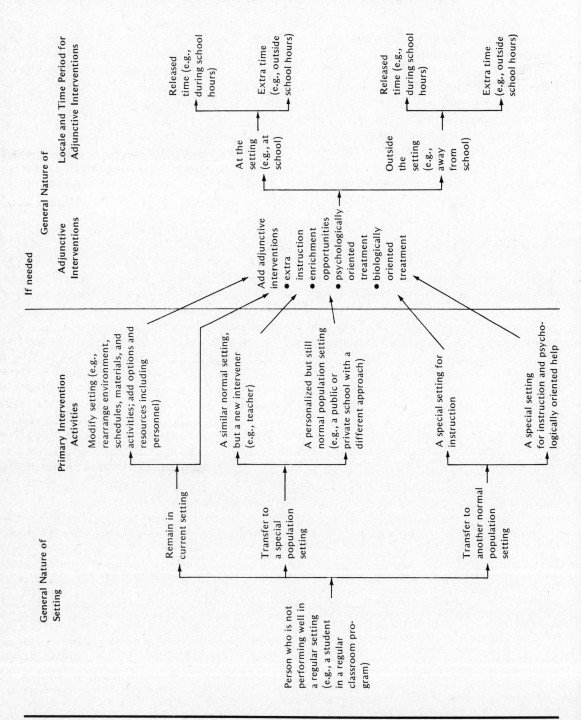

of concern is how to accomplish desired changes with no more disruption and restriction of options than is necessary.

Various writers have attempted to conceptualize a continuum of placements from most to least restrictive (e.g., Chaffin, 1975; Deno, 1970; Reynolds, 1962). Cruickshank (1977) cites one school system's efforts at such a ranking: (1) residential or institutional programs, (2) special schools in public systems, (3) special classes in public schools, (4) resource rooms, (5) tutorial programs, (6) itinerant teaching programs and (7) regular class placement. He then raises the issue that the least restrictive setting may prove to be the most restrictive in the long run if it can-

not meet the needs of the individual placed there. For one student with learning or emotional problems, the most efficacious program might be one designated above as least restrictive, such as a tutorial program. For another, however, such a minimal program might never ameliorate, and indeed might compound, the student's problems.

At its foundation, the dilemma remains that of how to match the person to the correct type and degree of intervention, while at the same time balancing the rights of the individual and the needs of society (Kittrie, 1971). Strongly associated with this dilemma is the confusion over what problems and tasks require what kinds of approaches and

FOR EXAMPLE

PLACEMENT PRACTICES

The way we professionalize any educational task is to administer these scientific instruments, called occupational interest inventories, to make scientific predictions about what we would really be happy doing. So [George] walks into the counselor's office, and he comes out with a score on a test. This is supposed to tell him how he should spend the rest of his life. He then gets placed in school programs according to this score and other scores like IQ and grade averages, and he is already programmed to go in a certain direction at 12 or 15 years of age.

Unfortunately, we also have scientific information telling us that about 80 percent of our population is unhappy in their work. It seems to me we either need a better interest test or a way of finding out who a person is that uses less science and a little more humanity.

Talking about tests reminds me of a conversation with George right after he had been professionally sorted out into the vocational curriculum. He came into my office feeling very low and had some trouble raising his eyes or his head. I asked him what had happened, and he told me. He said that he had taken all

these tests and the counselor was sending him to industrial arts.

"What do you mean?" I asked him. "That's not for you."

"Well, I don't know," he said. "I saw the scores."

"Do you believe them?" I asked.

"Well," he said, after a thoughtful moment, "I don't see why tests would lie."

I felt as if I just had eaten about a dozen rotten eggs: I knew George was feeling bad because he believed he had just learned something very disappointing about himself, not just because he was being sent into the shops where he didn't want to be.

"George," I said, "tests aren't mind readers. There can be mistakes."

"That's what I thought, and I told the counselor, but she told me she was getting her license as a school psychologist so she knew about things like that and I didn't."

I nodded my head. That's a tough combination to beat: a test and a psychologist. It took us a year to straighten out this particular problem for George.

Weinberg (1974, pp. 81–82)

the lack of demonstrated effectiveness of many psychoeducational interventions.

Efforts to implement the principle of least intervention needed already appear to have outstripped the ability of professionals to develop innovations in keeping with this potentially valuable guideline. As research and related activity are pursued, the principle should become more useful (e.g., Heron & Skinner, 1981). In this connection, an important question for study is whether presumptive decisions to focus interventions on individuals are inherently in conflict with this concept.

Three Sequential Decisions

Understanding options and sequences of interventions and the principle of least intervention needed are important bases for placement decisions. Placement considerations related to individuals with learning problems can be explored with reference to three sequential decisions:

1. What is the general nature and form of the intervention needed?
2. Given there is a range of specific persons, places, and times available with regard to providing needed interventions, which should be pursued, for example, where and how to apply for the needed intervention.
3. If all preferences or applications cannot be fulfilled, which should be selected?

Key concepts and concerns related to these considerations and the current status of assessment procedures used for making placement decisions are discussed below.

Nature and form of intervention needed.

As can be seen from Figure 7–1 and Table 7–3, the first placement decision encompasses decisions about (1) whether an individual should transfer from the current setting to another and what general in-

tervention activity should be pursued and (2) whether adjunctive interventions are needed and which should be pursued.

Decisions to remain in a setting or transfer to another are based on whether the problem is viewed as mild to moderate or severe and pervasive, and whether it is related to learning, behavior, or "emotional" functioning (see Table 7–3). Determining severity and pervasiveness may be based on recent samples of performance/learning/behavior in various settings (e.g., classroom, home, recreation centers) and on indices of intellectual capabilities. Such data may have been gathered as part of the screening process. Contrary to the approach reflected in the fairly standard use of test batteries, additional data should be gathered when available data are insufficient for judging problem severity and pervasiveness and when an assessment procedure that can provide the needed data is available.

When data indicate a person is not making appropriate progress, whatever the cause, the tendency is to consider use of special services and placements. Persons with severe and pervasive problems often are placed in special population settings such as special classrooms and institutions; mild to moderate problems are supposed to be dealt with in normal population settings. Individuals with mild to moderate problems may be transferred from one normal population setting to another if they cannot be maintained in the current setting by either appropriately modifying the setting or adding adjunctive services or both.

After major interventions are chosen, decisions are made about which, if any, adjunctive interventions are needed. In many cases, such decisions are best made after major interventions have a sufficient trial period and are evaluated as appropriate but insufficient.

As indicated in Figure 7–1, adjunctive interventions can involve (1) extra instruction such as tutoring, (2) enrichment opportunities including an expanded range of choices with regard to nonproblem-oriented activities such as projects, learning by discovery, arts and crafts, and recreation, (3) psychologically oriented treatments such as individual and family therapy, and (4) biologically oriented treatments such as medication, diet, and megavitamins.

Assessment data for making each of these general decisions are not complex. Extra instruction clearly is indicated whenever participants (e.g., teacher or student) in the primary setting state that not enough time and resources are available for instruction. Specific prescriptions (e.g., a specific skill focus or technical approach) are likely to be determined by the professionals and clients involved in the decision-making process and generally reflect their beliefs. Specific tests and data may be a featured aspect of the decision-making process.

Decisions to offer enrichment opportunities may be the result of regular programming in a setting or may be a prescribed adjunct. In either case, the major reason for offering them is theory or belief about the value of expanding options and choices beyond problem-oriented interventions.

Decisions about psychologically and biologically oriented adjunctive activities reflect the judgment that the problems are due to factors that "block" learning and performance or represent behaviors that should not be accommodated. Here, too, the need for, and the specific nature of, such specialized treatment more likely will reflect professional decision maker's and/or client's beliefs than valid assessment data.

Decisions as to the locale and time for adjunctive services usually are based on feasibility factors rather than evaluation of the pros and cons of each option. Relevant data and criteria for such decisions are the client's preferences and information about cost and benefits.

Client decision making.   Given the range of persons, places, and times available with regard to providing needed interventions the second placement decision which should be pursued is, for example, where and how to apply (see Table 7-4). Historically, consumer concerns with regard to psychoeducational interventions have been de-emphasized. Increasingly, however, ethical and legal issues have been raised about the role of clients in decision making.

As with other consumer concerns, assessment can provide basic information, that is, assessment procedures can be used systematically to gather information for consumer education on such matters as: What is available? What best meets the consumer's needs in terms of location, cost, and appropriateness of intervention approach? and How should the consumer successfully proceed to get what the consumer wants (e.g., get accepted by a desired program)?

Unfortunately, even where a broad range of resources is available, as in large urban centers, systematic information rarely is presented to aid consumers in selecting services. Most often professionals refer to those few professionals or agencies with whom they have become acquainted through someone else's "endorsement," by their own impressions based on brief personal encounters, or because of friendships ("old boy" networks).

Professional and agency decisions. The third placement decision shifts attention from the consumer to the service providers (see Table 7-5). From this perspective, assessment data are needed for selecting among applicants. Obviously, professionals and programs are not usually willing or able to accept everyone. Sometimes applicants are rejected because they do not fit established eligibility criteria. At other times, acceptable applicants must be rejected be-

TABLE 7-3

First Consideration in Placement Decision Making

Selection Decision

What is the general nature and form of the interventions needed? (See Figure 7–1)

Assessment Focus

Primary Assessment Questions	Relevant Data	Type of Assessment Procedures	Source of Data
How severe and pervasive is the problem with regard to • learning? • behavior? • "emotional" functioning?	Recent samples of task performance and/or learning and of behavior in various settings	Requests for available records	Persons maintaining files
		Observation ratings	Consumers, providers of interventions, knowledgeable others
		If needed: Standardized achievement tests	Tests and assessors
		Personality tests and projective techniques	Tests and assessors
	Current intellectual functioning[a]	Requests for available records on previous IQ testing and/or, *if needed*, an individual IQ test[a]	Persons maintaining files
			Tests and assessors
		Interview and personal reports	Consumers, providers of interventions, knowledgeable others
	Data for comparison purposes regarding performance, learning, and behavior of an appropriate normative, referent group	Location of and requests for summary reports and available records on an appropriate referent group (including test norms)	Providers of interventions
			Published norms (e.g., in test manuals and other published sources)

Bases for Decisions

1. Mild-moderate learning problem—Intellectual functioning and academic performance are not judged to be significantly below average, but academic performance is still viewed as mild-moderately below norm (e.g., up to a year below the norm in reading for the referent group used). In such cases, regular programs usually are seen as appropriate but setting modifications or transfers (e.g., a new teacher, new materials and activities, transfer to a more personalized regular school program) and/or the addition of adjunctive services may be recommended (e.g., resource help for the teacher, tutoring for the student).

2. Mild-moderate behavior problem—Behavior is judged as not being extreme (e.g., not uncontrollably disruptive, dangerously aggressive, or pathologically withdrawn) but still is seen as significantly different from the norm for the referent group used. In such cases, regular programs are seen as appropriate but a change in setting and/or the addition of adjunctive services may be recommended, such as a more personalized regular program, resource help for the teacher, counseling for the student and/or parents, medication, diet.

3. Mild-moderate "emotional" problems—Emotional states (e.g., anxiety, fear, unhappiness) are judged as being a minor side effect and secondary factor (overlay) to learning and/or behavior problems. In such cases, often no additional adjunctive service may be recommended or else the recommendation may be for counseling or psychotherapy for the student and/or the family.

4. Severe and pervasive problems—A problem will be judged severe and pervasive when inadequate performance at school and/or in other major activities is associated with one or more of the following:
   • intellectual functioning judged to be significantly below average (e.g., below IQ 80)
   • academic skills judged to be significantly below norm for the referent group being used (e.g., 1–1½ years below the norm in reading, math, and language skills) although intellectual functioning is at or above average
   • behavior is judged to be extreme (e.g., uncontrollable, dangerously aggressive, severely withdrawn, phobic)
   • extreme fear, anxiety, depression, bizarre actions, and/or loss of contact with reality
   In such cases, a special class/school/institutional placement is likely to be recommended. If the special setting does not treat behavior and "emotional" problems as part of its program, adjunctive services will likely be recommended as well.

a. Gathering data on intellectual functioning of problem populations is difficult, controversial, and critical. In general, the lower the intellectual functioning is judged to be, the more the problems are likely to be judged severe. However, since problem populations often perform poorly on formal IQ tests, there usually is a need to seek any evidence that suggests intellectual functioning may be higher than test performance. Thus, when available test scores indicate below-average IQ, supplemental procedures should be initiated in an attempt to see if there is disconfirming evidence. In particular, an individual IQ test may help to disconfirm implications of previous low scores (but often is equally suspect when clients perform poorly). Interviews and personal reports from professionals who have had close contact with an individual also may provide useful data suggesting a higher level of intellectual functioning.

cause too many have applied. Essentially, discussion of whom to select usually stresses data on type, severity and pervasiveness of a problem, and, where relevant, demographic factors.

As Cronbach and Gleser (1965) suggest, selection decisions in general and placement decisions in particular involve institutional or individual values or both. Data and criteria used in accepting and rejecting applicants usually reflect institutional values. For example, a professional or an agency

TABLE 7-4

Second Consideration in Placement Decision Making

Selection Decision

Given there is a range of specific persons, places, and times available with regard to providing needed interventions, which should be pursued, e.g., where and how to apply?

Assessment Focus

Primary Assessment Questions	Relevant Data	Type of Assessment Procedures	Source of Data
(A) What is desired?	Information on individual needs and wants	Interviews and personal reports	Prospective consumers
		Requests for available records	Professionals, agencies
(B) What is available?	Information on what resources exist (e.g., persons, agencies) for a specific type of problem (including sex, age, and ethnic considerations)	Requests for available records	Professionals, agencies
		Interviews and personal reports	Consumers
			Published directories and directory services
(C) What is accessible to a particular prospective consumer?	Information on financial, geographical, and demographic considerations	As above	As above

may want only persons with characteristics which are viewed as maximizing the service's efficacy, efficiency, or reputation. These factors, as well as locale and costs, may result in socioeconomic or racial imbalances.

Placement Practices
The literature on actual placement practices is sparse. Validation studies are confounded by the present state of corrective efforts. If a person placed in a service does not improve, usually it is unclear whether this results be-

Primary Assessment Questions	Relevant Data	Type of Assessment Procedures	Source of Data
(D) What is the nature of the intervention offered?	Information on the underyling rationale, objectives, and procedures related to the intervention and data on its efficacy	Location of and requests for summary reports and available records	Professionals, agencies
		Interviews and personal reports	Professionals, consumers
		Observation ratings	Professionals, consumers
		Tests (used for evaluation)	Evaluation personnel
(E) How to apply	Information on specific application steps	Requests for information	Professionals, agencies

Bases for Decisions

(A) What is desired? Key criteria are that the prospective consumer actually wants help or is under external compulsion to proceed and has specified the nature of the intervention desired or has indicated willingness to take whatever is available and accessible.

(B) What is available? Key criteria are that space and/or resources exist for the type of problem identified.

(C) What is accessible? Key criteria are that interventions are available without fees or that private and public resources are available to pay fees and that the intervention is geographically and demographically accessible.

(D) What is the nature of the intervention? Key criteria are that, in the decision makers' view, the intervention has a satisfactory rationale, objectives, and procedures and is sufficiently effective.

(E) How to apply? Key criteria are that application steps are specified and in the decision makers' view can be pursued effectively.

TABLE 7-5

Third Consideration in Placement Decision Making

Selection Decision

   When all preferences or applications cannot be fulfilled, which should be selected?

Assessment Focus

Primary Assessment Questions	Relevant Data	Types of Assessment Procedures	Source of Data
What type of problem is it and how severe and pervasive is it with regard to • learning • behavior • "emotional" functioning?	As described in Tables 7-1 to 7-3	As described in Tables 7-1 to 7-3	As described in Tables 7-1 to 7-3
When there are demographic considerations, questions will be asked about such matters.	Information as to age, sex, ethnicity, etc., as specified by the particular professional or agency	Interviews and personal reports	Applicants

Bases for Decisions

   Each professional and agency (intervener) specifies criteria as to which applicants are eligible. Such criteria are generated from the underlying rationale, objectives, and procedures of the intervention, data on current case load, resource availability, and so forth. Variables often considered are type, severity, and pervasiveness of a problem and, where relevant, demographic factors.

cause (1) the wrong type of placement was selected, (2) the type of placement is the best choice, but the problem is one for which current knowledge is inadequate, or (3) the particular professional or agency chosen was not prepared to provide the best available corrective services.

   Comprehensive research studies directly dealing with placements related to learning disabilities are yet to be initiated. Perhaps the most extensive bodies of literature of relevance are those focused on statistical versus clinical prediction, personnel selection, and treatment efficacy studies. Conclusions based on the literature in these areas suggest that assessment data can help improve placement accuracy. However, there continues to be raging arguments over what data are most helpful—that is, valid— given a specific decision. For example, Cronbach (1970) emphasizes that experts agree that procedures with predictive validity coefficients as low as .30 can be of definite practical value in any selection decision. In other words, where selection is necessary and procedures in current use have very low predictive validity, a procedure that contributes even a little incremental validity may be worth adding. Of course, a small increase in validity may not be judged as worth the additional costs, either financially or in terms of side effects.

FOR EXAMPLE

PARENTAL CONSENT AND DUE PROCESS IN PLACEMENT DECISIONS

Due process is a safeguard provided by the 14th Amendment and stressed in Public Law 94–142. It refers to the procedures which protect the rights of every person, and insure that every person is treated fairly. In education, due process is necessary when and if significant changes are made, or even proposed in a student's educational placement. Listed below are some of the important things you should know about due process and procedural safeguards.

1. Parents must be notified whenever the school
   • Plans to conduct a special evaluation of their child
   • Wants to change their child's educational placement
   • Refuses to conduct an evaluation or make a change in placement.
2. Parent consent must be obtained before the school conducts the evaluation.

3. Parents have the right to obtain an independent educational evaluation of their child.
4. Parents must be informed by the school of their right to examine school records which relate to their child's identification, evaluation, and educational placement.
5. Parents must receive a full explanation from the school of all of the procedural safeguards provided by the law.
6. Parents have the right to participate in the meeting when their child's educational program is designed.
7. Parents have the right to an impartial hearing if they disagree with the decision of the school. The schools also have the right to request a hearing.
8. Parents and the schools have certain rights in hearing procedures.

A Law Concerning You and Your Child, *Directions* (1978, p. 2)

Moreover, while procedures with low predictive validity coefficients may be useful, the fact remains that the lower the predictive validity of the total set of procedures, the more false positives and/or negatives there will be. In this connection, it is important to realize that assessment procedures currently used for placement decisions are essentially those used for screening (see Table 6–1). Based on our earlier discussion, it should be evident, therefore, that procedures currently in use do not have high predictive validity.

Even if the validity of selection procedures were higher, errors would be inevitable and any particular option might prove to be unsatisfactory for a variety of reasons. As a result, decisions must be reassessed after implementation so that adjustments can be made. That is, satisfaction should be assessed employing the type of data outlined with regard to the first screening consideration (see Table 5–1). In effect, this approach to assessment used for placement purposes constitutes a sequential selection strategy. Use of such a strategy can correct errors stemming from earlier procedures and, in general, can help to insure that inappropriate decisions are reconsidered. Again, it is important to emphasize that data cannot clearly indicate why the decisions turned out to be unsatisfactory. The general type of intervention chosen might be the right decision, but the problem may be intractable given current knowledge. Regardless of why the decision was unsuitable, sequential selection strategies have the potential to increase significantly the predictive validity of intervention decisions.

CONCLUDING COMMENTS

Diagnosis, screening, and placement practices are the foundation of current efforts to answer the questions Who is learning disabled? and What should be done to help such persons? As there are no widely agreed upon answers to these questions, there are no widely agreed upon diagnostic, screening, and placement practices. In this and the preceding chapter, we have highlighted basic features and concerns associated with such practices.

What should now be clear is that diagnosis, screening, and placement are complex topics. Moreover, the absence of agreed upon practices ensures continuing controversy. Yet, despite the complexities and controversies, each day professionals are called upon to diagnose, screen, and place learning disabled individuals. It is one of the ironies of the field that in such instances those of us in practitioner roles often are called upon to do more than we can know, and at other times we know more than we can do. Yet, do we must. Decisions must be made. While there may be major concern about specific practices, there can be no doubt that persons with problems can and must be helped.

In current daily practice, psychoeducational assessors generally must operate on a knowledge base that is so weak that it often constitutes little more than clinical lore. Inadequate knowledge does not, however, alter the pressure on professionals to act. Assessors are expected to diagnose, screen, and refer. In doing so, the assessment practices prevalently used focus on the person and on pathology. As a result, the bias from the onset is toward localizing the source of the problems within the person and focusing intervention almost exclusively on remediation, treatment, and rehabilitation of the person. Almost by presumption, environmental variables are exonerated as causal factors and as the focal point of interven-

FOR EXAMPLE

SCREENING

In the early 1970s, we embarked on a five-year federally funded project designed to study the prediction and prevention of learning problems (Adelman & Feshbach, 1971; Feshbach, Adelman, & Fuller, 1977). While we set out to explore an interactional model of screening, our efforts were frustrated by measurement problems related to assessing instructional effects. Thus, the relevance of our findings is limited to screening based on person variables.

In essence, we cross-validated the psychometric predictive index developed by de Hirsch and her colleagues (de Hirsch et al., 1966; Jansky & de Hirsch, 1973) and compared that procedure with an alternative strategy that we developed and cross-validated. The first kindergarten sample consisted of 888 children and the cross-validation sample consisted of 844 children. (Of course, there was some attrition over the years.) The procedure we developed was based on a behavioral analysis and ratings made by the kindergarten teacher of relevant behaviors and skills manifested by the child in the classroom situation over several months. The Student Rating Scale (SRS) that we developed for the teachers to use consisted of 41 items in its final versions. The

tion. Also ignored is the potential importance of a person's strengths and interests with regard to formulation of differential diagnoses and intervention plans.

Ultimately, the predictive validity of assessment for any classification and selection decision is limited by the inability of practitioners and researchers to assess validly causality, current capabilities, and motivation, and to determine the efficacy of many instructional and treatment interventions. Without valid information about the cause and status of a problem or about an intervention's ability to deal with a problem successfully, decisions can be expected to scale was factor-analyzed and yielded five factors: attention and behavior control, language skill, visual-auditory perceptual discrimination, perceptual-motor coordination, and memory (only the first three were replicated in the cross-validation sample). Moreover, the teachers rated each child using the Kohn Social Competence Scale (Kohn & Silverman, 1966; Kohn, 1968). This scale, factor-analyzed by Kohn, yielded two factors: interest-participation versus apathy-withdrawal and cooperation-compliance versus anger-defiance. Also, demographic and medical history data were obtained from school records and, for a subsample of children, from questionnaires completed by the parents.

Criterion variables included a self-concept measure, appropriately grade-modified versions of the Student Rating Scale (SRS) for teachers to fill out, and the Cooperative Primary Reading Tests—all administered in the first through the third grade. (An individualized reading inventory was also developed in an effort to provide a criterion- rather than norm-referenced index of reading competence. Periodic writing samples were also obtained.) Findings were analyzed by employing stepwise multiple regression procedures.

The central technical question, of course, is, How good were the predictions and identifications? The answer is that there was a moderate percentage of accurate identifications, but there were still too many false positive and negative errors. From 46 to 66 percent of the students who were predicted to have problems actually were having problems at the end of grade two, depending on the criterion variable and standard used. Both the psychometric procedures and the teacher ratings showed about the same results, but the teacher's ratings produced slightly fewer false positives. We found that the small number of youngsters who were predicted as "future" problems by both the psychometric tests and the teachers' ratings were already manifesting problems at home and at school to such a significant degree that it was clear the procedures were not so much predicting problems as simply identifying or validating currently acknowledged severe problems.

Other studies report comparably disquieting results. Obviously, we all have a long way to go before satisfactory screening can be done on a large scale.

produce a significant number of errors. Obviously, research on diagnostic, screening, and placement decisions is closely tied to research on these other matters.

Given the complex intertwining of research problems, it is likely that progress in eliminating classification and selection errors will be slow. There are, however, a number of conceptual and technical mistakes that might be reduced rapidly if research data were generated and used to publicize their prevalence and impact. Examples of such fundamental process mistakes include failure to consider a broad range of relevant variables (e.g., environ-

mental and interactional factors, strengths and interests, etc.), use of invalid procedures, basic errors in scoring and interpretation of tests, and so forth. Furthermore, since decision makers appear to weight certain factors differentially, research is needed to clarify what factors are weighted most heavily and why, and what the impact is on screening and general intervention decisions.

Even if current approaches did have proven validity, from a practical perspective it is clear that new approaches must be developed. Commitment to providing appropriate educational opportunities for all persons makes it unfeasible to administer

VIEWPOINT

ASSESSMENT FOR CLASSIFICATION AND SELECTION

Based on analysis of the state of the art, it seems reasonable to conclude at this time that:

Despite the importance of valid diagnostic classification, current assessment procedures are not capable of producing appropriate differential diagnoses among persons with learning problems nor do they lead to valid corrective prescriptions.

Overemphasis on assessment practices which focus only on person-assessment and test procedures hinders development of procedures for assessing the environment or complex interactions. A broader base of assessment data might lead to valid diagnoses and to an expanded range of appropriate interventions.

These concerns also apply to assessment strategies aimed at "early identification" or prediction of learning problems, i.e., such procedures are not seen as having sufficient validity to warrant large-scale implementation as is widely advocated and legislated.

Alternative assessment procedures are needed, are being developed, and deserve serious consideration.

comprehensive individual test batteries to all who are referred as problems. Ysseldyke and Algozzine (1979) report on one large, urban school system where there is a backlog of sixteen thousand students awaiting evaluation to determine eligibility for special services. More testing hardly seems to be the answer to problems of this magnitude. Alternatives have been proposed and a few are discussed in Chapter 8 and in Parts 3 and 4.

Chapter 8
Toward Improving Classification and Selection

I have known a number of learning-disabilities specialists and clinical staff who give little credence to neurological interpretations of academic underachievement, but who continue to diagnose children in those terms because they believe that their superiors expect this kind of diagnosis. To do otherwise would place the diagnostician's professional competence and standing in jeopardy. Others have reluctantly diagnosed children as neurologically impaired primarily because only with this diagnosis could children be placed in a Neurologically Impaired (NI) class that had a better curriculum than they could obtain in a regular classroom. Their view of the NI classroom was not that it was particularly good at remedying problems of neurological impairment, but that it used a method of instruction beneficial to all kinds of underachievers.
Coles (1978, p. 335)

It is easy to be critical of prevailing assessment practices. Suggestions about how to improve current procedures and develop promising alternatives are considerably harder to formulate. One key to stimulating such suggestions is to take a broader perspective about the focus of intervention and the concepts of screening and placement.

ADOPTING A BROAD PERSPECTIVE

The manner in which most assessment presently is done reflects the prevailing causal model, which locates learning and behavior problems within the person. Thus, decisions as to the focus of intervention tend to be predetermined. Assessment processes are directed at the person. Decisions to be made about future courses of action are guided by intent to change the person. The terms screening and placement generally refer to decisions made about persons. The types of questions asked are: Should an individual be placed in a special setting? Is resource help needed to maximize the likelihood that appropriate interventions will be provided for the individual? Are tutoring, medication, a special diet, or counseling indicated?

Expanding the Focal Point of Intervention

Because of the person-focused bias, the possibility that environmental or person-environment interactions are the problem and should be the focal point of intervention generally is ignored. When the environment is altered it usually is done as a means of shaping individual behavior in ways desired by teachers, parents, and others in authority. As Rhodes (1970) states:

> In our present practices of providing for . . . children, we might be accused of displacing the problem upon the least protected part of the microcommunity in which the problem is manifested. We might also be accused of working with that sector of the problem which can least resist our intervention attempts, and which has the least capacity to defend its right against intrusion. We are tackling that part of the community which is least able to point out the complicity of the rest of the community in the problem. It is much easier to practice our intervention upon the child alone because [the child] is helpless to resist our intrusion. The rest of the community resists reciprocal change. . . . From both an ethical and a practical point of view, this is a very limited solution to the total problem (p. 313)

The underlying bias is not surprising. Psychologically, there is the tendency of observers to attribute causes to stable dispositions within the actor. The fact that those experiencing a particular psychoeducational problem are in a minority (i.e., most other people do not have the problem) becomes supporting evidence for observers' beliefs that the cause must be within the actor. Social and political forces further this bias. The almost inevitable result has been that the greatest portion of the problem-oriented literature on psychoeducational intervention theory and methods assumes a person is behaving inappropriately or inadequately. From this perspective, the object of change is the person.

A smaller portion of the problem-oriented literature emphasizes that in many cases the person should not be viewed as behaving inappropriately (e.g., Goodwin, 1973; Hobbs, 1975a; Kelley, Snowden, & Muñoz, 1977; Kessler & Albee, 1975; Laing & Esterson, 1970; Rhodes & Tracy, 1972). Rather, "environments" such as home, school, and society are seen as establishing standards and limiting choices in ways that result in the person's behavior being labeled as inappropriate. From this perspective, the proper intervention is one that changes the environment in appropriate ways to accommodate either a specific person or a wider range of individual differences—as contrasted with changing the person (see Figure 8–1).

Given the range of ways interveners discuss "changing the environment," it is important to clarify the differences between environmental changes designed to accommodate rather than change individuals. Instructing parents and teacher to be more discriminating in their use of reinforcement contingencies is not the same as helping them see implications of offering additional options whenever appropriate and feasible, such as greater choice in what a child can do and how the child can do it. It also is not the same as helping them understand the impact of appropriately changing their expectations regarding acceptable behavior, performance, and rate of progress (Nicholls, 1979). While this example involves what we have designated as the primary or immediate environment (e.g., home, classroom), often

Figure 8-1

Options related to focal point of intervention.

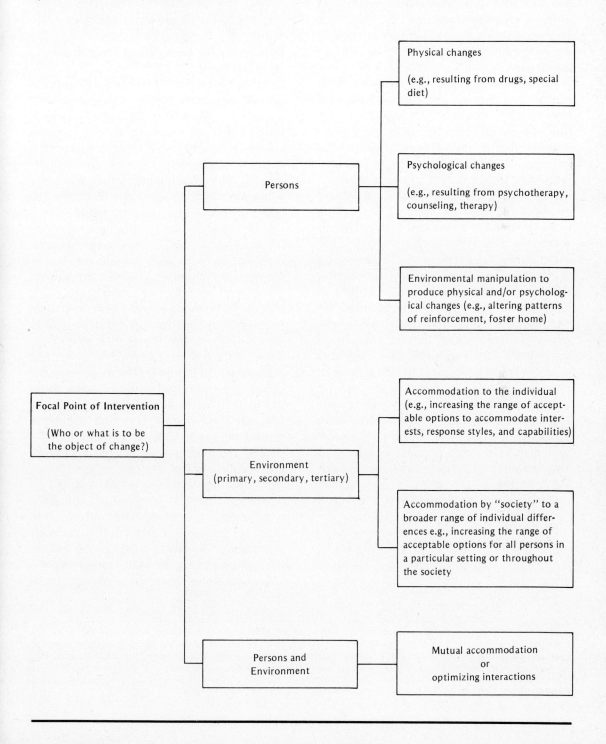

what appears to be a unique problem may be an indication of a more widespread malaise. An unhealthy milieu affecting more than a few individuals suggests the need for changes in the larger environment such as the neighborhood, school, and even the total society.

Rather than emphasizing person or environment, change on the part of both may represent an appropriate or necessary solution. It certainly is a more satisfactory compromise than an intervention that forces the individual to accommodate to an inappropriate or "pathological" situation. Furthermore, even if it is a person who is the primary object of change, concomitant changes that make the environment more supportive and accommodating often are warranted.

Expanding the focal point of intervention clarifies that there are actually three rather than two major screening considerations as discussed in Chapter 7. That is, before other decisions are considered, a preliminary decision is made about the focal point of screening activity (see Table 8-1). Decisions resulting in the selection of the focal point of intervention are shaped profoundly by who the decision makers are and by the criteria and rationale they use. The critical question in this context is, Who should determine such matters and on what basis or rationale? This question once again highlights the political nature of the decision making and underscores the concerns over the "political power balance" among involved parties.[1]

In general, contemporary selection activity surrounding learning and behavior problems often is extremely limited in its focus because of the nature of prevailing models, political power imbalances, and related factors. As a step toward altering this state of affairs, it is important to broaden understanding of the nature of selection activity.

Broadening the Concepts of Screening and Placement

Once the focal point for intervention is expanded, selection activity also must be expanded to encompass the environment. With regard to screening, this is a simple matter conceptually. Rather than understanding screening as a process for identifying persons with problems, screening can be viewed as a process appropriately applied to detecting problems in environments.

With regard to placement, the term makes no sense as applied to environments; one does not place an environment into an intervention program. In a broadened context, placements are only one group of decisions that might be made about a general change in intervention status. The term we use to designate the entire gamut of selection options portrayed in Figure 8-1 is *general intervention decisions*. (These general decisions are contrasted with decisions about the *specific* nature and form of an intervention, such as which theory and technique should be used. Specific intervention decisions and related assessment procedures are discussed in Part 3.

All other things being equal, it would be desirable if general intervention decisions were delayed until specific intervention plans are formulated. Indeed, this currently is advocated by law (Public Law 94-142) in the United States. The logic underlying this sequence stems from instructional, treat-

[1]For instance, in attempting to solve a problem when a person's behavior or performance is identified as deviant, it is likely that those representing normative behavior have the greatest power and make the decisions. This may lead to good and just actions. However, power is not necessarily to be equated with objectivity and competence in making decisions. Power imbalances are typical between teachers and students, parents and their children, psychologists employed by schools or parents to intervene with children, and so forth. (These concerns are discussed further in Parts 3 and 5.)

TABLE 8-1

A Preliminary Screening Consideration

Selection Decision
What should be the focal point of screening activity?

Assessment Focus

Primary Assessment Questions	Relevant Data	Type of Assessment Procedures	Source of Data
Should screening focus on the •environment •interaction of environment and person •person and which specific variables should be assessed?	Not an assessable question using current practices		
	Information to clarify whether prevalent, current practices are inappropriately focused (e.g., only on persons)	Validity research studies using multi-method, multivariate approaches (investigating current assessment practices, policy commitments and priorities, and negative conse-sequences)	Applied and basic theorists and researchers who, in turn, draw from consumers, providers of interventions, published records, and so forth
	If current practices are inappropriate, data are needed to develop effective procedures and strategies for answering the primary assessment question	Validity research studies	Applied and basic theorists and researchers

Bases for Decisions
Focus of screening currently appears to be decided on the basis of society's political policies and referrer and assessor "model" biases. That is, assessment data usually are not considered because prevailing policies, biases, and economic considerations generally preclude alternatives being evaluated in specific cases. In most cases, the focus is on the individual. While assessment does not currently play a role in this decision making, theoretically it could. Research is needed both to clarify the inappropriateness of current decision-making practices and to help develop new procedures and strategies.

ment, and administrative perspectives. The desire to clarify specific plans prior to general intervention decisions, especially placement decisions, also reflects an attempt to avoid past abuses, such as instances where poor instruction and treatment followed special classroom or institutional placement.

Unfortunately, the logic and good intentions ignore assessment considerations that have a powerful logic of their own, as discussed in Chapters 5 through 7. Assessment of problem populations cannot be presumed valid prior to major changes in a currently unsatisfactory intervention. The fact that current teaching and treatment are not satisfactory suggests that individuals will not be very positively motivated and, indeed, probably are negatively motivated toward tasks and activities associated with the intervention. Therefore, their performance on tests or as reflected in observation ratings done in the intervention setting is unlikely to represent their current capabilities. Until they are in a situation that reduces avoidance and increases approach motivation, it is doubtful that assessment data should be used for determining specific plans. Such practices probably are responsible for a significant number of major errors, wasteful prescriptions, and other negative consequences.

Obviously, if assessment data gathered at this time are not valid for use in specific planning, they cannot be valid for general intervention decisions. Thus, after screening has identified the current intervention as unsatisfactory, the best that can be done is to make *initial* decisions about the general form of intervention needed, after gathering only the data necessary for making such decisions.

The simple sequences usually advocated and debated are schematically represented in Figure 8-2. In contrast, valid decision making regarding such matters appears to require the complex series of events represented in Figure 8-3.

Given a broad perspective of selection activity, it is suggested that a complex series of steps is involved in efforts to arrive at valid intervention decisions. Screening and initial decision making about interventions logically occur prior to implementing interventions; in turn, intervention should occur prior to planning specifics.

IMPROVING CURRENT APPROACHES

Sequential assessment, such as that described above, appears to be a key procedure in addressing predictive validity problems encountered in selection and other intervention decisions (Adelman, 1971; Adelman & Taylor, 1977a; Cronbach, 1970; Wedell, 1970; Wissink, Kass & Ferrell, 1975). However, a comprehensive sequence of events

Figure 8-2

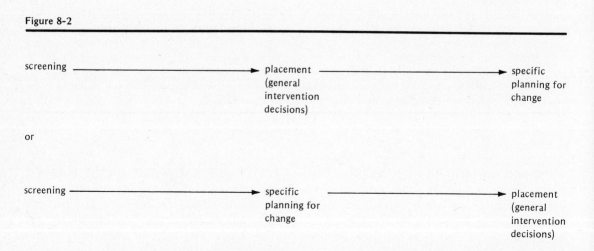

Figure 8-3

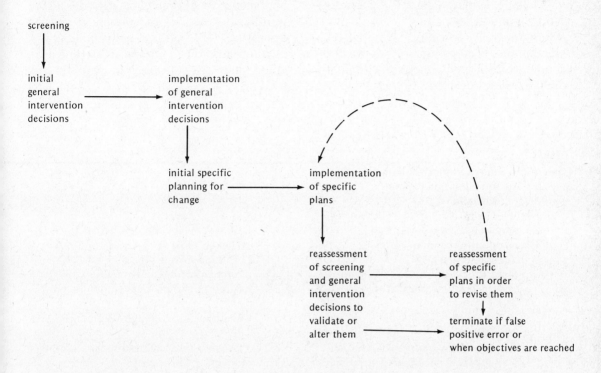

designed to improve decision making begins with the idea of *improving environments* and ongoing support systems in order to reduce the need for identifying problems (Hobbs, 1975a; Rhodes, 1970).

Improving Environments: An Alternative to Assessment

Screening provides a good example of the importance of environmental changes as a precursor of assessment. Prior to planning mass screening, improved and augmented programs for psychoeducational and health maintenance are needed. It makes little sense to wait for problems or try to predict specific problems if they can be averted by general preventive action.

With regard to school learning and behavior problems, it is widely acknowledged that many, perhaps most, classrooms are less than optimal learning environments. Some function considerably below acceptable standards. Prominent among the most discussed system deficiencies are poor methods and facilities, inexperienced or incompetent personnel, and unsatisfactory teacher-student ratios. Many preventive and early age intervention steps simply are not taken, thereby guaranteeing continuation of certain types of learning and behavior problems. Thus, a significant number of children probably manifest psychoeducational problems in the primary grades because of school-system deficiencies.

More generally, it should be noted that several of the recommendations of the Project on Classification of Exceptional Children emphasize steps designed to improve environments as a way "to minimize inappropriate classification, labeling, stigmatization, and alienation of the child" (Hobbs, 1975a, p. 223). Included are recommendations for improving (1) resources to help families help children, (2) education and treatment programs, and (3) personnel availability and training.

TABLE 8-2

Types of Procedures and Instruments for Assessing Environments and Person-Environment Interactions[a]

I. Assessment of Environments
  A. Observations or rating by observers
    1. In natural settings
      a. Assessment Checklists and Environmental Profiles (Smith et al., 1978)
      b. Home Observation for Measurement of the Environment Inventory (Caldwell & Bradley, 1979)
      c. Henderson Environmental Learning Process Scale (Henderson, Bergen, & Hunt, 1972)
      d. Target behavior observation (Cartwright & Cartwright, 1974)
      e. Ecological field study approaches (Barker, 1968)
      f. Availability and organization of equipment and materials (Kritchevsky & Prescott, 1969)
    2. In special assessment situations
      a. Simulation studies of environments (Kuethe, 1962)
      b. Laboratory studies of territoriality (Altman & Haythorn, 1967)
      c. Impact of noise levels on task performance (Slater, 1968)
      d. Single unit interventions with pre/post or time-series measures (Weinstein, 1977)
  B. Ratings by participants
    1. Classroom Environment Scales (Moos & Tricket, 1974)
    2. Attitude surveys regarding environmental preferences (Myers, 1971)
    3. Classroom Climate Inventory (Barclay, 1974)
    4. Learning Structure Questionnaire (DiMarco, 1974)
    5. Origins Climate Questionnaire (Koenigs & Hess, 1976)
  C. Interviews or written personal reports
    1. Diagnosing professional climates of schools (Fox, Schmuck, vanEgmond, Ritvo, & Jung, 1975)
    2. Life-space interviews (Lewin, 1951)
    3. Survey of territoriality (Rosenblatt & Budd, 1975)
    4. Content analysis of neighborhood drawings by children (Ladd, 1970)
  D. Available records and data
    1. Past
      a. Analysis of daily logs or records (Brandt, 1972)
      b. Use traces (Webb, 1966)
      c. Comparison of performance measures in different environments (Horowitz & Otto, 1973)
    2. Current
      a. Analysis of thema and stereotypes in

It is increasingly being recognized that, instead of conceiving the immediate need as one of screening, there is value in first considering how to upgrade learning and treatment environments. After the best that can be done to improve environments and programs is accomplished, there should be significantly less need for screening.

Improving Assessment

When screening and general intervention decisions are indicated, the following steps can help minimize the impact of systematic bias and invalid assessment data. First, the focal point of intervention need not be presumed to be persons. Research directly investigating environmentally and interac-

---

textbooks (Weitzman, Eifler, Hokada, & Ross, 1972)
b. Relation of current grades and absentee rates to classroom social climate (Moos & Moos, 1978)

II. Assessment of specific person-environment interactions[b]

A. Observations or ratings by observers
1. In natural settings
a. Teacher-Attention Scale (Smith et al., 1978)
b. Interaction Analysis in the Classroom (Flanders, 1974)
c. Anecdotal recording (Wright, 1967)
d. Observation schedule and record (Medley, Schluck, & Ames, 1968)
2. In special assessment situations
a. Laboratory studies of interpersonal reactions to infringement of personal space (Meisels & Dosey, 1971)
b. Reactions in density experiments (Loo, 1973)
c. Students' preferences for classroom layout as a function of their interpersonal needs (Feitler, Weiner, & Blumberg, 1970)

B. Ratings by participants
1. Student Questionnaire on Classroom

Norms (Fox, Luszki, & Schmuck, 1966)
2. Sociograms and sociometric questionnaires (Moreno, 1953)
3. Self-report Scales (Gordon, 1966)
4. Purdue Teacher Evaluation Scale (Bentley & Starry, 1970)

C. Interviews or written personal reports
1. Systematic description of coping strategies (White, 1974)
2. Behavior-Person-Environment analysis (Hunt & Sullivan, 1974)
3. Learning Style Inventory (Kolb & Fry, 1975)

D. Available records and data
1. Past
a. Records of books used by subgroups of students (Elmore, 1967)
b. Analysis of routine records (Webb, 1966)
2. Current
a. Comparisons of achievement performance in different learning environments using IQ or ability scores as independent variables (Ward & Barcher, 1975)
b. Case study analysis relating use of space and mental health (Paluck & Esser, 1971)

---

a. Examples and specific references cited when relevant and available.
b. These measures focus specifically on interactions. Obviously one might use person measures (Table 7-1) in conjunction with environment measures to arrive at interpolations of person-environment interactions.

tionally determined problems can be especially helpful because recently developed procedures for assessing environmental and interactional variables provide tools for counterbalancing biases stemming from overreliance on person-oriented procedures (e.g., see Table 8–2).

Second, assessment procedures used for decision making can be conceived as a series of sequential steps. For example, screening is the initial step in a sequence of assessment. Those individuals identified as problems subsequently can be assessed (1) to determine the validity of screening conclusions, particularly decisions about the focal point of intervention and (2) to facilitate initial general intervention decision making.

Third, the impact of differences in observer-actor perceptions of cause should be examined.

Fourth, pathological bias can be countered by shifting criteria to favor errors in the opposite direction, that is, to minimize false positives by maximizing false negatives.

Fifth, assessors should avoid overreliance on any one source of data and use of highly unreliable and invalid test procedures, and concomitantly, should alert consumers to limitations of data gathered under less than optimal motivational conditions.

Sixth, as the Project on the Classification of Exceptional Children (Hobbs, 1975a) recommends, the harmful effects of categories and labels can be reduced by (1) improvements in classification systems, (2) placing constraints on the use of psychological tests, (3) improvements in procedures for early identification of children of developmental risk, (4) placing safeguards on the use of records, and (5) paying attention to due process in classifying and placing exceptional children.

Finally, assessment and consultation processes are interventions and should reflect basic ideas about what makes intervention efficacious. This is particularly critical in maximizing follow-through by individuals on decisions they make during assessment and consultation activity.

While this last point is discussed in detail in Part 3, at this time it is worth briefly noting three basic ideas related to intervention theory. These ideas have been conceived in terms of establishing (1) an optimal accommodative *match*, (2) a valid *contract*, and (3) an appropriate *supportive structure* (Adelman & Taylor, 1977).

Current discussions of the problem of the match tend to be based on developmental theories (as discussed in Chapters 2 and 3). Implications for intervention are emphasized in our work and in that of J. McV. Hunt (1961), and D. Hunt and Sullivan (1974), among others. Essentially, the concept assumes that the information, tasks, affect, and so forth, related to exploration of new decision options be disparate, but not too much so, from the "client's" current way of understanding and coping. A major objective of assessment and consultation activity is to facilitate the occurrence of such a match.

The problem of a valid contract arises whenever an intervener (e.g., assessor) enters the picture. Initially, it is the problem of eliciting truly informed consent and mutual agreement about objectives and procedures for achieving them. Subsequently, it is the problem of establishing a mutual, active commitment from all parties involved in the interaction to take responsibility for achieving objectives effectively and efficiently. Cognitive theories and related research suggest that it is important for persons to be actively involved in choice making and to experience feelings of control, self-determination, and competence (Deci, 1975; Mahoney, 1974; Perlmuter & Monty, 1979).

The problem of establishing an appropriate supportive structure is related closely to that of developing an optimal match and valid contract. It involves providing support and direction (as contrasted with control and surveillance).

In developing an appropriate structure (and, by implication, a good match and mutually agreeable contract), the focus, at first, is on minimizing nonfacilitative anxiety and establishing a mutually satisfactory interpersonal relationship and pattern of communication. At this stage, the emphasis is on providing a bridge between the establishment of a working agreement and the effective procedures for decision making. Concern about anxiety, relationship, and communication, of course, continue through the interaction because they are keys to maintaining task focus and perseverance.

DEVELOPING ALTERNATIVE STRATEGIES

For many years, the clinic with which we are associated pursued a process that has become fairly standard practice for clinical assessment services in the field of learning disabilities. The assessment format available to clients was lengthy, costly, and test oriented. Reports were requested from physicians, schools, and other relevant professional sources. Adult clients and parents of minors filled out extensive questionnaires on medical and developmental history and current life status. Clients were administered an assessment battery focusing on

intelligence (e.g., Wechsler, Stanford-Binet);

achievement (e.g., California, Stanford, Iowa);

perceptual motor functioning (e.g., Bender Visual-Motor Gestalt, Frostig Developmental Test of Visual Perception, Wepman Auditory Discrimination Test);

language functioning (e.g., Illinois Test of Psycholinguistic Abilities);

memory (e.g., Graham-Kendall Memory for Designs Test); and

social and emotional functioning (e.g., sentence completion, Draw-A-Person, House-Tree-Person, Rorschach, Thematic Apperception Test).

Furthermore, many clients were referred for a neurological evaluation, including an EEG. After all data were analyzed, the psychologist met with the parents to report results and recommendations. Decisions were made about diagnoses, specific prescriptions for remediation, and where to go for services.

As we came increasingly to understand implications of the concepts and concerns related to this approach to assessment, we looked for promising alternatives. In the process, we have dramatically reduced emphasis on batteries of tests, diagnoses, specific prescriptions, and unilateral decision making.

Several examples based on our research are discussed below. The intent in presenting specific examples is to illustrate the features and feasibility of alternatives, not to encourage premature application.

Classification: A Sequential Approach
A differential diagnosis of learning disabilities requires not only evidence that a person should be *excluded* from other categories but indicators that unequivocally *include* the person in the learning disabilities category. A great deal of research in this area has focused on trying to establish inclusionary criteria. Much of this activity has been confounded by lack of adequate exclusionary criteria; the likelihood of identifying a group of persons whose learning problems are caused by minor cerebral dysfunctioning might be increased significantly if those whose problems do not stem from

such a cause were removed from the research samples. It seems research is needed to improve exclusionary procedures as a first step toward improving research on inclusionary criteria.

Several researchers have suggested some type of sequential screening (Adelman, 1971; Wissink et al., 1975) or ongoing hypothesis verification (Lindsay & Wedell, 1982; Wedell, 1970) to filter out individuals with cerebral dysfunctions. Such approaches eventually may lead to valid diagnosis of learning disabilities and may even distinguish several other significant subgroups within that category. At the very least these alternatives should help reduce the number of persons erroneously diagnosed as learning disabled.

One aspect of our research has focused on pursuing a sequential and hierarchical strategy for diagnostic classification. The assumption underlying this strategy is that those learning problems caused by factors other than neurological dysfunctions and severe emotional disturbance respond relatively quickly to personalized instruction. When learning activity accommodates *both* the current motivation and developmental levels of such students, they learn as readily as those without learning problems. Thus, while they may have a great deal of catching up to do, they can be reasonably excluded from disability and disorder categories. The remaining, reduced pool of problem learners then can be systematically studied with regard to the relationship of their symptomatic behaviors to brain functioning (Gaddes, 1980; Rourke, 1975).[2]

Our emphasis on improving programs prior to classifying individuals also leads us to classify and screen settings. Data for describing whether a setting may be a problem come mainly from cumulative findings related to each individual's progress. Findings of dissatisfaction and unreasonably slow progress on the part of a significant percentage of students can be used as a probable key screening indicator of setting problems. To classify school settings as problems, we propose the following: that when 5 to 10 percent of the students in a school are not making appropriate progress, the degree to which the school setting is a problem is classified *mild*; 11 to 30 percent, *moderate*; and over 30 percent, *severe and pervasive*.

Selection as an Initial Assessment and Consultation Process

One process we are researching related to screening and general intervention decision making is designated as *initial assessment and consultation* (Adelman & Taylor, 1979). In brief, the general nature of the process can be described as *shared problem solving*. A number of psychologists and educators have suggested that the process of problem solving provides a useful framework to guide and improve assessment and other intervention thinking and activity (e.g., Urban & Ford, 1971).[3] Figure 8–4 presents an outline

---

[2] This sequential strategy is discussed in greater detail in Part 4.

[3] Analyses of various formulations indicate the essential features of systematic problem solving include: (a) stimulus inputs experienced as a problem, (b) problem-solving activity that can be described in phases or stages, including steps and tasks, and (c) motivation and developmental capability to problem solve. The essence of the major phases or stages of problem-solving activity are

• a "set" to problem solve;

• a reasonably thorough understanding of important characteristics of the problem;

• choice behavior which includes generating and evaluating alternatives and decision making as to which to act upon;

• action; and

• evaluation of outcomes to decide whether additional problem solving is needed.

While an outline of systematic problem solving is logically appealing, there appears to be a tendency for people not to proceed in such a step-by-step sequence in everyday problem solving. Whether they can and whether it would be more effective as yet are unanswered empirical questions.

of our view of key steps and tasks of assessment and consultation—and intervention in general—using a shared problem-solving paradigm.

While most professional assessment and consultation can be seen as problem solving, such activity may or may not be *shared*. We stress the shared nature of the process to emphasize that the objective is to help interested parties arrive at their own decisions, rather than passively adopt the professional's recommendations and referrals.

As with all assessment involved in decision making, the assessment aspect of initial assessment and consultation is conceived as having three major facets: (1) an implicit or explicit *rationale* that determines what is assessed (including views of desired outcomes and facilitative processes based on philosophical, theoretical, empirical, and pragmatic considerations), (2) "measurement" or *data gathering*, in the form of tests, analyses of records, observations, personal descriptions and perspectives, and so forth (related to antecedent, transactions, and/or outcome conditions), and (3) *judgments* of the meaning of what has been "measured" based on norms or standards (e.g., standardized or unstandardized norms, personal standards).

The consultation aspect also has three major facets: (1) an implicit or explicit *rationale* that determines the focus of consultation activity, (2) *exploration of relevant information* (including "expert" information) and (3) *decision making* (by the student and parents).

The specific procedures of initial assessment and consultation include:

initial screening, usually via a phone conversation;

questionnaires filled out by all concerned regarding individual perceptions of cause and correction;

gathering records and reports from other professionals or agencies, as determined by the student and parents;

analysis—with the student and parents—of questionnaires, reports, and records to determine whether there is a need to correct or corroborate indices of deficits and disorders or both;

brief, highly circumscribed testing if necessary and desired by the student and parents;

conference(s) with immediately concerned parties to analyze problem(s) and in the process to determine whether other information is needed to complete the analysis;

additional brief and specific information gathering through testing, teaching, or counseling if needed;

conference(s) with the immediately concerned parties to (1) arrive at an agreement about how the problem will be understood for purposes of generating alternatives, (2) generate, evaluate, and make decisions about alternatives to be pursued, (3) formulate a plan for pursuing alternatives and for any support needed; and

follow-up via telephone or conference to evaluate success of each pursued alternative and satisfaction with the process. Problem analysis and decision making can be accomplished in one session, but if additional assessment data are needed, one or two assessment sessions and a subsequent conference are planned.

A shared problem-solving approach eliminates a number of problems encountered in prevailing approaches: the service costs about a tenth of what prevailing approaches charge; it avoids making "expert" prescriptions that go beyond the validity of assessment procedures; and it avoids refer-

Figure 8-4

Key steps and tasks in problem solving intervention.

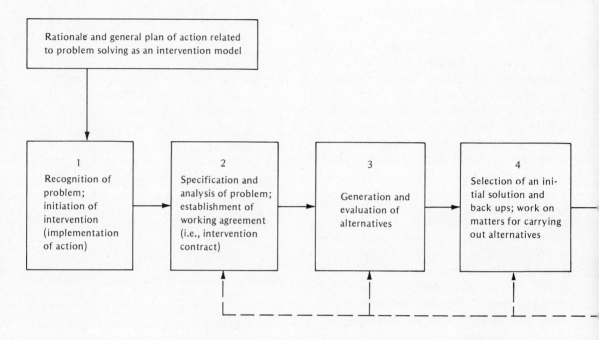

Tasks—step 1	Tasks—step 2	Tasks—step 3	Tasks—step 4
a) Initial awareness of the problem	a) Mutual assessment of the problem	a) Work through to shared understanding of alternatives for solving the problem, deferring judgment as much as is reasonable	a) Work through to a shared understanding of proposed solution, (e.g., implications and subtleties)
b) Awareness that intervention help is needed	b) Work through to a shared understanding of the problem, including diagnostic classification if needed and cause-effect (functional) analyses if feasible	b) Use of any new information arising from process to further clarify problem	b) Evaluate additional alternatives arising from process
c) Intervention tentatively initiated	c) Work through to shared understanding of expectations for work together	c) Develop criteria for evaluating pros and cons of alternatives	c) Choose primary and back up solutions
d) Relationship building, (e.g., trust and respect)	d) Develop attitudes related to effective problem solving, (e.g., openness to innovative solutions, deferring judgments)	d) Apply criteria	d) Develop plan for achieving selected alternatives, (e.g., identify support and skill needs)
e) Deal with emotional charge, (e.g., fears, anger, anxieties)			e) Develop needed skills
f) Initial awareness of mutual expectations related to intervention			f) Develop criteria for decision making about whether problem is resolved or whether to shift to back up solution

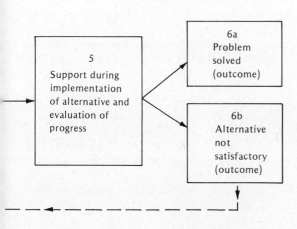

Tasks—step 5	Tasks—step 6
a) Deal with emotional charge	a) Formative and summative evaluation (stimulus inputs from outcomes)
b) Continue development of needed skills	b) Apply criteria regarding whether other alternatives are needed
c) Formative evaluation	c) If alternative has not been satisfactory, analyze feedback to determine whether information suggests additional alternatives not previously realized or perspectives of the problem which were not previously understood and may lead to new alternatives
d) Apply criteria to decide whether to shift to back up solution	

rals based on "old boy" networks or other biases of the professional referrer who either likes a specific approach or a specific person or place, but who is rarely in a position to have adequately evaluated many of these resources.

While avoiding a number of serious problems confronting diagnostic testing and professional referral procedures currently in vogue, the process described raises other problems. The most common and difficult of these stem from the fact that so many clients have come to overrely on experts for diagnoses and prescriptions (Illich, 1976). Thus, they expect and believe tests that provide definitive answers exist, and they want professionals to make decisions about courses of action. When they expect expert advice and instead encounter a process that encourages them to make their own decisions, they may feel frustrated and angry. Fortunately, and perhaps surprisingly, we have experienced this problem with only a few clients to date. Another major problem is that of facilitating articulation and clarification of client perceptions, especially with very young children and those who feel inhibited talking to professionals or talking while their parents are present. As we have encountered and investigated such problems, they appear solvable, and we are developing ways to cope with them.

CONCLUDING COMMENTS

Again, it should be noted that our intent here is not to argue for a particular alternative or model—the point is to provide some ideas about developing and evaluating alternative procedures and strategies.

Given the state of the LD field, charges of ethical and legal impropriety have been raised, and increases in malfeasance and malpractice suits can be expected. The key to ethical practice is to avoid procedures demonstrated to be invalid for the purpose, to mediate against misuse of valid data, and

FOR EXAMPLE

IMPROVING CLASSIFICATION

The Report of the Project on Classification of Exceptional Children (Hobbs, 1975a, pp. 233–36) states the following with regard to improving classification systems:

> Available classification systems are gross and inadequate. They obscure both the uniqueness of individual children and the similarities of children assigned to various categories. Gross classification leads to gross and inadequate solutions to problems at every level of concern. Federal, state, and local governments are organized on the basis of outmoded classification concepts. . . .
>
> The way a problem is defined will determine the way it is solved. It is thus a matter of utmost importance that there be made available an adequate system for defining exceptionality, for classifying with precision children loosely called handicapped, disadvantaged, or delinquent. . . . An adequate definition of the problem can lead to new solutions at all levels of concern with it—from how federal programs for children should be organized to how a teacher should conduct his or her class.
>
> 2.1.1 RECOMMENDATION The Secretary of Health, Education, and Welfare should contract with appropriate institutions or agencies to develop a comprehensive diagnostic and classification system for handicapped, disadvantaged, and delinquent children.
>
> (1) The classification system should embrace the full range of conditions in children who need special services; it should emphasize services required, not types of children; it should link etiology, current status, intervention, and outcome; it should identify assets as well as liabilities; it should be sensitive to the developmental status of the child, to his strengths as well as weaknesses; it should include the matrix of other persons significant in the life of the child, as well as settings; and it should be dated and its validity bound to a limited period of time. The system should be kept as simple as possible and potential users should be involved in all phases of its development.
>
> (2) The system should deemphasize the familiar but gross categories of exceptionality. It should specify instead the services required to assist the child or [the child's] family and school in the interest of the child's fullest development. The system should provide ways to monitor the achievement of specified treatment goals in specified periods of time.
>
> (3) The system should make maximum use of computer technology. It should provide compatible information on service requirements for use at all levels of public responsibility for the child: neighborhood school, school system, community health department, city, state, and federal government. The system must provide wholly dependable safeguards for the confidentiality of records of individual children.
>
> (4) While the system should emphasize the classification of children in ways that will facilitate the delivery of services to them, it should also yield information illuminating the etiology of handicapping conditions. Understanding of etiology is essential to prevention and may eliminate or reduce the incidence of a handicapping condition, thus altering radically the requirements for service. Finally, the sys-

to use unvalidated procedures conservatively and in a controlled, experimental fashion. Moreover, from both an ethical and practical perspective, development and investigation of new procedures and strategies is indicated (e.g., Bagnato, 1981). Specifically, new strategies that recognize the impor-tance of environmental change as a precursor and first step in an ongoing sequence of assessment activity must be developed. At the same time, new approaches must guard against presumptions that an individual referred as a problem should be the focal point of intervention.

tem should facilitate epidemiological studies to provide information essential to large-scale program planning and for the evaluation of the outcomes of intervention efforts.

(5) The project to develop a comprehensive classification system should be guided by a national advisory committee composed of experts in educational, psychological, medical, social, and legal aspects of exceptionality. The project should involve the major professional and voluntary organizations concerned with exceptional children, as well as representative parents, and to the extent feasible, children themselves. Its work should be coordinated with relevant projects of the World Health Organization. Approximately five years would be required to complete the formulation of a new system, and the estimated cost is five million dollars. Provision should then be made for its periodic revision.

2.1.2 RECOMMENDATION The Secretary of Health, Education, and Welfare should encourage, through grants and contracts with appropriate agencies, the development of standardized, quantitative, ecologically oriented profiling systems for work with individual handicapped, disadvantaged, or delinquent children, and the development of models of intervention programs embracing ecological concepts.

The familiar categories of exceptionality have limited value in planning education or treatment programs for most exceptional children. Assessment of and programming for individual children should be based on periodic analyses of the assets and liabilities of the child and his immediate world, which considered

together may be thought of as a circumscribed ecological system, with the child the center. The state of our knowledge at present permits the construction of profiles of the child in relationship with important other people in particular settings, and the specification of actions to be taken on behalf of the child. The goal is to make the system function in satisfactory and rewarding ways by giving specific assistance to the child and to people essential to [the child's] healthy development—parents, siblings, teachers, neighbors, agency personnel. Intervention should be focused on reducing disturbance within the system as a whole, not just on doing something to the child. The system must be continuously monitored and profiles revised as the child learns and [the child's] world changes; intervention strategies must be adapted or discarded as the system changes. Without constant monitoring and adaptation, these procedures can become as encumbering as the labels they supplant.

The profiling system should be compatible with the general classification system recommended in 2.1.1, but research on this important aspect of the problem (improving procedures for working with individual children) should proceed separately. While it is difficult to estimate costs of research and development work, an investment of three million dollars in this important undertaking should be sufficient to provide a constructive alternative to our current inefficient and sometimes deleterious classification and labeling procedures.

One of the sad ironies surrounding psychoeducational assessment and consultation is that practitioners and consumers remain so committed to existing practices that there is strong resistance to change. Nevertheless, as Coles (1978) states, there is little doubt that most of the tests currently used in batteries for diagnosis, screening, and placement eventually will be discarded since the evidence against them is mounting. The critical concern is over what will replace them. Little progress will have been made if they are simply replaced with equally invalid approaches.

IMPROVING SELECTION PRACTICES

Mercer (1979) has developed The System of Multicultural Pluralistic Assessment (SOMPA) to provide comprehensive, nondiscriminatory assessment data which can be used to improve placement decisions for students from lower socioeconomic, and certain ethnic, groups. SOMPA was developed to counter frequent mislabeling and misplacement of such students in special education classrooms. Its premise is that, in assessing intelligence, comparisons must be made between children of comparable ethnic and sociocultural backgrounds. To date, norms have been established for black, Hispanic, and white samples using 2,085 California children ages 5 to 11.

SOMPA gathers data on the extent to which an individual meets the expectations of his or her social system, on biological conditions (e.g., biological anomalies, sensory and motor impairments), and on learning potential. More specifically:

1. Data are gathered on family size, structure, socioeconomic status, and urban acculturation to assess the degree of difference from the "American core culture" and the "socioeconomic status of the family within the ethnic group." The information is elicited from the child's mother using standard English or Spanish.

2. The Bender Visual Motor Gestalt Tests, physical dexterity tests, and a health history inventory are administered and measures are taken of weight and visual acuity (i.e., the Snellen Chart).

3. The Wechsler Intelligence Scale for Children-Revised (WISC-R) and the Adaptive Behavior Inventory for Children (ABIC) are administered. The latter is a 242-item questionnaire focusing on family, peer relations, nonacademic school roles, earner/consumer, and self-maintenance functioning.

The data are used to generate a score of Estimated Learning Potential (ELP), which represents a statistical adjustment of the child's WISC-R and is intended to be a fairer estimate of intelligence for students from certain ethnic and from lower socioeconomic groups. This adjusted score is seen by many as a more appropriate basis for selection decisions in such cases.

While it is too early to judge its contribution in improving selection practices, SOMPA represents a major experimental effort to improve the nature of assessment data used in making placement decisions. Moreover, it highlights the critical need for additional research designed to develop and evaluate alternatives to prevailing practices.

PART 3
PLANNING AND IMPLEMENTING CHANGE

Before one can begin to change a condition one must believe in the possibility of change.
Lauter and Howe (1970, p. 282)

Good ideas and missionary zeal are sometimes enough to change the thinking and actions of individuals; they are rarely, if ever, effective in changing complicated organizations (like the school) with traditions, dynamics, and goals of their own.
Sarason (1971, p. 213)

Although they are known by several names—special education, educational therapy, psychobehavioral approach, perceptual-motor training, remediation, diagnostic remedial process, remedial diagnosis, rehabilitation, correction, helping relationships, reeducation, prescriptive teaching, precision teaching, clinical teaching, diagnostic teaching, task analysis, process analysis, individualized education program, personalization—corrective interventions share the common purpose of playing a decisive role in taking care of problematic conditions.

There is no dearth of literature describing and advocating approaches to correcting problems. A great deal of what has been written stresses the *special* nature of the interventions described. Advocates of such approaches, however, often presume a specialness yet to be demonstrated. We assume that understanding how to correct learning problems begins with understanding the general principles involved in any intervention designed to facilitate learning. While additional concepts and activities may be involved, we see no reason to postulate new principles for understanding them.

Three basic questions related to intervention provide a starting point: What changes are desired?, How can the desired changes be accomplished?, and How can one know the desired changes have been accomplished? The first question has to do with decision making about intended *content and outcomes,* the second with decision making about intended *processes,* and the third with decision making about *efficacy.* The first two questions are the central focus of Part 3.

No matter how altruistically based, decisions to intervene have potential for doing harm as well as good. This is true not only for those directly involved, but for others in the immediate environment, and ultimately for society. Psychoeducational interventions, then, must be well planned and carefully monitored. The purpose in

Part 3 is (1) to review prevailing LD approaches and highlight critical concerns, (2) to discuss the concept of motivation in some detail because of the central role it plays in planning and implementing change, and (3) to provide a general analysis of intervention outcomes, content, and procedures.

Our aims are not only to provide a picture of current approaches, but to suggest some ideas for how they can be improved and eventually transformed. "No approach is more impractical," says Silberman in *Crisis in the Classroom*,

than one which takes the present arrangements and practices as given, asking only, "How can we do what we are now doing more effectively?" or "How can we bring the worst institutions up to the level of the best?" These questions need to be asked, to be sure; but one must also realize that the best may not be good enough and may, in any case, already be changing. Thus, it is useful to work on two levels simultaneously: a level of short-run reform, where one works within the existing system, and a longer-run concern with the transformation of the system. (1970, p. 4)

Chapter 9

Interventions for Learning Disabilities: Prevailing Orientations

*The problem of determining how educa-
tional objectives should be stated or used is
not simply a question of technique but a
question of value. The differences between
individuals regarding the nature and the use
of educational objectives spring from differences in their conceptions of education;
under the rug of technique lies an image of
[people].*
Eisner (1969, p. 8)

Planning and implementing interventions
for individuals identified as learning disabled raises complex questions: What
changes are desired? Which areas of development and what types of competence
should be focused upon? How should needs
be assessed? What is the role of motivation
and affective variables? What should be the
goals and content of intervention? How
should outcome objectives be formulated?
How much should an intervention be expected to accomplish? Are short- or long-
term outcomes the major aim?

In this chapter, we present an overview of
intervention outcomes, content, and procedures currently used in programs for individuals designated as learning disabled.
Rather than a detailed description of the
many programs that are advocated, our intent is to provide a synthesis of prevailing
orientations.

OUTCOMES AND CONTENT

Because the focus in the LD field is on
problematic conditions of persons, the focal
point for change is persons. The outcomes

TABLE 9-1

Content Areas in the Learning Disabilities Field and Prominent Names Associated with Each Area[a]

Content (problem) Areas[b]	Prominent Names
Perceptual/Motor[c] • Motor skills and patterns • Perception, i.e., ability to recognize and interpret sensory stimuli • Perceptual motor integration, i.e., organization and coordination of sensory stimuli with motor activity and use of motor activity to monitor and correct perceptions • Relationship of motor and perceptual development to more complex cognitive development	Kurt Goldstein (e.g., 1936, 1939) shortly after World War I found brain-injured veterans hyperactive and easily distractible. They had difficulty differentiating figure and ground, dealing with abstract concepts, and delaying responses to stimuli. He observed an automatic compensatory ability that allowed them to reduce environmental stimuli. His clinical research provided a foundation for much of the field of LD. Heinz Werner and Alfred Strauss (e.g., 1940, 1941; Strauss, 1943) applied Goldstein's observations to their research differentiating exogenous (brain-injured) from endogenous (nonbrain-injured) retarded children. They recommended reducing unessential stimuli and increasing saliency of what is to be learned, e.g., looking at or touching a stimulus and responding with motor movement.
Specific examples of intervention content and outcomes: • Laterality and directionality • Body image and differentiation • Balance and posture • Locomotion • Gross and fine motor coordination • Ocular control • Figure-ground perception • Constancy of shape • Position in space • Spatial relationships • Perceptual motor coordination • Auditory and visual integration • Tactile and kinesthetic integration • Multisensory integration • Rhythm • Agility • Strength, endurance, flexibility • Catching and throwing	Alfred Strauss and Laura Lehtinen (1947) developed additional educational strategies designed to facilitate perceptual organization. Besides Strauss's other recommendations (e.g., reduced environmental stimuli), they stressed basing educational plans on analysis of specific task performance. They advocated use of specially selected and prepared materials and teaching strategies to compensate or avoid areas of weakness and capitalize on strengths. Newell Kephart (e.g., 1960, 1971), a colleague of Strauss (Kephart & Strauss, 1940; Strauss & Kephart, 1955), applied the view that motor and perceptual development are the basis for later conceptual learning. He designed techniques to enhance gross motor and perceptual motor functioning to the "slow learner in the classroom." He was particularly concerned with body image (emphasizing laterality and directionality), balance, locomotion, perceptual motor coordination, and use of kinesthetic feedback in spatial and temporal functioning. William Cruickshank (e.g., Cruickshank, Bentzen, Ratzeburg, & Tannhauser, 1961), also a colleague of Strauss, further refined the educational methods employed by Strauss and Lehtinen. His work focused especially on distractability and hyperactivity in children, including those functioning in normal range of intelligence. He stressed reduced environmental stimuli, multisensory methods, and structured educational programming.

Content (problem) Areas[b]	Prominent Names
The most prominent programs in the 1940s and 1950s espoused perceptual motor areas. Until recently, the evolution of the LD field has been dominated by such interventions and those persons associated with them. In addition to the psychoeducational interventions for perceptual motor problems, other professional groups have been involved in offering treatments, e.g., occular training and prescription of stimulant drugs.	Marianne Frostig (e.g., Frostig & Horne, 1961) developed a test of visual perception and a corresponding perceptual motor training program. She divides perception into 5 areas: eye motor coordination, figure-ground, constancy of shape, position in space, and spatial relationships. Gerald Getman (e.g., 1965), an optometrist, developed a visuomotor model and with several colleagues devised structured perceptual motor training techniques. These include general coordination, balance, eye-hand coordination, eye movements, form perception, and visual memory (Getman, Kane, and McKee, 1968). Ray Barsch (e.g., 1967) developed a perceptual motor training program called "movigenics" which stresses a spatial approach to teaching basic academic skills. Glen Doman, a physical therapist, and Carl Delacato, an educational psychologist (e.g., Delacato, 1959; 1966) have developed models and methods based on their view of neurological organization. They argue for a "patterning" approach for neural retraining. For those with motor (mobility) problems, including severely retarded individuals, they focus on development through a hierarchical sequence of 13 stages ranging from rolling over through creeping and crawling to walking cross pattern. Jean Ayres (e.g., 1965, 1973) also is interested in neural retraining. She believes intersensory integration of the modalities of visual, tactile, and kinesthetic perception is essential for reading. Her methods are designed to integrate sensory systems. She advocates activities for controlling sensory input through vestibular and somatosensory systems. Bryant Cratty (e.g., 1967, 1973) has developed movement activities and games of use in physical education to improve motor skills and patterns. His focus is on perception of the body and its position in space, balance, locomotion, agility, strength endurance, flexibility, catching and throwing, manual abilities, and moving and thinking. He has also developed a series of activity games to enhance academic abilities (Cratty, 1971).

continued

TABLE 9-1 *continued*

Content Areas in the Learning Disabilities Field and Prominent Names Associated with Each Area[a]

Content (problem) Areas[b]	Prominent Names
Language and Psycholinguistics • Listening Skills • Speaking Skills • Reading Skills • Writing Skills • Spelling Skills • Grammar • Usage (written expression) • Processing abilities underlying language Specific examples of intervention content and outcomes: • Basic skills related to each of the above, e.g., with regard to reading the focus might be on sound-symbol associations, word recognition, phonics and structural analysis, and comprehension. • Underlying abilities related to each of the above, e.g., with regard to psycholinguistics the focus has been on such factors as auditory and visual reception, association, closure, and sequential memory.	Samuel Orton, (e.g., 1937) from about 1925 to 1948, studied reading processes of brain-injured adults and concluded that specific location of damage is critical. This led to the view that reading problems resulted from mixed cerebral dominance. He advocated right-handed and right-sided practice to establish dominance. His approach to reading was essentially an individually paced phonics approach with kinesthetic aids. Grace Fernald (e.g., 1943) officially established her clinical laboratory in 1921. Her work focused on remediation of basic academic skills without great concern over specific causes or internal deficits. She proposed a variety of remedial approaches for all basic academic subjects. She stressed that learning could be improved through enhancing the vividness of stimulus inputs. A major way to do this was through multisensory methods in teaching language, reading, spelling, writing, and math. Also in this connection she stressed meaningful content, high-interest activities, and learning as a function of the whole person. Anna Gillingham and Bessie Stillman (e.g., 1936, 1966), following Orton's lead, stressed language development through associations with visual, auditory, and kinesthetic mechanisms in the dominant hemisphere. They developed techniques to strengthen these associations which emphasize phonics, multisensory techniques, repetition, and drill. Joseph Wepman (e.g., Wepman, Jones, Bock, & Van Pelt, 1960), developed a language model based on modality bound transmission, the importance of memory in perceptual and conceptual language, and the role of internal and external feedback. He is directly responsible for several tests in the area. His work has been used by others to develop tests and treatment approaches. Samuel Kirk (e.g., 1962) attempted to operationalize the models formulated by Osgood (1957) and Wepman. He and his colleagues developed the Illinois Test of Psycholinguistic Abilities (ITPA) which focuses on channels of communication, psycholinguistic processes, and levels of organization. The test was designed to guide instructional planning related to identifying strengths and weaknesses. Specific training programs have been developed to correct disabilities identified by the test.

Content (problem) Areas[b]	Prominent Names
Language and Psycholinguistics	Helmer Myklebust (e.g., 1954) worked initially with deaf children. This work led to his interest in the development of auditory or receptive language and in the diagnosis and remediation of auditory disorders. This interest drew him into theorizing about learning disabilities and along with Doris Johnson, he developed intervention approaches.

Doris Johnson and Helmer Myklebust (e.g., 1967) working with a theory of sequential levels of language acquisition advocated specific training procedures designed to strengthen deficit areas and teaching through intact modalities.

Siegfried Engelmann and Elaine Bruner (1969), working with behaviorist and programmed instruction ideas, have developed DISTAR Reading I & II, an intensive and highly structured, step-by-step instructional system. It modifies traditional print, and stresses early letter recognition and phonics. |
| **Math**

• Computational skills
• Conceptual processes associated with quantitative relationships

Specific examples of intervention content and outcomes:

• Shape and size discrimination
• Sets and numbers
• One to one correspondence
• Counting
• Place value
• Measurement
• Money and time concepts
• Word problems

In addition to basic skills, emphasis is often on prerequisite skills and/or underlying abilities related to perceptual motor development, language, cognition, and motivation. | Although long a remedial concern (e.g., Fernald, 1943; Strauss & Lehtinen, 1947), it is only recently that comprehensive efforts have been made to relate this content area to the LD field. For example: Jack Cawley and his colleagues (e.g., Cawley, Fitzmaurice, Goodstein, Lepore, Sedlak, & Althaus, 1976) have developed a programmed kit for instruction of exceptional children through sixth grade. Six areas are stressed: patterns, sets, geometry, measurement, fractions, and numbers.

Other approaches have been described as readily adaptable for use with children with learning problems, for example, basal texts, such as those developed by Duncan and his colleagues (Duncan, Copps, Dolciani, Quast & Zweng, 1970), a K–6 text series that uses a spiralled discovery approach to mathematics to help students discover patterns and build on concepts previously mastered. Second, programmed materials such as Sullivan Programmed Math (Behavioral Research Laboratories), Programmed Math 2/e (McGraw-Hill), and kits developed by Siegfried Engelmann and Douglas Carnine (1972). The latter, entitled DISTAR Arithmetic (K–3) parallels other DISTAR programs in design. It focuses on ordinal counting, signs, addition, subtraction, multiplication, money concepts, fractions, factoring, word problems, and algebraic addition. |

continued

TABLE 9-1 *continued*

Content Areas in the Learning Disabilities Field and Prominent Names Associated with Each Area[a]

Content (problem) Areas[b]	Prominent Names
Cognitive Prerequisites • Attentional skills, i.e., short-term and sustained voluntary attention • Memory, i.e., organization (coding), storage (retention), and retrieval of information • Conceptual skills, i.e., cognitive structuring of perceived stimuli and operations to order, sequence, classify, etc. In addition, prerequisites for cognitive development such as motivation and perceptual motor and language development are relevant. Specific examples of intervention content and outcomes: • Attention to task • Following directions • Rote memory • Short term or immediate memory • Serial or sequential memory • Long term memory • Spatial and temporal sequential ordering • Classification to understand relationships	Most research on attention has been basic rather than applied. Implications for content and outcomes in LD have been developed by individuals who have been concerned with interfering behaviors, especially hyperactivity, impulsivity, and distractibility. While of increasing interest, memory problems and how to improve memory have not been a central focus in the field of LD. A few individuals have reviewed the topic and it has been a focal point for assessment and some remedial activity (e.g., Benton, 1963; Chalfant, 1977; Chalfant & Scheffelin, 1969; Graham & Kendall, 1960; Kirk, McCarthy, & Kirk, 1968; Torgesen & Kail, 1980; Wepman, 1951). The feasibility of improving memory processes has been judged unlikely. However, compensatory strategies are seen as useful. Moreover, many memory problems are viewed as simply lack of specific skills and strategies that can be learned. Maria Montessori (e.g., 1912, 1964) was an early advocate of specific methods to facilitate development of basic conceptual skills. Her ideas are reflected in many remedial programs and related to all areas of development. One example is the use of concrete materials that represent abstract principles for use in teaching arithmetic and science.

Content (problem) Areas[b]	Prominent Names
Interfering Behaviors • Actions which compete with intended learning activities Specific examples of intervention content and outcomes: • Impulse control • Selective attention • Sustained attention and follow through • Perseverance • Frustration tolerance • Appropriate interactions with others With specific regard to those children diagnosed as hyperactive, there have been a number of controversial nonpsychoeducational interventions, e.g., use of stimulant drugs, special diets to avoid chemical additives in food.	Throughout the 1950s and 1960s the following individuals focused on a range of "interfering behaviors" in a number of contexts. Their various influences can be seen in many current programs for learning and behavior problems. The work of William Cruickshank and his colleagues (see above) can be seen to have influenced ideas about work with those seen as hyperactive and distractible. Richard Whelan (e.g., 1966) developed a highly structured, behavior modification oriented classroom program for severely disturbed children in the late 1950s and 1960s. The focus was on both improving behavior and academic remediation. Norris Haring (e.g., Haring & Phillips, 1962; Haring & Whelan, 1965), a student of Cruickshank, also developed a program emphasizing operant conditioning principles to improve behavior and academic problems. He joined forces with Whelan in 1962 and they further refined the use of operant methods in classrooms. Frank Hewett (e.g., 1968; Hewett & Taylor, 1980) in the early 1960s, designed what he called the "engineered classroom" based on behavior modification methods and a developmental sequence of educational goals. Recently, he has replaced the concept of "engineering" success with that of "orchestration" of success. In doing so, he is placing greater emphasis on the importance of attitudes, feelings, and self-concepts. Virginia Douglas (e.g., 1972, 1974) has emphasized both lack of impulse control and problems in sustaining attention. She has advocated teaching children, especially hyperactive children, to "stop, look, and listen." Donald Meichenbaum (e.g., Meichenbaum & Goodman, 1971; Meichenbaum, 1977) represents the trend to cognitive behavior modification concepts and methods. He stresses teaching children to use self-instruction strategies, which may include simple instructions such as "stop and look" and more complex sets of procedures, to control behavior and approach learning. He stresses overt verbalization of instruction initially, and covert verbalization in later stages.

continued

TABLE 9-1 *continued*

Content Areas in the Learning Disabilities Field and Prominent Names Associated with Each Area[a]

Content (problem) Areas[b]	Prominent Names
Social/Emotional • Interpersonal (e.g., social perception) • Intrapersonal (e.g., self-concept) Specific examples of intervention content and outcomes: • Awareness of self • Awareness of others • Mastery of interpersonal skills • Empathy training • Choice and decision making • How to cope • Assertion training • Intra and interpersonal problem solving	An early concern related to learning and behavior problems, these areas were somewhat de-emphasized with the advent of the LD movement in the late 1960s and the early 1970s (e.g., Dahlberg, Roswell, & Chall, 1952; Connolly, 1971). Practices in this area are drawn from a wide range of concepts and methods advocated in psychology over many years related to self-concept, anxiety, dependency, aggression and withdrawal, social perception, interpersonal relationships, and moral development. Particularly influential have been the vast literature on psychotherapy and behavior change (e.g., Garfield & Bergin, 1978).
Intrinsic Motivation • Increasing feelings of self-determination • Increasing feelings of competence and expectations of success • Increasing range of interests and satisfactions	While motivation always has been a process concern, a very recent addition to the LD literature has been an emphasis on intrinsic motivation as a content and outcome area. This work draws on various psychological theorists (e.g., Atkinson, 1964; Bruner, 1966; Berlyne, 1960; Deci, 1975; DeCharms, 1972; Hunt, 1965; Nicholls, 1979; Weiner, 1980; White, 1959). One recent review (Ruble & Boggiano, 1980) focuses on the topic of "optimizing motivation in an achievement context." While the emphasis is on process, the review is almost unique in broadly applying the topic to special education. Moreover, since a number of content and outcome concerns can easily be extrapolated, the review may help to increase the interest in this area as it applies to learning and behavior problems.

sought are usually formulated in specific terms based on the way the individual's problems are conceived. In turn, the content of remedial programs is shaped by the way intended outcomes are formulated. Table 9–1 presents content areas related to psychoeducational interventions described in the LD literature, lists key individuals associated with each area, and provides an overview of major perspectives predominant in the LD field.

Two Prevailing Orientations
Underlying most of the approaches listed in

Content (problem) Areas[b]	Prominent Names
Intrinsic Motivation Specific examples of intervention content and outcomes: • Learning to make appropriate choices and accept responsibility for choice • Awareness of motives and true capabilities • Learning to set valued and appropriate goals	Also see Chapter 10 (and Adelman, 1978a) for discussion of (a) the importance of methods designed to enhance intrinsic motivation and (b) the necessity of enhancing motivation as an area of content and outcome focus for those with learning and behavior problems. Environmental accommodation and enrichment activities are discussed.

a. The presentation is limited to those persons most associated with the evolution or current advocacy of approaches used with persons labeled *LD*. Obviously there are many other pioneers and leaders who could be cited with regard to understanding basic academic skills such as reading and math, and areas of human development such as cognitive, social, and emotional functioning. The emphasis here is on individuals who have been concerned primarily with problems in functioning and their correction.

It should also be noted that Weiderholt's (1974) brief historical summary suggests that three types of disorders shaped most of the development of the LD field: disorders of spoken language, of written language, and of perceptual and motor processes. He divides the evolution of the LD field into three phases. First, the foundation phase (up to about 1930) was characterized by studies of brain-behavior relationships with brain-damaged adults. Theoretical formulations were proposed regarding the nature and cause of learning disabilities. During this phase prominent planners included Goldstein, Strauss, Werner, and Orton. Second, was the transition phase (1920-1962) during which time attempts were made to translate theoretical formulations into remedial practices. During this phase the work of Wepman, Myklebust, Kirk, Fernald, Cruickshank, Frostig, and Kephart was prominent. Third, the integration phase (1963 on) reflects a merging of information into comprehensive diagnostic-remedial approaches. During this phase the number of professionals in the field has grown quickly and new attempts at theoretical formulations, further proliferation of diagnostic-remedial approaches, and basic and applied research have appeared. Lerner (1981) proposes that 1980 marked the beginning of a fourth phase, the contemporary phase. This phase is characterized as emerging toward broadening the definition of individuals served, provision of services across categories, involvement with students in the mainstream, and increased organizational activity.

b. As indicated in the text, many of the areas and the interventions developed to treat them, do not have a sound theoretical or research base. Their continued practice and claims of efficacy are extremely controversial.

c. Perceptual problems differ from sensory acuity problems, e.g., a person may have 20/20 vision and thus be able to receive visual stimuli quite well, but still have trouble interpreting what is seen. While a sensory deficit obviously could lead to other problems, these deficits have not been the main concern for psychoeducational interveners.

Table 9-1 are two basic orientations toward understanding causes and planning treatment of learning problems. One orientation stresses psychological processing abilities and related motor functioning. The other is a behavioristic skill orientation. The orientations differ because they stem from contrasting views of human development and functioning. The first is rooted in psychological theories of cognitive and perceptual processing and related language and motor functioning. The second perspective stems from behaviorism and focuses directly on observable skills and behaviors. For convenience, the view emphasizing psychological processing abilities is referred to simply as the *underlying abilities orientation* and the other perspective is designated the *observable skills orientation*.

As might be expected, each orientation has developed its own assessment procedures for remedial prescriptions. These have been designated by such terms as *the diagnostic-prescriptive approach, the diagnostic-remedial approach, ability assessment, task analysis, functional analysis, skill assessment,* and *applied behavioral analysis.* Such assessment strategies appear to have been shaped by one of the two prevailing orientations, and they, in turn, shape the planning of remedial content and outcomes.

The following brief review highlights the nature of the content, outcomes, and approaches to assessment associated with the two prevailing orientations. It should be noted that those who advocate underlying abilities (cognitive-perceptual theories) have tended to assimilate the observable skills orientation or behaviorist view. Strong advocates of the behaviorist view, however, remain very critical of assessment and corrective strategies that focus on underlying abilities.

Underlying abilities. An underlying abilities orientation emphasizes problems in the development of psychological processing and integrative functioning. In particular, underlying receptive, integrative, and expressive dysfunctions or deficits are postulated for such areas as perception, memory, and linguistic and motor functioning. Problems in these areas are seen as interfering with learning and performance in reading, oral and written language, mathematics, and so forth. As practiced, this approach is commonly called the *diagnostic-remedial approach, diagnostic-prescriptive teaching,* or the *ability model.*

From this perspective, underlying abilities

FOR EXAMPLE

CONTRASTING PERSPECTIVES

To illustrate the differences between the *underlying abilities* and *observable skill* orientations, consider Alice, a second-grader who has not been making satisfactory progress in arithmetic. She is the only one in the class who still cannot count and group objects.

The underlying abilities orientation would be concerned with whether a basic psychological process such as visual and auditory sequential memory might be dysfunctional and in need of remediation. If so identified, remediation might include efforts to improve short-term memory by having Alice do such things as repeat numbers, letters, words, and tapped patterns, and pursue other objectives to improve sequencing abilities.

The skill orientation would be concerned with directly teaching Alice such observable precomputational prerequisite skills as the rote learning and recitation of the numbers one to ten, eleven to twenty, and so forth.

naturally are viewed as the appropriate outcomes and content, for example, visual and auditory perception, short-term memory, psycholinguistics, and gross motor abilities. More specifically, this approach proposes that the underlying dysfunctions and deficits must be corrected or compensated for through remediation to enable those with learning problems to acquire basic academic skills. For example, learning in school requires making many perceptual discriminations—auditory, visual, tactile, and kinesthetic—as well as discriminations that require various combinations of these modalities. Therefore, when reading problems or other basic academic problems occur, many advocates of the diagnostic-remedial approach look for perceptual problems. They believe that, if there is a perceptual dysfunction or deficit, it must be remedied in order

VIEWPOINT

AN UNDERLYING PROCESSES PERSPECTIVE

Any disturbed brain function that finds its expression in a behavior change will probably cause other behavior changes as well. Treatment directed solely to isolated behavior or disabilities will probably not carry over to other situations. On the other hand, sometimes seemingly unrelated behaviors have a common origin in the same brain function. For example, difficulties in verbal logical behavior, mathematical skills, and spatial orientation may be overcome if the perception of spatial relationships is improved.

Frostig & Maslow (1979, p. 543)

to correct the academic problem.

An alternative underlying ability view avoids assumptions that such problems can be corrected directly. Instead, these abilities are assessed only as a basis for determining strengths and weaknesses to be considered in designing instruction. This view argues that an academic problem is best corrected by avoiding areas of weakness (e.g., handicapping conditions) such as visual perception, building on strengths, and teaching compensatory strategies, such as simultaneous use of visual, auditory, tactile, and kinesthetic senses.

In general, the underlying abilities orientation to specific planning assumes (1) the basis for the learning problem may be a disorder or disability within the individual; (2) dysfunctions, or some other developmental factors, have produced deficits interfering with learning and performance; (3) dysfunctions and deficits can be assessed;

(4) valid assessment instruments (including valid norms) are available;[1] and (5) dysfunctions and deficits can be corrected or circumvented and must be before learning and performance related to academics can be improved.

Observable skills. This perspective maintains a direct content focus on basic academics. Skills are viewed as hierarchical in nature. The appropriate outcomes of intervention are seen as mastery of any missing skills. This includes "readiness" behaviors. Remediation is continued until the learner has worked her or his way up to the appropriate level of skill development.

In this orientation, assessment for planning specific remediation usually is designated as task or functional analysis or the skill model. Assessment and prescribed outcomes and content focus on functions currently needed for effective learning and performance in the classroom. Specific needs are determined by (1) analyzing what is to be learned or done and then (2) assessing the individual to detect the absence of immediate prerequisite knowledge and skills and the presence of interfering behaviors. The hierarchical analysis of what is to be learned is used to aid both assessment and remediation. For example, to do long division requires the ability to multiply and subtract. An individual having trouble with division would be assessed to determine whether these and other apparent prerequisite skills have been acquired. If they have not, they would be taught.

In general, the observable skill orientation to specific planning assumes that (1) the person does not have a disorder, but simply has not acquired specific behaviors (knowl-

---

[1]Commonly used tests in underlying abilities assessments include the Developmental Test of Visual Perception (Frostig), Developmental Test of Motor Integration (Beery-Buktenica), Illinois Test of Psycholinguistic Abilities (ITPA), Wechsler Scale of Intelligence for Children-Revised (WISC-R), Wepman Auditory Discrimination Test, and standardized achievement tests, as well as case histories, interviews, and observations.

edge and skills); (2) assessment should focus only on observable behavior associated with hierarchies of knowledge and skills required for learning and performance (e.g., in the classroom); and (3) valid assessment procedures (including valid norms) are available;[2] and (4) assessed problems can be corrected by focusing directly on behavior change (e.g., acquisition of needed knowledge and skills).

Commonalities and criticisms. While the orientations differ markedly in their explanations of the bases for a person's problems, they share the assumption that the person is the appropriate object to be changed, and the *cognitive* and *psychomotor domains* are the primary areas for deriving content and outcomes. (The *affective domain* is treated only tangentially.)

With regard to assessment, both orientations assess present functioning to determine specific areas and the degree of performance deficiency, analyze how the individual is learning and why he or she is not learning, and formulate specific corrective intervention plans.

Both approaches recognize the necessity for continuous revision and modification based on data collected after implementation of intervention, especially information about what seems to work and what doesn't. At the same time, both recognize that assessments that focus specifically on what can be changed by corrective intervention are more appropriate for purposes of intervention planning than those that describe any or all correlates of the referral problem.

Some writers from each orientation also have emphasized that all assessment should be broadened to identify strengths related to performance and learning. Their intent is to capitalize not only on modality strengths, but on areas of competence and interests, and in general to improve the match between corrective interventions and the individual.

In practice, both orientations operate as if their assessment procedures, prescriptions, and corrective strategies are valid. Moreover, when a person overcomes her or his problems, the tendency has been to view such outcomes as evidence validating the strategy and orientation.

Of the two orientations, the underlying abilities, or diagnostic-remedial, approach has been most widely taught and practiced (see Table 9–1) and most severely criticized. In particular, it is argued that the assumptions underlying this approach are not only tenuous from the standpoint of theory, but that evidence that contradicts them is accumulating (e.g., Arter & Jenkins, 1979). Bypassing theoretical issues, some critics argue that most procedures used to assess underlying abilities are technically inadequate (e.g., Coles, 1978). Acceptance of the underlying abilities approach rests on belief in the validity of postulated causal relationships between a particular construct, such as visual perception, and remediation of a current problem, such as difficulty learning to read.

Critics of skill-oriented approaches point to what they see as the superficiality of the central assumptions, especially the restricted focus on a delimited set of behavioral symptoms and associated environmen-

---

[2]Skill-oriented assessments use procedures such as standardized achievement tests, unstructured, informal skill-diagnostic tests, observations, and criterion-referenced measures. One highly structured form of skills assessment is called applied behavior analysis. This involves simultaneous, direct, continuous, and discrete measurement of several designated behaviors, intervention procedures, or environmental variables and often incorporates machine processing of data.

More extensive listing of specific assessment procedures and instruments used by both approaches has been presented in Chapter 5. The major criticisms and concerns related to these procedures have been clarified throughout Part 2.

VIEWPOINT

A PRAGMATIC MATRIX FOR CONCEPTUALIZING CURRENT ASSESSMENT PROCEDURES USED IN PLANNING SPECIFIC INTERVENTION CONTENT AND OUTCOMES

Although different orientations advocate different assessment procedures and instruments, they share the intent of assessing present functioning in order to plan the specifics of intervention. Given the great many instruments propounded for this purpose (see Table 7-1), we find it helpful to reconceptualize and synthesize approaches to assessment for planning specifics. By adapting a two-dimensional schema suggested in another context by Popham (1971), assessment procedures can be categorized with regard to (a) the nature of the stimulus conditions presented and (b) the types of responses used as data (see Figure 9-1).

Cell A of the matrix in Figure 9-1 represents product responses to manipulated stimuli—the most frequently used data for initially prescribing specific interventions. The prototype of this approach is administration of psychometric tests ("diagnostic battery") and analyses of test scores and patterns (profiles) to plan remediation.

During testing or under other artificial conditions such as an interview, the person's actions and performance processes are observed and analyzed as an additional and sometimes as a primary basis for planning remediation, here represented by Cell B.

Cell C represents products prepared under natural conditions. A common example is daily classroom work analyzed to detect problems and progress, with findings used for planning.

The actions and performance processes of an individual in natural situations, represented by Cell D, also may be systematically observed, recorded, and analyzed. The data can be used as indices of problems and progress and the findings used to plan future work. While not always used systematically, teachers certainly rely heavily on such in situ data.

Findings based on all four approaches represented by Figure 9-1 can provide a wide range of data for planning. The particular procedures administered and the interpretation of findings, of course, continue to vary with the orientation of the professionals involved.

There also are variations in how the data are used. Some professionals use the data to determine *what* must be remedied. The same data also may be used to specify *how* to proceed with intervention.

Figure 9-1

		Stimulus Conditions	
		Manipulated/Simulated	Natural
Type of Responses	Product	A	C
	Actions and Performance Processes	B	D

VIEWPOINT

ON THE UNDERLYING ABILITIES APPROACH

In their review of diagnostic-prescriptive approaches in special education, or what they call Differential Diagnosis-Prescriptive Teaching (DD-PT), Arter and Jenkins (1979) conclude:

> *In summary, it is not surprising that DD-PT has not improved academic achievement, since most ability assessment devices have inadequate reliability and suspect validity. Moreover, abilities themselves have resisted training, and given the low correlations between ability assessments and reading achievement, it is not surprising that modality-instructional matching has failed to improve achievement.*
>
> *The repeated failure to support the basic assumptions underlying the DD-PT model casts doubt on the model's validity. We do not intend to suggest that the model is theoretically untenable, or that it may not one day be effectively implemented. Rather, we believe that with the current instructional programs and tests, this model is not useful. A number of authors who have reviewed specific aspects of the DD-PT model have arrived at a similar conclusion (Hammill & Larsen, 1974b; Sedlack & Weener, 1973; Silverston & Deichman, 1975; Ysseldyke, 1973). For example, with reference to psycholinguistic training, Newcomer et al. (1975) write, "We cannot help but conclude that psycholinguistic training based on the Kirk-Osgood model is not successful because it does not help children to increase their ability to speak or understand language, nor does it aid them in academic skills such as reading, writing or spelling. . . . the wrong skills are being remediated" (p. 147).*

> *Unfortunately, this view does not represent that held by most authorities and practioners in special education: the DD-PT model is preferred by the vast majority of special education teachers (Arter & Jenkins, 1977). In a statewide survey of Illinois, it was found that 82% of special education teachers believed that they could, and should, train weak abilities, 99% thought that a child's modality strengths and weaknesses should be a major consideration when devising educational prescriptions, and 93% believed that their students had learned more when they modified instruction to match modality strengths. The same survey provided data to suggest that teacher training programs were, to a large degree, responsible for these views and practices. Unsupported expert opinion and teacher training programs resulting from this opinion appear to have a direct, deleterious effect on teacher behavior and an indirect effect on children's learning. Not only are teachers adhering to an unvalidated model, but because they have been persuaded that the model is useful, they are less apt to create variations in instructional procedures which will result in improved learning. We believe that until a substantive research base for the DD-PT model has been developed, it is imperative to call for a moratorium on advocacy of DD-PT, on classification and placement of children according to differential ability tests, on the purchase of instructional materials and programs which claim to improve these abilities and on coursework designed to train DD-PT teachers.*
>
> Arter and Jenkins (1979, pp. 549–50)

---

tal variables. As discussed below, concern has been raised over this orientation's assumptions about what are appropriate intervention outcomes and content.

In answering criticisms, defenders of each orientation argue that their approach needs further development before it can be fairly evaluated. From this perspective, it has been proposed that both approaches have utility and promise (Smead, 1977).

Major perspectives on outcomes and content for individuals with learning and behavior problems highlight many of the issues involved in planning specific intervention.

Unfortunately, despite the best intentions on the part of their advocates, prevailing orientations have tended to introduce prematurely, and to perpetuate the use of, strategies of questionable validity. Moreover, prevailing orientations have colluded with the bias that focuses intervention on the individual as the object to be changed.

The Trend Toward Behavioral and Criterion-Referenced Objectives

For many years, educators have devoted a great deal of attention to the nature of objectives and procedures through which they are formulated (e.g., Popham, Eisner, Sullivan, & Tyler, 1969). Clinical psychologists have been much less concerned with these matters, but are beginning to consider them (e.g., Garfield & Bergin, 1978; Gurman & Razin, 1977).

The recent emphasis in education is on formulating objectives in highly concrete terms and only for outcomes. These types of outcome statements are designated as behavioral and criterion-referenced objectives. While there are times these are appropriate, it has been argued that not all objectives can or should be stated in this manner. Moreover, some critics point out there are times when only activities, and not outcomes, should be identified.

Arguments over how to approach the formulation of objectives reflect different philosophical orientations to psychoeducational intervention. For example, behavioral and criterion-referenced objectives not surprisingly tend to be based on a behaviorist metaphor or model of the basic nature of intervention.

The movement toward individual education plans for students with psychoeducational problems has accelerated the statement of short-term objectives in behavioral terms.[3] Such objectives describe:

client behavioral outcomes rather than intervener behavior (i.e., how a client should perform after an intervention activity rather than what the purposes or procedures of intervention should be);

both the intended behavior and the context in which the behavior is to occur;

only one unit of behavior at a time;

behavior that can be realistically attained; and

behavior stated with a level of specificity and precision that makes it readily recognizable should it be displayed (thus avoiding inferences to nonempirical phenomena such as mental events). Usually it is emphasized that the statement of the objective should begin with an active verb indicating the specific behavior that the client is to display.

As an illustration, Wallace and McLoughlin (1979) state, "An example of an *annual goal* is: 'The student will be able to sound out initial consonants in words,'" and they give two examples of specific objectives for this goal:

(1) Given a list of words with the initial consonant sounds /b/, /d/, /f/, and /h/, the student will decode them with 90% accuracy; or (2) Given a list of words with initial consonant sounds /k/, /m/, /n/, /p/, and /q/, the student will decode them with 90% accuracy. (p. 97)

Increasing emphasis on stating short-term outcome objectives in behavioral terms has led to increasing use of criterion-referenced tests and taxonomies of skills as aids in enumerating such objectives. Commercially prepared tests and programmed materials also delineate sequences of skills so that each skill a student has not yet acquired can be sequentially specified as an objective; the

---

[3]In the United States, Public Law 94–142 requires Individual Education Programs or IEP's. Among other requirements, the IEP is to provide statements of goals and objective criteria for determining whether short-term instructional objectives are being achieved (*Federal Register*, 1977, Vol. 42, No. 163, p. 42491).

earliest "deficits" become the immediate short-term objectives. Given the difficulties associated with specifying objectives, criterion-referenced tests and reading, math, and language programs such as DISTAR (e.g., Engelmann & Bruner, 1969) and System FORE (Bell, 1972) are undeniably attractive to many professionals. These materials provide not only the procedures for teaching skills, but a simple way to specify objectives and procedures for evaluating whether the objectives have been met. In general, where there is pressure for explicit objectives and accountability, it is likely that programs designed with observable and easily measured objectives will be adopted.[4]

Two major examples related to special education are Meyen's Instructional Based Appraisal System or IBAS (Meyen, 1976) and Hewett's hierarchy of learning competence ("the ABC's of the IEP", Hewett & Taylor, 1980).[5] Each of these provides goals and short-term outcome objectives emphasizing measurable behaviors for use in planning and implementing both instruction and evaluation.

While intuitively appealing and quite pragmatic, behavioral and criterion-referenced objectives raise serious concerns. No one denies that formulation of objectives in this fashion clearly can guide planning of content, intervention procedures, and evaluation. No one denies that objectives should be stated in a way that guides intervention toward major aims and goals. No one denies that aspects of some major goals and aims can be appropriately stated as behavioral and criterion-referenced objectives and that such objectives greatly help simplify outcome evaluation. However, there is considerable concern that important facets

FOR EXAMPLE

INSTRUCTIONAL OBJECTIVES FOR EXCEPTIONAL CHILDREN

Hewett's (Hewett & Taylor, 1980) formulation of objectives begins with a conceptualization of six hierarchical levels of learning competence: attention level, response level, order level, exploratory level, social level, and mastery level.

Each of these levels is developed through three stages (A, B, C) with each stage or skill area moving progressively toward specific "functional" descriptions that can be used as short-term objectives.

Listed below, as an example, are the first and last of the specific objectives formulated for each stage of the attention level.

ATTENTION LEVEL
A. Vision and visual perceptual skills
    B. Vision
        C1. Able to identify familiar objects
        •
        •
        •
        C5. Able to read or write without the aid of optical or other visual enlarging devices
    B. Visual discrimination skills
        C1. Follows moving object with eyes
        •
        •
        •
        C11. Identifies look-alike words
    B. Visual memory skills
        C1. Select, match, and reproduce previously viewed shapes, designs, letters, and numbers from memory
        C2. Other _____
A. Hearing and auditory perceptual skills
    B. Hearing
        C1. Able to hear only noise-type sensations

---

[4]There is an indication that most of the major group achievement tests are developing objective referenced formats. This reflects a trend toward what is being called "objective referenced assessment."

[5]Both Meyen and Hewett present their lists of objectives within more comprehensive systems for planning and implementing instruction and evaluation. Meyen's system, for instance, encompasses six activities ranging from diagnostic worksheets through evaluation and referral formats. Each activity is associated with a printed format and several information banks, e.g., there are a total of 73 objectives for reading and 100 for math.

- •
- •
    C5. Able to hear most sounds without amplification
- B. Auditory discrimination skills
    C1. Matches environmental sounds
- •
- •
- •
    C12. Identifies and forms words that rhyme
- B. Auditory memory skills
    C1. Chooses from groups of sounds the one previously presented.
- •
- •
- •
    C6. Repeats numbers, letters or words backwards
- A. Task attention skills
- B. Task attention skills (visual)
    C1. Makes eye contact with task
- •
- •
    C6. Pays attention to relevant details of task
- B. Task attention skills (auditory)
    C1. Listens to teacher
- •
- •
    C3. Profits from instruction delivered verbally by teacher
- B. Retention
    C1. Has immediate accurate recall for what was presented in lesson
    C2. Can accurately recall what was presented in lesson over varying periods of time (e.g., several days, one week, etc.)

of major aims and goals cannot be stated in behavioral terms, and that there are facets of intervention that should not be guided by specific objectives.

More specifically, concern is not with the technical and pragmatic features of behavioral and criterion-referenced objectives—it centers on the nature of intervention prescriptions that overemphasize such objectives. Philosophically such prescriptions are seen as representing a model that is too mechanistic. Critics argue that it will not facilitate development of affective (attitudinal, value, motivational, creative) dimensions of humanity, that it will not, for example, help individuals realize their unique potential. In the case of learning and behavior problems, the concern is compounded because mechanistic approaches tend to ignore the importance of affective dimensions that may be crucial in unblocking learning and performance and expanding interests.

In Chapter 12, we explore the general nature of intended outcomes and offer an analysis of the problems involved in specifying objectives. At this point, we can simply note that, empirically, neither the long-term power nor the utility of behavioral objectives has been demonstrated. What appears potent and useful in the short run might appear so only because the complex nature of intervention processes and outcomes has been grossly oversimplified.

REMEDIAL PROCEDURES

Remedial and treatment programs for students with psychoeducational problems have many vivid features that differentiate them from regular developmental programs. For instance, special classes focus on problems and tend to have more staff and varied material and fewer students than regular classes. Lerner (1976) recognizes these differences in distinguishing "clinical" (remedial) teaching from regular teaching. She describes clinical teaching as a cycle of five ongo-

VIEWPOINT

STATING OBJECTIVES

If education is conceived of as shaping behavior, then it is possible, indeed appropriate, to think of teachers as behavioral engineers. If the process of education is designed exclusively to enable children to acquire behaviors whose forms are known in advance, then it is possible to develop product specifications, to use quality control standards, and to identify terminal behaviors which students are to possess after having been processed properly. In this view the task of the teacher is to use scientifically developed materials which reduce error and thus make [one's] task as a behavioral engineer more efficient. If the child is not interested in doing the task we set . . . , the teacher's problem is not to find out what [the child] is interested in but to motivate [the child]. By establishing the appropriate reinforcement schedule we can mold the child in the image identified previously. In this view, it is not crucial to distinguish between the process of education and the process of training. The process of education enables individuals to behave intelligently through the exercise of judgment in situations that demand reflection, appraisal, and choice among alternative courses of action. The process of training develops specific types of behavioral responses to specific stimuli or situations.

If, however, education is viewed as a form of experience that has something to do with the quality of an individual's life, if it involves helping the child learn to make authentic choices, choices that are a result of . . . reflection and which depend upon the exercise of free will, then the problem of educational objectives takes a different turn.

What I am arguing is that the problem of determining how educational objectives should be stated or used is not simply a question of technique but a question of value. The differences between individuals regarding the nature and the use of educational objectives spring from differences in their conceptions of education; under the rug of technique lies an image of [people].

Eisner (1969, pp. 7–8)

---

ing phases: diagnosis, planning, implementation, evaluation, and modification of diagnosis. This cycle repeats until the problem is ameliorated. It differs from regular teaching by being planned for an atypical person rather than for an entire class. The individual "may be taught within a group setting," according to Lerner (1981),

but, even so, clinical teaching implies that the teacher is fully aware of the individual student's learning style, interests, shortcomings and areas of strength, levels of development and tolerance in many areas, feelings, and adjustments to the world. With such knowledge, a clinical teaching plan that meets the needs of a particular child can be designed and implemented. An important aspect of clinical teaching is the skill in interpreting feedback information and the need for continuous decision making. (p. 125)

The bulk of the LD literature stresses content, outcomes, and general phases of intervention. Procedural matters, when presented, are described in specific and technical terms, often like cookbook recipes, rather than discussed with reference to underlying models, mechanisms, and principles.

Bateman (1967) recognized the need to categorize processes as well as content when she described "three approaches to diagnosis and educational planning for children with learning disabilities" (p. 215); that is, the etiological, diagnostic-remedial, and task analysis approaches. Hewett (1968) also recognized this need when he outlined three "strategies" used in selecting procedures and goals for problem students; that is, the psychodynamic-interpersonal, sensory-neurological, and behavior modification strategies. In their classifications, both Bateman and Hewett recognized that, in practice, the categories are not mutually exclusive or irreconcilable. With this in mind, Hewett proposed what he called a "developmental" strategy, and Bateman and her colleague, Haring, have suggested a category described as akin to "aptitude-treatment interaction" approaches (Haring & Bateman, 1977). All such categories reflect that different formal models for understanding the causes and correction of psychoeducational problems underlie intervention processes. The added fourth category in both instances reflects the increased recognition that procedural planning must account for individual differences.

In contrast to textbook categories, LD practitioners rarely limit themselves to one approach. Most are ready to use "anything that works" and would probably describe themselves as eclectic. Nevertheless, specific procedures do differ in important conceptual ways. From our perspective, one of the most important differences relates to the focus of change. Prevailing procedural models are oriented to changing persons. Alternatively, a minority view advocates procedures focused on interaction and environments as the object of change. Using both the prevailing and minority perspectives, remedial procedures are recategorized and analyzed below.

Person Models

Differences among models that emphasize change in the person can be highlighted by contrasting prevailing psychoeducational *procedural* orientations either as (1) therapy-oriented or (2) behavior-change oriented. Not surprisingly, those who have adopted the underlying abilities orientation to content and outcomes tend to pursue therapy-oriented procedures. Those who stress observable skills as outcomes logically tend to use behavior modification procedures.

Therapy. Therapy-oriented approaches appear to have their roots in medical, psychotherapeutic, and pedagogical concepts. These include the notions that prescriptions should be based on diagnostic testing designed to analyze psychoneurological and/or psychodynamic functioning and that ability training, therapeutic relationships, and structure will be key factors in treatment. For example, therapy-oriented approaches have tended to stress the need to assess dysfunctions and deficits related to the development of psychological processing and motor functioning. This emphasis is based on assumptions that dysfunctions and deficits are at the root of learning and behavior problems and that they need to be "remedied" to ameliorate these problems. Procedures for remediation usually have been developed and advocated by clinicians. (See Table 9–1 for references to clinicians who have developed popular remedial approaches.) Procedures are conceived as improving underlying abilities or helping the individual compensate for the lack of such abilities or both.

The conceptual underpinnings for using these procedures range from traditional learning principles, such as reinforcement theory, to psychotherapeutic concepts, such as rapport building, collaboration, and ego enhancement. Interveners who systematically apply traditional psychotherapeutic concepts and those who draw on recent cognitive research stress the importance of thoughts and feelings, including attitudes and motivation, in improving learning and behavior.

Behavior change. Approaches that emphasize behavior change are based on behavior modification concepts, particularly those associated with operant conditioning, cognitive behavior modification, and operationism. Such approaches emphasize that what is to be changed is some observable behavior. The process by which change is accomplished is systematic application of techniques derived from learning theory and experimental research, especially work related to operant and respondent conditioning, for example, shaping and desensitization. In general, the reason for insisting that the behavior changed must be observable is based on the belief that intervention effectiveness cannot be evaluated stringently unless more than one person can agree that the frequency, rate, intensity, duration, or pattern of behavior has been affected (e.g., Mahoney, 1974; O'Leary, 1972).

The major principles of behavior change stress that individuals learn because of environmental stimuli. Two general principles can be specified: (1) scheduling of reinforcement, which is seen as the way in which a reinforcer is made contingent upon a response, and (2) satiation and deprivation, which are seen as the ways to maximize the power of a reinforcer. Applying these principles, interveners manipulate events preceding or following behavior or both.

With reference to basic behavior modification procedures, O'Leary and O'Leary state "all such procedures can be viewed as concerted attempts either to increase or decrease behavior" (p. 26). However, "such a dichotomy is somewhat arbitrary, since certain procedures may be used to increase some behavior while on other occasions the same procedures may be used to decrease behavior" (p. 26). They categorize the following as procedures used to increase behavior: praise and approval, modeling, shaping, passive shaping, token reinforcement programs, programmed instruction, self-specification of contingencies, self-reinforcement, and establishing clear rules and directions. Procedures to decrease behavior are categorized as: extinction, reinforcing behavior incompatible with a de-

sired behavior, soft reprimands, time-out from reinforcement, relaxation, gradual presentation of fearful stimuli in vivo, desensitization, response cost, medication, self-instruction, and self-evaluation.

Hewett and Taylor (1980) discuss types and schedules of reinforcement in terms of four possible consequences, which can follow behavior in the classroom setting: "(1) giving children something they want, (2) taking away something children don't want, (3) taking away something children want, and (4) giving children something they don't want" (p. 112). In this context, six types of positive consequences are identified: acquisition of knowledge and skills, knowledge of results, social approval, multisensory stimulation and activity, task completion, and tangible rewards. Punishing consequences are categorized as response cost, time out, and overcorrection. While categorizing positive and negative consequences, many behaviorally oriented writers now emphasize that whether the consequence is positive or negative depends on the perspective of the recipient, not that of the intervener.

Recognition that "an individual responds —not to some *real* environment—but to a *perceived* environment" has led to what has been dubbed "cognitive behavior modification" (Mahoney, 1974, p. 5). Cognitive behaviorists focus on identifying and controlling significant mediating behaviors, including thoughts and feelings. Mahoney (1974) categorizes cognitive behavioral interventions as (1) covert conditioning therapies (e.g., covert counterconditioning, thought stopping, coverant control, covert desensitization, reinforcement, extinction, and modeling) and (2) cognitive therapies (e.g., coping, skills training, and problem solving).

Commonalities and criticisms. Historically, behavioral approaches have been applied normatively, without regard to assessment of individuals, as in the use of token economies. In contrast, therapy approaches have tended to emphasize individual testing for prescriptive purposes, implying that intervention procedures are keyed to individual differences. However, given that the decision to administer "diagnostic" tests tends to reflect a practitioner's orientation, therapy approaches often are applied in as normative a fashion as behavioral approaches. An example of this occurs when all clients receive visual perception training or are taught to read using multisensory techniques.

Currently, both types of approaches use assessment for specific planning, but, as discussed earlier, they rely on different assessment procedures. Both use specialized techniques and materials—often the same ones— but different explanatory mechanisms in interpreting why the technique was chosen and why it "works." Both sets of approaches might emphasize techniques involving the simultaneous use of several sensory modalities (auditory, visual, tactile, kinesthetic) in learning vocabulary words. A therapy-oriented intervener might claim learners need multisensory inputs whenever there is a specific sensory modality preference or weakness. A behaviorist might explain the technique's worth in terms of its ability to make cues more vivid and because the procedures associated with the technique provide explicit directions, systematic practice, and immediate feedback on performance.

Both procedural orientations have relied on models of developmental stages and skill hierarchies. They have been criticized by those who question the validity of such models, for example, whether remediation is needed with reference to certain stages and skills hypothesized as necessary prerequisites for learning academic skills, such as reading and math (e.g., Goodman & Hammill, 1973; Hammill, Goodman, & Wiederholt, 1974; Keogh, 1974; Kleisius, 1972; Mann & Phillips, 1971; Newcomer, Hare, Hammill, & McGettigan, 1974; Sabatino, 1973; Sedlack & Weener, 1973).

Neither type of approach favors a particular administrative arrangement for providing services. Both can be seen as favoring a range of interveners and procedures that can provide the least intervention needed. As discussed in Chapter 7, this has become an administrative matter of whether a problem is to be dealt with in, or outside of, the "mainstream." (When is an individual to be removed to a special setting for help?)

In summary, therapy-oriented approaches explain the need for certain procedures in terms of the presence of individual predilections and problems, such as modality preferences and perceptual-motor deficits, assumed to require use of specialized remedial strategies. In contrast, approaches oriented toward behavior change explain all procedures in terms of normative behavioral principles; that is, therapy approaches assume remedial procedures are special, implying that different principles underlie these procedures than underlie those used with persons who have no problems. Behavioral approaches make no such assumptions, but do claim that systematic application of behavior modification procedures is critical in remediation. Both sets of approaches have been criticized for overrelying on inadequate models of human development, learning, and motivation.

Environment and Interaction Models

Since Part 4 is devoted to a presentation of those facets of our work that are based on interactional and environment-change models, our purpose in this section is simply to draw attention to the nature of these orientations and approaches. At the outset, it should be noted that, because behavior-change models stress manipulating environmental variables, they often are confused with the type of environment-change models discussed here. Consequently, it is important to reemphasize that the purpose of *behavior-change models* in altering the environment is to *change* individuals; the intent of *environment-change models* is to accommodate individual differences (see Figure 8-1).

Changing the environment. As we have discussed throughout this book, there are several levels of intervention with regard to the environment. Secondary and tertiary environmental levels, such as sociopolitical perspectives and policies, are crucial. Relevant procedures in this context are those of social and political action and are discussed in Parts 4 and 5. At this point, discussion is limited to procedures affecting the primary environment (e.g., home and classroom) since these are the ones stressed in the remediation and therapy literature (e.g., Muñoz, Snowden, & Kelly, 1979).

Four nonmutually exclusive ways in which persons with learning and behavior problems are accommodated by changes in the environment are (1) rearrangement of physical and social environment variables, (2) individualized intervention, (3) personalized intervention, and (4) introduction of special services.

1. Rearrangements of physical and social environments are common to all psychoeducational interventions. They represent a major area of overlap between efforts to change persons and intentions to accommodate individual differences.

   Physical rearrangements encompass ways the setting is furnished and equipped, including architectural design and decor (Holahan, 1979). Variables include crowding, proximity, privacy, distractions, access, traffic patterns, visibility, types and range of work space and materiel, cleanliness and aesthetic features, and so forth.

   Social environment variables that might be rearranged can be categorized as the personal and behavioral characteristics of the milieu inhabitants, numbers in the setting, and standards for interpersonal contact. Specific exam-

FOR EXAMPLE

DISRUPTIVE CLASSROOM BEHAVIOR: AN ENVIRONMENTAL ALTERNATIVE TO BEHAVIORAL AND PSYCHOPHARMA-COLOGICAL MANAGEMENT

Some student behaviors viewed as problematic within the context of the classroom are not inherently undesirable. For example, physical abuse of other children would be considered undesirable irrespective of context. In contrast, talking to peers is an important socialization skill and yet may be viewed negatively in a structured classroom environment.

[We describe] a classroom intervention which recognizes two distinct goals: (1) elimination of inherently problematic behaviors, and (2) accommodation to other behaviors which are labeled, yet not intrinsically, problematic. . . . [Our] basic premise . . . is that efforts to modify the setting should precede efforts to modify children's behavior whenever possible and especially in cases where the behavior could be viewed positively in other contexts. An environmental intervention avoids the negative labeling consequences of individually focused interventions.

This study was conducted in a classroom for children identified as having learning or behavior problems. The classroom was organized around five activity centers as well as individual student desks. Students were free to move between activity centers according to their individualized study plans.

Pre-intervention observations through a one-way mirror and a series of teacher consultations permitted identification of structural variables that appeared to maximize the disruptive consequences of some student behaviors.

In particular, the teacher reported greatest

ples are sex, age, social class, ethnic status, and behavior groupings, intervener-client ratios, and milieu rules as these matters relate to support, guidance, crowding, noise, disruption, and so forth.

difficulty working with students during the period just before lunch when half of the students were returning from physical education. As you can imagine this period was characterized by considerable student restlessness, compounded by the boisterousness and high energy of the students entering the class from an outdoor playing field where running and yelling were appropriate behaviors.

After observation, we recognized that task centers compatible with the state of these returning students were poorly located. The teacher had struggled with various ways of calming these students. We proposed as an alternative to structurally rearrange the classroom by placing activity centers for which a high level of student energy and camaraderie were appropriate—such as arts and crafts—near the entrance of the classroom so that re-entering students could quickly get involved in learning tasks compatible with their energy. . . .

The intervention involved rearranging the classroom task centers and furniture to change traffic flow patterns and the physical proximity of preferred activities. The purposes of the intervention were to (1) increase task involvement, (2) decrease aggressive behavior, and (3) alter the disruptive consequences of student movement in the classroom while allowing the frequency of movement to remain the same. Behavioral observations were made pre- and post-intervention over a one-month period to record the frequencies of four relevant behaviors. Two of these target behaviors—disrupting other students and being disrupted—were considered undesirable irrespective of situational context and we therefore hoped to decrease their frequency. One target behavior —task involvement—was considered positive and we hoped to increase its frequency. The fourth target behavior—gross movement—was considered inherently neutral and we expected its frequency would remain the same while we hoped the disruptive consequences of such behavior would decrease. . . .

In general, our measures indicated behavior change in the desired directions; that is, task involvement increased, disruptive behavior decreased, and frequency of movement within the classroom remained the same while having fewer disruptive consequences. . . .

The present study represents both a conceptual and pragmatic alternative to traditional methods of managing disruptive classroom behavior. It extends the conceptual framework of intervention from a focus on person variables to a consideration of person-environment interaction variables. As a consequence of relocating the site of treatment from the individual to the environment, the stigmatizing effects of labeling are avoided. Consideration of environmental factors also broadens the definition of "treatment"—to include accommodation of behavior in addition to behavior change. Furthermore, compared with the more traditional approaches applied to this population, this study was cost efficient in terms of both professional time and material resources needed."

Rook, Padesky, and Compas (1979, pp. 2–5)

In general, rearrangement of physical and social environments potentially can have a major impact on whether an environment creates problems or appropriately accommodates those who use it, for example, when physical environments are rearranged to accommodate handicapping conditions, such as when ramps are provided for those in wheelchairs. Two other examples are redesigning classrooms so that children, especially those who tend to be very active and gregarious, can do their work and move about with reduced probability of distracting others, and grouping individuals who can work appropriately together.

2. The term *individualized intervention* describes efforts to design intervention procedures to accommodate the *developmental* functioning of specific clients. The importance of accounting for individual differences in rate and amount of performance and progress typically is considered. A wide range of differences in quality of performance and stylistic ways of approaching tasks and activities also may be allowed. In addition to rearrangement of physical and social environments—and, if needed, special services—prominent examples of individualization include stocking classrooms with a wide range of graduated and programmed materials and audio-visual devices, and providing for self-pacing and specific feedback.

3. The term *personalized intervention* is used here to differentiate efforts to accommodate *developmental* functioning from approaches that attempt systematically to accommodate individual differences in both *motivation and development*. Personalized intervention encompasses and expands the notion of individualized intervention. The importance of systematically accounting for extrinsic and intrinsic motivation is discussed in detail in Chapter 10. In brief, besides the procedures described above, personalized interventions attempt to accommodate and build upon a wide range of interests, desires, and expectations and to provide opportunities for a wide range of satisfactions.

4. Special services include provision for intervention in special settings (such as special classrooms, home, and hospital), special administrative groupings for all or part of the intervention, and addi-

tional professional and paraprofessional personnel as supplementary resources to add enrichment opportunities and appropriately accommodate extreme individual differences. Several models outline the range of special services and propose ways such services might be provided in keeping with the principle of least intervention needed discussed in Chapter 5 (see Chaffin, 1975; Deno, 1970; Dunn, 1973; McCarthy, 1973; Reynolds, 1962; and Schworm, 1976).

Reciprocal change. Interactional or transactional models related to learning and behavior problems have been gaining acceptance in recent years (Apter, 1982). The influence of community, environmental, and transactional psychologists and of the ecology movement are reflected in this trend (Adelman, 1971; Cowen, Gardener, & Zax, 1967; Lewis, 1967; Rhodes, 1967; 1970). However, in some cases, terms such as *ecological* and *ecosystem models* are used to encompass procedures involving no more than modifying environments to accommodate bothersome behavior. Some even misuse such terms to describe environmental manipulations designed to change individuals. Reciprocal change models are more appropriately viewed as referring to approaches that stress transactional procedures and mutual accommodation; that is, the approaches encompass a series of reciprocal person-change and environment-change procedures. In everyday experience, this is exemplified when each of us makes allowances for a particular characteristic of a friend (such as someone who, we think, uses profanity excessively) and have allowances made for us by that friend (such as when we are repeatedly late for appointments). In a classroom, teachers and students make many such informal mutual accommodations, but also often agree on formal compromises. For instance, a teacher may offer not to lower grades for spelling and punctuation errors if the student will write longer papers. On an ongoing basis, a teacher and student engaged in an activity should modify each step based on reciprocal feedback.

TEACHER: Let's pick up in reading where we left off yesterday.

STUDENT: I really don't like this book.

TEACHER: Well, let's look for one that interests you.

STUDENT: I have a book at home on animals that I'd like to read.

TEACHER: Bring it in tomorrow. Also, let me show you some of the books on animals we have here at school.

The substantive and complex nature of such transactions can hardly be captured by simple examples. However, mutual reassessments and accommodations clearly are the heart of interactional models, as we will discuss in Part 4.

CONCLUDING COMMENTS

The LD field has grown rapidly. In many ways, the prevailing orientations have been useful frames of reference for both research and practice. While useful, however, they are not sufficient. The status quo must be understood and that understanding must be used as a springboard for change, but not change for the sake of change, and not simply more growth. What is needed now is a transformation of major proportions, such as is occurring currently in the field of psychology. It is time to consider new concepts, develop new frames of reference, and explore new approaches.

Chapter 10

Motivation: A Key Concept

Philip Jackson (1968) asked a group of elementary school teachers who were rated as outstanding how they judged when they were teaching effectively. Unlike most educational researchers, who would seek objective evidence of student learning or cognitive development, these teachers said they used evidence of motivation—signs of student interest during lessons and of interest that endured beyond lessons.

I argue that we would do well to follow these teachers and acknowledge optimum student motivation as a justifiable educational goal. . . . When any children are not optimally motivated, we are making less than desirable progress.

Nicholls (1979, p. 1071)

There is no way to know what people are capable of unless they want to show us their best. If a person is motivated to learn something, he or she often can do much more than anyone would have thought possible. Conversely, if a person is not interested in learning something, levels of performance may be no indication of ability (Adelman & Chaney, 1982; Haines & Torgensen, 1979). Teachers and parents commonly lament that a child could do much more *if only the child wanted to.* In many test situations involving measures of achievement, intelligence, and perceptual motor or language functioning, it is assumed that the scores represent actual capabilities, an assumption that is wrong when individuals are not motivated to capacity performance.

From a motivational perspective, the first question one needs to ask in planning interventions for school learning problems is, Does the student want to learn? If the answer is no, the student probably will not want to engage in learning activities, and it becomes almost inconsequential whether he or she has the capability. While the teacher and others may view the situations and tasks as worthwhile and as something the student can do, such perceptions may be irrelevant to facilitating learning.

For those who understand that motivation is the key to effective learning, the prevailing dilemma is, How does one *tap into* such motivation in the classroom? We emphasize the phrase *tap into* because we start with the assumption that students come to school motivated in some areas—things they want to know more about, activities they like to do because they produce feelings of competence and self-determination.

The above concerns are of tremendous importance in terms of intervention processes and outcomes. However, one probably would not arrive at this conclusion based on a review of the prevailing LD literature.

MOTIVATION AND LD LITERATURE

A significant body of psychological literature that discusses extrinsic and intrinsic motivation as an important influence on behavior has major implications for understanding learning and learning problems. But motivation—especially intrinsic motivation—virtually has been ignored by the LD field, which is apparent from the lack of discussion of the construct in basic LD textbooks and the dearth of empirical and conceptual papers discussing motivation in connection with learning problems. Why has the construct been ignored by the field? One probable reason is that widely accepted definitions of learning disabilities stress that such problems are developmental and are related to central nervous system dysfunctioning. The thrust of the first works specifically dealing with learning disorders or disabilities was therefore on developmental concepts in discussing etiology, diagnosis, and treatment.

A second probable reason the construct of motivation has been relatively ignored by the LD field stems from the popularity of behavior modification techniques in the 1960s and 1970s. As professionals set out to apply what early textbooks advocated, it became clear that identifying a child's problem as developmental did not eliminate the fact that many children with learning problems also manifested behavior problems. The need to deal with behavior problems, regardless of whether they were a cause or result or were independent of the learning problems, led to widespread adoption of *behavior control* techniques. For those who viewed classroom management and behavioral control as a function of contemporary reinforcement contingencies, the construct of motivation seemed unnecessary.

Given the dominance of developmental and behaviorist perspectives, it is not surprising that the LD literature rarely discusses motivation in any systematic detail and almost completely ignores the concept of intrinsic motivation. This state of affairs, of course, is not unique to the LD field. Motivation, particularly intrinsic motivation, has only slowly come to the forefront of scientific and practical inquiry in psychology over the past twenty-five years. Currently, there is increasing recognition among psychologists of the role of thoughts and feelings in affecting motivation and thus behavior.[1]

Efforts to highlight the importance of motivation for psychoeducational intervention have stressed the concept of intrinsic motivation and the relevance of theories that suggest thoughts and feelings can be de-

---

[1]Historical perspectives related to the increasing interest in cognitive approaches to motivation are offered in Deci (1975), Hunt (1965, 1971), Mahoney (1974), and Weiner (1972, 1980).

VIEWPOINT

THE WILL TO LEARN

The will to learn is an intrinsic motive, one that finds both its source and its reward in its own exercise. The will to learn becomes a "problem" only under specialized circumstances like those of a school, where a curriculum is set, students confined, and a path fixed. The problem exists not so much in learning itself, but in the fact that what the school imposes often fails to enlist the natural energies that sustain spontaneous learning—curiosity, a desire for competence, aspiration to emulate a model, and a deep-sensed commitment to the web of social reciprocity.

Bruner (1966, p. 127)

MOTIVATIONAL READINESS

There are those who see no alternative between forcing the child from without, or leaving [the child] entirely alone. Seeing no alternative, some choose one mode, some another. Both fall into the same fundamental error. Both fail to see that development is a definite process, having its own law which can be fulfilled only when adequate conditions are provided.

Dewey (1902, p. 17)

terminers of behavior (Ruble & Boggiano, 1980). The purpose of Chapter 10 is to build on these efforts in highlighting the topic of motivation and the crucial role it plays in learning and learning problems.

INTRINSIC AND EXTRINSIC MOTIVATION

Why is it that someone thinks and behaves as he or she does? This is the conceptual problem the study of motivation attempts to solve; the problem can be further divided into components: How does behavior get initiated? energized? directed? maintained? terminated? A related motivational question

of particular importance to learning and performance is, How is the probability increased that the behavior will be pursued in the future?

Theorists attempting to answer these questions have found it necessary to distinguish between extrinsic and intrinsic motivation. Extrinsics include both physical and social reinforcers such as material rewards, praise, physical punishment, censure, and so forth. The motivational qualities of extrinsics are seen to arise from establishing causal connections between the extrinsics and behavior; that is, a person's behavior is assumed to be shaped by the way positive and negative reinforcers are related to the behavior, for example, positive reinforcers following a given behavior should increase the likelihood that the behavior will be repeated. Thus, a child's current behavior is viewed as fully determined by his or her reinforcement history and current contingencies (within obvious biological limits). Changes in behavior are seen as best accomplished by systematically manipulating current environmental contingencies, including scheduling positive reinforcers, threatening loss of positive reinforcers, or administering negative consequences (see Chapter 9).

Because of the prevalence of programs emphasizing extrinsics in the LD field, the following points are worth noting. In general, it is clear that extrinsic rewards will increase the likelihood of a response and even improve performance under some circumstances. As Bruner (1966) has stated, however,

External reinforcement may indeed get a particular act going and may lead to its repetition, but it does not nourish, reliability, the long course of learning by which [one] slowly builds in [one's] own way a serviceable model of what the world is and what it can be. (p. 128)

Extrinsic rewards are complex phenomena and produce complex effects. As Deci (1975) points out:

Every reward (including feedback) has two aspects, a controlling aspect and an informational aspect which provides the recipient with information about his [or her] competence and self-determination. . . . If the controlling aspect is more salient, it will initiate the change in perceived locus of causality. . . . If the informational aspect is more salient, the change [will be initiated] in feelings of competence and self-determination. . . . (p. 142)

A generous interpretation of the literature on engineered and token reward approaches to learning problems suggests that such programs reduce disruptive behavior and increase orienting behaviors toward tasks while the youngsters are in the programs. When the tasks have involved rote learning or memorization, task improvement has been found (e.g., O'Leary & Drabman, 1971). Critics point out, however, that improvements in behavior have not been found to generalize in the ways desired. There also is widespread concern that the objectives of such programs, as practiced, seem limited to controlling behavior rather than to educating children in terms of developing cognitive structures, problem-solving abilities, and intrinsic motivation (Bruner, 1966; Illich, 1970; Robinson, 1974; Schrag & Divoky, 1975; Silberman, 1970).

Intrinsic motivation includes the psychological concepts of curiosity, striving for competence and self-determination, pursuing a positive affect such as happiness, and avoiding a negative affect such as anxiety. These cognitive and affective constructs are reflected in formal definitions of intrinsic motivation. For example, Deci (1975) proposes that intrinsically motivated behaviors are those in which a person engages to feel competent and self-determining. They are of two general kinds: (1) the seeking of stimulation and (2) the conquering of challenges or reducing incongruity or dissonance. Deci stresses that feelings of competence and self-determination are primary needs of human beings and suggests such needs are met by engaging in *seeking* and *conquering* be-

FOR EXAMPLE

STUDENT MOTIVATION

I'll try to achieve more. I'm going to try to get out of school as soon as possible. I'm going to try to give it everything I've got: that's all I got. Since the end of last year, I think I want to learn more. I have more of a craving since last year.
Richard

haviors, for example, seeking out optimal stimulation (challenges) and dealing effectively with the challenges created or encountered, thus reducing incongruity, uncertainty, or dissonance, and so forth. These primary needs are viewed as innate; all humans are assumed to be "born with the basic and undifferentiated need for feeling competent and self-determining" and "active organisms in continual interaction with their environment" (p. 65).

Such cognitive-affective approaches to motivation assume that individuals act on their environments rather than being passively controlled by previous reinforcers and current environmental contingencies. A cognitive-affective, as contrasted with a mechanistic, approach to explaining behavior, introduced in Chapter 2, is discussed in several basic works (de Charms, 1968; de Charms & Muir, 1978; Deci, 1975, 1980; Hunt, 1965, 1971; Skinner, 1971; Staw, 1975; Weiner, 1980). For our purposes here, it is sufficient to recognize that cognitive-affective approaches assume that thoughts and feelings play a primary role as *determiners* of behavior. This proposition, of course, like the opposite assumption which underlies behavioristic approaches, is not testable. It is a philosophical proposition about the basic nature of people, which science can neither prove nor disprove (e.g., Matson, 1973; Skinner, 1971). At its core, this assumption views people as having the ability to choose.

Applying a cognitive-affective orientation

to the study of human motivation, especially related to children's learning and learning problems, raises a number of more specific questions: How does the way children perceive and think about a learning situation (e.g., tasks, materials, teacher, classroom) affect their learning and performance? How do children's views of the causes of their problems (or for that matter a teacher's or parent's views of such causes) affect learning and performance? How do students' perceptions of choice in the classroom affect learning and performance? These questions assume that the child's perceptions and thoughts play a key role, and thus that significant aspects of his or her behavior are determined by factors in the child. In a discussion of motivation, then, theories about the relationship of cognitions, affect, and motivation are of central importance, and specific information about an individual's thoughts and feelings are indispensable in understanding his or her behavior.

INTRINSIC VERSUS EXTRINSIC MOTIVATION

A commonly held assumption in education is that intrinsic and extrinsic motivation complement each other. If a child is interested in reading and the teacher gives a gold star for each completed book, it is believed the interest in reading will increase. While this assumption has been used to shape psychoeducational programs for years, current research suggests that the two are not complementary; their interaction is so complex that at times the use of extrinsics may decrease intrinsic motivation.

With regard to the relationship between intrinsic and extrinsic motivation, Weiner (1980) states:

> Perhaps the most well-documented findings in the psychological literature is that pairing a behavior with a reward increases the likelihood that the behavior subsequently will be repeated. This principle of reinforcement was first articulated by Thorndike and later was elaborated in Skinnerian behaviorism. . . . However, there are data that call into question the all-powerful reward principle. For example, Atkinson's theory of achievement motivation and the empirical findings concerning the consequences of success and failure clearly demonstrate that persons desire intermediate risk. Hence, success (a reward) at an easy task should not augment the probability of undertaking the task again. . . . Consistent with the data questioning the positive effects of reward, there is a growing literature documenting that children with initial interest in a task (intrinsic motivation) lose some of that interest when an external reward (extrinsic motivation) is promised for performing that task (Deci, 1975). Stated somewhat differently, when a goal becomes construed as only a means to an end, then that goal loses some of its value (Kruglanski, 1975). (p. 257)

The literature on the negative relationship between extrinsic rewards and intrinsic motivation is extensive. What has been most emphasized by reviewers (Deci, 1975; Lepper & Greene, 1978; Levine & Fasnacht, 1974; Notz, 1975) is that use of extrinsic rewards may (a) produce only token learning and (b) mask and undermine a student's intrinsic motivation. Conversely, it has been suggested that insufficient extrinsic rewards may increase intrinsic motivation (Deci, 1975).

Research related to cognitive dissonance theory (Festinger, 1957), inequity theory (Adams, 1965), and cognitive evaluation theory (Deci, 1975) emphasizes the role played by a person's perceptions of personal causality and personal responsibility (e.g., self-determination, choice) in enhancing and diminishing intrinsic motivation. For example, intrinsic motivation is seen as enhanced when a person feels personally responsible for a consequence. Conversely, intrinsic motivation is seen as negatively affected when persons feel they do not have choice and thus have no sense of personal responsibility for consequences.

Not only are intrinsic and extrinsic moti-

VIEWPOINT

THE "BENEFITS" OF BRIBERY

In a little Southern town where the Klan was riding again, a Jewish tailor had the temerity to open his little shop on the main street. To drive him out of the town the Kleagle of the Klan set a gang of little ragamuffins to annoy him. Day after day they stood at the entrance of his shop. "Jew! Jew!," they hooted at him. The situation looked serious for the tailor. He took the matter so much to heart that he began to brood and spent sleepless nights over it. Finally out of desperation he evolved a plan.

The following day, when the little hoodlums came to jeer at him, he came to the door and said to them, "From today on any boy who calls me "Jew" will get a dime from me." Then he put his hand in his pocket and gave each boy a dime.

Delighted with their booty, the boys came back the following day and began to shrill, "Jew! Jew!" The tailor came out smiling. He put his hand in his pocket and gave each of the boys a nickel, saying, "A dime is too much—I can only afford a nickel today." The boys went away satisfied because, after all, a nickel was money, too.

However, when they returned the next day to hoot at him, the tailor gave them only a penny each.

"Why do we get only a penny today?" they yelled.

"That's all I can afford."

"But two days ago you gave us a dime, and yesterday we got a nickel. It's not fair, mister."

"Take it or leave it. That's all you're going to get."

"Do you think we're going to call you "Jew" for one lousy penny?"

"So don't."

And they didn't.

Ausubel (1948, pp. 440-41)

---

vation seen as nonadditive, they are viewed as motivating behaviors toward different goals (e.g., Calder & Staw, 1975; Deci, 1975; Notz, 1975). For example, because of overreliance on rewards and punishments, learning in school often becomes directed toward getting rewards, (e.g., stars, grades, diplomas). Indeed, learning frequently gets redefined as something that gets rewards. Thus, activities originally involving an internal locus of causality become externally oriented. In contrast, Bruner (1962) suggests

to the degree that one is able to approach learning as a task of discovering something rather than "learning about" it, to that degree there will be a tendency for the child to work with the autonomy of self-reward or, more properly, be rewarded by discovery itself. (p. 88)

Bruner represents a long list of psychologists who emphasize the importance of providing school learning opportunities that capitalize on intrinsic motivation and thus maintain and enhance motivation of behavior directed toward learning for its own sake.

Finally, we should note that not only rewards, but the very act of "surveillance," may negatively affect motivation (e.g., Lepper & Greene, 1975). For example, research by Kipnis (1972), Kruglanski (1970), and Strickland (1958) suggests an attributional cycle in which surveillance first produces a sense of distrust, which, in turn, produces further surveillance. The objects of surveillance may think surveillance is an indication that they are performing poorly (i.e., negative reinforcement), resulting in the concomitant effects of such perceptions (Lepper & Greene, 1975). A separate line of investigation focuses on the contrasting reinforcing effects of surveillance on those with and without learning problems (Adelman, 1969).

In general, along with whatever degree of skill students acquire, overreliance on extrinsics may also result in students acquiring a pronounced distaste for that particular area of learning. The use of extrinsics often is justified by equating skill building with tasks that must be done whether or not they are liked, for example, unrewarding jobs or chores. Such comparisons are misleading. Unfortunately, many students and teachers are led to equate learning opportunities with drudgery and to de-emphasize the potential role of intrinsic motivation, which may then be diminished. Reinforcements that lead to memorizing vocabulary words, for example, not only may fail to sustain interest in reading, but may reduce intrinsic motivation or increase disliking for reading, a large price to pay for an expanded vocabulary. For every person for whom the strategy of using extrinsics seems to have worked, there appear to be a great number of others for whom it may have produced negative consequences, for example, those who learn to add, subtract, multiply, and divide, but fear and hate math. Moreover, it is doubtful that those who have become very skillful in reading, math, or playing a musical instrument went through the many hours of practice needed to develop such skills simply because they were extrinsically rewarded or threatened with punishment.[2]

IMPLICATIONS FOR LEARNING PROBLEMS

An understanding of the cognitive-affective view of motivation outlined above further broadens perspectives about learning problems. The following discussion explores (1) motivational factors that can cause learning problems, (2) the impact of low or negative motivation on assessment, and (3) the role of motivation in correcting learning problems.

Motivational Factors as a Cause of Learning Problems

In Chapter 2, we examined how learning problems can result from a poor match between a child's level of development and the demands of the school setting. The longer the child is confronted with these conditions, or the more the failure is made salient, the greater the likelihood of a negative motivational impact on future learning and performance.[3]

Learning problems also may stem directly from a poor match between the child's level of intrinsic motivation and the demands of the school setting. From this perspective, a child's level of intrinsic motivation in school learning is viewed as a particularly important determinant of learning and performance. If a child has a low level of intrinsic motivation in a specific area such as reading or math for whatever reasons, that child is unlikely to

---

[2]The above examples can be contrasted with situations where an extrinsic reward is used briefly to elicit a behavior so that an individual can become aware of interest in the area. Such a brief use of rewards can be conceptualized as a process by which an activity is made salient by capitalizing on the informational aspects of rewards. According to cognitive evaluation theory (Deci, 1975, 1980) information about learning and performance (e.g., feedback about success and failure) can strengthen intrinsic motivation, while rewards which are controlling (not perceived only as information) can have a negative effect on such motivation.

[3]Such youngsters often are characterized as having poor self-concept and low self-esteem. Recent theories have argued that such youngsters come to perceive themselves as having little or no control over certain situations and outcomes. They are described as having an external locus of control (Crandall, 1967), making external attributions of cause (Weiner, 1974), or as experiencing learned helplessness (Dweck and Goetz, 1978). That failure has a negative impact on motivation and on perceptions of personal competence and control is not a controversial point. However, explanations for these effects, which hypothesize stable dispositions within persons such as external locus of control and learned helplessness, are quite controversial. The notion of learned helplessness, in particular, seems to be an inappropriate model for all but the most extreme psychoeducational problems, and even then, only for those who have almost completely stopped coping with learning tasks.

VIEWPOINT

INTRINSIC v. EXTRINSIC MOTIVATION

The "undermining" effect of extrinsic reward appears to be a robust and a powerful phenomenon. The implications of such a finding for the practices of teachers in the classroom, behavior modification procedures, and even for business management are staggering.
Weiner (1980, p. 259)

CONTINUING MOTIVATION

It may well be that it is equally important, if not more so, for the school to foster the continued willingness of students to learn than it is to insure the fact that they have learned some particular things at a certain point in time.
Maehr (1976, p. 444)

direct behavior toward performing in that area and may direct behavior away from it.

What produces a low level of intrinsic motivation? Cognitive evaluation theory (Deci, 1975) suggests that such areas as reading may be perceived by a child as not potentially satisfying. This would be the case, for example, if the child perceives an area or activity as unable to fulfill the need for feeling competent and self-determining, and especially when a stimulus is also associated with a negative affect such as anxiety.

If there is no awareness of potential satisfaction related to activities, it is unlikely that behaviors will be directed toward achieving goals associated with such activities. Thus, skill in performing these activities is unlikely to increase very quickly. This is not to say that no development will occur; after all, there is great overlap in the skills involved in the variety of tasks a child encounters daily, both in and out of school.

Finally, as discussed above, it is hypothesized that using extrinsic rewards often in-

terferes with learning. That is, when learning is dependent upon rewards, students may focus primarily on getting the reward in the easiest way (Deci, 1975). The more salient the extrinsic factor, the more likely the interference with learning (Ross, 1975). One major exception related to this appears to be if "rewards" are perceived as an indication of competence (Deci, 1971; Karniol & Ross, 1977; Swann & Pittmann, 1977). However, even this exception seems to depend on the developmental level of the child (Boggiano & Ruble, 1979; Ruble & Boggiano, 1980).

Environmental variables can affect a person's motivation in ways that result in learning problems. This may occur whenever there are insufficient opportunities for a person to behave in ways that produce feelings of competence and self-determination. In this connection, an environment may be (1) passive, for example, simply not offering opportunities, (2) subtly undermining, for example, overemphasizing extrinsics, or (3) actively hostile, for example, making demands which the person is expected to meet, but is unlikely to want or be able to fulfill at the time the demands are made. Such circumstances interact with person variables including, but not limited to, any major developmental deficits and disorders. This interaction generally produces thoughts, feelings, and overt actions incompatible with accomplishment of long-range educational aims (e.g., Bandura, 1978, 1982).

Impact of Motivation on Assessment

As with etiology, the implications of motivational factors must be recognized in assessment. Despite the intriguing patterns that can be charted using test data, the findings may not allow for valid interpretations if the performance is not motivated. For example, procedures have not yet been found for validly identifying whether the cause of a youngster's uneven performance is due to minimal neurological dysfunctions interfering with development of certain skills or low motivation and lack of opportunity, which kept the youngster from putting in the time and effort needed to learn and practice many of the skills assessed.

More specifically, it is likely that the cumulative performance of many children (e.g., the total IQ score) is diminished because of the long-term impact of reduced motivation. Furthermore, it is suggested that unevenness in the performance of some children with learning problems is due to motivational factors. Such children will perform poorly in areas where motivation is low, but may perform comparatively well in areas where motivation and thus development is positive. The more complex the area being assessed, such as reading or intelligence, the more likely that specific facets of the child's performance will be relatively good when the items sample general skills developed as part of natural and motivating life experiences.

Of course, areas of relative strength only can be assessed if the youngster is highly motivated to perform well in the assessment situation. How to determine whether this is the case, unfortunately, is by no means simple.

When a youngster refuses to do a task, the motivational problem is evident and performance findings can be judged accordingly. However, when a child does the work, it is extremely difficult to judge whether the behavior is directed toward performing up to fullest capabilities or toward simply satisfying what appear to be the technical requirements of the situation, for example, giving a "reasonable" response, putting out "reasonable" effort, and "going through the motions."

Bruner (1966) has suggested that many children who have had problems in school are motivated to learn a variety of defensive coping strategies for dealing with the demands of adults. Many of these strategies are incompatible with performing at one's full-

est capabilities. Thus, it is likely that efforts to assess such children will overidentify deficits: many skills the youngster has in fact developed will appear undeveloped as assessed by test/task performance. Such performances can result in prescriptions for unnecessary instruction.

A related concern arises: will children who have had problems in school come to perceive most test-like tasks and situations as threatening and expect to do poorly? If so, they may value the tasks and situations, but they may perceive them as beyond their control and therefore not be motivated to put forth their best effort. Conversely, they might perform closer to their capabilities whenever tasks are perceived as within their control (Lefcourt, 1976; Weiner, 1974). Studies by Lefcourt (1967) and Taub and Dollinger (1975) do suggest that some of the avoidance behavior of persons who perceive task performance as beyond their control might be eliminated by providing explicit information about the task's purpose and methods for doing it successfully.

Role of Motivation in Correcting Learning Problems

Whether perceptions of lack of competence and control are accurate, they seem to affect motivation and performance (e.g., Stipek & Weisz, 1981). As long as a person does not intrinsically value and expect to succeed in pursuing a learning activity, one can expect to see learning and performance that is less than optimal. These motivational considerations are often discussed, but they are almost systematically ignored in assessing and treating learning disabilities.

Optimal performance and learning requires motivational readiness. However, such readiness should not be viewed in the old sense of waiting until an individual is interested. It should be understood in the contemporary sense of offering stimulating environments that can be perceived by stu-

VIEWPOINT

OPTIMIZING MOTIVATION
IN AN ACHIEVEMENT CONTEXT

What do the various theoretical formulations, separately or together, tell us about the processes which optimize the motivational aspect of performance in achievement situations? Are there several variables or a constellation of factors that provide guidance for decisions regarding educational programs? On at least a surface level there seems to be considerable agreement across theories about what are the major determinants of achievement orientation. Every model contains, explicitly or implicitly, three factors: (1) individual differences, (2) expectations or probability of success and (3) incentive values of outcomes. Although the specific relationship among these factors varies across models, their universal presence is worth noting. . . .

Specifically, individuals are seen to differ in their cognitions or self-perceptions in achievement situations. Thus, optimization can be affected not only by means of modifying situational factors to suit individual perceptions but also by modifying cognitions about the self.

Two interrelated self-perceptions seem to emerge most consistently as critically related to achievement orientation: the perception of competence and the perception of personal control over outcomes. . . .

The analysis of points of integration across theories suggests that attempts to make specific predictions become extremely complicated because of confounds and interactions across variables. It is clear that we are not dealing with three totally separate constructs that make independent contributions to achievement orientation. Nevertheless, one may conclude that motivation can be enhanced in at least the following ways: (1) increasing perceptions of competence and personal control over outcomes; (2) providing challenging tasks, in which the optimal difficulty of the task depends on both individual (e.g., perceptions of competence) and task (e.g., multiple trials) parameters; and (3) providing additional incentives, such as matching the nature of the task to individual interests or providing an orientation to future goals.

Ruble and Boggiano (1980, pp. 193–98)

dents as vivid and valued options leading to successful learning and performance.

Although individuals with negative perceptions can be expected to perform below their full response capabilities, diminished performance often is used as assessment data to prescribe specific corrective objectives. When this occurs, corrective interventions may prove wasteful and less effective than if the initial emphases were on systematically addressing the motivational "deficit." Many of the objectives prescribed to remedy an individual's developmental deficits may be superfluous once the person is highly motivated to perform.

Efforts to facilitate motivation take many forms: systematic manipulation of extrinsics (O'Leary & Drabman, 1971), attributional retraining (Dweck, 1975), "misattribution" approaches (Weiner & Sierad, 1975), personal causation training (de Charms, 1972, 1976), teaching achievement motivation (Alschuler, Tabor, & McIntyre, 1970), and the mastery approach (Torshen, 1977). The following implications for correcting learning problems reflects our synthesis of these applications and other recent discussions of motivation.

The first major implication is that practitioners must not only be concerned with increasing motivation, but also must avoid practices that decrease motivation. For example, they must be careful not to overrely on extrinsics to entice and to reward because to do so may decrease motivation.

Second, it is important to recognize that motivation represents both a process and an outcome concern. Interveners, of course, must use processes that increase motivation toward objectives such as reading improvement and appropriate interpersonal behavior. At the same time, however, maintenance, enhancement, and expansion of intrinsic motivation also are major intended outcomes and thus are significant content areas.

Third, increasing motivation as a process and outcome concern involves procedures designed to affect a learner's thoughts, feelings, and decisions (see Figure 10-1). Procedures should clarify, modify, and enhance specific cognitions and feelings prior to, during, and after a task or activity. Of particular importance are perceptions of competence (including expectancies and attributions of success and failure), personal valuing, commitment to perform up to capacity, personal choice, personal responsibility, effectiveness (e.g., self-evaluations of impact), and self-determination.

A related implication is that procedures may be required to clarify and modify specific negative cognitions and affects that may interfere with pursuing, and successfully completing, a task or activity. For example, if individuals have strong beliefs about the likelihood of failure or that success is beyond their control, intervention procedures designed to modify these perceptions may be necessary. Similarly, if an individual strongly values, and feels committed to, incompatible behaviors, intervention would need to address these matters.

Finally, there are implications about methods for enhancing motivation both in terms of process and outcome. To provide significant guideposts in selecting relevant methods, four procedural objectives are suggested:

FOR EXAMPLE

TRAINING PERSONAL CAUSATION

De Charms (1976) reports on a large scale, four-year field project involving inner-city schools and a group of sixth- and seventh-grade black teachers. In-service programs focused on training the teachers to treat their students in ways designed to enhance perceptions of personal control.

In the practical world of the school, the problem is to create conditions that will stimulate commitment and responsible choice felt to be originating from within the individual.

The conditions that promote commitment, internal choice and responsibility within a person . . . have four basic elements. The person should be encouraged to consider carefully his [or her] basic motives (self-study) in a warm atmosphere of acceptance by others in the group. The setting should help . . . to translate his [or her] motives into realistic short- and long-range goals (internal goal setting) and to plan realistic and concrete action to attain the goals (planning and goal-directed behavior). Finally, the setting should help him [or her] learn to accept responsibility for selected goals as well as for the success and failure of . . . attempts to reach them (personal responsibility). (p. 6)

While de Charms's findings indicate positive outcomes related to this project, the large number of variables at work in such a comprehensive effort precludes clarifying the specific mechanisms producing effects. Nevertheless, it is an interesting pioneering effort in the area of systematic interventions designed to enhance motivation. The work reflects the trend toward including motivation as a content focus, as well as a process concern in education.

clarifying and expanding intrinsic justifications for pursuing positive learning and behavior;

eliciting public declarations of realistic and valued choices with regard to immediate objectives and longer range goals;

developing a mutual agreement about, and implementing, realistic methods (e.g., materials, support, direction, formative feedback), with particular emphasis on techniques to enhance motivation during the process (e.g., nurturance, permission, protection, and effectiveness); and

providing summative feedback in the form of information (sometimes packaged as awards and other indications of competence).

Figure 10-1 and the following consolidation of the above points provide a summary of our discussion of motivation. To increase motivation during an intervention and to enhance intrinsic motivation as an outcome, methods are selected to achieve four procedural objectives. The intent is to clarify, modify, and enhance cognitions and affects prior to, during, and after a task or activity (see arrow [a]). If an individual has poor self-concept, low self-esteem, or is committed to incompatible behavior, these conditions are of particular concern. Furthermore, strategies are chosen to affect the individual's actions as well as outcomes (see arrows [b] and [c]). Such strategies are viewed as transactions modulated on the basis of formative evaluation data, for example, observations of a student's behavior. Thoughts, feelings, and decisions are posited as leading to actions and outcomes (see arrows [d], [e], and [f]). As diagrammed, some outcomes occur as the result of overt actions; some are direct cognitive and affective changes, such as expanded learning and enhanced intrinsic motivation. In turn, overt actions and outcomes are viewed as transacting with thoughts, feelings, and decisions and thus as affecting perceptions during the intervention, at its termination, and even later.

Obviously, pursuit of each of the procedural objectives outlined above involves many specific planned actions on the part of the intervener. Space does not allow us to pursue each here. Two key elements that deserve special attention, however, are the range of available choices and support. That is, it seems critical that the intervention should incorporate a wide range of substantive choices when motivation to learn is low or there is avoidance motivation. Regardless of theoretical explanations, experimentally it has been demonstrated that even the illusion of choice and personal control can facilitate performance, while the opposite perception can have a debilitating effect (e.g., Perlmuter & Monty, 1977, 1979). For example, in classrooms the wider the range of substantive choices, the more likely the student will find something to perceive as worthy of attention and the more likely the experience will result in learning. Others may feel they know what the student needs to learn, that is, what is good for the student, what skills are needed, and what society will demand. In the final analysis, however, it is the student who decides what he or she wants to learn and can accomplish at a particular time, which alone makes any overreliance on extrinsic rewards and consequences seem unsound.

Of course, providing a good range of substantive options does not necessarily result in effective choice making or follow-through. Interveners must provide information and support as needed. In particular, as the studies by Lefcourt (1967) and Taub and Dollinger (1975) suggest, providing information about the purpose of, and methods for, succeeding at a given task may help overcome avoidance motivation. Moreover, as we discuss in Chapter 13, such information and support are necessary for arriving at mutually agreeable outcomes and procedures. Such agreements are seen to increase expectancy of success and personal valuing, commitment, and responsibility, all of which should enhance intrinsic motivation for learning and performance.

Figure 10-1

A cognitive-affective perspective on corrective procedures designed both to increase motivation during intervention and enhance intrinsic motivation as an outcome.

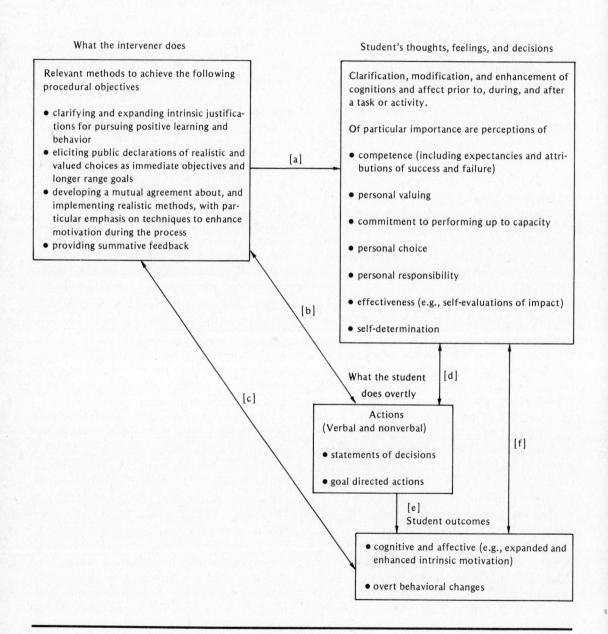

What the intervener does

Relevant methods to achieve the following procedural objectives

- clarifying and expanding intrinsic justifications for pursuing positive learning and behavior
- eliciting public declarations of realistic and valued choices as immediate objectives and longer range goals
- developing a mutual agreement about, and implementing realistic methods, with particular emphasis on techniques to enhance motivation during the process
- providing summative feedback

[a]

Student's thoughts, feelings, and decisions

Clarification, modification, and enhancement of cognitions and affect prior to, during, and after a task or activity.

Of particular importance are perceptions of

- competence (including expectancies and attributions of success and failure)
- personal valuing
- commitment to performing up to capacity
- personal choice
- personal responsibility
- effectiveness (e.g., self-evaluations of impact)
- self-determination

[b]

[c]

What the student does overtly   [d]

Actions
(Verbal and nonverbal)

- statements of decisions
- goal directed actions

[e]
Student outcomes

[f]

- cognitive and affective (e.g., expanded and enhanced intrinsic motivation)
- overt behavioral changes

FOR EXAMPLE

ENHANCING MOTIVATION

As outlined in Figure 10-1, to enhance motivation the intervener's initial procedures focus on (1) clarifying and expanding intrinsic justifications for pursuing positive learning and behavior and (2) eliciting public declarations of realistic and valued choices as immediate objectives and longer-range goals, (3a) developing a mutual agreement about, and (3b) implementing, realistic methods while emphasizing techniques that enhance motivation during the process, and (4) providing feedback on progress. With regard to these four objectives, the following are examples of procedures we have adapted or developed in our current work.

Intrinsic justifications. With regard to intrinsic justifications, the essence of intervener activity is to provide a wide range of options related to both content and procedures and then to assist students in actively exploring the options as a stimulus for clarifying activities the student has intrinsic reasons for pursuing. Included are options about materials and when, where, and with whom learning activities are to be pursued. Discussion and active exploration occurs at formally designated times each day and on an informal basis in other activities. (Activities and exercises to facilitate active exploration by students, with emphasis on clarifying intrinsic reasons for selecting particular options, have been described by de Charms, 1976.) During discussions and active exploration, the student identifies self-initiated activities: those that have been pursued for intrinsic reasons, those in which they are presently involved, those they perceive as currently available, and those they would like to add (see Kruglanski, 1975). They also are asked to clarify how much they value such activities. To counter negative effects due to perceptions of surveillance, external monitoring is minimized and the use of confidential logs kept by the student is encouraged (de Charms, 1976).

Public declarations of realistic and valued personally chosen objectives. The essence of intervener activity related to this objective is to follow the preceding clarification and expansion of intrinsic justifications with a discussion period during which the student openly explores the feasible options, identifies those which he or she values to a significant degree, and explicitly indicates those which he or she has a strong desire to pursue. Students are encouraged to identify only those learning activities they both value and feel relatively competent to pursue. (On a few occasions students have only been able to identify one such activity at first, but the average has been about five to begin with.) As a first step, such declarations may be made in individual contact with the intervener. This is done to minimize anxiety. Potential threats to perceptions of competence that may result from students choosing activities and outcomes far above their current ability are minimized by helping them identify prerequisites and specific sequential steps toward reaching long-range goals. Delineating steps that can be accomplished successfully provides statements of initial objectives and is the basis for developing mutual agreements.

Mutual agreements. The essence of intervener activity related to this objective is to assist the student in making personal choices and mutual and explicit agreements about specific activities and resources (personnel and materials) to be used and times for working on declared goals and objectives (Adelman & Taylor, 1977). To evolve a mutually satisfying or valued agreement, students need to be informed of the available alternatives in support, instruction, and materials. Initial agreements and schedules formulated are flexible in order to accommodate fluctuations in students' interests and to capitalize on new information about activities and outcomes a student highly values and is committed to. The first period of implementation is formally designated a period of adjustment and further assessment during which agreements are explored and, if necessary, altered daily. Moreover, it is always emphasized that agreements can be renegotiated as needed and can include a temporary "escape clause" for both positive and negative unexpected events. Through this ongoing refinement of explicit and mutual agreements, students are able to identify valued content and can help develop alternative opportunities they would like added.

continued

FOR EXAMPLE   *continued*

Implementing realistic and motivationally en-hancing methods. The essence of intervener activity related to this objective is to facilitate the student's daily activity in keeping with her or his current developmental and motiva-tional status and in ways that can enhance mo-tivation, for example, providing ready access to a wide range of materials and ensuring support and direction are available when needed, but only when needed. The interveners attempt to pro-vide resource materials related to subject matter in such a way that students are appropriately chal-lenged to accommodate new information and feel a growing sense of competence and mastery from not only accomplishing specific outcomes, but from the initial act of choosing materials, goals, and objectives. Interveners also attempt to make available a continuum of structure that will ensure that instructional resources are available when needed, and that there are suf-ficient opportunities for independent and small-group work, which can enhance feelings of competence and self-determination. The amount and type of support and direction are based on students' requests and feedback. Decisions to work on areas of skill deficiency are made mutually and are based, in part, on the finding that a student perceives a lack of competence and capability for independent performance and desires greater competence and independence; formal instruction related to skill deficiencies is keyed to areas where students do not, but want to, feel efficacious. Assessment of specific in-structional needs is done through conferences es-tablished to provide feedback on progress.

Feedback on progress. The essence of intervener activity related to this objective is to assist stu-dents in assessing progress toward planned goals and objectives in ways that highlight not only the student's effectiveness, but also the role the stu-dent is now playing in making decisions. The in-tervener then relates the outcomes back to the student's intrinsic reasons for pursuing the out-comes: an effort is made to elicit from students their perceptions of feelings of competence and self-determination. Feedback is provided during formal and informal conferences at which time (1) products and work samples are analyzed, (2) content, process, and outcome objectives are re-viewed, and (3) agreements and schedules are evaluated and if necessary revised. Regardless of the form in which feedback is given, the empha-sis is on conveying information and avoiding procedures that will be perceived as efforts to entice or control. To these ends, interveners guide students in developing self-monitoring techniques and record keeping, which provide desired information about progress and effec-tiveness while minimizing the potential negative effects of external surveillance and evaluation and overreliance on rewards (e.g., Lepper & Dafoe, 1979).

CONCLUDING COMMENTS

In conclusion, a broad perspective of the complex phenomenon of motivation sug-gests its pervasive effects in terms of causes and corrections of learning problems. In this chapter, we have explored some basic con-cepts and outlined some major implications for practice. Key areas for research on moti-vation as related to learning problems are cited in Adelman (1978a) and Ruble and Boggiano (1980).

In Part 4, we present an intervention model that attempts to incorporate motiva-tional strategies in a comprehensive and systematic manner. It is offered as a po-tentially useful framework for research and practice that emphasizes the relation-ship of motivation, environment and pro-gram changes, and remediation of learning problems.

Chapter 11

The Nature of Intervention

Alfred Adler is quoted as saying that schooling is the process of transferring the notes of the teacher to the notebook of the pupil without passing through the head of either.

Given any sort of reasonable opportunity, most people learn to read, complete an educational program, and function successfully in society. For some, however, something more is needed. That "something" is not easy to identify. Psychoeducational interventions indeed remain controversial because it is unclear why some work for some individuals and none seem effective for others.

Each of us has our own ideas about how learning happens and how it can be influenced. There are great pressures on interveners to claim that what they believe has been proven effective. Think of a time you tried unsuccessfully to help someone learn, when you used a strategy which had worked successfully in a previous situation. Such thoughts can lead to a nagging awareness that less is known about teaching and learning than most of us like to admit.

Clearly, there is a need to improve understanding of what works, what does not, and why. For some problem learners nothing seems successful and, for them at least, new approaches must be investigated. To provide a basis for understanding the specific "active ingredients" of currently effective approaches and for developing promising new strategies, we begin by exploring the general nature of intervention.

183

FRAMEWORK FOR ANALYZING INTERVENTION

Are there important similarities among and between the various approaches to remediation, psychotherapy, schooling, rehabilitation, social welfare, parenting, and so forth? While there have been numerous efforts to conceive specific interventions (e.g., a particular approach to teaching or psychotherapy) and classes of intervention (e.g., systems of education or psychotherapy), discussion of intervention as a generic phenomenon remains relatively ignored. As a result, important similarities and differences are not understood, and discussion of issues and problems related to such activities are more parochial than they need be.

If an improved understanding of how interveners should proceed is to be developed, a fundamental analysis of the commonalities among educational and psychological interventions is needed. As one step in this direction, we offer a general definition of intentional intervention and a broad formulation of major intervention phases and tasks.

Intervention Defined

In the context of psychoeducational practices, intervention generally is defined with reference to its positive objectives. "Intervention is a general term that refers to the application of professional skills to maintain or improve a child's potential for ongoing healthy development" (Suran & Rizzo, 1979, p. 79). Such definitions are relevant, but incomplete.

As a starting point for developing a general perspective of intervention, let's look at the essential components of a comprehensive definition of the term. *Webster's New World Dictionary* (1970) defines intervention as "the act of intervening; any interference in the affairs of others." Intervene is defined as "to come, be, or lie between . . . as something unnecessary or irrelevant . . . as an influencing force . . . to modify, settle, or hinder some action." What the dictionary

THE RELATIONSHIP AMONG INTERVENTIONS

We share with a growing body of scholars the conviction that the heterogeneity of theory and method [related to therapeutic intervention] that has taken place over the last century obscures some underlying interrelationships, and that the task at this juncture is one of sorting out the interrelationships which are presumed to exist. We believe that interrelationships do exist and that they will be identified and verified if they are sought. The most likely outcome of such a search would appear to be more adequate and comprehensive theoretic formulations.
Urban and Ford (1971, p. 6)

definition implies is that as much as professionals may intend interventions to have positive outcomes, it is a distinct possibility that an intervention may be "unnecessary," "irrelevant" or a hindrance. It also identifies the *interference nature* of interventions.

What the definition does not clarify are other important components implied by the way the term is commonly used in fields such as psychology, education, public health and welfare, law and law enforcement, the military, and so forth. In such fields, intervention seems to refer to planned *actions* that are intended to produce desired *changes* in existing *conditions* of a person or environment—often with the condition being identified as a problem in need of correction, improvement, or prevention.

As an aid in theory building and analysis, we propose that actions (interferences), changes (outcomes), and conditions be viewed as primary facets in defining intervention. An adequate, general definition of intentional intervention must incorporate references as to whether the actions and changes are intended or not and whether the conditions are problematic or

Figure 11-1

Essential features of a definition of intentional intervention.

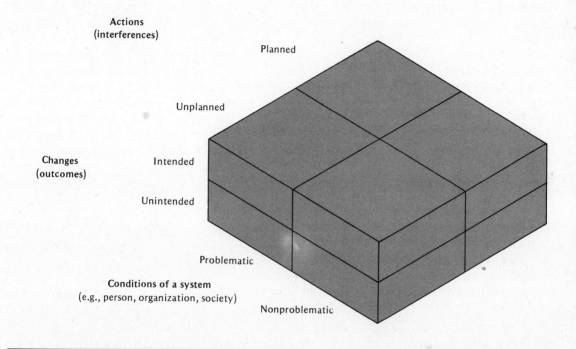

nonproblematic. The focus on intentionality guarantees that unplanned actions and unintended changes, such as positive and negative side effects, are not ignored. The inclusion of nonproblematic conditions provides a reminder about the relevance of actions and changes related to such matters as positive growth and enrichment. It should be noted that conditions can refer broadly to any system including a person, an organization, an institution, society, and so forth.

In summary, then, as a broad working definition, intentional intervention can be viewed as any planned or unplanned actions that result from a desire to produce changes in existing problematic or nonproblematic

conditions of a system (person, environment, or an interaction of both). Such actions may or may not produce changes, and resultant changes may include unintended outcomes (see Figure 11-1).[1] From this perspective, any formal school program is an intervention. Whenever an individual or group seeks help, they are requesting an intervention. When society dictates that a person should be "helped," intervention is occurring.

The above definition is meant to be one aid in analyzing interventions. It can be used, for instance, in systematically formulating basic questions that must be answered about any intervention, What are the bases

---

[1] While it generally is implied that intervention actions come from outside the system which is to change, such a view reflects specific theoretical positions and is not implied by the definition presented here.

for the actions?, How do the actions produce change?, What is the nature of the changes produced?, and so forth. Other major aids in analyzing intervention are formulations that outline tasks and phases, which are discussed next.

Major Tasks Related to Services for Learning Problems

The most compelling and visible features of psychoeducational interventions are the specific programs and services which are implemented. These may be designated as intervention tasks. For example, with reference to learning and behavior problems, we have identified six major interrelated tasks:

initial assessment and consultation (e.g., screening and placement decisions),

transition into corrective intervention,

assessment and consultation for planning specific changes,

corrective intervention (e.g., teaching, enrichment, treatment),

reassessment and consultation, and

transition from the intervention.

Figure 11–2 shows how we conceive the relationship among the six tasks. Such a formulation highlights the sequence and the connections between the various interventions, all of which may be needed to produce effective change.

Since each task has a comprehensive rationale and extensive planning and evaluation requirements associated with it, we can describe only the essence of each below.[2]

1. *Initial assessment and consultation.* When someone is experiencing a problem related to learning, there is an immediate need to determine (1) the general scope of the problem (severity and pervasiveness), (2) the appropriate focal point of the intervention (person, environment, person-environment interaction), and (3) what general types of corrective steps might be appropriate, such as changes in the environment to accommodate an individual, changes in a specific aspect of a person-environment interaction, or special forms of schooling, tutoring, and therapies to change individuals. It is important to stress that the immediate focus is on the *general* nature of the services needed, such as a school remedial program to improve basic academic skills, and not on a specific prescription, such as a detailed remedial plan to be carried out by a school with a particular orientation to teaching skills.

The focus of consultation is not only on clarifying assessment findings, but also on clarifying appropriate and feasible alternatives and arriving at a decision. With regard to students, for example, the range of alternatives and decisions may include staying in a current setting with appropriate modifications, transferring to another nonproblem population setting that provides a broader range of options, or transfer to a special population setting for part- or full-time instruction and/or psychologically oriented help.

2. *Transition into corrective interventions.* Once a decision has been made to pursue a service alternative, the task focus shifts to implementing the decision (see Table 7–4). However, in implementing intervention decisions, significant practical and psychological barriers usually confront the involved parties. When asked to make changes, most in-

---

[2]Chapter 8 and Part 4 detail some of the specific services we are developing and evaluating in connection with the tasks described here.

Figure 11-2

Major tasks related to services for learning problems.

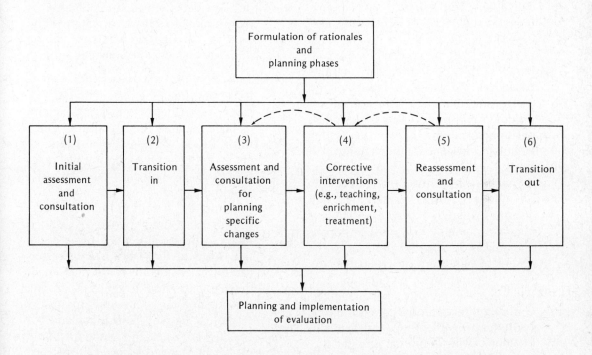

dividuals are anxious, and for some the step from decision making to successfully initiating a new program proves to be altogether too difficult. Such instances indicate the need for transition services encompassing such activities as (1) clarifying application procedures, funding, and transportation, (2) orientation discussions and visits to demystify as much of the new program as is feasible and to develop positive expectations, (3) personalized contact to provide support and assurance to the participants when needed, and (4) monitoring and facilitating the initial implementation in order to identify any selection (screening and placement) errors and to mediate any initial adjustment problems. In other words, the task

is to implement procedures that lead to an effective beginning.

3. *Assessment and consultation for planning specific changes.* Corrective interventions are shaped by ongoing assessment and decision-making processes. The initial focus is on assessing present status of the person or environment to be changed and deciding on initial objectives. Subsequent emphasis is on refining plans based on new assessment data. The intent is to guide daily intervention actions toward systematic accomplishment of intended outcomes.

Formulating specific objectives is most appropriately accomplished at the time a program is initiated and by those who implement it. Those involved in implementing a program are in the best position to assess changes as an intervention proceeds and to formulate daily plans. To do so, various combinations of the types of procedures discussed in Part 2 may be used. What occurs is that the intervener then (1) initiates the best program feasible, based on the program rationale and whatever preliminary data appear appropriate and useful, and (2) monitors performance in the intervention setting to gather relevant data for planning next steps.

Specific intervention plans obviously are influenced by assessment data, but also are shaped by all active participants in such planning. In most instances planning is done with reference to the desires of significant others such as the State, administrators, parents, and students. Since conditions change regularly during intervention, there is ongoing consultation with others and mechanisms for arriving at mutual agreements.

4. *Corrective interventions.* While there is a wide range of specific corrective services in terms of orientations and methods, the types of activities can be categorized as teaching, enrichment, and treatment. Simply stated, the task involves implementing the planned actions in order to accomplish the intended outcomes. (Chapter 12 details the complexities of this task.)

5. *Reassessment and consultation.* After corrective interventions have been implemented beyond an appropriate "transition in" period, there is a need to reconsider such matters as: Was the selection decision appropriate?; If problems are occurring at this stage, how can the difficulties best be understood and dealth with?; Is progress adequate?; and, If goals are reached, what is the

next step? In essence, decisions are made about whether a program should be continued, changed, or discontinued. The data used are a combination of daily evaluations and an updating of the type of information gathered during initial assessment and consultation.

6. *Transition from the intervention.* An intervention may be discontinued because it was inappropriate, insufficient, or because goals were achieved. Once this decision is made, the next task focuses on the same administrative, practical, and psychological concerns that arise during initial assessment and consultation and transitions into the intervention. For example, when it is decided that a student will leave a special class, the range of appropriate programs is carefully considered. If the decision is made to return to the regular classroom, the intervention focus shifts to anxiety related to the move and anticipation of specific activities the student should master in order to succeed in the next program (e.g., "survival skills"). Also often appropriate are plans for ongoing support until students are successfully assimilated into the new program.

An Overview of Major Phases of Intentional Intervention

In addition to knowledge about major tasks, understanding the basic nature of intentional interventions requires appreciation of the general phases of such activity. Elsewhere, Adelman (1974) has presented a framework discussing seven phases and detailing sequential activities involved in each. Stated simply, the general phases are:

formulation of an overall rationale,

normative planning (e.g., a generalized plan of intervention strategies, a curriculum plan),

evaluation planning,

VIEWPOINT

PLANNING

The learning characteristics of exceptional children and youths translate into a wide range of instructional challenges for classroom teachers. While some instructional needs are met through minor modifications in materials, scheduling changes, or through corrective devices, most instructional needs require a major investment in instructional planning by teachers and support personnel.

Until recently, instructional planning as a basis for special education programming has been something for which educators acknowledged the need, but something which was accomplished rarely. At the least, relatively little evidence is apparent of systematic instructional planning on behalf of exceptional children and youth. Certainly, some planning has been carried out—but not at a level many would consider sufficient.

Meyen (1979, p. 139)

administrative planning,

planning for specific changes (e.g., a plan for personalizing intervention),

implementation, and

evaluation.

As indicated in Figure 11–3, these phases do not occur in a strictly sequential order.

What Figure 11–3 perhaps illustrates most vividly is that intentional intervention requires planning. Planning may be unilateral or participatory in nature and can provide ways to ensure that implementation is dynamic, innovative, and purposeful rather than static and reactive. The following sections will show that planning represents an attempt to organize an intervention's content and procedures in ways that are consistent with the underlying rationale and that incorporate appropriate evaluation.

RATIONAL BASES FOR INTERVENTION

Intentional interventions are rationally based; that is, underlying such activity, there is a rationale—whether or not it is explicitly stated.

Conceptual and Empirical Sources

An intervention rationale shapes intervention purposes and procedures. It is a framework regarding the nature of intervention *aims and practices*. It consists of views derived from theoretical, empirical, and philosophical sources.

While rationales shape intervention, it is rare to find them systematically formulated and explicitly stated. Even when not explicitly stated, however, rationales stimulate the thoughts and actions of those involved.

In their discussion of factors that shape intervention, Rossi, Freeman, and Wright (1979) suggest that interventions are based on a set of hypotheses drawn from causal and predictive studies, from logical theories, and from clinical impressions. With regard to instruction, Bruner (1966) has stated that such intervention reflects "a theory of how growth and development are assisted by diverse means" (p. 1). With regard to psychotherapy, Howard and Orlinsky (1972) indicate that such interventions imply

some conception of human nature or personality (the 'material' to be worked with), human fulfillment (the ideal to be sought), human vulnerability (psychopathology), of therapeutics, and of the therapeutic profession. Taken together, they comprise . . . the Therapeutic Belief-Value Complex. (p. 617)

In general, philosophical and theoretical concepts and data are amalgamated into a psychoeducational intervention rationale. They may be drawn from a variety of disciplines and fields, such as basic and applied psychology, the biological sciences and medicine, education, sociology, philosophy, and social welfare. A rationale also reflects com-

Figure 11-3

The process of planning, implementing, and evaluating intervention.

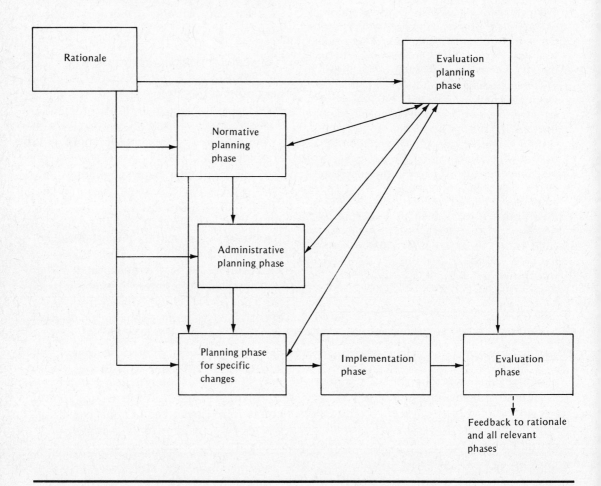

mitment to general orientations or *models* of the causes of problems, of tasks to be accomplished, and of the appropriate outcomes and processes of intervention.

With regard to models of cause, three basic orientations can be seen to underlie a great deal of intervention research and practice: (1) the disordered or "ill" person (medical) model, (2) the lack of developmental readiness or slow maturation model, and (3) an interactional model emphasizing the

interplay between person and environment. As discussed in Part 1, the prevailing orientation related to learning and behavior problems is a tendency to see the locus of causality as centered in persons, for example, disorders and developmental lags. For those who favor one or the other of these causal models, their concept of appropriate tasks, outcomes, and procedures logically are derived from their preferred model; adherence to any particular model of causality,

VIEWPOINT

IMPLICIT RATIONALES

Getzels (1974) focused on the idea that varied architectural arrangements of classrooms imply varied images of the student. The rectangular classroom in which pupils' chairs are bolted to the floor in straight rows and the teacher's desk is front and center fits the image of the "empty organism" that learns only from the teacher. The square classroom in which pupils' chairs are movable and the teacher's desk is in a corner fits the image of the "active organism" participating in the learning process. The classroom without a teacher's desk, in which the pupils' desks are trapezoidal (to make a circle when placed next to one another), fits the image of the "social organism" learning primarily from peers. The open classroom, featuring several activity and resource centers and no desks at all, fits the image of the "stimulus-seeking organism" searching for the novel, challenging experiences by which learning takes place. Thus, the physical organization of the classroom is shaped by particular values about the learning process and in turn, shapes how students learn.

Moos (1979, p. 7)

TABLE 11-1

Parties directly and indirectly interested in intervention decisions

I. Directly involved interested parties
   A. *Subscribers*—including private individuals and representatives of organized bodies who are seeking intervention for themselves, others, or both
   B. *Objects to be changed*—including individuals and those in settings who seek change or are referred by others
   C. *Interveners*—those who, in addition to whatever self interests are involved, may base their activity on the stated desires or interpreted needs of subscribers, the objects of change, or both.
II. Indirectly involved interested parties, i.e., those whose influence has the potential to produce a major impact on the intervention
   A. *Immediate or primary environmental influences*—e.g., family, friends, employers, teachers, co-workers, local representatives of funding sources
   B. *Secondary and tertiary environmental influences*—governmental agents related to health, education, welfare, and law enforcement; professional and lay organizations; theorists, researchers, and instructors; i.e., those who lobby for, underwrite, study, evaluate, and teach about intervention.

correction, or evaluation both guides and limits the nature of the rationale and subsequent intervention activity.[3]

Whose Rationale?

What is finally incorporated into a particular rationale is largely dependent upon who is doing the incorporating and what are the forces influencing that person or persons. It is important to be aware that intervention programs are of concern to a variety of persons and groups. This point has been demonstrated for many years in the "mental health" field (e.g., Krause, 1969; Parloff, Kelman, & Frank, 1954; Smith, 1963). For instance, in 1977 Strupp and Hadley stressed that there are three "interested parties" involved in intervention decision making—the client, society, and the intervener.

For purposes of this discussion, the interested parties are categorized into two not mutually exclusive groups: (1) those who are most directly involved in the activity and (2) those not directly involved, but whose influence is felt (see Table 11-1).

[3]Interventions and their underlying rationales, of course, also are affected by pragmatics, absence of data, and other factors not very rationally and ethically rooted.

Thus, it may appear at first glance that the intervener is the only party concerned with intervention rationales, but, sophisticated or not, directly involved or not, with or without control, each of the interested parties is likely to have beliefs and values about causes, corrections, and what constitutes progress. Given the range of concepts, data, and general orientations from which "interested parties" can make choices, the questions arise: How greatly do rationales differ? Who decides what theory, data, and philosophy should be incorporated into any specific rationale? How are such decisions made? Because rationales for currently prominent psychoeducational interventions are not systematically formulated, these questions are not easily studied. A major area in need of research involves clarifying the content of divergent rationales of interested parties and related decision-making processes.

PLANNING FOR INTERVENTION

Rationales are translated into action through the formulation of specific plans. Planning has been formally defined as the task of "relating means to ends, formulating rationally feasible courses of action through systematic considerations of alternatives" (Hartley, 1968, p. 256). In the context of psychological intervention, Urban and Ford (1971) emphasize that:

> Ideally, . . . procedures for affecting behavioral change will be formulated in orderly, systematic, and explicit fashion; the more this is done, the more successfully some other person (therapist or researcher) can replicate them, and the more successfully the effects of the specific procedures can be studied. (p. 16)

System management theorists have been among the most active in delineating what a plan of action might encompass. For example, Hartley (1968) includes as aims of educational planning the formulation of gen-

VIEWPOINT

EXPLICATING A RATIONALE

Intervention models, implicit or explicit, are predicated on some notion of cause and effect. But, because of the present state of knowledge in the social and behavior sciences, models are rarely based upon a set of principles and generalizations which are grounded in definite evidence. . . .

The absence of an explicitly stated intervention model prevents replication of the program and severely limits the opportunities for controlling its quality and evaluating its effectiveness. If the parties involved in program development and implementation fail (or refuse) to apply themselves to unraveling and specifying the assumptions and principles underlying the program, there is no basis for understanding what they are doing, why they are doing it, or for judging whether or not they are doing what they intend to do (Freeman and Sherwood, 1965). Even if their program is capable of achieving the objectives set for it without an explicit model there is no basis for understanding why it worked or for reproducing it and its effects on a broader scale and in other communities.

Rossi, Freeman and Wright (1979, pp. 66–67)

eral goals and objectives, organization of relevant data, determination of personnel, space, and material requirements, examination of alternative procedures and establishment of priorities, provision for communications and information retrieval for the system, analysis of financial resources, evaluation of how well objectives are being met, anticipation of future needs, and continuous review of the system so that objectives are reformulated to prevent the system from becoming static and rigid.

As represented in Figure 11-2, four of the intervention phases address planning—normative, evaluative, administrative, and a phase for planning specific changes. It is

VIEWPOINT

RATIONAL PLANNING

Carried to an extreme, the order implied in a rational system fails to square with what we know about human beings and human resources. Both are marked by irrationality, a substantial measure of which may be desirable. But there is little danger of the decision-making process in education becoming overly rationale. When it does, I shall be delighted to argue the case for irrationality.
Goodlad (1966, p. 8)

To some persons, planning conjures up the image of a totalitarian society embracing centrally planned economic objectives and activities. In this case, self-expression and human freedom may approach a kind of universal triviality. The requisite assumption for the use of economic models in education is that some planning is desirable; exactly how much is less clear . . . [Planning] is a way of attempting to somewhat control the future instead of merely reacting to it and being controlled by it.
Hartley (1968, pp. 2-3)

during these phases that an intervention's underlying rationale is translated from abstract ideals into a practical plan of action. Because many planners who apparently subscribe to similar aims advocate different objectives and practices, it seems clear that the translation process involves interpretation. Understanding the nature of the four planning phases clarifies not only that interpretation is necessary, but that a variety of socioeconomic-political factors play a significant role in shaping and delineating interventions. A few brief comments should suffice to highlight these points.

The *normative* planning phase involves translating comprehensive and highly abstract theories, beliefs, and values into *general* approaches to intervention. This type of

"planning" is reflected in the work of (1) authors of texts on teaching (e.g., reading, math), counseling, psychotherapy, and behavior change, (2) curriculum developers, (3) academics who prepare practitioners (e.g., teachers, psychologists), and (4) individual interveners who formulate generalizations about how they will approach their work.

For instance, legislation may be passed to help a specific group such as those with learning disabilities. Following the legislative mandate, agencies and individuals draw upon current theories, beliefs, and values to develop programs (e.g., Meyen, 1982). They rely on prevailing views of causes and correction of learning disabilities. Such views reflect the weak knowledge base and psychological and societal biases we discussed in Part 2. Thus, efforts to translate normative plans into specific objectives and activities inevitably are subjective.

To reduce variability in normative planning, government agencies and curriculum developers attempt to standardize outcomes and procedures. The effect of this standardization is to institutionalize a particular set of theories, beliefs, and values. Standardization is an appropriate strategy when it is done in order to evaluate a particular approach to compare it with reasonable alternatives. Such research is sorely needed to strengthen the weak knowledge base related to psychoeducational interventions. However, more often than is desirable, such standardization is not motivated by proposed research, but by sociopolitical forces. When sociopolitical influences result in standardized intervention outcomes and procedures, those who control the political decision-making processes are in a position to shape a field in the image of any model they propound, or in accord with current fashions and fads. The inherent dangers are obvious.

Appropriate *administrative* planning involves selection considerations and deployment of resources, such as finances, personnel, and space. The intent is to facilitate translating rational *ideals* into practice, but *real world* considerations often interfere. Most common are lack of finances and limitations in the competence and motivation of personnel. An important basis for administrative planning is assessment information regarding needs and available resources. In some extreme cases, the rationale is inadequately attended to because administrative cost-accounting has become the prime determiner of intervention activity. With regard to schools, educationally desirable programs often have been jettisoned because of lack of funds or because quantitative analysts have been allowed to establish a "cult of efficiency." Administrative planning, then, becomes a primary referent and reshaper of intervention rationales, which can subvert or facilitate intervention aims.

A third phase of planning involves translating normative, and usually administrative, plans into a *specific* plan of intervention. Given a specific person (or group), environment, or person-environment interaction, it is necessary to plan specific objectives and processes for a particular intervention effort, such as a specific session or day. This is the process implied whenever an intervention is described as individualized.

A critical facet is some form of assessment to guide specific planning for change. Data are needed to clarify such antecedent conditions as (1) current motivational and developmental levels of intervention participants and (2) available resources. Data gathered can be limited to that required for planning objectives and processes that are logically consistent with the rationale underlying the intervention.

Logically, *evaluation* planning immediately follows each of the other planning phases. The first objective of this phase is to determine the appropriateness and adequacy of the other planning phases, especially their congruence with the rationale and their logical consistency with each other. The second objective is to formulate an evaluation design for describing and judging the effectiveness of the intervention.

With increasing demands for accountability, evaluation activities are increasing. Not surprisingly, the first reaction to pressure for accountability has been to focus on the measurement of outcomes. Thus, evaluation planning often is discussed narrowly in terms of the procedures and instruments available for measuring objectives.

Few would argue with the idea that outcomes should be evaluated or that such evaluation requires measurement procedures. The problem is that overemphasis on what currently is measurable can have a devastating effect on efforts to appropriately translate a rationale into practical activity. There are several important points that one should remember:

Many important facets incorporated into an intervention rationale are not readily measurable, for example, self-concept, attitudes toward learning, expectancies, problem solving capabilities, and creativity.

Available measures purporting to measure the same areas of performance often reflect very different content and constructs, for example, standardized achievement tests.

Once a particular evaluation instrument has been designated, intervention practices often are reshaped subtly to ensure that what the instrument actually measures is accomplished. For example, teachers often are tempted "to teach to the test" and, in order to do so, may de-emphasize whatever is not being evaluated.

Judgments about the efficacy of an intervention will be based on what is measured; therefore, "survival" of specific approaches often is dependent on accountability measures. For instance, political and economic support may be based primarily on the ability to demonstrate improvement on a particular measure, such as a reading achievement test.

In general, while evaluation planning logically flows from efforts to translate an intervention rationale into specifics, evaluation planners and those who are being evaluated may ignore many facets of a rationale and inappropriately reshape planning and implementation. In such cases, current measurement capability rather than an intervention rationale appears to be the primary shaper of specific intervention approaches. This is backwards. Intervention objectives and activities must be rationally based on theoretical and philosophical considerations related to understanding the cause and correction of problems and the developmental aims of individuals and society. Evaluation plans can then be formulated with due recognition of current limitations and needs to advance evaluation capabilities, which is discussed at greater length in Chapter 17.

Finally, it should be noted that plans are made by people and the key components of an intervention generally are people. The range of interested parties presented in Table 11-1 indicates the large number of persons who may be involved and who may have to be considered in planning. This point involves more than the conventional warning not to exclude significant persons—such as the family of clients—from intervention activity. Simply involving persons in an intervention is not the same as logically planning objectives and actions that will be a good match for such persons and will have a high probability of being achieved. For example, if an intended activity assumes the persons involved have particular skills or attitudes which they do not have,

the planned action is illogical and unlikely to be effective.

Planning raises major theoretical, methodological, and ethical concerns regarding the appropriate relationship of means to ends, the desirability of specific ends, the processes by which ends and means of any given intervention are decided upon, the degree to which planning should be participatory rather than unilateral, and so forth. Subsequent chapters will elaborate on these points. Before proceeding, however, it is necessary to stress the topic of planning for certain unintended and undesired outcomes.

IATROGENIC EFFECTS

Intervention can produce iatrogenic effects.[4] Iatrogenic effects refer to problems that result from the methods used by interveners, that is, negative effects such as errors in identification, self-fulfilling prophecies, increases in dependency, or somatic residual effects. Our purpose here is to highlight the need to anticipate such effects and plan steps to minimize them. The importance of doing so relates both to intervention efficacy and ethical considerations. For this brief presentation, examples are grouped under three sources of negative effects: (1) technical deficiencies, (2) interpersonal dynamics, and (3) misuses of intervention procedures.

1. Technical deficiencies related to intervention probably have been discussed more than any other type of procedural concern. The most frequently cited example of these deficiencies is the use of assessment procedures that have poor reliability and validity and lack appropriate norms for use as standards (e.g. Cronbach, 1970). Technical deficiencies related to prevailing assessment prac-

---

[4]*Iatrogenesis* comes from *iatros*, the Greek word for *physician*, and *genesis*, meaning *origin*. As used here, *iatrogenic* means any negative consequence resulting from an intentional intervention (Illich, 1976).

tices play a major role in generating problems in identification and placement (e.g. false negative and false positive errors) and also are responsible for many of the problems encountered in planning specific changes and evaluating the efficacy of interventions. Overcoming such problems remains one of the most complex and vexing challenges confronting researchers and interveners. In planning, generally the major recourse open to the intervener is to avoid methods which are extremely deficient and to develop strategies to minimize inevitable negative effects.

2. Interveners, of course, rely heavily on the dynamics of intervention to produce desired outcomes. Some of these dynamics also produce undesired effects. Furthermore, other dynamics often arise which, at best, are not facilitative and may be counter-productive. These undesired outcomes represent serious problems to be overcome, that is, the intervener must plan how to avoid or eliminate the interaction.

    For instance, the rescue phenomenon is a frequently encountered transaction experienced by interveners (e.g., therapists, parents, teachers) and those they set out to help. This dynamic, described by Karpman (1968), is one which often arises when an intervention is provided to an individual who has not asked for help and does not want to change. It may occur also when an intervener acts as if he or she knows what others should do, sets out to "save" them or mainly gives "good advice." Such circumstances frequently result in frustration, disappointment, and anger building up among participants. This, in turn, results in accusations of blame and termination of the activity. Awareness of the possibility of this dynamic allows interveners to plan steps to ensure that

VIEWPOINT

THE RESPONSIBILITY OF INTERVENING

The recovery of the power to learn or to teach means that the teacher who takes the risk of interfering in somebody else's private affairs also assumes responsibility for the results. Similarly, the student who exposes himself [or herself] to the influence of a teacher must take responsibility for his [or her] own education.
Illich (1977, p. 85)

individuals want help in overcoming a problem and that help involves more than giving advice.

Another common problem that requires the intervener's vigilance and planning is dependency. If a student or client is becoming overly dependent, the intervener must determine ways to counteract this trend, usually by planning ways to develop greater independence, for example, by teaching independence skills and reducing the amount of support and direction the intervener provides.

Even when interpersonal dynamic problems have been addressed and interventions are effective in producing intended changes, the very changes produced can result in negative effects. These can be designated the *dynamics of change*. For example, students who have participated in programs that have taught them to make independent choices and express their preferences often are frustrated on finding that those in their environment (e.g., teacher, family, or friends) are unwilling or unable to respond positively to their new skills. Intervention planning that anticipates such dynamics not only benefits the student, but can minimize problems for others who may be involved.[5]

3. Finally, there are misuses of intervention procedures, examples of which include (1) premature application of inadequately validated procedures (Adelman, 1978d; Adelman & Compas, 1977; Elinson, 1967; Ward & Kassebaum, 1972; Weiss, 1975), (2) limiting interventions to what can be measured by available assessment procedures (Cohen, 1972; Sjoberg, 1975), (3) inappropriate restrictions of choices and participation (Bierman, 1969; Ellsworth, Maroney, Klett, Gordon & Gunn, 1971; Moos and MacIntosh, 1970; Rosenshine, 1971), (4) inappropriate information gathering and usage (Anastasi, 1966; Mercer, 1972; Wasserstrom, 1976; Willingham, 1967), and (5) inappropriately assigning the locus of causality to an individual when environmental (e.g., societal) factors are responsible (Ryan, 1971). The negative consequences of such misuses involve the whole spectrum of practical and ethical iatrogenic concerns. The primary recourse for dealing with such problems is planning ways to avoid creating them. For this to occur, however, interveners must be aware of the forces that perpetuate such misuses, and they must be committed to combating them.

CONCLUDING COMMENTS

The purpose of this chapter has been to introduce some ways to think about psychoeducational interventions systematically and in general terms so that common ideas and concerns can be highlighted. As we proceed with the discussion of intervention outcomes, content, and procedures in Chapter 12, we intend to continue to stress commonalities as well as significant differences. There are distinct practical advantages to be gained from the systematic understanding of general concepts that underlie a variety of apparently discrete theories and practices. Of greater importance, however, are the potential benefits of refining research and theory, thus advancing the LD field.

---

[5]Examples of other positive and negative dynamic phenomena discussed in the literature are the Hawthorne, placebo, and persuasion effects (Beecher, 1955; Bergin, 1971; Frank, 1961; Roethlisberger & Dickson, 1939; Rosenthal, 1966; Trouton, 1957), transference, counter transference, and resistance (Brammer & Shostrom, 1977; May, 1967; Rapaport, 1960; Rogers, 1951; Schuldt, 1966), the expert trap (Taylor & Adelman, 1977), and reactions to change (Baldridge, 1972; Bennis, Benne, & Chin, 1969; Haley, 1977; Lippitt, Watson & Westley, 1958; Sarason, 1971).

Chapter 12

Intervention Outcomes and Procedures:
A General Analysis

*If you don't care where you get to, then it
doesn't matter which way you go.*
Nay, Scalon, Schmidt, and Wholey (1976, p. 97)

*I hear, and I forget;
I see, and I remember;
I do, and I understand.*
Old Chinese proverb

*Let the main object . . . be as follows: To seek
and to find a method of instruction, by
which teachers may teach less, but learners
learn more; by which schools may be the
scene of less noise, aversion, and useless la-
bour, but of more leisure, enjoyment, and
solid progress. . . .*
Comenius, 1632

One reason so many issues and problems
continue to plague the LD field is that certain conceptual concerns are treated sim-
plistically and remain poorly defined. Planning and implementing psychoeducational
interventions can be enhanced greatly by
an expanded understanding of the nature
of intended outcomes, the importance of
breadth of content, and the value of conceiving procedures in generic terms. Moreover, the scope of various issues associated
with formulating objectives and selecting
methods are best appreciated from the perspective of a general analysis. Therefore,
to encourage a sophisticated approach to
planning and implementing outcomes, content, and procedures, this chapter is devoted
to discussing basic concepts and frameworks. In Part 4, these basic ideas are incorporated into presentation of a model of

instruction for persons experiencing learning problems.

OUTCOMES

Because of increasing interest in accountability, specifying discrete outcomes has become the central focus in planning. The benefits of clarifying specific outcomes are not to be denied. There is, however, danger that the broad and substantive nature of desired goals will be lost in the emphasis on easily measurable, behavioral objectives. Many of the highly specific intervention outcomes being described and promoted may only be a small, unrepresentative, and unimportant segment of the most valued aims and goals that society has for its citizens—and that citizens have for themselves.

Nature of Intended Outcomes

The rationale underlying intervention (see Chapter 11) encompasses its purposes and is the primary referent for planning specific outcomes. An intervention's purposes are major long-range *aims* that are assigned or adopted. For instance, a major aim of psychotherapy is to promote "mental health"; a major aim of formal schooling is to facilitate development of children in a manner that prepares them to be effective citizens. It is from such extremely abstract statements of desired aims that interveners first derive a range of general *goals* and then short-term and immediate *objectives*. The process of concretizing the nature of a particular intervention's outcomes involves translating highly abstract and normative goals into less abstract supraordinate goals, subordinate goals, and ultimately into a statement of relatively specific intended outcome objectives (see Figure 12–1). This process is analogous to operationally defining highly abstract psychological concepts, such as intelligence, in order to clarify subconcepts and corresponding sets of related observable variables (Nunnally, 1967). Figure 12–1 por-

trays the idea that long-range aims and supraordinate goals are the ultimate and most appropriate reference for specifying objectives and evaluating whether an intervention is achieving intended outcomes.

In practice, many intervention objectives are formulated unsystematically and may be related only tangentially to the underlying intervention rationale. School programs frequently provide examples of how policies proposed to improve the planning of outcomes may be counterproductive. It is commonplace for legislators and administrators to require school personnel responsible for students with psychoeducational problems to list instructional objectives for each student. Individual educational planning (e.g., the *IEP*) of specific outcome objectives already has been mandated for some educators. Furthermore, the mandate for specific objectives frequently is translated into a demand that they be specified in highly concrete, behavioral terms. The result, of course, is that school personnel do provide lists of objectives in the form demanded. It should not be surprising that such outcome statements often do not reflect an adequate understanding of what is involved in ameliorating the student's problems. Too often, the primary factors shaping the nature of the objectives formulated are evaluation criteria and measures that have been introduced to achieve narrowly defined demands for accountability. Undeniably school programs need to be held accountable. However, appropriate evaluation involves considerably more than requiring specific outcome objectives to be formulated and evaluated using available procedures. More importantly, appropriate intervention stems not only from clarity of intended outcomes, but from qualitative content and procedures.

Specifying Objectives

Even after clarifying the general nature of intended outcomes, there remain issues and problems related to formulating specific ob-

Figure 12-1

Translation of long-range aims into goals and objectives.

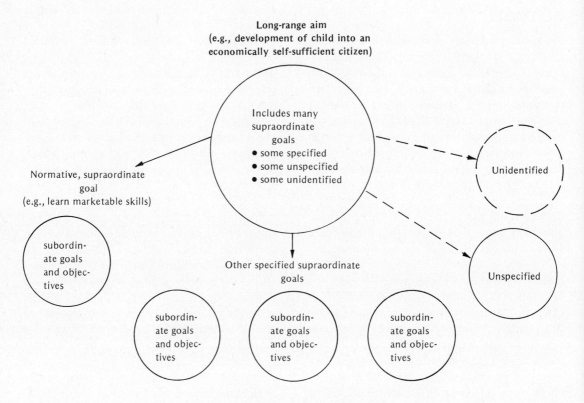

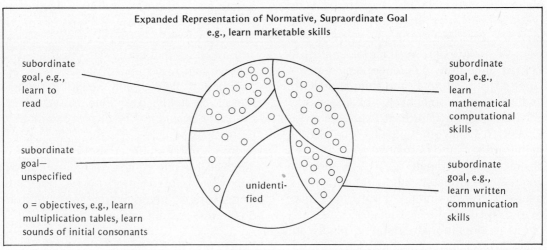

jectives. The debate that has raged around this topic involves major philosophical, theoretical, and practical considerations. At the heart of the matter lies the most basic and profound concerns associated with psychoeducational interventions. Therefore, it is imperative that these matters be underscored. To highlight the central issues and problems, this section presents a brief discussion of (1) criteria for determining level of abstraction in specifying objectives and (2) unspecified objectives.

Criteria for determining level of abstraction. Specifying objectives is not synonymous with stating them at a high level of specificity. Whether they are stated as behavioral objectives, there remains the problem of determining degree of specificity.

> On the one hand, the statement of an objective should not be so general and global as to be meaningless, nor, on the other hand, should the statement be so narrow and specific that the educational process seems to be made up of isolated bits and pieces. In the latter case an adequate list of objectives becomes too long and too unwieldy to use effectively. (Thorndike & Hagen, 1977, p. 202)

Ultimately both the nature and scope of intervention are determined by the decision-making process that leads to adopting certain objectives and rejecting others. Deciding what constitutes an appropriate objective involves the application of criteria for judging the *utility* (i.e., potency, power) and *economy* of what is specified. An objective that has high utility is one that, once acquired, significantly increases competence, or in the case of an activity, may lead to outcomes that can significantly increase competence. The economy of a set of intervention objectives is determined by how much time, space, intervener competence, and so forth, are needed.

Logically, objectives of potentially high utility and economy encompass more than one observable behavioral outcome or activ-

VIEWPOINT

THE UTILITY AND ECONOMY OF OBJECTIVES

> There are too many particulars to teach and to master. If we are to do justice to our evolution, we shall need, as never before a way of transmitting the crucial ideas and skills, the acquired characteristics that express and amplify [individual's] powers. We may be sure that the task will demand our highest talents. I would be content if we began, all of us, by recognizing that this is our task, as learned [individuals] and scientists, that discovering how to make something comprehensible to the young is only a continuation of making something comprehensible to ourselves in the first place—that understanding and aiding others to understand are both of a piece.
> Bruner (1966, p. 38)

ity and are stated at a somewhat low level of specificity. (The lower the level of specificity, the higher the level of abstraction.) From this perspective, the view that all intervention objectives should be stated with a high degree of specificity is seen as incorrect. What is important for measurement or evaluation purposes is only that the observables encompassed by an objective be identified and understood. In contrast to suggestions that all objectives be stated in highly specific behavioral terms, outcome objectives should be stated with a low level of specificity (1) whenever it is more economical to do so, such as when there is high likelihood of "transfer of training" or generalization of learning (e.g., when the "whole" or a general principle can be taught appropriately rather than having to teach each separate part or instance), and (2) in the many situations where only a low level of competence or involvement is to be attained. Furthermore, it is evident that objectives must be stated with a low level of specificity whenever they are associated with goals and aims that have not been well defined and when complex activities must be pursued.

In general, minutely detailed itemizations of skills as presented in many basal textbooks, programmed materials, and as advocated by some proponents of behavioral objectives usually are unnecessary. They may be harmful when they lead teachers to believe that students must be *taught* every one of the skills. Students do not need to have everything taught. They often learn skills independently. Rigidly conceived procedures and materials ignore this fact as well as a variety of other individual differences and may result in lost time and negative attitudes that result from the error of "teaching" a student something he or she already knows or by forcing a student to cope with something which he or she cannot learn or is determined not to learn at the time.

Unspecified outcomes. Given the current state of knowledge, it seems safe to conclude that not all outcomes are, can be, or should be specified. Two types of very important and contrasting unspecified outcomes can be briefly highlighted: (1) unplanned positive outcomes, such as serendipitous learning, and (2) unstated or unintended negative consequences (negative side effects).

1. *Unplanned positive outcomes.* Almost everyone can point to unplanned experiences that led to unexpected positive benefits that were among the most important events in one's life. Sometimes an outcome was important in and of itself, and sometimes it was the key to motivating profound changes in attitudes, learning, and performance. The more highly prescribed an intervention is, the less opportunity there may be for such serendipity.

   All important facets of an intervention's aims and goals need not be and, given the limitations of current knowledge, often cannot be translated into objectives. The more an intervention prescribes objectives that fill up available time, the less opportunity there is for unprescribable, but still extremely important, events. There will be little opportunity, for instance, for the types of exploration that allow individuals to accomplish outcomes not well enough understood to be programmed or that cannot be achieved through programming since their very essence depends on autonomous choice and self-discovery. Specific examples of such outcomes may be the development of high self-esteem, high order interpersonal skills associated with empathy and altruistic values, ability to make one's own decisions and effectively solve personal and interpersonal problems, enjoyment of literature and fine arts, and so forth.

   With particular reference to learning and behavior problems, any tendency to use all available intervention time to pursue prescriptions related only to remedying identified problems risks enshrouding the activity in a pall of pathology and having it experienced as a "grind." Major interventions, such as school programs, cannot justify being narrowly focused on problem remediation; to do so may be counterproductive to even accomplishing their narrow focus. Most school and institutional programs are responsible for more than remedying problems. They also are responsible for ongoing development in nonproblem areas. In either connection, it can be argued there should be the type of developmental, recreational, and enrichment experiences that make the painstaking effort to overcome one's problems and learn basics at least tolerable and perhaps even increasingly desirable. Moreover, both an organismic approach to human motivation and a humanistic orientation to development suggest such experiences should provide the opportunity for problem students to find areas where they can be competent and even excel and areas where they can feel self-determining and joyful. In a humane society all persons are seen as entitled to opportunities for finding their individuality. They must not be deprived of this right because they are seen as special, exceptional, and so forth. Clearly, what is being suggested· in no way contradicts the need for planning outcomes and activities; the point is simply that there also must be time and opportunities for unplanned positive outcomes and activities.

2. *Unstated or unintended negative consequences.* Few, if any, major interventions can claim to have no negative features. Even when negative consequences are known, they often go unstated and thus plans are not made for dealing with them. Obviously, there is little justification for this and in most cases such action is unethical. (A contemporary example of this is the growing concern over negative consequences, both physical and psychological, of treating "hyperactivity" with stimulant drugs.)

Of equal ethical concern are those unintended negative consequences that are not known and thus cannot be foreseen. The possible occurrence of such negative outcomes, however, should be expected. Some evaluation models set out to measure not only intended outcomes, but all outcomes of major consequence. Such approaches can be used informally to monitor behavior for signs of iatrogenic effects. The need for research to identify as yet unknown negative outcomes is indisputable. In

FOR EXAMPLE

UNINTENDED OUTCOMES

Evaluators seem more attentive to possible program side effects . . . than they were a few years ago, partly because of the emphasis placed on side effects by such authors as Messick (1970), Scriven (1967), and Suchman (1967). This concern with side effects is more novel among those working in the educational and social-action fields than those in medical fields, where researchers have long attended to the issue even when distributors and practitioners appeared to ignore their warnings. Of course, not all side effects are negative. When early Head Start advocates could find little comfort in the size of IQ increments among their charges (an inappropriate major criterion of effectiveness of that program in any case, but one used simply because 'the tests were there'), they could point with some pride to the involvement of enormous numbers of parents and to the diagnosis and treatment of medical defects for many, many children (Temp and Anderson, 1966; Grotberg, 1969).

Anderson and Ball (1978, pp. 29–30)

Chapter 16 we explore such ethical concerns in a broader context; in Chapter 17 we discuss this as a major concern related to evaluation.

To have identified, inductively or deductively, as many objectives as is feasible is an invaluable aid to planning, implementation, and evaluation. Moreover, for evaluation, it is undeniably important that observable and measurable facets be delineated. Listings of outcome objectives, however, are meant only as a general aid, not as specific prescriptions of intervention content and outcomes. Obviously many more specifics can be delineated than can, or should, be the focus of intentional interventions. For example, if a teacher tries to teach too many specifics related to any one goal, other goals will be slighted due to time constraints. Ultimately, the range of content taught and outcomes achieved will be altered drastically.

Our intent in the next section is to broaden the preceding discussion by highlighting a wider range of content and outcomes for persons and environments. The general frameworks presented can be used to generate specific objectives related to comprehensive intervention efforts.

Broadening Outcomes and Content

In the LD field, objectives usually are limited to a rather narrow range of intervention outcomes focusing on developmental problems in individuals. Motivational and attitudinal outcomes are seldom systematically delineated, which is ironic because, in many learning and behavior problems, low motivation and negative attitudes are a central feature of the problem. It is more than ironic, however, when objectives continue to be formulated for individuals in cases where the focal point of intervention should be the environment. For example, given that a classroom or home situation is identified as culpable, environmental variables logically should be the focal point of intervention at least some of the time. At such times, objectives should be formulated with reference to desired environmental changes. Similarly, if the focal point of intervention should be the interaction of person and environment, then objectives need to be formulated for both.

In this section, we first explore how outcomes and content can be expanded with regard to person-focused interventions. Then we outline some key variables which might be considered in broadening the focus of interventions designed to improve environments and interactions.

In general, to facilitate planning of person-focused intervention, aims and goals can be translated into major *areas of development* and *types of content and outcomes*. Such areas and types are widely discussed in the psychoeducational literature in terms of general domains of human functioning, such as cognitive, affective, and psychomotor domains (Bloom, Engelhart, Furst, Hill, & Krathwohl, 1956; Kibler, Barker, & Miles, 1970; Krathwohl, Bloom, & Masia, 1964). Each domain has been delineated taxonomically to identify component parts and to reduce the level of abstraction. This work synthesizes a broad range of person-focused outcomes and demonstrates how highly abstract aims and goals can be translated into components and continuously subdivided (see Appendix B). Carried to its logical end, the minutest and most concrete behaviors can be identified.[1]

For persons manifesting learning problems, intervention outcomes also may be conceived in terms of different *levels of intervention focus*. Intervention may focus on any or all of three levels. At the most direct, and thus highest, level in the hierarchy, objectives address the pursuit of current life tasks and interests. Examples include learning to multiply, memorization of multiplication tables, learning initial consonant sounds, learning to work independently and to relate effectively to others, increasing

---

[1]For the most part, the works cited reflect deductive approaches to identifying relevant content and outcomes, that is, the specific components are deduced by rationally dividing each supraordinate goal into subgoals and then into specific objectives. In contrast, an inductive approach to planning outcomes and content could be used to specify as completely as feasible the objectives encompassed by each goal, group them into appropriate subsets of one or more objectives, and then label the subsets.

In addition to the references cited in this chapter, demonstrations of attempts to translate highly abstract aims and goals into specifics are found in curriculum guides, teacher manuals, and outlines and charts (e.g., taxonomies, scope and sequence charts) published by textbook companies and by education and evaluation centers and agencies.

motivation for learning, and expanding areas of interest (Cartledge & Milburn, 1980; Kohlberg & Mayer, 1972; Mercer & Mercer, 1981). At this level, if the intent is to help a student overcome a reading problem, the objectives formulated are related to motivation, attitudes, behavior, skills, and knowledge directly associated with the current reading curriculum.

At the next level, objectives emphasize acquisition of prerequisites not adequately developed and needed for pursuing current life tasks and interests. Instead of teaching comprehension of the main idea in a paragraph or the steps in a math problem, the focus might be on learning to order and sequence events, or follow directions, or, alternatively, on basic motivation and attitudes toward learning and schooling (Feldman, 1981; Gresham, 1981; Harris & Sipay, 1980; Hewett & Taylor, 1980).

At the most indirect and lowest level, objectives for students with learning problems address incompatible behaviors and interests and underlying psychological processing dysfunctions and resulting deficits presumed to interfere with pursuit of current life tasks and interests. Such objectives have as their focus ways to improve and compensate for attentional, perceptual, and psycholinguistic deficits, eliminate avoidance motivation and antisocial interactions, and so forth (Hewett & Taylor, 1980; Lerner, 1981; Mann, Goodman, & Weiderholt, 1978; Myers & Hammill, 1976).

The areas of development, types of content and outcomes, and levels of intervention focus are viewed as interacting dimensions (see Figure 12–2) reflecting a wide range of intervention content for persons with psychoeducational problems. The matrix produced by these interacting dimensions provides a framework for generating intervention objectives. Each cell in the matrix can be used to deduce and clarify subgoals, outcome objectives, and content to be

pursued. The products of this activity are obvious aids for evaluation.

The matrix presented in Figure 12–2, however, still does not capture the total complexity of formulating intervention outcomes. Another major dimension to be considered is the *degree of intended learning and change*. For example, in presenting ideas, the intended learning can range from budding awareness to an in-depth understanding. Objectives associated with skill competence can range from developing minimal ability to perfecting a high level of performance capability. Motivational and attitudinal objectives can range from awakening interest to stimulating a high degree of appreciation, personal valuing, and expectation of success. Decisions about the degree of intended learning and change clearly are critical in shaping the content and outcomes to be pursued. When the time available for intervention is short, this dimension is a major determinant of the range of content the intervention can pursue.

Formulation of any intervention objectives involving the *environment* requires an understanding of environmental facets that might be causing problems and of those seen as the appropriate objects of change in ameliorating problems. In effect, what is needed is knowledge of significant environmental variables and their impact. Such knowledge includes delineation of key characteristics of persons, tasks, and processes in immediate behavioral settings and surrounding contexts. Table 12–1 represents one attempt to outline key variables hypothesized to be of major significance in understanding the impact of environments.

The variables in Table 12–1 represent factors that need to be considered in developing content, outcome objectives, and procedures for interventions designed to change environments. As is evident, some of these factors are conditions that may have to be accommodated, but many are variables

Figure 12-2

A matrix for generating a wide range of intervention content and objectives for students manifesting learning problems.

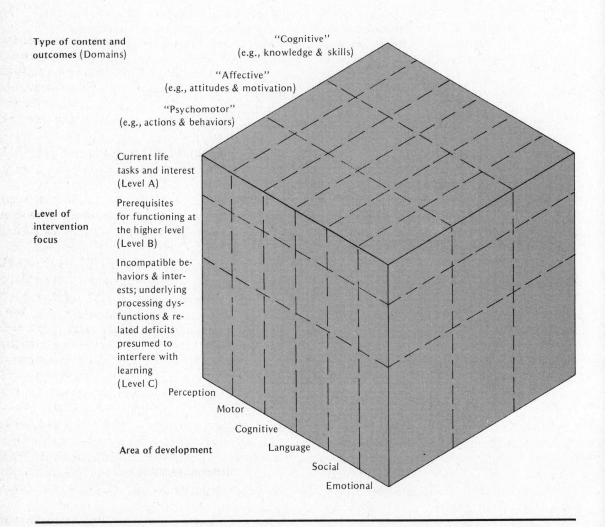

Type of content and outcomes (Domains)

"Cognitive" (e.g., knowledge & skills)

"Affective" (e.g., attitudes & motivation)

"Psychomotor" (e.g., actions & behaviors)

Current life tasks and interest (Level A)

Level of intervention focus

Prerequisites for functioning at the higher level (Level B)

Incompatible behaviors & interests; underlying processing dysfunctions & related deficits presumed to interfere with learning (Level C)

Perception

Motor

Cognitive

Area of development

Language

Social

Emotional

that can be manipulated to produce potent effects—which are discussed later in this chapter.

Steps for Planning Specific Outcomes and Content

It is worth stressing that most groupings of goals and objectives constitute theories and hypotheses. The relationships among many sets of goals and objectives have not been empirically demonstrated and many are not amenable to construct validation. Thus, a significant probability exists that content and outcomes that merit intervention focus are unknown or are being ignored. All systems and ways of categorizing intervention outcomes and content risk distorting and masking the full nature of complex human

TABLE 12-1

Relevant environmental variables for planning intervention[a]

I. Setting and context characteristics
   A. Organizational format
      (e.g., personnel patterns, client/student groupings)
   B. Locale, nature, and scope
      (e.g., geographic context, architectural features, availability and use of materials and furnishings, population "density")
   C. Climate
      (e.g., perceptions of physical, social, intellectual, political, and moral atmosphere)
II. Characteristics of the participants
   A. Formal role identification
      (e.g., intervener, client, student, parent, societal agent, and/or association with specific organizations)
   B. Demographics
      (e.g., urban/rural, ethnicity, socioeconomic status, sex and age distribution, association with specific groups)
   C. Individual differences in current motivation and development
      (e.g., competence, commitment, perceptions of self and others)
   D. Criteria and standards used in judging person characteristics
      (e.g., absolute or relative standards about good-bad, normal-abnormal, success-failure; psychological, socioeconomic-political criteria; cutoff points altering the number of false negatives and false positives)

III. Task-process-outcome characteristics
   A. General features
      1. Quantitative
         (e.g., amount to be accomplished; sequencing, duration, pacing, and rate; number of persons required or involved)
      2. Qualitative
         (e.g., underlying rationale; intrinsic and extrinsic value; cooperative or competitive; actual and perceived difficulty)
   B. Specific types, areas, and levels of tasks and outcomes
      (e.g., current system tasks; prerequisites needed to perform current tasks; remediation; development; enrichment)
   C. Specific processes
      1. Procedural methods and models
         (e.g., helping or socialization; mechanistic-behavioral, industrial, humanistic; role of participants; nature of structure)
      2. Tools (actions/experiences/materials)
         (e.g., communication, practice, learning; printed material such as texts and workbooks; audiovisual—including computer—presentations; games)
      3. Techniques
         (e.g., variations in the characteristics of a tool or the way it is applied such as varying intensity, duration, patterning, and cuing; systematic or unsystematic feedback, rewards, punishments)

a. While primary, secondary, and tertiary environments might each be the focus of change, the examples here emphasize variables in the primary environment.

behavior, environments, and their interaction. Given that theory is a primary basis for formulating and translating underlying intervention rationales, improvement in planning involves considerably more than requiring interveners to formulate outcome objectives. Significant progress in the field requires comprehensive and systematic efforts at theory building and concomitant empirical investigation, for example, to clarify desired aims and translate them into feasible plans of action.

Planning intervention not only requires major applications of theory, but inevitably reflects major philosophical and theoretical biases. One such bias currently in vogue is

FOR EXAMPLE

DIFFERENTIAL IMPACT OF ENVIRONMENTS
ON STUDENT GAINS

Primary grade students make the greatest gains in reading and mathematics in classes that are warm, task oriented, and systematic and orderly, that is, classes that emphasize all three learning environment domains. Students in these classes do as well on such outcome criteria as creativity and positive self concept as do students in classes that are warm and flexible but less task oriented and structured. However, children show higher scores on nonverbal reasoning, have lower absence rates, and display greater willingness to work independently when in flexible classroom settings that provide more exploratory materials and allow more individual freedom. Furthermore, students in classes that emphasize task orientation and structure but that are relatively low in warmth do well on standard achievement test measures but less well on indexes of creativity and self esteem (see Bennett, 1976; Kennedy, 1978; Soloman and Kendall, in press; Stallings, 1975). . . .

Rosenshine (1978) . . . suggested that stu-dents in formal classes obtain better achievement test results because teachers use instructional techniques that require more time devoted to academics and greater coverage of content. Students in formal classes where academics are not emphasized (such as control oriented classes) should not do particularly well on achievement indexes, whereas students in informal classes with much academically engaged time and content covered (such as supportive task oriented classes) should show high performance gains. These ideas are supported by recent work showing that children in open program classes with enthusiastic teachers and a high press for achievement do better in mathematics (Eshel and Klein, 1978) and by studies noting the importance of signal input continuity by other students and the teacher and of fewer 'call outs' (interruptions) during academic discussions (see, for example, Crawford and others, 1977; Kounin and Doyle, 1975).

Moos (1979, pp. 195–98)

the view that all intervention objectives should be stated in highly concrete behavioral terms and focus on outcomes for specific individuals. While each planning phase can be greatly facilitated by identifying all observable components, this is not a sufficient argument for restricting the planning of intervention objectives to discrete and limited behavioral outcomes. On the contrary, many objectives can only be formulated at a rather high level of abstraction and ambiguity given that so many important components of desired intervention outcomes are poorly understood and not readily observable or measurable. Moreover, where positive outcomes are anticipated as a result of certain activities, but cannot be specified in advance, objectives can only be stated in terms of activities to be implemented.

In general, then, specifications of outcomes and content inevitably involves the use of philosophical and theoretical standards regarding what is desirable and desired, as well as what is most feasible, useful, and economical. Unavoidably, there are instances where many of the observable components of an outcome are unknown. In such instances, objectives will be imprecisely understood and subjected to varying interpretations, thereby producing significant and often undesired variations in implementation and resulting outcomes.

Given that planning intervention outcomes involves considerably more than specifying objectives, the following steps are offered as broad guidelines for planning specific content and outcomes.

1. Determine desired changes and who or what is to be the focal point of intervention, that is, whether person, environment, or both are to change.

2. Clarify long-term *aims* to be accomplished related to the object of change.

3. With reference to goals, clarify possible short-term and immediate *outcome objectives* and *activity objectives* (e.g., content and procedures).

4. Formulate specific intervention plans including short-term and immediate outcome and activity objectives to be pursued in accomplishing intended changes. This involves three major tasks: first, assessment of present functioning to determine areas and degree of strength, weakness, and limitation, as well as preferred modes and interfering factors; second, decision making as to immediate changes to be made; and third, decisions about appropriate level of specificity of objectives based on judgments of utility and economy.

5. Determine that opportunities exist for acquisition of unspecified positive outcomes and that plans are made to deal with negative consequences.

6. Use data collected during intervention to revise and modify immediate outcome and activity objectives to keep them consistent with long-term aims and goals.

Probably all this sounds as if it is so difficult and so much work that it could not be important enough to be worth all the trouble. Planning appropriate content and outcomes is complex and it is hard work, but it is worth it. Planning can provide conceptual clarity about the content one is working with and

VIEWPOINT

EDUCATIONAL OBJECTIVES

What the best and wisest parent wants for his [or her] own child that must the community want for all of its children. Any other idea for our schools is narrow and unlovely.
Dewey (1889, p. 7)

outcomes to be achieved. Planning establishes specific road signs for reassurance that one is headed in the right direction. Planning is the sine qua non of *intentional* intervention. If one is going to "interfere" in someone else's life, one has the responsibility for doing so with explicit clarity of purpose and a sophisticated approach. Moreover, in providing interventions for those with psychoeducational problems, as John Dewey (1899) implied, we should set out with the intent of providing a richness and quality of experience that matches the best we provide for those without problems.

PROCEDURES CONCEIVED IN GENERIC TERMS

Given that certain content and outcomes are to be implemented, the focus of intervention planning turns to procedures for accomplishing these in an *optimal* manner, that is, in a manner that is more than efficient. Efficiency is important, but it is meaningless in the absence of effectiveness. The intent is to be effective, efficient, and to avoid, or at least minimize, negative side effects.

Considerable controversy exists over which psychoeducational methods and settings, if any, are effective. The status of applied research in psychology and education is such that questions of efficacy probably will remain without satisfactory answers for a long time (Glaser, 1982). What is clear is that many appropriate changes occur and many problems are overcome regardless of the method used: some appropriate changes and resolutions of problems occur without formal intervention; some problems continue despite the best intervention procedures.

Because there is no definitive set of psychoeducational procedures or procedural principles, the emphasis here is on synthesizing current thought. The intent is to underscore a wide range of procedural options and point to directions for advancing the field. The premise is that, at this time, a scholarly and sophisticated eclecticism (as contrasted with either a grab-bag approach or a highly doctrinaire orientation) probably is the best strategy for practitioners and for some stages of research.

Underlying the concepts and suggestions discussed in this chapter are the following assumptions: (1) intervention procedures for learning and behavior problems are intended to lead to significant, long-term improvements for those experiencing problems; (2) means should be as consistent with ends as is feasible; and (3) means should be qualitatively satisfying ends in themselves —psychoeducational procedures should improve the immediate quality of daily experiences.

Assumptions that *remedial* and *regular procedures* are based on different psychological principles obscures important similarities and implications. Efforts are being made in psychology and education to explore the commonalities and to clarify the critical procedural components in contrasting in-

VIEWPOINT

ECLECTICISM

Increasingly, when asked their orientation, interveners seem to be responding that they take an "eclectic" view. Having said this, some can list many specific theories and techniques they use; other know much less. We have come to distinguish three types of eclecticism:

Naive eclecticism—The tendency to assimilate indiscriminately and use each new perspective, viewpoint, concept, and technique one learns is naive eclecticism; the intervener is rather casual in adopting ideas and procedures. It is this casual and indiscriminate approach that results in eclecticism being viewed negatively by some professionals.

Professional/empirical eclecticism—Having years of experience, professional practitioners have encountered and tried many procedures. They differentiate among those practices that never

seem to work for them and thus should be avoided and those that are likely to be useful in a particular situation. In some instances, professionals develop a philosophical (as contrasted with a theoretical) stance and try to use only those practices that fit their philosophy.

Scholarly eclecticism—Based on systematic investigation and theoretical and philosophical analyses, some professionals evolve a set of procedures that is comprehensive, integrated, and consistent. Scholarly eclecticism consists of a comprehensive set of philosophical, theoretical, and empirical principles applied in a coordinated and integrated fashion.

While all of us would like to claim a scholarly view, all three types of eclecticism are likely to be found in any large intervention program.

terventions (e.g., Adelman & Taylor, in press; Garfield & Bergin, 1978; Howard & Orlinsky, 1972; Rhodes & Tracy, 1972; Sundberg, Tyler, & Taplin, 1973; Urban & Ford, 1971; Westbury & Bellack, 1971).

Based on our analysis of the literature and our experiences in the field, we suggest that all psychoeducational interveners manipulate the same types of variables. Table 12–1 represents our initial grouping of such variables (i.e., characteristics of participants, task-process-outcome characteristics, and setting and contextual characteristics). We also find it helpful to conceptualize the intent of procedural planning as that of accomplishing six comprehensive objectives:

- to establish and maintain an appropriate working relationship (e.g., trust, communication, support, overcoming emotional inhibitors, and fostering motivation) among those directly involved in the intervention;

- to clarify the purpose (aims or outcomes) of the intervention and particularly any specific problems that are to be solved;

- to clarify the intervention procedures to be used and the reasons they can be expected to be effective (e.g., structure, sequence, and consequences);

- to clarify any other procedures, such as evaluative measures, and why they are necessary;

- to produce the changes; and, finally,

- to terminate the intervention appropriately.

In exploring commonalities and critical differences a procedure is defined very broadly as any variable (such as those in Table 12–2) that can be manipulated in an effort to facilitate intended changes in the condition of a system (either person or setting or both).

Of course, efforts to stimulate intended changes in an optimal manner require concepts or principles to guide manipulation of key variables. In particular, optimal use of material, activities, and techniques in a planful way requires understanding why they are needed and why they should work in a given instance. The concept of the *match* is helpful in this regard and, therefore, is reviewed prior to discussion of methods and setting characteristics.

Motivational and Developmental Match

Since the concept of the match is outlined in Chapter 3, only a brief additional discussion is needed. The earlier presentation explored individual learning; the focus is broadened here to include organizational and interactional changes.

Psychoeducational interventions often are described as starting from "where the client is." In a commonsense way, this maxim suggests the essence of the need for well-planned intervention procedures. For many interveners, however, this phrase means simply not requiring responses beyond present developmental levels (e.g., Hunt & Sullivan, 1974; Miller, 1981). For some the phrase may mean matching current motivational levels. For a few, the idea is understood to mean there is a need to match both motivation and development in the sense of personalized intervention within an interaction model. To convey the fullest sense of this important topic, the last of these positions is described below.

From an interaction perspective, decisions about procedural variables are guided by a desire to establish environmental opportunities (e.g., tasks, activities, settings) which maximize the likelihood of a good motivational and developmental match. In teaching, for instance, the intent is to establish an environment that evokes an optimal match with the concepts, skills, and attitudes a student has assimilated. Such an optimal match is seen as appropriately challenging the individual's assimilated way of adapting to environmental circumstances, which leads to accommodative modification and growth as manifested in the way a system (e.g., individual or organization) copes and functions. Assimilation of new ways of coping and functioning are assumed to follow if there are sufficient opportunities for use. Thus, planning for an optimal match also means that procedures are planned to encourage use. It should be noted that an optimal match implies that many aspects of the system's current functioning will be accepted as they are and not challenged.

Efforts to establish and maintain an optimal match are complicated by continuous changes resulting from experience and maturation. Further complications arise because of the varying degrees of understanding, access, and control interveners have over relevant environmental circumstances. Because of such complications, procedures to establish and maintain an optimal match are based on trial and appraisal. Some direction is provided by knowledge of the *general* trends and stages of human and organizational development and functioning. Further direction is provided when the intervener has acquired *specific* knowledge about particular objects of intervention as the result of assessment. Ideally, then, procedures are planned with reference to both a general and specific knowledge base, which, from a psychological perspective, includes major facets of human functioning such as motivation, attention, information processing, decision making, and interpersonal dynamics.[2]

Most practitioners recognize the impact of individual differences. There is little doubt that normative strategies often are indicated, as when general setting and contextual variables are mostly responsible for the existence of a problem. However, there also is little doubt about the frequency with which normative strategies do not work. It is for this reason that all intervention requires plans for modifying normative ideas. The guiding principle is to approximate an optimal match. Recognition of this need is reflected in the increasing emphasis on individualization and personalization of psychoeducational intervention.

Unfortunately, sophisticated research on subtle interactions and transactions associated with change processes has proven difficult to accomplish. Research on aptitude-treatment interactions sometimes is cited in this connection as the most relevant evidence of both the problems and promise of concepts such as the match (e.g., see research discussed by Arter & Jenkins, 1979; Berliner & Cahen, 1973; Bracht, 1970; Cronbach & Snow, 1977; Garfield & Bergin, 1978; Hunt & Sullivan, 1974; Janicki & Peterson, 1981; Reed, Rabe, & Mankinen, 1970; and Salomon, 1972). However, aptitude-treatment interaction research generally has not focused on a broad range of person variables, especially motivational variables and nonproblematic conditions, nor has it considered interventions designed to change settings. While such research is of potential importance, it is but one line of investigation

---

[2] These psychological constructs encompass such topics as the role of realistic goals, choice, commitment, incentives, curiosity, strivings for competence, schedules of reinforcement, negative consequences, feedback, expectation and set, intensity and vividness, cues, stimuli covariation, life circumstances, active participation, massed versus distributed practice, overlearning, memory and assimilated schemata, group dynamics in informal and formal settings, sense of community, task focus versus ego-oriented communication, leadership styles, and so forth.

VIEWPOINT

MOTIVATIONAL MATCH

We let the individual read and write anything he [or she] wishes, and in this way get the various elements as parts of meaningful wholes. . . . [A] profile of errors . . . is not essential for our technique except as a means of obtaining scientific records. . . .

The rapid reader who has no difficulty in learning to read attains skill through much reading of material that is of interest to him [or her]. As ability to read develops, the individual turns to books and other writings for information and amusement. In attempting to obtain information or to get the outcomes of a story, *he [or she] reads as rapidly as possible and so develops all the necessary apperceptive and physiological adjustments. . . . The slow reader will improve in speed and comprehension if he [or she] develops sufficient recognition of words and phrases to make out what is on the printed page and then reads sufficient material that possesses a high degree of interest for him [or her]. Final success in any remedial work in reading can be achieved only if it includes much reading in which interest in content is the pacer.*

Fernald (1943, pp. 73–75)

bearing on the planning of procedures to optimize intervention. Two key examples of other potentially relevant research areas are psychological studies on the reciprocal determinism of behavior (e.g., Bandura, 1978) and on organizational changes (e.g., Fullan, Miles, and Taylor, 1980). At this time, however, research unfortunately has neither clarified the efficacy of any specific procedures in ameliorating severe learning problems nor the general mechanisms that make any of a range of procedures appear to produce satisfactory changes in the majority of mild-moderate cases. It has proven far easier to create and develop procedures than to provide satisfactory data on their effectiveness and underlying mechanisms. Thus, a solution to the problem of the match is still elusive.

Methods

The focus in planning procedures is not on isolated events. Instead of considering manipulating one procedure at a time, interveners usually have some overall method or implementation plan that guides the se- lection of certain procedures and the rejection of others. Procedures are not only guided by concepts such as the match but by general methods subscribed to by an intervener.

In discussing methods, the following definitions are used. Intervention *methods* are the regular, systematic, and orderly use of *tools* and *techniques*, based on a general *model* of intervention. A *model* is an overall pattern or plan that guides the course of intervention. It usually incorporates both content and the kinds of procedures (tools and techniques) to be pursued. *Tools* are the specific instruments or types of actions, experiences, or materials used to implement an intervention. *Techniques* are planned variations in the characteristics of a tool or the way it is applied, the immediate intent of which is to increase attraction and acceptability and decrease avoidance and distraction.

A brief analysis of the essential features of models, tools, and techniques provides an understanding of the range of procedural options.

Individual practitioners often simply want

VIEWPOINT

ACTIVE METHODS

The use of active methods . . . gives broad scope to the spontaneous research of the child or adolescent and require that every new truth to be learned be rediscovered or at least reconstructed by the student and not simply imparted to him [or her]. Two common misunderstandings however have diminished the value of the efforts made in this field up to now. The first is the fear (and sometimes hope) that the teacher would have no role to play in these experiments and that their success would depend on leaving the students entirely free to work or play as they will. It is obvious that the teacher as organizer remains indispensable in order to create the situations and construct the initial devices which present useful problems to the child. Secondly, he [or she] is needed to provide counter-examples that compel reflection and reconsideration of over-hasty solutions. What is desired is that the teacher cease being a lecturer, satisfied with transmitting ready-made solutions; his [or her] role should rather be that of a mentor stimulating initiative and research.

Piaget (1973, pp. 15–16)

a set of "practical" procedures. It should be clear by this point, however, that the creation and development of overall procedural strategies require a rationale including theoretical and philosophical propositions, as well as data indicating the appropriateness of such propositions. Cookbook recipes may be sound places for practitioners to learn how to proceed. Advancement of a field and avoidance of inappropriate fads and panaceas, however, require an understanding and critical evaluation of underlying models.

Applied to methods, a *model* provides systematic guidance for specific procedural choices. For example, with regard to teaching, Joyce and Weil (1972) have proposed

that there are four families of models that have "much to say about the kinds of realities which will be admitted to the classroom and the kinds of life-view which are likely to be generated as teacher and learner work together" (p. 3). The four families of models encompassing sixteen separate, but not mutually exclusive, models are classified as

(1) those oriented toward social relations and toward the relation of [persons] and [their] culture and which draw upon social sources; (2) those which draw on information processing systems and descriptions of human capacity for processing information; (3) those which draw on personality development, the processes of personal construction of reality, and the capacity to function as an integrated personality as the major source; (4) those developed from an analysis of the processes by which human behavior is shaped and reinforced. (p. 8)

What becomes clear from such a classification is that adherents of different models often plan and implement very different procedures in keeping with their orientations. For example, advocates of social relations models are likely to generate procedures involving group interactions as an integral part of most classroom activity, but with no intention of manipulating social reinforcers and without much concern about social reinforcement influences. In contrast, those whose models emphasize the shaping and reinforcement of behavior are likely to stress contingency management procedures and might only inaugurate group interactions as part of a management strategy.

The models Joyce and Weil categorize apply to interventions for students with and without problems. In addition, as outlined earlier, various models of cause and correction also profoundly shape methods for learning and behavior problems. For instance, in Chapter 9 we explored the differences in assessment procedures selected by those who subscribe to (1) an underlying abilities orientation (e.g., a disordered-person model) or (2) a skill deficiency view (e.g., seen as caused by developmental lag). Similarly, in that chapter we clarified that interveners associated with one or the other orientation select different corrective procedures (i.e., one group stresses therapy procedures, the other pursues behavior modification approaches). In contrast, those who adopt environment and interaction models choose assessment and corrective procedures which seem most consistent with their perspective, such as rearranging physical and social environmental variables or strategies emphasizing mutual accommodation of person and environment.

Tools are the specific instruments or types of actions/experiences/materials used to implement an intervention. All packaged and published materials—such as the DISTAR materials and programs (e.g., Engelmann & Bruner, 1974) for teaching reading, language, and math skills—are tools. However, these types of materials also prescribe specific content and outcomes, reflect specific models of intervention, and incorporate a particular set of techniques.

There is a variety of ways to categorize tools. A quick perusal suggests that tools in common use might be grouped rather simply by

purpose (e.g., communication, learning, practice, construction, creative expression, enrichment, recreation, and entertainment);

form (e.g., printed material such as texts, workbooks, and library materials; audiovisual, including computer, presentation; lectures; one-on-one group discussions; role playing; games; and machines, instruments, and equipment for cooking, science, music, art, athletics, electronics, photography, animal care, woodworking); and

source (e.g., publishers, community resources, and intervener-made materials).

The tendency in education is to group tools in terms of activities. A number of efforts have been made to categorize specific types of activities (e.g., Burton, 1962; Hyman, 1970; Hough & Duncan, 1970; and Joyce & Weil, 1972). Diedrich (reported in Burton, 1962) lists about one hundred eighty activities organized into eight groupings: visual, oral, listening, writing, drawing, motor, mental, and emotional. Darrow and Van Allen (1961) group activities, which students can do independently, into four categories: searching, organizing, originating, and communicating. Means (1968) discusses activities as well as techniques under the general rubric of methodology and organizes them as: group, dramatic, student-oriented, teacher-initiated, material-focused, and equipment-centered. Lerner (1976) groups activities used in the LD field into areas of human dysfunctioning (see Appendix C).

Although each categorization of activities is helpful, classification by activity fails to distinguish among procedural components and between processes and content. The various groupings of *activities* camouflage conceptual distinctions of importance in planning. Thus, tools should be viewed as more than activities. To this end, tools are viewed as encompassing all noncontent facets of activities, materials, and so forth. While some of the ways activities are categorized could be used in classifying tools, a broader approach seems necessary. From our perspective, tools might be classified by purpose, form, and source in terms of different focal points of intervention. Thus, they could be grouped with regard to those which are focused on producing (1) physical changes in the person, such as drugs and diets, (2) psychological changes in the person, such as cognitive strategies and counseling, (3) environmental changes to produce person changes, such as teaching parents and teachers to use behavior modification approaches, and (4) environmental changes to accommodate a wider range of individual differences, such as adding materials to accommodate a broad range of motivational differences.

Another way tools might be classified is with reference to the type of intervention activity for which they are designed, that is, assessment, instruction, treatment, enrichment. For instance, a wide range of remedial and psychotherapeutic treatments could be classified in terms of traditional and contemporary therapy or behavior-oriented approaches (e.g., Kanfer & Goldstein, 1980; Sabatino, Schmidt, & Miller, 1981). Similarly, assessment, instructional, and enrichment approaches could be classified into major groupings.

Our intent here is not to argue for a particular way of categorizing tools. Almost any way they are grouped will benefit interveners by increasing their awareness of a range of procedural options. Given that such categorization is worth pursuing, we suggest that the initial focus should be on general categories in order to highlight the potential breadth of use.

Psychoeducational *techniques* are viewed as the way in which tools (e.g., materials, activities, tasks) are developed and used. For instance, the same activity can be pursued under different degrees of guidance and support by varying the amount of cueing and prompting. More specifically, with regard to immediate intent, techniques can be viewed as planned variations in the characteristics of a tool or the way it is applied. These variations are designed to increase attraction and accessibility and decrease avoidance and distraction. That is, the intent is to enhance (1) motivation (attitudes, commitment, approach, follow-through), (2) sensory intake (perceptual search and detection of external stimuli intended to initiate action and pro-

VIEWPOINT

SHOULD THE STUDENT ADAPT TO THE LESSON OR SHOULD THE LESSON ADAPT TO THE STUDENT?

Our hypothesis is that the so-called aptitudes of "good" students in mathematics or physics, etc., consist above all in their being able to adapt to the type of instruction offered them, whereas students who are "bad" in these fields, but successful in others, are actually able to master the problems they appear not to understand—on condition that they approach them by another route. What they do not understand are the "lessons" and not the subject . . . many failures in school are due to this. . . .
Piaget (1973, p. 14)

vide feedback), (3) processing and decision making (evaluation and selection of stimuli and feedback), and (4) output (practice, application, and demonstration).

Techniques may be a standardized feature of the procedure or an intentional and systematic adaptation introduced by an intervener. (Of course, other variations in the characteristics of a tool or the way it is used may result from serendipity). Standardized features include (1) formal characteristics incorporated into materials, such as special formats for printed material as occurs in programmed texts and tachistoscopic presentations, and (2) specified procedures for administration, such as the directions for presenting material and guiding students provided in teachers' manuals for basal textbooks. Adaptations can be made in almost any material and activity so that formal characteristics and specified administrative procedures are varied.

To the observer, techniques appear as verbal and nonverbal stimuli, such as direct communications of fact or interpretation, demonstrations and models, guided exploration, and changes in demand and feedback characteristics. In this context, they often are described as *guidelines*. For example, Wood (1969) suggests as remedial guidelines such ideas as (1) working with a child's own speech and language, rather than using formal lists, (2) giving the child the feeling you are interested in what he or she is attempting to say, (3) working from concrete to abstract, (4) capitalizing on strengths, (5) using stimuli natural to each child's own environment, and (6) keeping careful records of the child's progress.

Table 12–2 represents an attempt to clarify some categories for organizing thought about techniques and offers some major examples. (More on this in Part 4). We present these in terms of effects the intervener is interested in achieving. From a psychological perspective, however, the variations are best understood in terms of how they are perceived by both the intervener and those who are to be affected by the techniques.

Also, in this connection, it may be noted that "qualities" or characteristics of interveners when used intentionally and systematically as part of an intervention strategy are "adaptive variations." For instance, when interveners systematically try to convey accurate empathy, nonpossessive warmth, and genuineness (Truax & Carkhuff, 1967), these are not simply fortuitous intervener characteristics, but intentional applications of techniques. In contrast, when these or other qualities are manifested as a natural characteristic of the intervener and not as techniques, their influence is seen as serendipitous and sometimes negative.

Some confusion has arisen from the indiscriminate way terms such as *procedures*, *methods*, *techniques*, and *activities* have been used. For example, some rather complex procedures are referred to simply as techniques despite the fact they incorporate both tools (activities/experiences/materials) and a complex set of techniques, for example, kinesthetic techniques. We call these *technical methods* as a concession to the fact they often are called *techniques* in the psychoeducational literature.

Confusion also has arisen because of the failure to recognize that methods (especially technical methods) may be designated with the same label and yet differ in critical ways. That is, while they share commonalities in the characteristics of the tools and techniques used, they are being guided by very different models due to the respective orientations of the interveners using them. A good example is the use of "problem-solving" strategies. The specific features of such strategies can vary significantly depending on whether they are being used from the perspective of radical behaviorism, cognitive behaviorism, or a cognitive-affective orientation, or from the viewpoint of utilitarian or humanistic philosophies.

Setting and Intervener Role Variations
No effort to formulate an understanding of procedures in generic terms can be complete without categorizing the various settings in which interventions are offered and the range of roles interveners may assume. As seen in Table 12–1, setting and contextual characteristics can be classified in terms of organizational format (e.g., personnel staffing patterns, and client/student groupings), locale, nature and scope (e.g., geographic context, architectural features, and availability and use of material), and climate (e.g., perceptions of physical, social, intellectual, political, and moral atmosphere).

Among the most discussed with regard to school settings are organizational variations. A major concern over the years has been whether to segregate (to group homogeneously) or to integrate (to group heterogeneously) based on such factors as age, sex, race, intelligence, learning and behavior problems. Until recently, students with certain types of psychoeducational problems and physical handicaps tended to be homo-

TABLE 12-2

Categorizing techniques

Techniques are defined as planned variations in the characteristics of a tool or the way it is applied, the immediate intent of which is to increase attraction and accessibility and decrease avoidance and distraction. Ultimately, these variations are meant to enhance one or more of such facets of human functioning as motivation, sensory intake, processing, decision making, and output. Techniques are categorized below in terms of specific objectives they are intended to achieve.

I. Techniques to enhance *motivation*
   A. *Nurturance* (including positive regard, acceptance and validation of feelings, appropriate reassurance, praise, and satisfaction)
      Specific examples:[a]
      - eliciting and listening to problems, goals, and progress
      - statements intended to reassure clients that change is possible
      - increasing the number of interpersonal, but nonauthority and supervisory, interactions
      - increasing the frequency of positive feedback and positive public recognition
      - reducing criticism, especially related to performance
      - avoiding confrontations
   B. *Permission* for exploration and change (including encouragement and opportunity)
      Specific examples:
      - increasing availability of valued opportunities
      - establishing and clarifying appropriate expectations and "set"
      - modeling expression of affect (self disclosing) when relevant
      - encouraging pursuit of choices and preferences
      - reducing demand characteristics such as expanding behavioral and time limits, reducing the amount to be done

   C. *Protection* for exploration and change (including principles and guidelines—rights and rules—to establish "safe" conditions)
      Specific examples:
      - reducing exposures to negative appraisals
      - providing privacy and support for "risk taking"
      - statements intended to reassure clients when risk taking is not successful
      - reducing exposure to negative interactions with significant others through eliminating inappropriate competition and providing privacy
      - establishing nondistracting and safe work areas
      - establishing guidelines, consistency, and fairness in rule application
      - advocating rights through statements and physical action
   D. *Facilitating effectiveness* (See techniques presented below for enhancing sensory intake, processing, decision making, and output)
II. Techniques for *sensory intake, processing, decision making,* and *output*
   A. *Meaning* (including personal valuing and association with previous experiences)
      Specific examples:
      - using stimuli of current interest and meaning
      - introducing stimuli through association with meaningful materials, such as analogies and pictorial representation of verbal concepts, stressing emotional connections
      - presenting novel stimuli
      - participating in decision making

a. While we have attempted to conceptualize discrete categories, all the examples are not mutually exclusive.

B. *Structure* (including amount, form, sequencing and pacing, and source of support and guidance)
Specific examples:
- presenting small amounts (discrete units) of material and/or information
- increasing vividness and distinctiveness of stimuli through physical and temporal figure-ground contrasts (patterning and sequencing) such as varying context, texture, shading, outlining, use of color
- varying levels of abstraction and complexity
- multi-sensory presentation
- providing models to emulate such as demonstrations, role models
- self-selection of stimuli
- using prompts and cues such as color coding, directional arrows, step by step directions
- verbally mediated "self"-direction ("stop, look, and listen")
- grouping material
- using formal coding and decoding strategies such as mnemonic devices, word analysis and snythesis
- rote use of specified study skill and decision making sequences
- allowing responses to be idiosyncratic with regard to rate, style, amount, and quality
- reducing criteria for success
- using mechanical devices for display, processing, and production, such as projectors, tape recorders, and other audio visual media, typewriters, calculators, computers, and so forth
- using person resources such as teachers, aides, parents, peers to aid in displaying, processing, and producing

C. *Active Contact and Use* (including amount, form, and sequencing and pacing of interaction with relevant stimuli)
Specific examples:
- immediate and frequent review
- allowing for self-pacing
- overlearning
- small increments in level of difficulty such as in "errorless training"
- use of play, games, and other personally valued opportunities for practice
- role playing and role taking
- use of formal reference aides, such as dictionaries, multiplication charts
- use of mechanical devices and person resources to aid in interactions

D. *Feedback* (including amount, form, sequencing and pacing, and source of information/rewards)
Specific examples:
- feedback in the form of information/rewards
- immediate feedback provided related to all processes and/or outcomes or provided on a contingency basis (reinforcement schedules or need)
- peer and/or self-evaluation
- use of mechanical monitoring and scoring

III. "Technical methods" Sometimes groups of techniques are combined into comprehensive and complex sets of tools (activities/experiences/materials and techniques). Despite the fact they are complex methods, they usually are referred to simply as *techniques* as they are communicated from intervener to intervener.
Specific examples:
- kinesthetic techniques (Fernald, 1943)
- desensitization and relaxation techniques (Wolpe, 1958)
- problem-solving strategies (see Chapter 8)

VIEWPOINT

FAVORED METHODS

Each week the staff of We-Cure-Em Remedial School meets to discuss the students and focus on difficult cases. Principal Brown chairs the meetings, and this week the sixth-grade teachers, Ms. Black and Mr. White, are presenting.

PRINCIPAL BROWN: What student has given you the most difficulties this week, Ms. Black?

MS. BLACK: Well, early in the week John wouldn't follow his scheduled activities and frequently misbehaved.

PRINCIPAL BROWN: What did you do about it?

MS. BLACK: I used my *staring hard* technique.

PRINCIPAL BROWN: I'm not sure I know that approach.

MS. BLACK: Well, I did my masters thesis on it and use it all the time. I've been staring hard at John as much of the time as I could over the past few days.

PRINCIPAL BROWN: How's it working?

MS. BLACK: Fine! Besides I never cared much for teaching reading.

PRINCIPAL BROWN: Reading?

MS. BLACK: Well, Johnny can't read.

PRINCIPAL BROWN: I see. How about the rest of the class?

MS. BLACK: I'm beginning to stare long and hard at several others who won't do their work.

PRINCIPAL BROWN: Good work, Ms. Black. Reminds me of when I began teaching. The big thing then was the belt technique.

MS. BLACK: Bend 'em and buckle 'em, right?

PRINCIPAL BROWN: Yep. I developed quite a backswing. Well, Mr. White, how about your students?

MR. WHITE: At the beginning of the week, I had four who were major problems. One was always late, another was getting into fights daily, and two just wouldn't do any work.

PRINCIPAL BROWN: What did you do?

MR. WHITE: I did what I do with all problem students. Research indicates that clarifying rules and expectations can reduce behavior problems, so I had each of them write the classroom rules a hundred times.

PRINCIPAL BROWN: Not only improves their behavior, but their handwriting too, right? That's applying the old research findings, White.

MR. WHITE: Thanks, but I had a bit of bad luck. Three of the students dropped out of school.

PRINCIPAL BROWN: Not bad luck, White, bad students. Neither good teachers nor good techniques can help bad students.

MR. WHITE: Yes, but I worry that perhaps rule writing wasn't the answer, that there might have been something better.

PRINCIPAL BROWN: Don't be foolish! Good techniques don't fail. Carry on, White, and don't trouble yourself. When students drop out, it isn't because we did the wrong thing; it's because they don't want to get better.

---

geneously grouped by problem classification in institutions, special schools, or special classes. Those who try to integrate such students into regular classes and noncategorical special programs are confronted with issues as to who can be successfully grouped together or mainstreamed. Do these students still need to spend some part of the day in special classes? How many and what type of problems can be accommodated appropriately in a given classroom? Does the success of mainstreaming depend on the number and type of nonproblem students? Does success depend on the availability of special resource teachers and the ratio of adults to students? and so forth.

The focus on problem populations has highlighted the need for a variety of persons to take roles in intervention processes. A major problem related to the various interveners available in public and private settings is the confusion for the general public due to overlapping roles and functions. Another problem is "the danger of creating a chaos of titles and training programs" (Sundberg et al., 1973, p. 474). The current level of confusion and chaos is reflected in the ongoing debate over who is qualified to intervene and how to maintain standards of performance.[3] As a result, persons seeking help have no satisfactory criteria for selecting the most appropriate or effective intervener.

In addition to regular and specialized personnel, it is increasingly recognized that paraprofessionals, "natural helpers," and persons with special talents also can enrich an intervention significantly.

Professionals involved in psychoeducational intervention represent a wide spectrum of educational and mental health personnel, such as teachers, counselors, administrators, psychologists, psychiatrists, and community mental health workers, who work in schools, clinics, hospitals, mental health and counseling centers, welfare agencies, correctional institutions, and private practice. When the "general practitioners" are unable to provide a satisfactory intervention, specialists usually are seen as necessary.

Specialists who deal with particularly complex problems and exceptional populations generally have had lengthy specialized training. Unfortunately, the limited number of such professionals and the costs related to the services they provide make them relatively inaccessible to many who need their

VIEWPOINT

Life as a whole is too complicated to teach to children. The minute it is cut up they can understand it, but you are liable to kill it in cutting it up.
Beeby in Ashton-Warner (1963, p. 46)

services. The fact of limited accessibility is an important one because it emphasizes that while theoretically there is a large range of interveners, in practice, some clients have no range of options at all.

In order to increase the number of personnel and hopefully the range of options, there has been renewed interest in paraprofessional and natural "helpers." These interveners may be neighbors, friends, or relatives who informally intervene or who staff formally organized activities, such as classroom programs, tutorial projects, and self-help groups (Brammer, 1973; Illich, 1976).

Despite the possible range of setting and intervener variations, many service placements are determined primarily by administrative realities such as what settings and personnel are available or, more generally, by current socioeconomic-political policies. For example, discussions of mainstreaming seem concerned more with administrative pros and cons related to efficient service systems than with such central psychoeducational questions as How wide a range of individual differences can and should be appropriately accommodated in a regular classroom? and How many problems cur-

---

[3] This debate often gets sidetracked into squabbling over field boundaries. In this context, certification and licensure have been advocated ostensibly as a means for allowing only the qualified to practice. Such gatekeeping devices, however, have been no guarantee of competence. Credentialing also has restricted access to professional jobs in various fields and thus has limited the range of differences among professional interveners, e.g., in terms of sex, socioeconomic, and minority status.

rently are caused by the inability of regular classrooms to facilitate the learning of certain individuals?

Cautions

Several cautions related to planning procedures are worth underscoring. Both the emphasis on procedures as individual units and the distinction between procedures and content can be misleading. Several education writers have identified an intervention concept called an *organizing center* which, in effect, highlights that procedures and content are integrally interwoven and that procedures rarely are used one at a time. In particular, it is stressed that procedures are means to an end and that the end is best served if the means are seen as rationally related to the ends. As McNeil (1965) states with regard to classroom learning, an organizing center is

> the theme, topic, problem, or project which gives immediate purpose and direction to the undertaking of a number of learning experiences. The popularity of an organizing center stems from the assumption that learning best occurs when the learner is confronted with a problematic situation. In the resolution of the problem, relevant information, methods, and details acquire significance. Further, the tension generated by the problem is believed to "motivate" the learner. (p. 79)

The concept of an organizing center also highlights the assumption that all learning that occurs in a classroom (or other intervention setting) is not, will not, and should not be the result of an intervener's efforts to provide formal instruction. For example, it seems evident that no university instructor is able to teach successfully all the skills that can be detailed and sequenced for career preparation in education, psychology, or medicine. Even if it were possible, there is no satisfactory evidence that this type of ap-

VIEWPOINT

PLANNING AND IMPLEMENTING CHANGE

Based on analysis of the state of the art and our experiences, it seems reasonable to conclude the following:

Intervention is an interference in the affairs of others which may lead to positive outcomes but may also be unnecessary, irrelevant, or even a hindrance.

Intentional intervention should be a rationally based set of activities involving several planning phases and systematic implementation and evaluation. Instead it is frequently a set of ad hoc procedures based on naive eclecticism.

Prevailing approaches have failed to substantively resolve most concerns related to planning valid content and outcomes for individuals with learning and behavior problems. New alternatives must take a broader perspective which not only focuses on individuals, but systematically directs intervention towards changing environments and person-environment interactions. Moreover, the focus should not only be on developmental variables, but on motivation as conceived in cognitive-affective theories.

Specialized procedures, including "remedial" techniques, can and should be reconceptualized in a generic manner. To do so helps clarify the wide range of procedural options available and should improve current practices and suggest directions for advancing the field.

proach to the instructional and learning processes is necessary or desirable. In keeping with this assumption, the instructor's function is viewed not only as that of instruction, but of facilitation as well, that is, a person who leads, guides, stimulates, clarifies, and supports. Consequently, the instructor must know when, how, and what to teach *and* when and how to structure the situation so that students can learn on their own. This implies that intervention planners know what conditions facilitate learning.

(We all know from experience that much more learning than instruction takes place in some classrooms and much more instruction than learning in others.)

CONCLUDING COMMENTS

We concur with colleagues such as Koppitz (1973) who suggest that

learning disabilities cannot be corrected or "cured" by a specific teaching method or training technique. It is imperative that teachers have a wide range of instructional materials and techniques at their disposal and that they are imaginative and flexible enough to adapt these to the specific needs of their pupils. (p. 137)

To be appropriately flexible and imaginative, however, requires a comprehensive and generic understanding of intervention planning and implementation. Like creative improvisation and new forms in the arts, a solution to the problem of planning and implementing appropriate interventions requires a sound grounding in fundamentals.

PART 4

PERSONALIZATION AND REMEDIATION: A SEQUENTIAL INTERVENTION MODEL

Once upon a time, the animals decided that their lives and their society would be improved by setting up a school. The basics identified as necessary for survival in the animal world were swimming, running, climbing, jumping, and flying. Instructors were hired to teach these activities and it was agreed that all the animals would take all the courses. This worked out well for the administrators, but it caused some problems for the students.

The squirrel, for example, was an A student in running, jumping, and climbing, but had trouble in flying class, not because of an inability to fly, for she could sail from the top of one tree to another with ease, but because the flying curriculum called for taking off from the ground. The squirrel was drilled in ground to air take-offs until she was exhausted and developed charley horses from overexertion. This caused her to perform poorly in her other classes, and her grades dropped to D's.

The duck was outstanding in swimming class—even better than the teacher. But she did so poorly in running that she was transferred to a remedial class. There she practiced running until her webbed feet were so badly damaged that she was only an average swimmer. But since average was acceptable, nobody saw this as a problem—except the duck.

In contrast, the rabbit was excellent in running, but, being terrified of water, he was an extremely poor swimmer. Despite a lot of make up work in swimming class, he never could stay afloat. He soon became frustrated and uncooperative and was eventually expelled because of behavior problems.

The eagle naturally enough was a brilliant student in flying class and even did well in running and jumping. He had to be severely disciplined in climbing class, however, because he insisted that his way of getting to the top of the tree was faster and easier.

It should be noted that the parents of the groundhog pulled him out of school because the administration would not add classes in digging and burrowing. The groundhogs, along with the gophers and badgers, got a prairie dog to start a private school. They all have become strong opponents of school taxes.

By graduation time, the student with the best grades in the animal school was a compulsive ostrich who could run superbly and also could swim, fly, and climb a little. She, of course, was made class valedictorian and received scholarship offers from all the best universities.[1]

---

[1]Benjamin (1949) credits George H. Reavis with giving this parable to American educators.

The discussion in the preceding chapters has been designed to place learning disabilities in a broad perspective. It is from such a vantage point that, in Part 4, we discuss interventions for learning problems in classroom settings.

As a starting place, it may be recalled that in Chapter 3 the heterogeneity of the learning problem population was classified with reference to causality. Specifically, three types of learning problems were designated along a continuum: *Type I* is used as a designation for those individuals without internal disorders whose problems primarily stem from the deficiencies of the learning environment; *Type II* designates those with minor disorders, which are readily compensated for under appropriate conditions; and *Type III* learning problems designate those who do have fairly severe disorders, which predispose them to school difficulties.

In this context, the label *LD* or *specific* or *severe learning disabilities* (*SLD*) is viewed as appropriate only for Type III learning problems. Given the low validity of prevailing assessment practices, however, it is highly probable that many Type I and II learning problems have been, and continue to be, misdiagnosed as Type III problems. As a result, those currently labeled *SLD* or *LD* represent a heterogeneous group with regard to causality and probably with regard to the nature and scope of corrective interventions needed.

Ironically, misdiagnoses which lead to misprescription of corrective practices do result in improvement for some persons. For instance, treatments may be prescribed based on the view that the observed learning problems stem from a neurological disorder. These treatments may lead to positive changes for some individuals, including many whose problems were caused only by poor teaching and not by neurological disorders. In such instances, this may be because the intervention improves the overall teaching process or because of placebo effects. Even more ironic is the possibility that the practices may be effective only in those cases where the LD diagnosis is in error (e.g., those cases which actually represent Type I and II problems). In fact, their continued use with persons correctly diagnosed as LD may be a waste of time and resources and even may be harmful. Misdiagnosis and misprescription related to Type I and II problems are major factors impeding progress in the field.

While such matters are acknowledged by most professionals, awareness has not led to the dramatic action that seems indicated. In particular, corrective interventions for those diagnosed *LD* must be designed to *disconfirm*, if at all possible, both the diagnosis of underlying process deficits and the need for remediation at this level. Such an approach would reflect true commitment to instituting the essence of the principle of least intervention needed.

Exploring alternatives to current corrective strategies, we have been developing an intervention model that deals both with environment and person causal factors, can aid in differentially diagnosing learning problems, and can be used in meeting the needs of the full continuum of problem learners. The model uses two sequential sets of intervention strategies (see Figure 1). The first emphasis is on personalizing the environment and program as a means of dealing with Type I learning problems. Then, the focus expands to provide remedial treatment for those individuals who still manifest problems.

More specifically, the first set of strategies (Step 1) is directed at (1) altering learning environments and programs to accommodate systematically a wider range of individual differences in motivation *and* development and (2) stimulating learning by establishing an appropriate learner-environment match. The intended effect of such accommodation on learner perceptions is referred to as *personalization*. In personalized classrooms, a major ingredient is programming designed to enable each student to select options that he or she values and believes he or she can accomplish.[2]

If needed, the second set of strategies, (Step 2), is directed at person remediation. After environment and programmatic changes are initiated to personalize the learning situation, the intervener proceeds, if necessary, with remedial strategies. Such remediation is necessary only for those who continue to manifest minor-occasional or severe and pervasive problems related to learning at school.

The sequential and hierarchical strategies for use during the second step focus on three different levels of intervention (see Figure 1). The sequence is determined by the success or failure of each attempted strategy. Level A emphasizes maintaining the focus of instruction on current tasks and interests and on expanding the learner's areas of interest. The procedures involved are (1) continued adaptation of methods to match and enhance current levels of motivation and development and (2) reteaching specific knowledge and skills when the youngster has difficulty. For students who continue to have problems learning, Level B emphasizes development of missing prerequisites needed for functioning at the higher level. Again procedures

---

[2]While personalized classrooms represent a possible approach for improving the learning of any student, they are seen as particularly important for students who find regular programs insufficiently accommodating.

Figure 1

Sequential and hierarchical corrective intervention strategies for psychoeducational problems.

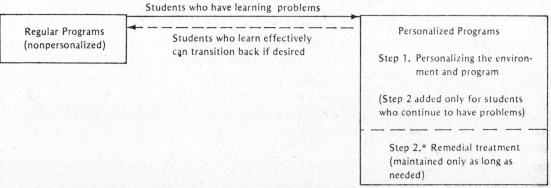

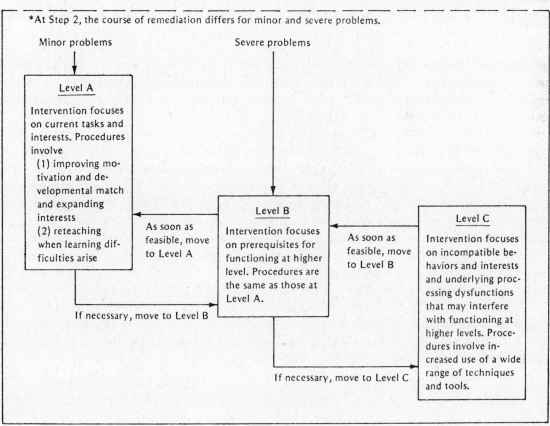

are adapted to improve the match; reteaching is used when the learner has difficulty. Level C attempts to deal with any incompatible behaviors and underlying processing deficits that may interfere with functioning at higher levels. At this level, there is an increased use of a wide range of psychoeducational techniques (see Table 12-2).

At Step 2, the sequence for those with minor-occasional problems differs from that used for those who continue to manifest severe and pervasive problems. For the former group, the sequence begins with Level A, drops to Level B if necessary, and returns to A as soon as feasible. For the latter group, the sequence begins with Level B, if necessary shifts to Level C, and returns to Level B and on to Level A as soon as feasible. Step 2 is maintained as long as necessary and reinstituted if problems arise.

It should be noted that in this model no standardized tests are employed to specify the etiology or level of remedial need. The corrective interventions themselves provide a sequential assessment clarifying both the level of intervention focus and the specific needs. In effect, both the identification of specific or severe learning disabilities and of intervention needs occur only after the impact of each intervention strategy becomes apparent.

It also may be noted that the model is being used to test our hypothesis that the best strategy for investigating whether a person has a learning disability is to begin by investigating the possibility that the individual does not need specialized remedial interventions to correct her or his learning problems; that is, we place a group of persons with learning and behavior problems (including possible specific or severe learning disabilities) in an environment that can accommodate their individual differences in motivation and development and find that a significant number begin to learn effectively without special remediation. These persons can reasonably be viewed as not having specific disorders—leaving only those who continue to have problems to be studied for possible internal disorders.

Chapters 13 and 14 are devoted to a detailed presentation of the strategies we have evolved to date for personalizing the learning environment and for person remediation. We offer the model and the strategies in the hope that they will prove heuristic for research and practice.

Chapter 13

Personalizing the Environment and Program: Step 1

We must take the learner into account in teaching and planning for teaching. This platitude covers up the complexity of the problems involved, however. The learner, obviously, is not the only data-source to which one turns in making curricular decisions. Awareness of this fact, when coupled with an inadequate conception of the total context of educational decision-making, leads us to scream, "You've forgotten the children" when someone attempts to analyze the place of subject matter, and "You've forgotten the subject matter!" when someone seeks to analyze the place of the learner. Thus, a sterile debate arises out of our inability to see two quite different parts as essential to a larger whole as well as unique within themselves.
Goodlad (1966, p. 157)

Most tactics the school uses are intended to minimize the nuisance of individual differences so that it can go on teaching the same unaltered course. This is true also of remedial instruction which adds onto the common program rather than redesigning it. Remedial work takes it for granted that the classroom work is largely a fixed program. Many a pupil needs help that a standard program does not give . . . , and supplementary instruction is therefore provided, with the intention of repairing the gaps in skill. . . . That is to say, remedial instruction attempts to erase individual differences.
Cronbach (1967, p. 27)

In presenting personalization and remediation as sequential steps, we have three objectives: (1) to describe the general features of the approach, (2) to clarify the value of viewing cause and intervention from interactional and motivational perspectives, and (3) to demonstrate the utility of conceiving corrective strategies in sequential and hierarchical terms. The underlying message is that broader perspectives than those currently dominating the LD field are needed if intervention efficacy is to be significantly increased.

As represented in Figure 1, the necessary first step in the sequential model is to change the learning environment so that it is personalized. Personalizing the classroom environment and program is not viewed as a remedial or special education approach, per se; it is seen as an alternative, regular approach intended to enhance learning and to correct learning problems. Personalization can be accomplished either by altering existing programs or, if necessary, by moving problem learners to personalized programs. In school settings, personalization can be accomplished in either regular or special classrooms.

Implementation of Step 1 of the sequential model should be a sufficient strategy for many of those individuals we have described as Type I learning problems. Obviously, they will have to make up developmental deficiencies in areas where learning was arrested or disrupted. However, these deficiencies are not disorders, and regular instruction in the personalized setting should prove to be a sufficient remedy. Only when Step 1 of the sequential model proves insufficient does the learner require additional specialized, remedial strategies, which are discussed in Chapter 14.

PERSONALIZATION DEFINED

Personalization is a psychological construct referring to a person's cognitive-affective appraisal of the match between an intervention and his or her current level of motivation and development. It is the emphasis on the *perceived match* and on *motivation* which distinguishes personalization from other individual-oriented instructional approaches. Specifically, a personalized program is one where the learner perceives the environment and program as accommodating her or his current developmental capabilities and motivation, especially intrinsic motivation.

In contrast, individualized school programs are not defined in terms of learner perceptions and tend to be planned solely with regard to a student's current developmental status. (Some individualized programs do no more than accommodate differences in rate of performance.) Such efforts do provide for developmental differences and thus are an improvement over practices that ignore such variations in human learning and performance. However, by failing to account for individual differences in motivation and the significance of learner perceptions, such approaches do not systematically take into account situations where, for example, a student is able, but unwilling, to perform the prescribed lesson. (This type of situation occurs in many individualized programs, especially after the novelty of new materials and procedures diminishes.)

Personalized classrooms are intended to accommodate a wider range of individual differences in motivation and development than occurs in most classrooms. This accommodation involves (1) accepting a greater degree of variation from the norm with regard to behavior and learning and (2) establishing learning opportunities designed to improve the *perceived match*. Such accommodation focuses on the learning environment[1] as the object of change (see Figure 8-1) and is accomplished initially in a normative fash-

---

[1] By *learning environment* we mean physical, interpersonal, organizational, and programatic aspects, especially content, process, and structure.

VIEWPOINT

PERSON-ENVIRONMENT FIT

Still unasked is the question that may be of greatest significance to prevention, namely, "How can we fit different individuals or, better still, how can individuals learn to fit themselves to settings optimal for them at specific periods in their development?. . ."

One possible strategy might be to develop competence-building interventions that teach the individual to recognize and select personally optimal environments (cf. Hunt, 1975).

Levine and Perkins (1980, p. 154)

ion—the changes made in the environment are based first on general information about individual differences. Subsequent changes are pursued with reference to specific individuals.

How wide a range of individual differences any classroom can accommodate under any given circumstances has yet to be determined empirically. However, our research (Adelman,1971; Feshbach & Adelman, 1971, 1974) suggests that the range can be significantly increased when alternatives to current instructional approaches, staffing patterns, and in-service training are used.

In our work, we find personalized classroom programs are feasible and promising approaches to the correction of learning problems. To provide an image of the nature of such programs, the rest of Chapter 13 is devoted to discussion of (1) the major elements involved in personalizing a classroom and (2) the general aims of personalized classrooms.

PERSONALIZING THE CLASSROOM: MAJOR ELEMENTS

Drawing on relevant psychological research, it seems the following elements are essential features of a personalized classroom:

The importance of *learner perceptions* is acknowledged in relation to all facets of the environment and program.

A wide variety of content and process *options* are offered as one basis for establishing an appropriate motivational and developmental match.

A *continuum of structure* is provided to ensure communication, support, direction, and limits in the form needed and as needed, including periods during which students work either independently or in small groups without adult supervision.

Each learner takes an active role in making *choices* related to major intervention decisions as a way to increase the learner's perception of commitment, control, and personal responsibility.

Informal and formal *conferences* are held regularly as a key mechanism for communication about, and enhancing, learner perceptions of options, decisions, contracts, and so forth.

Contractual agreements are evolved and renegotiated as necessary to enhance commitment and motivation by clarifying intrinsic justifications, personal choice and responsibility, availability of external support and direction, and so forth.

Ongoing assessment and formative evaluation are implemented to monitor progress and negative effects, and to modulate plans in order to improve the perceived match.

In this section, we briefly explore each of these elements.

Learner Perceptions, Options, and Preferences

What makes personalized classroom programs good is never a matter of what the content, process, or overall structure looks like to the teacher or even what has worked previously. Ultimately, what makes a program a good match is that it is perceived as such by the student and that it facilitates intended changes. While the teacher may view situations and tasks as worthwhile and as something the student can do, insisting that students share this view may lead to frustration, anger, anxiety, or boredom for all involved. For example, the teacher or parent who keeps offering a youngster a chance to be involved in "exciting" activities may become very aggravated when the youngster consistently refuses. What the teacher and parent are ignoring is that their view of what is exciting or important and within the student's capabilities may not be the youngster's view. They also may be ignoring the possibility that the pressure they exert may lead the student to express dislike for the task and perhaps the persons and situation associated with it.

Rather than choosing *for* students, personalized programs emphasize students choosing from among a variety of relevant options. To maximize the likelihood that there will be relevant options for all students in a classroom, it seems evident that classroom programs must encompass a large variety of content and procedures, including structure. For example, there must be varied projects, learning centers, materials, and options about when, where, and with whom learning is to be pursued. Providing options, however, is no guarantee that the learner will perceive them positively. The manner in which options are presented and choices facilitated is critical to positive learner perceptions and pursuit of preferences.

Learner perception.   It is important that a

VIEWPOINT

LEARNER PERCEPTION

To a grown up person who is too absorbed in his [or her] own affairs to take an interest in children's affairs, children doubtless seem unreasonably engrossed in their own affairs.
Dewey (1961, p. 44)

student view a classroom learning situation not only as one in which he or she can perform successfully, but as one that is interesting and worthwhile. More is involved than providing students with easy tasks. A task perceived as too easy often is devalued—seen as boring—and avoided.

The task of the intervener is to present options in a way that ensures they are noticed and in a way that ensures there will be some that are perceived and responded to positively. To understand how this might be accomplished requires some general understanding of the processes of perception and cognition.[2]

Although there is controversy over whether people have a finite capacity for perceiving and retaining input, it is clear that only a limited amount of the stimuli impinging on a person at a given time is attended to (Neisser, 1976). Theories of attention attempt to explain why this is so. Currently, the majority of theories postulate a mechanism that filters out certain stimuli (e.g., Deutsch & Deutsch, 1963; Treisman, 1964, 1969). Neisser (1976), on the other hand, has suggested that perception is active and selective, that is, a student only experiences stimuli that he or she is equipped, and has the skill, the schemata, to perceive. Also,

---

[2]To achieve a working understanding of perception requires at least some notion of contemporary psychological theory regarding cognition. Cognition usually refers to "the activity of knowing" (Neisser, 1976; Reid, Knight-Arest, & Hresko, 1981), e.g., how knowledge is acquired, organized, stored, transformed, created, evaluated, and used by the organism. Even more broadly, understanding perception involves assimilation of ideas about how human behavior is motivated, organized, expressed, and experienced. Such theory encompasses explanations of how biological, pychological, social, and physical systems interact with their subsystems and each other. The focus here is restricted to a limited set of psychological considerations to illustrate the point.

each of us functions differently at different times depending on external conditions, such as intensity of stimuli, and on our internal states, such as how capable, anxious, or frightened we are. Any intended intervention has to account for these facts and attempt to facilitate the perception and retention of relevant stimulus inputs.

Like a number of earlier theorists (e.g., Bartlett, 1932; Piaget, 1952), a central assumption of Neisser's model is that "the perceiver has certain cognitive structures, called *schemata*, that function to pick up the information that the environment offers" (p. xii). Unlike other theories of perception (e.g., Gibson, 1966), Neisser's view sees mental events playing an active role. That is, students have definite structures (i.e., anticipatory schemata, cognitive maps) that prepare them to accept certain kinds of information and to notice certain aspects of the environment. These structures are modified as perception occurs and are part of a continuously interactive process.

Neisser's model, with its view of perception as determined by an interplay between schemata and situation, is quite useful in pointing to factors that may affect the processing of inputs. Similarly, models discussing other constructs, such as motivation (see Chapter 10) and memory[3] and how they interact with perception, suggest areas for investigation and practices for facilitating retention of important inputs.

Given the range of topics relevant to any discussion of perception and cognitive processing in general, it is clear that a unifying concept would be helpful. The concept of the "match" as summarized in preceding chapters seems quite useful. It captures the essence of how the interaction between a student's current schemata and the existing environment determines learning. In a personalized classroom, the problem of facilitating the processing of inputs can be seen as one of establishing an environment that evokes an *appropriate match* with the student's assimilated schemata. The more optimal the match, the more likely it is that some, but certainly not all, ways of perceiving and adapting to environmental circumstances will be challenged and result in accommodative growth, learning, and change.[4]

A teacher planning for personalization must consider a two-fold question: Is it likely that students can find a sufficient range of options (both in terms of processes and outcomes) that they will perceive as (1) neither too hard nor too easy? (2) worth the effort (i.e., of personal value)? If the answer is "no," it is unlikely the student will want to be in the situation—it becomes almost irrelevant whether the student has the capability to perform. If the answer is "yes," then the teacher can proceed to determine if the student actually does perceive the situation as it was planned. It is unlikely that students can be tricked or forced into such perceptions. Rather the process is seen as involving presentation of the options, assessment of whether the student perceives the options as a good motivational and developmental match, and facilitation of the student's active choice making.

---

[3]Unfortunately, most contemporary theories are based not on how memory operates in ordinary circumstances, but on phenomena observed under highly artificial laboratory conditions. A critical theoretical concern from the perspective of psychoeducational intervention is how sensory and short-term memories are transferred to long-term memory. What do theories and empirical findings currently suggest about memory which may have relevance for learner perceptions? The literature indicates that the coherence of the material to be remembered, the degree of organization, the strategies used for storing it and the modes for eliciting it (e.g., recognition, recall) are the major factors that can be manipulated to facilitate retention and performance based on retained information (Kagan & Lang, 1978).

[4]Remember: An appropriate match for learning involves an accommodatable discrepancy or incongruity between current ways of understanding the world and the pattern of stimulation experienced. An optimal match means that the discrepancy demands the fullest use of one's accommodative capacity.

Content and process.   Ideally, the students and the teacher in a personalized classroom should perceive themselves as participants in an educational enterprise which encourages innovation and continued experimentation. It is such a perception that contributes greatly to increased enthusiasm and additional expenditures of effort. Since few activities and tasks will elicit the same degree of motivation from every student, the teacher must allow for choice and self-selection, and there must be a variety of possibilities from which to choose.[5] The point is to provide enough variation so that each student can find an activity or task that he or she will pursue vigorously and persistently.

In personalizing learning, teachers capitalize on basic psychological *needs* that seem to operate in normal development, for example, wanting to know about the world around one and to see order and meaning in it; wanting to see oneself as being of worth and wanting to enhance self-worth; wanting to have a sense of direction, with hope of success in one's efforts; wanting to develop and use one's potential. Obviously, such needs are not independent of each other nor are they independent of the social context in which they evolve and are expressed. The challenge, then, can be seen as one of providing a classroom program that maximizes the impact of motivationally relevant factors in ways that are congruent with attaining intended goals.

It should be clear that it is harder and relatively uninteresting for a student to focus on things that appear to be unrelated to his or her key motives. In contrast, a student will devote extraordinary time and energy to activities he or she views—for whatever reasons—as meaningful, interesting, worth the effort, and attainable. The likelihood that a student will find such activities is increased when options are presented that emphasize substantive content rather than simply skills to be learned. Centers and projects, for example, not only allow for the practice of acquired skills and the acquisition of new skills, but also for motivated exploration and breadth of learning. Centers and projects can be restricted to activities directly related to such basic school subjects as reading, science, and math, or the activities can be broadened to encompass carpentry, cooking, art, drama, job training, and so forth. (See Chapter 12 for examples of specific options.)

Structure.   In addition to options for content and process, the concept of structure suggests a complementary set of options that must be available to enhance learning. The term has been used in a variety of ways. Some describe structure as the degree to which the teacher is in control. Others talk about seating arrangements, the extent to which participants interact, differentiated roles and functions of the participants, use of materials to structure interpersonal contacts, and so on. Structure has also been discussed as the general pattern of communication in a setting. McGrath (1972), in applying systems theory to schooling, discusses a "structures component" composed of three subsystems: (1) roles and positions, (2) communication networks, and (3) work flow. From his perspective, structure is seen as how an organization is put together to do the job.

With regard to personalized classrooms, we define structure as the degree and type of communication, support, direction, and limits or external controls needed to facilitate an individual's learning and performance.

---

[5]It should be noted that too many materials introduced all at once can be confusing. Therefore, a limited number of materials can be introduced initially and, as new materials are added, materials that have been in the room awhile can be rotated out. Some of these materials can be returned at a later date if it is felt that there will be renewed interest in them.

VIEWPOINT

STRUCTURE

Haring and Phillips have defined structure as "the clarification of the relationship between behavior and its consequences" (1962, p. 9). We have previously defined it as consisting of "teacher expectations associated with the task assigned the child which determine the conditions under which a reward will be provided" (Hewett, 1968, p. 62).

Among the considerations Haring and Phillips took into account in developing their structured educational program for disturbed children were the following:

1. Maintaining a definite and dependable classroom routine

2. Starting with specific and limited tasks and extending these when the child is ready

3. Maintaining consistency on the part of the teacher

4. Forwarding the impression to children that they are at school for work

Gallagher (1979) has developed a structured program along these same lines but has expanded the Haring and Phillips definition to include clarification of the relationship between behavior and stimuli such as curriculum materials, teacher instruction, and room furnishings.

We are in general agreement with these definitions of structure. Our definition is, however, "the orchestration of success." . . . We do not need a curriculum task that is harmonious with the child's level of functioning or a set of conditions that produce a harmonious working situation for the child or consequences harmonious with what is meaningful and motivating to the child, we need total harmony among all three. The potentially effective task presented under inappropriate conditions leads to disharmony. The ideal working conditions are of little effectiveness if a disharmonious task is involved.

Harmony. You can tell when it is there in a classroom. Things are in tune. Tasks, working conditions, and consequences are synchronized with the children. The teacher conducts. Everyone is playing their part. You can also recognize disharmony in the classroom. Things are out of tune. Tasks, working conditions, and consequences are not synchronized with the children. The teacher may be trying to conduct, but the results are off-key.

Hewett and Taylor (1980, p. 123)

When there is a classroom of students involved, the provision of appropriate structure is made more difficult, but the nature of the concept does not change. (Unfortunately, when classrooms contain students who do not respond readily to staying within limits, the emphasis often shifts from two-way communication and support for learning to enforcement of limits and directed performance.)

Ideally, structure need not be prescribed solely by the intervener. In order to maximize motivation, the intent in a personalized classroom is for students to take as much responsibility as they can for identifying the type and degree of support, direction, and limits they require. The objective is to help students "know their own minds" and make their own decisions. Thus, the structure is designed to facilitate movement toward this objective. This means approaches that allow students to take as much responsibility as they are ready for in choosing the support and direction they require. More generally, this means finding some way to match the structure to each student's current motivational and developmental status.

How this can be accomplished in classrooms is the intriguing problem which must be solved before personalization can be maximized in classrooms. Working on this problem, we have arrived at a few insights we want to share. (While the emphasis is on classrooms, we believe the points have relevance for interventions in general.)

First, we find that a personalized classroom must be able to offer a wide range of support and direction. For example, some students request a great amount of direction, while others prefer a structure that allows them to work autonomously.

Second, because the continuum of structure encompasses a wide variety of options, the personalized environment appears less confining. However, it is not an *open classroom* or *open structure* as these terms are widely understood (e.g., Marshall, 1981). There is the danger in some programs designated as open classrooms that youngsters will be deprived of the structure that they require. On the other hand, one must be careful about the tendency to hold on to a tight and controlling structure. There appears to be a tendency to see tight control as the structure which must prevail if students are to learn, rather than seeing it as a starting point—for very dependent and uninterested learners—from which they should move as rapidly as they can. Limits and external controls will be discussed in more detail in Chapter 15.

As long as a student does not value the classroom, the teacher, and the activities, then the teacher is likely to believe that the student requires a great deal of direction and support. In general, the less the student is motivated, the more it is necessary to teach and control behavior, and the less successful the whole enterprise of schooling appears to be. Conversely, the more the student is motivated, the less it is necessary to teach and control, and the more likely the student will learn.

Choice and commitment. Given the learner perceives a range of attractive options, how does he or she become engaged in pursuing learning activities? Choice, re-

VIEWPOINT

OPTIMIZING MOTIVATION

If we could recognize optimum motivation and produce it, there would be no more that could or should be done.
Nicholls (1979, pp. 1079–80)

The whole art of teaching is only the art of awakening the natural curiosity of young minds for the purpose of satisfying it afterwards.
Anatole France (1881, p. 178)

sponsibility for decision making, and commitment are viewed by most cognitively oriented psychologists as critical to any comprehensive understanding of behavior, behavior change, and resistance to change. There are impressive lines of research related to each (e.g., Brehm, 1976; Deci, 1975; Gerard, Conolley, & Wilhelmy, 1974; Janis & Mann, 1977; Kiesler, 1971; Lepper & Greene, 1978; Perlmuter & Monty, 1979). Of interest here are the implications for psychoeducational practices (e.g., Hresko & Reid, 1981; Kosiewicz, Hallahan & Lloyd, 1981).

Recent literature has emphasized that persons' perceptions of the degree to which they have choice and control can significantly affect performance related to various tasks and situations. In general, the illusion of control is seen as related to improved performance; the opposite perception is seen as often debilitating (e.g., Perlmuter & Monty, 1977). Unfortunately, these relationships are not simple, to which any parent or teacher who has tried to allow children to choose for themselves or has tried to limit freedom as a way of inducing better behavior would attest. Nevertheless, choice is seen as having incentive value and reinforcing properties under some conditions and as a potentially critical determiner of the success or failure of interventions.

A wide variety of investigations studying choice have concluded that, when people believe they have control, commitment and motivation are enhanced resulting in better effort, learning, and performance. Conversely, proceeding without consent and active involvement in decision making probably results in a low degree of commitment to participate and to act upon decisions. It has also been suggested that one major way to enhance learners' perceptions of control is to involve them in decision-making processes.

Of course, once involved in an activity, the learner may quickly decide that the alternative chosen is a poor match in terms of perceived value or expectancy of success. The fact that students often change their minds is sometimes interpreted as evidence that they do not know what they want or what is best for them and are ill-prepared to make choices. We are not suggesting that all students are equipped to make sound choices or that intervention should be student-centered in a philosophical sense; we are stressing that one reality of dealing with the problem of the match is that the learner's perception of choice is a critical determinant. Furthermore, we suggest that the process of choosing increases not only the likelihood students will perceive the situation positively, but the likelihood that they also will learn to make meaningful choices, which is an important and basic skill in effective daily functioning.[6]

Conferences, Contracts, and Evaluation

The key mechanism for identifying learner perceptions and facilitating decision making is a dialogue between the student and teacher. We refer to this dialogue as a conference. Conferences are important not only for choosing options, but for establishing contractual agreements, and for ongoing assessment and formative evaluation.

Conferences and personalized planning.

In a personalized classroom, a conference is a beginning and ongoing point of contact between teacher and student (and parents). The purposes of a conference may include

giving, sharing, and clarifying information;

initiating and building a working relationship;

making agreements regarding program plans; and

evaluating progress and problems.

In theory then, there can be four types of conferences, although in practice any particular conference may be directed at several purposes simultaneously.

It should be emphasized that conferences are not designed simply to get the involved individuals meeting together. Conferences, as we are discussing them, also are not intended as one way communication mechanisms. Teachers can use such times to clarify expectations, rules, limits, and so forth. However, sessions that emphasize only authority are seen as counterproductive to minimizing the negative stereotypes the participants may have regarding each other.

A conference should be a time for *each* person to say what they need, want, and are hoping for from each other. This should be accomplished in an atmosphere where assumptions based on previous negative experiences are avoided. The intended outcome of any particular conference may be

---

[6]There is a parallel between discussions of problem solving and choice behavior as applied to psychoeducational interventions (e.g., Adelman & Taylor, 1978b; Davis, 1973; Mahoney, 1974; Spivack, Platt, & Shure, 1976; Urban & Ford, 1971). In particular, such discussions emphasize that effective intervention seems to require first an awareness of alternatives followed by judicious decisions from among identified alternatives. Furthermore, there is a tendency to relate the adequacy of such awareness and decision making primarily to developmental variables (e.g., skills). From our perspective, however, motivational variables (e.g., extrinsic and intrinsic valuing, expectancies of success, feelings of competence and self-determination) may be as, or more, potent in determining choice.

designated as general communication of information, planning, or evaluation. The impact of the process, however, always is intended to maintain or improve the working relationship through positive rapport and working agreements arrived at collaboratively. The emphasis is on motivation and development and on mutuality in effort and decision making.

Conferences are held on a regular basis with additional conferences as needed. Table 13-1 provides an example of activities typically addressed during a personalized classroom conference. Table 13-2 presents a list of conditions found to facilitate conferences.

While conferences are thought of in terms of formal times and places, any of the purposes of a conference can be pursued as part of numerous daily informal classroom contacts. Indeed, sometimes the purposes are best accomplished in this manner with young children and those whose behavior precludes lengthy, formal conferences. For instance, a teacher might simply sit down at a student's desk at any time that seems mutually appropriate and initiate a brief "conference."

The first teacher-student contacts are of particular importance. During the first weeks in the classroom, each student is still involved in a *transition in* process designed to establish a positive attitude toward the learning environment and build positive working relationships. Conferences between the students and teacher at this stage focus on identifying what, if anything, each student is *now* interested in learning in school.

A facet of these conferences is initial *needs assessment* to determine what objectives (content, process, and outcome) are appropriate. A particular focus of these conferences is the determination of how best to establish the following motivational objectives:

TABLE 13-1

Example of personalized conference activities

I. Information giving, sharing, clarifying, informal conversation

II. Mutual evaluation of previous plans, starting with student's self-evaluation; review and analysis of
   A. Records,
   B. Products (including tests),
   C. Formal behavior observations, and
   D. Informal personal perceptions

III. Conclusions about learning and progress: What objectives have been met? ⟶ Progress Recorded
   Any acute or chronic problems interfering with progress?

IV. Planning of next steps
   Content, process, and outcome objectives ⟶ Objectives Recorded
   (The focus remains on regular as contrasted with remedial programming unless progress indicates there are barriers to learning and performance. If there is such an indication and there is sufficient information to analyze the problem, a special intervention is planned. If the available information is insufficient, some specific special assessment activity designed to provide a better analysis of the problem is planned).

V. Next evaluation conference is scheduled

---

positive relationships between staff and student and between students;

student and staff awareness of what learning opportunities the student values pursuing and what the student can expect to attain in the current learning environment;

student awareness of what staff and parents value regarding student pursuits and what the staff and parents expect the student to attain;

a mutually positive agreement between staff and student regarding the student's program at school; and

TABLE 13-2

Conditions to facilitate conferences

I. Establishment of a special space and time
  A. Quiet area where others will not interfere or be distracted by conference
  B. Time scheduled when other students are involved in independent activities and/ or there are others present to help (e.g., aides, peers, volunteers)
II. Preparing the class (transition to classroom conference activity)
  A. Explanation to class regarding importance of conference times and the need to avoid interruptions
  B. Enthusiastic communication to students regarding the special opportunity a conference provides, e.g., a special time set aside just for the student, etc.
  C. Students taught to be relatively self-sufficient (e.g., independent activities including transitioning from activities on own)

and to ask others (aides, peers, volunteers) for help when necessary
  D. Aides, peers, volunteers taught how to provide the help which may be needed by other students while conferences are held
  E. Trial runs to evaluate if students, aides, etc. can function effectively during conference time; continue training and trial runs until all are fairly self-sufficient during conference times
  F. First conferences should be particularly oriented to building a valuing of conference times by the student
III. Materials
  A. Record keeping materials for both student and teacher
  B. Objectives checklists
  C. Records from last conferences
  D. Products, work samples, test materials, etc.

positive valuing and expectation of success with reference to chosen areas of participation.

Along with the above motivational objectives, conferences should focus on identifying developmental needs within a motivational context. The conceptual basis for such objectives are provided in Chapter 10. The assessment process remains one of verbal interchanges and analyses of work and performance during formal and informal conferences, which are held as frequently as necessary.

Many school-age youngsters, especially those who have had problems in school, have learned not to value or to expect to succeed in classrooms. During the initial stages of working with such youngsters, conferences may be difficult to implement. In such cases, it is often necessary to provide a high degree of structure (e.g., support, direction, or limits) in exploring areas of con-

tent and preferred modes for learning. Such external structuring of behavior clearly is not a procedure which should be maintained longer than is necessary since it may undermine intrinsic motivation and independence in learning.

Contractual agreements. Another important purpose of conferences arises when learning experiences involve working with others. The manner in which an agreement evolves determines both its validity and whether learner commitment is increased. That the learner may enter a learning situation without a formal agreement does not mean that none is implied. A contract is implicit in all interactions. For example, in most school situations the implied contract is that students will do assignments and will behave in accordance with school rules. This implied contract is often invalid since many students may not understand the expectations or do not have any intention of meeting them. The contract is invalid not so much because it lacks explicit statement, but because the parties involved have not actually agreed to undertake specific activities and to interact with each other in mutually acceptable ways.

Even explicit contracts may be invalid because only the form and not the substance of an agreement has been addressed. For example, when the teacher asks the student to agree to pursue a teacher-planned program, the teacher may get a signed contract, but not a mutual agreement. Personalization requires explicit efforts and care in (1) evolving a valid contract and (2) facilitating renegotiation when necessary.

Evolving the contract. To evolve a valid learning contract, it is first necessary to clarify the available learning alternatives in terms of goals, activities, and facilitation of learning. Clarification is initiated by a counselor meeting with the student to work out the general nature of a program and then further developed through conferences with the teacher.

In clarifying appropriate goals, it is important to explore both what the student should and wants to learn. The more the *should* and *wants* overlap, the more satisfactory the situation. (We do not mean to suggest that the task of determining what the learner wants to learn is a simple one.)

With reference to activities, exploration specifically focuses on what will be learned, how it will be learned, and the context for such learning. Different activities require different commitments from the learner in terms of the rate, style, amount, and quality of performance. Since the same goals can usually be accomplished by participating in any of several different activities, the learner must have alternative activities from which to choose. The more alternatives, the more likely a satisfactory contract can be evolved.

With reference to the facilitation of learning, the facilitator clarifies the demands made as a part of any commitment to help the learner. Here again alternatives will increase the likelihood of an appropriate match and a satisfactory contract.

Negotiating contract changes. All parties should be in a reasonable position to determine whether the learning experiences being offered and chosen are satisfactory. If an unsatisfactory situation cannot be avoided, then it is necessary to negotiate a compromise. If the learner is forced into the situation, it is highly probable that there will be conflict between facilitator and learner. It is an act of provocation for a facilitator to expect a learner to perform in agreed upon ways. (If the intent is coercion, justification should be explicitly stated so that it can be evaluated, and reacted to, by those responsible for the learner's rights.) If a valid contract cannot be negotiated, the facilitator simply is not in a position to work effectively with the learner—another facilitator with different expectations and willingness to negotiate in different ways might be able to establish a valid learning agreement.

Since a student may not fully understand the implications of what has been agreed to, it is important that learning contracts be subject to renegotiation. By recognizing the likelihood of such circumstances, the parties involved can minimize feelings of failure, disappointment, and anger because some facet of the contract did not work out. After an initial period, the implications of the contract should be clear and the contract can be viewed as valid.

To summarize, evolving a valid learning contract involves first clarifying desired goals, activities, and modes for facilitating learning. A personalized program offers a variety of meaningful and feasible alternatives so that the student can find compatible procedures and a person with whom he or she can work successfully. After an initial contract is made, there must be a period of adjustment and assessment to clarify the contract's various implications. Finally, there must be procedures for renegotiat-

VIEWPOINT

COMMITMENT

As an aid in distinguishing commitment from motivation, Keisler and Sakumura (1966) suggest the following working definition: commitment is "the pledging or binding of the individual to behavioral acts" (p. 349). In explorations of factors that affect a person's degree of commitment to act, the following factors have been stressed: (1) the importance of the behavior for the person, (2) the explicitness of the behavior which reflects the commitment, (3) the degree to which the behavior is irrevocable, (4) whether the behavior is performed, the number of times it is repeated, and the amount of effort expended, and (5) the degree of volition perceived by the persons related to the act. In applying such factors, the major emphasis has been on the importance of choice and acceptance of responsibility for having made a particular choice and for the consequences of the act. A sense of sufficient internal justification (low external justification) for behaving in a given manner has been viewed as contributing to one's sense of responsibility for one's behavior.

Among the practical implications that can be extrapolated from the literature on commitment, then, are that psychoeducational procedures need to result in students perceiving high internal justification and choice related to the behavioral acts involved in the intervention. If the procedures are effective, the students should experience a high sense of responsibility for, and a high commitment to, attitudes and behaviors that facilitate intended intervention processes and outcomes. (Of course, it is also recognized that, as a prerequisite, psychoeducational practices often first need to reduce justifications, responsibilities, and commitment to existing nonfacilitative attitudes and behaviors).

With regard to the relationship of commitment to motivation, it has been assumed that commitment to change is not a sufficient condition for producing change (Kiesler, 1971). The forces needed to instigate and maintain change are viewed as motivational. With reference to motivation, the recent reemergence of a cognitive perspective in psychology has stressed the importance of intrinsic motivation and cognitive mediation of extrinsic reinforcers and of the inverse relationship which exists between intrinsic and extrinsic motivation (see Chapter 10).

---

ing the contract, and, if feasible, a temporary "escape clause" should be included.

Ongoing assessment and formative evaluation. From the moment an intervention is initiated, there is a need to monitor its impact, especially its progress and negative effects. Data on these matters are necessary to determine whether initial plans are still appropriate, to refine objectives, and to specify next steps.

Data gathered during the first weeks and months in a program are of particular importance. It is difficult to determine a student's motivation and developmental level until he or she has settled into a program, especially when the student has experienced learning problems. Therefore, during the initial period of adjustment in a personalized classroom, the major assessment activity is to have the student identify what he or she wants to learn. Then, as the student becomes adjusted to, and involved in, the routines, the focus is on determining *with the student* her or his developmental needs and objectives. Students' initial decisions about objectives, of course, may not reflect well-informed choices and strong commitments. It is through the ongoing conference dialogues that stated intentions and actual follow-through are explored and an appropriate set of objectives evolved.

If the student identifies nothing he or she wants to work on when first entering the program, the intervention focus is on motivation, that is, identifying things of personal value and interest that can be pursued in the program. At the end of the initial period of adjustment, which can vary from a week to several months, a reassessment is made to determine whether the initial choice to enter this particular program was a good one.

Essentially, we are describing what most experienced professionals do in some form or another—they establish a highly motivating program, make a daily assessment of a client's performance in the natural setting of the program (as contrasted with testing), and plan accordingly. Where this process so often goes astray is that many programs do not tap into a student's intrinsic motivation and the student remains rather immobilized and appears to be less competent than he or she is. This leads to identifying developmental problems that are more apparent than real and to ignoring and perhaps worsening the motivational problems.

As the above suggests, the assessment procedures initially do not involve formal testing. Rather, teacher and student have formal and informal conferences during which interests and capabilities are discussed; products and work samples analyzed; content, process, and outcome objectives formulated; and plans for formative evaluation made. Ongoing assessment and formative evaluation also rely heavily on conferences and reviews of daily work as a collaborative basis for analyzing current status and deciding on future directions.

Tests may be used as another product generated periodically as part of regular classroom activity. As with other work samples, tests help clarify progress and outline possible areas for future work.

Cumulative information about whether objectives have been accomplished provides one index for use in evaluations of the program's overall efficacy. At the same time, in order to have some comparative norms, a standardized achievement test of reading, math, and language skills is administered at the beginning and end of each year (or sooner if the student leaves the program).[7]

For those students who continue to have difficulty, task and behavioral analyses are used in an attempt to identify the specific nature and scope of the problem. If additional data are required, marketed and experimental tests focusing on underlying abilities may be administered on a research basis (see Chapter 14) in connection with Step 2 of the sequential model.

In one sense, implementation of the various elements involved in personalizing a classroom may be viewed as an institutionalization of the *Hawthorne effect*.[8] The Hawthorne effect usually denotes a temporary and deceptive effect. However, there is no theoretical necessity for the positive attitudes and increased behavioral output, which result from perceptions of being part of an experimental program, to be temporary

---

[7]The sequential approach to needs assessment described above is seen as a potential research strategy for investigating the type and amount of needs assessment required in planning intervention programs for different types of problems.

[8]The term comes from a series of studies done at the Western Electric Company's Hawthorne plant between 1927 and 1933. The investigations were designed to determine the impact of changes in the physical environment upon worker productivity. However, the findings were interpreted as demonstrating the potent impact of social organization as overshadowing physical surroundings in determining productivity, e.g., production increases were attributed to increased morale (positive attitudes and motivation) among the workers, which was attributable to the special attention they were receiving as participants in the investigation. Although the findings and their interpretation have been challenged (Bramel & Friend, 1981), the term *Hawthorne effect* has come to denote a source of experimental error, i.e., temporary effects resulting from factors not intrinsically associated with the variables under investigation. For example, in education, *Hawthorne-type* phenomena (motivational factors) often account for the initial success of new materials, methods, and curriculum content that later are found to lose their potency.

or deceptive in nature. The personalized classroom lends itself to the inclusion of such phenomena as a stable and positive aspect of the learning situation. What is being advocated is not complete novelty or novelty for its own sake, but a continuing emphasis on innovative options in the classroom to help elicit and maintain teacher and student interest and effort.

To this end, the teacher in a personalized classroom facilitates a variety of options and a structure that makes them accessible. The intent is (1) to arouse positive feelings associated with doing something important and "special" (in a positive sense), (2) to arouse such intrinsic motives as curiosity and competence, (3) to focus attention on relevant stimuli, and (4) to minimize boredom and tedium (and generate excitement and interest). If the teacher's efforts are successful in getting the student to feel that the program is of personal interest, relevance, and importance, then the classroom should tend to maximize Hawthorne-type phenomena and be effectively personalized.

AIMS OF A PERSONALIZED CLASSROOM

In implementing a personalized classroom or any type of formal public schooling, it is assumed that the organization's long-range goals are, and will remain, oriented to society's needs. For example, three major aims have been recognized as basic to society's desire to prepare children for adult roles through schooling: (1) to maintain order by socializing children to function within the society's current legal and customary boundaries, (2) to guarantee society's economic survival by preparing children for appropriate roles as producers and consumers in the marketplace, and (3) to preserve the prevailing political system by inculcating children with a positive understanding of the society's political doctrines and mechanisms (Ehman, 1980; Wisconsin v. Yoder, 1972). Pursuit of these aims has been trans-

lated into curricular goals as reflected in taxonomies associated with cognitive, affective, and psychomotor domains. Specific objectives, including behavioral objectives, have been formulated for most of the population and for exceptional individuals These curricular formulations along with professional preparation programs, school board policies, and parent and voter mandates guarantee that personalized classrooms will not differ too substantively from other approaches in terms of the intent to develop awareness of societal and political norms, literacy, and vocational skills.

However, statements of aims do not tell the total story. Schools do more than develop basic skills and general awareness of norms. They critically shape motivation, attitudes, and post school learning. Evidence suggests that students often learn as much or more from the processes used in teaching as from the manifest curriculum content (e.g., Ehman, 1980; Illich, 1977; Nicholls, 1979; Overley, 1970). However, this type of learning usually has not been discussed and often is unintended. This is evident from the terms used by researchers who have investigated such phenomena, for example, unstudied, hidden, covert, implicit, latent, or tacit curriculum. The major implication of the fact that "process teaches" is that procedures (means) should be consistent with content and desired outcomes (ends).

Understanding the aims of personalization and how the intended processes differ from other approaches requires more than comparison of stated aims. It also requires analyses of the processes themselves and the aims they convey. To avoid masking any of the aims of personalization, we want to specify three major outcomes the process itself is intended to produce.

1. *Acceptance and even valuing of individual differences*—Since the most fundamental facet of personalization is accommodation of individual differences,

FOR EXAMPLE

THE INTERACTION OF THE TEACHER AND THE CURRICULUM: CLASSROOM CLIMATE INFLUENCES

The general argument can be made that it is not who teaches, nor what is taught, as much as how the teaching is carried out which makes an impact on student political orientations.

Classroom climate refers to how teaching is carried out. When students have an opportunity to engage freely in making suggestions for structuring the classroom environment, and when they have opportunities to discuss all sides of controversial topics, the classroom climate is deemed "open." When these conditions do not prevail, and when the teacher uses authoritarian classroom tactics, it is considered "closed."

Open classroom climate has been found to foster a range of positive political attitudes, and a closed climate is associated with negative attitudes. Torney, Oppenheim, and Farnen (1975) analyzed their national sample of 9-, 12-, and 17-year-olds to determine the effects of specific civic education practices on political attitudes and beliefs. . . .

Some specific factors appearing to be related to low authoritarianism were (1) encouragement of independence of opinion expression, (2) infrequent participation in patriotic rituals, (3) emphasis on nonWestern cultures in social studies classes, (4) infrequent use of printed drill, and (5) willingness of teachers to discuss sensitive issues in class. These same factors appear to be related to student participation in political discussions, both in and out of school. It was only classroom climate, however, that appeared related in a positive way to all of the desired civic outcomes under study. . . .

In a different, 13-school, 2-year longitudinal study of classroom climate effects, Ehman . . . found very consistent, positive effects of open-class climate variables on political trust, social integration, and political interest, and negative effects on political efficacy. The three climate indicators in this study were (1) frequency of controversial issues exposure, (2) range of viewpoints encouraged by teacher, and (3) openness of student opinion expression. . . .

Although there are a few contradictory studies, it is impressive that the evidence from a variety of studies lines up solidly in support of classroom climate as a potent correlate of student political attitudes. The different studies use different indicators of this rather vague construct, but the relationships show remarkable consistency. Open-classroom climate generally is related to higher political efficacy and trust, and lower political cynicism and alienation—to more democratic attitudes.

Ehmen (1980, pp. 108–10)

---

the benefits and fairness of such accommodation are stressed and meant to be learned.

2. *Intrinsic valuing and acceptance of personal responsibility for learning*—By stressing motivation, including choice behavior, and avoiding overreliance on extrinsics, the process intends to facilitate commitment to personal learning and development of a sense of self-determination and competence.

3. *Independent and cooperative functioning and problem solving*—The structure in a personalized classroom is designed specifically to facilitate these outcomes.

In addition to the above intended outcomes, it should be noted that personalized classrooms, as we conceive them, differ from most other approaches in the importance placed on offering enrichment opportunities that do not have planned outcome objectives. This is not a hidden curriculum. Rather, the intent is to recognize the value of positive serendipity. (In doing so, the risks inherent in its pursuit also are recognized.)

Both the emphasis on accommodating an individual's intrinsic motivation and on offering enrichment means that the idiosyncratic interests of learners are encouraged. This results in a variety of major outcomes that cannot be planned. While it usually is possible to keep these serendipitous outcomes within positive boundaries, the learner may choose to pursue certain areas and reject others with regard to his or her predilections and best interests. At times what is chosen will not be consistent with areas or limits prescribed by society's current priorities.

Whether personalized classrooms will be as, or more, effective in producing individuals the society values is an as yet unanswered question. Clearly, a great number of those who are products of nonpersonalized school programs are not valued and indeed are seen as major problems by the society. This may be significant evidence that current processes are inappropriate for such individuals. Personalization is seen as a concept and approach worth investigating—at least with regard to those for whom current approaches have proven to be unsatisfactory.

CONCLUDING COMMENTS

It should be clear that personalizing a classroom calls for dramatic modification in the way teachers think about, and provide, learning opportunities. We recognize it is particularly difficult to think in terms of the environment as the primary object of change. However, as outlined in Step 1 of the sequential model, accommodating students' motivation and development can improve learning for a significant number of individuals who have experienced learning problems. Personalizing learning environments and programs as the first step in the intervention sequence, therefore, should reduce the number labeled *learning disabled*. After Step 1 is implemented, we proceed to Step 2 of the model and offer specialized remedial help to those students who continue to have problems learning.

Remedial Treatment: Step 2

Remedial teaching has sometimes been used as a palliative, whereas more radical remedies are needed. This is not to say that remedial teaching, especially when it includes an advisory element, does not provide a very useful service. But the training and experience of remedial teachers should perhaps be focused increasingly on the children who have specific and severe learning disabilities—children for whom something more than good teaching seems to be needed.
Guillford (1971, p. 13)

To help another . . . you have to know what the other needs, and the only way to find out what the other needs is for him to tell you. And he won't tell you unless he thinks you will listen . . . carefully. And the way to convince him that you will listen carefully is to listen carefully.
Nyberg (1971, p. 181)

A significant number of learning problems can be corrected and others can be prevented by personalizing the classroom. The remaining problems require additional specialized interventions usually referred to as *treatment, remediation,* or *therapy.* Our focus here is on the specialized psychoeducational interventions that can be described as *remediation* and not on other specialized treatments such as psychotherapy and drugs.

Whether remedial approaches should be administered in special or regular classrooms frequently is the first concern raised. From our perspective, this concern is secondary. The primary problems are to clarify the nature of effective interventions, to provide competent interveners, and to establish conditions that enable them to pursue promising approaches. In this chapter, we take as given that (1) it is always preferable not to segregate individuals who require specialized interventions, and (2) students who need remediation must have a teacher who has the competence and time to work individually with them. (If these two factors are mutually exclusive in a given situation, then the interests of such students cannot be served in an optimal manner. Solutions to this type of dilemma obviously are political and economic, not psychoeducational.)

There is a multitude of unresolved psychoeducational issues and problems to be explored in relationship to remedial efforts. Step 2 of the sequential model diagrammed at the beginning of Part 4 in Figure 1 represents our current framework for investigating such concerns. Before we discuss the specifics of this second step, however, we will offer a few definitional statements about remediation.

REMEDIAL PRACTICES

Remediation usually designates interventions applied when there is a problem to be corrected. Remedial practices have been discussed in terms of both the methods and the settings in which they are employed, and have been contrasted with regular or *developmental* approaches. As a result the impression has been conveyed that there are substantive differences between remedial and regular practices. However, as discussed in Part 3, the similarities may be greater than has been implied.

Differentiating Remedial and Regular Teaching

The general features that distinguish remedial from regular teaching—at least as experienced in applying Step 2 of the sequential model—are:

Teacher competence and time   Probably the most basic feature differentiating remedial and regular practices is the need for a competent teacher[1] who has time to provide one-to-one instruction when necessary for students manifesting learning problems. Establishing an appropriate match for such students is more difficult than for successful learners. Indeed, a great deal of this process remains essentially a matter of empirical trial and appraisal.[2] Thus, there must be additional time to develop an understanding of the student (e.g., strengths, weaknesses, limitations, likes, dislikes). There also must be access and control over a wide range of relevant environmental circumstances, especially any methods that have been found effective.

Sequence of application   Remedial practices are pursued after the best available regular or nonspecial practices have been attempted and found insufficient.

Outcomes and content   While remedial efforts may continue to stress similar skills and knowledge, the focus often is shifted to include additional content and outcome objectives. These are related to different levels of functioning, such as missing prerequisites, underlying processing deficits, or interfering behaviors and attitudes.

---

[1]See Adelman (1974a) for a discussion of competence as related to teaching students with learning problems.

[2]Such a process is akin to what Miller, Galanter, and Pribram (1960) describe as the TOTE model. (TOTE stands for test, operate, test, exit.) The model describes a feedback mechanism which can be applied to ongoing intervention actions (trials) and the appraisal of their effects. That is, as a first step, the need for action is determined; actions are implemented and observed; if they are unsatisfactory, new procedures are initiated and so on until satisfactory outcomes are achieved.

Processes   While essentially the same instructional principles are invoked in establishing remedial and regular procedures, remediation usually emphasizes an extreme application of these principles. Such applications may include major reductions in levels of abstraction, intensification of the way stimuli are presented and acted upon, and increases in the amount and consistency of direction and support, including added reliance on technical aides and other resources.

Resource costs   Because of additional objectives and the need for extreme applications in implementing procedures, remediation usually requires a greater amount of one-to-one student-staff interactions than do regular approaches. Remedial practices generally are associated with personnel who have special training and often are provided in spaces other than regular classrooms. These factors continue to make remediation more costly than regular practices with regard to time, personnel, materiel, and space.

Psychological impact   The above features are highly visible to students, teachers, and others. They likely are perceived, at least in part, in stigmatizing terms, for example, "different" in a negative sense. As a result, it is probable that the psychological impact of remediation has a negative component, which makes remediation such a psychologically sensitive practice, only to be implemented when necessary. This feature also underscores the need for actions to make remediation different in a positive sense, that is, perceived by the learner as a special *and* positive opportunity.

VIEWPOINT

PERSONALIZING REMEDIAL PRACTICES

For some children, presentation of a single problem on a page may be necessary so that "the end is in sight." For others, pages may have to be torn out of workbooks one by one, rather than assigning the entire book and expecting the child to work systematically through it.
Hewett and Taylor (1980, p. 176)

There is a super-abundance of materials on the market specifically designed for remedial work with children with learning disabilities. Much of it is overpriced, superficial, shoddy or boring. Prefabricated materials are a luxury, not a necessity. With a little imagination, a good remedial teacher can teach reading, writing and arithmetic, using nothing more than pencil and paper and ordinary household objects.
Golick (1978, p. 203)

Commonalities Among Teaching Practices

Techniques and materials designated as remedial approaches often have much in common with each other and with regular teaching practices. Some are nothing more than adapted regular procedures. Others are specially developed packaged programs, materials, and methods for problem populations. These are often based on specific theoretical formulations. For example, procedures emphasizing stimulus bombardment, stimulus simplification, modality isolation or multisensory integration have been designed particularly for problem learners. In our work, such procedures are occasionally used, but not because of the "theories" upon which they are based. Rather, we suggest that these specialized procedures can be reanalyzed and evaluated in terms of their motivation, attention, and performance inducing properties. Such an analysis and evaluation allows for use of the same general

Type III learning problem). To allow for common fluctuations in retention however, remediation is not implemented unless retention is below criteria for at least two weeks. As a further precaution against misidentification, daily performances (e.g., work samples) are analyzed to determine whether a retention problem manifests itself in other than test and formal review sessions.[3]

Breadth of interest and learning. The final index of need for initiating or expanding remediation is whether the student eventually demonstrates a breadth of interest, learning, or both. This index is used only after the student has been in the program for about a year. With regard to *interests*, the criterion for initiating remediation is that the student is not actively pursuing at least five major areas of interest (skills or content or both). Because of the importance of basic reading, math, and language skills, the criterion for inadequate breadth of *learning* is the amount of learning in these areas after a year in the program. The same process for determining amount of learning described above is used. By the end of a second year in the program, data from standardized achievement tests are used to evaluate whether the student has made at least three-quarters of a year's gain, for example, seven month's progress for the year on a standardized reading achievement test. If the student has not been identified previously as in need of remediation, the problem is classified as *motivational* (mild to severe). Again, daily performance is analyzed as a check on the accuracy of test findings.

Obviously, the criteria described above are debatable and fallible. At the same time,

we can report that our pilot work indicates they have promise, especially with regard to reducing the number of diagnostic errors currently made using psychometric procedures.

The same assessment procedures and criteria are used to determine the success or failure of the specific remedial interventions. If the findings indicate the problem is corrected, remediation is terminated. If the problem continues unabated, there is a shift in the level of remedial intervention focus as described in the next section.

Sequencing of Hierarchical Strategies

When a youngster manifests a problem, the teacher and student must decide whether intervention in that area should be delayed until learning might be easier. This occurs frequently with young children (5–8 year olds) whose perceptual development may be slower than the mean for their age group. It also occurs for students whose anxiety and motivational levels make them unready to pursue vigorously any learning in a particular area. Remediation is initiated at this point for all students who indicate a desire for help in order to improve functioning.

Once the need for remediation is indicated, the teacher may employ up to three hierarchical strategies. However, the sequence and level of these three strategies differ depending on whether the student is manifesting only minor or occasional (Type II) problems or is found to have severe and pervasive (Type III) problems.

For students manifesting minor or occasional problems, the initial emphasis of in-

---

[3] Because assessment and evaluation are essential ingredients in the program, we have been concerned particularly about how to integrate performance checks, record keeping, and ratings. Our intent is to have these activities experienced as procedures to facilitate self-evaluation, rather than as surveillance and teacher evaluation. In this way, we hope to avoid undermining motivation and perhaps even to enhance it. The procedures stressed are meant to be natural and unobtrusive ways of gathering and sharing information—daily informal and formal conferences have proven to be indispensible. We have found that, properly gathered and used, this kind of data can facilitate aspects of specific daily planning, and as data accumulates, they can aid in selection decisions (about changes in status) and in classification. These data along with standardized achievement test data, and pre-post ratings by teachers, students, and parents provide the nucleus of our evaluation findings on intervention effectiveness.

Figure 14-1

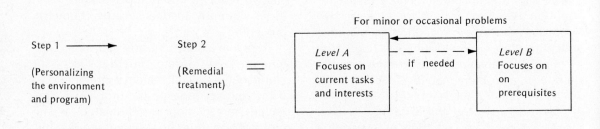

struction is on current tasks and interests and expanding areas of interest. The procedures involve (1) continued adaptation of methods to match and enhance current levels of motivation and development and (2) reteaching specific skills and knowledge when the youngster has difficulty. This level of focus is designated as "A" in Figure 1, reproduced as Figure 14-1.

If the problem continues unabated and is assessed as severe using the criteria cited above, the emphasis shifts to assessment and development of missing prerequisites (Level B) needed for functioning at the higher level. Again procedures are adapted to optimize the match, and reteaching is used when the learner has difficulty. If missing prerequisites are successfully developed, the focus returns to Level A—current tasks and interests.

By proceeding in this sequential and hierarchical way, our intention is to use the simplest and most direct approaches first, and to avoid having to focus on missing prerequisites (Level B) and incompatible behaviors or dysfunctions (Level C) whenever problems appear to be minor. However, if available data indicate the presence of severe and pervasive motivation or developmental problems, Level B interventions are implemented immediately (see Figure 14-2). If these interventions are not effective, Level C interventions are initiated. It is only at this

level that the emphasis is on factors that may interfere with functioning at higher levels, that is, incompatible behaviors and interests and/or underlying processing dysfunctions and related deficits. At this level, there is increased and intensified use of a wide range of psychoeducational tools and techniques (e.g., see Table 12-2). As soon as it is feasible, the focus shifts back to prerequisites (B) and on to current tasks and interests (A). Step 2 is maintained as long as necessary and reinstituted if problems arise.

To further clarify aspects of this sequential and hierarchical approach, the example of a *minor* reading problem can be used. When criteria are reached designating the problem as minor, remediation first involves reteaching, which is not a matter of trying more of the same—for example, more drill—but using qualitatively different instructional approaches. The teacher adds procedures that range from commonly used, but alternative, explanations, techniques, and materials (such as another example or analogy or a *concrete* demonstration) to less common specialized *remedial techniques* (such as a multisensory method).

If the teacher finds that reteaching at Level A does not work, then he or she assesses whether the student lacks a necessary prerequisite and, if so, attempts to correct the deficiency (Level B). For example, if a young-

Figure 14-2

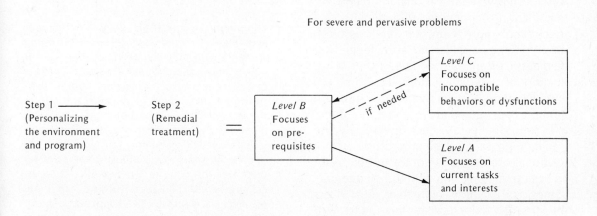

For severe and pervasive problems

Step 1 ⟶
(Personalizing
the environment
and program)

Step 2
(Remedial
treatment)

=

Level B
Focuses
on pre-
requisites

if needed

Level C
Focuses on
incompatible
behaviors or dysfunctions

Level A
Focuses on
current tasks
and interests

ster has difficulty with reading comprehension, the teacher might find the student has little awareness of such underlying concepts as the relationship between the spoken and printed word, or the student may be deficient with regard to such basic educational skills as the ability to follow directions, answer questions, and order and sequence events. If the teacher is able to detect and correct such deficiencies, then he or she is in an improved position to remedy the original problem at Level A.

In contrast to those who have minor learning problems, there are those who continue to manifest *pervasive* and *severe* motivational problems, developmental deficits, or both even after several weeks in the personalized classroom program. (These are the most likely candidates for a diagnostic classification of Type III learning problems or specific learning disabled, seriously emotionally disturbed, etc.) For these students, remediation begins with prerequisites at Level B.

If this proves unfruitful, the teacher proceeds to level C, which involves the assessment and remediation of interfering behaviors and attitudes or underlying process deficits, such as behavioral, motivational, perceptual motor, or linguistic problems.[4] As some success at Level C is achieved, the sequence reverses so that needed prerequisites and basics related to current tasks and interests can be acquired.

Even among those with pervasive and severe problems, there are likely to be some areas where the problem is not severely handicapping and where learning can proceed without remedial interventions or, at least where remediation can be focused more directly and simply on Level B or A. It seems probable that these students can pursue learning at several levels simultaneously. On the other hand, it should be emphasized that there is a small percentage of students whose chronic learning difficulties will require ongoing remediation at Level C in specific areas.

---

[4]There seems to be an unfortunate tendency for some educational, medical, and psychological specialists to begin at this level when working with any child who has been categorized as a school problem.

ATTITUDE AND MOTIVATION PROBLEMS

As with all psychoeducational interventions, remediation is concerned directly with attitudes and motivation, as well as with development of skills and knowledge. Remediation often has to deal with the reduction of avoidance motivation and the enhancement of approach motivation. In doing so, the immediate intervention objectives should reflect this fact. Specifically, the initial emphasis must be on attitudinal/motivational objectives as contrasted with objectives specifying skill and knowledge outcomes. For example, objectives must stress the intent (1) to increase motivation to learn and perform during intervention, (2) to enhance intrinsic motivation as an outcome, and, where necessary, (3) to decrease negative attitudes about schooling and attraction toward behaviors which maintain learning problems.

We do not mean to suggest that developmental objectives are unrelated to motivation. On the contrary, if a student's capabilities increase, it is reasonable to expect that his or her expectations of succeeding may significantly reduce avoidance and increase approach tendencies with regard to the area of increased competence. However, it is not reasonable to expect major shifts in negative attitudes and avoidance tendencies simply as the result of inducing students to perform under conditions designed to ensure success. Human functioning, especially well-established attitudes and behaviors, is too complex to be so easily altered. This is true whether the student is induced to perform using sink-or-swim approaches, desensitization techniques, or subtle do-it-because-you-like-me enticement. Indeed, these approaches, at best, seem to lead to slight improvements in immediate post-test scores, but do not lead to long-term improvement. The reason for this may be that the intervention results in the short-

VIEWPOINT

IS SUCCESS ALWAYS A MOTIVATOR?

One might assume at first glance that failure-avoiding tactics could be reversed by providing students with their fair share of successes. It makes sense, after all, that if a scarcity of success experiences is the original culprit, then providing compensatory rewards should set things right. Moreover, according to reinforcement theory, individuals ought to seek out success once they find how satisfying it can be. Yet, despite this logic, things do not always work out this way. Failure-avoiding students are largely unresponsive to success, something teachers know only too well. Indeed, such pupils seem almost calculating in their disregard for the success experiences that teachers carefully set up for them. Another puzzling observation is that failure, far from discouraging success-oriented students, actually appears to motivate them to greater effort! This also runs counter to the strict reinforcement view of learning, which predicts that failure ought to inhibit achievement. These apparent paradoxes are resolved when we realize that there are other important factors in learning beyond the sheer frequency and strength of rewards and punishments. There are also the person's beliefs about what cause his [or her] successes and failures. As is often true in psychology, the way a person perceives an event can be as important as the fact that it occurred in the first place.

Covington and Beery (1976, p. 66)

term practice of a few skills, such as learning new vocabulary, but does not increase, and may decrease, motivation toward comprehensive activities, such as reading. Without positive motivation, a student is unlikely to pursue learning independently—for example, a student will not choose to read at home or during noninstructional times at school. Therefore, skill gains related to major areas of achievement remain minimal.

Avoidance and Interfering Behavior

For some students with severe and pervasive skill problems, the psychological impact of past school failure produces a generalized pattern of negative attitudes and avoidance behavior related to schools, teachers, class-work, books, and so forth. The avoidance behavior may take a variety of forms, all of which interfere with learning at school. In such cases, the problem is further com-pounded if the student has found some of the interfering behaviors *attractive* alterna-tives to school learning, as is often the case. For example, we find a significant number of adolescent students seem much more in-terested in the *negative* excitement of tru-ancy, peer interactions including gangs and the drug culture, baiting authority, and so forth, than in anything a teacher can offer in the way of learning activities. For every suc-cess among such cases, many more go un-changed, which is evident from the lack of efficacy in programs for juvenile delinquents. It is one thing to try to reduce avoidance motivation and increase approach motiva-tion related to literacy skills. It is quite an-other problem also to have to reduce ap-proach motivation related to behaviors that others designate as interferences, but which the student values and even views as an area of competence.

In instances where a student has strong avoidance motivation toward a task, activity, or situation, or is strongly motivated to pursue interfering behavior, efforts to en-hance motivation generally are inhibited. For such students, these motivational "prob-lems" usually must be addressed directly and prior to efforts to remedy academic and developmental deficits. For example, if students have strong beliefs about the like-lihood of failure or that success is beyond their control, intervention procedures de-signed to modify these perceptions may be necessary. Similarly, if a student strongly values and feels committed to incompatible behaviors, intervention should address these matters.

Attitudinal and motivational problems are the focus of ongoing applied research in our laboratory. In particular, specific procedures for affecting commitment and motivation are being explored. What follows are some ideas from our work to date, which seem worth sharing.

Procedural Objectives

There is a variety of specific theoretical models for understanding avoidance moti-vation and interfering behavior. In general, cognitive and affective theories related to correcting such problems stress changes in affective states, cognitive states, and coping behaviors. More specifically, the ideas out-lined in Chapter 10 provide guidelines for evolving strategies to identify negative states and coping patterns and for planning ways to produce appropriate changes. Additional guidelines are provided by problem-solving, psychotherapeutic, and cognitive behavior modification models (e.g., Adelman & Tay-lor, 1978b; Mahoney, 1974; Meichenbaum, 1977; Spivak et al., 1976; Urban & Ford, 1971). In essence, the intervener employs pro-cedures to reduce negative and increase positive affects, cognitions, and coping strategies. Concomitantly, the intervener at-tempts to identify and minimize experiences that might maintain or increase negative affects, cognitions, and coping strategies.

The point about minimizing experiences that evoke negative associations and actions deserves particular emphasis. Students with extremely negative perceptions of teachers and programs are not likely to be amenable to these interventions if they are perceived as more or less the same as those experi-enced in the past. Unless there are major differences, it seems unlikely that the stu-dent will even perceive a difference—let alone modify negative perceptions. For ex-ample, if the intent is (1) to have the teacher perceived as supportive rather than controlling and indifferent, (2) to have options perceived as of substantive value, and (3) to have activities perceived as feasible and likely to be satisfying, the intervention strategies must convey this intent vividly.

To this end, our initial efforts involve procedures for enhancing motivation (see Chapters 10 and 13).[5] In addition, the following three procedural objectives are used as guidelines in planning subsequent strategies for reducing avoidance motivation, interfering behavior, and negative attitudes: (1) establishment of a noncoercive approach including the broadening of limits to accommodate a greater range of attitudes and actions in the classroom, (2) expansion of the range of learning options, incorporating as many as feasible, that have a known, high probability of being valued by the student and presentation of the options in a vivid and accessible manner, and (3) provision and clarification of mutually acceptable alternatives for behaviors that cannot be accommodated.

Noncoercion/Broadened limits. The essence of activity in this regard is (1) to establish voluntary participation, (2) to arrange the classroom environment and program in ways that provide structure as needed and minimize situations that stimulate behavior problems, and (3) to deal with problems which arise in a manner that is nonauthoritarian and adheres to psychotherapeutic principles when appropriate (Holahan, 1979; Levine & Perkins, 1980; Rook, Padesky, & Compas, 1979). A few specifics should illustrate these points.

We do not proceed unless a student clearly understands available options

and has made a public, unambiguous agreement to proceed. At all times, our intent is to underscore the fact that any choice to participate has been made by the student. This is done by clarifying options and eliciting the student's perceptions of intrinsic reasons for pursuing them. It also is indicated to each student that he or she can choose not to participate—this choice is reiterated whenever students do not participate in agreed-upon ways. If a student feels there is no reasonable alternative but to participate, that is, if the student feels coerced, the reasons for this perception are explored and, if possible, changed.

We also provide information about the purposes and ways of succeeding (especially clarifying available support). This is intended to improve students' expectations of success. While no learning objective or procedure is beyond a student's capabilities, it is expected that individuals will feel they need various forms of help and feedback at different times. No more support and direction is provided than is requested, and all help and feedback also involves noncoercive efforts to teach ways the student can function autonomously, for example, teaching coping skills and self-control techniques.

Schedules and locations of activities are organized to avoid creating situations where student interactions will be problemsome. For example, curriculum is designed to anticipate waning interests at certain times, such as before lunch and at the end of the school day. Sufficient space is maintained between desks to accommodate students' sense

---

[5]As outlined in Figure 10-1, efforts to enhance motivation include (a) clarification and expansion of intrinsic justifications for change, (b) elicitation of public declarations of realistic and valued choices with regard to immediate and longer range procedures and outcomes, and (c) development of a mutual agreement about, and implementation of, realistic methods, including formative and summative feedback.

of crowding. Active centers are established in areas where they will not distract nonparticipants.

Learning activities are planned to accommodate specific students' needs, interests, and styles. For example, talkative students are assigned to work in small discussion groups. Students with high activity levels work with manipulable materials. Students with limited attention work on discrete, time-limited units. Partitions provide privacy and quiet for students who prefer it.

Classroom rules and standards are redefined so that nondisruptive talking and movement are appropriate.

Consequences for violating essential classroom rules are applied on a principle of distributive justice emphasizing individual need. Students who do manifest problem behaviors are encouraged to discuss and explore the reasons for the event and related matters in a fashion similar to discussions of progress as described above. The concluding focus of such discussions is to clarify alternative ways to handle the situation next time.

Our emphasis is on maximizing student perception of self-control by minimizing external control and increasing areas of independence, autonomous functioning, competence and responsibility, and self-determination.

Expanding options.   The essence of the intervener activity in connection with expanding the range of valid options, vividly and accessibly, is to explore with the student a much more comprehensive and vivid range of activities than are usually available in classroom programs. This is done in order to increase the probability of finding a valued option. These alternatives may include work

or career-related learning opportunities, such as participatory learning experiences in the community (e.g., apprenticeships). Projects can be initiated that focus on such applied skills as auto mechanics, animal husbandry, and videocommunications. Special resource personnel, such as skilled crafts persons, can be contacted to help initiate a chosen and valued project.

The intent is to find an activity for which the student has little or no avoidance or negative attitudes. When students participate in such activities, generally we find they do not manifest interfering behaviors or blocks in learning, even though they may lack certain skills. Moreover, we find a student's involvement in one such activity provides a foundation upon which to build positive working relationships and to expand involvement to other learning activities in ways that can enhance motivation.

Mutually acceptable alternative behaviors. When there is a frequent occurrence of behavior that cannot be accommodated, mutually acceptable alternatives are sought. In general, we initiate intervention without prejudging the commitment of students. If the interventions appear seriously hampered by a student continuing to manifest behaviors that are directly incompatible with staying in the program, the focus shifts to this problem. An example would be a student who spends no time on activities related to learning and instead spends the time in disruptive or destructive ways such as hitting others, stealing, or selling drugs.

Among students who manifest such behavior, we have distinguished three groups to date: those who say they want to change and do; those who say they want to change, but behaviorally do not follow through; and those who say they do not want to change. Students who initially or eventually indicate little or no commitment to maintaining negative behaviors are involved immediately in

FOR EXAMPLE

PROVIDING A NONCOERCIVE PROGRAM WITH BROADENED LIMITS AND EXPANDED OPTIONS

As a central aspect of overcoming severe attitudinal and motivational problems, we have found it essential not to insist that a student continue to work in areas where avoidance motivation is manifested. A major reason for this strategy is to avoid increasing avoidance, either in the form of withdrawal (including passive performance) or active resistance (e.g., disruptive behavior). We also want to avoid *psychological reactance* which is the term Brehm (1972) uses to describe motivational arousal, which occurs when a person thinks one of his or her freedoms is threatened and is moved to react against the threat.

Thus, if a student initially indicates that he or she does not wish instruction in a specific area, even if it is a basic area such as reading or math, our approach has been to set it aside temporarily. We use the time to explore other areas of positive and appropriate interest.

We recognize this is a controversial and for some an alarming strategy. It is not one we adopt lightly or naively. From a motivational perspective, it is clearly rational to pursue areas of positive and appropriate interest. However, ignoring avoidance areas as a step in developing positive interest probably goes against common sense.

Indeed, if an area were completely ignored, the best outcome an intervener should expect is that avoidance motivation would not be significantly increased. For many persons, this might be an acceptable outcome with regard to "esoteric" and nonfundamental areas such as art and music. It would not be acceptable to the majority with

regard to basic literacy skills, such as reading, math, and language skills. Fortunately, what makes these skills *basic* is that most facets of daily living call for their application (e.g., Bruner, 1966; Dewey, 1938; Fernald, 1943). Moreover, that they are designated as basic makes them a pervasive point of focus by almost everyone in the society. Both of these factors result in frequent natural encounters by students with the need for, and expectation that they have, such skills. For example, our students build models, play games, look at comics, and do a variety of special projects related to electronics, science, and so forth. In each activity, they encounter the need to read and often to write and compute. In addition, they are constantly aware of others who have acquired such skills and the value society places on them. Our role is to help them explore their feelings and attitudes when these natural encounters occur.

Our work suggests that during the course of natural encounters teachers can (1) facilitate student discovery or rediscovery of personal reasons for learning basics, (2) provide a variety of options and aid in pursuit of personal projects, and (3) elicit choices that reduce avoidance and increase approach motivation. As a result, skills improve due to both informal teaching during natural encounters and to students seeking formal instruction as they come to intrinsically value the skills. As importantly, positive attitudes are developed and motivation for improving basic skills such as reading is maintained and manifested outside the framework of formal instruction.

procedures to establish commitment and motivation for a mutually satisfactory alternative pattern of behavior. Those who seem committed to negative behavior require the use of additional intervention strategies. In discussing their behavior with such students, some indicate the behavior represents the

way they want to act ("It's too bad if others don't like it"); some see the behavior as a problem, but see it as caused by others or by factors beyond their control; and some readily agree that the behavior is a problem and that they are at fault. In this last instance, the lack of desire to change is manifested in one of two ways: either they give many reasons that alternatives to the negative behavior will not work ("I've tried that." "Others won't cooperate." "Yes, but—"), or they quickly acquiesce to ideas about how to improve the behavior and then do not follow through.

The essence of activity related to reducing incompatible behavior is (1) to explore with the student whether there is mutual agreement that an ongoing behavior problem exists and, if so, (2) to begin to understand better the problem and determine mutually acceptable alternative courses of action. To accomplish this systematically, problem-solving steps are used (e.g., see Figure 8–2). The student's perception of the causes of the behavior are assessed. Alternative behaviors that would prevent or reduce the problem are identified. If it is unclear whether the student wants to discontinue the problem behavior, this is explored. The consequences of not finding an alternative are clarified, as is the student's role in controlling subsequent decisions that must be made. Among the specific messages given are that: (1) the behavior has been identified as going beyond the limits that were established as a prerequisite for continuing in the program; (2) the program cannot maintain the student much longer if the identified behavior continues unabated; and (3) the student is making a choice about continuing in the program by either maintaining or changing the identified behavior.[6] Finally, the student is asked to choose an alternative from those that have been identified, and plans are made for implementing and evaluating it.

If the student is not willing to compromise in some fashion, the scheduled program is halted. In its place, we offer the student three or four hourly sessions with a staff member to explore whether the student wants to identify ways to stay in the program.

If all else fails, behavior-shaping procedures such as systematic manipulation of of external reinforcement contingencies (rewards and punishments) are sometimes tried in hopes of decreasing the negative behaviors. The full range of behavior modification strategies can be invoked.[7] Where necessary and appropriate, parents are called upon to enlist their systematic cooperation in following through in the manipulation of reinforcement contingencies.

PROBLEMS RELATED TO SKILLS AND KNOWLEDGE

After the motivational status of the learner is appropriately addressed, the focus shifts to developmental problems affecting acquisition of skills and knowledge. Remedial approaches are designed to overcome deficiencies by directly correcting them or indirectly compensating for them. Direct strategies involve (1) increasing efforts to personalize the environment and program, including reteaching as needed, to enhance learning and (2) use of psychoeducational treatments, where necessary and feasible, to correct problems blocking acquisition of desired skills and knowledge. Indirect approaches emphasize (1) helping the learner evolve ways to compensate for handicap-

---

[6]This last point often requires considerable clarification. It is emphasized that maintenance of the identified behavior is a choice, albeit not verbalized as such, to leave the program. It is explicitly stated that the program staff cannot accept the behavior, and therefore the student is choosing not to work with the available staff by avoiding a compromise. For most students, leaving the program also means being transferred to another program by their parents, the school district, or a judge. Thus, the student is asked to understand that the behavior is a choice that has these specific consequences as well.

[7]The literature on behavior modification strategies is extensive and does not bear repeating here. However, it can be noted that the approaches described by Kopel and Arkowitz (1975), Mahoney (1974), Mahoney and Arnkoff (1978), and Meichenbaum (1977) provide both prescriptive steps and relevant principles.

ping conditions and (2) nonpsychoeducational treatments.[8]

There is considerable debate as to what is directly correctable, what needs to be compensated for, and what compensatory mechanisms are appropriate and effective. While the issues are intriguing, their persistence as issues is one indication that they are unresolvable given the current state of knowledge about human functioning. At this point, we take the pragmatic position that if direct approaches do not remedy the problem, compensatory approaches should be pursued. Moreover, treatment activity aside, most direct and indirect psychoeducational approaches appear to differ primarily in degree rather than in form and substance. While direct and indirect approaches make different assumptions about whether a student has a handicap, the emphasis in both cases is on initiating strategies to accommodate the student or teaching the student self-strategies to accommodate the demands of a learning situation.

Since *direct* approaches do not assume the student has a handicap, the strategies tend not to differ significantly from nonremedial strategies. They often amount to no more than taking additional time to support the student's efforts and use of alternative, but rather standard, sets of materials, activities, and so forth (see Chapter 12).

Indirect approaches involve teacher or student *compensating* for what may be temporary or permanent learning handicaps. For our purposes, a person has a learning handicap whenever he or she is expected to learn and perform, but cannot because of inadequate development (a delay or a disorder) related to *sensory intake systems*, especially those involved in perceptual search and detection of external stimuli intended to initiate learning or provide feed-

back; *processing and decision-making systems*, especially those involved in cognitive evaluation and selection of stimuli and feedback; and *output systems*, especially those involved in practicing, applying, and demonstrating what is learned.

Fortunately for them, but unfortunately for assessors, individuals with the types of learning problems we are discussing do not have gross problems related to these systems. Thus, as stressed in Parts 2 and 3, the subtle disorders they do have cannot be validly diagnosed with available psychometric procedures. Some experienced teachers and clinicians appear able to make educated guesses as to whether the problem is associated with some facet of intake, processing, or output. At least for now, expert analyses seem to be the best practical and research strategy for assessing such needs.

Whatever the problem, compensatory remedial approaches essentially are rather delimited. As suggested above and represented in Figure 14–3, an intervener may (1) manipulate the environment in relatively extreme ways in efforts to accommodate the learner's handicap and (2) teach the learner compensatory strategies which can be self-initiated whenever needed. In both cases, the strategies pursued involve increased reliance on tools and increased emphasis on formal techniques.

No new principles need to be invoked in understanding direct and indirect remedial approaches. What characterizes them is the extreme degree to which, and consistency with which, strategies must be used.

CONCLUDING COMMENTS

Personalized classroom programs seem to us a reasonable alternative to current regular school programs for students who find reg-

---

[8]The major treatments in this area are biologically oriented, involving the use of drugs, special diets, and recommendations regarding rigid scheduling of sleep, play, television, and so forth. While such treatments appear to have some effects on behavior, evidence does not support their efficacy in improving learning.

FOR EXAMPLE

PERSONALIZED CORRECTIVE AND COMPENSATORY PRACTICES

The child who cannot perform arithmetic operations with the class following oral directions may be able to do so if the teacher provides a visual demonstration; or a child who cannot work independently because he [or she] cannot read directions can do quiet seatwork if directions are put on tape and given to him [or her] through earphones. Most remedial learners will require considerable use of audio-visual aids. Some may be candidates for the multisensory systems of integrated reading, writing and spelling instruction. Decisions will have to be made in regard to providing group experiences for children on prescription, so that they do not find themselves working in isolation on seatwork activities for much of the day. Peer tutoring and paraprofessional aides have a place in prescriptive programming. . . .

Usually, only portions of adopted basal readers, arithmetic, social studies, and spelling texts are appropriate for children with skills deficits. Texts must be supplemented by skill-building activities selected from a variety of sources, as well as by teacher-made materials. Because development of materials is often prohibitive in terms of time, many teachers find that they can adapt available materials to meet special needs.

Simple adaptation measures might include reducing the number of arithmetic problems on a page by cutting the page into four parts to be presented separately or making a task more concrete by supplementing a word problem involving addition of sets. Moderate levels of adaptation could include recording word problems on tape and permitting the child to listen to rather than read them or preparing a set of questions for a page of social studies material to be studied before the page is read as an aid to comprehension. More complex adaptations are such measures as the application of readability formulas in order to match the reading level of materials in content areas to the child's instructional reading level or, alternatively, arranging for another child or an aide to put content-area materials such as social studies chapters on tape.

Teachers who are well-acquainted with a variety of materials can usually locate a published lesson which can serve a particular purpose. Just as an automobile mechanic might 'cannibalize' several cars to find parts to repair one automobile, so the teacher must take apart published materials to find appropriate parts to repair skills deficits.
Moran (1979, p. 179)

---

ular classes insufficiently accommodating. For those manifesting learning problems, we think personalization is a necessity. Perhaps even more importantly, if our hypotheses about Type I and II learning problems are anywhere near the mark, applying this type of approach to the early elementary grades should prove to be a major step forward in primary prevention.

With reference to remediation, it is critical to recognize that reliance on extreme measures and, indeed, use of any measure perceived as remedial has the potential to produce negative consequences. These in turn become another set of problems to be addressed. Because of their prevalence, we want to highlight three problems in particular: negative motivational impact, narrowness in learning, and dependency.

Paradoxically, the very process that is intended to remedy a person's problems and thereby result in increased feelings of competence can also be perceived by the person as another indication of lack of competence.

Figure 14-3

Compensatory remedial intervention approaches.

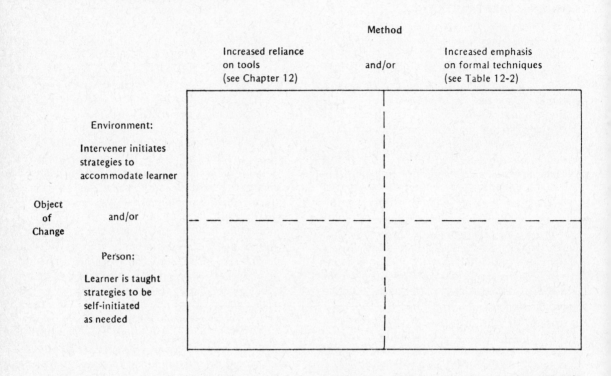

Thus, in some instances, remediation actually may result in increased feelings of incompetence and reduced motivation. The challenge is to find procedures for remedial use that are not associated with remediation, or to introduce remedial procedures in ways that minimize stigmatizing features.

Because remedial approaches are specialized, take added time, and stress problem amelioration, *what* is learned and *how* to learn are often viewed from a very narrow perspective. As a result, there often is little opportunity to facilitate transfer and generalization. Provision of extra support and direction and increased use of staff resources, in general, are conditions likely to foster excessive dependency. These outcomes mediate against students understanding

the connections between what they have learned and other phenomena in the world and learning how to learn without assistance. As long as these conditions go uncountered, many students can be expected not to be able to pursue successfully a nonremedial, normative existence in school and community.

Our approach to dealing with such problems has had three facets. First, remediation always is treated as but one aspect of the program, pursued only when absolutely necessary. Second, all intervention is designed to facilitate the development of independence. When assistance is required for a particular activity, part of the intervention is designed to teach independence related to future encounters with the activity. In

Figure 14-4

Major tasks as related to Fernald's service programs.

A. Major Tasks (see Figure 11-2)

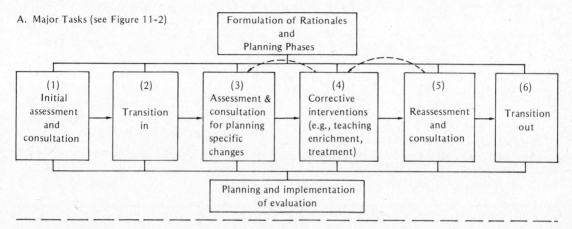

B. Fernald Services

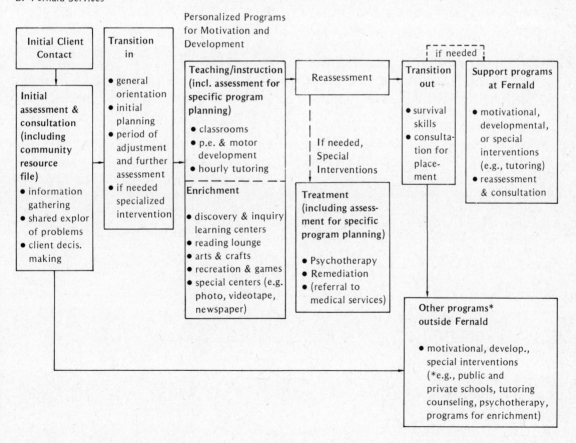

VIEWPOINT

PERSONALIZATION AND REMEDIATION

Based on our analyses of the state of the art and our work in the field, it seems reasonable to conclude the following:

Correction of learning problems has inappropriately focused primarily on presumed developmental needs and has not systematically addressed motivation.

Corrective interventions for those diagnosed as *LD* must be designed with the possibility of *disconfirming* both the diagnosis and necessity for remedial procedures aimed at improving underlying process deficits.

In correcting learning problems, the first emphasis should be on environmental and programmatic changes, then on person remediation if still needed.

In correcting learning problems, it is necessary to deal systematically first with individual differences in motivation, especially intrinsic motivation, then with individual differences in development, and finally with any problems interfering with learning.

---

general, an intervener should be a catalytic stimulus and provide specific help only when it is essential. Third, as a direct approach to ensuring that students have the necessary skills to survive in the "real world," we have developed transition activities specifically focused on teaching these skills (see *transition out* task in Chapter 11).

Solutions for the complex learning and behavior problems manifested by most persons seeking special help require a comprehensive and integrated package of services (see Figure 14-4). Many of these have been discussed in detail in the preceding chapters. (Elsewhere, we have outlined the nature and scope of such interrelated services as developed at Fernald; see Adelman and Taylor, 1978a; Taylor and Adelman, 1980). As can be seen in Figure 14-4, services such as transition activities, personalized programs, and special interventions—including remediation—are embedded in an interrelated set of interventions. Ultimately, the efficacy of the practices discussed above, or any other classroom model, must be evaluated in the context of a well-developed, comprehensive, and integrated set of intervention programs.

Epilogue to Part 4:
Change in Systems and Organizations

Environment and program changes, of course, are easier to advocate than accomplish, especially when what is to be changed is a public school classroom. Classrooms are organizational subsystems of schools that are subsystems of larger organizations, such as school districts. Because efforts to change these environments must pursue processes appropriate for changing organizational systems, they are confronted by the multitude of problems related to all organizational change (Brookover, 1981.). A brief review of some general points about such processes and problems is presented below.

Organizational change in schools encompasses efforts ranging from changing standard ways furniture is arranged to changing curriculum and staffing patterns. In terms of such notions as mainstreaming exceptional children, obviously major organizational changes are required, for example, class size, staffing patterns, and materials. Regardless of the specific nature of the intended changes, altering schools requires awareness of the issues and problems involved in organizational change processes. Of particular concern are those related to comprehensive *diffusion* of new approaches and those associated with organizational development.

The term *diffusion* as used here means the process by which a prototype (e.g., of personalized classrooms) not only is disseminated for others to hear and read about, but is installed and maintained in other situations. The literature in this area, while hardly definitive, provides a number of ideas about how diffusion may be accomplished (e.g.,

Adelman, 1974b; Alderfer, 1977; Baldridge, 1972; Berman & McLaughlin, 1977; Fullan, Miles, & Taylor, 1980; Fuller, Wood, & Dornbusch, 1982; Guba, 1968; Havelock, 1973; Havelock & Havelock, 1973; Huse, 1975; Keys & Bartunek, 1979; Sarason, 1971, 1972).

Based on the pertinent literature and relevant personal experiences, it seems that any proposed strategy for institutional change must provide at least for the following if an appropriate climate for change is to be created:

appropriate incentives for change (e.g., intrinsically valued outcomes, expectations of success, recognitions, and rewards);

the presentation of an appropriate range of relevant alternatives for change so that an institution may select one that is workable within the institution's context and is acceptable to those who will carry it out;

establishment of mechanisms (e.g., participatory decision making, special training, resources, rewards, procedures designed to improve organizational health) to facilitate the effective functioning of any person who takes, or is given, responsibility for installing changes;[1]

persons who perform the role of change agents in a pragmatic manner rather than as utopian advocates;[2]

appropriate feedback regarding progress of change activity;

appropriate structuring of the scope and timing of change (e.g., establishing or facilitating readiness, planned transition or phasing in of changes);

appropriate feedback regarding progress of change activity; and

ongoing, supportive mechanisms to maintain substantive changes as long as they remain appropriate.

As can be seen, organizational change involves more than a set of procedures.[3] As with any substantive environmental or person change, the motivation and developmental readiness of those involved is funda- mental. Motivation and competence remain critical factors in ongoing maintenance of change.

We do not mean to suggest that awareness of the above factors is sufficient to produce and maintain changes in school settings. Indeed, some writers (e.g., Derr, 1976) speculate that certain properties of schools make them incompatible with successful organizational development. Others have implied that, as with persons, planning for organizational change can be more successful if done in a manner that accommodates key differences among classrooms and schools and their socioeconomic-political contexts (Fullan et al., 1980; Safer, Kaufman, Morrissey, & Lewis, 1979), which fits our perspective that all planning for intended change has to reflect personalization.

Organizational change does not come easily. It is hard work. Progress usually is slow and difficult to measure. Frustration and disappointment are common. On the other hand, as long as organizational changes are desirable and possible, they are worth pursuing. In the process, it is well to remember the immortal words of whoever said it first: *"illegitimati non carborundum"*; "don't let the bastards grind you down."

---

[1] Such mechanisms may be directed at change agents or at persons who are to change. For example, the change agent may need special training regarding how to facilitate a particular change; at the same time, persons who are to change may need training to develop prerequisite knowledge, skills, and attitudes before they can be expected to carry out a particular change. Examples of other mechanisms which may be needed are: released time, extra clerical help, in situ demonstrations, communication-oriented meetings, frequent indications of support for a given change by the organization's leaders, "influentials," gatekeepers, and by relevant professional associations.

[2] Gallaher (1965) states that there is "a large body of research to support the basic assumptions underlying the pragmatic model, that is that people will more readily accept innovations that they can understand and perceive as relevant, and secondly, that they have had a hand in planning" (pp. 41–42).

[3] Another way to think about the characteristics of a change process is in terms of the inhibiting factors that must be overcome. Miller (1967) suggests (a) three general inhibiting factors—traditionalism, laziness, and fear and insecurity, and (b) seven less general educational factors inhibiting change—rut of experience, administrative reticence, educational bureaucracy, insufficient finances, community indifference and resistance, inadequate knowledge about the process of change, and inadequate teacher-education programs.

VIEWPOINT

ON THE PROCESS OF CHANGE

Havelock (1973) summarizes six research-identified phases in the process of individual adoption of an innovation: awareness, interest, evaluation, trial, adoption, and integration. He then indicates that the change agent's activities should be designed to *coordinate* with these six phases, that is, be designed so that the change agent is with, not ahead or behind, the individual adopter. Thus, he suggests the process occurs in the following way:

Coordinating change agent activities with the client's adoption activities

Change Agent Activities   **Client Activities**

Havelock (1973, p. 115)

PART 5

EMERGING CONCERNS FOR THE LD FIELD: SOCIAL CONTROL, ETHICS, AND ACCOUNTABILITY

Improvement in the quality of life must begin with changes in the behavior of individuals, specifically greater concern about others, coupled with a willingness to devote considerable effort and energy to promoting the well-being and happiness of others—to insuring that all humans enjoy basic dignity, freedom, rights, and opportunities.

Mussen and Eisenberg-Berg (1977, p. 172)

One thing all children know is that adults are there to help them. They hear it all the time. "I am here to help you." "I want to help you." "I am doing it for your good."

Children can take only so much help of the kind that most school personnel have to offer. "If you are here to help me," a child might ask, "why must I do everything your way?"

Weinberg (1974, p. 15)

How well do the host of programs, new and old, succeed in achieving the goals for which they were established? That seems a rational question, but not everyone is interested in the answers. Some people justify a program because it is "doing something" to deal with an obvious need. Others declare themselves content if a program saves one youth from crime, prepares one pupil for college.

Weiss (1972a, p. 4)

Learning problems exist in the context of society. Ultimately, consideration of such problems brings us in touch with some basic concerns about learning and teaching, education and training, helping and socializing, democracy and autocracy. Schools, in particular, are places where choices about each of these concerns arise daily.

Because these concepts reflect major issues in any society, schools are always surrounded by controversy and crisis. Educators have had to learn to live with a chronic negative reputation and cyclical crises of confidence. Because changes in most societies are accelerating, the cycles seem to occur more frequently and last longer. In recent years litigation, legislation, and tax-payer rebellions all have converged into a set of conflicting mandates. These include simultaneous demands for increased and better student services, greater protection of student rights, more specific accountability for outcomes, and reduced financial outlay. At the same time, there has been increased vandalism and violence in schools, large numbers of students graduating with minimal literacy skills, teacher burn-out, and student dropouts. How such variables are related to each other has not been established by research. Perhaps there is no cause-and-effect connection. However, given that schools are instruments of society and reflect and shape socio-cultural thought and actions, the possibility of causal connections cannot be ignored.

Over the years, we have seen the number of students with learning problems increase well beyond the resources available to help them. When we first began our work, our primary interest was in those individuals who might appropriately be labeled *specific learning disabled* (Type III). We wanted to understand their problems and *help* them, and, in doing so, demonstrate respect for rights, liberties, dignity, and worth. We also saw our work as a way to serve society and perhaps improve the quality of education and psychoeducational practices in general. Such straightforward motives were soon confounded. We discovered that learning problems were often *schooling* and *societal* problems and that it was impossible to identify and thus limit our focus to any one subgroup of learning problems. We also found that schooling and helping are very complex phenomena, which sometimes are compatible, but very often come into conflict.

These realities led us to reflect on the role of school environments and professional "helpers" in contributing to the cause of learning problems. It did not take long to realize that blaming professionals was to miss the point that there are pervasive circumstances that may make schooling and helping incompatible, especially for those students who do not fit in.

Professionals working in schools struggle against horrendous odds to make programs work for most students. Even the most successful teacher, however, has a few problem students who almost inevitably are a source of anxiety and guilt. In some school districts, there are large numbers of students for whom no one seems to know what to do. While one can debate what labels and definitions seem appropriate, what is beyond debate is that such students need help, and they need systems that can provide it. Many interveners who could provide such help, and want to, indicate that conflicting societal priorities and pressures on school systems prevent them from doing so. They are asked increasingly to assume functions other than helping, such as activities related to managing, record keeping, evaluating, and policing.

Despite the many pressures and conflicting priorities, however, as interveners we must take responsibility for our actions and their impact. To better understand our obligations, we have found it essential to clarify the needs and expectations of individuals and of society, and to understand whose interests we have been contracted to represent. If both, we must determine whether the respective expectations are compatible. We have come to recognize the importance of distinguishing between helping and socializing. To appreciate the critical differences, it has been necessary to analyze the sociopolitical, social philosophical, and moral underpinings of psychoeducational interventions. These matters are the focus of Chapters 15 and 16.

The final chapter is devoted to evaluating intervention efficacy. Until recently, the question of how to evaluate, systematically and comprehensively, the nature and worth of psychoeducational interventions was relatively ignored. Currently, it is one of the most discussed, and least understood, concerns in the field.

While some professionals would prefer to ignore the topic, two facts make this impossible. One, evaluation is essential to the improvement of interventions related to learning problems. Two, this is an age of accountability, and therefore evaluation increasingly is mandated by legislation and regulations.

Unfortunately, the great need for evaluating intervention effectiveness has outstripped the field's readiness to meet the need. Comprehensive evaluation models and procedures that can be applied on a wide scale are yet to be evolved. But important new starts have been made and deserve attention before we conclude. Therefore, Chapter 17 presents a conceptual framework for evaluating efficacy. Specifically, the purposes and processes of evaluation are outlined and major factors and critical problems delineated.

Evaluation is a key to the future. It may be a difficult process, which many would prefer to avoid, but it is a process that can improve programs, protect consumers, and advance knowledge.

Most interveners would like the opportunity to reflect on what would be in students' and society's long-range best interests. However, they usually have to settle for a plan to get through the next day. To those in this position, discussions of theory, social philosophy, ethical issues, and evaluating intervention efficacy seem almost tangential and certainly esoteric given the facts of life in the "real world" of the public school. From the perspective of immediate survival, they are right. In terms of changing things for the better, however, the narrow focus on survival probably tends to perpetuate the status quo with all its problems, including the need to settle for survival.

As the LD field moves toward maturity, many professionals are finding that understanding the topics of social control, ethics, and accountability is a necessity. These matters permeate every facet of daily practice and research. Because of their profound and pervasive influence, they are emerging as major topics of concern. The time devoted to understanding such concerns can be viewed as essential if day-to-day activity in classrooms and clinics is to advance.

Chapter 15

Social Control and Helping Individuals Overcome Learning Problems

"Annoying behavior" is legislated out of existence by the authoritarian teacher, pretended out of existence by the permissive teacher, and dealt with as a fact of existence by the open teacher.
Kohl (1969, p. 15)

In a chaotic society that sometimes seems bent on its own destruction, it is no longer possible for any professional to hide behind the myth of political neutrality.
Halleck (1971, p. xvi)

As if dealing with the complexities of learning and learning problems were not enough, psychoeducational interveners often find their work confounded by students' behavior problems, which also demand attention. Students behind in reading also may have trouble with peers, their family, and even with legal authorities. Older students may be involved with drug or alcohol abuse and truancy. It seems, at times, as if teachers and other school personnel are being asked to solve some of society's most intractable problems—illiteracy, delinquency, racial prejudice, and poverty. Most school professionals are aware of the complexity of each of these problems. Often in the face of tremendous odds, they persevere because they *want to help*. The desire to help is particularly strong when children are involved. Unfortunately, sometimes the desire to help is so strong that the consequences of a particular intervention are not fully comprehended.

Whether the focus is on the learning problem, related behavior problems, or both, the following implications must be considered by anyone who sets out to help another:

Help is not always helpful.

Help is not always wanted, even though apparently needed.

Interventions designed to help usually have some negative consequences and sometimes these outweigh the benefits.

Some ways of providing help are inappropriate even if effective in achieving desired ends.

What is defined as help by one person may not be seen as help by another.

Sometimes interventions are used to serve the interests of one person or group at the expense of another.

To understand these matters and how they relate to those with learning problems, it is necessary to comprehend (1) the difference between helping and social control and (2) the social philosophical and moral underpinnings of psychoeducational interventions. The first topic is the focus of this chapter, the second the focus of Chapter 16.

HELPING RELATIONSHIPS VERSUS SOCIALIZATION

Psychoeducational programs for students with problems are established by a variety of persons and groups to meet varying, and at times conflicting, needs and ends. Major differences in perspective are viewed as stemming from whether intervention decisions are made with reference to the interests of (1) clients,[1] (2) society, or (3) interveners (see Table 11–1).

Each of the interested parties may perceive the nature of intervention different-

ly. For example, whether explicitly stated or not, school personnel generally are aware that they are expected both to help and socialize students. School systems are established by society as socializing agencies with helping services tacked on whenever feasible. Parents of students experiencing learning problems generally want greater emphasis on helping by the school, but usually also want the socializing functions. The students generally do not like the socializing facets of school and often seem not to perceive school programs as helpful.

While the difference between helping and socialization is intriguing, grappling with these distinctions has not been simply an intellectual exercise for us. Our concern with these matters was necessitated by our experiences in working with students who saw their problems and the "help" needed in very different ways than the schools who referred them or the specialists who treated them. These students often felt they were not in control of decisions affecting their lives. In such instances, a great deal of valuable time and energy was wasted because students and teachers were engaged in a struggle over whose rationale, interests, and criteria should prevail.

As a result of our experiences, we came to recognize that many students referred as *learning disabled* were, in fact, individuals who had not responded to the socialization efforts of public schools. We also noted that the learning problems of students often went uncorrected because so much teacher effort was devoted to social control.

Concerns related to the major interested parties and factors that differentiate helping relationships and socialization are highlighted in Figure 15–1. The following comments should clarify key points.

First, the various parties probably employ different criteria in evaluating the need for

---

[1] In this section, the term *client* is used mostly to designate students with psychoeducational problems. However, more broadly, the term encompasses any object of change (e.g., individuals, groups, a family, or an environment.)

Figure 15-1

Basic concerns related to helping relationships and socialization.

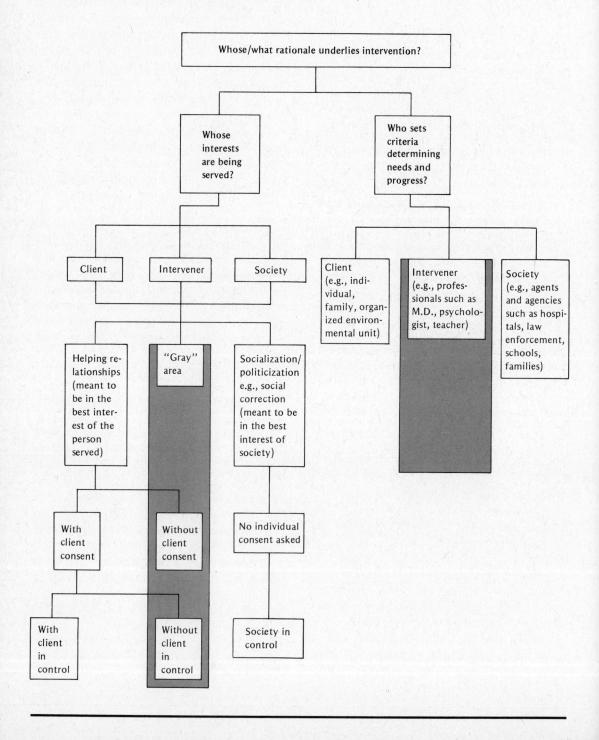

and effectiveness of interventions. More-over, it often is unclear whether the criteria are the client's, the society's, the profession's, or the intervener's personal standards.

Second, the matter of whose interests are being served should be recognized as the key to differentiating helping and social control. We propose that only when the client's interests are served is it proper to designate the intervention as a *helping relationship*. In contrast, when the society's interests are served, the intervention probably is better viewed as *socialization/politicization*. When clients' and society's interest do not coincide, this distinction has critical significance.

Third, in *helping*, client consent for, and control over, intervention is desirable. In this regard, two points should be particularly noted. (1) Client control over intervention is by definition a matter of ensuring that key decisions are made collaboratively with no action proceeding without the client's approval. (In contrast, socialization presumes general consent under implied "social contracts," i.e., individual consent is not seen as necessary, and control is in the hands of the socializing agent.) (2) Interveners often presume that clients with problems, especially children, do not have the competence to know what is in their long-range interest. This presumption bypasses several critical issues related to determination of incompetence and adoption of a paternalistic stance.[2] For example, problems arise because of the lack of satisfactory empirical criteria for determining competence, the possibility of situations existing where the best interests of the client are not served by decisions made for them, and the likely infringement on individual rights.

Fourth, we recognize there are many times interveners must attempt to help even though consent of the individual has not been given. When "help" proceeds without

VIEWPOINT

PATERNALISM AND LIBERTY— THE "HARM PRINCIPLE"

The object of this Essay is to assert one very simple principle. . . . That principle is, that the sole ends for which mankind are warranted, individually or collectively, in interfering with the liberty of action of any of their number, is self-protection. That the only purpose for which power can be rightfully exercised over any member of a civilized community, against [one's] will, is to prevent harm to others. [One's] own good, either physical or moral, is not a sufficient warrant. [One] cannot rightfully be compelled to do or forbear because it will be better for [individuals] to do so, because it will make [them] happier, because in the opinion of others, to do so would be wise, or even right. These are good reasons for remonstrating . . . or reasoning . . . or persuading . . . or entreating . . . , but not for compelling . . . or visiting [them] with any evil in case [they] do otherwise. To justify that, the conduct from which it is desired to deter [them] must be calculated to produce evil to someone else. The only part of the conduct of anyone, for which [one] is amenable to society, is that which concerns others. In the part which merely concerns . . . self, . . . independence is of right, absolute.

J. S. Mill, 1859

client consent and control, the intervention is seen to fall into a gray area. At such times, an intervener wittingly or unwittingly may be acting more as a societal agent (e.g., socializing a problem *citizen*) than as an agent of the client.

Finally, even when a client provides consent and exercises a degree of control, the intervener is in a very powerful position. Interveners, such as teachers and psychologists, almost always have a significant degree

---

[2] The problem of competence and the corollary problem of paternalism are discussed further in Chapter 16.

VIEWPOINT

COMPETENCE AND INCOMPETENCE

The vast majority of cases that confront us will be borderline—cases in that greyish area between full competence and obvious incompetence. The real problem that will face us, then, is what to do in the borderline cases. When in doubt, which way should we err—on the side of safety or on the side of liberty? It is vital that we do not adopt analyses of "incompetence" or patterns of argument that obscure the obviously moral nature of this question.

Murphy (1974, p. 469)

of control over those they teach and treat. Thus, in most situations, interveners find themselves operating in somewhat of a gray area.

For at least two groups, the matter of society's, or a particular professional's, ability to exercise control over others is a nonissue. At one extreme there are those who hold the attitude that society needs to do what society judges it needs to do; at the other extreme, are those who espouse the view that coercion and invasion of privacy are never justified. For many persons, however, neither extreme is acceptable; thus this matter is a complex ethical and legal dilemma.

Compulsory education, mandatory inoculations to prevent disease, mass screening of kindergartners to identify potential learning problems, involuntary treatment of the "insane," are all examples of programs seen as so beneficial to the individuals involved and to society that they often are not even viewed as coercive. Indeed, they usually are discussed in altruistic terms such as *helping*, *caring for*, and *protecting*. Some of these and other comparable interventions, such as achievement and scholastic aptitude testing, simply are seen as necessary to the socio-economic-political functioning of society—they are viewed as helping the society

and generally are not seen as very harmful to individuals.

Social critics have been less generous than the general public in evaluating the types of compulsory and mandatory programs exemplified above. Without agreeing or disagreeing with any particular critic's position, one can appreciate the importance of the body of criticism in raising public consciousness. Specifically, the polemic discourse serves to heighten awareness that (1) no society is devoid of some degree of corecion in dealing with its members (e.g., no right or liberty is absolute) and (2) consent and due process of law are central to the protection of individuals.

Control over others implies the possibility of coercion and invasion of privacy, and more generally, loss of freedoms and rights. These are disturbing implications. In a free society, coercion and invasion of privacy are repugnant concepts, and the general public is rightly shocked when evidence of such activity is brought to light. At the same time, consent and individual control over decision making are valued concepts for protecting individuals from abuses by those with power to exercise control over them. Major legislation in the United States, such as the Family Rights and Privacy Act and the Education for All Handicapped Children Act, highlight the increasing value placed on these matters.

In our work, we have found that understanding the above concepts and the concerns associated with them is essential. Furthermore, our efforts have led us not only to distinguish helping relationships from socialization, but to differentiate between helping and the use of power and influence to produce change.

POWER, INFLUENCE, AND HELPING

Implied by the phrase "control over others" and the terms *coercion* and *invasion of privacy* is the concept of power. *Power* refers to the ability to control others so that they do,

VIEWPOINT

ABOUT SCHOOL

He always wanted to say things. But no one understood. He always wanted to explain things. But no one cared. So he drew.

Sometimes he would just draw and it wasn't anything. He wanted to carve it in stone or write it in the sky.

He would lie out on the grass and look up in the sky and it would be only him and the sky and the things inside that needed saying.

And it was after that, that he drew the picture. It was a beautiful picture. He kept it under the pillow and would let no one see it.

And he would look at it every night and think about it. And when it was dark, and his eyes were closed, he could still see it.

And it was all of him. And he loved it.

When he started school he brought it with him. Not to show anyone, but just to have with him like a friend.

It was funny about school.

He sat in a square, brown desk like all the other square, brown desks and he thought it should be red.

And his room was a square, brown room. Like all the other rooms. And it was tight and close. And stiff.

He hated to hold the pencil and the chalk, with his arm stiff and his feet flat on the floor, stiff, with the teacher watching and watching.

And then he had to write numbers. And they weren't anything. They were worse than the letters that could be something if you put them together.

And the numbers were tight and square and he hated the whole thing.

The teacher came and spoke to him. She told him to wear a tie like all the other boys. He said he didn't like them and she said it didn't matter.

After that they drew. And he drew all yellow and it was the way he felt about morning. And it was beautiful.

The teacher came and smiled at him. "What's this?" she asked. "Why don't you draw something like Ken's drawing? Isn't that beautiful?"

It was all questions.

After that his mother bought him a tie and he always drew airplanes and rocket ships like everyone else. And he threw the old picture away.

And when he lay out alone looking at the sky, it was big and blue and all of everything, but he wasn't anymore.

He was square inside and brown, and his hands were stiff, and he was like anyone else. And the things inside him that needed saying didn't need saying anymore.

It had stopped pushing. It was crushed. Stiff. Like everything else.

Mukerji (1970, p. 2)

---

knowingly or unknowingly, what they do not really want or prefer to do, whether it is in their best interests or not. Power stems from the political nature of the relationships (1) between society and its citizens, (2) between organizations and groups and their membership, (3) among small interpersonal units such as families and friends, and (4) between professionals and their clients.

As Rogers (1977) states:

Politics in present-day psychological and social usage, has to do with power and control: with the extent to which persons desire, attempt to obtain, possess, share, or surrender power and control over others and/or themselves. It has to do with the maneuvers, the strategies and tactics, witting and unwitting, by which such power and control over one's life and others' lives is sought and gained—or shared or relinquished. It has to do with the locus of decision-making power: who makes the de-

cisions which, consciously or unconsciously, regulate or control the thoughts, feelings, or behavior of others or oneself. (p. 4)

In our growing understanding of the uses and abuses of power, we have become aware that the sources of power can sometimes be overt, legislated rulings and sometimes covert practices and interpersonal maneuverings and inequalities. More specifically, power can be exercised through legislative and judicial actions, economic sanctions (rewards, salaries, allowances, fines, unemployment), sociopsychological pressures (cultural mores and societal norms, interpersonal influence and persuasion, ostracizing and isolation), and physical force. Whether overt or covert, consciously or unconsciously perpetrated, the source of power can be identified by clarifying who makes the decisions, especially those decisions that have the greatest influence over processes and outcomes (e.g., situations, events, thoughts, feelings, actions). Most of us can easily identify situations where we feel coerced; it is, however, more difficult to recognize situations where we are coercive.

Psychoeducational interventions, including assessment, involve numerous decisions about procedural matters and about future courses of action. The politics of psychoeducational intervention arises out of such decision making. Whoever makes the decisions potentially has a great deal of power in relation to others involved. We find that one of the most striking and frequent examples of this occurs in the assignment of diagnostic labels. Most of the widely used labels, such as *learning disabled, hyperactive, mentally retarded,* and *juvenile delinquent,* have been developed to designate behaviors society finds unsatisfactory and wants to "take care of." Toward this end, there usually are substantive prescriptions associated with the labels, such as assignment to special classrooms or other institutional programs, psychotherapy, and drug treatments. When interveners are employed by government-funded agencies (e.g., schools, public clinics, and hospitals), they are contracted to act for society, sometimes in helping ways, usually as agents of socialization. In general, any psychoeducational intervention may become an act of overt political power through the use of particular types of labeling and programs.

A less obvious example, involving power of a more covert nature, is academic and vocational counseling. For many years (and, probably, still in some places), it was common practice for counselors to decide, based on prevailing biases and procedures, which students should be "guided" into vocational and which into college preparatory courses. The total number of students and the proportion of women and racial minorities "detoured" from going to college as a result is unknown, and while relevant, is not the point of the example. The point is that counselors who make such unilateral decisions are exercising control over others even though they and the persons whose lives are being shaped may not think of the activity in terms of covert political power.

Rather than thinking in terms of politics and power, teachers, counselors, psychologists—indeed, most of us—are more likely to see ourselves as *influencing* others through advice, guidance, instruction, modeling, and so forth. Indeed, influence has been formally contrasted with power. Influence and power can be exercised through the same mechanisms (ranging from advice and persuasion to force). The distinction depends on whether those affected indicate the decisions made reflect their preferences rather than mere acquiescence. Obviously clarifying that a person is not being controlled, but has been persuaded and is now pursuing a preference, is a distinction which is easier to make conceptually than to validate in practice. Often the means for influencing others are identical to those involved in directly controlling others (e.g., strong recommendations). Therefore, some forms of influence raise the issue of whether accomplishment of desirable ends justifies use of any means.

The concept of *helping* represents a contrast to power both in terms of means and ends. In helping, all key decisions are "ends" and should be controlled by the clients. To ensure this is the case, the processes (means) used to arrive at decisions must be under the control of the clients. Thus, interveners must not exercise more power than is absolutely necessary to facilitate decisions. Again, these distinctions are easier to state than to translate into practice. At the same time, it should be clear that many who see themselves as "helping professionals" do not fit the concept of helping as defined here.[3] Ironically, it is their professional expertise that often interferes with their ability and desire to equalize power and influence.

EXPERTS AND EXPERTISE

Expertise is a specific form of power and influence. Expertise is defined broadly as the quality of having particular skills and knowledge, especially related to a professional field of activity. Implicit is that others may want or need to avail themselves of the expertise and thus may be controlled or influenced by it.[4] While persons with expertise are frequently described as experts, the quality of being expert is perhaps best reserved for the most knowledgeable or skillful persons in areas where there is a strong knowledge base or a definite set of skills and related standards for validly judging masterful performance.

When the term *expert* is used too freely, it can result in a variety of problems and embarrassments to a profession and to individual professionals. A frequent embarrassment, for example, is the conflicting testimony of professionals in court cases and at legislative hearings. The embarrassment arises not from the conflicting perspectives. It stems from the confusion that results when opinionative statements based on expertise are offered by a respected professional, but are not identified as opinion to differentiate them from definitive knowledge. Given the relatively weak nature of the knowledge base in psychology and education, psychoeducational interveners probably should be seen as having expertise, but not as being experts.

Expertise puts educators and psychologists in a potentially powerful role vis-à-vis others. In particular, we are in a position to invade privacy and to make decisions for and about others in the absence of true consent. This is not to imply a malicious intent, but to recognize the realities and ambiguities that arise in many intervention situations.

When asked to help, psychoeducational practitioners certainly are ready to do so. However, from experience we know that while we believe we are helping (i.e., acting in the best interests of clients), we often cannot be certain this is the case. The frequency with which professionals rely on power and influence (expertise and expert images) makes it difficult for any of us to avoid acting at times as agents of society or in our self-interests, albeit unintentionally.[5] Many examples of this problem occur in

---

[3]The perspective of a *helping relationship* as presented here is sociopolitical. A psychological definition might describe a helping relationship as one that the client perceives as helpful. Given these two perspectives, four possible situations emerge. Two represent no conflict: one where a helping relationship is present sociopolitically and psychologically, and one where there is not a helping relationship in either sense. There are two conflicting situations: one where the relationship is not helping in the sociopolitical sense, but is experienced as helpful, and one where a helping relationship has been contracted, but is not experienced as helpful.

[4]Expertise usually is associated with persons. However, it is a quality available through a variety of reference sources, such as libraries and computerized systems.

[5]See Appendix D for a discussion of "The Expert Trap," which can result from overselling expertise.

relation to interventions for clients with learning problems. For instance, it is common for professionals to advise parents, on the basis of test scores, that enrollment in a LD or other special program is essential. Yet, how confident can a professional be that such decisions are best for the client and will, for example, lead to maximum positive outcomes and minimal harm?

In general, expertise is a two-edged sword. To help students overcome learning problems, teachers are expected to have specialized knowledge and skills. At the same time, a student's awareness of the teacher's expertise creates interpersonal dynamics, which makes it difficult to equalize power and counteract influence. If teachers intend both to help and enhance students' abilities to take responsibility for themselves, they must adopt strategies that are compatible with these intentions and avoid relying on power and influence in implementing programs—examples of such strategies were discussed in Part 4. It should also be stressed that a redefinition of *limits* may be required. We turn to this topic next.

REDEFINING LIMITS FOR HELPING STUDENTS WITH PROBLEMS

In recent years, it has become clear to us that the limits imposed in order to manage classrooms and schools often conflict with helping. For example, one teacher of students with learning problems tells them not to talk with each other during assignments, to ask permission to move about, and insists that assignments be completed as prescribed. Another teacher works with students to evolve a setting where they can talk quietly while they work, move about as needed, and add personal experiences and interests to assignments as they desire. We have found that teachers—and parents—who opt for defining limits narrowly, as the first case portrays, tend to be concerned primarily with socialization. The teacher in the

VIEWPOINT

SOCIETY AND THE INDIVIDUAL

The most important kind of tolerance, therefore, is tolerance of the individual by society and the state. The state is certainly necessary, in order to give the individual the security he [or she] needs for his [or her] development. But when the state becomes the main thing and the individual becomes its weak-willed tool, then all finer values are lost. Just as the rock must first crumble for trees to grow on it, and just as the soil must first be loosened for its fruitfulness to develop, so too can valuable achievement sprout from human society only when it is sufficiently loosened so as to make possible to the individual the free development of his [or her] abilities.
Einstein (1950, p. 15)

The interests of society can, on balance, come into conflict with and sometimes override substantial individual interests. It is quite plausible, however, to suppose that the interests of society in general are best served by rigid observation of principles protective of individual rights. Whether or not this view is correct, it is arguably the case—to take one example—that the long-term interests of society cannot ever be served by weakening fundamental human rights. . . .
Beauchamp and Childress (1979, p. 145)

second example is seen as establishing limits conducive to both a helping relationship and maintenance of appropriate social standards.

For our purposes, *limits* are defined as the degrees of freedom or range of choices allowed to an individual in any given situation. Stated differently, limits are the restraints placed on an individual's freedom of choice and action. It is in this context that permissiveness and license may be differentiated. License implies that the individual is ignoring (and perhaps is being encouraged to ignore) commonly accepted limits—going beyond the bounds of consensually approved behavior. Permissiveness often is used to describe any effort to expand limits beyond what the observer considers appropriate. For some, permissiveness is seen as a move toward greater freedom and liberty; for others, it is seen as a step toward license.

Figure 15–2 graphically suggests that varying criteria may be used in establishing limits. That varying criteria are used in different situations is demonstrated by the fact that individuals are expected to alter their behavior, often dramatically, in going from one setting to another. What is appropriate on the playground usually is not appropriate in the livingroom. As outlined in Figure 15–2, some agencies often set very narrow limits for the individual (schools and particularly special classrooms are good examples).

When an agency's limits are narrower or broader than those currently supported by the majority of citizens in the society, socialization efforts within that agency are based more on the agency's than on society's current rules. In such instances, socialization should be justified on some other basis than the notion that individuals must function within the limits set by society.

In pursuing their role in the socialization of the young, schools often impose much narrower limits than are actually required by society. In some cases this may cause or exacerbate learning and behavior problems. Nevertheless, they justify these narrow limits according to their interpretation of what society demands. It is arguable that a great deal of time in school is spent socializing children to function within the limits that those who establish the rules for a particular school or district find necessary or wish to impose, for example, lining up for dismissal, dress codes, and so forth. It is clear that once out of school the limits society demands are much less restrictive than those of the school.

At the same time, it is clear that the limits

Figure 15-2

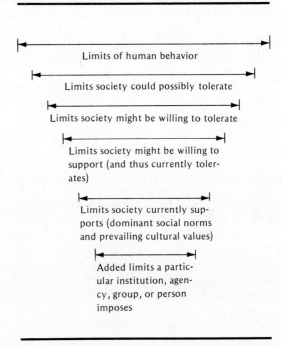

currently advocated by the majority in a free society are narrower than those that are *tolerated*. Some writers have suggested that the limits we learn to accept through our socialization are recipes for maintaining the status quo and that progress demands expanding current limits. As Sarason (1976) states:

> Somehow, we have to learn that our accustomed beliefs are literally more a matter of custom than they are the consequences of thinking. We are unaware of this until that point (which may never come) when, for one or another reason, custom loses its believability for us. It is only then that we see that, in a sense, our world has been made for us, and we are now in the process of creating our own. As a consequence, that other world looks radically different than custom has taught us. (p. 258)

Psychoeducational interveners often feel conflict over what role they should play in

VIEWPOINT

SOCIAL CONTROL AND RULES

It is often well in considering educational problems to get a start by temporarily ignoring the school and thinking of other human situations. I take it that no one would deny that the ordinary good citizen is as a matter of fact subject to a great deal of social control and that a considerable part of this control is not felt to involve restriction of personal freedom . . . let us note some examples of social control that operate in everyday life, and then look for the principle underlying them. Let us begin with the young people themselves. Children at recess or after school play games, from tag and one-old-cat to baseball and football. The games involve rules, and these rules order their conduct. The games do not go on haphazardly or by a succession of improvisations. Without rules there is no game. If disputes arise there is an umpire to appeal to, or discussion and a kind of arbitration are means to a decision; otherwise the game is broken up and comes to an end.

There are certain fairly obvious controlling features of such situations to which I want to call attention. The first is that the rules are a part of the game. They are not outside of it. No rules, then no game; different rules, then a

different game. As long as the game goes on with a reasonable smoothness, the players do not feel that they are submitting to external imposition but that they are playing the game. In the second place an individual may at times feel that a decision isn't fair and he [or she] may even get angry. But he [or she] is not objecting to a rule but to what he [or she] claims is a violation of it, to some one-sided and unfair action. . . .

Now, the general conclusion I would draw is that control of individual actions is effected by the whole situation in which individuals are involved, in which they share and of which they are co-operative or interacting parts. For even in a competitive game there is a certain kind of participation, of sharing in a common experience. Stated the other way around, those who take part do not feel that they are bossed by an individual person or are being subjected to the will of some outside superior person. When violent disputes do arise, it is usually on the alleged ground that the umpire or some person on the other side is being unfair; in other words, that in such cases some individual is trying to impose his [or her] individual will on someone else.

Dewey (1938, pp. 52–53)

maintaining or expanding limits in their own work, in the organization in which they are employed, and in the society in which they live. For example, a teacher or psychologist in a publicly funded agency is expected to pursue the intervention purposes formulated by the institution. These usually involve the teaching and enforcement of limits currently supported by society and possibly even a narrower set of limits advocated by the institution itself. In effect, interveners in these positions are contracted by society to accomplish the purposes as formulated by

the institution, not to pursue their own values.

This is the type of conflict situation in which teachers working with students with learning and related behavior problems consistently find themselves caught. They are expected to socialize the child to prevailing rules, and simultaneously they are expected and want to establish a helping relationship so that problems can be corrected. For the most part, they find the two roles incompatible. The need to enforce the narrow limits reflected by most classroom

VIEWPOINT

SOCIAL CONTROL IN THE CLASSROOM

I do not wish to refer to the traditional school in ways which set up a caricature in lieu of a picture. But I think it is fair to say that one reason the personal commands of the teacher so often played an undue role and a reason why the order which existed was so much a matter of sheer obedience to the will of an adult was because the situation almost forced it upon the teacher. The school was not a group or community held together by participation in common activities. Consequently, the normal, proper conditions of control were lacking. Their absence was made up for, and to a considerable extent had to be made up for, by the direct intervention of the teacher, who, as the saying went, "kept order." He [or she] kept it because order was in the teacher's keeping, instead of residing in the shared work being done. . . .

I am not romantic enough about the young to suppose that every pupil will respond or that any child of normally strong impulses will respond on every occasion. There are likely to be some who. . . . because of previous experience, are bumptious, and unruly and perhaps downright rebellious. But it is certain that the general principle of social control cannot be predicated upon such cases. It is also true that no general rule can be laid down for dealing with such cases. The teacher has to deal with them individually. He or she cannot, if the educational process is to go on, make it a question of pitting one will against another in order to see which is strongest, nor yet allow the unruly and non-participating pupils to stand permanently in the way of the educative activities of others. Exclusion perhaps is the only available measure at a given juncture, but it is no solution. For it may strengthen the very causes which have brought about the undesirable antisocial attitude. . . .

Dewey (1938, p. 55–57)

We like children who are a little afraid of us, docile, deferential children, though not, of course, if they are so obviously afraid that they threaten our image of ourselves as kind lovable people whom there is no reason to fear. We find ideal the kind of "good" children who are just enough afraid of us to do everything we want, without making us feel that fear is what is making them do it.

Holt (1964, pp. 167–68)

rules interferes with establishing a helping relationship. Enforcement of narrow limits can lead students (and teachers) to perceive the teacher as a police officer or warden rather than as someone who has the student's *best interest* at heart. Unable to establish a helping relationship, the teacher finds that behavior problems and classroom management become the total focus of the job. Among the consequences are that the students' learning problems are not corrected, and many students become societal problems (despite the socialization processes which were, ironically, imposed to prevent this).

It has been suggested by many writers that the limits set in current classroom programs may be counterproductive to the proper education *and* socialization of the young. Whether this is the case, we suggest that this seems a particularly relevant concern for programs for those with psychoeducational problems. We are neither advocating license nor permissiveness in some naive sense. We are suggesting the necessity of environments and programs that are more permitting in the sense of an increased range of valued options and realistic choices. There is a need to rid ourselves of limits that interfere, and to expand the degrees of freedom in ways that can increase intrinsic motivation and enable teachers to establish effective helping relationships. The alternative to moving in this direction seems to be perpetuation of a large number of student and teacher dropouts, psychologically if not physically.

CONCLUDING COMMENTS

Both the processes of helping and social control are needed in any society. However, there are times when the two processes are in conflict and times when one or the other or both are inappropriate.

How does one decide when it is appropriate to use power, influence, or a helping relationship? The answer to this obviously depends on one's conceptual, methodological, and ethical perspectives. From an ethical point of view, the crux of the matter centers on principles and rules related to social philosophy and morality, which we will discuss in the next chapter.

Chapter 16

Ethical Concepts and Concerns in Helping Individuals Overcome Learning Problems

There is a substantial community-serving component in policies and procedures for classifying and labeling exceptional children and in the various kinds of institutional arrangements made to take care of them. "To take care of them" can and should be read with two meanings: to give children help and to exclude them from the community.
Hobbs (1975, p. 21)

The two besetting sins in our prevailing habits of ethical thinking are our ready acquiescence in unclarity and our complacence in ignorance. . .
Frankena (1973, p. 8)

Awareness of the plight of those with psychoeducational problems leads to a desire to help. In helping, the intention always is to behave ethically—to respect individual rights, liberties, dignity, and worth. Unfortunately, these rather straightforward aims have proven easier to espouse in codes of professional ethics and standards for practice than they have been to accomplish in daily actions.

Psychoeducational practices have been criticized by political conservatives, liberals, and civil libertarians. Ethical concerns have been raised over such practices as diagnostic test batteries for prescribing instruction, early age screening of learning problems, restrictive special class placement, and use of stimulant drugs for hyperactivity.

Some critics have stressed the psychological, social, and possible physical negative effects on individuals. Others have pointed out that subgroups may be unfairly discriminated against. Still other critics have raised the spectre that the society as a whole may be negatively affected.

In contrast to the critics are those professionals who underscore positive values of psychoeducational interventions. While acknowledging the potential for abuse, they stress the obligation of professionals (1) to advance knowledge and skills related to intervention activity and (2) to use practices in ways which maximize benefits and minimize negative effects. To do otherwise ignores the duty to help those with learning problems and denies the rights of those who want help.

The problem of balancing iatrogenic effects and the benefits of psychoeducational intervention represents one set of ethical conflicts. Another stems from the tension between social control and individual freedom.

Critics have pointed to a tendency for individual rights and liberties to be insufficiently considered and safeguarded during many psychoeducational interventions. The demand has been for greater concern for human dignity. Legally, this demand has been reflected in an emphasis on protection of rights and due process.[1] Ethically, the concern has been to improve consent procedures and clarify the bases for mandatory assessment and treatment.

In dealing with ethical concerns, there are no simple answers, only broad principles to be applied when clarifying the issues. As suggested by Beauchamp and Childress (1979), the principles of beneficence, nonmaleficence, justice, and autonomy provide a foundation for understanding major ethical dilemmas related to services, research,

FOR EXAMPLE

PREAMBLE TO THE AMERICAN PSYCHOLOGICAL ASSOCIATION "ETHICAL PRINCIPLES OF PSYCHOLOGISTS" (1981)

Psychologists respect the dignity and worth of the individual and strive for the preservation and protection of fundamental human rights. They are committed to increasing knowledge of human behavior and of people's understanding of themselves and others and to the utilization of such knowledge for the promotion of human welfare. While pursuing these objectives, they make every effort to protect the welfare of those who seek their services and of the research participants who may be the object of study. They use their skills only for purposes consistent with these values and do not knowingly permit their misuse by others. While demanding for themselves freedom of inquiry and communication, psychologists accept the responsibility this freedom requires: competence, objectivity in the application of skills, and concern for the best interests of clients, colleagues, students, research participants, and society.

and public policy. In the following sections, we explore these principles and their application to learning problems with reference to three topics: utility and equity, consent, and demystification.

UTILITY AND EQUITY

Traditionally, the most critical concern in providing programs to correct learning problems has been that of ensuring that

---

[1]Stier (1978, p. 53) reports from a recent case law review describing the legal rights of children in the United States as enunciated by the courts: *(1) Children are persons and enjoy constitutional rights and protections. (2) The children's interests have generally been seen as allied with those of their parents. (3) In conflicts between the interests of parents and children, the rights of children and the role of the state are still without clear delineation. (4) The state may act to limit parents' discretion with regard to their child. When it does, its interests are twofold: (a) protecting the interests of the child, and (b) furthering general societal interest in the well-being of its youth. (Ellis, 1974, pp. 875–76).*
Reviews of the rights of children and adults as defined in litigation and legislation in the United States can be found in works by Buss, Kirp, and Kurlioff, 1975; Ellis, 1974; Feshbach and Feshbach, 1978; Haubrich and Apple, 1975; Kirp, 1974; Kirp, Kurlioff, and Buss, 1975; Rodham, 1973; and Tapp and Levine, 1977.

benefits outweigh *costs*. Recent legal emphasis on *rights to treatment* and *right of all children to an education* also have highlighted the moral obligation to ensure that services are allocated fairly. The directness with which such obligations can be stated tends to make them sound less complex to implement than they are.

Costs Versus Benefits

Those of us who work with learning problems confront the cost-versus-benefits dilemma every day. Should we proceed with an intervention? Will the special program help the child? If so, will the amount of help justify the pain, loss, and other potential negative effects the individual may experience on being *labeled* and differentiated?

It would be nice if professional training prepared us to deal with these concerns. Our training programs did not, and perhaps could not, have done so. After grappling with the issues for many years on an ad hoc basis, we finally realized the usefulness of going beyond our profession's ethical code-books to the ethical *principles* underlying our concerns. With regard to cost-benefit dilemmas, this meant grasping the principles of beneficence, nonmaleficence, and their relationship to the principle of utility: *beneficence* refers to one's duty to act positively in the interests of others; *nonmaleficence* refers to one's duty to avoid acting negatively in relation to others; and *utility* refers to the obligation to produce the greatest possible balance of positive to negative effects for all persons affected.

A maxim associated with medical practice, "above all, do no harm" (*"primum non nocere"*), as incorporated into the Hippocratic oath, accompanies the expressed duty to beneficence: "I will apply . . . measures for the benefit of the sick according to my ability and judgment; I will keep them from harm and injustice." The ideal of help without harm must, however, sometimes be compromised. Negative consequences, costs, risks, or harm may be side effects of

VIEWPOINT

WHAT IS IN A PERSON'S BEST INTERESTS?

Until recently, codes of ethics were formulated primarily by professional organizations as rules to govern their members. The Hippocratic oath is an example. Advocates of the public interest have demanded more. Private consumer groups and government agencies have formulated guidelines focused on the rights and autonomy of those receiving services rather than solely on the obligations and paternalistic wisdom of professionals (Adams & Orgel, 1975; Auerbach & Bogue, 1978; Lazare, 1975; Reeder, 1972; Thompson & Zimmerman, 1969).

The positive intent of most advocates is to act in the best interests of the general public, especially children. Unfortunately, in their enthusiasm to improve policies and programs, advocates often oversimplify the problem of deciding what is in a person's best interests. As Mnookin (1978) notes: "in many critical areas what is best for an individual child or for children in general is usually indeterminate or speculative, and is not demonstrable by scientific proof, but is instead fundamentally a matter of values" (p. 163). Even when what best serves the child's welfare is evident, there are times the only way to ensure welfare is to deny some rights. Because of such considerations, the issue often is not *what is best*, but *who should decide*.

---

many positively intended interventions. (Harm also may result from unintended actions, including acts of omission.) Deciding to label a child *learning disabled* is an example of a positively intended act that can give rise to negative consequences. The decision to proceed with such a compromise is made by applying the principle of utility. Do possible benefits outweigh possible harm?

Costs and benefits encompass more than financial considerations and often are not readily quantifiable. Besides finances, the costs and benefits most frequently discussed are psychological and physical effects on individuals. Unfortunately, the sparsity of data demonstrating intervention effectiveness and clarifying negative effects makes it difficult to specify benefits and costs, let alone determine net gains or losses. Thus, current efforts to resolve ethical dilemmas by considering cost benefits for the individual must decide how heavily to weigh the potential—but unproven—positive and negative effects.

From a broader perspective, it has been suggested that cost-benefits also should be analyzed with reference to the societal *biases* perpetuated by intervention practices. For example, it has been contended that children whose backgrounds differ from the dominant culture will be classified and treated as deficient to the extent that their values and norms, and thus their behaviors and performance, are incompatible with those of the dominant culture. Whether intentional or not, beneficial practices also can collude with biases against subgroups in society. Thus, the iatrogenic effects on such subgroups must be considered in cost-benefit appraisals.

The point is that the perspective can no longer remain oriented only to individuals. The concern over IQ testing related to minority students is a recent dramatic illustration of this point. Litigants have argued that minority populations have been inappropriately served by most IQ tests and resulting labeling (e.g., in California, Diana v. State Board of Education, 1970; Larry P. v. Riles, 1972). Court cases have led to the position that intelligence testing should be culture fair, including use of the individual's "home language," and that tests alone should not be used to classify students. Such litigation highlights the concern that the benefits of some school practices for any individual may be considerably less than the costs to a particular subgroup of the society, for example, perpetuation of racial injustices in the form of additional discrimination, stigmatization, and restriction of educational opportunities.

Another broad ethical perspective, best

VIEWPOINT

SOCIETY AND MORALITY

Moral principles are not disembodied rules, cut off from their cultural setting. Most, if not all, of our moral beliefs have arisen from shared experiences and tacit social agreements and arrangements. Morality is by its very nature not an individual-centered phenomenon. . . .

Beauchamp and Childress (1979, p. 61)

articulated by Illich (1976), focuses on the iatrogenic effects of professional practices to the culture. He warns that the public's mystified reliance on professionals, who often overstate their expertise, is growing. The negative effect of this trend for the entire culture is a general loss of people's ability to cope with their problems. As a result, society is manifesting an ever-increasing, distressing, and unnecessary overdependence on professionals, which, with regard to learning disabilities, is illustrated by the increasing number of parents and students who simply accept the LD label and special interventions with little or no questioning and understanding. Ethically, professionals are expected to avoid contributing to such widespread, inappropriate surrendering of individual responsibility and initiative. In general, then, this perspective suggests that professionals must judge the ethics of their activities not only in terms of the impact on an individual and the validity of their own and society's biases, but with regard to the impact on the entire culture.

While balancing costs against benefits is important, the complexity of determining that costs outweigh benefits makes the utility principle difficult to apply. Even when the principle can be used effectively, it is still only one of the ethical guidelines to be considered. Decisions that overemphasize utility at the expense of fairness, in particular, have been criticized.

VIEWPOINT

CULTURAL IATROGENESIS

Schools fail, however, less because of maliciousness than because of mindlessness. Like Procrustes stretching his guests or cutting off their limbs to make them fit the standard-size bed his inn provided, educators and scholars, frequently with the best of intentions, have operated on the assumption that children should be cut or stretched or otherwise "adjusted" to fit the schools, rather than adjusting the schools to fit the children. And most of us have tended to accept this without question.

Silberman (1970, p. 81)

Fairness

It's not fair is a common complaint. We often feel situations and people aren't being fair. Students want privileges, rules, and punishments administered fairly. One student must neither get more nor get away with more than another. We all want to see injustices corrected. The underdog should win at least some of the time. If someone is afflicted with a handicap or a learning problem, it seems only fair that they be helped. In providing help, interveners are expected to be just and fair. But how do we decide what is fair?

Beauchamp and Childress (1979) provide what they describe as a standard list of *principles* of distributive justice, which are relevant to decisions about what is fair:

to each person an equal share;

to each person according to individual need;

to each person according to individual effort;

to each person according to societal contribution; and

to each person according to merit.

Each principle considered alone is compelling. However, each may conflict with the others, and any one may be weighted more heavily than another, depending on an individual's social philosophy.[2]

As the above list suggests, the matter of fairness involves such questions as : (1) Fair for whom? (2) Fair according to whom? and (3) Fair using what criteria and what procedures for applying the criteria? Obviously what is fair for the society may not be fair for an individual; what is fair for one person may cause an inequity for another. To provide special services for learning problems raises the taxes of all citizens. To deny such services is unfair and harmful to those who, because of their problems, need more help.

One basic guideline for use in making fair and just decisions is that similar cases should be treated alike and dissimilar cases should be treated differently. However, since we are all similar and dissimilar in so many ways, the factors to be considered must be relevant variables.

A second guideline with direct application to helping those with learning problems is the fair opportunity principle. This principle stresses that no one should be denied benefits on the basis of either *disadvantageous or advantageous properties* for which they are not responsible. Fairness demands that those with *disadvantageous properties* be given special aid. The duty to identify those who should be helped constitutes an ethical reason *for* classifying or labeling individuals. However, fairness requires that the need for help not become a basis for stigmatizing and isolating individuals and groups.

---

[2]For example, *"Egalitarian* theories emphasize equal access to the goods in life that every rational person desires; *Marxist* theories emphasize need; *Libertarian* theories emphasize contribution and merit; and *Utilitarian* theories emphasize a mixed use of such criteria so that public and private utility are maximized" (Beauchamp & Childress, 1979, p. 173).

Decisions based on the fairness principle often call for unequal allocations and affirmative action in distributing resources and applying rules. Thus, although they are intended to result in just and fair distinctions, such decisions can be quite controversial, especially when resources are scarce.

There are always conflicting views as to which of many injustices should be assigned highest priorities in allocating limited resources. In a tight economy, controversies over fairness are likely to be extremely prevalent. Should school programs be cut back in favor of increasing welfare benefits? Should programs for the gifted be cut more than programs for students with learning problems? Should school athletic teams be cut more than vocational programs? For the most part these are decisions made in the political arena with ethical concerns playing a small role. However, even if they were made strictly on ethical criteria, the issues obviously would involve debate over the appropriateness of any particular principle and over the definition of such notions as *individual need* and *societal contribution*.

On a more individual level, parents, teachers, psychologists, and other interveners consistently are confronted by the problem of applying rules differently. For example, should different consequences be applied for the same offense when the students involved differ in terms of problems, age, levels of competence, and so forth?

Some persons try to simplify matters by avoiding making distinctions and treating everyone alike. Some advocates of mainstreaming students in public schools, for example, seem to be suggesting this course of action. In general, however, while a no-exceptions approach represents a simple solution to resource allocation and rule application, it perpetuates injustices.

We recall many instances where teachers of problem populations have insisted on enforcing rules without regard for the nature of a particular student's social and emotional problems. They usually argued that it was

FOR EXAMPLE

FAIRNESS

In indicating the fairness of the late football coach, Vince Lombardi, one of his players, Henry Jordan, said: "He treated us all the same. Like dogs."
Newsweek (September 14, 1970, p. 123)

unfair to other students if the same rule was not applied in the same way to everyone. Initially, our response simply was to argue that such indiscriminate applications perpetuate the student's problem—they undermine helping in the pursuit of social control and superficial fairness. These days, we also work with teachers and students to expand understanding of different principles for judging fairness. It seems likely that in the absence of simple prescriptions, only a very strong commitment to understanding and applying ethical principles can advance the cause of justice in working with learning problem populations.

CONSENT

There was a time not so long ago when assigning students with problems to special programs was done matter-of-factly. Most professionals believed we knew who needed help and what help was needed. It was a relatively simple administrative matter to inform parents that a problem existed and what was to be done.

It was a naive era, a time we assumed benefits outweighed harm and inequity. Currently, however, such matters are not routine. Parent and student consent have emerged as crucial components of such decisions. The concept of consent is a primary consideration in discussions of individual rights and professional ethics, especially with reference to children, which in part represents a backlash to past abuses and in part reflects a new awareness of the relevance of the concept.

In a society that values fairness and personal liberty, consent is of paramount importance. An appreciation of why this is so requires some understanding of the principle of *autonomy*.

Autonomy and Informed Consent

As Beauchamp and Childress (1979) state:

> The autonomous person is one who not only deliberates about and chooses ... but who is capable of acting on the basis of such deliberations.... A person's autonomy is his or her independence, self-reliance, and self-contained ability to decide. A person of diminished autonomy, by contrast, is highly dependent on others and in at least some respect incapable of deliberating or acting on the basis of such deliberations. (pp. 56–57)

Children and individuals with problems often are treated in ways that diminish their autonomy, which occurs because of assumptions about their relative lack of competence and wisdom. Even when they are treated autonomously, their decisions may not be respected.

> It is one thing to be autonomous and to apprehend that others are acting autonomously, but quite another to be respected as an autonomous agent and to respect the autonomy of others. To respect autonomous agents is to recognize with due appreciation their own considered value judgments and outlooks even when it is believed that their judgments are mistaken. (Beauchamp & Childress, 1979, p. 58).

It is the idea that autonomy should be respected which has made consent not only a legal, but a major, moral concern. It is the fact that liberty is not absolute in any society and the problem that some individuals are not able to act autonomously that has made consent a major sociopolitical issue.

Maintenance of autonomy in professional-client relationships depends on autonomous acceptance of authority by clients and ongoing respect for clients' autonomy by professionals. The legal and moral mechanism for maintenance of autonomy usually is designated *informed consent*. Capron (1974) suggests six major functions served by the consent mechanism: (1) promotion of individual autonomy; (2) protection of patients (e.g., clients, students) and subjects; (3) avoidance of fraud and duress; (4) promotion of rational decisions; (5) encouragement of self scrutiny by professionals; and (6) involvement of the public in promoting autonomy as a general social value and in controlling professional practices and research. The desirability of such outcomes seems evident. The problems and issues involved in appropriately eliciting consent have to do with such matters as: When is consent needed? When is it justified for one person to consent for another? Who decides when consent is needed and when one person can represent another? What information must be given in eliciting consent? How can anyone be certain that consent has been voluntarily given? Each of these questions raises significant dilemmas for professionals, for consumers of psychoeducational services, and for society.

In the following sections, we highlight major concerns associated with the concept of consent for psychoeducational interventions. Specifically, the focus is on (1) competence and paternalism as they affect decisions about when consent must be elicited and from whom, (2) the nature of relevant information and voluntary consent, and (3) the ethics of not obtaining informed and voluntary consent and thus coercing others.

The Question of Competence and the Problem of Paternalism

Capacity or *competence* in the context of consent essentially means the ability to understand, which implies the ability to receive and process information, and to make decisions, choosing from among alternatives. Criteria for deciding about the adequacy of these abilities are difficult to specify. There-fore, global, undifferentiated criteria usually are established, such as age and mental sta-tus. Children and those diagnosed as men-tally retarded, autistic, or insane are often seen as incompetent in a legal sense and in need of surrogates (e.g., surrogate parents, guardians, and courts) to give consent. Historically, but not that long ago, women and racial minorities also were seen as in-competent in a similar sense.

Decisions about incompetence and who shall act for those judged as incompetent continue to be primarily defined by legisla-tion and court actions. While the bases for these actions can be found in social philo-sophy, they are also shaped by practical pol-itics. As a result, current legal criteria that guide professional practice may be viewed as providing a rather conservative ethical perspective. Advocates for those seen as le-gally incompetent seek a more liberal stance with regard to appropriate criteria and due process protections related to judging in-competence and allowing someone to give consent for another.

The bases for deciding what constitutes competence and when others should act re-main controversial. The example of chil-dren's consent illustrates just how difficult the problem is: at what age should it be necessary to ask a child's consent before in-volving the child in a psychoeducational in-tervention (including testing)? With regard to mandatory school attendance, the legal answer is that no individual consent is needed from either parents or child during the age period when attendance is com-pelled by the State. With regard to special-ized interventions such as psychological

testing, special class placement, and thera-peutic treatments, the common answer is that only the parents' consent is needed—and in some cases not even their consent is sought.[3]

Until recently a similar stance prevailed with regard to the participation of school children in research projects. In the United States, Federal guidelines now indicate that valid consent for participation in research is to be solicited not only from parents, but from all children age 12 or older. Moreover, there is discussion about the possibility of lowering to 7 the age for consent for re-search participation. The pros and cons of this matter are debated heatedly. In the pro-cess, of course, the question of what consti-tutes competence is raised, but so are im-portant questions about society's preroga-tives, responsibilities, and needs.

It should be noted that the question of competence is strongly related to the prob-lem of *paternalism*. It is no surprise that professionals, parents, governmental agents, and many others in society have opinions as to what is good for various groups and indi-viduals. Opinions backed up by the power to impose them on others may lead to the problem of paternalism.

The teacher or parent who must decide whether to intervene in order to help or protect a child from the consequences of his or her autonomous choice is confronted by this problem. For example, it is a paternalistic action to stop a child from pursuing a chosen activity because the activity is viewed as not being in the child's "best interests." When such actions are taken, the child's autonomy is seen as less important than (1) the possi-ble harm, nuisance, or offensiveness of the

---

[3]In the United States, federal legislation has been enacted, e.g., Public Laws 93-380 (1974) and 94-142 (1975), designed to establish procedures to curtail placement of children in special school programs without due process. As safeguards related to student evaluations and placements, it is specified in law that parents have the right to be notified in their native language about proposed changes in their child's school program, to examine records, to have the child evaluated in a culturally normative manner and/or have an independent evaluation, to register complaints, and to have appeals and impartial hearings. In place of parents, a suitable surrogate (e.g., child advocate) is to be appointed to protect the child's rights.

VIEWPOINT

CHILDREN'S WELFARE v. RIGHTS

My objections to positions taken by child liberators which would (a) add to the rights of children by increasing the responsibilities of their elders and (b) sacrifice the welfare of children to their presumed rights are both scientific and ethical, and the ethical are based on the scientific. To grant that children should have all the rights now possessed by adults contradicts four propositions which have gained wide popular and scientific support.

1. Children undergo successive qualitative transformations requiring commensurate changes in social status as they pass from one stage of development to the next. (Developmental Issue)

2. Children are inferior to adults in the competencies required to survive independently and therefore require special protection. (Instrumental Competence Issue)

3. Self-determination in adulthood is a product of maturation and not a gift bestowed by permissive caretakers. (Self-Determination Issue)

4. Adult authority properly exercised in the early years is positively related to later independence. (Parental Authority Issue).

The ethically insupportable feature of the children's liberation movement is its failure to acknowledge that dependent status precludes possession of the full rights of the emancipated person; the principle of reciprocity in parent-child relations is thereby rejected. Holt and Farson affirm the duty parents have to nurture the dependent child, but reject as oppressive the duty of the dependent child to conform to parental standards. Indeed, adults are expected to assume new duties so that children may exercise new rights.

Baumrind (1978, pp. 181–82)

---

child's chosen activity, (2) the possible benefits to be gained if the child were allowed to pursue the autonomous course of action, or (3) the benefits to be gained from pursuing the alternative course of action the child is directed to pursue.

When a paternalistic intervention occurs with relatively little complaint and reaction from the child, or when major health and safety considerations are at stake, paternalism is unlikely to be much of an issue. However, there are times the only way for the paternalistic intervention to prevail is by the exercise of major physical or psychological force. In such instances, paternalism becomes an extremely controversial consent

issue, separable, but usually quite related to the problems and issues regarding competence.

It is not uncommon, for example, for those who wish to act in a paternalistic way to argue that persons who resist the judgments of those in authority are incompetent (e.g., immature, ignorant, or incapacitated) or are unduly influenced by others (e.g., under the influence of bad values and models). As long as there is a lack of objective criteria for what constitutes competence, the problems and issues associated with paternalism and decisions about who is competent to choose will continue to be major ethical concerns.[4]

---

[4]Some writers have distinguished between *strong* and *weak* paternalism. Feinberg (1973) sees the former as the decision to intervene even when an individual's choices are informed and voluntary. Weak paternalism involves intervening only when the individual's conduct is substantially nonvoluntary or when the intervention is a brief one designed to determine whether the conduct is voluntary.

VIEWPOINT

FREEDOM AND INFORMATION

The connection between freedom of choice and access to valid information is fundamental; one cannot meaningfully exist without the other. This poses a particularly acute danger to freedom in contemporary society, in which various kinds of middlemen and media control our access to important facts.

Neisser (1976, p. 186)

Relevant Information and Voluntary Consent

Whenever consent is to be elicited, relevant information must be provided and decisions must be made voluntarily. In order to have *relevant* information, the information must be provided in an understandable manner—a requirement that is difficult to meet the more complex and unspecifiable the key intervention procedures and outcomes are. Cultural and language differences also may be barriers in making the information understandable.

Levine (1975) enumerates eleven elements of information, which should be communicated and understood: (1) statement of overall purpose; (2) definition of the role of the subject; (3) informing the prospective subject why he or she has been selected; (4) fair explanation of the procedures, including the setting, the time involved, with whom the subject will interact; (5) description of discomforts and risks; (6) description of benefits; (7) disclosure of alternatives; (8) offer to answer questions; (9) offer of consultation; (10) noncoercive disclaimer; and (11) consent to incomplete disclosure. To facilitate communication and understanding, such information may need to be presented in a variety of ways. Repeated verbal or written communications, translations, media presentations, question-and-answer follow-ups to evaluate whether information was understood, and feedback from other consumers all may be relevant at

various times.

Provision of relevant information does not guarantee that consent is given voluntarily. In many situations, consent is given because people feel they have no meaningful alternative. For example, parents and children in special school programs may consent to additional assessment, therapy, medication, and so forth because they fear refusal will result in exclusion from the rest of the program. In some cases, the fear is a correct perception.

When is voluntary consent needed? In addition to legal and ethical guidelines, voluntary consent is needed whenever the intent is to establish a helping relationship. Power relationships and situations where influence is relied upon do not involve the consent of participants. By definition, helping relationships are based on voluntary consent. It is the obtaining of informed and voluntary consent which defines whether the intent is to base a relationship on power or helping.

A related question is: When may consent be waived (as contrasted to withholding consent)? The answer to this question seems clearest when a problem is extremely threatening or an activity is designated as extremely unthreatening.

Thus, persons who are seen as imminently dangerous to others or as incapable of protecting or caring for themselves generally are accepted as likely candidates for waivers of consent. In contrast, activities that are common facets of everyday living—for example, much of the assessment and evaluation activity which permeates all our lives—usually are not understood or discussed in these terms. They are, however, instances of de facto waived consent.

In sum, where consent is withheld, given by a surrogate, or waived, helping is not an option. Under such circumstances, implementation of psychoeducational interventions is based on power or influence and thus is coercive.

Ethics of Coercion

The reason that concern over waived consent and coercion may seem abstract and even irrelevant to learning problems is that the ethical principles related to autonomy and consent have not been well assimilated in the LD field. In an effort to clarify such matters, social philosophers have extensively discussed the grounds for coercion, and various applications have been made to psychological and educational practices. For example, to clarify the major philosophical principles related to what he calls the "ethics of coercion," Robinson (1974) draws heavily on the philosophical synthesis done by Feinberg (1973). As Feinberg states, philosophers have clarified a number of valid grounds for coercion:

> One might hold that restriction of one person's liberty can be justified:
>
> (1) To prevent harm to others, either
>   (a) injury to individual persons (The Private Harm Principle), or
>   (b) impairment of institutional practices that are in the public interest (The Public Harm Principle);
> (2) To prevent offense to others (The Offense Principle);
> (3) To prevent harm to self (Legal Paternalism);
> (4) To prevent or punish sin, i.e., to "enforce morality as such" (Legal Moralism);
> (5) To benefit the self (Extreme Paternalism);
> (6) To benefit others (The Welfare Principle). (p. 33)

As Robinson (1974) states:

> None of these justifications for coercion is devoid of merit nor is it necessary that any one of them exclude the others in attempts to justify actions against the freedoms of an individual. . . . It is one thing to assert that each of these justifications enjoys some merit but quite another to suggest that they are all equally valid. And it is manifestly the case that they do not share equally in the force of law. Yet, while not sharing equally, they have all, on one occasion or another, been relied on to validate a legal judgment. (p. 234)

VIEWPOINT

THREE KEY ELEMENTS OF CONSENT

With regard to the processes associated with the consent mechanism, Biklen (1978) stresses that the term *informed* consent probably somewhat misrepresents the nature of what is involved:

> It suggests that the key element of consent is the provision of information to people who are giving consent. Consent is a legal concept that has been referred to and implicitly defined in court cases and in legislation. It has three major aspects: capacity, information, and voluntariness. All three elements are equally relevant to any consent procedure or decision. Simply stated, one must have the ability to give consent in order to do so; one must have adequate information to do so in a knowledgeable way; and one must be free from coercion or any other threat to one's voluntariness. (p. 99)

Robinson provides ample examples of judicial cases to support his point and to clarify that the courts (and legislatures) can only provide the broadest guidelines. Ultimately, every citizen must personally come to grips with what he or she views as right in balancing the respective interests of society and an individual when those interests are in conflict. For example, when a student is seen as needing a special education program, but he or she refuses to enroll in it, how is the dilemma to be resolved?

It has been argued by some writers that involuntary psychoeducational intervention is never justified. Others have argued that various forms of majority disapproved behavior (ranging from illegal acts through immoral and deviant behaviors to compulsive negative habits) produce enough social harm, offense, and nuisance to warrant compulsory treatment. Examples of such behavior which have been cited with regard to children are drug and alcohol abuse, homosexuality, truancy, aggressive behavior towards peers and teachers, and low self-esteem.

VIEWPOINT

WHO DECIDES?

We deny the rights of any portion of the species to decide for another portion, or any individual for another individual, what is and what is not their "proper sphere." The proper sphere for all human beings is the largest and highest which they are able to attain to.

Harriet Mill

For behavior that is illegal or in violation of organizational rules, it has been suggested that the person be compelled, or at least "encouraged," to enroll in treatment rather than go to jail or be expelled. When treatment is offered as an alternative to punishment, the choice between the lesser of two evils may seem clear and devoid of coercion. A chronically truant and "incorrigible" student might indeed prefer a "diversion" treatment program to juvenile detention. However, given a third, more desirable alternative, such an individual might not choose to attend a remedial reading or a psychotherapy treatment program.

Even the most dramatic behaviors cited above raise serious ethical concerns about compulsory interventions. The tendency to extrapolate the need for coercion from such dramatic cases to less extreme behaviors, such as reading problems, minor speech problems, and high activity level, raises even greater ethical concern

The reason that the coercive nature of some psychoeducational interventions may not be evident is that they simply are viewed as helpful and unlikely to be harmful. If this tendency were allowed to proceed unchecked, the danger is that any minor learning and behavior problem eventually might be seen as justification for bypassing *informed* and *voluntary* consent for treatment.

The morality of compulsory treatment and diversion programs clearly is related to one's social philosophy and view of deviancy. In this connection, we are struck by Robinson's (1974) warning that: "Transferring moral paternalism from the legislature to the counseling room (or surgical theater) can have only monstrous consequences" (p. 237).

DEMYSTIFICATION: BEYOND INFORMED CONSENT

In our discussion of autonomy, utility, and equity, we have underscored that ethical concerns go beyond the individuals directly involved in a particular practice. However, because there has been limited awareness of ethical responsibilities to the society and culture, we want especially to highlight the obligation to demystify the public.

Nonprofessionals usually are uncertain about what can and cannot be accomplished by formal psychoeducational practices. There is little appreciation of the limitations of current practices or the scope of misuses, abuses, and premature applications.

The obligation to demystify is viewed as an extension of educators' and psychologists' comprehensive duty to honesty. Besides providing relevant information in eliciting consent, this duty involves an affirmative, ethical commitment to avoid mystifying others (Bazelton, 1982).

It is risky to be truthful, but we must be aware of the risks of not being honest. Such consequences include (1) oppressing others by mystifying them, (2) being oppressed in return by the backlash that inevitably occurs when the public becomes enlightened or disillusioned, and (3) holding back systematic inquiry by encouraging premature closure on complex questions. In the LD field, in education in general, in medicine, and in related fields, the failure to demystify the public probably is accountable for the perpetuation of fads and panaceas, the movement toward naive accountability measures, the increased numbers of malpractice suits, and the widespread use of relatively unvalidated practices, such as preschool and kindergarten screening for learning problems

FOR EXAMPLE

DEMYSTIFICATION

Principle 4. Public Statements

Public statements, announcements of services, advertising, and promotional activities of psychologists serve the purpose of helping the public make informed judgments and choices. Psychologists represent accurately and objectively their professional qualifications, affiliations, and functions, as well as those of the institutions or organizations with which they or the statements may be associated. In public statements providing psychological information or professional opinions or providing information about the availability of psychological products and services, psychologists base their statements on scientifically acceptable psychological findings and techniques with full recognition of the limits and uncertainties of such evidence.

American Psychological Association (1981, pp. 634–35)

---

and stimulant drugs for treating children labeled *hyperactive.*

The duty to honesty raises questions about nondisclosure and deception in practice and research. It has been argued that too much information can interfere with helping individuals or can cause them discomfort, that is, "What they don't know can't hurt them." Sometimes it is argued that nonprofessionals do not have the ability to understand the complexities involved or that they do not really want to know.

In fact, some people are annoyed when professionals ask that they become more involved in making decisions. There are, indeed, instances when other ethical principles should prevail. However, the likelihood is that these instances are comparatively few. Therefore, the apparent proclivity of professionals to use and justify nondisclosure and deception on a broad scale is seen as a political act involving intentional mystification to maintain a power imbalance

(e.g., Halleck, 1971; Laing, 1967; Rogers, 1977; Szasz, 1969).

Studies of the nature and scope of intentional mystification by professionals are not readily available. However, it may be noted that in a review of complaints about practices of psychologists, Sanders (1979) states that violations of one or more sections of the "Principle on Public Statements," which stresses, among other matters, the responsibility to clarify the limits and uncertainties of present psychological knowledge and techniques, are the violations about which the APA's Committee on Scientific and Professional Ethics and Conduct is most frequently notified.

A major way interveners mystify others is by the use of jargon and special professional language. Jargon not only mystifies, but perhaps makes professionals feel superior—and nonprofessionals feel inferior. In turn, this perpetuates tendencies toward paternalism and away from demystification. As Wasserstrom (1975) states:

If there is, in fact, an area in which one does know things that the client doesn't know, it is extremely easy to believe that one knows generally what is best for the client.... In addition there is the fact . . . the client has a serious problem or concern which has rendered the client weak and vulnerable. This, too, surely increases the disposition to respond toward the client in a patronizing, paternalistic fashion. The client of necessity confers substantial power over his or her well-being. . . . Invested with all of this power both by the individual and the society, the . . . professional responds to the client as though the client were an individual who needed to be looked after and controlled, and to have decisions made for him or her . . . with as little interference from the client as possible (pp. 21–22).

The need for demystification highlights once again that psychoeducational interventions raise not only moral but broad socioeconomic-political concerns. Educators and psychologists daily are confronted by problems related to conflicts between the interests

VIEWPOINT

PUBLIC ACCEPTANCE OF MYSTIFICATION

Ironically, not only is there a tendency for professionals to mystify the public, the public seems more than ready to be mystified by "experts":

> Some academic disciplines breed obscurity. Much of American behavioral psychology, for instance, has achieved the rather dumbfounding condition of being at the same time trite and inaccessible. . . . These disciplines presently enjoy a certain deferential reverence-from-a-distance, an uncritical acceptance from outsiders. This deference comes not so much of understanding as it does from a willingness to praise those who make us feel ignorant. Confronted with one expert or another who proceeds to confound us . . . we blame ourselves for not understanding . . . and assume [it was] right because an expert said it. (Nyberg, 1971, pp. 67–70)

In turn:

> Overconfidence in "better knowledge" becomes a self-fulfilling prophecy. People first cease to trust their own judgment and then want to be told the truth about what they know. Overconfidence in "better decision making" first hampers people's ability to decide for themselves and then undermines their belief that they can decide. (Illich, 1973, p. 93)

of society and the individual and their own professional and personal interest as well. It is in meeting the duty to demystification that many professionals confront their vested interests in being perceived as an expert and in maintaining power, for example, institutionalized special credentials, roles, privileges, and rewards. At such times, the basic question often amounts to whose interests should be allowed to prevail. In effect, social justice and morality come face-to-face with political and economic interests.

CONCLUDING COMMENTS

Figure 16–1 outlines the major perspectives and ethical principles discussed in this chapter. Understanding ethical concepts and concerns, however, is no guarantee they will be adhered to. Indeed, ethical considerations often appear to be honored more in discussion than in practice.

While most professional organizations have committees to deal with reports of ethical lapses, no one claims that such committees create ethical practitioners. Ultimately, ethical practice is a matter of individual understanding, conscience, and action. At the same time, it must be recognized that learning problems are a societal concern. Programs designed to deal with such problems require the support of the general public and their elected representatives. The impact of the programs and the professionals who staff them is not only on individuals, but on major subgroups of the society and on cultural thought and attitudes. A significant part of the foundation of future societal priorities and policies is being laid by current psychoeducational interventions. Consequently, from both an ethical and a pragmatic perspective, such interventions can be seen to be socioeconomic-political acts.

Recognition of the social action nature of professional intervention increasingly is being recognized and indeed advocated. As Hobbs (1965) states:

> A mature profession does not simply respond to the needs of society but claims a role in determining what society should need and how social institutions, as well as individual professional careers can be shaped to the services of an emerging social order . . . the responsible professional person becomes the architect of social change.

Since we do not believe there is any way to escape the socioeconomic-political nature of interventions related to learning prob-

Figure 16-1

Ethical principles and perspectives involved in psychoeducational interventions.

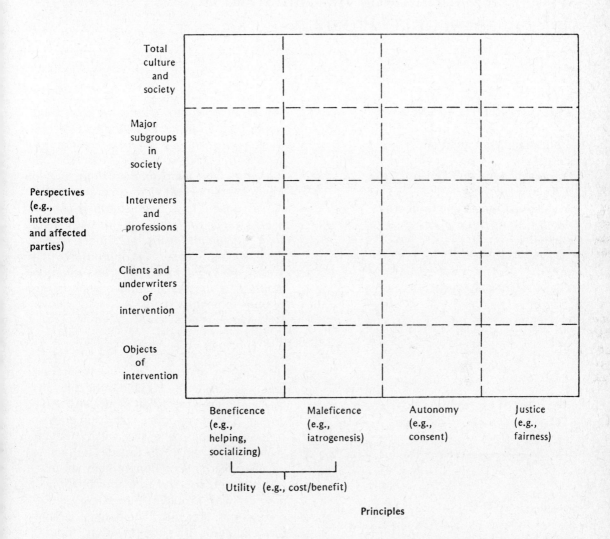

lems, we think Hobb's point is well taken. If all we had to contend with were specific learning disabilities, perhaps the point would be less compelling. However, as we have discussed, the majority of learning problems probably reflect schooling and societal deficiencies. It seems evident, there-fore, that those who want to reduce signifi-cantly the number of psychoeducational problems must participate in efforts to change prevailing perspectives, practices, priorities, and policies. To do any less is to continue to deal with the problem in a con-text that is too narrow.

Chapter 17

Toward Comprehensive Evaluation of Effectiveness of LD Programs

We are all too apt to measure the gains of our pupils by their proficiency in directly reproducing in a recitation or an examination [of] such matters as they may have learned. . . . Be patient . . . and sympathetic with the type of mind that cuts a poor figure in examinations. It may, in the long examination which life sets us, come out in the end in better shape than the glib and ready reproducer, its passions being deeper, its purposes more worthy, its combining power less commonplace, and its total mental output consequently more important.
William James, 1892

One of the reasons many divergent perspectives exist in the LD field is the difficulty of clearly showing what works and what does not. While informal evaluation goes on continually, comprehensive and systematic evaluation is rare. For decades efforts to measure learning of nonproblem students was rudimentary, and formal evaluation of progress with problem learners was almost nonexistent. Recently, increasing demand for evaluation has come from funding agencies wishing to monitor their financial outlay. This thrust has led to mandated accountability and has contributed to an increasing emphasis on translating intervention aims and goals into concrete and observable objectives to facilitate program evaluation. Since accountability requirements and procedures can easily reshape the intervention, there is a danger that many longer-range goals and complex aims will be subverted unless evaluation is done comprehensively.

There is an obvious need for LD interveners to improve their practices and to be accountable. There is an equally obvious need for improving current evaluation practices. Toward this end, this chapter presents a conceptual framework for systematic and comprehensive evaluation, and highlights major concerns.

EVALUATING EFFECTIVENESS

Space does not allow for an extensive review of the literature related to evaluation. Therefore, in discussing a broad conceptual basis for evaluation, we must settle for (1) a brief discussion of purposes, approaches, dimensions, and a conceptual framework for understanding evaluation, (2) an outline of major areas of choice and concern, and (3) a synthesis of key steps in planning evaluation.

Understanding Evaluation

The essence of evaluation is the determination of worth or value. Beeby (1979) defines evaluation as "the systematic collection and interpretation of evidence leading, as part of the process, to a judgment of value with a view to action" (p. 3).

In the following discussion, evaluation is defined as a systematic process designed to describe and judge the overall impact and value of an intervention for purposes of decision making and advancing knowledge. As discussed in Chapter 5, evaluation is one of several assessment activities related to psychoeducational interventions (see Figure 5–1).

Purposes. Brinkerhoff (1979) proposes four broad goals for evaluating programs: (1) to clarify and communicate the expectations, or standards for the program; (2) to document operation of the program particularly those phases of operation requiring legal compliance; (3) to assess impact of the program on its intended recipients; and (4) to provide information to revise and improve the program.

From an administrative-societal perspective, the purpose of evaluation is to provide information for policy decisions. Levine (1975) distinguishes three types of policy considerations: *cost benefit, cost effectiveness,* and *cost utility analysis*. The management or traditional administrative criteria of *cost benefit* assigns a monetary value to both benefits and costs and weighs the outcome. The broader perspective of *cost effectiveness* allows the effectiveness of a strategy to be expressed in terms of its psychological or physical outcomes as well as monetary benefits. Finally, a *cost utility analysis* goes one step further and includes the decision maker's subjective views in determining the value of intervention outcomes.

Consistent with our discussion of assessment in Chapter 5, we specify the goals and objectives of evaluation as follows:

to *describe* an intervention's (1) rationale, (2) intended and actual antecedents, transactions, and outcomes, and (3) standards for making judgments;

to *judge* an intervention's (1) planning and implementation, (2) intended and unplanned positive impact, (3) anticipated and unanticipated negative impact, and (4) costs in relation to benefits, effectiveness, and utility;

to *make decisions* about the future of an intervention with regard to (1) a particular object of change and (2) a program; and

to *advance knowledge* about interventions to improve (1) practices, (2) training, and (3) theory.

As the statements of goals cited above indicate, evaluation should be focused broadly. In practice, unfortunately, evaluations usually are restricted to determining whether programs produce a delimited set of desired changes, and which programs produce these outcomes for the largest number of participants.

Special education programs, in particular, need to be evaluated more comprehensively. For instance, in addition to pupil achievement in the *3 Rs* and per capita cost with reference to immediate pupil benefits, evaluation should focus on changes in student attitudes and the program's general contribution to improving professional practice through training or research activity.

In general, a comprehensive evaluation of effectiveness encompasses both immediate and long-term data on the breadth of impact. Moreover, the focus is on both direct and indirect program effects, such as student cognitive and affective growth, changes in district practices, and shifts in social policy.

Because evaluations have been narrowly focused (e.g., Arter & Jenkins, 1979; Bergin & Lambert, 1978; Horan, 1980; Weiss, 1972b) many educators and psychologists argue that current interventions are judged unfairly. These professionals tend to reject negative findings and are quite critical of current evaluation purposes and practices.

Approaches and dimensions.   Because evaluations differ in purpose, they differ with regard to general approaches and the dimensions they incorporate. Stake (1976) charts nine contemporary approaches to evaluation: student gain by testing, institutional self-study by staff, blue-ribbon panel, transaction-observation, management analysis, instructional research, social policy analysis, goal-free evaluation, and adversary evaluation. The approaches differ in objectives, in key elements evaluated, in whose perspective is emphasized, and in the "risks and payoffs" that result.

For example, the objective of the student-gain-by-testing approach is to measure student performance and progress. The key elements are statements of goals, analysis of test scores, and the discrepancy between the two. The perspective emphasized is that of educational psychology. The payoff is that it identifies student progress. It does so, how-

ever, at the risk of oversimplifying educational aims and ignoring processes.

A variety of dimensions have been described as facets of evaluation. Based on analyses by Anderson and Ball (1978), Scriven (1967), Stake (1976), Worthen and Sanders (1973), the following is our synthesis of the key dimensions.

Evaluations differ in terms of the degree to which they are designed to be

formative-summative (focused on interventions in operation v. completed programs)

formal-informal

case specific-generalizable

product-process oriented

descriptive-judgmental

preordinate-responsive (oriented to objectives, hypotheses, and prior expectations vs. organized around phenomena encountered as the program proceeds)

wholistic-analytic

internal-external with regard to evaluation personnel and use of findings

phenomenological-behavioral

absolute-theoretical

narrow-broad in scope

high-low in intensity

The various approaches and dimensions reflect differing evaluator and consumer objectives and values. Some are mutually exclusive, most are not. Decisions about each shape evaluation design, the type of information sought, and how data are gathered and weighed.

Knowledge of the major approaches and dimensions related to evaluation is a helpful conceptual aid. Of greater use, however, is working from a conceptual model that serves both to outline key facets and clarify

FOR EXAMPLE

ON FORMATIVE AND SUMMATIVE EVALUATION

Scriven (1967) descirbes two types of evaluation that occur at different points of intervention. Evaluation that occurs while the program is in operation and is still capable of being modified he calls *formative* evaluation. In contrast, he designates assessment of the worth or merit of the completed intervention or treatment as *summative* evaluation. Formative evaluation might include a range of measures used to monitor implementation, change, and unintended outcomes with a view toward deciding whether to change the intervention. Summative evaluation may occur immediately at the conclusion of the intervention or at a later time to evaluate long term impact. As Stake (1976, p. 19) says,

> *when the cook tastes the soup it is formative evaluation and when the guests taste the soup it is summative. The key is not so much when as why. What is the information for, for further preparation and correction or for savouring and consumption? Both lead to decision-making, but toward different decisions.*

their relationships. There is a variety of evaluation models and frameworks available for consideration (see reviews by Popham, 1975; Stake, 1976; Weiss, 1972a).[1]

A framework. As an example, we present the evaluation framework formulated by Stake (1967). This model offers a graphic and comprehensive picture of evaluation facets and their relationships (see Figure 17-1). In brief, Stake emphasizes that "the two basic acts of evaluation" are description and judgment. Descriptions take the form of data gathered by formal or informal measurements and reporting. Judgments take

the form of interpretive conclusions about the meaning of the data, such as whether a phenomenon is good or bad, above or below norm, pathological or not. In practice, judgments are used for purposes of decision making.

Stake stresses that proper evaluation of intervention requires data and criteria (absolute or relative) for analyzing (1) the functional contingencies between antecedent conditions, transactions, and outcomes, and (2) the congruence between what is intended and what occurs. The overriding intent is to describe and judge phenomena about which decisions are to be made.

Stake's framework makes it clear that appropriate understanding of any intervention begins with comprehension of the intervention's rationale, intended antecedents, intended transactions, and intended outcomes. These considerations create the context for gathering descriptive data (observations) and making decisions (judgments). Such decisions encompass whether the intervention should be continued, modified, or terminated. In general, such a matrix of data would provide a wealth of information for use in describing, demonstrating the effectiveness of, and improving intervention.

Evaluation Choices and Concerns

In planning the evaluation of psychoeducational intervention, decisions must be made regarding five major areas. As outlined in Table 17-1, these areas are (1) the focus of evaluation, (2) the role of various interested parties, (3) specific objectives of evaluation, (4) appropriate methodology and measures, and (5) ethical considerations. Each area involves major choices for the evaluator. The following discussion is designed to clarify the significance of these choices by high-

---

[1]Wolf (1979) has grouped evaluation models into four general classes: goal attainment models, judgmental models emphasizing intrinsic criteria, judgmental models emphasizing extrinsic criteria, and decision facilitation models.

Figure 17-1

Stake's graphic representation of his conceptual framework for evaluation.

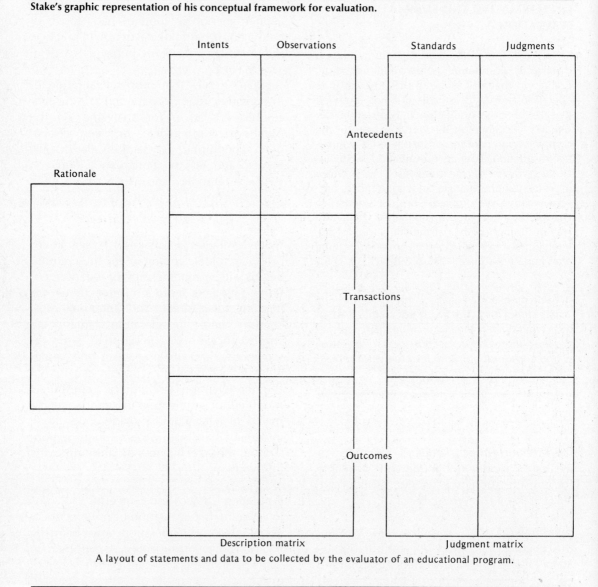

A layout of statements and data to be collected by the evaluator of an educational program.

lighting a few key concerns. Appendix E provides a more extensive presentation.

Focus. There are five sets of choices or decisions to be made regarding the focus of evaluation. The first set involves determining who or what is to be the object(s) of evaluation. Specifically, one must decide to focus on one or a combination of the following:

Person—one person, a subgroup, an entire school population;

FOR EXAMPLE

CLARIFYING THE DIMENSIONS
OF STAKE'S FRAMEWORK

Popham (1975) uses the example of a high-school government course to illustrate each cell in Stake's framework:
Rationale
Mr. Vine has decided to emphasize the distinctions between functions of local, state, and federal government because he believes that these distinctions are pivotal in one's understanding of citizenship responsibilities.

Intents

Antecedents:	*Mr. Vine knows that chapter 9 has been assigned for Tuesday.*
Transactions:	*He plans to have a lecture plus discussion on Tuesday.*
Outcomes:	*He estimates what students will be able to do on a quiz Wednesday.*

Observations

Antecedents:	*He observes that six students were absent on Tuesday.*
Transactions:	*His lecture took so long that there was little time for discussion.*
Outcomes:	*On Wednesday's quiz well over half the students answered an important question incorrectly.*

Standards

Antecedents:	*He expects a few absences on non-quiz days such as Tuesday.*
Transactions:	*He believes his lectures are clear enough for 80 percent of the class to understand them.*
Outcomes:	*His fellow government teachers believe three-fourths of their students should do well on these kinds of quizzes.*

Judgments

Antecedents:	*Mr. Vine retrospectively judges the chapter 9 reading assignment to be somewhat confusing.*
Transactions:	*Several of his weaker students told him his lecture was unclear.*
Outcomes:	*A teacher's aide assigned to grade the quiz papers said too many students performed poorly on the quiz.*

Popham (1975, pp. 31–32)

Environment—one specific intervention program or instructional approach, a setting, or a general context, e.g., to improve the environment to prevent or solve problems (Moos, 1979; Illich, 1970; Whitall, 1969); or

Person-environment interaction—one particular person and environment, e.g., to identify and arrange optimal person-environment interactions (Bandura, 1978; Cronbach & Snow, 1977; Hunt & Sullivan, 1974).

Since the intent may be to change any or all of the above, in theory any or all might be the focal point of evaluation. The obvious concern is that this choice can collude with prevailing biases about cause and correction.

A second example of choices and concerns involves whether the evaluation is to

TABLE 17-1

Major areas of choice and concern in evaluation

I. Focus of evaluation
  A. Object of change
    1. Person
    2. Environment
    3. Person-environment interaction
  B. Scope of interest
    1. Narrow band
    2. Broad band
  C. Classes of intervention variables
    1. Antecedents
    2. Transactions
    3. Outcomes
  D. Level of effects
    1. Micro-macro effects on person (e.g., current life tasks and interests, prerequisites, underlying processing abilities)
    2. Effects on primary-secondary-tertiary environmental variables (e.g., community field, social policy and thought)
  E. Specificity and immediacy of outcome
    1. Long-range aims
    2. Intermediate goals
    3. Immediate objectives
II. Evaluation perspectives
  A. Those directly involved in the intervention
    1. Subscriber
    2. Object of change
    3. Intervener
  B. Interested parties not directly involved
    1. Primary environmental influences (e.g., family, friends, etc.)
    2. Secondary and tertiary environmental influences (e.g., governmental agencies including funding sources)
III. Goals and objectives (reflecting the perspectives of one or more interested parties)
  A. To describe (clarify, document, communicate) an intervention
    1. Rationale (including objects of change and scope of interest)
    2. Intended and actual antecedents, transactions, and outcomes
    3. Standards for judgment
  B. To judge an intervention
    1. Functional contingencies and congruence among variables
    2. Intended and unplanned positive impact (progress/success)
    3. Anticipated and unanticipated negative impact (problems/failure)
    4. Cost analyses
  C. To make decisions about the future of an intervention
    1. A particular object of change
    2. A program
  D. To advance knowledge about interventions and evaluation (evaluation research)
    1. Improve practice
    2. Improve training
    3. Improve theory
IV. Methodology
  A. Designs
    1. Pre-experimental
    2. Experimental
    3. Quasi-experimental

have a narrow or broad focus. Involved are decisions about (1) the number of units to be evaluated, such as a single case, a total program, or some subcomponent, and (2) the number and types of variables to be measured in relation to each unit, for example, one or more areas of achievement, and attitudes toward one or more of these areas.

In practice, because of cost factors, a broad scope in terms of units usually means that only a few complex variables can be measured. The fewer the units, the more feasible in-depth evaluation is likely to be. In general, the scope of evaluation interest is directly related to the scope of the generalizations that can be made.

A final example of options regarding evaluation focus involves the level of evaluation. For example, students with learning and behavior problems might be evaluated with reference to impact on any of three levels: (1) the remediation of underlying

B. Design problems
   1. Insufficient evaluation of implementation
   2. Threats to validity
   3. Lack of control or comparison groups
   4. Lack of pre-post measures
C. Procedures for collecting data and judging findings
   1. Measures (see Table 6-1 and 8-2)
   2. Standards or criteria
      a. Absolute ("ideal", criterion referenced)
      b. Relative (e.g., age related, pre-post treatment)
D. Limited measures and criteria and their effects
   1. Difficulty of translating goals into measures
   2. Tendency of measurement capability to reshape goals
   3. Individual differences not accounted for
   4. Overemphasis on cost accounting standards
   5. Lack of clarity and range related to intervention's objectives
E. Nontechnical problems
   1. Negative attitudes toward evaluation and the impact of political pressures
   2. Limited financial support for comprehensive evaluation
   3. Inappropriate use of evaluation feedback

V. Sources of ethical concerns and their efforts
   A. Limited knowledge base
      1. Many intervention procedures and outcomes unidentified, especially negative effects
      2. Limited understanding of how to measure many significant effects
      3. Narrow range of measures and criteria developed to date
   B. Biases
      1. Psychological, e.g., actor-observer perspectives
      2. Societal, e.g., social definitions of problems and progress
      3. Professional, e.g., assumptions about objectives of evaluation
      4. Personal, e.g., vested financial interests
   C. Conflicts among interested parties
      1. Whose perspective should prevail?
      2. How should conflicts be resolved?
   D. Iatrogenic effects of evaluation
      1. Abuses, e.g., infringements on privacy, coercion, misuses of findings, overselling of expertise
      2. Shaping influence on specific interventions, fields, and on society in general
      3. Backlash on evaluation
      4. Undermining self-evaluation
   E. Responsibility to improve evaluation
      1. Improve knowledge base for evaluation
      2. Control biases
      3. Develop effective and ethical procedures

processing abilities, interfering behaviors, or both (e.g., perceptual deficits, extreme withdrawal, and passivity), (2) the acquisition of needed prerequisites (e.g., attending and listening), (3) achievement in basic school subjects (e.g., reading and language, mathematics) and relevant other behaviors and attitudes (e.g., self-direction, self-evaluation, interstudent cooperation, interests, values, and feelings toward school).

With reference to impact on the environment, effects might be evaluated in terms of primary, secondary, or tertiary levels. For instance, on the primary and secondary levels, the evaluation might focus on the number of persons, groups, agencies, or associations served directly or indirectly in the community. On a tertiary level, the focus might be on the impact on the fields of psychology and education and on social policy. Examples include direct and indirect program influences on (1) the quantity and quality of available personnel, (2) policies and practices of specific school districts (e.g., related to methods, staffing patterns, and inservice training), (3) policies and practices of specific institutions of higher education and government agencies (e.g., related to training personnel to serve LD populations), and (4) social thought in general (e.g., changes in views regarding problem populations and specific interventions).

Methods. Discussion of methods used for evaluation implies that evaluation is a carefully anticipated part of planning interventions. Those who evaluate and those who implement programs in schools and clinics know that this is seldom the case. A pressing problem demands a response, a good idea becomes a "pilot" program, along the way people try to justify or demonstrate the effectiveness of what was done. The realities of applied settings create methodological problems (Cronbach, 1980).

The most basic concern related to evaluation methodology is development of an evaluation plan that specifies how to proceed and what specific procedures to use. The complexities of this concern are great (see Appendix E). A few comments should suffice to illustrate this fact.

There is a great deal to be learned about the causes and correction of psychoeducational problems. Evaluation should help us determine not only outcomes, but also antecedent conditions and transactions that led to these outcomes.

To this end, evaluation and research overlap. To qualify as research, evaluation efforts must include methods that allow for analyzing cause and effect and for making generalizations. Research that focuses on evaluation may be viewed as a process by which information is systematically gathered using carefully controlled procedures and appropriate comparisons, thereby producing information that may have widespread

VIEWPOINT

EVALUATION AS RESEARCH

[We are] committed to the experiment: as the only means for settling disputes regarding educational practice, as the only way of verifying educational improvements, and as the only way of establishing a cumulative tradition in which improvements can be introduced without the danger of a faddish discard of old wisdom in favor of inferior novelties.
Campbell and Stanley (1963, p. 2)

implications (Wolf, 1979). To accomplish this, all programs would have to be evaluated using a research design.

An evaluation design is the organization or overall plan for pursuing specific evaluation objectives and general purposes. The design is intended to facilitate controlled measurement and unambiguous interpretation by specifying the kinds of data to be gathered and the conditions that will allow for desired analyses, judgments, and generalizations.

Most evaluation designs focus on outcome measures. However, at this point in the development of psychoeducational interventions, it is equally important to evaluate process. In discussing their survey of program evaluations, Hetherington, Greathouse, O'Brien, Matthias, and Wilner (1974) emphasize the importance of describing at least what was done, how often, by whom, and in what setting. The Stake evaluation model (see Figure 17–1) investigates not only processes and outcomes, but antecedent conditions in order to understand the intervention's impact and factors that may account for it.

Both a poor evaluation design and confounding factors can subvert valid interpretation of findings. Cook and Campbell (1979) discuss design relevant threats to valid inference in evaluation. These threats refer to extraneous variables which may effect the validity of the evaluation.

The confirmation needed in evaluating effectiveness is to know what would have happened to participants if they had not been in the program. The best way to answer this is to assign randomly participants to control and treatment groups. Because we cannot ethically deprive anyone of needed services, ideal control groups are seldom available. Hetherington et al. (1974) found only 15 percent of all program evaluations they surveyed had such random assignments. Absence of appropriate comparison using control or contrast groups can make it virtually impossible to use collected data to answer questions of major concern: What should be measured? What criteria should be used in judging findings? How large an effect is needed to decide whether the intervention outcome is greater than chance or no effect? Will the results generalize if the program is continued or applied in different settings? Are the outcomes large enough to warrant policy decisions and commitment of resources on an ongoing, long term basis? (Rossi et al., 1979). In this connection, appropriate standards (e.g., comparison groups) and stringent tests of statistical significance are necessary.

While many of the choices and concerns illustrated above reflect pragmatic considerations, evaluation practices encompass significant ethical and sociopolitical matters as well. (See Appendix E.)

Steps in Planning

By way of summary, the following is a list of some key steps in evaluation planning:

1. Clarify intended use of information. The total nature and scope of the evaluation depends on the intended use of evaluation information (e.g., decisions to be made). Potential audiences may include funding agencies, program administrators or management staff, relevant political bodies, interested community groups, current or prospective clients, and providers of service.

2. Understand intervention rationale. It is important to start with a detailed appreciation of the underlying intervention rationale, especially purposes (What is the problem addressed? What is the hypothesis to be tested?).

3. Formulate evaluation questions. The rationale and purposes are translated into a set of major questions, which the evaluation is to be designed to answer (e.g., How effective is the intervention with regard to correcting learning problems? Do kindergartners with perceptual motor problems have more difficulty learning to read than those without such problems? What is the impact of using resource teachers?).

4. Specify data to be gathered. As a first step in answering the formulated questions, it is necessary to specify the relevant descriptive data (e.g., intended and unintended antecedents, transactions, and outcomes) that have a bearing on the questions.

5. Specify procedures. After specifying the data, it is necessary to specify the procedures that can be used to gather such data, for example, rating scales, observations, checklists, questionnaires, and surveys (see Tables 6-1 and 8-2).

6. Specify design. In addition to designating procedures for gathering desired data, it also is necessary to specify an evaluation design (e.g., case study, one group pre-test–post-test design, post-test only control or contrast group design, etc., see Cook & Campbell, 1979). As discussed in Appendix E, designs are based on decisions regarding the range and type of conclusions and generalizations under consideration.

FOR EXAMPLE

STIMULANT DRUGS AND LEARNING PROBLEMS

In examining studies purporting to evaluate the effectiveness of stimulant medication with learning problems, Adelman and Compas (1977) highlight serious design and measurement problems:

Subject selection—Subjects referred to drug treatment programs are very heterogeneous with regard to critical dimensions (such as the cause of their problems). This subject variability limits analyses and generalization of findings.

Controls—Observers used to rate behavior in drug studies are, by design, "blind" to the treatment condition. The "blind" however is easily broken as experimenters (and often subjects themselves) note physical or behavioral cues of drug effects. The impact may be to bias evaluation studies in favor of expected outcomes. Investigation of placebo controls and spontaneous remission also complicates the evaluation picture.

Measurement—Development of reliable and valid instruments to measure change have been discouraging. Identifying relevant behaviors in home and school situations has not been dealt with systematically. Which behaviors are problematic (i.e., interfere with learning) is not yet clear.

Relevant criteria—Outcomes related to change in academic learning and performance may or may not relate to classroom and home behavior outcomes. Well-designed studies have not yet consistently shown that stimulant medication with learning problem students produces reliable or valid changes in either. Evaluation of negative outcomes is equally inconclusive.

The authors conclude that "research findings do not indicate the general efficacy and therefore do not support the widespread use of stimulant drugs as a treatment of learning problems" (1977, p. 406).

---

7. Designate time and place for data collection. These matters are determined, in part, by the design and, in part, by pragmatic factors, for example, available person and material resources, and co-operation of the people who are the sources of data.

CONCLUDING COMMENTS

Overselling expertise by practitioners and researchers alike in the LD field is becoming pervasive. As one facet of overselling expertise, there has been a trend toward large-scale, premature application of interventions prior to appropriate validation. A major example has been widespread use of stimulant drugs on youngsters with learning problems, even though research evidence does

not warrant this type of unrestricted practice (e.g., Cohen, Sullivan, Minde, Novak, & Helwig, 1981).

Besides ethical concerns, such trends raise the practical likelihood of increased demands for professional accountability, subsequent escalation of malpractice charges, and general backlash from the public and its elected representatives. Reactions of this nature seldom produce carefully formulated reforms. Indeed, they usually are quite harmful to a field. To prevent these kinds of reactions, it is extremely important for professionals in the field to move quickly to (1) establish higher standards for practice and (2) clarify for the general public that available evaluation findings are limited and must be interpreted cautiously.

The problem with clarifying evaluation findings is that there are so many studies

VIEWPOINT

TESTING EDGES OUT TEACHING

[A] cost-benefit system will always be a sub-system controlled by the master social and political system in which it is embedded and will therefore always be used and compromised by the prevailing practices and values of this larger context. . . .

[D]espite the fantasy of omnipotence, you have very little control over the "input" and "output" of kids and therefore not the least chance of controlling experimental variables. Input affecting language performance, for example, extends back to infancy and occurs daily outside of school. What kids put out to you depends on motives and other features of their ongoing inner life that may be comically out of key with your testing and research intentions.

If scores rise, you still do not know what to attribute this to because so many things happen in a week, even just counting what was controlled within school. Did scores rise because of certain texts, certain discussions, certain exercises, or what? Well, we'll control for that by testing daily. Same problem. Well, a 20-minute lesson, then. But even that lesson consists of several steps. Which steps caused the happy effects and which got in the way or were irrelevant? So for feedback purposes, learning must be broken down into absurdly small pieces that can be controlled one at a time. But then how do you sequence these

mini-steps? Nobody knows because the steps aren't learning units in the first place, they are artificial . . . units. Besides, the sequence would be different for different kids. After all this, suppose kids scored high because they already knew how to do what the lesson was supposed to teach. To control for that you have to test before and after the lesson.

So testing edges out teaching, leaving less to test for. Generally, for me to see kids learn I must make them do something that turns their heads inside out. Overt behavior, you know. And of course effects that show up later will be lost. The lesson may have temporarily set a student back by complicating his mental life in a good way that pays off later, but no one will ever know that. Those later effects will be attributed instead to some later lesson that happened to fall on the day some score rose. And, conversely, as we finally learned in reading research, what look like good effects in second grade often disappear by third. This is science?

No, but it is something else very familiar, isn't it? Recognize the itsy-bitsy steps laid out in an invented sequence, the take-a-step, take-a-test format? By a remarkable coincidence, what is good for the nation's youth is also good for manufacturers of programmed materials. It all comes full circle because the same mentality produced both the mode of evaluation and what is to be evaluated.

Moffet (1970, pp. 6–7)

---

reporting on interventions for learning problems that it is difficult to develop an overall view. An important perspective can be gained, however, from reviewing the follow-up studies, which are of particular interest because of their special focus on long-term effectiveness.

Compared to the total body of efficacy literature, follow-up studies are relatively rare. In a cursory review of work published

over the last fifteen years, we found about thirty titles that seemed potentially relevant. Thirteen of these had sufficient data and procedures to warrant serious attention. Of these, three report statistically significant positive results, for example, the majority of individuals were doing satisfactorily in later schooling, older students had completed high school. Two studies report mixed results, for example, satisfactory school progress, but other psychological problems. The remaining eight indicate negative results.

Each of the follow-up studies, like their shorter term counterparts, suffers from major methodological problems.[2] These include overreliance on parent interview data, failure to delineate important variables in the sample that could significantly account for differential effects, lack of control or contrast groups, and so forth. Rather than critique any investigation individually, we simply report that the internal validity of each was seriously compromised.

Earlier, we did a comparable analysis of research on stimulant drug efficacy related to individuals manifesting learning problems (Adelman & Compas, 1977). The research in this area also reflected major methodological problems and did not warrant claims of efficacy in treating learning problems.

Because of the difficulties inherent in evaluating intervention efficacy, many individuals and groups would prefer to see no evaluation rather than take a chance that a program will be evaluated in an inadequate fashion. These critics point to instances when evaluation procedures and data have been misused and abused. It is true that current approaches to evaluation in the LD field tend to reflect the type of naive accountability that endangers individuals, the field, and social action programs. This is lamentable. Equally lamentable, however, is the tendency to suggest that such misuses of the evaluation process justify the continuing absence of formal evaluation, which characterizes so many psychoeducational interventions. Evaluation is an essential and indispensable phase of intervention.

---

[2]We have not cited references because they are not necessary to the point being made. Any attempt to conduct a follow-up study or any evaluation of intervention effectiveness is costly and difficult. We would not want to demean any specific effort, and we certainly are not interested in singling out any study as a bad example.

Conclusion

"Well, you've pointed out this issue, illustrated that problem, and highlighted more concerns than I care to know. Now what is the answer?"

The questioner had just heard us talk about learning disabilities and was half joking, but only half. Parents, professionals, and anyone who has a learning problem need to do something now. The plaintive cry of teachers coming out of training workshops is often, "But what do I do on Monday?"

We are not unmindful of the importance of specific methods. They are essential and a considerable part of this book has focused on them. But methods are only part of the answer. The *way* problems are approached is equally, if not more, important. Let us illustrate.

Below are nine dots:

The problem you must solve is how to connect all nine dots with four straight, connecting lines, without removing your pencil from the page or retracing any line.

Most people cannot solve this problem. We hope you did, but in case you did not, the answer appears on the following page. The solution to the problem is not found in methods per se; we all know how to use a pencil and draw straight lines. The solution requires being able to see beyond the dots—to get out of the nonexistent square box—to see the problem from a different perspective.

The tendency has been to perceive the problem of learning disabilities as another type of physical handicap, much like not being able to see or hear. Thus, the methods chosen and the way they are used have reflected this perspective. The emphasis has been almost completely on remediation. Our intent has been to suggest a different perspective for dealing with the problem.

Will Rogers stated, "We are all ignorant on different subjects." Similarly, we are all vulnerable in different areas. Some people find mathematics intimidating. Some are poor at sports. Some cannot carry a tune. Others find it hard to make friends. Left-handed students have difficulties when in classrooms set up for right-handed students and taught by right-handed teachers. At the same time, we all have areas where we do just fine.

The same is true for those persons who are called *learning disabled*. A major ingredient in understanding learning disabilities is to accept a wide range of individual differences (areas of competence and vulnerability) as

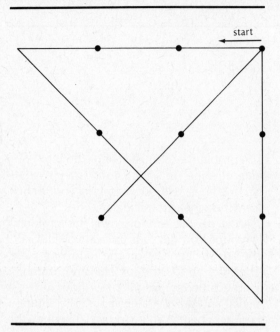

start

part of the natural order of everyday living. One of the keys to helping others overcome their learning problems is for helpers to understand our own experiences of competence and vulnerability. Do we consider all our vulnerabilities as problems? Do we want to spend most of our time working on those we do consider problems? What have we found that works best for us?

One of the important strategies in helping is to capitalize on areas people enjoy, where they can succeed. This means not excluding activities where they do just fine. Another important strategy seems to be not aggravating vulnerability. In particular, this means not insisting that people spend too much time in areas where they lack competence. This includes changing situations to minimize vulnerability. Few people who do not do arithmetic very well want to spend most of their time in situations where they are required to rely on mathematical skills.

A critical component in helping others is understanding what help a person wants. Since most people's learning problems have not affected their competence to communicate and make choices, a good way to begin to understand these matters is to ask the person about the problem and what he or she wants to do about it.

For those who continue to have a lot of trouble staying tuned in to a task and who learn slowly, helping means providing more support and guidance and trying to improve the teaching-learning match. This includes exploring different methods to find a combination of learning activities and techniques that a particular individual can do and wants to do. And so on.

Thus, when individuals with learning problems are not viewed first and foremost as handicapped, important implications for teaching emerge. From a perspective which views such individuals as competent with some vulnerability, teaching stresses areas of competence first, greater acceptance of the naturalness of some areas of weakness, greater involvement of individuals in identifying problems and choosing which to work on, and the search for a good teacher-learner match as one of continuing exploration. To this kind of help, even the most severely learning disabled seem to respond.

relevance, (2) freedom from bias, (3) reliability, and (4) availability. While such qualities can be defined in ways that make them ideal goals to be pursued, in practice the criterion chosen must be measurable. Thus, it often is simply an existing assessment method. The irony is that, in efforts to validate a new procedure, one may be forced to use as criteria procedures that have low reliability and validity, such as observer ratings of complex phenomena and many existing tests.

The above problems highlight a key assumption underlying methodology for establishing criterion-related validity. It is assumed that an appropriate, measurable, highly valid criterion *is* available. With regard to psychoeducational assessment procedures, this is never the case when the phenomenon of interest is complex. At best, what is available will be of moderate validity. As a result, if high correlations are found, they may be spurious and only indicative of the fact that the new procedure is as fallible as the criterion measure. Ironically, a procedure that is highly related to a criterion *variable* may not be very highly correlated with existing *measures* of that variable. More generally, spurious validity correlation coefficients may result because of the reliability or validity characteristics of the procedures, including the possibility that they both validly measure some unspecified component not of interest (Proger, Cross, & Burger, 1973; Ysseldyke, 1973).

Other factors that may affect correlations between current assessment data and a criterion are sample homogeneity, sample size, and time separation between procedure and criterion. As a general rule, the more homogeneous and smaller the samples with regard to the phenomenon being assessed, the lower the validity coefficient. Similarly, the greater the time lapse, "the less the correlation" (Cronbach, 1970; p. 133), which em-

phasizes that concurrent validity coefficients, although still not much higher than .77, usually will be the highest. Predictive and postdictive[3] coefficients will be lower and decrease with the time separation between current data and the future or past criterion of interest. Future criteria may change significantly over time; past criteria may become less reliable and less accessible over time.

A final critical set of factors that should be mentioned as influencing validity coefficients is individual differences in, and unique interactions between, people and situations. For many years, for example, efforts to predict reading failure ignored this point. As a result, studies consistently found that large numbers of kindergarteners who performed poorly on a particular "readiness" skill were subsequently as successful in reading as those who performed well (Adelman & Feshbach, 1971). The reason was that predictions based on a readiness index failed to account for differences in instruction, in student development and motivation, and so forth.

Since there is no single best criterion with which to validate current assessment data, the developers and users of assessment procedures again are caught in a judgmental situation. Not only must judgment be made as to whether a validity coefficient is high enough, but whether a particular criterion used in arriving at the coefficient is compatible with the types of decisions to be made. Furthermore, since the validity coefficient is established with reference to samples, it must be recognized that the validity of the procedure in any given instance is never known. Thus, because all assessment procedures have far from perfect validity, decisions made about a particular person or environmental component always may be in error. Each specific decision has a probability

---

[3]The term *postdictive validity* is used to encompass assessment data that focuses on identifying previous causes of current circumstances.

FOR EXAMPLE

VALIDITY FOR WHAT?

Discussion between a younger and older psychologist regarding labeling minority children:

Younger Psychologist: I don't hesitate to give standardized IQ tests when I diagnose minority children.

Older Psychologist: Recent research and legislation indicate the tests aren't measuring intelligence and lead to over prescribing remedial programs for minority children.

Younger Psychologist: But they're very good at predicting how well a child will do in regular school settings.

Older Psychologist: It's true that the correlation with regular classroom performance is high, that's no surprise, but if we're implying they validly measure the child's potential, we're wrong. Perhaps we should work with the environment to accommodate a broader range of individual differences.

Younger Psychologist: I can't change the world, I can only work with my client. If the child will fail in regular programs, it's better to be in a special program.

The logic and the conclusions of the young psychologist are not unique. That the young psychologist was from a minority group makes the implications of the argument especially poignant.

---

of being 100 percent right or 100 percent wrong. In choosing a procedure then, the question is not which procedure will avoid *all error* but which will produce the *smallest number of errors*. Finally, one must be careful not to confuse criterion-related validity, such as a test's ability to predict, with content validity. Because a test predicts a future event does not necessarily mean that what it measures is the cause of that event. Again, cautions about the difference between observing correlates and proving cause and effect apply. Delineation of cause-effect connections requires construct validation.

Construct Validity

Construct validity refers to the extent to which an assessment procedure measures some theoretical concept or abstraction which is not directly observable, such as intelligence, anxiety, perception, motivation, or a relationship among concepts. Such a theoretical or hypothetical idea is called a construct because it is constructed by scientists to help organize thinking about unobservable phenomena, including the nature of the relationship among observ-

ables (Nunnally, 1967). In effect, a construct is a myth that is found to be a useful and convenient way to understand and communicate about a theoretical notion, but it is rarely treated as a myth as long as enough scientists continue to find it useful.

Since constructs are not directly observable, they are not directly measureable. Thus to establish that a procedure is assessing phenomena of interest, the theoretical idea must be clearly delineated, and measures must be developed with reference to the indicators and relationships described. For example, the idea of intelligence has been constructed to represent an internal attribute of people. Theories suggest the nature of this attribute and the behaviors that should be directly and indirectly associated with it, such as the ability to reason using verbal, graphic, and mathematical symbols. It is hypothesized that some groups of persons such as university students are likely to be more intelligent than high-school dropouts. Efforts to determine construct validity, then, might involve relating the procedure to be validated with one or more measures of the specified behaviors or comparing hypothesized group performance differences. No one behavior or group comparison constitutes sufficient validation. Convergence of relatively high positive correlations and consistency in factor analyses based on a variety of studies (along with low correlations with behavior and factors that are not theoretically related to the construct) builds a sense of confidence in the procedure's construct validity and contributes to the belief that the constructed quality indeed exists. "Construct validity," according to Cronbach (1970), "is established through a long-continued interplay between observation, reasoning, and imagination. . . . The process of construct validation is the same as that by which scientific theories are developed" (p. 142).

Thus, rather than being a straightforward empirical process, reasoning and judgment play as major a role in the validation of a procedure for assessing a construct as in content and criterion-related validation. That is, delineation of the theory related to a construct to be validated and the ways to test the theory clearly are elaborate, rational exercises. Also, as with content validity, it is evident that no single summary index is available to describe degree of validity.

An even greater problem arises from the fact that different definitions are often used for a given construct and therefore validation studies often are testing ideas that differ in major ways. In such cases, findings are not really comparable. This can lead to major misinterpretation with regard to how adequately a construct has been validated.

In the end, the assessor must know whether the procedure has been validated by a large body of convergent and divergent multitrait and multimethod research (Cronbach, 1970) or the assessor must rely on expert judgment that such research has been done. Expert judgment that a procedure has construct validity despite the fact that only minimal research has been accomplished to date is not sufficient. Given the difficulty in validating procedures for diagnosis, screening, and placement, it must be expected that most psychoeducational assessment procedures require additional validation.

NORMS AND STANDARDS

One of the most basic aspects of human behavior is that people try to make sense out of what they see. In the process, complex phenomena are sized up and conclusions are made: the new neighbor appears to be wholesome and friendly; the person walking behind you in an unlit parking lot at night looks like a mugger or worse; students are judged by their teachers to be smart or not too smart; teachers are judged by students to be good or terrible; classroom environments quickly are evaluated as conducive or a hindrance to learning. To arrive at such conclusions, people obviously are influenced by the sample of information immediately available in the situation. They also draw on past experiences, general models and theories they have assimilated and use in understanding the world, current attitudes, values, and beliefs, and so forth. Because of differences in information samples, information processing, and motivation, people often arrive at diverse conclusions about the same complex phenomenon. In effect, they are using different norms and standards.

Differentiating Norms and Standards

For our purposes, the term *standard* can be understood broadly to mean a theoretical or value referent used as a basis for making judgments about whether a phenomenon is as it *should* be, for example, whether the phenomenon is a problem or not, good or bad, or consistent with theory. Norms are not standards. Norms are not theoretical. Norms are not value statements. They are empirically based referents, such as a set of previously gathered data on the phenomenon, that can be used for comparison with current assessment findings. Norms are an indication of the distribution of samples of behavior, performance, learning, environmental physical characteristics, and so forth. Norms provide assessors with a basis for interpreting whether a phenomenon is typical of a certain class of phenomena, such as whether it is above or below the median for a sample group. It is common for findings of above and below average, typical and atypical, to be quickly judged in terms of *good* and *bad*—so quickly in some cases that it is not apparent that judgments have been made. Whether it is explicitly stated, conclusions about findings are judgments and stem from application of some standard, that is, a theoretical or value referrent. The assessor might not even be able to say what standard was applied.

An example of this distinction is given in Chapter 7 with reference to diagnosing hyperactivity. Another example of the differences between norms and standards is provided by standardized achievement tests. In discussing such tests, the difference between the test's norm and norms also needs to be underscored. The test's norm is the median score of the standardization sample. The norms are the total distribution of scores from the standardization sample. Let us assume we have norms for a national sample of sixth-graders. When the test is given to a new sample, not all students are expected to score at the national norm or median established for sixth-graders. If the sample is comparable to the standardization sample, about half the students will fall below, and half above, the norm. Just where they fall in relation to the norm is determined by the test's norms. Other sixth-grade samples may have many more or fewer students scoring above the norm. In judging whether the number of students scoring above or below norm is satisfactory, a standard must be used. For instance, in higher socioeconomic neighborhoods, parents, teachers, students, and indeed the society all are unlikely to be satisfied with a distribution of scores that are similar to national norms. They want and expect a higher proportion than 50 percent of the students to score above the norm. The basis for this standard probably derives from both a theoretical and value belief supported by a variety of data which indicates that most students in the neighborhood are able to learn and perform at a higher-than-average level. A quite different standard is widely applied to students in low socioeconomic neighborhoods.[4]

As the above discussion emphasizes, standardized norms and standards make explicit the specific criteria for interpreting and making judgments about assessment findings. With reference to psychoeducational assessment, criteria are always relative in that they are derived from comparisons with data on past grouped or individual phenomena or with future expectations (which usually are based on previously gathered data or theory-based predictions). One exception to this is when an absolute value is used as a standard, such as "Thou shall not kill."

Reliable and Valid Norms

The desirability of adequate norms is evident. Establishing an adequate set of standardized, published norms is, however, as

---

[4]With regard to assessment of the degree to which significant skills and knowledge are mastered, criterion-referenced tests often are used. Instead of using norms to interpret performance, these procedures simply describe performance or, more typically, a level of expected performance is specified for defined skills or content. Assessment focuses on the degree to which an individual approximates the expected performance level. While criterion-referenced procedures are contrasted with norm-referenced procedures, expected performance levels on criterion-referenced tests at times are based on comparisons with the performance of others. The only time such comparisons are not involved is when performance is simply described or when skills and content are defined in terms of standards that require absolute levels of mastery, for example, can the student add 2 + 2?

costly as it is desirable. As a result, manuals and tables of norms and expectancies primarily are available with tests standardized and sold by publishing companies or actuarial reports developed by major businesses such as insurance companies. Of course just because norms are published is no guarantee they are appropriate and adequate. A dramatic example of this fact is provided by the original Wechsler Intelligence Scale for Children (WISC). As published in 1949, the sample used to standardize the procedures and establish norms included only "white" children. In the years prior to the 1974 publication of the revised and restandardized version (WISC-R), countless individuals were tested and decisions made based on norms from this extremely skewed sample. Apparent bias in the test's content and obvious inadequacy of the norms for interpreting intelligence of individuals from subgroups not represented in the standardization sample led to enormous criticism, including judicial action. The new version has been standardized with samples reflecting the same proportion of population subgroups indicated in the 1970 U.S. Census. However, while content also has been revised, construct validity remains unestablished for many subgroups.

In general, frequently used psychoeducational procedures, such as many so-called diagnostic tests related to academic skills and psychological projective tests, either do not have published norms or the norms associated with the procedure are grossly inadequate and are potentially more harmful than helpful. When there are no published norms—and sometimes even when there are—assessors either rely on self-established norms assimilated from their professional and personal experiences or directly apply standards based on theory and value orientations.

Where nonstandardized norms are used, they vary markedly in reliability and validity. Both reliability and validity are diminished,

in part, by unsystematic gathering and application of normative data. Even when a standardized approach is taken in establishing norms, their reliability and validity depend greatly on the adequacy of the standardization methodology. Briefly, adequate norms evolve from data gathered on a sample which is

recent;

representative in kinds and proportions of the phenomenon of interest (e.g., if the phenomenon is person-related, a variety of characteristics may need to be considered, such as sex, age, race, acculturation; variations in physical settings, which may determine representativeness, include size and space dimensions, furnishing, etc.);

large enough to minimize errors in measurement; and

relevant to the purposes, such as types of interpretations and ultimately decisions, for which the norms are to be used.

Development of comprehensive norms involves a great deal of practical and technical activity. Samples have to be defined and cooperation solicited. Procedures have to be administered and data analyzed in a standardized manner. Even with recent, representative, large, and relevant samples, it is to be expected that control over data collection and differences in technical decisions about such matters as sample stratification characteristics will produce variations in norms for procedures that may be similar in most other ways.

When there is a choice among procedures with different norms, a procedure may be chosen primarily because the norms allow assessors to interpret data in a desired way, rather than in terms of validity of the norms with reference to making appropriate decisions. Cronbach (1970) provides an example of this with regard to the use of achievement tests.

> The national average in fifth-grade arithmetic reported for one test may be higher than the average performance reported for a similar test. When the State of California directs every school district to give a nationally standardized test and report publicly how well its fifth-graders are doing, and leaves the choice of test to the school district, there is an understandable tendency for teachers to select the test whose national norms set "average performance" at a low figure. The marketplace may thus tend to reward the publisher who has been less careful than others to obtain accurate norms. (p. 105)

In addition to problems related to standardizing norms, their reliability and validity are limited by the many problems illustrated above, that is, problems related to establishing the reliability and validity of data gathered by available psychoeducational procedures. Obviously, data used as norms cannot be more reliable and valid than the best data generated by the instrument used. Reliability and validity are further diminished when standardized norms are applied in an unstandardized way.

While the above discussion emphasizes norms as related to formal assessment procedures, the desirability of "normative" data for interpreting all assessment findings should be evident. For example, interpretation of evaluative data on a variety of changes resulting from instruction or treatment generally requires a basis for comparison. Such comparisons may be made with reference to previous status of the person or environment or in terms of some criterion-referenced objective such as learning the multiplication tables. Ideas about appropriate types of comparison data have been extrapolated from use of control and contrast groups in experimental designs (e.g., Cook & Campbell, 1979). A common approach to establishing a basis for comparison has been to assess average base-level behavior or preintervention status. These data then are treated as the norm with which post intervention status measures are compared.

As with the other technological concerns, norms and standards represent another hurdle that must be overcome if psychoeducational assessment and decision-making practices are to be improved. Such hurdles are not insurmountable. An understanding of each ensures that the limitations of prevailing practices will be understood; such understanding provides a basis for improvement.

Outline of Goals of Elementary Education

The following outline was developed by the Evaluation Technologies Program, Center for the Study of Evaluation, UCLA.[1] It provides a useful example of a broad range of outcomes and content which might be incorporated into any school program, including programs designed for students identified as *learning disabled*.

I. Affective and personality traits
  A. Personal temperament
    1. Self-assertion
    2. Emotional stability
    3. Responsibility and self-control
  B. Socialization
    1. Social awareness
    2. Social values and conduct
  C. Attitudes, values, and motivation
    1. School orientation
    2. Self-esteem
    3. Achievement motivation
    4. Interests

II. Arts and crafts
  A. Valuing art
    1. Appreciation of art
    2. Internalization of art
  B. Producing art
    1. Representational skill in art
    2. Expressive skill in art
  C. Understanding art
    1. Art analysis
    2. Developmental understanding of art

III. Career education
  A. Career values and understanding
    1. Knowledge of vocations and careers
    2. Interest in vocations and careers

IV. Cognitive and intellectual skills
  A. Understanding and reasoning
    1. Classification
    2. Comprehension of information
    3. Logical reasoning
    4. Spatial reasoning
  B. Creativity and judgment
    1. Creativity
    2. Evaluative judgment
  C. Memory
    1. Rote memory
    2. Meaningful memory
  D. Foreign language skills
    1. Reading comprehension in a foreign language
    2. Knowledge of elements of a foreign language
    3. Conversation in a foreign language
    4. Writing in a foreign language
  E. Valuing foreign language and culture

---

[1]This material is also presented in CSE Elementary School Test Evaluations, 2nd ed., (Los Angeles: Center for the Study of Evaluation, UCLA, 1976), edited and prepared by R. Hoepfner, M. Bastone, V. Ogilvie, R. Hunter, S. Sparta, C. Grothe, E. Shari, L. Hufano, E. Goldstein, R. Williams, and K. Smith. The original source is out of print but can be retrieved through the ERIC system (ED 143670).

1. Cultural insight and values
2. Enjoyment and application of a foreign language

V. Language arts
  A. Writing skills
    1. Spelling
    2. Punctuation and capitalization
    3. Grammatical skills in writing
    4. Penmanship
    5. Purpose and organization in writing
    6. Expression in writing
  B. Reference and study skills
    1. Reference and library skills
    2. Personal study skills and habits

VI. Mathematics
  A. Understanding math
    1. Knowledge of numbers and sets
    2. Knowledge of numeral systems and number principles
    3. Knowledge basic to algebra
  B. Performing arithmetic operations
    1. Whole number computation
    2. Computation with fractions
    3. Decimal and percent computation
  C. Applying and valuing mathematics
    1. Solution of word problems
    2. Personal use and appreciation
  D. Geometry and measurement skills
    1. Knowledge of geometric objects and relations
    2. Measurement knowledge and skills
    3. Use of tables, graphs, and statistical concepts

VII. Music
  A. Valuing music
    1. Appreciation of music
    2. Internalization of music
  B. Performing in music and dance
    1. Singing
    2. Instrument playing
    3. Dancing
  C. Understanding music
    1. Music analysis
    2. Developing understanding of music

VIII. Perceptual and motor skills
  A. Sensory perception
    1. Visual and tactile perception
    2. Auditory perception
  B. Psychomotor skills
    1. Fine motor skills
    2. Gross motor skills

IX. Physical education and health education
  A. Sports skills
    1. Athletic skills and physical condition
    2. Sports knowledge
  B. Valuing physical education
    1. Sportsmanship
    2. Sports enjoyment and participation
  C. Health habits and understanding
    1. Health and safety behavior and attitudes
    2. Knowledge of health factors
    3. Knowledge of life functions
    4. Knowledge of human sexuality
  D. Understanding hazards and diseases
    1. Knowledge of safety precautions
    2. Knowledge of habit-forming substances
    3. Knowledge of disease and disability

X. Reading
  A. Reading readiness skills
    1. Listening
    2. Speaking
    3. Word attack skills
  B. Familiarity with literature
    1. Recognition of literary devices and qualities
    2. Knowledge of literature
  C. Reading with understanding
    1. Recognition of word meanings
    2. Reading comprehension
  D. Reading interpretation and criticism
    1. Oral reading
    2. Reading interpretation
    3. Critical reading
  E. Valuing literature and language
    1. Response to literature and language
    2. Personal use of reading and language skills

XI. Religion and ethics
  A. Understanding religion
    1. Knowledge of own religion
    2. Knowledge of religions of the world
  B. Personal ethics and religious belief
    1. Ethical code and practice
    2. Religious belief and practice
XII. Science
  A. Investigating the environment
    1. Scientific observation and description
    2. Generalization and hypothesis
       formulation in science
    3. Experimentation
  B. Understanding science
    1. Knowledge of different life forms
    2. Knowledge of ecology
    3. Knowledge of physical science
    4. Knowledge of the foundations
       of science
  C. Valuing and applying science
    1. Science interest and appreciation
    2. Application of scientific methods
       in everyday life

XIII. Social studies
  A. Understanding history and civics
    1. Knowledge of history
    2. Knowledge of government and civics
    3. Knowledge of current events
  B. Understanding geography
    1. Knowledge of physical geography
    2. Knowledge of anthropology and
       cultural geography
    3. Knowledge of economic processes
       and geography
  C. Understanding social relationships
    1. Knowledge of family life
    2. Knowledge of social control
       and conflict
    3. Knowledge of social groups
  D. Valuing and applying social studies
    1. Social studies interest and
       appreciation
    2. Citizenship
    3. Ethnic and cultural appreciation

Appendix C

Lerner's Categorization of Activities for Teaching in LD Areas[1]

I. Activities for motor development
  A. Gross motor
    1. Walking activities (e.g., forward, backward, sideways, and variations; animal walks; cross-pattern walking; stepping stones; line and ladder walks)
    2. Floor activities (e.g., angels in the snow, crawling, obstacle crawl)
    3. Balance beam (e.g., forward, backward, sideways, and variations)
    4. Other (e.g., skateboard, stand-up, jumping jacks, hopping, bouncing, galloping steps, skipping, hopscotch, hoop games, rope skills)
  B. Body-image and body-awareness activities
    (e.g., point to body parts, robot man, Simon Says, puzzles, life-sized drawings)
  C. Fine motor
    1. Throwing and catching (e.g., objects, ball games)
    2. Eye-hand coordination (e.g., tracing, cutting, stencils, lacing, paper and pencil activities, paper folding)
    3. Chalkboard (e.g., dot-to-dot, geometric shapes, letters and numbers)
    4. Eye movement (e.g., ocular pursuit, visual tracking)
II. Perception
  A. Visual perception
    (e.g., pegboard, block, and bead designs; puzzles; classification; finding, matching, sorting, grouping, tracing, and reproducing shapes, letters, and numbers)
  B. Auditory perception
    1. Auditory sensitivity to sounds (e.g., listening and identifying different sounds of objects and events)
    2. Auditory attending (e.g., responding to rhythmic patterns)
    3. Discrimination of sounds (e.g., near and far; loud and soft; high and low)
    4. Awareness of phonemes or letter sounds (e.g., initial consonants; consonant blends; rhyming words)
  C. Haptic perception: tactile and kinesthetic skills
    (e.g., feeling and touching textures and shapes, perceiving temperature and weight differences)
  D. Cross-modal perception
    (e.g., perceiving and reproducing rhythms, shapes, sounds across modalities such as visual to auditory, tactile to visual, and so forth)
III. Memory
  A. General memory
    (e.g., frequent reviewing; organizing material; mnemonic strategies)
  B. Auditory memory
    (e.g., practice with simple and increasingly complex letter and number retention; following directions)

[1]Appendix C outlines the activity headings from Part 3 of Lerner's (1976) textbook.

C. Visual memory
(e.g., practice with simple and then increasingly complex recall of objects, designs, letters, numbers, tachistoscopic presentations)

IV. Oral language
A. Listening
1. Auditory perception of nonlanguage sounds (see activities listed above for perception)
2. Auditory perception and discrimination of language sounds (e.g., recognition and discrimination of initial consonants; blending of phonemes; identifying rhyming sounds and syllables)
3. Understanding words (e.g., object naming; verb meanings; object classification)
4. Understanding sentences and other linguistic units (e.g., following simple directions; learning function words)
5. Auditory memory (see activities listed above for memory)
6. Listening comprehension (e.g., listening for details; sequencing events; following directions; getting the main idea; making interpretations and drawing conclusions)
7. Critical listening (e.g., recognizing absurdities; analyzing advertisements and propaganda)
B. Speaking
1. Building a speaking vocabulary (e.g., naming objects; supplying missing words)
2. Producing speech sounds (e.g., exercising speech muscles and organs; feeling vibrations and observing sounds)
3. Learning linguistic patterns (e.g., morphological generalizations through auditory and visual presentations)
4. Formulating sentences (e.g., practice with simple to complex sentences)
5. Practicing oral language skills (e.g., conversations; discussions; telephoning; reports; role playing; telling jokes and riddles; questions and answers)

V. Reading
A. "Decoding" approaches to beginning reading
(e.g., phonics; linguistics; modified alphabet)
B. Language-experience approach
(e.g., building on basic language skills and personal experience)
C. Multisensory approach
(e.g., using procedures for teaching reading vocabulary that incorporate use of auditory, visual, kinesthetic, and tactile modalities)
D. Individualized reading
(e.g., reading materials chosen to match individual needs)
E. Programmed reading instruction
(e.g., materials designed to be self-instructional, self-pacing, self-corrective)
F. Basal reading series
(e.g., graded sets of readers intended to cover basic reading skills in sequence)
G. Behavior modification approaches
(e.g., establishing specified, observable, and measurable objectives and structuring the environment through contingency management)
H. Technological approaches
(e.g., computer instruction and various types of audiovisual teaching machines)
I. "Systems" approaches
(e.g., packaged multimedia materials including books, games, puzzles, tape cassettes, practice sheets, tests, etc.)

VI. Written language
  A. Handwriting
     (e.g., chalkboard; holding pencil correctly; tracing; dot-to-dot; tracing with cues; unlined paper; template lines)
  B. Spelling
     (e.g., auditory and visual perception and memory of sounds; multisensory practice; programmed spelling materials; use of dictionary including *Bad Speller's Dictionary*)
  C. Written expression
     (e.g., composing and dictating to others; copying; taking dictation; rewriting)
VII. Cognitive development
  A. Arithmetic
     (e.g., practice with basic counting and computational skills; use of materials and apparatus such as counting materials and measuring instruments; practice with matching and sorting; discriminating relationships using concepts of size, length, part-whole, serial order, time, space)
  B. Reading comprehension
     (e.g., noting facts and details; main idea; following sequence of events; drawing inferences; organizing ideas; applying ideas; critical evaluation)
VIII. Self-concept and emotional attitudes
     (e.g., bibliotherapy; classroom group discussion; self-understanding exercises and creative materials; counseling and psychotherapy)
IX. Social perception skills
  A. Body image and self-perception
     (e.g., body-image motor activities cited above)
  B. Sensitivity to other people
     (e.g., drawing or gathering pictures of others who are expressing various emotions; analyzing body and voice communications)
  C. Social situations
     (e.g., use of pictures and stories to focus on understanding social situations and events; differentiating between real and make-believe; practicing comprehension of time, space, and direction)
X. Behavior modification techniques
     (e.g., monitoring behavior; systematic use of reinforcers; modeling; precision teaching)

Appendix D

The Expert Trap[1]

What ever happened to cautious optimism, self-criticism, and professional standards?

Of course we want to provide effective services to Learning Disabled children!

Of course we want to do important research!

Of course we have expertise that makes us a valued resource to others who know little about our field!

But in offering our services, research, and training, we need to avoid the *Expert Trap*!

The expert trap is a term my colleagues and I have adopted to describe the phenomenon whereby the pressures to provide immediate answers to the public lead us to overstate our expertise—overselling the effectiveness of our services, overgeneralizing the implications of our research, dogmatically teaching theories and methods. A major symptom of this tendency to overstate is seen in what I view as the widespread and pervasive failure of professionals, especially researchers, to carefully spell out the limitations of their techniques and procedures. This is not too surprising since there is great pressure from a variety of sources to extrapolate practical implications from every bit of experience and data regarding the possible efficacy of a procedure. Unfortunately, the result is the mystification of the public and professionals alike with the concomitant abusive premature application of procedures such as has been recently experienced with regard to the use of stimulant drugs as a treatment for learning problems.

Besides the overriding ethical concerns raised by overstating our expertise, there are a number of serious negative side effects which, if ignored, will severely hamper our growth as a field. For example, the tendency to overstate expertise appears to be highly related to the tendency of our field to foster fads, "panaceas", and mystical thinking. Such fads and panaceas reflect an uncritical acceptance of what are often marginal services and thus lead to many unfullfilled promises which can result in "backlash" from a disappointed public. I believe that we are seeing such backlash in the form of the malpractice problem in medicine, the naive accountability measures being enacted related to education, the overly restrictive federally mandated guidelines for researchers, and such outcries as Schrag and Divoky's *The Myth of the Hyperactive Child*.

What is to be done?

My colleagues and I have been trying to curb this tendency in our own activities, and our experiences lead us to suggest:

(1) Professionals responsible for teacher education and graduate programs need to put greater emphasis on their students understanding that the current state of the art in the field of Learning Disabilities is still quite limited. The products of such programs need to come out with a greater appreciation that what they have learned is but a prologue to what we all still need to learn. In particular, they need to realize that not only don't we know all the answers, but as Lee Cronbach has suggested, we don't even know many of the important questions.

[1]H. S. Adelman, The expert trap. *Journal of Learning Disabilities,* 1978, *11,* 465–66.

(2) Professionals providing services and who have a direct influence on public policy and thinking, such as the leadership of BEH, DCLD, ACLD, need to take a more active role in demystifying the general public; in particular, this means at the very least a greater readiness to acknowledge limitations and to share ideas, data, and approaches with *cautious* optimism. Despite current impressions among the general public, we can't validly assess the cause of most individuals' learning problems, and we haven't satisfactory evidence of the efficacy of the intervention programs currently being offered. We have responsibility for the fact that so many people hold erroneous impressions regarding our level of expertise as individuals and as a field.

(3) Professionals who write and/or provide editorial services need to be more severe in their criticism of work being submitted for publication. Because of design, sampling, and other procedural limitations, rarely do the findings of a particular study have widespread implications, and yet the introduction and discussion sections of most studies related to learning problems seem to suggest the research is a major contribution to the state of the art and often recklessly specify immediate applications. Textbooks are an even greater problem in this connection. By uncritically synthesizing and summarizing various sources (e.g., limited research findings, naive theories, unvalidated clinical procedures) they tend to reify both the promising and worthwhile and the worthless and potentially harmful.

None of the above ways of curbing the tendency to overstate expertise need diminish our stature. Indeed, our openness and candor can accelerate the positive growth of the field by maintaining public confidence in the fact that we have the competence to train professionals (a) who can and do systematically evaluate their activities to accurately identify the strengths, weaknesses, and limitations of our field and (b) who can use this information to actively pursue the directions which need to be taken in order to advance the state of the art. Ultimately, our stature will be determined by the standards to which we adhere in this connection. As individuals who collectively comprise the field of Learning Disabilities, we need to employ the highest standards in evaluating our ability to be self-critical and to use that criticism productively in improving our service, research, and training activities.

The field is at a critical stage in its development. In the last few years, we have had a great deal of the public's "good will". This has helped us in many ways. If we don't take steps to avoid the expert trap, we are quite likely not only to lose that good will, but to experience a very painful backlash. I believe the most appropriate way to demonstrate our expertise is to take responsibility for not overstating it. This is not only an ethical stance, although the ethics of the situation should be a compelling enough reason for taking such responsibility. In the long run, it may be a most practical consideration in preventing the loss of much needed support and avoiding the enactment of overly restrictive, mandated guidelines on services and research activity which can adversely effect our efforts to advance the state of the art.

Major Choices and Concerns in Planning and Implementing Evaluation

METHODS
Evaluation Designs
Varying designs for various purposes
Threats to validity
Collecting Data and Judging Findings
What should be measured?
What criteria should be used?

ETHICAL CONCERNS
Bias in Evaluation
Iatrogenic Effects of Evaluation
Conflicts of Interest

I made one hundred and ten decisions today—all of them wrong!

In planning the evaluation of psychoeducational intervention,[1] choices and concerns arise with regard to five areas: (1) the focus of evaluation, (2) the role of various interested parties, (3) specific objectives of evaluation, (4) appropriate methodology and measures, and (5) ethical considerations (see also Table 17-1). The emphasis here is on exploring choices and concerns related to methods and ethical considerations.

METHODS

As stated in Chapter 17, there are great complexities involved in planning how to proceed and what specific procedures to use in an evaluation. The essence of what is involved can be clarified, however, by understanding (1) evaluation designs and (2) procedures and problems related to gathering data and judging findings.

Evaluation Designs
An evaluation design is the organization or overall plan for pursuing specific evaluation objectives. The design is intended to facilitate controlled measurement and unambig-

---

[1] It should be noted that most of the current emphasis on evaluation is described as *program evaluation. Program* can be used to refer to an organizational arrangement, a system of instruction, or a piece of instructional material used only with one child (Whelen, 1979). The term *program evaluation* has become widely used to refer to any educational evaluation. In practice, the term often is used to describe very specific and narrow evaluations, such as cost effectiveness of service delivery or efficacy of specific materials and techniques. Furthermore, the focus usually is on efficacy for the majority, thus overlooking subtle variations due to individual and subgroup differences and problems. This type of limited evaluation contributes very little to understanding what accounts for differences in effectiveness. In this chapter, we use the term *program evaluation* only when referring to such a narrow focus.

uous interpretation by specifying the kinds of data to be gathered and the conditions that will allow for desired analyses, judgments, and generalizations.

While all programs ideally should be comprehensively evaluated using a research design, different designs are required for different evaluation situations. This is the matter to which we turn first. Then, we explore various design relevant factors that can undermine the validity of evaluation findings.

Varying designs for various purposes.   Most evaluation designs focus on a limited range of immediate outcome measures. For example, since most educational programs do not have well-delineated objectives in the affective domain, data regarding the program's impact in this area often are not collected. This is unfortunate since two programs that produce equal ability with respect to stated performance criteria may produce individuals with very different attitudes toward learning.

Moreover, at this point in the development of interventions for learning problems, it is equally important to evaluate process. The Stake evaluation model (see Figure 17-1) stresses the importance of investigating not only processes and outcomes but antecedent conditions in order to understand the intervention's impact and factors that may account for it. That is, from this perspective, an evaluation design should ensure that data are gathered (1) to determine congruence between what is intended and what occurs and (2) to investigate unintended occurrences such as incidental and serendipitous learning, changes in attitude, and negative effects.

Related to the matter of outcome evaluation is the choice of focusing on immediate or long-term outcomes. Evaluations done at the point at which intervention is completed represent minimal evidence of intervention efficacy. While most evaluators would acknowledge that long-range aims and major

VIEWPOINT

LONG-TERM IMPACT

Most psychoeducational programs are lengthy and most interventions should be planned with reference to long-range goals rather than immediate instructional objectives. Indeed, the most relevant criterion for evaluating a program's success is the long-range impact, and thus the use of immediate objectives as criteria may be misleading. For example, the positive or negative impact of something learned today may only be reflected at a later time; furthermore, the fact that something is not learned at a particular moment is not tantamount to saying that it should have been learned at that moment. It well may be that it will be more easily mastered at a subsequent time. In view of such temporal factors, it is evident that the differences between two individuals, two groups, two organizations, and so forth, may not be apparent at the conclusion of intervention, but may be very evident two years later.

goals are the ultimate and most appropriate referents for judging efficacy, follow-up studies are rare and usually not done very well because they are costly and difficult to implement.

Researchers (e.g., Campbell & Stanley, 1963; Cook & Campbell, 1979) group various designs in the categories of pre-experimental, experimental, and quasi-experimental. Pre-experimental evaluation designs are useful for suggesting new ideas but not sufficient for permitting strong tests of causal hypotheses. Such designs include one-group posttest-only designs, one-group pretest-posttest designs, and static group comparisons. These three designs are weak because of the lack of control groups, lack of pretest data (except for the one-group posttest-only design) and lack of data regarding other factors that may influence variability. In marked contrast, experimental designs are used in evaluations of interventions in which variables are systematically manipulated and their effects on other variables observed. Examples of true experimental designs include pretest-posttest control group designs, Solomon group design, and posttest-only control group designs.

Carefully controlled evaluation research, however, is likely to occur only under laboratory conditions. Therefore, evaluation researchers have had to expand design concepts to deal with the realities of applied settings. This has led to development of quasi-experimental research designs that are used when nonequivalent groups are included and random assignment is not feasible (Cook & Campbell, 1979). These types of designs are designated time series, equivalent time sample designs, equivalent materials sample designs, nonequivalent control group designs, counterbalanced designs, and separate-sample pretest-posttest designs.

Threats to validity.   Both a poor evaluation design and confounding factors can subvert valid interpretation of findings. Based on the work of Campbell and Stanley (1963), Cook and Campbell (1979) refer to three types of design-relevant threats to valid inference in evaluation: (1) ability to control the situation in which a treatment is conducted to keep out extraneous forces, (2) ability to determine which units receive a particular treatment at a particular time, and (3) ability through design, implementation, or analysis of procedures to rule out threats to valid inferences. These threats refer to extraneous variables that may affect the internal validity of the evaluation. That is, Did the treatment make a difference in this particular instance? They also may affect external validity. That is, To what population, setting, treatment variables, and measurement variables can this effect be generalized?

It is worth highlighting the problem of appropriate control and comparison groups in applied settings. The confirmation needed

FOR EXAMPLE

FACTORS JEOPARDIZING INTERNAL AND EXTERNAL VALIDITY

Cook and Campbell discuss a variety of factors jeopardizing internal and external validity. Among the factors which threaten internal validity are maturation, effects of repeated testing, changes in instrument calibration, statistical regression, selection biases, ambiguity about the direction of causal influence, compensatory rivalry by respondents receiving less desirable treatments. For example, we might want to believe that the effects of our intervention over the period of a year are responsible for the positive changes in a youngster's ability to pay attention and follow directions. We cannot ignore, however, an alternative maturational explanation. That is, the observed changes may be due to the youngster "growing older, wiser, stronger, more experienced and the like between pretest and posttest . . ." (Cook and Campbell, 1979, p.52).

Even if effects can be shown to be due to the intervention in a particular case, this is no guarantee that this intervention would be effective in other cases. Unique facts of a particular sample, setting, or history which interact with the intervention under evaluation jeopardize generalization or external validity.

If there is an interaction between, say, an educational treatment and the social class of children, then we cannot say that the same result holds across social classes. We know that it does not. Where effects of different magnitude exist, we must then specify where the effect does and does not hold and, hopefully, begin to explore when these differences exist. (Cook & Campbell, 1979, p. 73)

in evaluating effectiveness is to know what would have happened to participants if they had not been in the program. The best way to approximate this is to assign clients randomly to control and treatment groups. Because we cannot ethically deprive clients of needed services, ideal control groups are seldom available. Therefore, it is more likely that contrast groups are used. Thus, participants in a given treatment are compared to persons with similar characteristics participating in alternative interventions. The absence of appropriate comparison (control, contrast) groups can make it virtually impossible to use collected data to answer questions of major concern.

Collecting Data and Judging Findings

Two of the most vexing evaluation concerns are choosing measures and establishing appropriate criteria for interpreting data. Underlying these seemingly practical choices are a multitude of sociopolitical issues.

What should be measured?   The breadth of possible assessment and thus evaluation measures is outlined in Tables 6–1 and 8–2. As discussed in Chapter 5, the types of procedures used may be standardized, or unstandardized instruments such as interviews and written personal reports, observations, verbal and performance measures, biological tests, and analyses of available records and data. In practice, these procedures may vary from normative to personalized, vary in the degree of involvement of those being evaluated, and vary in terms of stimulus and response conditions (see Table 5–1). The most commonly used measures for evaluating psychoeducational interventions appear to be paper and pencil tests of ability, self-reports, ratings, systematic observations, interviews, and performance tests (Popham, 1975).

The limits of current measurement capability raise questions as to the technical adequacy (i.e., reliability and validity) of available data. The specificity (or lack thereof) of clearly stated goals and objectives raises concerns about the criteria and standards used in interpreting data. For evaluation purposes, it is important that the concrete, observable, and measurable facets of intervention aims be delineated. The observ-able facets of specific objectives become the first level of criteria for evaluation. However, the problems associated with evaluating only these facets deserve consideration so their impact can be understood and, if possible, minimized.

As suggested above, accountability pressures on psychoeducational interveners have led to overemphasis on measuring immediate outcomes for which there already are available measures. While it is preferable to use standardized instruments whenever possible, most available measures not only have a narrow content focus, but are limited by important reliability and validity constraints (see Chapter 5 and Appendix A). It is practically impossible to translate a broad rationale and many long-term aims into easily observable behaviors. Consequently, facets of a program's rationale are not readily measureable (e.g., self-concept, attitudes toward learning, expectancies, problem-solving capabilities, creativity).

Further complications in measurement arise from the impact of individual difference variables. A procedure may prove to be more effective for an individual with a certain history of success and failure than for a person with a different pattern. If the effects of individual differences are great, the data may need to be viewed in an interactional perspective, that is, with regard to what types of interventions are most effective with what types of learners. This is a major limitation on understanding and generalizing evaluation findings.

Since there is a significant possibility that unintended outcomes may occur, objective assessment of such outcomes is of critical importance. While unintended positive effects are delightful to find and do not cause problems, negative effects do. Anderson and Ball (1978) believe evaluators are becoming more sensitive to such possible effects. In alerting professionals to types of negative effects that deserve to be addressed, they refer to three classes of effects: "drop-out (client drop out, program personnel turnover), attitudes (of those who receive the program, those who deliver it, and those who are excluded from it for one reason or another), transfer effects (to other content areas or areas of activity)" (p.30). Other examples of possible negative effects of major concern in interventions for learning problems are drug dependency and negative physical effects of stimulant drugs used in treatment of hyperactivity, the development of dependency in programs that overrely on one-to-one tutoring models, and the compounding of developmental deficits for students removed from mainstream programs.

What criteria should be used?   Criteria appropriate for judging intervention effectiveness are reflected by such questions as: How large an effect is needed to decide whether the intervention outcome is greater than chance or no effect? Will the results generalize if the program is continued or applied in different settings? Are the outcomes large enough to warrant policy decisions and commitment of resources on an ongoing, long-term basis? (Rossi et al., 1979). In this connection, appropriate comparison groups and stringent tests of statistical significance are necessary.

Ultimately, evaluation questions have to do with whether an intervention should be modified, continued, or terminated. Some of the criteria used for making such decisions are political. They go beyond the data on intervention effectiveness per se and reflect prevailing political policies and priorities. The evaluation data from one particular program or a set of similar programs may be factors in the decision to fund or terminate a general type of intervention on a local or national level. Influencing decisions at these levels are fiscal matters, political philosophy, pragmatics, and special criteria valued by those in power. For example, accountability pressures have led to a trend (e.g., on the

VIEWPOINT

POLITICAL CONTEXT FOR JUDGING FINDINGS

Evaluation, as some recent commentators have pointed out, produces information which is at least potentially relevant to decision-making (Stufflebeam, 1967; Guba, 1968). Decision-making, of course, is a euphemism for the allocation of resources—money, position, authority, etc. Thus, to the extent that information is an instrument, basis, or excuse for changing power relationships within or among institutions, evaluation is a political activity.
Cohen (1972, pp. 139–39)

part of legislatures) to judge a program's benefits in terms of immediately measurable academic improvement. In some instances, it has been suggested that the amount of improvement should be judged with reference to whether it warrants the fiscal expenditure per teacher and per pupil. On the surface such criteria may appear to be reasonable. However, in light of current limited knowledge regarding effective strategies for educating many groups of children, e.g., exceptional children, this level of evaluation is probably premature and is certainly not comprehensive enough.

A broad perspective for judging intervention efficacy requires understanding the total range of content and outcomes being pursued. As long as interveners specify only a narrow range of outcomes to satisfy accountability requirements, a broad perspective will not be available.

Comprehensive evaluation requires careful planning and a financial commitment. Unfortunately, it often is difficult to gain acceptance for inclusion of meaningful evaluation activity in program budgets. Evaluation competes for scarce financial resources. Overhead costs for qualified evaluation personnel, material, and resources can be a

FOR EXAMPLE

UNINTENDED OR NEGATIVE EFFECTS

With respect to goal orientation, students learn more in classes that emphasize difficulty and competition, but these classes also have high absenteeism rates. Task orientation and competition encourage cognitive growth for some students, but for others they can result in absenteeism, poor grades, and an increased chance of dropping out. Furthermore, attention to academic tasks and extrinsic rewards (such as grades) can have the opposite of the intended effect; that is, it may decrease interest in the material outside of class and inhibit intrinsic motivation to learn, particularly for achievement oriented students (Maehr, 1976). Individual competition, at least as typically implemented in classrooms, can be ineffective for many students. Low-ability students who need to try hardest are given the least incentive to do so. Less able students experience more failure in competitive reward structures and therefore are more anxious, less self-assured, and less likely to benefit from mistakes, because they often hide them to avoid ridicule. Johnson and Johnson (1974) argued that these students will become oriented toward avoiding failure, will perform more poorly in subsequent competition, will try to obstruct other students' academic accomplishments, and eventually will become less achievement oriented.

Moos (1979, p. 199)

significant part of intervention planning and budgeting. If evaluation results are to be widely disseminated, the costs can run even higher. Because of the costs, evaluation usually remains a token item in many budgets. While costly, evaluation need not be prohibitively expensive. That is, there are many ways to reduce costs, such as sampling if a large population is being studied, using existing appropriate validated instruments when possible rather than developing new ones, gearing small-scale evaluations to size by using already existing procedures, and carefully evaluating the need for computer access and analyses (Stake, 1976).

ETHICAL CONCERNS

Many of the negative effects discussed with regard to assessment and corrective interventions can arise as a result of evaluation, since it too is an intervention. Therefore, ethically, evaluators also must be concerned about various sources of bias, about poten-

tial iatrogenic effects stemming from evaluation itself, and about conflicts of interest.

Bias in Evaluation

The prevailing assumption shaping most evaluations of psychoeducational intervention is that positive intended outcomes are the primary and often sufficient objective of evaluation. This assumption parallels the presumption of many interveners that their actions are unquestionably helpful and not harmful. Its impact is twofold: it limits the focus to a narrow range of positive outcomes and de-emphasizes evaluation of negative effects. This impact is even greater in evaluating intervention for learning and behavior problems because focus is narrowed to positive outcomes in designated problem areas.

Limiting the focus to a narrow range of positive outcomes prevents analyses of whether negative effects outweigh positive gains. In addition, differences among interventions with regard to unspecified positive outcomes are ignored, preventing evaluation of which interventions provide the most benefits.

On the other hand, we recognize there are times evaluators are interested in investigating the inadequacies of an intervention. This occurs when an agency has the responsibility to evaluate and uncover negative side effects, for example, for drug treatments, or when an evaluator is sent out to justify terminating a program that is in disfavor politically. Under such circumstances, the ethical concern obviously is that negative facets will be overstressed and positives underemphasized.

In general, all biasing assumptions shaping the data gathered and their interpretation and use reflect the perspectives of those who underwrite, plan, and implement the evaluation. Of critical importance in this connection is the impact of society as an interested party. For example, Weiss (1975) suggests

> Political considerations intrude in three major ways and the evaluator who fails to recognize their presence is in for a series of shocks and frustrations. First, the policies and programs with which evaluation deals are the creatures of political decisions. . . . Second, because evaluation is undertaken in order to feed into decision-making, its reports enter the political arena . . . Third, . . . evaluation itself has a political stance [and] makes implicit political statements about such issues as the problematic nature of some programs, and the unassailableness of others, the legitimacy of program strategies, the utility of strategies of incremental reform." (pp. 13–14)

In choosing what they look at, how they look, what they see, and what they report, most evaluators are strongly influenced by the society's values, policies, priorities, and rewards. These influences, of course, usually are mediated by the predilections of those who employ the evaluator and by the evaluator's personal and professional code of

FOR EXAMPLE
POLITICS AND EVALUATION

The controversial history of evaluating "Head Start" in the USA reflects the ethical dilemma that evaluators can find themselves in when interventions embody popular ideology. This prevention program was a response to a rising social awareness regarding both civil rights and educational needs of children of poverty. At the time of implementation the programs were undisputedly appropriate and favored by the populace and their political representatives.

The first evaluation of the program, however, was unfavorable and particularly questioned lasting effects. A less popular program probably would have experienced reduced funding or termination. Instead a phalanx of experts launched major evaluations of the evaluation. They criticized it for methodological design and measurement problems. The initial evaluators conceded some of the methodological criticism. At the same time, they stressed they had operated under restrictions preventing ideal design. "Nevertheless, it appears likely that the critisism was motivated more by ideology than by methodology—that critics wanted to protect a popular program. Had the evaluation results been favorable, it is hard to imagine a similar outcry." (Weiss, 1972b, p. 115).

Whatever the merits, or lack thereof, of the various evaluations of Head Start, the ongoing scenario represents an intriguing example of political and ethical dilemmas in evaluation.

ethics and values, favored models, and so forth.

As long as biases reflect prevailing attitudes, values, beliefs, and policies, they are unlikely to be seen as producing errors. When such biases are challenged, those who hold them may grant that alternative views can be used in interpreting the findings. After all, they say, there are always competing orientations and perspectives. We think this way of resolving the matter bates the issue and encourages perpetuation of fads, panaceas, and naive eclecticism. All biases should not be viewed as competing perspectives; some competing perspectives are not valid. All sources of systematic bias in evaluation must be recognized and either eliminated, minimized and guarded against, or appropriately justified.

Iatrogenic Effects of Evaluation

Evaluators must be aware of the range of iatrogenic effects their practices can produce, take steps to minimize these effects, inform those who may be affected, and determine whether evaluation benefits outweigh costs. Among the common iatrogenic effects are such abuses as failure to get informed consent, infringements on privacy, overselling of expertise, and misuses of findings. Also, any assessment procedure used in evaluation may produce distress reactions; the ethical evaluator should anticipate such reactions and introduce appropriate safeguards.

On another level, there is concern over the shaping influence evaluation can have on specific interventions, on the learning disabilities field, and on society in general. For example, programs for learning and behavior problems increasingly appear to be reflecting the narrow scope of available evaluation measures rather than broad rational aims. As a result, programs often are maintained and expanded inappropriately, and the reasons for a student's ongoing problems frequently are misidentified.

VIEWPOINT

SHAPING INFLUENCE OF EVALUATION

Elementary school students almost invariably regard mathematics as the most important subject in the curriculum—not because of its elegance, but because math has the most homework, because the homework is corrected the most promptly, and because tests are given more frequently than in any other subject. The youngsters regard spelling as the next most important subject, because of the frequency of spelling tests. "To a pupil," Professor White explains, "the workload and evaluation demands obviously must reflect what the teacher thinks is important to learn."
Silberman (1970, p. 147)

Perhaps the most devastating iatrogenic effect of professional evaluation of programs has been the tendency of teachers and students to surrender evaluation responsibility. This trend makes little sense ethically or practically. The facts are that (1) the sampling, design, and measurement capabilities of professional evaluators in this area are not very sophisticated or comprehensive and (2) nonparticipants are not necessarily more "objective" or accurate than participants in their evaluations. Students, in particular, should be encouraged to improve their ability to self-evaluate and actively participate in making decisions.[2]

---

[2]There are obvious problems with client self-reports and self-ratings. For example, research suggests that (a) students with learning problems tend to underestimate the severity of their problems (e.g., Adelman et al., 1979) and (b) individuals generally tend to attribute the causes of success to internal factors, such as skill and ability, and the causes of failure to external factors, such as task difficulty and interferences from others in the environment (e.g., Compas, Friedland-Bandes, Bastien, & Adelman, 1981). The reasons for these biases may be due to the nature of the information available to the individual or may be motivated by psychological self-protection, or both. Despite these problems it is hard to justify neglecting self-reports since they represent an important evaluative perspective. The recent development of cognitive behavior modification strategies with children (e.g., self-instruction) emphasizes self-evaluation and self-monitoring as important components in both intervention planning and ongoing evaluation. How this will affect the student's stated perceptions is an intriguing question for research.

Perhaps the most ironic iatrogenic effect of current evaluation practices has been the backlash to program evaluation efforts. This reaction is not only a self protective stance, but a response to the inadequacies of many facets of evaluation efforts. It must be recognized, however, that the inadequacies of evaluation do not justify abandoning evaluation efforts.

Conflicts of Interest

Psychological and educational interventions often begin with broad goals that everyone supports, such as teaching students to read, reducing behavior problems, or providing a supportive environment for positive change. After a time, however, differences in opinion often arise and those initially in agreement may end up adversaries. This change usually reflects the realization by various interested parties that the broad goals are not being pursued in the specific ways they had anticipated. That is, as different evaluative criteria are applied, those involved often find they disagree about specific changes and timetables. The more diverse the perspectives of the involved parties, the more conflict. This is what has occurred in relation to such psychoeducational programs as "third party"-payments—from public funds and insurance companies—which have become common.

Given the range of interested parties in most evaluations of intervention effectiveness, the probability of frequent conflicts of values and interests is quite high. For example, it is not uncommon for teachers and their students to be convinced that an intervention for a learning problem is effective while an outside evaluator concludes that progress is insufficient and continuation of the program is unwarranted. As with all interventions, this raises the ethical concern over whose perspective should prevail—that of teachers, students, parents, society, or perhaps that of an independent "objective" evaluator.[3] It also raises concern about how conflicts should be ethically resolved.

Evaluators obviously must favor not vested interests, but objectivity and professional ethics and standards for practice. Unfortunately, very difficult ethical dilemmas often arise in absence of a strong knowledge base concerning what is being evaluated and the evaluation itself.

Other dilemmas arise when conflicts are between competing vested interests. In such instances, control is usually retained by those with greatest authority in the situation. Perhaps the ultimate in such conflicts occurs when the rights and liberties of individuals are challenged by society. Evaluators frequently find themselves enmeshed in such conflicts and confronted with the ethical dilemma of whose rights they should support. For instance, evaluators hired by government agencies or supported by public funds have an ethical requirement to fulfill their contracts. However, they may feel it is unethical to do so if it becomes clear that the policies that led to the evaluation, or the way the findings will be used, are antithetical to certain values the evaluator holds about the respective rights of the society and the individual.

In general, evaluators need to be concerned about who initiated the evaluation, why it was initiated, and the potential audiences and uses they have for the information (e.g., clients seeking refunding, funding

---

[3]In a radical move to enhance evaluation objectivity and free evaluation from its narrow focus, Scriven (1972) proposed a model of goal-free evaluation. He suggested evaluators enter a setting "blind" to the specific plans and objectives of the interveners and instead assess processes and outcomes using a checklist sensitive to a wide range of indications of effectiveness. Stake (1976) and others have raised major issues—some ethical—related to this proposal.

agencies seeking to justify termination, media seeking an exposé of fiscal misappropriation). Clarifying as fully as possible the audience and use of the data is an important contractual step for the evaluator and those being evaluated. This is a particularly important step whenever economic and political considerations are prominently involved.

Evaluators need to understand that evaluation is fundamentally a sociopolitical process. "Evaluation is implicit in all social orders," says Sjoberg (1979).

A society's status or stratification system rests upon some form of evaluation. Men and women are evaluated in one way or another throughout their entire lifetime. And this evaluation process is fraught with tensions and dilemma . . . . I would not impose upon social life an evaluation process that demands uniformity or unidimensionality . . . . Ultimately, I am more concerned with the consequences of evaluation than with the narrow technical proficiency that has all too frequently dominated efforts in this significant social realm. (pp. 33–49)

References

ABROMS, K. I. Service delivery networks. In K. I. Abroms & J. W. Bennett (Eds.), *Issues in genetics and exceptional children*. San Francisco: Jossey-Bass, 1981.

ADAMS, J. S. Inequity in social exchange. In L. Berkowitz (Ed.), *Advances in experimental psychology*, Vol. 2. New York: Academic Press, 1965.

ADAMS, S., & ORGEL, M. *Through the mental health maze: A consumer's guide to finding a psychotherapist, including a sample consumer/therapist contract.* Washington, D.C.: Public Citizen's Health Group, 1975.

ADELMAN, H. S. Reinforcing effects of adult nonreaction on expectancy of underachieving boys. *Child Development*, 1969, *40*, 111–22.

ADELMAN, H. S. Learning problems: Part I, An interactional view of causality. *Academic Therapy*, 1970–71, 6. 117–23.

ADELMAN, H. S. Learning problems: Part II, A sequential and hierarchical approach to identification and correction. *Academic Therapy*, 1971, *VI*, 287–92.

ADELMAN, H. S. Competency-based training in education: A conceptual view. Monograph published by ERIC (ED 090214), 1974a.

ADELMAN, H. S. Facilitating educational change and preparing change agents. Monograph published by ERIC (ED 090207), 1974b.

ADELMAN, H. S. The concept of intrinsic motivation: Implications for practice and research with the learning disabled. *Learning Disability Quarterly*, 1978a, *1*, 43–54.

ADELMAN, H. S. Predicting psychoeducational problems in childhood. *Behavioral Disorders*, 1978b, *3*, 148–59.

ADELMAN, H. S. Diagnostic classification of learning problems: Some data. *American Journal of Orthopsychiatry*, 1978c, *48*, 717–26.

ADELMAN, H. S. The expert trap. *Journal of Learning Disabilities*, 1978d, *11*, 10–12.

ADELMAN, H. S. Diagnostic classification of LD: Research and ethical perspectives as related to practice. *Learning Disabilities Quarterly*, 1979, *2*, 5–16.

ADELMAN, H. S., & CHANEY, L. A. Impact of motivation on task performance of children with and without psychoeducational problems. *Journal of Learning Disabilities*, 1982, *15*, 242–44.

ADELMAN, H. S., & COMPAS, B. Stimulant drugs and learning problems. *Journal of Special Education*, 1977, *11*, 377–416.

ADELMAN, H. S., & FESHBACH, S. Predicting reading failure: Beyond the readiness model. *Exceptional Children*, 1971, *37*, 349–54.

ADELMAN, H. S., & FESHBACH, S. Early identification of children with learning problems: Some methodological and ethical concerns. Paper presented at the meeting of the Society for Research in Child Development, Denver, April, 1975.

ADELMAN, H. S. & TAYLOR, L. Two steps toward improving learning for students with (and without) "learning problems." *Journal of Learning Disabilities*, 1977, *10*, 455–61.

ADELMAN, H. S., & TAYLOR, L. Learning problems and the Fernald laboratory: Beyond the Fernald techniques. Presented at the World Conference of the Council for Exceptional Children, Stirling, Scotland, 1978a.

ADELMAN, H. S., & TAYLOR, L. Problem solving as a model for intervention. Paper presented at the annual meeting of the Association for Children with Learning Disabilities, Kansas City, 1978b.

ADELMAN, H. S., & TAYLOR, L. Initial psychoeducational assessment and related consultation. *Learning Disabilities Quarterly*, 1979, *2*, 52–64.

ADELMAN, H.S., & TAYLOR, L. Toward integrating intervention theory, research, and practice. In S. Pfeiffer (Ed.), *Clinical child psychology: Contemporary perspectives*. New York: Grune & Stratton, in press.

ADELMAN, H., TAYLOR, L., FULLER, W., & NELSON, P. Discrepancies among student, parent and teacher ratings of the severity of a student's problems. *American Educational Research Journal*, 1979, *16*, 38–41.

ADELMAN, H. S., ZIMMERMAN, I. L., & SPERBER, Z. Psychological testing in the schools: A position paper. In E. P. Torrance & W. F. White (Eds.), *Issues and advances in educational psychology*. Itasca, Ill.: Peacock, 1969.

ALDERFER, C. P. Organization development. *Annual Review of Psychology*, 1977, *28*, 197–223.

ALGOZZINE, B. The emotionally disturbed child: Disturbed or disturbing? *Journal of Abnormal Child Psychology*, 1977, *5*, 205–11.

ALGOZZINE, B., & YSSELDYKE, J. E. Special education services for normal children: Better safe than sorry? *Exceptional Children*, 1981, *48*, 238–43.

ALSCHULER, A. S., TABOR, D., & MCINTYRE, J. *Teaching achievment motivation*. Middletown, Conn.: Educational Ventures, 1970.

ALTMAN, I. *The environment and social behavior*. Monterey, Calif.: Brooks-Cole, 1975.

ALTMAN, I., & HAYTHORN, W. W. The ecology of isolated groups. *Behavioral Sciences*, 1967, *12*, 169–82.

AMERICAN PSYCHIATRIC ASSOCIATION. *Diagnostic and statistical manual of mental disorders*, 3rd ed.

(D.S.M. III). Washington, D.C.: American Psychiatric Association, 1980.

AMERICAN PSYCHOLOGICAL ASSOCIATION. Ethical principles of psychologists. *American Psychologist*, 1981, *36*, 633–38.

AMERICAN PSYCHOLOGICAL ASSOCIATION, AMERICAN EDUCATIONAL RESEARCH ASSOCIATION, & NATIONAL COUNCIL ON MEASUREMENT IN EDUCATION. *Standards for educational and psychological tests*. Washington, D.C.: American Psychological Association, 1974.

ANASTASI, A. (Ed.). *Testing problems in perspective*. (Twenty-fifth anniversary volume of topical readings from the invitational conference on testing problems.) American Council on Education, 1966.

ANDERSON, C. *Society pays: The high costs of minimal brain damage in America*. New York: Walker, 1972.

ANDERSON, S. B., & BALL, S. *The profession and practice of program evaluation*. San Francisco: Jossey-Bass, 1978.

APTER, S. J., *Troubled children/troubled systems*. New York: Pergamon Press, 1982.

ARTER, J. A., & JENKINS, J. R. Examining the benefits and prevalence of modality considerations in special education. *Journal of Special Education*, 1977, *11*, 281–98.

ARTER, J. A., & JENKINS, J. R. Differential diagnosis—Prescriptive teaching: A critical appraisal. *Review of Educational Research*, 1979, *49*, 517–55.

ASHTON-WARNER, S. *Teacher*. New York: Simon & Schuster, 1963.

ATKINSON, J. W. *An introduction to motivation*. Princeton, N.J.: D. Van Nostrand, 1964.

AUERBACH, M., & BOGUE, T. *Getting yours: A consumer's guide to obtaining your medical record*. Washington, D.C.: Public Citizen's Health Research Group, 1978.

AUSUBEL, N. (Ed.). Applied psychology. In *A treasury of Jewish folklore*. New York: Crown, 1948.

AYRES, A. J. Patterns of perceptual-motor dysfunction in children: A factor analytic study. *Perceptual and Motor Skills*, 1965, *20*, 235–368.

AYRES, A. J. *Sensory integration and learning disorders*. Los Angeles: Western Psychological Services, 1973.

BADIAN, N. A. Early prediction of academic underachievement. Paper presented at the meeting of the 54th Annual International Convention of the Council for Exceptional Children, Chicago, 1976. (ERIC Document Reproduction Service No. ED 122 500).

BAGNATO, S. J. Developmental diagnostic reports: Reliable and effective alternatives to guide individualized intervention. *Journal of Special Education*, 1981, *15*, 65–76.

BALDRIDGE, V. J. Organizational change: The human relations perspective versus the political systems perspective. *Educational Researcher*, 1972, *1*, 4–10, 15.

BALOW, B. Perceptual-motor activities in the treatment of severe reading disability. *The Reading Teacher*, 1971, *24*, 513–25.

BALOW, H., HOGAN, T. P., FARR, R. C., & PRESCOTT, G. A. *Metropolitan Achievement tests: Language instructional battery*. New York: Psychological Corporation, 1978.

BANDURA, A. Behavior theory and the models of man. *American Psychologist*, 1974, *29*, 859–69.

BANDURA, A. *Social learning theory*. Englewood Cliffs, N.J.: Prentice-Hall, 1977a.

BANDURA, A. Self-efficacy: Toward a unifying theory of behavioral change. *Psychological Review*, 1977b, *84*, 191–215.

BANDURA, A. The self system in reciprocal determinism. *American Psychologist*, 1978, *33*, 344–58.

BANDURA, A. Self-efficacy mechanism in human agency. *American Psychologist*, 1982, *37*, 122–47.

BANDURA, A., & WALTERS, R. H. *Adolescent aggression*. New York: Ronald Press, 1959.

BARATZ, S. S., & BARATZ, J. C. Early childhood intervention: The social science base of institutional racism. *Harvard Educational Review*, 1970, *40*, 29–50.

BARCLAY, J. Needs assessment. In H. J. Walberg (Ed.), *Evaluating Educational Performance*, Berkeley, Calif.: McCutchan, 1974.

BARKER, R. G. *Ecological psychology: Concepts and methods for studying the environment of human behavior*. Stanford, Calif.: Stanford University Press, 1968.

BARSCH, R. *Achieving perceptual-motor efficiency: A space-oriented approach to learning*. Seattle: Special Child Publications, 1967.

BARTLETT, F. C. *Remembering*. Cambridge, England: Cambridge University Press, 1932.

BATEMAN, B. Three approaches to diagnosis and educational planning for children with learning disabilities. *Academic Therapy Quarterly*, 1967, *2*, 215–22.

BAUMRIND, D. Reciprocal rights and responsibilities in parent-child relations. *Journal of Social Issues*, 1978, *34*, 179–96.

BAZELTON, D. L. Veils, values, and social responsibility. *American Psychologist*, 1982, *37*, 115–21.

BEAUCHAMP, T. L., & CHILDRESS, J. F. *Principles of biomedical ethics*. New York: Oxford University Press, 1979.

BECKER, H. S. *Outsiders: Studies in the sociology of deviance*. New York: Free Press, 1963.

BEEBY, C. E. *The meaning of evaluation*. Paper presented at Evaluation Conference, Dept. of Education, Wellington, New Zealand (as cited in Wolf, 1979).

BEECHER, H. K. The powerful placebo. *Journal of the American Medical Association*, 1955, *159*, 1602–06.

BEERY, K. E., & BUKTENICA, N. *Developmental test of visual-motor integration*. Chicago: Follett, 1967.

BELL, B. A. (Coordinator). *System FORE*. Los Angeles: Foreworks, 1972.

BELLAK, C., & BELLAK, S. *Children's apperception test*. New York: C. P. S., 1965.

BEM, D. J., & ALLEN, A. On predicting some of the people some of the time: The search for cross-situational consistencies in behavior. *Psychological Review*, 1974, *81*, 506–20.

BENDER, L. A visual-motor gestalt test and its clinical use. *American Orthopsychiatric Association Research Monograph*, 1938, *3*.

BENDER, L. Childhood schizophrenia: Clinical study of one hundred schizophrenic children. *American Journal of Orthopsychiatry*, 1947, *17*, 40–55.

BENDER, L. Neuropsychiatric disturbances. In A. H.

Keeney & V. T. Keeney (Eds.), *Dyslexia*, St. Louis: Masby, 1968.

BENEDICT, R. *Patterns of culture.* Boston: Houghton Mifflin, 1934.

BENJAMIN, H. *The cultivation of idiosyncracy.* Cambridge, Mass.: Harvard University Press, 1949.

BENNETT, N. *Teaching styles and pupil progress.* Cambridge, Mass.: Harvard University Press, 1976.

BENNIS, W. G., BENNE, K. D., & CHIN, R. (Eds.). *The planning of change,* 2nd ed. New York: Holt, Rinehart & Winston, 1969.

BENTLEY, R. R., & STARRY, A. R. *The Purdue teacher evaluation scale.* Lafayette, Ind.: Purdue Research Foundation, Purdue University, 1970.

BENTON, A. L. *The revised Benton visual retention test.* New York: Psychological Corp., 1963.

BERGIN, A. E. The evaluation of therapeutic outcomes. In A. E. Bergin & S. L. Garfield (Eds.), *Handbook of psychotherapy and behavior change: An empirical analysis,* New York: Wiley, 1971.

BERGIN, A. E., & LAMBERT, M. J. The evaluation of therapeutic outcomes. In S. L. Garfield & A. E. Bergin (Eds.), *Handbook of psychotherapy and behavior change: An empirical analysis,* 2nd ed. New York: Wiley, 1978.

BERLINER, D. C., & CAHEN, L. S. Trait-treatment interaction and learning. In F. N. Kerlinger (Ed.), *Review of Research in Education,* Vol. 1. Itasca, Ill.: Peacock, 1973.

BERLYNE, D. *Conflict, arousal, and curiosity.* New York: McGraw-Hill, 1960.

BERLYNE, D. E. Attention as a problem in behavior theory. In D. I. Mostofsky (Ed.), *Attention: Contemporary theory and analysis.* New York: Appleton-Century-Crofts, 1970.

BERLYNE, D. E. What next? Concluding summary. In H. I. Day, D. E. Berlyne, & D. E. Hunt (Eds.), *Intrinsic motivation: A new direction in education,* Toronto: Holt, Rinehart & Winston, 1971.

BERMAN, P., & MCLAUGHLIN, M. *Federal programs supporting educational change: Factors affecting implementation and continuation* Vol. 7. Santa Monica, Calif.: Rand Corporation, 1977.

BERMANT, G., & WARWICK, D. P. The ethics of social intervention: Power, freedom, and accountability. In G. Bermant, H. C. Kelman, & D. P. Warwick (Eds.), *The ethics of social intervention.* Washington, D. C.: Hemisphere, 1978.

BERNE, E. *Games people play.* New York: Grove, 1964.

BERSCHIED, E., & WALSTER, E. Physical attractiveness. In L. Berkowitz (Ed.) *Advances in experimental psychology* Vol. 7. New York: Academic Press, 1974.

BIERMAN, R. Dimensions of interpersonal facilitation in psychotherapy and child development. *Psychological Bulletin,* 1969, *72,* 338-52.

BIKLEN, D. Consent as a cornerstone concept. In J. Mearig & Associates (Ed.), *Working for children: Ethical issues beyond professional guidelines.* San Francisco: Jossey-Bass, 1978.

BLOOM, B. S., ENGLEHART, M. D., FURST, E. J., HILL, W. H., & KRATHWOHL, D. R. *Taxonomy of educational objectives: Handbook I: Cognitive domain.* New York: McKay, 1956.

BLOOM, R. *Stability and change in human characteristics.* New York: Wiley, 1964.

BOEHM, A. *Boehm Test of Basic Concepts.* New York: Psychological Corporation, 1970.

BOGGIANO, A. K., & RUBLE, D. N. Competence and the overjustification effect: A developmental study. *Journal of Personality and Social Psychology,* 1979, *37,* 1462-68.

BORING, E. G. The role of theory in experimental psychology. *American Journal of Psychology,* 1953, *66,* 169-84.

BOWER, E. M. *Early identification of emotionally handicapped children in school.* Springfield, Ill.: Charles C. Thomas, 1960.

BOWERS, K. S. Situationism in psychology: An analysis and a critique. *Psychological Review,* 1973, *80,* 307-36.

BRACHT, G. H. Experimental factors related to aptitude-treatment interactions. *Review of Educational Research,* 1970, *40,* 627-45.

BRADLEY, G. W. Self-serving biases in the attribution process: A re-examination of the fact or fiction question. *Journal of Personality and Social Psychology,* 1978, *36,* 56-71.

BRAMEL, D., & FRIEND, R. Hawthorne, the myth of the docile worker, and class bias in psychology. *American Psychologist,* 1981, *36,* 867-78.

BRAMMER, L. M. *The helping relationship: Process and skills.* Englewood Cliffs, N.J.: Prentice-Hall, 1973.

BRAMMER, L. M., & SHOSTROM, E. L. *Therapeutic psychology* (4th ed.). Englewood Cliffs, N.J.: Prentice-Hall, 1982.

BRANDT, R. M. *Studying behavior in natural settings.* New York: Holt, Rinehart & Winston, 1972.

BREHM, J. W. (Ed.). *A theory of psychological reactance.* New York: Academic Press, 1966.

BREHM, J. W. *Response to loss of freedom: A theory of psychological reactance.* Morristown, N.J.: General Learning Press, 1972.

BREHM, S. S. *The application of social psychology to clinical practice.* New York: Wiley, 1976.

BRIGANCE, A. *Brigance diagnostic inventory of basic skills.* North Billerica, Mass.: Curriculum Associates, 1977.

BRIGANCE, A. *Brigance diagnostic inventory of early development.* North Billerica, Mass.: Curriculum Associates, 1978.

BRIGANCE, A. *Brigance diagnostic inventory of essential skills.* North Billerica, Mass.: Curriculum Associates, 1980.

BRINKERHOFF, R. O. Evaluating full service special education programs. In E. L. Meyen, G. A. Vergason, & R. J. Whelan, *Instructional planning for exceptional children: Essays from focus on exceptional children.* Denver: Love Publishing Co., 1979.

BROOKOVER, W. B. (Ed.). Changing school social systems. *The Generator,* 1981, *11.*

BROWN, F. G. *Principles of educational and psychological testing,* 2nd ed. New York: Holt, Rinehart & Winston, 1976.

BRUNER, J. S. *On knowing: Essays for the left hand.* Cambridge, Mass.: Harvard University Press, 1962.

BRUNER, J. S. *Toward a theory of instruction.* Cambridge, Mass.: Belknap Press of Harvard University Press, 1966.

BRYAN, T. An observational analysis of classroom behaviors of children with learning disabilities. *Journal of Learning Disabilities*, 1974, *7*, 26–34.

BRYAN, T. H., & BRYAN, J. H. *Understanding Learning Disabilities*, 2nd ed. Sherman Oaks, Calif.: Alfred Publishing Co., 1978.

BRYANT, N. D. Recommendations for programmatic research. *Final report: Leadership Training Institute in Learning Disabilities*, Contract No. 0 EG-0-71-4425-604, U.S. Office of Education, Dept. of Special Education of the University of Arizona, Tucson: University of Arizona, 1972.

BUHLER, C., & ALLEN, M. *Introduction to humanistic psychology*. Monterey, Calif.: Brooks-Cole, 1972.

BURKE, A. A. Placement of black and white children in educable mentally handicapped classes and learning disability classes. *Exceptional Children*, 1975, *41*, 438–39.

BURKS, H. *Burks' behavior rating scales*. El Monte, Calif.: Arden Press, 1969.

BUROS, O. K. (Ed.). *Seventh mental measurements yearbook*. Highland Park, N.J.: Gryphon Press, 1972.

BUROS, O. K. (Ed.) *Tests in print II*. Highland Park, N.J.: Gryphon Press, 1974.

BUROS, O. K. (Ed.). *The eighth mental measurements yearbook*. New York: Gryphon Press, 1978.

BURTON, W. H. *The guidance of learning activities*. New York: Appleton-Century-Crofts, 1962.

BUSS, W. G., KIRP, D. L., & KURILOFF, P. J. Exploring procedural modes of special classification. In N. Hobbs (Ed.), *Issues in the classification of children*, Vol. 2. San Francisco: Jossey-Bass, 1975.

CALDER, B. J., & STAW, B. M. Self-perception of intrinsic and extrinsic motivation. *Journal of Personality and Social Psychology*, 1975, *31*, 599–605.

CALDWELL, B. M., & BRADLEY, R. H. *Home observation for measurement of the environment*. Little Rock, Ark.: University of Arkansas at Little Rock, Center for Child Development and Education, 1979.

CAMPBELL, D. T., & STANLEY, J. C. *Experimental and quasi-experimental design for research*. Chicago: Rand McNally, 1963.

CAPRON, A. Informed consent in catastrophic disease and treatment. *University of Pennsylvania Law Review*, 1974, *123*, 364–76.

CARTLEDGE, G., & MILBURN, J. F. (Eds.), *Teaching social skills to children: Innovative approaches*. New York: Pergamon, 1980.

CARTWRIGHT, C. A., & CARTWRIGHT, G. P. *Developing observation skills*. New York: McGraw-Hill, 1974.

CASSEL, R. N. *The Child Behavior Rating Scale*. Los Angeles: Western Psychological Services, 1962.

CAWLEY, J. F., FITZMAURICE, A. M., GOODSTEIN, H. A., LEPORE, A. V., SEDLAK, R., & ALTHAUS, V. *Project MATH*. Tulsa, Okla.: Education Development Corporation, 1976.

CHAFFIN, J. D. Will the real "mainstreaming" program please stand up! (or ... should Dunn have done it?) In E. L. Meyen, G. A. Vergason, & R. J. Whelan (Eds.), *Alternatives for teaching exceptional children*. Denver: Love Publishing Co., 1975.

CHALFANT, J. C. Improving the memory process. Paper presented at the annual meeting of the Association for Children with Learning Disabilities, Washington, D.C., March, 1977.

CHALFANT, J. C., & SCHEFFELIN, M. A. Central processing dysfunction in children: A review of research. *NINDS Monograph* No. 9. Bethesda, Md.: U.S. Department of Health, Education, and Welfare, 1969.

CHALL, J. S., & MIRSKY, A. F. (Eds.). *Education and the brain*. Chicago: National Society for the Study of Education, 1978.

CHASE, A. *The legacy of Malthus: The social costs of the new scientific racism*. New York: Knopf, 1977.

CHASE, S. *Guides to straight thinking*. New York: Harper & Brothers, 1956.

CHESLER, P. *Women and madness*. Garden City, N.Y.: Doubleday, 1972.

CHUN, K., COBB, S., & FRENCH, J. R. P., Jr. *Measures for psychological assessment*. Ann Arbor, Mich.: Institute for Social Research, The University of Michigan, 1975.

CLEMENTS, S. M.B.D. in children. Terminology and identification. NINDW³, Monograph #3, U.S. Department of Health, Education and Welfare, 1966.

COAN, R., & CATTELL, R. *Early School Personality Questionnaire*. Champaign, Ill.: Institute for Personality and Ability Testing, 1970.

COATES, B. White adult behavior toward black and white children. *Child Development*, 1972, *43*, 143–54.

COHEN, D. K. Politics and research: Evaluation of social action programs in education. In C. H. Weiss (Ed.), *Evaluating action programs: Readings in social action and education*. Boston: Allyn & Bacon, 1972.

COHEN, N. J., SULLIVAN, J., MINDE, K., NOVAK, C., & HELWIG, C. Evaluation of the relative effectiveness of methylphenidate and cognitive behavior modification in the treatment of kindergarten-aged hyperactive children. *Journal of Abnormal Child Psychology*, 1981, *9*, 43–54.

COLES, G. S. The learning disabilities test battery: Empirical and social issues. *Harvard Educational Review*, 1978, *48*, 313–40.

COMENIUS, J. S. *The great didactic*, 1632. Translated into English and edited by M. W. Kentinge. New York: Russell & Russell, 1967.

COMPAS, B. E., & ADELMAN, H. S. Clinicians' judgments of female clients' causal attributions. *Journal of Clinical Psychology*, 1981, *37*, 456–60.

COMPAS, B. E., ADELMAN, H. S., FREUNDL, P., NELSON, P., & TAYLOR, L. Parent and child causal attributions during clinical interviews. *Journal of Abnormal Child Psychology*, 1982, *10*, 77–84.

COMPAS, B. E., FRIEDLAND-BANDES, R., BASTIEN, R., & ADELMAN, H. S. Parent and child causal attributions related to the child's clinical problems. *Journal of Abnormal Child Psychology*, 1981, *9*, 389–97.

COMREY, A. L., BACKER, T. E., & GLASER, E. M. *A sourcebook for mental health measures*. Los Angeles: Human Interaction Research Institute, 1973.

CONDRY, J. Enemies of exploration: Self-initiated versus other-initiated learning. *Journal of Personality and Social Psychology*, 1977, *35*, 459–77.

CONE, T.E., & WILSON, L. R. Quantifying a severe discrepancy: A critical analysis. *Learning Disabilities Quarterly*, 1981, *4*, 359–71.

CONNERS, C. K. A teacher rating scale for use in drug studies with children. *American Journal of Psychiatry*, 1969, *126*, 884–88.

CONNERS, C. K. Symptom patterns in hyperkinetic, neurotic, and normal children. *Child Development*, 1970, *41*, 667–82.

CONNOLLY, C. Social and emotional factors in learning disabilities. In H. Mykelbust (Ed.), *Progress in learning disabilities*, Vol. 2. New York: Grune & Stratton, 1971.

COOK, T. D., & CAMPBELL, D. T. *Quasi-experimentation: Design and analysis issues for field settings.* Chicago: Rand McNally, 1979.

COVINGTON, M. V., & BEERY, R. C. *Self-worth and school learning.* New York: Holt, Rinehart & Winston, 1976.

COWEN, E. L., GARDNER, E. A., & ZAX, M. *Emergent approaches to mental health problems.* New York: Appleton-Century-Crofts, 1967.

CRANDALL, V. C. Achievement behavior in the young child. In W. W. Hartup (Ed.), *The young child: Reviews of research.* Washington, D.C.: National Association for the Education of Young Children, 1967.

CRATTY, B. J. *Developmental sequences of perceptual-motor tasks.* Freeport, Long Island, New York: Educational Activities, 1967.

CRATTY, B. J. *Active learning: Games to enhance academic abilities.* Englewood Cliffs, N.J.: Prentice-Hall, 1971.

CRATTY, B. J. *Intelligence in action.* Englewood Cliffs, N.J.: Prentice-Hall, 1973.

CRAVIOTO, J., & DELICARDIE, E. Environmental and nutritional deprivation in children with learning disabilities. In W. M. Cruickshank & D. P. Hallahan (Eds.), *Psychoeducational practices: Perceptual and learning disabilities in children*, Vol. I. Syracuse, N.Y.: Syracuse University Press, 1975.

CRAWFORD, J., & OTHERS. Classroom dyadic interaction: Factor structure of process variables and achievement correlates. *Journal of Educational Psychology*, 1977, *69*, 761–72.

CRINELLA, F. M. Identification of brain dysfunction syndromes in children through profile analysis: Patterns associated with so-called "minimal brain dysfunction." *Journal of Abnormal Psychology*, 1973, *82*, 33–45.

CRONBACH, L. J. The two disciplines of scientific psychology. *American Psychologist*, 1957, *12*, 671–84.

CRONBACH, L. J. How can instruction be adapted to individual differences. In R. M. Gagné (Ed.), *Learning and individual differences.* New York: Macmillan, 1967.

CRONBACH, L. J. *Essentials of psychological testing*, 3rd ed. New York: Harper & Row, 1970.

CRONBACH, L. J. Beyond the two disciplines of scientific psychology. *American Psychologist*, 1975, *30*, 116–27.

CRONBACH, L. J., & ASSOCIATES, *Toward reform of program evaluation: Aims, methods, and institutional arrangements.* San Francisco: Jossey-Bass, 1980.

CRONBACH, L. J., & GLESER, G. C. *Psychological tests and personnel decisions* (2nd ed.) Urbana, Ill.: University of Illinois Press, 1965.

CRONBACH, L. J., & SNOW, R. E. *Aptitudes and instructional methods.* New York: Irvington, 1977.

CRUICKSHANK, W. M. Least-restrictive placement: Administrative wishful thinking. *Journal of Learning Disabilities*, 1977, *10*, 193–94.

CRUICKSHANK, W. M., BENTZEN, F. A., RATZEBURG, F. H., & TANNHAUSER, M. T. *A teaching method for brain-injured and hyperactive children.* Syracuse, N.Y.: Syracuse University Press, 1961.

DAHLBERG, C., ROSWELL, F., & CHALL, J. Psychotherapeutic principles as applied to remedial reading. *The Elementary School Journal*, 1952, *53*, 213.

DALBY, J. T. Deficit or delay: Neuropsychological models of developmental dyslexia. *Journal of Special Education*, 1979, *13*, 239–64.

DARROW, H. F., & VAN ALLEN, R. *Independent activities for creative learning.* New York: Teachers College Press, 1961.

DAVIS, G. S. *Psychology of human problem solving: Theory and practice.* New York: Basic Books, 1973.

DAWES, R. M. The robust beauty of improper linear models in decision making. *American Psychologist*, 1979, *34*, 571–82.

DE CHARMS, R. *Personal causation: The internal affective determinants of behavior.* New York: Academic Press, 1968.

DE CHARMS, R. Personal causation training in the schools. *Journal of Applied Social Psychology*, 1972, *2*, 95–113.

DE CHARMS, R. *Enhancing motivation.* New York: Irvington Publishers, 1976.

DE CHARMS, R., & MUIR, M. S. Motivation: Social approaches. *Annual Review of Psychology*, 1978, *29*, 91–113.

DE HIRSCH, L., JANSKY, J., & LANGFORD, W. S. *Predicting reading failure.* New York: Harper & Row, 1966.

DE LA CRUZ, F. F., FOX, B. H., & ROBERTS, R. H. Minimal brain dysfunction. *Annals of the New York Academy of Sciences*, 1973, *205*.

DECI, E. L. Effects of externally mediated rewards on intrinsic motivation. *Journal of Personality and Social Psychology*, 1971, *18*, 105–15.

DECI, E. L. *Intrinsic motivation.* New York: Plenum Press, 1975.

DECI, E. L. *The psychology of self-determination.* Lexington, Mass.: Lexington Books, 1980.

DELACATO, C. H. *The treatment and prevention of reading problems: The neurological approach.* Springfield, Ill.: Charles C. Thomas, 1959.

DELCATO, C. H. *The diagnosis and treatment of speech and reading problems.* Springfield, Ill.: Charles C. Thomas, 1963.

DELACATO, C. H. *Neurological organization and reading.* Springfield, Ill.: Charles C. Thomas, 1966.

DELGADO, J. M. W. *Physical control of the mind: Toward a psychocivilized society.* New York: Harper & Row, 1971.

DELOACH, T. F., EARL, J. M., BROWN, B. S., POPLIN, M. S., & WARNER, M. M. LD teachers' perceptions of severely learning disabled students. *Learning Disabilities Quarterly*, 1981, *4*, 343–58.

DENO, E. Special education as developmental capital. *Exceptional Children*, 1970, *37*, 229–37.

DERR, C. B. "O.D." won't work in schools. *Education and Urban Society*, 1976, *8*, 227–41.

DESHLER, D. D. Psychoeducational aspects of learning-disabled adolescents. In L. Mann, L. Goodman, & J. L. Wiederholt (Eds.) *Teaching the learning-disabled adolescent.* Boston: Houghton Mifflin, 1978.

DEUTSCH, J. A., & DEUTSCH, D. Attention: Some theoretical considerations. *Psychological Review*, 1963, *70*, 80–90.

DEWEY, J. *The child and the curriculum.* Chicago: University of Chicago Press, 1902.

DEWEY, J. *The quest for certainty.* New York: Minton Balch & Co., 1929.

DEWEY, J. *Experience and education.* New York: Collier Books, 1938.

DEWEY, J. *Democracy and education.* New York: Macmillan, 1961.

DEWEY, J. *Lectures in the philosophy of education,* 1899. R. D. Archambault, (Ed.). New York: Random House, 1966.

DIANA v. STATE BOARD OF EDUCATION, No. C–70–37 (N.D. Cal. 1970).

DIEDRICH, P. B. A master list of types of pupil activities. *Education Research Bulletin* Vol. 15, College of Education, Ohio State University, 1936. (Reported in Burton, 1962).

DIMARCO, N. Life style, learning structure, congruence, and student attitudes. *American Educational Research Journal*, 1974, *11*, 203–09.

DOHRENWEND, B. P., & DOHRENWEND, B. S. Social and cultural influences on psychopathology. In M. R. Rosenzweig & L. W. Porter (Eds.), *Annual Review of Psychology*, Vol. 25. Palo Alto, Calif.: Annual Review, 1974.

DOLL, E. *Measurement of social competence: A manual for the Vineland social maturity scale.* Princeton, N.J.: Educational Testing Service, 1953.

DOUGLAS, V. I. Stop, look and listen: The problem of sustained attention and impulse control in hyperactive and normal children. *Canadian Journal of Behavior Science*, 1972, *4*, 259–81.

DOUGLAS, V. I. Sustained attention and impulse control: Implications tor the handicapped child. In J. A. Swets & L. L. Elliott (Eds.) *Psychology and the handicapped child.* Washington, D.C.: U.S. Department of Health, Education, and Welfare, 1974.

DREW, A. L. A neurological appraisal of familiar congenital word blindness. *Brain*, 1956, *79*, 440–60.

DUDLEY-MARLING, C. C., KAUFMAN, N. J., & TARVER, S. G. WISC and WISC-R profiles of learning disabled children: A review. *Learning Disabilities Quarterly*, 1981, *4*, 307–19.

DUFFEY, J. B., SALVIA, J., TUCKER, J., & YSSELDYKE, J. Nonbiased assessment: A need for operationalism. *Exceptional Children*, 1981, *47*, 427–34.

DUNCAN, E. R., COPPS, L. R., DOLCIANI, M. P., QUAST, W. G., & ZWENG, M. J. *Modern school mathematics: Structure and use K-6.* Boston: Houghton Mifflin, 1970.

DUNN, L. M. Special education for the mildly retarded—Is much of it justifiable? *Exceptional Children*, 1968, *35*, 5–22.

DUNN, L. M. (Ed.). *Exceptional children in the schools*, 2nd ed. New York: Holt, Rinehart & Winston, 1973.

DUNN, L., & DUNN, L. *Peabody picture vocabulary test–revised.* Circle Pines, Minn.: American Guidance Service, 1981.

DUNN, L. M., & MARKWARDT, F. C. *Peabody individual achievement test.* Circle Pines, Minn.: American Guidance Service, 1970.

DWECK, C. S. The role of expectations and attributions in the alienation of learned helplessness. *Journal of Personality and Social Psychology.* 1975, *31*, 674–85.

DWECK, C. S., & GOETZ, T. E. Attributions and learned helplessness. In J. H. Harvey, W. Ickes, & R. F. Kidd (Eds.), *New directions in attribution research* Vol. 2. Hillsdale, N.J.: Erlbaum Associates, 1978.

DYKMAN, R. A., ACKERMAN, P. T., CLEMENTS, S. D., & PETERS, J. E. Specific learning disabilities: An attentional deficit syndrome. In H. R. Myklebust (Ed.), *Progress in learning disabilities*, Vol. 2. New York: Grune & Stratton, 1971.

DYKMAN, R. A., WALLS, R., SUZUKI, T., ACKERMAN, P., & PETERS, J. E. Children with learning disabilities: Conditioning, differentiation, and the effect of distraction. *American Journal of Orthopsychiatry*, 1970, *40*, 766–81.

EBEL, R. L. The social consequences of educational testing. *College Board Review*, Winter, 1964, 10–14.

EHMAN, L. H. The American School in the political socialization process. *Review of Educational Research*, 1980, *50*, 99–120.

EINHORN, H. J., & HOGARTH, R. M. Confidence in judgment: Persistence of the illusion of validity. *Psychological Review*, 1978, *85*, 395–416.

EINSTEIN, A. *Out of my later years.* New York: Philosophical Library, 1950.

EISNER, E. W. Instructional and expressive educational objectives: Their formulation and use in curriculum. In W. J. Popham, E. W. Eisner, H. J. Sullivan, & L. L. Tyler, *Instructional objectives.* AERA Monograph Series on Curriculum Evaluation. Chicago: Rand McNally, 1969.

ELINSON, J. Effectiveness of social action programs in health and welfare. In *Assessing the effectiveness of child health services* (Report of the Fifty-sixth Ross Conference on Pediatric Research). Columbus, Ohio: Ross Laboratories, 1967.

ELLINGSON, R. J. Relationships between EEG and test intelligence: A commentary. *Psychological Bulletin*, 1966, *65*, 91–98.

ELLIS, J. W. Volunteering children: Parental commitment of minors to mental institutions. *California Law Review*, 1974, *62*, 840–916.

ELLSWORTH, R. B., MARONEY, R., KLETT, W., GORDON, H., & GUNN, R. Milieu characteristics of successful psychiatric treatment programs. *American Journal of Orthopsychiatry*, 1971, *41*, 427–41.

ELMORE, M. C. A comparison of children's use of hard cover versus soft cover library books. Unpublished manuscript. 1967.

ENDLER, N. S., & MAGNUSSON, D. (Eds.). *Interactional*

psychology and personality. Washington, D. C.: Hemisphere, 1975.

ENGELMANN, S., & BRUNER, E. *Distar reading I and II: An instructional system.* Chicago: Science Research Associates, 1969; 1974; 1975.

ENGELMANN, S., & CARNINE, D. *Distar® Arithmetic Level III.* Chicago: Science Research Associates, 1972.

ESHEL, Y., & KLEIN, Z. The effects of integration and open education on mathematics achievement in the early primary grades in Israel. *American Educational Research Journal,* 1978, *15,* 319–23.

EUSTIS, R. S. The primary etiology of specific language disabilities. *Journal of Pediatrics,* 1947, *31,* 448.

EYSENCK, H. *The scientific study of personality.* London: Routledge & Kegan Paul, 1952.

FARR, R. C., PRESCOTT, G. A., BALOW, I. H., & HOGAN, T. P. *Metropolitan achievement tests: Reading instructional battery.* New York: Psychological Corporation, 1978.

FAUST, M. Cognitive and language factors. In B. K. Keogh (Ed.), Early identification of children with potential learning problems. *Journal of Special Education,* 1970, *4,* 335–46.

FEDERAL REGISTER. U.S. Office of Education. Education of handicapped children. *Federal Register,* 1976, *41,* 52405.

FEDERAL REGISTER. U.S. Office of Education. Education of handicapped children. *Federal Register,* 1977, *42,* 65082–85.

FEINBERG, J. *Social philosophy.* Englewood Cliffs, N.J.: Prentice-Hall, 1973.

FEINGOLD, B. F. Hyperkinesis and learning disabilities linked to the ingestion of artificial food colors and flavors. *Journal of Learning Disabilities,* 1976, *9,* 551–59.

FEITLER, F. C., WEINER, W., & BLUMBERG, A. The relationship between interpersonal relations orientations and preferred classroom physical settings. Paper presented at the annual meeting of the American Educational Research Association, Minneapolis, 1970. (ERIC Document Reproduction Service. No. ED 039 173).

FELDMAN, D. H. Beyond universals: Toward a developmental psychology of education. *Educational Researcher,* 1981, *10,* 21–31.

FERGUSON, L. R. The competence and freedom of children to make choices regarding participation in research: A statement. *Journal of Social Issues,* 1978, *34,* 114–21.

FERNALD, G. M. *Remedial techniques in basic school subjects.* New York: McGraw-Hill, 1943.

FESHBACH, S., & ADELMAN, H. S. An experimental program of personalized classroom instruction in disadvantaged area schools. *Psychology in the Schools,* 1971, *8,* 114–20.

FESHBACH, S., & ADELMAN, H. S. The remediation of learning problems among the disadvantaged. *Journal of Educational Psychology,* 1974, *66,* 16–28.

FESHBACH, S., ADELMAN, H. & FULLER, W. Prediction of reading and related academic problems. *Journal of Educational Psychology,* 1977, *69,* 299–308.

FESHBACH, N. D., & FESHBACH, S. (Eds.) The changing status of children: Rights, roles, and responsibilities. *Journal of Social Issues,* 1978, *34.*

FESTINGER, L. *A theory of cognitive dissonance.* New York: Harper & Row, 1957.

FISCHOFF, B. Attribution theory and judgment under uncertainty. In J. H. Harvey, W. J. Ickes, & R. F. Kidd (Eds.), *New directions in attribution research,* Vol. 1. Hillsdale, N.J.: Lawrence Erlbaum Associates, 1976.

FLANDERS, N. A. Interaction analysis: A technique for quantifying teacher influence. In H. G. Clarizio, R. C. Craig, & W. A. Mehrens. *Contemporary issues in educational psychology,* 2nd ed. Boston: Allyn & Bacon, 1974.

FOOTE, F. M., & CRANE, M. M. An evaluation of vision screening. *Exceptional Child,* 1954, *20,* 153–61.

FOSTER, G., YSSELDYKE, J., & REESE, J. I never would have seen it if I hadn't believed it. *Exceptional Children,* 1975, *41,* 469–73.

FOUCALT, M. *Madness and civilization.* New York: Random House, 1965.

FOX, R., LUSZKI, M. B., & SCHMUCK, R. *Diagnosing classroom learning environments.* Chicago: Science Research Associates, 1966.

FOX, R. S., SCHMUCK, R., VANEGMOND, E., RITVO, M., & JUNG, C. *Diagnosing professional climates of schools.* Fairfax, Va.: NTL Learning Resources Corporation, 1975.

FRANCE, A. *The crime of Sylvestre Bonnard.* Translated by L. Hearn. New York: Harper & Brothers, 1890.

FRANK, J. *Persuasion and healing.* Baltimore: Johns Hopkins Press, 1961.

FRANKENA, W. K. *Ethics,* 2nd ed. Englewood Cliffs, N.J.: Prentice-Hall, 1973.

FRANKENBURG, W., DODDS, J., FANDALL, A., KAZUK, E. & COHRS, M. *Denver developmental screening test, reference manual, revised, 1975 edition.* Denver: LA–DOCA Project and Publishing Foundation, 1975.

FRANKS, D. J. Ethnic and social status characteristics of children in EMR and LD classes. *Exceptional Children,* 1971, *37,* 537–38.

FREEDMAN, M. H. A plea to professional psychologists. *American Psychologist,* 1965a, *20,* 877–79.

FREEDMAN, M. H. Testimony. *American Psychologist,* 1965b, *20,* 923–31.

FREEMAN, H. E., & SHERWOOD, C. C. Research in large-scale intervention programs. *Journal of Social Issues,* 1965, *21,* 11–28.

FREUND, J. H., BRADLEY, R. H., & CALDWELL, B. M. The home environment in the assessment of learning disabilities. *Learning Disabilities Quarterly,* 1979, *2,* 39–51.

FROSTIG, M., & HORNE, D. *The Frostig program for the development of visual perception: Teacher's guide.* Chicago: Follett, 1964.

FROSTIG, M., LEFEVER, W., & WHITLESEY, J. *Developmental test of visual perception.* Palo Alto, Calif.: Consulting Psychological Press, 1964.

FROSTIG, M., & MASLOW, P. Neuropsychological contributions to education. *Journal of Learning Disabilities,* 1979, *12,* 538–52.

FULLAN, M., MILES, M. B., & TAYLOR, G. Organization development in schools: The state of the art. *Review of Educational Research,* 1980, *50,* 121–84.

FULLER, B., WOOD, K., RAPOPORT, T., & DORN-BUSCH, S. M. The organizational context of individual efficacy. *Review of Educational Research*, 1982, 52, 7–30.

GADDES, W. H. *Learning disabilities and brain function: A neuropsychological approach.* New York: Springer-Verlag, 1980.

GALLAGHER, J. The future special education system. In E. Meyen (Ed.), *Proceedings—The Missouri Conference on the Categorical/Non-categorical Issue in Special Education.* Columbia, Mo.: University of Missouri Press, 1971.

GALLAGHER, J. J., & BRADLEY, R. H. Early identification of developmental difficulties. In I. J. Gordon (Ed.), *Early childhood education.* Chicago: University of Chicago Press, 1972.

GALLAGHER, P. A. *Teaching students with behavior disorders: Techniques for classroom instruction.* Denver: Love Publishing Co., 1979.

GALLAHER, JR., A. Directed change in formal organizations: The school system. In R. O. Carlson, A. Gallaher, Jr., M. B. Miles, R. J. Pellegrin, & E. M. Rogers, *Change processes in the public schools.* Eugene, Oregon: Center for the Advanced Study of Educational Administration, 1965.

GARFIELD, S. L., & BERGIN, A. E. (Eds.). *Handbook of psychotherapy and behavior change: An empirical analysis* (2nd ed.). New York: Wiley, 1978.

GARRETT, H. E. *Statistics in psychology and education.* New York: Longmans Green, 1954.

GERARD, H. D., CONOLLEY, E. S., & WILHELMY, R. A. Compliance, justification, and cognitive change. In L. Berkowitz (Ed.), *Advances in experimental social psychology* Vol. 7. New York: Academic Press, 1974.

GERSTEN, J. C., LANGNER, T. S., EISENBERG, J. G., SIM-CHA-FAGAN, O., & MCCARTHY, E. D. Stability and change in types of behavioral disturbance in children and adolescents. *Journal of Abnormal Child Psychology*, 1976, 4, 111–27.

GESCHWIND, N. Neurological foundations of language. In H. R. Myklebust (Ed.), *Progress in learning disabilities*, Vol. 1. New York: Grune & Stratton, 1968.

GESCHWIND, N. Specializations of the human brain. *Scientific American*, 1979, 241, 180–201.

GESELL, A., & AMATRUDA, C. S. *Developmental diagnosis: Normal and abnormal child development*, 2nd ed. New York: Harper & Row, 1947.

GESSELL, J. K. *Diagnostic mathematics inventory.* Monterey, Calif.: CTB/McGraw-Hill, 1977.

GETMAN, G. N. The visuomotor complex in the acquisition of learning skills. In J. Hellmuth (Ed.), *Learning disorders*, Vol. 1. Seattle: Special Child Publications, 1965.

GETMAN, G., KANE, E. R., & MCKEE, G. W. *Developing learning readiness: A visual-motor tactile skills program.* Manchester, Mo.: Webster Division, McGraw-Hill, 1968.

GETZELS, J. Images of the classroom and visions of the learner. *School Review*, 1974, 82, 527–40.

GIBSON, J. J. *The senses considered as perceptual systems.* Boston: Houghton Mifflin, 1966.

GILES, M. T., MEIER, J. H., & CAZIER, V. O. *Individual learning disabilities classroom screening instrument.* Evergreen, Colo.: Learning Pathways, Inc., 1973.

GILLINGHAM, A., & STILLMAN, B. W. *Remedial work for reading, spelling and penmanship.* New York: Sachett & Wilhelms, 1936.

GILLINGHAM, A., & STILLMAN, B. *Remedial training for children with specific disability in reading, spelling, and penmanship*, 7th ed. Cambridge, Mass.: Educators Publishing Service, 1966.

GLASER, R. Instructional psychology: Past, present, future. *American Psychologist*, 1982, 37, 292–305.

GOFFMAN, E. *Asylums: Essays on the social situation of mental patients and other inmates.* Garden City, New York: Doubleday, 1961.

GOLDBERG, L. R. Man versus model of man: A rationale, plus some evidence, for a method of improving on clinical inferences. *Psychological Bulletin*, 1970, 73, 422–32.

GOLDSTEIN, K. The modifications of behavior consequent to cerebral lesions. *Psychiatric Quarterly*, 1936, 10, 586–610.

GOLDSTEIN, K. *The organism.* New York: American Book, 1939.

GOLICK, M. She thought I was dumb, but I told her I had a . . . Learning Disability. In *Readings in Learning Disabilities*, Guilford, Conn.: Special Learning Corporation, 1978.

GOMEZ, E. H. Minimal cerebral dysfunction (Maximum neurological confusion). *Clinical Pediatrics*, 1967, 6, 589–91.

GOODLAD, J. I. *School, curriculum, and individual.* Waltham, Mass.: Blaisdell Publishing Co., 1966.

GOODLAD, J. I., KLEIN, M. F. & ASSOCIATES. *Behind the classroom door.* Worthington, Ohio: C. A. Jones Publishing Co., 1970.

GOODMAN, L., & HAMMILL, D. The effectiveness of the Kephart-Getman activities in developing perceptual-motor cognitive skills. *Focus on Exceptional Children*, 1973, 9, 1–9.

GOODWIN, L. Bridging the gap between social research and public policy: We have a case in point. *Journal of Applied Behavioral Science*, 1973, 9, 85–114.

GORDON, E. W., & SHIPMAN, S. Human diversity, pedagogy, and educational equity. *American Psychologist*, 1979, 34, 1030–36.

GORDON, I. J. *Studying the child in school.* New York: Wiley, 1966.

GOUGH, H. G. Clinical versus statistical prediction in psychology. In L. Postman (Ed.), *Psychology in the making: Histories of selected research problems.* New York: Knopf, 1962.

GOUGH, H. Some reflections on the meaning of psychodiagnosis. *American Psychologist*, 1971, 26, 160–67.

GRAHAM, F. K., & KENDALL, B. S. *Memory for designs test.* Missoula, Mont.: Psychological Test Specialist, 1960.

GREEN, O. C., & PERLMAN, S. M. Endocrinology and disorders of learning. In H. R. Myklebust (Ed.), *Progress in learning disabilities*, Vol 2. New York: Grune & Stratton, 1971.

GRESHAM, F. M. Social skills training with handicapped

children: A review. *Review of Educational Research,* 1981, *51,* 139–76.

GROTBERG, E. (Ed.) *Critical issues in research related to disadvantaged children.* Princeton, N.J.: Educational Testing Service, 1969.

GUBA, E. G. Development, diffusion, and evaluation. In T. L. Eidell & J. M. Kitchell (Eds.), *Knowledge production and utilization in educational administration.* Eugene, Oregon: University Council for Educational Administration and Center for the Advanced Study of Educational Administration, 1968.

GUILFORD, J. P. *Fundamental statistics in psychology and education.* New York: McGraw Hill, 1956.

GUILLFORD, R. *Special educational needs.* London: Routledge & Kegan Paul, 1971.

GURMAN, A. S., & RAZIN, A. M. (Eds.), *Effective psychotherapy: A handbook of research.* Oxford: Pergamon Press, 1977.

GUSKIN, S. L., BARTEL, N. R., and MACMILLAN, D. L. Perspective of the labeled child. In N. Hobbs (Ed.), *Issues in the classification of children,* Vol 2. San Francisco: Jossey-Bass, 1975.

HACKETT, M. G. *Criterion reading: Individualized learning management system.* Westminster, Md., Random House, 1971.

HAINES, D. J., & TORGENSEN, J. K. The effects of incentives on rehearsal and short-term memory in children with reading problems. *Learning Disabilities Quarterly,* 1979, *2,* 48–55.

HALEY, J. *Problem solving therapy.* San Francisco: Jossey-Bass, 1977.

HALLAHAN, D. P., & CRUICKSHANK, W. M. *Psychoeducational foundations of learning disabilities.* Engelwood Cliffs, N.J.: Prentice-Hall, 1973.

HALLAHAN, D. P., & KAUFFMAN, J. M. *Introduction to learning disabilities: A psychobehavioral approach.* Englewood Cliffs, N.J.: Prentice-Hall, 1976.

HALLECK, S. L. *The politics of therapy.* New York: Perennial Library, 1971.

HAMMILL, D., GOODMAN, L., & WIEDERHOLT, J. L. Visual-motor processes: What success have we had in training them? *The Reading Teacher,* 1974, *27,* 469–78.

HAMMILL, D. D., & LARSEN, S. C. The relationship of selected auditory perceptual skills and reading ability. *Journal of Learning Disabilities,* 1974, *7,* 40–46.

HAMMILL, D., & LARSEN, S. *Tests of written language.* Austin, Tex.: Pro-Ed, 1978.

HAMMILL, D. D., LEIGH, J. E., MCNUTT, G., & LARSEN, S. C. A new definition of learning disabilities. *Learning Disabilities Quarterly,* 1981, *4,* 336–42.

HANEY, W. Validity, vaudeville, and values: A short history of social concerns over standardized testing. *American Psychologist,* 1981, *36,* 1021–34.

HARBER, J. R. Assessing the quality of decision making in special education. *Journal of Special Education,* 1981, *15,* 77–90.

HARDY, W. G. Dyslexia in relation to diagnostic methodology in hearing and speech disorders. In J. Money, *Reading disability: Progress and research needs in dyslexia.* Baltimore: Johns Hopkins Press, 1962.

HARING, N. G., & BATEMAN, B. *Teaching the learning disabled child.* Englewood Cliffs: Prentice-Hall, 1977.

HARING, N. G., & PHILLIPS, E. L. *Educating emotionally disturbed children.* New York: McGraw-Hill, 1962.

HARING, N. G., & PHILLIPS, E. L. *Analysis and modification of classroom behavior.* Englewood Cliffs, N.J.: Prentice-Hall, 1972.

HARING, N. G., & WHELAN, R. J. Experimental methods in education and management. In N. J. Long, W. C. Morse, & R. G. Newman (Eds.), *Conflict in the classroom.* Belmont, Calif.: Wadsworth, 1965.

HARRIS, A. Lateral dominance, directional confusion and reading disability. *Journal of Psychology,* 1957, *44,* 283–94.

HARRIS, A. J., & SIPAY, E. T. *How to increase reading ability: A guide to developmental and remedial methods,* 7th ed. New York: Longman, 1980.

HARRIS, D. B. *Children's drawings as measures of intellectual maturity: A revision and extension of the Goodenough draw-a-man test.* New York: Harcourt, Brace & World, 1963.

HARTLEY, H. J. *Educational planning-programming-budgeting: A systems approach.* Englewood Cliffs, N.J.: Prentice-Hall, 1968.

HAUBRICH, V. F., & APPLE, M. W. (Eds.). *Schooling and the rights of children.* Berkeley: McCutchan, 1975.

HAVELOCK, R. G. *The change agent's guide to innovation in education.* Englewood Cliffs, N.J.: Educational Technology Publications, 1973.

HAVELOCK, R. G., & HAVELOCK, M. C. *Training for change agents.* Ann Arbor, Mi.: Center for Research on Utilization of Scientific Knowledge, Institute for Social Research, University of Michigan, 1973.

HEIDER, F. Social perception and phenomenal causality. *Psychological Review,* 1944, *51,* 358–74.

HEIDER, F. *The psychology of interpersonal relations.* New York: Wiley, 1958.

HENDERSON, R., BERGAN, J., & HUNT, M. Development and validation of the Henderson Environmental Learning Process Scale. *Journal of Social Psychology,* 1972, *88,* 185–96.

HERMANN, K. *Reading Disability.* Copenhagen: Munksgaard, 1959.

HERON, T. E., & SKINNER, M. E. Criteria for defining the regular classroom as the least restrictive environment for Learning Disabled students. *Learning Disabilities Quarterly,* 1981, *4,* 115–20.

HERSCH, S. P., & ROJCEWICZ. S. (Eds.). *Health care screening and developmental assessment.* Proceedings of First National Institute of Mental Health/Medical Services Administration Conference on Developmental Assessment under Medicaid's Early and Periodic Screening, Diagnosis, and Treatment Program, Washington, D.C.: U.S. Government Printing Office, 1974.

HERSEN, M., & BELLACK, A. S. (Eds.). *Behavioral assessment: A practical handbook,* 2nd ed. New York: Pergamon Press, 1981.

HETHERINGTON, R. W., GREATHOUSE, V., O'BRIEN, W., MATTHIAS, R., & WILNER, D. M. The nature of program evaluation in mental health. *Evaluation,* 1974, *2,* 78–82.

HEWETT, F. M. *The emotionally disturbed child in the classroom.* Boston: Allyn & Bacon, 1968.

HEWETT, F. M., & TAYLOR, F. D. *The emotionally disturbed child in the classroom: The orchestration of success,* 2nd ed. Boston: Allyn & Bacon, 1980.

HIERONYMUS, A. N., LINDQUIST, E. F., & HOOVER, H. D. *Iowa tests of basic skills.* Lombard, Ill.: Riverside Publishing Co., 1978.

HINSHELWOOD, J. *Congenital word-blindness.* London: H. K. Lewis, 1917.

HOBBS, N. Ethics in clinical psychology. In B. B. Wolman (Ed.), *Handbook of clinical psychology.* New York: McGraw-Hill, 1965.

HOBBS, N. An interview. *The Directive Teacher,* 1979, *1,* 8–9.

HOBBS, N. *The futures of children: Categories, labels, and their consequences.* San Francisco: Jossey-Bass, 1975a.

HOBBS, N. (Ed.) *Issues in the classification of children,* 2 vols. San Francisco: Jossey-Bass, 1975b.

HOGAN, T. P., FARR, R. C., PRESCOTT, G. A., & BALOW, I. H. *Metropolitan achievement tests: Mathematics instructional battery.* New York: Psychological Corporation, 1978.

HOLAHAN, C. J. Redesigning physical environments to enhance social interactions. In R. F. Muñoz, L. R. Snowden, & J. G. Kelley and Associates, *Social and psychological research in community settings.* San Francisco: Jossey-Bass, 1979.

HOLT, J. *How children fail.* New York: Pitman Publishing, 1964.

HOLT, R. R. Formal aspects of the TAT: A neglected resource. *Journal of Projective Techniques,* 1958, *22,* 163–72.

HOLT, R. R. Diagnostic testing: Present status and future prospects. *Journal of Nervous and Mental Disease,* 1967, *144,* 444–65.

HOLT, R. R. Yet another look at clinical and statistical prediction: Or is clinical psychology worthwhile? *American Psychologist,* 1970, *25,* 337–49.

HORAN, J. J. Experimentation in counseling and psychotherapy Part I: New myths about old realities. *Educational Researcher,* 1980, 9, 5–10.

HORNER, M. S. Toward an understanding of achievement-related conflicts in women. In J. Stacey, S. Gereaud, & J. Daniels (Eds.), *And Jill came tumbling after: Sexism in American education.* New York: Dell, 1974.

HOROWITZ, P., & OTTO, D. *The teaching effectiveness of an alternative teaching facility.* Alberta, Canada: University of Alberta, 1973. (ERIC Document Reproduction Service No. ED 083 242).

HOUGH, J. B., & DUNCAN, J. K. *Teaching: Description and analysis.* Reading: Addison-Wesley Publishing Co., 1970.

HOWARD, K. I., & ORLINSKY, D. E. Psychotherapeutic processes. In P. Mussen & M. R. Rosenzweig (Eds.), *Annual Review of Psychology,* Vol. 23. Palo Alto, Calif.: Annual Reviews, Inc., 1972.

HRESKO, W. P., & REID, D. K. Five faces of cognition: Theoretical influences on approaches to learning disabilities. *Learning Disabilities Quarterly,* 1981, *4,* 238–43.

HUNT, D. E. Person-environment interaction: A challenge found wanting before it was tried. *Review of Educational Research,* 1975, *45,* 209–30.

HUNT, D. E., & SULLIVAN, E. V. *Between psychology and education.* Chicago: Dryden Press, 1974.

HUNT, J. MCV. *Intelligence and experience.* New York: Ronald Press, 1961.

HUNT, J. MCV. Intrinsic motivation and its role in psychological development. *Nebraska Symposium on Motivation,* 1965, *13,* 189–282.

HUNT, J. MCV. Toward a history of intrinsic motivation. In H. I. Day, D. E. Berlyne, & D. E. Hunt (Eds.), *Intrinsic motivation: A new direction in education.* Toronto: Holt, Rinehart & Winston, 1971.

HUSE, E. F. *Organization development and change.* New York: West Publishing Co., 1975.

HYMAN, R. T. *Ways of teaching.* Philadelphia: Lippincott, 1970.

ILG, F. L., & AMES, L. B. *School readiness: Behavior tests used at the Gesell Institute.* New York: Harper & Row, 1964.

ILLICH, I. *Deschooling society.* New York: Harper & Row, Publishers, 1970.

ILLICH, I. *Tools for conviviality.* New York: Harper & Row, Publishers, 1973.

ILLICH, I. *Medical nemesis.* New York: Pantheon Books, 1976.

ILLICH, I. *Toward a history of needs.* New York: Pantheon Books, 1977.

INSEL, P. M., & MOOS, R. H. Psychological environments: Expanding the scope of human ecology. *American Psychologist,* 1974, *29,* 179–88.

JAMES, W. Talks to teachers, 1892. Reprinted in *Talks to teachers on psychology and to students on some of life's ideals.* New York: Norton, 1958.

JANICKI, T. C., & PETERSON, P. L. Aptitude-treatment interaction effects of variations in direct instruction. *American Educational Research Journal,* 1981, *18,* 63–82.

JANIS, I. L., & MANN, L. *Decision making: A psychological analysis of conflict, choice, and commitment.* New York: Free Press, 1977.

JANSKY, J., & DE HIRSCH, K. *Preventing reading failure: Prediction, diagnosis, and intervention.* New York: Harper & Row, 1973.

JASTAK, J. F., & JASTAK, S. R. *The wide range achievement test,* rev. ed. Wilminton, Del.: Guidance Association of Delaware, 1965; 1963; 1978.

JENSEN, A. R. How much can we boost IQ and scholastic achievement? *Harvard Educational Review,* 1969, *39,* 1–123.

JOHNSON, D., & MYKLEBUST, H. R. *Learning disabilities: Educational principles and practices.* New York: Grune & Stratton, 1967.

JOHNSON, D. W., & JOHNSON, R. Instructional goal structure: Cooperative, competitive, or individualistic. *Review of Educational Research,* 1974, *44,* 213–40.

JOHNSON, O. G., & BOMMORITO, J. W. *Tests and measurements in child development: A handbook.* San Francisco: Jossey-Bass, 1971.

JONES, E. E. The rocky road from acts to dispositions. *American Psychologist,* 1979, *34,* 107–17.

JONES, E., & NISBETT, R. The actor and the observer: Divergent perceptions of the causes of behavior. In E. E. Jones, D. E. Kanouse, H. H. Kelley, R. E. Nisbett, S. Valens, & B. Weiner. *Attribution: Perceiving the causes of behavior.* Morristown, N.J.: General Learning Press, 1971.

JOYCE, B., & WEIL, M. *Models of teaching.* New York: Prentice-Hall, 1972.

KAGAN, J., & LANG, C. *Psychology and education.* New York: Harcourt Brace Jovanovich, 1978.

KALUGER, G., & KOLSON, C. J. *Reading and learning disabilities,* 2nd ed. Columbus, Ohio: Merrill, 1978.

KAMIN, L. J. *The science and politics of I.Q.* New York: Wiley, 1974.

KANFER, F. H., & GOLDSTEIN, A. P. (Eds.). *Helping people change: A textbook of methods,* 2nd ed. New York: Pergamon Press, 1980.

KARNIOL, R., & ROSS, M. The effect of performance-relevant and performance irrelevant rewards on children's intrinsic motivation. *Child Development,* 1977, *48,* 482-87.

KARPMAN, S. Script drama analysis. *Transactional Analysis Bulletin,* 1968, *7,* 39-43.

KASS, C. E. Psycholinguistic disabilities of children with reading problems. *Exceptional Children,* 1966, *32,* 533-39.

KAUFMAN, A. S. The WISC-R and learning disabilities assessment: State of the art. *Journal of Learning Disabilities,* 1981, *14,* 520-26.

KAUFMAN, M. J., & MONA, L. G. The least restrictive environment: A major philosophical change. In E. L. Meyen *Exceptional children and youth: An introduction.* Denver: Love Publishing Co., 1978.

KELLEY, J. G., SNOWDEN, L. R., & MUÑOZ, R. F. Social and community interventions. In M. R. Rosenzweig & L. W. Porter (Eds.), *Annual review of psychology,* Vol. 28. Palo Alto, Calif.: Annual Reviews Inc., 1977.

KENNEDY, M. Findings for the follow-through planned variation study. *Educational Researcher,* 1978, *7,* 3-11.

KEOGH, B. K. Optometric vision training programs for children with learning disabilities: Review of issues and research. *Journal of Learning Disabilities,* 1974, *7,* 219-31.

KEOGH, B. K., & BECKER, L. D. Early detection of learning problems: Questions, cautions, and guidelines. *Exceptional Children,* 1973, *40,* 5-11.

KEPHART, N. C. *The slow learner in the classroom.* Columbus, Ohio: Merrill, 1960; 1971, 2nd ed.

KEPHART, N. C., & STRAUSS, A. A. A clinical factor influencing variations in I.Q. *American Journal of Orthopsychiatry,* 1940, *10,* 345-50.

KESSLER, M., & ALBEE, G. W. Primary prevention. In M. R. Rosenzweig & L. W. Porter (Eds.), *Annual review of psychology,* Vol. 26. Palo Alto, Calif.: Annual Reviews Inc., 1975.

KEYS, C. B., & BARTUNEK, J. M. Organization development in schools: Goals agreement, process skills, and diffusion of change. *Journal of Applied Behavioral Science,* 1979, *15,* 61-78.

KIBLER, R. J., BARKER, L. L., & MILES, D. T. *Behavior objectives and instruction.* Boston: Allyn and Bacon, 1970.

KIESLER, C. A. *The psychology of commitment.* New York: Academic Press, 1971.

KIESLER, C. A., & SAKUMURA, J. A. A test of a model of commitment. *Journal of Personality and Social Psychology,* 1966, *3,* 349-53.

KINSBOURNE, M. Cerebral dominance, learning, and cognition. In H. R. Myklebust (Ed.), *Progress in learning disabilities,* Vol. 3. New York: Grune & Stratton, 1975.

KIPNIS, D. Does power corrupt? *Journal of Personality and Social Psychology,* 1972, *24,* 33-41.

KIRK, S. A. *Educating exceptional children.* Boston: Houghton Mifflin, 1962.

KIRK, S. A. Behavioral diagnosis and remediation of learning disabilities. In *Proceedings of the Conference on Exploration into the Problem of the Perceptually Handicapped Child.* Chicago: Perceptually Handicapped Child, 1963. Reprinted in J. McCarthy & S. A. Kirk (Eds.), *Learning Disabilities: Selected ACLD Papers.* Boston: Houghton Mifflin, 1975.

KIRK, S. A., & GALLAGHER, J. J. *Educating exceptional children,* 3rd ed. Boston: Houghton Mifflin, 1979.

KIRK, S. A., & KIRK, W. D. *Psycholinguistic learning disabilities: Diagnosis and remediation.* Urbana, Ill.: University of Illinois Press, 1971.

KIRK, S. A., McCARTHY, J. J., & KIRK, W. D. *Illinois test of psycholinguistic abilities.* Urbana: University of Illinois Press, 1968.

KIRP, D. L. Student classification, public policy, and the courts. *Harvard Educational Review,* 1974, *44,* 7-52.

KIRP, D. L., KURILOFF, P. J., & BUSS, W. G. Legal mandates and organizational change. In N. Hobbs (Ed.), *Issues in the classification of children.* Vol. 2. San Francisco: Jossey-Bass, 1975.

KITTRIE, N. N. *The right to be different: Deviance and enforced therapy.* Baltimore, Md.: Johns Hopkins Press, 1971.

KLEISIUS, S. E. Perceptual-motor development and reading—A closer look. In R. C. Aukerman (Ed.) *Some persistent questions on beginning reading.* Newark, Del.: International Reading Association, 1972.

KNIGHTS, R. M., & BAKKER, D. J. (Eds.) *The neuropsychology of learning disorders.* Baltimore, Md.: University Park Press, 1976.

KOENIGS, S. S., & HESS, R. J. The origins climate questionnaire. In R. de Charms, *Enhancing motivation.* New York: Irvington Publishers, 1976.

KOHL, H. *The open classroom.* New York: Vintage, 1969.

KOHLBERG, L., & MAYER, R. Development as the aim of education. *Harvard Educational Review,* 1972, *42,* 449-96.

KOHN, M. *Competence and symptom factors in the preschool child.* New York: William Alamson White Institute, 1968.

KOHN, M. & SILVERMAN, H. W. A competence scale and a symptom checklist for the preschool child. Paper presented at the meeting of the Eastern Psychological Association, New York, 1966.

KOLB, D. A., & FRY, R. Toward an applied theory of experiential learning. In C. Cooper (Ed.), *Theories of group processes.* New York: Wiley, 1975.

KOPEL, S., & ARKOWITZ, H. The role of attribution and self-perception in behavior change: Implications for behavior therapy. *Genetic Psychology Monographs,* 1975, *92,* 175-212.

KOPPITZ, E. M. *The Bender Gestalt test for young children.* New York: Grune & Stratton, 1963.

KOPPITZ, E. Special class pupils with learning disabilities: A five year follow-up study. *Academic Therapy*, 1973, *13*, 133–40.

KOPPITZ, E. M. *The Bender Gestalt test for young children: Vol. II: Research and application, 1963–1973*. New York: Grune & Stratton, 1975.

KORCHIN, S. J. *Modern clinical psychology*. New York: Basic, 1976.

KOSIEWICZ, M. M., HALLAHAN, D. P., & LLOYD, J. The effects of an L. D. student's treatment choice on handwriting performance. *Learning Disabilities Quarterly*, 1981, *4*, 281–86.

KOUNIN, J. S., & DOYLE, P. H. Degree of continuity of a lesson's signal system and the task involvement of children. *Journal of Educational Psychology*, 1975, *67*, 159–64.

KRATHWOHL, D. R., BLOOM, B. S., & MASIA, B. B. *Taxonomy of educational objectives: Handbook II: Affective domain*. New York: McKay, 1964.

KRAUSE, M. S. Construct validity for the evaluation of therapy outcomes. *Journal of Abnormal Psychology*, 1969, *14*, 524–30.

KRITCHEVSKY, S., & PRESCOTT, E. *Planning environments for young children: Physical space*. Washington, D.C.: National Association for the Education of Young Children, 1969.

KRUGLANSKI, A. W. Attributing trustworthiness in supervisor-worker relations. *Journal of Experimental Social Psychology*, 1970, 6, 214–32.

KRUGLANSKI, A. W. The endogenous-exogenous partition in attribution theory. *Psychological Review*, 1975, *82*, 387–406.

KUDER, R. *Kuder personal preference record*. Chicago: Science Research Associates, 1954.

KUETHE, J. L. Social schemas. *Journal of Abnormal and Social Psychology*, 1962, *64*, 31–38.

LADD, F. Black youths view their environments. *Environment and Behavior*, 1970, *2*, 74–99.

LAING, R. D. *The politics of experience*. New York: Ballantine, 1967.

LAING, R. D. & ESTERSON, A. *Sanity, madness, and the family*. Baltimore, Md.: Penguin, 1970.

LAPOUSE, R., & MONK, M. A. Behavior deviations in a representative sample of children: Variation by sex, age, race, social class and family size. *American Journal of Orthopsychiatry*, 1964, *34*, 436–46.

LARRY P. v. RILES, 343 F. supp. 1306 (ND Cal. 1972).

LAUTER, P., & HOWE, F. *The conspiracy of the young*. New York: New World Publishing Co., 1970.

A LAW CONCERNING YOU AND YOUR CHILD. Directions, Los Angeles: Western Los Angeles Direction Service, Spring, 1978.

LAZARE, A. The customer approach to patienthood. *Archives of General Psychiatry*, 1975, *32*, 553–55.

LEE, S. D., & TEMERLIN, M. K. Social class, diagnosis, and prognosis for psychotherapy. *Psychotherapy: Theory, Research, and Practice*, 1970, *7*, 181–85.

LEFCOURT, H. M. Effects of cue explication upon persons maintaining external control expectancies. *Journal of Personality and Social Psychology*, 1967, *5*, 372–78.

LEFCOURT, H. M. *Locus of control*. Hillsdale, N.J.: Erlbaum Press, 1976.

LEIFER, R. *In the name of mental health: Social functions of psychiatry*. New York: Aronson, 1969.

LENNENBERG, E. H. *Biological foundation of language*. New York: Wiley, 1967.

LEPPER, M. R., & DAFOE, J. Incentives, constraints, and motivation in the classroom: An attributional analysis. In I. Frieze, D. Bar-Tal, & J. Carroll (Eds.), *Attribution theory: Applications to social problems*. San Francisco: Jossey-Bass, 1979.

LEPPER, M. R., & GREENE, D. Turning play into work: Effects of adult surveillance and extrinsic rewards on children's intrinsic motivation. *Journal of Personality and Social Psychology*, 1975, *31*, 479–86.

LEPPER, M. R., & GREENE, D. (Eds.) *The hidden costs of rewards*. Hillsdale, N.J.: Erlbaum Press, 1978.

LERNER, J. W. *Children with learning disabilities*, 2nd ed. Boston, Mass.: Houghton Mifflin, 1976.

LERNER, J. W. *Learning disabilities: Theories, diagnosis, and teaching strategies*, 3rd ed. Boston, Mass.: Houghton Mifflin, 1981.

LERNER, J., & JAMES, K. Systems and systems applications in special education. In L. Mann and D. Sabatino (Eds.), *The second review of special education*. New York: Grune & Stratton, 1974.

LEVINE, F. M., & FASNACHT, G. Token rewards may lead to token learning. *American Psychologist*, 1974, *29*, 816–20.

LEVINE, M., & LEVINE, A. *A social history of helping services: Clinic, court, school, and community*. New York: Appleton-Century-Crofts, 1970.

LEVINE, M., & PERKINS, D. V. Social setting interventions and primary prevention: Comments on the report on the task panel on prevention to the President's Commission on Mental Health. *American Journal of Community Psychology*, 1980, *8*, 147–57.

LEVINE, R. J. *The nature and definition of informed consent in various research settings*. Washington, D. C.: National Commission for the Protection of Human Subjects, 1975.

LEWIN, K. *Field theory and social sciences*. New York: Harper & Row, 1951.

LEWIS, W. W. Project Re-ED: Educational intervention in discordant child rearing systems. In E. L. Cowen, E. A. Gardner, & M. Zax (Eds.), *Emergent approaches to mental health*. New York: Appleton-Century-Crofts, 1967.

LINDSAY, G. A., & WEDELL, K. The early identification of educationally "at risk" children revisited. *Journal of Learning Disabilities*, 1982, *15*, 212–17.

LIPPITT, R., WATSON, J., & WESTLEY, B. *The dynamics of planned change*. New York: Harcourt Brace & Co., 1958.

LIPTON, M. A., & WHELESS, J. C. Nutrition and learning disabilities. In J. Gottlieb and S. S. Strichart (Eds.), *Developmental theory and research in learning disabilities*. Baltimore, Md.: University Park Press, 1981.

LOO, C. M. The effect of spatial density on the social behavior of children. *Journal of Applied Social Psychology*, 1973, *2*, 372–81.

LUICK, T. The relations of diagnostic profiles to academic achievement and remedial programming. Paper presented at the annual convention, Association for Children with Learning Disabilities, San Francisco, 1979.

LURIA, A. R., & MAJOVSKI, L. V. Basic approaches used in American and Soviet clinical neuropsychology. *American Psychologist*, 1977, *32*, 959–68.

MCCARTHY, D. *Manual for the McCarthy scales of children's abilities.* New York: Psychological Corporation, 1972.

MCCARTHY, J. M. Education: The basis of the triangle. *Annals of the New York Academy of Science*, 1973, *205*, 362–67.

MCGAHAN, F., & MCGAHAN, C. *Early detection inventory.* Chicago, Ill.: Follett, 1967.

MCGRATH, J. H. *Planning systems for school executives: The unity of theory and practice.* Scranton: Intext Educational Publishers, 1972.

MCGUINNESS, D. How schools discriminate against boys. *Human Nature*, 1979, 82–88.

MCINTYRE, C. W., MURRAY, M. E., BLACKWELL, S. L., & HARRIS, A. M. Visual search in learning disabled and hyperactive boys. Paper presented at biennial meetings of the Society for Research in Child Development. San Francisco, 1979.

MCNEIL, J. D. *Curriculum administration: Principles and techniques of curriculum development.* New York: MacMillan, 1965.

MCREYNOLDS, P. (Ed.). *Advances in psychological assessment*, vol. 3. San Francisco: Jossey-Bass, 1975.

MACGINITE, W. *Gates-MacGinite reading tests.* Boston, Mass.: Houghton Mifflin, 1978.

MADDEN, R., GARDNER, E. R., RUDMAN, H. C., KARLSEN, B., & MERWIN, J. C. *Stanford achievement test.* New York: Harcourt Brace Jovanovich, 1973.

MAEHR, M. L. Continuing motivation: An analysis of a seldom considered educational outcome. *Review of Educational Research*, 1976, *46*, 443–62.

MAHONEY, M. J. *Cognition and behavior modification.* Cambridge, Mass.: Ballinger Publishing Co., 1974.

MAHONEY, M. J., & ARNKOFF, D. Cognitive and self-control therapies. In S. L. Garfield and A. E. Bergin (Eds.), *Handbook of psychotherapy and behavior change*, 2nd ed. New York: Wiley, 1978.

MAKITA, K. The rarity of reading disability in Japanese children. *American Journal of Orthopsychiatry*, 1968, *38*, 599–614.

MANN, L., GOODMAN, L., & WIEDERHOLT, J. L. (Eds.) *Teaching the learning-disabled adolescent.* Boston, Mass.: Houghton Mifflin, 1978.

MANN, L., & PHILLIPS, W. A. Fractional practices in special education. In D. Hammill & N. Bartel (Eds.), *Educational perspectives in learning disabilities.* New York: Wiley, 1971.

MANOSEVITZ, M., LINDZEY, G., & THIESSEN, D. D. *Behavioral genetics: Methods and research.* New York: Appleton-Century-Crofts, 1969.

MARK, V. H., & ERVIN, F. R. *Violence and the brain.* New York: Harper & Row, 1970.

MARSHALL, H. H. Open classrooms: Has the term outlived its usefulness? *Review of Educational Research*, 1981, *51*, 181–92.

MARTIN, E. Mainstreaming as national policy. In P. H. Mann (Ed.), *Shared responsibility for handicapped students: Advocacy and programming.* Coral Gables, Fla.: University of Miami Training and Technical Assistance Center, 1976, 13–15.

MASLOW, A. *The psychology of science: A reconnaissance.* Chicago: Henry Regnery, 1969.

MATSON, F. W. (Ed.). *Without/within: Behaviorism and humanism.* Monterey, Calif.: Brooks-Cole, 1973.

MAY, R. *Existential Psychology*, New York: Random House, 1961.

MAY, R. *Psychology and the human dilemma.* Princeton, N.J.: D. Van Nostrand, 1967.

MEANS, R. K. *Methodology in education.* Columbus, Ohio: Merrill, 1968.

MEDLEY, D., SCHLUCK, C., & AMES, N. *Assessing the learning environment in the classroom: A manual for users of OSc Ars.* Princeton, N.J.: Educational Testing Service, 1968.

MEEHL, P. E. *Clinical versus statistical prediction.* Minneapolis, Minn.: University of Minnesota Press, 1954.

MEEHL, P. E. When shall we use our heads instead of the formula? *Journal of Counseling Psychology*, 1957, *4*, 268–73.

MEEHL, P. E. Seer over sign: The first good example. *Journal of Experimental Research in Personality*, 1965, *1*, 27–32.

MEEHL, P. E., & ROSEN, A. Antecedent probability and the efficiency of psychometric signs, patterns or cutting scores. *Psychological Bulletin*, 1955, *52*, 194–216.

MEICHENBAUM, D. *Cognitive-behavior modification: An integrative approach.* New York: Plenum Press, 1977.

MEICHENBAUM, D., & GOODMAN, J. Training impulsive children to talk to themselves: A means of developing self-control. *Journal of Abnormal Psychology*, 1971, *77*, 115–26.

MEIER, J. H. Screening, assessment, and intervention for young children at developmental risk. In N. Hobbs (Ed.), *Issues in the classification of children*, Vol. 2. San Francisco: Jossey-Bass, 1975.

MEISELS, M., & DOSEY, M. A. Personal space, anger arousal, and psychological defense. *Journal of Personality*, 1971, *39*, 333–34.

MENNINGER, K. A. *The vital balance.* New York: Viking Press, 1963.

MERCER, C. D., & MERCER, A. R. *Teaching students with learning problems.* Columbus: Merrill, 1981.

MERCER, J. R. *Labeling the mentally retarded: Clinical and social system perspectives on mental retardation.* Berkeley, Calif.: University of California Press, 1972.

MERCER, J. R. I.Q.: The lethal label. *Psychology Today*, 1973, *6*, 44–47, 95–97.

MERCER, J. *System of multicultural pluralistic assessment: Technical manual.* New York: Psychological Corp., 1979.

MERCER, J. R., & BROWN, W. C. Racial differences in I.Q.: Fact or artifact. In C. Seena (Ed.) *The fallacy of I.Q.* New York: Third Press, 1973.

MERCER, J. R., & LEWIS, J. F. *SOMPA: Parent Interview Manual.* New York: Psychological Corporation, 1977.

MERCER, J. R., & LEWIS, J. F. *System of multicultural pluralistic assessment: Technical manual.* New York: Psychological Corporation, 1979.

MERTON, R. K. The self-fulfilling prophecy. *Antioch Review*, 1948, *8*, 193–210.

MESSICK, S. Personality measurement and ethics of assessment. *American Psychologist*, 1965, *20*, 136–42.

MESSICK, S. The criterion problem in the evaluation of instruction: Assessing possible, not just intended, outcomes. In M. C. Wittrock & D. E. Wiley (Eds.), *The evaluation of instruction: Issues and problems.* New York: Holt, Rinehart & Winston, 1970.

MESSICK, S. The standard problem: Meaning and values in measurement and evaluation. *American Psychologist*, 1975, *30*, 955–66.

MESSICK, S. Evidence and ethics in the evaluation of tests. *Educational Researcher*, 1981, *10*, 9–20.

MEYEN, E. L. *Instructional based appraisal system.* Bellevue, Wash.: Edmark Associates, 1976.

MEYEN, E. L. Instructional planning. In E. L. Meyen, G. A. Vergason, & R. J. Whelan. *Instructional planning for exceptional children: Essays from focus on Exceptional Children.* Denver: Love Publishing Co., 1979.

MEYEN, E. L. *Exceptional children and youth: An introduction*, 2nd ed. Denver: Love Publishing Co., 1982.

MILL, J. S. On liberty, 1859. Reprinted in *Essential works of John Stuart Mill.* New York: Bantam Books, 1961.

MILLER, A. Conceptual matching models and interactional research in education. *Review of Educational Research*, 1981, *51*, 33–84.

MILLER, D. T., & ROSS, M. Self-serving biases in the attribution of causality: Fact or fiction? *Psychological Bulletin*, 1975, *82*, 213–25.

MILLER, G. A., GALANTER, E., & PRIBRAM, K. H. *Plans and the structure of behavior.* New York: Holt, 1960.

MILLER, R. I. An overview of educational change. In R. I. Miller (Ed.) *Perspectives on educational change.* New York: Appleton-Century-Crofts, 1967.

MISCHEL, W. Toward a cognitive social learning reconceptualization of personality. *Psychological Review*, 1973, *80*, 252–83.

MITCHELL, K. M., & NAMENEK, T. M. A comparison of therapist and client social class. *Professional Psychology*, 1970, *1*, 225–30.

MNOOKIN, R. Children's rights: Beyond kiddie libbers and child savers. *Journal of Clinical Child Psychology*, 1978, *7*, 163–67.

MOFFETT, J. Phony problems: Accountability and learning to read. Paper presented at the Conference of the Southern California Council of Teachers of English, Los Angeles, October 17, 1970.

MONEY, J. *Reading disability: Progress and research needs in dyslexia.* Baltimore: Johns Hopkins Press, 1962.

MONSON, T. C., & SYNDER, M. Actors, observers, and the attribution process: Toward a reconceptualization. *Journal of Experimental Social Psychology*, 1977, *13*, 89–111.

MONTESSORI, M. *The Montessori method.* A. E. George, trans. New York: Frederick Stokes, 1912.

MONTESSORI, M. *The Montessori method.* A. E. George, trans. New York: Shocken, 1964.

MOOS, R. H. *Evaluating educational environments.* San Francisco: Jossey-Bass, 1979.

MOOS, R. H., & INSEL, P. M. (Eds.) *Issues in social ecology: Human milieus.* Palo Alto, Calif.: National Press Books, 1974.

MOOS, R. H. & MACINTOSH, S. Multivariate study of the patient-therapist system: A replication and extension. *Journal of Consulting and Clinical Psychology*, 1970, *35*, 298–307.

MOOS, R. H. & MOOS, B. S. Classroom social climate and student absences and grades. *Journal of Educational Psychology*, 1978, *70*, 263–69.

MOOS, R. & TRICKETT, E. J. *Classroom environment scale—manual.* Palo Alto, Calif.: Consulting Psychologists Press, Inc., 1974.

MORAN, M. R. Nine steps to the diagnostic prescriptive process in the classroom. In E. L. Meyen, G. A. Vergason, & R. J. Whelan (Eds.), *Instructional planning for exceptional children.* Denver: Love Publishing Co., 1979.

MORENO, J. L. Who shall survive? *Foundation of Sociometry, Group Psychology and Sociodrama*, 2nd ed. New York.: Random House, 1953.

MOWRER, O. H. *Learning theory and the symbolic processes.* New York: Wiley, 1960.

MUEHL, S., & DINELLO, M. C. Early first-grade skills related to subsequent reading performance: A seven year followup study. *Journal of Reading Behavior*, 1976, *8*, 67–81.

MUKERJI, R. About school. *Colloquy*, 1970, *3*, 2.

MUÑOZ, R. F., SNOWDEN, L. R., KELLY, J. G., & Associates, *Social and psychological research in community settings.* San Francisco: Jossey-Bass, 1979.

MURPHY, J. Incompetence and paternalism. *Archiv für Rechts-und-sozialphilosophie*, 1974, *50*, 465–86. As cited in T. L. Beauchamp & J. F. Childress, *Principles of biomedical ethics*, New York: Oxford University Press, 1979.

MUSSEN, P., & EISENBERG-BERG, N. *Roots of caring, sharing, and helping: The development of prosocial behavior in children.* San Francisco: W. H. Freeman, 1977.

MYERS, P., & HAMMILL, D. *Methods for learning disorders.* New York: Wiley, 1976.

MYERS, R. E. A comparison of the perceptions of the elementary school children in open area and self-contained classrooms in British Columbia. *Journal of Research and Development in Teaching*, 1971, *9*, 100–106.

MYKELBUST, H. R. *Auditory disorders in children.* New York: Grune & Stratton, 1954.

MYKLEBUST, H. R. *The pupil rating scale revised.* New York: Grune & Stratton, 1981.

NATIONAL ADVISORY COMMITTEE ON HANDICAPPED CHIDREN. *First annual report, Subcommittee on Education of the Committee on Labor and Public Welfare, U. S. Senate.* Washington, D.C.: U.S. Government Printing Office, 1968.

NATIONAL COMMISSION FOR THE PROTECTION OF HUMAN SUBJECTS. *Children and the mentally disabled as research subjects* (Staff Report). Washington, D. C.: National Commission, October, 1975.

NAY, J. N., SCANLON, J. W., SCHMIDT, R. E., & WHOLEY, J. If you don't care where you get to, then it doesn't matter which way you go. In C. C. Abt (Ed.), *The evaluation of social programs.* Beverly Hills: Sage, 1976.

NEISSER, U. *Cognition and reality: Principles and implication of cognitive psychology.* San Francisco: W. H. Freeman & Co., 1976.

NEWCOMER, P., HARE, B., HAMMILL, D., & MCGETTIGAN, J. Construct validity of the ITPA subtests. *Exceptional Children*, 1974, *40*, 509-10.

NEWCOMER, P., LARSEN, S. C., & HAMMILL, D. D. A response to research on psycholinguistic training. *Exceptional Children*, 1975, *42*, 144-48.

NEWSWEEK, September 14, 1970, 123.

NICHOLLS, J. G. Quality and equality in intellectual development: The role of motivation in education. *American Psychologist*, 1979, *34*, 1071-84.

NORMAN, JR., C. A., & ZIGMOND, N. Characteristics of children labeled and served as Learning Disabled in school systems affiliated with Child Service Demonstration Centers. *Journal of Learning Disabilities*, 1980, *9*, 542-47.

NORTHERN, J. L., & DOWNS, M. P. *Hearing & Children.* Baltimore: Williams & Wilkins, 1974.

NOTZ, W. W. Work motivation and the negative effects of extrinsic rewards: A review with implications for theory and practice. *American Psychologist*, 1975, *30*, 884-91.

NUNNALLY, J. C. *Psychometric theory.* New York: McGraw-Hill, 1967.

NUNNALLY, J. C. *Psychometric theory*, 2nd ed. New York: McGraw-Hill, 1978.

NURSS, J. R., & MCGAUVRAN, M. E. *Metropolitan readiness tests, teacher's manual, Part II: Interpretation and use of test results (Level I & II).* New York: Harcourt Brace Jovanovich, 1976.

NYBERG, D. *Tough and Tender Learning.* Palo Alto, Calif.: National Press Books, 1971.

O'LEARY, K. D. The assessment of psychopathology in children. In H. C. Quay & J. S. Werry (Eds.), *Psychopathological disorders of childhood.* N.Y.: Wiley, 1972.

O'LEARY, K. D., & DRABMAN, R. Token reinforcement programs in the classroom: A review. *Psychological Bulletin*, 1971, *75*, 379-98.

O'LEARY, K. D., & O'LEARY, S. G. (Eds.). *Classroom management: The successful use of behavior modification.* New York: Pergamon, 1972.

OLMEDO, E. Testing linguistic minorities. *American Psychologist*, 1981, *36*, 1078-85.

ORNSTEIN, R. E. *The psychology of consciousness*, 2nd ed. New York: Harcourt Brace Jovanovich, 1977.

ORTON, S. T. Specific reading disability–strephosymbolia. *Journal of the American Medical Association*, 1928, *90*, 1095-99.

ORTON, S. T. *Reading, writing and speech problems of children.* New York: Norton, 1937.

OSGOOD, C. E. A behavioristic analysis of perception and language as cognitive phenomena. In J. S. Bruner (Ed.), *Contemporary approaches to cognition.* Cambridge: Harvard University Press, 1957.

OSS STAFF. *Assessment of men.* New York: Holt, Rinehart & Winston, 1948.

OWEN, F. W., ADAMS, P. A., FORREST, T., STOLZ, L. M., & FISHER, S. Learning disorders in children: Sibling studies. *Monographs of the Society for Research in Child Development*, 1971, *36*, serial no. 144.

PALMER, J. O. *The psychological assessment of children.* New York: Wiley, 1970.

PALUCK, R. J., & ESSER, A. H. Territorial behavior as an indicator of changes in clinical behavior condition of severely retarded boys. *American Journal of Mental Deficiency*, 1971, *76*, 284-90.

PARLOFF, M. B., KELMAN, H. C., & FRANK, J. D. Comfort, effectiveness, and self-awareness as criteria of improvement in psychotherapy. *American Journal of Psychiatry*, 1954, *3*, 343-51.

PENFIELD, W., & ROBERTS, L. *Speech and brain mechanisms.* Princeton, N.J.: Princeton University Press, 1959.

PERLMUTER, L. C., & MONTY, R. A. The importance of perceived control: Fact or fantasy? *American Scientist*, 1977, *65*, 759-65.

PERLMUTER, L. C., & MONTY, R. A. (Eds.). *Choice and perceived control.* Hillsdale, N.J.: Erlbaum Associates, 1979.

PHILLIPS, L., & DRAGUNS, J. G. Classification of the behavior disorders. In P. H. Mussen & M. R. Rosenzweig (Eds.), *Annual Review of psychology*, Vol. 22. Palo Alto, Calif.: Annual Reviews, 1971.

PIAGET, J. *Play, dreams, and imitation in childhood.* New York: Norton, 1951.

PIAGET, J. *The origins of intelligence in children.* New York: International Universities Press, 1952.

PIAGET, J. *To understand is to invent: The future of education.* New York: Grossman Publishers, 1973.

PIERS, E. & HARRIS, D. *The Piers-Harris children's self-concept scale.* Nashville: Counselor Recordings and Tests, 1969.

PIHL, R. O. Learning disabilities: Intervention programs in the schools. In H. R. Myklebust (Ed.), *Progress in learning disabilities*, Vol. 3. New York: Grune & Stratton, 1975.

PLOMIN, R., & FOCH, T. T. Hyperactivity and pediatrician diagnoses, parental ratings, cognitive abilities, and laboratory measures. *Journal of Abnormal Child Psychology*, 1981, *9*, 55-64.

POPHAM, W. J. *An evaluation guidebook.* Los Angeles: The Instructional Objectives Exchange, 1971.

POPHAM, W. J. *Educational evaluation.* Englewood Cliffs, N.J.: Prentice-Hall, 1975.

POPHAM, W. J., EISNER, E. W., SULLIVAN, H. J., & TYLER. L. L. *Instructional objectives.* AERA monograph Series on Curriculum Evaluation. Chicago: Rand McNally, 1969.

POSTMAN, W., & WEINGARTNER, C. *Teaching as a subversive activity.* New York: Delacorte Press, 1969.

PRESCOTT, G. A., BALOW, I. H., HOGAN, T. P. & FARR, R. C. *Metropolitan achievement tests: survey battery.* New York: Psychological Corporation, 1978.

PRESIDENT'S COMMITTEE ON MENTAL RETARDATION. *The six-hour retarded child.* Washington, D. C.: U.S. Government Printing Office, 1970.

PROGER, B. B., CROSS, L. H., & BURGER, R. M. Construct validation of standardized tests in special education: A framework of reference and application to ITPA research (1967-1971). In L. Mann & D. A. Sabatino (Eds.), *The first review of special education*, Vol. 1. Philadelphia: JSE Press, 1973.

QUAY, H. E., & PETERSON, D. R. *Manual for the behavior problem checklist.* Unpublished manuscript, University of Illinois, 1967.

RABINOVITCH, R. D. Reading and learning disabilities. In S. Arieti (Ed.) *American handbook of psychiatry,* Vol. 1. New York: Basic Books, 1959.

RAPAPORT, D. The structure of psychoanalytic theory: A systematizing attempt. *Psychological Issues,* 1960, *2,* 1–158.

RAVENS, J. C. *Progressive matrices.* London: H. K. Lewis, 1956.

REED, J. C., RABE, E. F., & MANKINEN, M. Teaching reading to brain-damaged children: A review. *Reading Research Quarterly,* 1970, *5,* 379–401.

REEDER, L. G. The patient-client as a consumer: Some observations on the changing professional-client relationship. *Journal of Health and Social Behavior,* 1972, *13,* 406–12.

REICHMANN, W. J. *Use and abuse of statistics.* Baltimore: Penguin Books, Inc., 1961.

REID, D. K., KNIGHT-AREST, I., & HRESKO, W. P. Cognitive development in learning disabled children. In J. Gottlieb & S. S. Strichart (Eds.) *Developmental theory and research in learning disabilities.* Baltimore: University Park Press, 1981.

REITAN, R. M., & BOLL, T. J. Neuropsychological correlates of minimal brain dysfunction. *Annals of the New York Academy of Sciences,* 1973, *205,* 65–88.

REITAN, R. M., & DAVISON, L. A. *Clinical neuropsychology: Current status and applications.* New York: Winston-Wiley, 1974.

RESCHLY, D. J. Psychological testing in educational classification and placement. *American Psychologist,* 1981, *36,* 1094–1102.

REYNOLDS, M. A framework for considering some issues in special education. *Exceptional Children,* 1962, *7,* 367–70.

RHODES, W. C. The disturbing child: A problem of ecological management. *Exceptional Children,* 1967, *33,* 449–55.

RHODES, W. C. A community participation analysis of emotional disturbance. *Exceptional Children,* 1970, *36,* 309–314.

RHODES, W. C., & TRACY, M. C. *A study of child variance: Intervention.* Vol. 2. Ann Arbor, Mich.: University of Michigan Press, 1972.

RIVERS, L. W., HENDERSON, D. M., JONES, R. L., LADNER, J. A., & WILLIAMS, R. L. Mosaic of labels for black children. In N. Hobbs (Ed.), *Issues in the classification of children,* Vol. 2. San Francisco: Jossey-Bass, 1975.

ROACH, E. G., & KEPHART, N. C. *The Purdue perceptual motor survey.* Columbus, Ohio: Merrill, 1966.

ROBINSON, D. N. Harm, offense, and nuisance: Some first steps in the establishment of an ethics of treatment. *American Psychologist,* 1974, *29,* 233–38.

RODHAM, H. Children under the law. *Harvard Educational Review,* 1973, *43,* 487–514.

ROETHLISBERGER, F. J. & DICKSON, W. J. *Management and the worker.* Cambridge, Mass.: Harvard University Press, 1939.

ROGERS, C. R. *Client-centered therapy.* Boston: Houghton Mifflin, 1951.

ROGERS, C. *On personal power: Inner strength and its revolutionary impact.* New York: Delacorte Press, 1977.

ROGERS, E. M. *Diffusion of innovations.* New York: Free Press, 1962.

ROGOLSKY, M. M. Screening kindergarten children: A review and recommendations. *Journal of School Psychology,* 1968–69, *7,* 18–27.

ROOK, K. S., PADESKY, C. A., & COMPAS, B. E. Disruptive classroom behavior: An environmental alternative to behavioral and psychopharmacological management. Paper presented at the meeting of the Western Psychological Association, San Diego, 1979.

ROSENBLATT, P. C., & BUDD, L. G. Territoriality and privacy in married and unmarried couples. *Journal of Social Psychology,* 1975, *97,* 67–76.

ROSENSHINE, B. Teaching behaviors related to pupil achievement: A review of research. In I. Westbury & A. A. Bellack (Eds.), *Research in classroom processes: Recent developments and next steps.* New York: Teachers College Press, 1971.

ROSENSHINE, B. V. Teaching styles and pupil progress. In *American Educational Research Journal,* 1978, *15,* 163–69.

ROSENTHAL, R. *Experimenter effects in behavioral research.* New York: Appleton-Century-Crofts, 1966.

ROSS, A. O. *Psychological aspects of learning disabilities and reading disorders.* New York: McGraw-Hill, 1976.

ROSS, A. O., & PELHAM, W. E. Child psychopathology. In M. R. Rosenzweig & L. W. Porter (Eds.), *Annual Review of Psychology.* 1981, *32,* 243–78.

ROSS, L. The intuitive psychologist and his shortcomings: Distortions in the attribution process. In L. Berkowitz (Ed.), *Advances in experimental social psychology,* Vol. 10. New York: Academic Press, 1977.

ROSS, M. Salience of reward and intrinsic motivation. *Journal of Personality and Social Psychology.* 1975, *33,* 245–54.

ROSSI, P. H., FREEMAN, H. E., & WRIGHT, S. R. *Evaluation: A systematic approach.* Beverly Hills: Sage Publications, 1979.

ROURKE, B. P. Brain-behavior relationships in children with learning disabilities: A research paradigm. *American Psychologist,* 1975, *30,* 911–20.

ROUTH, D. K., & ROBERTS, R. D. Minimal brain dysfunction in children. Failure to find evidence for a behavioral syndrome. *Psychological Reports,* 1972, *31,* 307–14.

RUBIN, R. A., KRUS, P., & BALOW, B. Factors in special class placement. *Exceptional Children,* 1973, *39,* 525–532.

RUBLE, D. N., & BOGGIANO, A. K. Optimizing motivation in an achievement context. In B. Keogh (Ed.), *Advances in special education: Basic constructs and theoretical orientations.* Greenwich, Conn.: JAI Press, 1980.

RUBOVITS, P., & MAEHR, M. Pygmalion black and white. *Journal of Personality and Social Psychology,* 1973, *25,* 210–18.

RUNION, H. Hypoglycemia—Fact or fiction. In W. Cruickshank (Ed.), *Approaches to learning, Vol. I. The best of ACLD*. Syracuse, N.Y.: Syracuse University Press, 1980.

RYAN, W. *Blaming the victim*. New York: Random House, 1971.

SABATINO, D. A. Auditory perception: Development assessment and intervention. In L. Mann & D. A. Sabatino (Eds.), *The first review of special education*, Vol. 1. Philadelphia: JSE Press, 1973.

SABATINO, D. A., SCHMIDT, C. R., & MILLER, T. L. *Learning disabilities: Systemizing teaching and service delivery*. Rockville, Md.: Aspen Systems Corp., 1981.

SAFER, N. D., KAUFMAN, M. J., MORRISSEY, P. A., & LEWIS, L. Implementation of IEP's: New teacher roles and requisite support systems. In E. L. Meyen, G. A. Vergason, & R. J. Whelan (Eds.), *Instructional planning for exceptional children*. Denver: Love Publishing Co., 1979.

SALOMON, G. Heuristic models for the generation of aptitude-treatment interaction hypotheses. *Review of Educational Research*, 1972, *42*, 327–43.

SALVIA, J., & YSSELDYKE, J. E. *Assessment in special and remedial education*, 2nd ed. Boston: Houghton Mifflin, 1981.

SANDERS, J. Complaints against psychologists adjudicated informally by APA's Committee on Scientific and Professional Ethics and Conduct. *American Psychologist*, 1979, *34*, 1139–44.

SARASON, S. B. *The culture of the school and the problem of change*. Boston: Allyn & Bacon, 1971.

SARASON, S. *The creation of settings and future societies*. San Francisco: Jossey-Bass, 1972.

SARASON, S. B. Community psychology and the anarchist insight. *American Journal of Community Psychology*, 1976, *4*, 246–59.

SARBIN, T. R. A contribution to the study of actuarial and individual methods of prediction. *American Journal of Sociology*, 1943, *48*, 593–602.

SARBIN, T. R. A role theory perspective for community psychology: The structure of social identity. In D. Adelson & B. L. Kalis (Eds.), *Community psychology and mental health: Perspectives and challenges*. Scranton, Pa.: Chandler, 1970.

SATTLER, J. M. *Assessment of children's intelligence and special abilities*, 2nd ed. Boston: Allyn & Bacon, 1982.

SATZ, P. & FLETCHER, J. Early screening tests: Some uses and abuses. *Journal of Learning Disabilities*, 1979, *12*, 56–60.

SATZ, P., FRIEL, J., & RUDEGEAIR, F. In J. Guthrie (Ed.), *Aspects of Reading Acquisition*. Baltimore: Johns Hopkins, 1976.

SAWYER, J. Measurement and prediction, clinical and statistical. *Psychological Bulletin*, 1966, *66*, 178–200.

SCANNELL, D. P. *Tests of achievement and proficiency*. Lombard, Ill: Riverside Publishing Co., 1978.

SCHAER, H. F., & CRUMP, W. D. Teacher involvement and early identification of children with learning disabilities. *Journal of Learning Disabilities*, 1976, *9*, 91–95.

SCHAIN, R. J. *Neurology of childhood learning disorders*. Baltimore: Williams & Wilkins, 1972.

SCHEFF, T. J. The labeling theory of mental illness. *American Sociological Review*, 1974, *39*, 444–52.

SCHILDER, P. *The image and appearance of the human body*. New York: International Universities Press, 1935.

SCHMIDT, F. L., & HUNTER, J. E. Racial and ethnic bias in psychological tests: Divergent implications of two definitions of test bias. *American Psychologist*, 1974, *29*, 1–8.

SCHRAG, P., & DIVOKY, D. *The myth of the hyperactive child and other means of child control*. New York: Pantheon Books, 1975.

SCHULDT, J. W. Psychotherapists' approach-avoidance responses and clients' expressions of dependency. *Journal of Counseling Psychology*, 1966, *13*, 178–83.

SCHWORM, R. Models in special education: Considerations and cautions. *Journal of Special Education*, 1976, *10*, 179–86.

SCRIVEN, M. The methodology of evaluation. In. R. W. Tyler, R. M. Gagné, & M. Scriven (Eds.) *Perspectives of curriculum evaluation*. AERA Monograph Series on Curriculum Evaluation No. 1. Chicago: Rand McNally, 1967.

SCRIVEN, M. The methodology of evaluation. *AERA Monograph Series on curriculum evaluation*, No. 1. Chicago: Rand McNally, 1967, 39–83.

SEASHORE, H. G., & RICKS, J. H., JR. Norms must be relevant. *Test Service Bulletin*, No. 39. New York: Psychological Corporation, 1950.

SEDLACK, R. A., & WEENER, P. Review of research on the Illinois test of psycholinguist abilities. In L. Mann & D. A. Sabatino (Eds.) *The first review of special education*, Vol. 1. Philadelphia: JSE Press, 1973.

SEIDEL, H. M. & ZIAI, M. Pediatric history and physical examination. In M. Ziai (Ed.) *Pediatrics*, Boston: Little, Brown, 1975.

SELYE, H. *The stress of life*. New York: McGraw-Hill, 1956.

SENF, G. M. An information-integration theory and its application to normal reading acquisition and reading disability. In N. D. Bryant & C. E. Kass (Eds.) *Leadership training institute on learning disabilities: Final report*, Vol. 2. Tucson: University of Arizona, 1972.

SILBERMAN, C. E. *Crisis in the classroom: The remaking of American education*. New York: Vintage Books, 1970.

SILVERSTON, R. A., & DEICHMANN, J. W. Sense modality research and the acquisition of reading skills. *Review of Educational Research*, 1975, *45*, 149–72.

SJOBERG, G. Politics, ethics, and evaluation research. In M. Guttentag & E. L. Struening (Eds.) *Handbook of evaluation research*, Vol. 2. Beverly Hills: Sage Publications, 1975.

SKAGER, R. W., & WEINBERG, C. *Fundamentals of educational research: An introductory approach*. Glenview, Ill.: Scott, Foresman & Co., 1971.

SKINNER, B. F. *Science and human behavior*. New York: Free Press, 1953.

SKINNER, B. F. *Contingencies of reinforcement: A theoretical analysis*. New York: Appleton-Century-Crofts, 1969.

SKINNER, B. F. *Beyond freedom and dignity*. New York: Knopf, 1971.

SLATER, B. Effects of noise on pupil performance. *Journal of Educational Psychology*, 1968, *59*, 239–43.

SLINGERLAND, B. H. *A multisensory approach to lan-guage arts for specific language disability children: A guide for primary teachers.* Cambridge, Mass.: Educators Publishing Service, 1971.

SLINGERLAND, B. H. *Slingerland screening tests.* Cambridge, Mass.: Educators Publishing Service, 1974.

SLOAN, W. *Lincoln-Oseretsky test of motor development.* Chicago: Stoelting, 1955.

SLOSSON, R. L. *Slosson intelligence test.* East Aurora, N.Y.: Slosson Educational Publications, 1971.

SMEAD, V. S. Ability training and task analysis in diagnostic/prescriptive teaching. *Journal of Special Education,* 1977, *11,* 113-25.

SMITH, D. E. P., & CARRIGAN, P. *The nature of reading disability.* New York: Harcourt, Brace & World, 1959.

SMITH, C. R., & KNOFF, H. M. School psychology and special education students' placement decisions: I.Q. still tips the scale. *Journal of Special Education,* 1981, *15,* 55-64.

SMITH, M. B. Personal values in the study of lives. In R. W. White (Ed.), *The study of lives.* Englewood Cliffs, N.J.: Prentice-Hall, 1963.

SMITH, R. M., NEISWORTH, J. T. & GREER, J. G. *Evaluating educational environments.* Columbus: Merrill, 1978.

SMITH, W. L. Forward. In W. A. Hunter (Ed.) *Multicultural education.* Washington, D.C.: American Association of Colleges for Teacher Education, 1974.

SOLOMON, D., & KENDALL, A. J. *Individual characteristics and children's performance in varied educational settings.* New York: Praeger, 1979.

SPIVAK, G. PLATT, J., & SHURE, M. *The problem solving approach to adjustment.* San Francisco: Jossey-Bass, 1976.

SPIVACK, G., & SPOTTS, J. *Devereux child behavior rating scale.* Devon, Pa.: Devereux Foundation Press, 1966.

SPIVACK, G., SPOTTS, J., & HAIMES, P. *Devereux adolescent behavior rating scale.* Devon, Pa.: Devereux Foundation Press, 1967.

SPRING, C., VERMEERSCH, J., BLUNDEN, D., & STERLING, H. Case studies of effects of artificial food colors on hyperactivity. *Journal of Special Education,* 1981, *15,* 361-72.

STAKE, R. E. The countenance of educational evaluation. *Teachers College Record,* 1967, *68,* 523-40.

STAKE, R. E. *Evaluating educational programs: The need and the response.* Paris: Organisation for Economic Cooperation and Development, 1976.

STALLINGS, J. Implementation and child effects of teaching practices in follow through classrooms. *Monographs of the Society for Research in Child Development,* 1975, *40.*

STAW, B. M. *Intrinsic and extrinsic motivation.* New York: General Learning Press Module, 1975.

STEVENSON, H. W. *Children's learning.* New York: Appleton-Century-Crofts, 1972.

STIER, S. Children's rights and society's duties. *Journal of Social Issues,* 1978, *34,* 46-59.

STIPEK, D. J., & WEISZ, J. R. Perceived personal control and academic achievement. *Review of Educational Research,* 1981, *51,* 101-137.

STRAUSS, A. A. Diagnosis and education of the cripple-brained, deficient child. *Journal of Exceptional Children,* 1943, *9,* 163-68.

STRAUSS, A. A., & KEPHART, N. C. *Psychopathology and education of the brain-injured child, Vol. 2, Progress in theory and clinic.* New York: Grune & Stratton, 1955.

STRAUSS, A. A., & LEHTINEN, L. E. *Psychopathology and education of the brain-injured child.* New York: Grune & Stratton, 1947.

STRAUSS, A. A., & WERNER, H. Disorders of conceptual thinking in the brain-injured child. *Journal of Nervous Mental Diseases,* 1942, *96,* 153-72.

STRICKLAND, L. H. Surveillance and trust. *Personality,* 1958, *26,* 200-215.

STRUPP, H. H., & HADLEY, S. M. A tripartite model of mental health and therapeutic outcomes with special reference to negative effects in psychotherapy. *American Psychologist,* 1977, *32,* 187-96.

STUFFLEBEAM, D. The use and abuse of evaluation in Title III. *Theory into Practice,* 1967, *6,* 126-33.

SUCHMAN, E. A. *Evaluative research: Principles and practice in public service and social action programs.* New York: Russell Sage Foundation, 1967.

SUNDBERG, N. D. *Assessment of persons.* Englewood Cliffs: Prentice-Hall, 1977.

SUNDBERG, N. D., TYLER, L. E., & TAPLIN, J. R. *Clinical psychology, Expanding horizons.* Englewood Cliffs, N.J.: Prentice-Hall, 1973.

SURAN, B. G., & RIZZO, J. V. *Special children: An integrative approach.* Glenview, Ill.: Scott, Foresman & Co., 1979.

SWANN, W. B., & PITTMAN, J. S. Initiating play activity of children: The moderating influence of verbal cues on intrinsic motivation. *Child Development,* 1977, *48,* 1128-32.

SWANSON, J., & KINSBOURNE, M. Food dyes impair performance of hyperactive children on a laboratory learning test. *Science,* 1980, *207,* 1485-86.

SZASZ, T. S. *The myth of mental illness.* New York: Harper & Row, 1961.

SZASZ, T. S. Psychiatric classification as a strategy of personal constraint. In T. S. Szasz (Ed.), *Ideology and insanity.* New York: Doubleday, 1969.

SZASZ, T. S. *Manufacture of madness: A comparative study of the inquisition and the mental health movement.* New York: Harper & Row, 1970.

TANSLEY, P., & PANCKHURST, J. *Children with specific learning difficulties: A critical review of research.* Windsor, Berkshire: NFER-Nelson, 1981.

TAPP, J. L., & LEVINE, F. J. (Eds.) *Law, justice, and the individual in society: Psychological and legal issues.* New York: Holt, Rinehart & Winston, 1977.

TARNOPOL, L., & TARNOPOL, M. *Reading disabilities: An international perspective.* Baltimore: University Park Press, 1976.

TAUB, S. I., & DOLLINGER, S. J. Reward and purpose as incentives for children differing in locus of control expectancies. *Journal of Personality,* 1975, *43,* 179-95.

TAYLOR, L., & ADELMAN, H. S. Myths, mystification, and magic in teaching. *Academic Therapy,* 1977, *12,* 343-52.

TAYLOR, L., & ADELMAN, H. S. Demonstration and research programs for learning problems at Fernald. *Journal of Learning Disabilities*, 1980, *13*, 47–52.

TEMP, G., & ANDERSON, S. B. *Final report Project Head Start—Summer, 1966, Section 3, pupils and programs.* Princeton, N.J.: Educational Testing Service, 1966.

TERMAN, L. M., & MERRILL, M. A. *Stanford Binet intelligence scale.* Boston: Houghton-Mifflin, 1973.

THOMPSON, A. C. Some counter thinking about learning disabilities. *Journal of Learning Disabilities*, 1981, *14*, 394–96.

THOMPSON, A., & ZIMMERMAN, R. Goals of counseling: Whose? When? *Journal of Counseling Psychology*, 1969, *16*, 121–23.

THORPE, L., CLARK, W., & TIEGS, E. *California test of personality.* Monterey, Calif.: California Test Bureau, 1953.

THORNDIKE, R. L., & HAGEN, E. P. *Measurement and evaluation in psychology and education*, 4th ed. New York: Wiley, 1977.

THURLOW, M. L., & YSSELDYKE, J. E. Current assessment and decision-making practices in model LD programs. *Learning Disabilities Quarterly*, 1979, *2*, 15–24.

TIEGS, E. W., & CLARKE, W. W. *California achievement test.* Monterey, Calif.: CTB/McGraw-Hill, 1978.

TOBACH, E. (Ed.). *The four horsemen: Racism, sexism, militarism, and social Darwinism.* New York: Behavioral Publications, 1974.

TOBIAS, S. Achievement treatment interactions. *Review of Educational Research*, 1976, *46*, 61–74.

TORGESEN, J. K. The role of nonspecific factors in the task performance of learning disabled children: A theoretical assessment. *Journal of Learning Disabilities*, 1977, *10*, 27–34.

TORGESEN, J., & KAIL, JR. R. V. Memory processes in exceptional children. In B. Keogh (Ed.), *Advances in special education: Basic constructs and theoretical orientations.* Greenwich, Conn.: JAI Press, 1980.

TORGESEN, J. K., & HOUCK, G. Processing deficiencies of learning disabled children who do poorly on the digit span test. Paper presented to biennial meeting of the Society for Research in Child Development, San Francisco, 1979.

TORNEY, J. B., OPPENHEIM, A. N. & FARNEN, R. F. *Civic education in ten countries.* New York: John Wiley & Sons, 1975.

TORRANCE, E. P. Different ways of learning for different kinds of children. In E. P. Torrance & R. D. Strom, *Mental health and achievement: Increasing potential and reducing school dropout.* New York: Wiley, 1965.

TORSHEN, K. P. *The mastery approach to competency-based education.* New York: Academic Press, 1977.

TREISMAN, A. M. Monitoring and storage of irrelevant messages in selective attention. *Journal of Verbal Learning and Verbal Behavior*, 1964, *3*, 449–59.

TREISMAN, A. M. Strategies and models of selective attention. *Psychological Review*, 1969, *76*, 282–99.

TROUTON, D. S. Placebos and their psychological effects. *Journal of Mental Science*, 1957, *103*, 344–54.

TRUAX, C. B., & CARKHUFF, R. R. *Toward effective counseling and psychotherapy.* Chicago: Aldine-Atherton, 1967.

TVERSKY, A., & KAHNEMAN, D. Judgment under uncertainty: Heuristics and biases. *Science*, 1974, *185*, 1124–31.

URBAN, H. B., & FORD, D. H. Some historical and conceptual perspectives on psychotherapy and behavior change. In A. E. Bergin & S. L. Garfield (Eds.), *Handbook of psychotherapy and behavior change.* New York: Wiley, 1971.

U.S. OFFICE OF EDUCATION. *Progress toward a free, appropriate public education: A report to Congress on the implementation of PL 94-142, The education for all handicapped children act.* Washington, D.C.: U.S. Department of Health, Education and Welfare, January, 1979.

VANDE VOORT, L., SENF, G. M., & BENTON, A. L. Development of audiovisual integration in normal and retarded readers. *Child Development*, 1972, *43*, 1260–72.

VELLUTINO, F. R. *Dyslexia: Theory and research.* Massachusetts Institute of Technology, 1979.

WADE, T., & BAKER, T. Opinions and use of psychological tests: A survey of clinical psychologists. *American Psychologist*, 1977, *32*, 874–82.

WALLACE, G., & LARSEN, S. C. *Educational assessment of learning problems: Testing for teaching.* Boston: Allyn & Bacon, 1978.

WALLACE, G., & MCLOUGHLIN, J. A. *Learning disabilities: Concepts and characteristics* (2nd ed.). Columbus: Merrill, 1979.

WALTON, H. N., & SCHUBERT, D. G. Vision-perception testing and training program: Clerical operations. *American Journal of Optometry*, 1969, *46*, 840–47.

WARD, W. D., & BARCHER, P. R. Reading achievement and creativity as related to open classroom experience. *Journal of Educational Psychology*, 1975, *67*, 683–91.

WARD, D., & KASSEBAUM, G. G. On biting the hand that feeds: Some implications of sociological evaluations of correctional effectiveness. In C. Weiss (Ed.), *Evaluating action programs: Readings & social action and education.* Boston: Allyn & Bacon, 1972.

WASSERSTROM, R. Lawyers as professionals: Some moral issues. *Human Rights*, 1975, *5*, 1–24.

WASSERSTOM, R. The legal and philosophical foundations of the right to privacy. Unpublished manuscript, University of California at Los Angeles, 1976.

WEBB, E. J., CAMPBELL, D. J., SCHWARTZ, R. D., & SECHRECT, L. *Unobtrusive measures: Nonreactive research in the social sciences.* Chicago: Rand McNally, 1966.

WEBSTER'S NEW WORLD DICTIONARY, 2nd college edition. Englewood Cliffs, N.J.: Prentice-Hall, 1970.

WECHSLER, D. *Manual for the Wechsler Adult Intelligence Scale.* New York: Psychological Corporation, 1955.

WECHSLER, D. *Manual for the Wechsler Preschool and Primary Scale of Intelligence.* New York: Psychological Corporation, 1967.

WECHSLER, D. *Wechsler Intelligence Scale for Chil-*

dren-Revised. New York: Psychological Corporation, 1974.

WEDELL, K. Diagnosing learning disabilities: A sequential strategy. *Journal of Learning Disabilities,* 1970, *3,* 311–17.

WEINBERG, C. *Education is a shuck: How the educational system is failing our children.* New York: Morrow, 1974.

WEINER, B. *Theories of motivation: From mechanism to cognition.* Chicago: Rand McNally, 1972.

WEINER, B. (Ed.) *Achievement motivation and attribution theory.* Morristown, N.J.: General Learning Press, 1974.

WEINER, B. *Human motivation.* New York: Holt, Rinehart & Winston, 1980.

WEINER, B., & SIERAD, J. Misattribution for failure and enhancement and achievement strivings. *Journal of Personality and Social Psychology,* 1975, *31,* 415–21.

WEINSTEIN, C. S. Modifying student behavior in an open classroom through changes in physical design. *American Educational Research Journal,* 1977, *14,* 249–62.

WEISS, C. H. *Evaluating action programs: Readings in social action and education.* Boston: Allyn & Bacon, 1972a.

WEISS, C. H. *Evaluation research: Methods of assessing program effectiveness.* Englewood Cliffs, N.J.: Prentice-Hall, 1972b.

WEISS, C. H. Evaluation research in the political context. *evaluation research,* Vol. 1. Beverly Hills, Calif.: Sage, 1975.

WEITZMAN, L., EIFIER, D., HOKADA, E., & ROSS, C. Sex-role socialization in picture books for preschool children. *American Journal of Sociology,* 1972, 1125–50.

WEPMAN, J. *Recovery from Aphasia.* New York: Ronald Press, 1951.

WEPMAN, J. *Wepman auditory discrimination test.* Chicago: Chicago Language Research Associates, 1973.

WEPMAN, J. M. Dyslexia: Its relationship to language acquisition and concept formation. In J. Money (Ed.), *Reading disability: Progress and research needs in dyslexia.* Baltimore: Johns Hopkins, 1962.

WEPMAN, J. M. Modalities and learning. In H. A. Robinson (Ed.), *Meeting individual difference in reading.* Supplementary Educational Monographs, 94. Chicago: University of Chicago Press, 1964.

WEPMAN, J., CRUICKSHANK, W., DEUTSCH, C., MORENCY, A., & STROTHER, C. Learning disabilities. In N. Hobbes (Ed.), *Issues in the classification of children,* Vol. 1. San Francisco: Jossey-Bass, 1975.

WEPMAN, J. M., JONES, L. V., BOCH, R. D., & VAN PELT, D. Studies in aphasis: Background and theoretical formulation. *Journal of Speech & Hearing Disorders,* 1960, *25,* 323–32.

WERNER, H., & STRAUSS, A. A. Causal factors in low performance. *American Journal of Mental Deficiency,* 1940, *45,* 213–18.

WERNER, H., & STRAUSS, A. Pathology of figure-background relation in the child. *Journal of Abnormal and Social Psychology,* 1941, *36,* 236–48.

WERNICKE, C. 1874. See G. H. Eggert, *Wernicke's Works on aphasia: A source book and review.* The Hague: Mouton Publishers, 1977.

WERRY, J. S. Organic factors in childhood psychopathology. In H. C. Quay & J. S. Werry (Eds.), *Psychopathological disorders in childhood.* New York: Wiley, 1972.

WERRY, J. S., & QUAY, H. C. The prevalence of behavior symptoms in younger elementary school children. *American Journal of Orthopsychiatry,* 1971, *41,* 136–43.

WESTBURY, I., & BELLACK, A. A. (Eds.), *Research into classroom processes: Recent developments and next steps.* New York: Teachers College Press, 1971.

WESTIN, A. F. *Privacy and freedom.* New York: Atheneum, 1967.

WHELAN, R. J. The relevance of behavior modification procedures for teachers of emotionally disturbed children. In P. Knoblock (Ed.), *Intervention approaches in educating emotionally disturbed children.* Syracuse, N.Y.: Syracuse University Press, 1966.

WHELAN, R. J. Evaluation. In E. Meyer, G. A. Vergason & R. J. Whelan (Eds.), *Instructional planning for exceptional children: Essays from focus on exceptional children.* Denver: Love Publishing Co., 1979.

WHITE, R. W. Motivation reconsidered: The concept of competence. *Psychological Review,* 1959, *66,* 297–333.

WHITE, R. W. Strategies of adaptation: An attempt at systematic description. In G. V. Coelhs, D. A. Hamburg, & J. E. Adams (Eds.), *Coping and Adaptation.* New York: Basic Books, 1974.

WIEDERHOLT, J. L. Historical perspectives on the education of the learning disabled. In L. Mann & D. Sabatino (Eds.), *The second review of special education.* Philadelphia: JSE Press, 1974.

WILHAMS, J. H. *Psychology of Women: Behavior in a biosocial context.* New York: Morton, 1974.

WILLINGHAM, W. W. (Ed.). Invasion of privacy in research and testing (Proceedings of a symposium sponsored by the National Council on Measurement in Education). Published as a supplement to the *Journal of Educational Measurement,* 1967, *4,* 1.

WILSON, E. O. *Sociobiology: The new synthesis.* Cambridge, Mass.: Harvard University Press, 1975.

WINKLER, A., DIXON, J. F., & PARKER, J. B. Brain function in problem children and controls: Psychometric, neurological, and electroencephalographic comparisons. *American Journal of Psychiatry,* 1970, *125,* 94–105.

WISCONSIN v. YODER, 406 U.S. 205 (1972).

WISSINK, J. F., KASS, C. E., & FERRELL, W. R. A Bayesian approach to the identification of children with learning disabilities. *Journal of Learning Disabilities,* 1975, *8,* 158–66.

WITELSON, S. F. Sex and the single hemisphere: Specialization of the right hemisphere for spatial processing. *Science,* 1976, *193,* 425–27.

WITELSON, S. F. Developmental dyslexia: Two right hemispheres and none left. *Science,* 1977, *195,* 309–11.

WOLF v. LEGISLATURE OF THE STATE OF UTAH. Civil no. 102626 3rd Jud. Dist. Ct. (Utah, January 8, 1969).

WOLF, R. The measurement of environments. In A.

Anastasi (Ed.), *Testing problems in perspective.* Washington, D. C.: American Council on Education, 1966.

WOLF, R. Data analysis and reporting considerations in evaluation. In W. J. Popham (Ed.), *Educational evaluation: Current applications.* Berkeley: McCutchan, 1974.

WOLF, R. M. Evaluation in education: *Foundations of competency assessment and program review.* New York: Praeger, 1979.

WOLFF, P. H., & HURWITZ, I. Functional implications of the minimal brain damage syndrome. In S. Walzert & P. H. Wolff (Eds.), *Minimal cerebral dysfunction in children.* New York: Grune & Stratton, 1973.

WOLPE, J. *Psychotherapy by reciprocal inhibition.* Stanford, Calif.: Stanford University Press, 1958.

WOOD, N. *Verbal learning.* Belmont, CA.: Fearon, 1969.

WOODCOCK, R. W., & JOHNSON, M. B. *Woodcock-Johnson psycho-educational battery.* Boston: Teaching Resources Corporation, 1977.

WORTHORN, B. R., & SANDERS, J. R. *Educational evaluation: Theory and practice.* Worthington, Ohio: Charles A. Jones Publishing Company, 1973.

WRIGHT, H. F. *Recording & analyzing child behavior.* New York: Harper & Row, 1967.

WUNDERLICH, R. C. Treatment of the hyperactive child. *Academic Therapy,* 1973, *8,* 375–90.

YARROW, M. R., CAMPBELL, J. D., & BURTON, R. V. Recollections of childhood—A study of the retrospective method. *Monographs of the Society of Research in Child Development,* 1970, *35,* No. 5.

YOUNG, P. T. *Motivation and emotion.* New York: Wiley, 1961.

YSSELDYKE, J. E. Diagnostic-prescriptive teaching: The search for aptitude-treatment interactions. In L. Mann & D. A. Sabatino (Eds.), *The first review of special education,* Vol. 1. Philadelphia: JSE Press, 1973.

YSSELDYKE, J. E., & ALGOZZINE, B. Perspectives on assessment of learning disabled students. *Learning Disability Quarterly,* 1979, *2,* 3–14.

YSSELDYKE, J. E., ALGOZZINE, B., REGAN, R., & POTTER, M. *Technical adequacy of tests used in simulated decision making* (Research Report No. 9). Minneapolis, Minn.: University of Minnesota, Institute for Research on Learning Disabilities, 1979.

YULE, W., & RUTTER, M. Epidemiology and social implications of specific reading retardation. In R. M. Knights & D. J. Bakker (Eds.), *The neuropsychology of learning disorders.* Baltimore: University Park Press, 1976.

ZIGLER, E., & PHILLIPS, L. Psychiatric diagnosis: A critique. *Journal of Abnormal and Social Psychology,* 1961, *63,* 607–18.

Index

Classroom
  elements of, 231–42
  learning problems in, 37–45
  "open," 236
  "personalized," 230–45
  redefining limits in, 280–84
  See also Intervention; School
Clements, S. D., 9, 10n
Clinical teaching, 159–60. *See also* Remediation
Coan, R., 87
Coates, B., 72
Cobb, S., 74
Cognition, 232n
Cognitive disability, 148
Cohen, D. K., 197
Cohen, N. J., 311, 337
Cohrs, M., 87
Coles, G. S., 66, 69, 72, 73, 89n, 93, 95, 96, 123, 138, 154
Commitment, 231, 236–37
Compas, B. E., 71, 165, 197, 256, 311, 312
Comrey, A. L., 74
Concurrent validity, 318–20
Condry, J., 39
Cone, T. E., 6n
Conners, C. K., 86, 93
Conolley, E. S., 236
Consent, to intervention, 290–96
Construct validity, 66, 82, 95, 206, 317, 323
Content validity, 66, 83, 95, 317–18
Contractual agreements, 231, 239–41
Cook, T. D., 308, 309, 324, 334, 335
Corrective intervention. *See* Intervention
Costs, of intervention, 287–90
Council for Learning Disabilities (CLD), 8
Cowen, E. L., 166
Crandall, V. C., 174n
Crane, M. M., 88
Cratty, Bryant, 145
Cravioto, J., 15
Crawford, J., 208
Crinella, F. M., 10n
Criterion-related validity, 66, 95, 317, 318–20
Cronback, Lee J., 39, 57, 62, 68, 75, 116, 118, 128, 195, 212, 229, 305, 308, 319, 321, 323–24, 331
Cross, L. H., 319
Cruickshank, William M., 5, 111, 144, 149
Crump, W. D., 101, 107

D

Dafoe, J., 182
Dalby, J. T., 17, 33
Darrow, H. F., 215
Davison, L. A., 89, 97
Dawes, R. M., 68, 69
de Charms, R., 171, 177, 178, 181
de Hirsch, K., 107, 120
de Hirsch, L., 86–87

de la Cruz, F. F., 14
De Licardie, E., 15
Deci, E. L., 23, 28, 39, 132, 169n, 170–71, 172, 173, 174n, 175, 236
Decision making
  in personalized classroom, 231, 236–37
  in placement, 112–17, 118
Delacato, Carl H., 14n, 145
Delgado, J. M. W., 73
DeLoach, T. F., 10n
Demystification, of LD practices, 296–99
Deno, E., 11, 166
Derr, C. B., 266
Deshler, D. D., 7
Determinism, 25
Deutsch, C., 5
Deutsch, D., 232
Deutsch, J. A., 232
Developmental aphasia, 4, 14
Developmental lag, 12, 15, 28, 51
Dewey, John, 49, 170, 209, 232, 258, 282, 283
Di Nello, M. C., 101
Diagnosis, of learning disabilities, 58, 84–99. *See also* Assessment; Labeling
Diagnostic testing, 58
Diagnostic validity, 318–20
Dickson, W. J., 197n
Diedrich, R. B., 215
Differential assessment, 93–95
Diffusion, 265
Discrimination, 77
Division for Children with Communication Disorders (DCCD), 8
Divoky, D., 101, 107n, 171, 331
Dixon, J. F., 96
Dodds, J., 87
Dohrenwend, B. P. 106n
Dohrenwend, B. S., 106n
Doll, E., 86, 87
Dollinger, S. J., 176, 179
Doman, Glen, 145
Dornbusch, S. M., 265
Douglas, Virginia, 149
Downs, M. P., 88
Doyle, P. H., 208
Drabman, R., 171, 177
Draguns, J. G., 88
Drew, A. L., 14n
Drugs
  and learning problems, 203, 311
Dudley-Marling, C. C., 95
Due process, 119, 292n
Duffey, J. B., 73–74
Duncan, J. K., 215
Dunn, L., 87
Dunn, L. M., 88, 92, 166
Dweck, C. S., 174n, 177
Dykman, R. A., 10n
Dyslexia, 4, 14, 16